A Compendium of
Neuropsychological Tests

A COMPENDIUM OF NEUROPSYCHOLOGICAL TESTS
Administration, Norms, and Commentary

Otfried Spreen
Esther Strauss

Department of Psychology
University of Victoria
Victoria, B.C., Canada

New York   Oxford
OXFORD UNIVERSITY PRESS
1991

Oxford University Press

Oxford   New York   Toronto
Delhi   Bombay   Calcutta   Madras   Karachi
Petaling Jaya   Singapore   Hong Kong   Tokyo
Nairobi   Dar es Salaam   Cape Town
Melbourne   Auckland

and associated companies in
Berlin   Ibadan

Library of Congress Cataloging-in-Publication Data
Spreen, Otfried.
A compendium of neuropsychological tests : administration, norms,
and commentary / by Otfried Spreen, Esther Strauss.
p. cm.   Includes bibliographical references.
Includes index.   ISBN 0-19-505439-3
1. Neuropsychological tests--Handbooks, manual, etc. I. Strauss,
Esther, II. Title.
[DNLM: 1. Neuropsychological Tests--handbooks. WL 396768c]
RC386.6.N48S67   1991
152--dc20   DNLM/DLC   90-7334

5 7 9 8 6 4

Printed in the United States of America
on acid-free paper

Preface

This manual is a compilation of the main selection of neuropsychological tests as they are currently used in the University of Victoria Neuropsychology Laboratory and its associated facilities. The need for a manual of this type will be obvious to the practicing clinician: Neuropsychological tests have been developed in numerous laboratories, but few of them have reached formal publication by commercial publishers. As a result, manuals of administration and norms are passed along among clinicians in mimeographed form and as in-house laboratory publications (e.g., Harley et al., 1980; Trites, 1977, 1985) like underground literature, and remain available only for short periods of time as authors move from place to place or in and out of the clinical field. Worse, in the process of exchanging manuals and normative data, inaccuracies and deliberate changes slip in, which modify the intent of the original investigator and render previously developed norms useless. Information on reliability and validity is scattered across both well-known and less accessible journals and conference reports (frequently unpublished) or are hidden in studies where these topics are not the primary objective.

Exceptions to this generalization are a number of formally published tests and the "fixed" test batteries: Reitan's battery of tests is still available in its original form from Tucson, Arizona, but even this battery has been modified in many laboratories, and interlaboratory differences in norms resulting from apparently minor changes are common. The Christensen–Luria battery, used relatively little in North America, and its North American amalgamation by Golden et al. (1976) are other examples of fixed batteries. Also commercially available are a few specific batteries for the assessment of aphasia (Goodglass & Kaplan, 1972; Kertesz, 1982; Porch, 1967, 1973). Clinicians who are satisfied with a "fixed" battery approach to neuropsychological examinations may not need this book, although normative data for the Reitan battery and its modifications are still difficult to find and some of its tests are included here.

Neuropsychological tests originate from several sources, including (1) the clinical neurological examination, (2) experimental psychology, (3) neuropsychological research, and (4) clinical psychology; only a small number of tests were originally designed for the neuropsychological clinician. As a result, the original descriptions of many of the procedures to be included here had to be traced to scattered and often obscure sources. Commercial distribution of such procedures was often not practical. We believe that with the growth of clinical neuropsychology as a discipline, a compendium of tests is essential at this stage, if only to form a common base of reference for the user and the researcher who wants to refer to available studies of validity, reliability, and norms.

For each test entry, information is provided under the following headings listed in the actual order of presentation: Test Name, Other Test Name(s), Purpose, Source, Description, Administration, Approximate Time for Administration, Scoring, Comment, Normative Data.

Because of the history of many of these tests, psychometric standards are not always met: A procedure developed for a single experiment or a clinical routine does not need a full psychometric development. However, once in use as a clinical instrument, such standards should be adhered to. In the Comment section, we have tried to provide as much documentation as was available at the time of writing. Notes on particular features, experiences with the test, and a comparison with similar tests are also frequently included. For unpublished tests, full descriptions of the test and test material as well as administration procedures, sample score sheets, norms, and data on reliability and validity are presented. Where copyrighted studies are used for the documentation, permission of the author and publisher has been obtained. The manual also includes a number of tests that are commercially available. These are described briefly, unless the administration manuals distributed with the test deviate from our use. Ordering information is provided, including prices most recently available to us. The user will have to obtain the material from the publisher or distributor. However, we have furnished norms and data from other studies if they were not included in the published version of the test. We have also included the approximate time required for the administration of each test under normal conditions in order to allow the user to plan an estimated timetable for a given patient. The time required may be considerably longer in patients with comprehension problems or with sensory or motor deficits.

A word of caution regarding the use of norms may be appropriate: Even if normative data have been meticulously collected for the general population, the use of such norms in populations with geographic and ethnic differences may, especially for verbal tests, be misleading. Similarly, the application of such norms to special populations with suspected handicap may lead to erroneous conclusions. For example, motor skill or motor speed in boxers with concussion may show no deficits, unless compared to norms from the same special population—that is, with other athletes.

The tests presented here constitute our most commonly used measures. Owing to limitations of space, less frequently used tests are not included. Our selection of tests is deliberately eclectic: Over the years, our laboratory has added and deleted many procedures, retaining what we hope is a useful selection for the practitioner. At the beginning of each chapter, we provide a rationale for our selection, including suggestions as to when a given test may be of particular use. Others may disagree with our selection. Nevertheless, we hope that this book may serve as a useful manual for neuropsychological clinicians, whether they choose to use this book for just a few of the tests ancillary to their own battery, or as a working manual supplementing details and norms of their own selection of tests, or as their main administration manual.

It should be explicitly stated that in our approach only a few tests are routinely used in most patients. Others are used rarely for the exploration of a specific problem. The selection presented here should not be mistaken as a "battery." The choice of tests is tailored to the specific questions raised in an individual's assessment.

Most tests allow administration by a psychometrician, although we do not advocate "blind" interpretation: The psychometrician administers tests carefully selected by the clinician in light of the referral question after the initial interview. The test selection for a given patient is revised as the results of earlier tests are considered midway through the examination. Some tests are self-administered, some of them by desktop computer; however, the same principles of test selection apply.

We would like to express our gratitude to the many colleagues in other institutions and to several former Victoria students who generously shared their published or unpublished data with us and frequently provided additional helpful comments. A special note of thanks goes to Linda Atwood, Mary Petersen, Maxine Stovel, and our graduate students who helped us in a preliminary version of the "Victoria Manual" and clarified many points of the test administration and the use of norms.

Victoria, B.C.   O.S.
June 1990   E.S.

REFERENCES

Golden, C.J., Hammeke, T.A., & Purisch, A.D. (1976). *Luria-Nebraska Neuropsychological Battery.* Los Angeles: Western Psychological Services.

Goodglass, H., & Kaplan, E. (1972). *The Assessment of Aphasia and Related Disorders.* Philadelphia: Lea & Febiger.

Harley, J.P., Leuthold, C.A., Matthews, C.G., & Bergs, L.E. (1980). Wisconsin Neuropsychological Test Battery T-Score Norms for Older Veterans Administration Medical Center Patients. Mimeo. Madison, WS.: Department of Neurology, University of Wisconsin.

Kertesz, A. (1982). *Western Aphasia Battery Test: Manual.* New York: Grune & Stratton.

Porch, B. (1967, 1973). *The Porch Index of Communicative Ability* (Vols. 1 & 2).

Palo Alto: Consulting Psychologists Press.

Trites, R.L. (1977, 1985). *Neuropsychological Test Manual.* Ottawa, Ont.: Royal Ottawa Hospital.

Contents

List of Acronyms, xiii

1. **History Taking,** 3

3. **General Intellectual Ability and Assessment of Premorbid Intelligence,** 17

2. **Profile of Test Results,** 10
   Category Test (HCT),21
      Adult Version: Victoria Revison, 24
      Adult and Intermediate Standard Versions, 26
      Children's Version, 26
   Mattis Dementia Rating Scale (MDRS), 39
   North American Adult Reading Test (NAART), 41
   Raven's Progressive Matrices, 45
   Stroop Test, 52
   Wechsler Intelligence Tests (WAIS-R, WISC-R, WPPSI-R), 56
   Wisconsin Card Sorting Test (WCST), 71

4. **Cognitive Tests for Children,** 77
   Bayley Scales of Infant Development (BSID), 78
   Kaufman Assessment Battery for Children (K-ABC), 81
   Stanford-Binet Intelligence Scale—Revised (SBIS-R), 88

5. **Achievement Tests,** 94
   KeyMath Diagnostic Arithmetic Test, 95
   Peabody Individual Achievement Test—Revised (PIAT-R), 100
   Stanford Diagnostic Reading Test (SDRT), 104
   Wide Range Achievement Test—Revised (WRAT-R), 107
   Woodcock–Johnson Psychoeducational Battery—Revised: Tests of
      Achievement (WJ-R ACH), 110

6. **Attention and Memory Tests,** 117

    Benton Visual Retention Test—Revised (BVRT-R), 118
    Buschke Selective Reminding Test (BSRT), 125
    Concentration Endurance Test (d2 Test), 138
    Paced Auditory Serial Addition Test (PASAT), 142
    Rey Auditory–Verbal Learning Test (RAVLT), 149
    Rey–Osterrieth Complex Figure Test, 157
    Rey Visual Design Learning Test (RVDLT), 168
    Sentence Repetition, 177
    Wechsler Memory Scale (WMS), 184
    Wechsler Memory Scale—Revised (WMS-R), 205

7. **Language Tests,** 210

    Boston Naming Test (BNT), 211
    Communicative Abilities in Daily Living (CADL), 215
    Controlled Oral Word Association (Word Fluency), 219
    Neurosensory Center Comprehensive Examination for Aphasia (NCCEA), 227
      Language Tests, 228
        Test 1. Visual Naming (VN), 228
        Test 2. Description of Use (DU), 230
        Test 3. Tactile Naming, Right Hand (TNR), 231
        Test 4. Tactile Naming, Left Hand (TNL), 233
        Test 6. Repetition of Digits (DRF), 234
        Test 7. Reversal of Digit (DRR), 234
        Test 9. Sentence Construction (SC), 236
        Test 10. Identification by Name (IN), 237
        Test 12. Oral Reading, Names (RNO), 238
        Test 13. Oral Reading, Sentences (RSO), 239
        Test 15. Reading Sentences for Meaning, Pointing (RSP), 239
        Test 14. Reading Names for Meaning, Pointing (RNP), 240
        Test 16. Visual–Graphic Naming (VGN), 241
        Test 17. Writing of Names (WN), 241
        Test 18. Writing to Dictation (WD), 244
        Test 19. Writing from Copy (WC), 245
        Test 20. Articulation (ART), 246
      Control Tests, 247
        Test C1. Tactile–Visual Matching, Right Hand (TMR), 247
        Test C2. Tactile–Visual Matching, Left Hand (TML), 249
        Test C3. Visual–Visual Matching (VVM), 249
        Test C4. Form Perception (FP), 251

Peabody Picture Vocabulary Test—Revised (PPVT-R), 262
Token Test, 266

8. **Visual, Visuomotor, and Auditory Tests**, 276
    Clock Drawing, 277
    Dichotic Listening, 280
      Words, 280
      Music, 283
    Developmental Test of Visual–Motor Integration (VMI), 287
    Embedded Figures Test, 291
    Facial Recognition Test, 296
    Hooper Visual Organization Test (VOT), 300
    Right–Left Orientation, 303
      Benton Form, 304
      Culver Form, 306
    Sound Recognition Test, 311
    Three-Dimensional Block Construction (3-D), 317
    Trail Making Test, 320

9. **Tactile, Tactile–Visual, and Tactile–Motor Tests**, 332
    Aesthesiometer, 333
    Finger Localization, 337
    Tactile Form Perception, 339
    Tactual Performance Test (TPT), 341
    Two-Point Discrimination, 355

10. **Motor Tests**, 359
    Finger Tapping Test (FTT), 360
    Hand Dynamometer, 365
    Hand Preference Test, 371
    Purdue Pegboard Test, 374

11. **Adaptive Behavior and Personality Tests**, 384
    Beck Depression Inventory (BDI), 385
    Geriatric Depression Scale (GDS), 390
    Minnesota Multiphasic Personality Inventory (MMPI), 394
    Personality Inventory for Children (PIC), 403
    Rorschach Test, 407
    Thematic Apperception Test (TAT), 413
    Vineland Adaptive Behavior Scales, 419
    Name Index, 423
    Test and Subject Index, 437

List of Acronyms

AAMD	=	American Association on Mental Deficiency
AL	=	Associate Learning (WMS subtest)
APM	=	Advanced Progressive Matrices (Raven's)
ART	=	Articulation (NCCEA subtest)
AVLT	=	Auditory–Verbal Learning Test (= RAVLT)
BDAE	=	Boston Diagnostic Aphasia Examination
BDI	=	Beck Depression Inventory
BNT	=	Boston Naming Test
BSID	=	Bayley Scales of Infant Development
BSRT	=	Buschke Selective Reminding Test
BVRT	=	Benton Visual Retention Test
CADL	=	Communicative Abilities in Daily Living
CF	=	Complex Figure Test (= RF)
CLTR	=	consistent long-term retrieval (Buschke)
CLTS	=	consistent long-term storage (Buschke)
CPM	=	Colored Progressive Matrices (Raven's)
D2	=	Concentration Endurance Test
3-D	=	Three-Dimensional Block Construction
DAT	=	dementia of the Alzheimer type
DSM-III	=	*Diagnostic and Statistical Manual of Mental Disorders*, 3rd ed.
DRF	=	Repetition of Digits (NCCEA subtest)
DRR	=	Reversal of Digits (NCCEA subtest)
DSp	=	Digit Span (WMS subtest)
DU	=	Description of Use (NCCEA subtest)
FAS	=	Controlled Oral Word Association (Word Fluency)
FOT	=	Finger Oscillation Test (= FTT)
FSIQ	=	Full Scale IQ (Wechsler)
FTT	=	Finger Tapping Test (= FOT)
FP	=	Form Perception
GDS	=	Geriatric Depression Scale (Mood Assessment Scale)

HCT   =   Halstead Category Test

IN   =   Identification by Name (NCCEA subtest)
ITPA   =   Illinois Test of Psycholinguistic Abilities

K-ABC   =   Kaufman Assessment Battery for Children

LM   =   Logical Memory (WMS subtest)
LTR   =   long-term retrieval (Buschke)
LTS   =   long-term storage (Buschke)

MC   =   Mental Control (WMS subtest)
MDI   =   Mental Development Index (BSID index)
MDRS   =   Mattis Dementia Rating Scale
MMPI   =   Minnesota Multiphasic Personality Inventory
MMSE   =   Mini–Mental State Exam
MNI   =   Montreal Neurologic Institute
MQ   =   Memory Quotient (WMS subtest)
MS   =   Memory Span (WMS subtest)

NAART   =   North American Adult Reading Test
NART   =   National Adult Reading Test
NCCEA   =   Neurosensory Center Comprehensive Examination for Aphasia

OR   =   Orientation (WMS subtest)

PAL   =   Paired Associates Learning (WMS subtest)
PASAT   =   Paced Auditory Serial Addition Test
PCI   =   Personal and Current Information (WMS subtest)
PDI   =   Motor Development Index (see BSID)
PI   =   Personal and Current Information (WMS subtest)
PIAT-R   =   Peabody Individual Achievement Test – Revised
PIC   =   Personality Inventory for Children
PIQ   =   Performance IQ (Wechsler)
PPVT   =   Peabody Picture Vocabulary Test
PR   =   percentile ranks

RAVLT   =   Rey Auditory–Verbal Learning Test
RF   =   Rey Figure Test (= CF)
RLTR   =   random long-term retrieval (Buschke)
RMI   =   Relative Mastery Indices (WJ-R ACH scoring system)
RNO   =   Oral Reading, Names (NCCEA subtest)
RNP   =   Reading Names for Meaning, Pointing (NCCEA subtest)
RPM   =   Raven's Progressive Matrices
RSO   =   Oral Reading, Sentences
RSP   =   Reading Sentences for Meaning, Pointing (NCCEA subtest)
RVDLT   =   Rey Visual Design Learning Test

SAS   =   Standard Age Scores (see SBIS score system)
SBIS(T)   =   Stanford–Binet Intelligence Scale (Test)

SC	=	Sentence Construction (NCCEA subtest)
SDRT	=	Stanford Diagnostic Reading Test
SPM	=	Standard Progressive Matrices (Raven's)
SRT	=	Selective Reminding Test (Buschke)
STR	=	short-term recall (Buschke)
TAT	=	Thematic Apperception Test
TML	=	Tactile Visual Matching, Left Hand (NCCEA subtest)
TMR	=	Tactile Visual Matching, Right Hand (NCCEA subtest)
TNL	=	Tactile Naming, Left Hand (NCCEA subtest)
TNR	=	Tactile Naming, Right Hand (NCCEA subtest)
TPT	=	Tactual Performance Test
VGN	=	Visual–Graphic Naming (NCCEA subtest)
VIQ	=	Verbal IQ (Wechsler)
VMI	=	Developmental Test of Visual–Motor Integration (Beery Test)
VN	=	Visual Naming (NCCEA subtest)
VOT	=	(Hooper) Visual Organization Test
VR	=	Visual Reproduction (WMS subtest)
VRT	=	Visual Retention Test (= BVRT)
VVM	=	Visual–Visual Matching (NCCEA subtest)
WAIS-R	=	Wechsler Adult Intelligence Scale – Revised
WC	=	Writing from Copy (NCCEA subtest)
WD	=	Writing to Dictation (NCCEA subtest)
WN	=	Writing of Names (NCCEA subtest)
WCST	=	Wisconsin Card Sorting Test
WISC-R	=	Wechsler Intelligence Scale for Children – Revised
WJPEB	=	Woodcock–Johnson Psychoeducational Battery
WJ-R ACH	=	Woodcock–Johnson Psychoeducational Battery – Revised: Tests of Achievement
WMS	=	Wechsler Memory Scale
WMS-R	=	Wechsler Memory Scale – Revised
WPPSI-R	=	Wechsler Preschool and Primary Scale of Intelligence – Revised
WRAT	=	Wide Range Achievement Test
WRAT-R	=	Wide Range Achievement Test – Revised

A Compendium of
Neuropsychological Tests

1

History Taking

A patient's account of his or her problems, and the patient's behavior during an interview, can provide a wealth of information about the presence and nature of cognitive disturbances. Consequently, taking a detailed history is essential to the neuropsychological evaluation, as it may yield important clues to a correct diagnosis and to the impact of the disorder on daily life. Sometimes the patient's account will have to be supplemented by information from other people since a patient's statements may prove misleading with regard to both the gravity of the symptoms and the time course of their evolution. For example, patients who have a memory disorder or who lack insight are likely to be poor informants.

The taking of a competent history is a skill that requires, in addition to a broad knowledge of neuropsychology, an awareness of interactions that may occur in interview situations. Often patients are tense and concerned about their symptoms. The clinician's job is to put the patient at ease and convey that the assessment is a collaborative venture to determine the presence and nature of the problem. The patient should be encouraged to relate the history in an unhurried manner. Introductory questions such as "How can I help you? Tell me about your problem" may be useful.

History taking does not follow a fixed format. Rather, the choice of questions and their order of presentation are guided by the patient's account. During this account, the following information should be obtained: basic descriptive data (age, marital status, etc.), description of the illness (nature of onset, duration, behavioral changes), relevant past medical history, relevant family history, educational and vocational history, and the effect of the disorder on daily life and personal relations. At the end of the history, the clinician may wish to go over the material with the patient to ensure that the details are correct and to check for additional information. Informal test questions about a patient's orientation, memory for current events, television shows, local politics, or geography may be included in the interview. We use two questionnaires, one designed for adult patients (Fig. 1–1) and the other for use with parents when the clients are children (Fig. 1–2).

3

History

PERSONAL HISTORY:

Name ————————————————————————————————
Address ——————————————————————————————
Phone No. ——————————————————————————
Sex M ———— F ————
Date of birth ————————————————————————
Age ————————————————————————————
Date tested ——————————————————————
Referred by ————————————————————
Referral question ————————————————————————————————

Family doctor ——————————————————————
Neurologist ————————————————————————
Psychiatrist ——————————————————————
Psychologist ————————————————————
Dates of previous psychological testing: ——————————————————
Education ————————————————————————————
Special training ————————————————————————
School problems ————————————————————————

Native language ————————————————————
Place of birth ——————————————————————
Handedness ——————————————————————
Occupation ————————————————————————
Current or last job ————————————————————
Previous work history ————————————————————————————
Marital status S ———— M ———— D ———— W ————
Relevant family history ————————————————————————————

MEDICAL HISTORY:

Previous hospitalizations/operations ——————————————————————————

Serious illnesses ————————————————————————————————

Family history of serious illness/neurological disease ——————————————————

Head injuries ————————————————————————————
Accidents/loss of consciousness ————————————————————————

Medications (type & dose) ————————————————————————————

Recent changes in medication ————————————————————————
Alcohol consumption ————————————————————————
Medical findings & dx: ————————————————————————

Figure 1–1.   History questionnaire for adult patients.

PHYSICAL/PSYCHOLOGICAL SYMPTOMS & CHANGES:

Weakness in any parts of your body _____

Numbness _____

Hearing _____ Ringing or buzzing _____

Vision _____ Blurred or double vision _____

Hear or see things that others do not _____

Balance _____

Change in ability to use hands _____

Hands tremble _____ Arthritis _____

Problem with taste or smell _____

Problem with nausea _____

Change in appetite/weight _____

Change in sexual responsiveness _____

Fainting spells _____

Dizziness _____

Headaches _____ Location _____

    Frequency _____ Time of day _____

Seizures _____ Type _____

    Warning _____ Frequency _____

    Time of day _____ Lose consc. _____

Blackouts _____

Depression _____

_____

_____

COGNITIVE CHANGES:

Any problems understanding what people say to you _____

_____

Any problems in finding the right word when you are talking to people _____

_____

Any change in your handwriting _____

Any problems understanding what you read _____

Any problems with calculating, handling money _____

Any problems in concentrating _____

Any periods of confusion _____

Any change in your ability to handle household chores or job _____

_____

Any changes in memory _____ What kinds of things do you forget _____

_____

Have you recently been disoriented _____

Have you been some place familiar recently and not known how to get home _____

_____

Any change in your mood or personality _____

Are you more irritable _____ Tense _____ Tired _____

Do you get depressed or cry more easily than before _____

_____

Has your sleep pattern changed _____

Any change in the way you get along with your wife/husband/family members ____

_____

Social activities _____

_____

Reason for referral (as reported by patient) _____

_____

_____

_____

Has daily living at home, at work or in social situations been affected by the complaints? How? ___

_____

_____

_____

History

Child's name _____ Sex M _____   F _____

Address _____

Phone No. _____ Mo (wk) _____ Fa (wk) _____

Referred by _____

Referral question _____
_____

Family doctor _____

Neurologist _____

Date of birth _____ Age _____

Date tested _____

Dates of previous psychological testing _____

Was this child adopted   Yes _____   No _____

Other children and relatives living with the child. (Indicate their names, relation, age, their health, or other problems) _____
_____
_____
_____

PREGNANCY WITH THIS CHILD:

Did mother suffer from anemia _____   high blood pressure _____

toxemia _____   swollen ankles __   kidney disease _____

heart disease __   bleeding _____   german measles _____

chronic illness such as diabetes, kidney failure, thyroid, etc. _____
_____

other illness(es) _____

Rh or other blood incompatibility _____

vomiting _____ hospitalization _____ when _____

why _____

operation _____

injury _____

threatened miscarriage or early contractions _____

BIRTH HISTORY:

Did mother have natural childbirth?   Yes _____   No _____

Was labor induced?   Yes _____   No _____

Was this a breech (feet first) delivery?   Yes _____   No _____

Were forceps used? If yes why _____

Did mother have a cesarean? If yes, why _____

Complications _____

Did mother have twins?   Yes _____   No _____   Which born first _____

Did this baby have breathing problems _____

Cord around neck _____

Did this baby cry quickly _____

Was the baby's color normal _____

Did the baby require transfusions _____ phototherapy _____

Was the baby premature? If yes, how early _____

Was the baby put on respirator _____

Birth weight _____

Did mother take the baby home with her from the hospital? If not, how long after _____

Figure 1–2. History questionnaire for parents of child patients.

Did baby have problems with feeding? If yes, describe _____

Was the cry weak _____

Was the baby normally active _____ limp _____

Did the baby have seizures _____

Did any of these problems occur with other pregnancies _____

DEVELOPMENT:

Is the development of this child different from that of brothers and sisters _____

Motor:

Age sat alone _____ Age walked without holding on _____

Age fed self _____ Age dressed self _____

Age rode bicycle _____ Drooling past 2½ _____

Difficulty sucking as infant _____ Difficulty chewing _____

Language:

Age spoke first words _____ Age 2–3 words together _____

Speech problems _____

Behavior:

Toileting problems _____

Bed wetting problems _____

Does child get along well with children _____

Does child get along well with adults _____

Is child shy _____ Of average intelligence _____

Immature _____ More active than other children _____

Well behaved _____ Clumsy in using hands _____

Clumsy in walking _____ Stubborn _____

Impulsive _____ Poor handwriting _____

Temper tantrums _____ Head banging _____

Sleep problems _____ Nightmares _____

Thumb sucking _____ Nail biting _____

Blank spells _____ Falling spells _____

Tics & twitching _____

Difficulty staying at one activity for reasonable length of time _____

Does (Did) child eat paint, paper, etc. _____

PAST MEDICAL HISTORY:

Has child had meningitis or encephalitis _____

Head injury _____ Other injury _____

Frequent ear infections _____ Visual defects _____

_____ Hearing defects _____

Allergies _____ Seizures _____

Episodes of unconsciousness _____

Hospitalization _____

Other illnesses _____

Has child had emotional, adjustment, or behavioral problems _____

Has child received psychological or psychiatric treatment _____

(continued)

Does child frequently complain of headache _____
dizziness _____ nausea _____
trouble with vision or hearing _____ weakness _____
stomach ache _____ other _____
Medications (type and dose) _____
Medical findings & dx _____

SCHOOL HISTORY:
Did child attend preschool (any problems) _____
Did child attend kindergarten (any problems) _____
Were there any school entry problems _____
_____

Present school and grade _____
Previous schools _____
Has the school reported problems with reading _____
writing _____ spelling _____
arithmetic _____ social adjustment _____
Does child like school _____
Results of previous psychological testing _____
_____
Has child had special tutoring _____

FAMILY HISTORY:
Father's age _____   education _____ occupation _____
Mother's age _____   education _____ occupation _____
Family history of serious illness/neurological disease/learning disorder _____
_____
_____

SOCIAL HISTORY:
Are there significant marital problems _____
Are there significant conflicts between parent and child _____
Are there significant conflicts between children _____
Does child have difficulty getting along with children his/her own age _____
_____
How does child occupy him/herself _____
How does child concentrate and pay attention (TV, games, etc.) _____
_____
How does child perform athletically _____
Is the child's problem getting worse _____
_____

Figure 1–2. (*Continued*)

These questionnaires should be used only as guides and not as a substitute for the interview, although the child questionnaire may in some cases be filled out by the parent alone. In this case, the interview can focus on the major questions concerning the child and need not touch on minor details already provided by the parent.

During the interview, much other information can be gleaned from (1) general appearance (e.g., eye contact present, modulation of face and voice, personal hygiene, habits of dress); (2) motor activity (e.g., hemiplegia, tics, tense, hyper- or hypokinetic); (3) mood; (4) degree of cooperation; and (5) abnormalities in language, prosody, or memory.

Computer-based interviews can be useful additions to the clinical interview, providing information about an individual's life not otherwise available. The Giannetti On-line Psychosocial History (GOLPH) is designed to gather information about an individual's life history and current circumstances. Its branching capabilities presents questions based on the responses to previous questions, resulting in individualized reports with a minimum of time (about 30 to 90 minutes) and effort. It can be ordered from National Computer Systems, P. O. Box 1416, Minneapolis, MN 55440. The cost is about $6.00 U.S. per report.

2

Profile of Test Results

For the purpose of interpretation, most clinicians prepare a summary or profile sheet of the test results obtained during the neuropsychological examination. It should be stressed that such a summary is no substitute for careful analysis of the patient's problem-solving approach or actual answers or behavior on a given test, which may reveal particular characteristics of psychopathology. However, a profile of test results can be the starting point of interpretative considerations for diagnostic as well as intervention and rehabilitation purposes.

For the convenience of the user, it is preferable to translate all test raw scores into standard scores, z-scores, T-scores, or percentile ranks. Our profile (Fig. 2–1), which we offer only as an example, uses percentile ranks and standard deviations, grouping tests by area in the same order in which they are described in this manual. The test descriptions in this book or the original test manuals frequently provide age-appropriate percentile ranks. Where these are not provided, deviations from the age-appropriate mean can be converted into percentile ranks by using Table 2–1, which shows the percentile ranks corresponding to portions or multiples of the standard deviation as they would be expected by the area under the normal curve. If test manuals transcribe test scores into T-scores, a similar conversion can be made using Table 2–1. It should be noted that such conversions are based on the assumption of a normal distribution of the ability measured, and are inappropriate if this assumption is not met. Few neuropsychological tests contain information about score distributions in a normal population. In fact, some tests are deliberately designed to measure deficit; these have a concentration of items in the low and very low range of abilities and have a ceiling score appropriate for a healthy person with average abilities. Such score distributions should therefore be considered in the interpretation of any of the tests. Since few personality tests yield scores that can be expressed in percentiles, a check mark or a brief remark on the appropriate line in the profile sheet is usually sufficient here.

It is our practice to start the interpretative process by marking in the profile the lowest test score obtained, and to look for similarly poor scores in the same area of

Table 2–1. Conversion of Standard Deviations and T-Scores into Percentile Ranks

Percentile	SD	T-score
99+	3.0	80
99	2.5	75
98	2.0	70
93	1.5	65
84	1.0	60
69	0.5	55
50	0.0	50
31	−0.5	45
16	−1.0	40
7	−1.5	35
2	−2.0	30
1	−2.5	25
<1	−3.0	20

deficit. This forms a first hypothesis about a patient's problem area. A second, third, or fourth area of deficit can often be hypothesized, again based on other poor scores and scores related to these areas of ability. Such hypotheses should be followed by a thorough review of the actual performance—that is, the actual responses of the patient. Following a similar line of deduction, areas of strength can be outlined by beginning with the highest test scores obtained, and considering the performance of the patient in related tests. This "syndromatic" approach ensures that each area of deficit is thoroughly explored, dissociation of individual deficits are discovered, and the remaining strong abilities of a patient are outlined in the final interpretation.

Figure 2–1. Profile of test scores, using percentile ranks and standard deviations.

Name ______________________ File # __________

Date of Test __________ Previous Tests __________

Date of Birth __________ Age ______ Handedness __________

Education __________ Examiner __________

Referred by __________

INTELLECTUAL ABILITY AND PREMORBID INTELLIGENCE

	Scaled S.	Age Cor.	Standard Deviation: 3 2 · 1 · .5 · 0 · .5 · 1 · 2 3 / Percentile Rank: 0 · 10 · 20 · 30 · 40 · 50 · 60 · 70 · 80 · 90 · 100
N.A.A.R.T. errors			
Estimated VIQ	____		
Estimated PIQ	____		
Estimated FSIQ	____		
Barona Index			
Estimated VIQ	____		
Estimated PIQ	____		
Estimated FSIQ	____		
WAIS-R/WISC-R	Scaled S.	Age Cor.	
Information	____	____	
Digit Span	____	____	
Vocabulary	____	____	
Arithmetic	____	____	
Comprehension	____	____	
Similarities	____	____	
Picture Compl.	____	____	
Picture Arrgm.	____	____	
Block Design	____	____	
Object Assmb.	____	____	
Digit Symbol/Codg.	____	____	
Full Scale IQ	____		
Verbal IQ	____		
Performance IQ	____		
Category Test, errors		____	
Mattis Dementia Rating Scale		____	
Raven Progressive Matrices		____	

Stroop Test   I
                     II
                     III
Wisconsin Card Sort Categories
                     Persev. Err.
                     Failure to Maint. Set

COGNITIVE TESTS FOR CHILDREN

Bayley Scale   Mental D.I.
                Motor D.I.
Kaufman ABC   Sequential
              Simultaneous
              Ment. Proc. Comp.
Stanford–Binet–R Comp. SAS

ACHIEVEMENT TESTS

KeyMath Diagnostic Arithmetic
    Content
    Operations
    Applications
Peabody Individual Achievement–R
    General Information
    Reading Recognition
    Reading Comprehension
    Mathematics
    Spelling
    Written Expression
Stanford Diagnostic Reading Test
    Reading Comprehension
    Fast Reading
Wide Range Achievement Test–R
    Reading
    Spelling
    Arithmetic
Woodcock–Johnson Battery
    Reading

(continued)

Figure 2-1. *(Continued)*

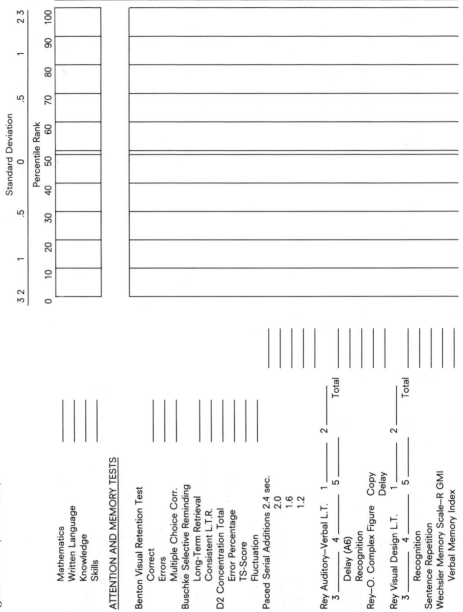

14

Visual Memory Index
Attention/Concentr. Index
Delayed Recall Index
Digit Span Forward
Digit Span Backward
Visual Span Forward
Visual Span Backward
Logical Memory I
Logical Memory II
Visual Reproduction I
Visual Reproduction II

LANGUAGE TESTS

Boston Naming Test
CADL Total Score
Controlled Word Assoc. FAS
  Animals
NCCEA
PPVT-R
Token Test

VISUAL, VISUAL–MOTOR, AUDITORY TEST

Dichotic Words   R   L
Dichotic Music   R   L
Devlopm. Test of Visual–Motor Integration
Embedded Figures
  Credit
Facial Recognition
Hooper V.O.T.
Right–Left Orientation   Benton   Culver
Sound Recognition
3-D Block Construction
Trail Making Test   A   B

(continued)

15

Figure 2–1. *(Continued)*

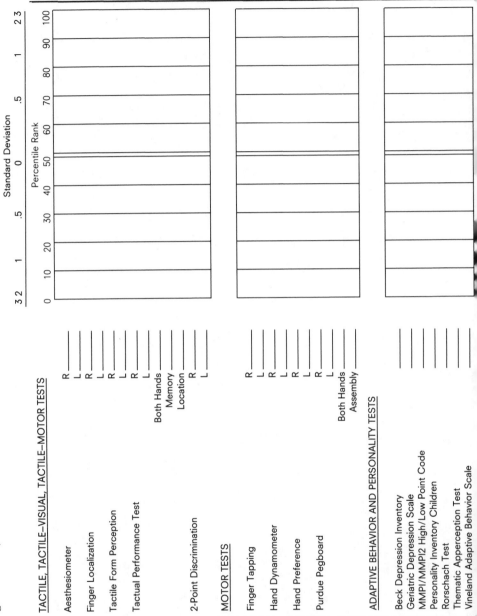

TACTILE, TACTILE–VISUAL, TACTILE–MOTOR TESTS

Aesthesiometer — R, L
Finger Localization — R, L
Tactile Form Perception — R, L
Tactual Performance Test — R, L
Both Hands
Memory
Location
2-Point Discrimination — R, L

MOTOR TESTS

Finger Tapping — R, L
Hand Dynamometer — R, L
Hand Preference — R, L
Purdue Pegboard — R, L
Both Hands
Assembly

ADAPTIVE BEHAVIOR AND PERSONALITY TESTS

Beck Depression Inventory
Geriatric Depression Scale
MMPI/MMPI2 High/Low Point Code
Personality Inventory Children
Rorschach Test
Thematic Apperception Test
Vineland Adaptive Behavior Scale

Standard Deviation
Percentile Rank

16

3

General Intellectual Ability and Assessment of Premorbid Intelligence

Although early psychologists treated intelligence as a unitary concept, subsequent work has suggested that intelligence is best considered a multiplicity of abilities, and therefore best evaluated with a multifaceted instrument. We present here a number of tests including the Wechsler Intelligence Scales (Wechsler, 1967, 1974, 1981) which are composed of a variety of subtests and are the most popular measures of general intellectual ability. We tend to give the Wechsler test early in the course of the assessment since it allows the examiner to observe how the patient behaves on a wide array of tasks. In this way, the examiner can develop hypotheses about the patient's spared and impaired abilities that can then be tested more thoroughly during the course of the assessment. Batteries developed specifically for children (as opposed to downward extensions of adult measures) are considered in the next section. When adults generate very few responses on the Wechsler Adult Intelligence Scale (WAIS), making it difficult to rank them according to the extent of their cognitive deficits, tests such as the Mattis Dementia Rating Scale (Mattis, 1976) or the Mini-Mental State Exam (MMSE; Folstein et al., 1975) may be preferred in order to provide gross estimates of cognitive functioning. We tend to use the MDRS more than the MMSE since the MDRS provides for a broader coverage of cognitive functions. Nonetheless, the clinician may prefer the MMSE, particularly with those individuals who have difficulty concentrating for extended periods of time; that is, longer than 5–10 minutes.

There are a number of clinical, medicolegal, and research situations where knowledge of premorbid IQ is important (Matarazzo, 1990). Since data from premorbid testing are rarely available, it becomes necessary to estimate an individual's premorbid level of functioning. Many investigators have relied on the

Vocabulary and Information subtest scores of the Wechsler Scales as the best indicators of premorbid intelligence. Although Vocabulary is among the most resistant of the Wechsler subtests, performance on the test is markedly impaired in a range of clinical conditions. It is therefore likely to underestimate premorbid intelligence seriously (Crawford, in press; Lezak, 1983). The Information subtest scores reflect a person's general fund of knowledge; however, this score may be misleading in clients with poor educational opportunities. Information scores may also be affected by a number of clinical conditions. Nelson and her colleagues (Nelson, 1982; Nelson & O'Connell, 1978) therefore proposed that a reading test for irregularly spelled words would be a better indicator of premorbid ability since it would assess the level of reading achieved before the onset of brain impairment. They developed in Britain a test called the National Adult Reading Test (NART). The NART consists of 50 irregular words (e.g., debt, naïve), has high internal and test–retest reliability, and does indeed provide a better estimate of WAIS-R IQ than Vocabulary subtest scores (Crawford, in press). Deterioration in NART performance, however, does occur in patients with cerebral dysfunction—for example, in cases of moderate to severe levels of dementia (Stebbins et al., 1988, 1990a). The NART also appears to underestimate IQ in patients with mild dementia who have accompanying linguistic deficits (Stebbins et al., 1990b). Thus the NART is *not* insensitive to cerebral dysfunction. Nonetheless, it may prove useful in providing a lower limit to the estimate of premorbid IQ (Stebbins et al., 1990a,b). One should also note that the NART cannot be used with aphasic or dyslexic patients, or with patients having significant articulatory or visual acuity problems (Crawford, in press). Finally, the test needs to be standardized on the WAIS-R, rather than the WAIS, and needs to be modified for use with North American populations. Blair and Spreen (1989) have adapted the NART for use with a North American population (North American Adult Reading Test, NAART), and this modified version is presented here.

The use of demographic measures to estimate premorbid IQ has also shown considerable promise, with education, race, and occupation being the most powerful predictors. A number of investigators (e.g., Barona et al., 1984; Reynolds & Gutkin, 1979; Wilson et al., 1978) have developed regression equations to calculate premorbid IQ. Wilson and colleagues regressed WAIS IQs on five demographic variables (age, sex, race, education, and occupation) with moderately favorable results. Barona and colleagues updated the formulas for the WAIS-R, again with promising results, although the standard errors of estimate for the regression equations were rather large (e.g., 12.14 for WAIS-R Full Scale IQ). The complete Barona Index equations and demographic variable weights are given in Table 3–1. These indices should be considered estimates of premorbid functioning, rather than exact indicators. In addition, in cases where the premorbid Full Scale IQ is above 120 or below 69, use of these formulas may result in serious under- or overestimation, respectively (Barona et al., 1984; Sweet et al., 1990).

Table 3–1.   Barona Index Equations and Variable Weights

Estimated VIQ = 54.23 + 0.49(age) + 1.92(sex) + 4.24(race) + 5.25(education) + 1.89(occupation) + 1.24(urban–rural residence). Standard error of estimate of VIQ = 11.79; R = .62.

Estimated PIQ = 61.58 + 0.31(age) + 1.09(sex) + 4.95(race) + 3.75(education) + 1.54(occupation) + .82(region). Standard error of estimate of PIQ = 13.23; R = .49.

Estimated FSIQ = 54.96 + 0.47(age) + 1.76(sex) + 4.71(race) + 5.02(education) + 1.89(occupation) + .59(region). Standard error of estimate of FSIQ = 12.14; R = .60.

Variables take the following values:
Sex
Female = 1   Male = 2

Race
White = 3   Black = 2   Other = 1

Occupation
Professional/Technical = 6
Managerial/Official/Clerical/Sales = 5
Skilled labor = 4
Not in labor force = 3
Semiskilled labor = 2
Unskilled labor = 1

Region (U.S.)
Southern = 1   North central = 2
Western = 3   Northeast = 4

Residence
Rural (<2,500) = 1   Urban (>2,500) = 2

Age
16–17 = 1	18–19 = 2	20–24 = 3
25–34 = 4	35–44 = 5	45–54 = 6
55–64 = 7	65–69 = 8	70–74 = 9

Education (years of school)
0–7 = 1	8 = 2	9–11 = 3
12 = 4	13–15 = 5	16+ = 6

Note: VIQ = Verbal IQ; PIQ = Performance IQ, and FSIQ = Full Scale IQ.

Source: Barona et al. (1984).

Demographic methods have the advantage that they are applicable to a wide variety of patients, and, unlike performance on cognitive tests (e.g., Vocabulary and Information Subtests, NART, NAART), they are not subject to decline in clinical conditions (e.g., dementia). Pairing test behavior (e.g., Vocabulary, Information, NART, NAART) or other patient information with data from demographic variables may increase the power of prediction (Crawford, in press; Sweet et al., 1990).

Patients may have difficulty in forming concepts, in maintaining the use of the principle while it is in effect, or in shifting from one principle to another according to situational demands. These problems may occur together, or they may also exist separately (Lezak, 1983). The Category Test (Halstead, 1947; Reitan & Davison, 1974) and Raven's Progressive Matrices (Raven, 1938, 1947, 1965) provide sensitive measures of abstraction ability, whereas the Stroop Test (Stroop, 1935) and the Wisconsin Card Sorting Test (Heaton, 1981) give better measures of mental flexibility. These popular tests of conceptual ability are also considered here.

REFERENCES

Barona, A., Reynolds, C.R., & Chastain, R. (1984). A demographically based index of pre-morbid intelligence for the WAIS-R. *Journal of Consulting and Clinical Psychology, 52*, 885–887.

Blair, J.R., & Spreen, O. (1989). Predicting premorbid IQ: A revision of the National Adult Reading Test. *Clinical Neuropsychologist 3*, 129–136.

Crawford, J.R. (in press). Estimation of premorbid intelligence: A review of recent developments. In J.R. Crawford & D.M. Parker (Eds.), *Developments in Clinical and Experimental Neuropsychology.* New York: Plenum Press.

Folstein, M.F., Folstein, S.E., & McHugh, P.R. (1975). "Mini-Mental State": A practical method for grading the cognitive state of outpatients for the clinician. *The Journal of Psychiatric Research, 12*, 189–198.

Halstead, W.C. (1947). *Brain and Intelligence.* Chicago: University of Chicago Press.

Heaton, R.K. (1981).*Wisconsin Card Sorting Test Manual.* Odessa, Fla.: Psychological Assessment Resources.

Lezak, M.D. (1983). *Neuropsychological Assessment* (2nd ed.). New York: Oxford University Press.

Matarazzo, J.D. (1990). Psychological assessment versus psychological testing. *American Psychologist, 45*, 999–1017.

Mattis, S. (1976). Mental status examination for organic mental syndrome in the elderly patient. In L. Bellak, & T.B. Karasu (Eds.), *Geriatric Psychiatry.* New York: Grune & Stratton.

Nelson, H.E. (1982). *National Adult Reading Test (NART): Test Manual.* Windsor, U.K.: NFER Nelson.

Nelson, H.E., & O'Connell, A. (1978). Dementia: The estimation of pre-morbid intelligence levels using the new adult reading test. *Cortex, 14*, 234–244.

Raven, J.C. (1938). *Progressive Matrices: A Perceptual Test of Intelligence.* London: H.K. Lewis.

Raven, J.C. (1947). *Colored Progressive Matrices Sets A, Ab, B.* London: H.K. Lewis.

Raven, J.C. (1965). *Advanced Progressive Matrices Sets I and II.* London: H.K. Lewis.

Reitan, R.M., & Davidson, L.A. (1974). *Clinical Neuropsychology: Current Status and Applications.* Washington, D.C.: V.H. Winston.

Reynolds, C.R., & Gutkin, T.B. (1979). Predicting the premorbid intellectual status of children using demographic data. *Clinical Neuropsychology, 1*, 36–38.

Stebbins, G.T., Wilson, R.S., Gilley, D.W., Bernard, B.A., & Fox, J.H. (1988). Estimation of premorbid intelligence in dementia. *Journal of Clinical and Experimental Neuropsychology, 10*, 63–64.

Stebbins, G.T., Wilson, R.S., Gilley, D.W., Bernard, B.A., & Fox, J.H. (1990a). Use of the National Adult Reading Test to estimate premorbid IQ in dementia. *Clinical Neuropsychologist, 4*, 18–24.

Stebbins, G.T., Gilley, D.W., Wilson, R.S., Bernard, B.A., & Fox, J.H. (1990b). Effects of language disturbances on premorbid estimates of IQ in mild dementia. *Clinical Neuropsychologist, 4*, 64–68.

Stroop. J.R. (1935). Studies of interference in serial verbal reaction. *Journal of Experimental Pychology, 18*, 643–662.

Sweet, J.J., Moberg, P.J., and Tovian, S.M. (1990). Evaluation of Wechsler Adult Intelligence Scale-Revised premorbid IQ formulas in clinical populations. *Psychological Assessment, 2,* 41–44.

Wechsler, D. (1967). *Manual for the WPPSI.* New York: Psychological Corporation.

Wechsler, D. (1974). *Manual for the WISC-R.* New York: Psychological Corporation.

Wechsler, D. (1981). *Manual for the WAIS-R.* New York: Psychological Corporation.

Wilson, R.S., Rosenbaum, G., Brown, G., Rourke, D., Whitman, D., & Grisell, J. (1978). An index of premorbid intelligence. *Journal of Consulting and Clinical Psychology, 46,* 1554–1555.

CATEGORY TEST (HCT)

Purpose

This test measures a patient's abstraction or concept formation ability.

Source

The manual version of the test can be obtained from Ralph Reitan, Ph.D, Neuropsychology Laboratory, 1338 Edison Street, Tucson, Arizona 85719, for about $665 U.S. The booklet versions of the Adult and Intermediate forms of the test are highly portable and can be ordered from Psychological Assessment Resources, P.O. Box 998, Odessa, Florida 33556, for $210 U.S., or from the Institute of Psychological Research, 34 Fleury Street West, Montreal, Quebec, H3L 1S9, for about $325 Cdn. Apple computer versions of the test are available from Psychological Assessment Resources, Inc. P.O. Box 998, Odessa, Florida 33556, for $195 U.S.

Description

The Category Test, developed by Halstead (1947), is also part of the Reitan test battery (Reitan & Davison, 1974). The original version involves the projection of seven sets of items, with a total of 208 items. Each set is organized on the basis of a different principle, such as number of objects, ordinal position of an odd stimulus, etc. Subjects must use feedback they receive from their correct and incorrect guesses on the series of items in each subtest to infer the rule behind the subtest. No clues are given as to what the rule might be. The adult version covers the age range 15:6 years and up. An intermediate version (Reed et al., 1965) covers the age range 9:0–15:6 years, and includes 168 items, divided into six subtests. A children's version (Reed et al., 1965), consisting of 80 items arranged into five subtests, is available for age 8 years and under or for individuals suspected of being mentally retarded.

Table 3–2.   Item Content for the Long and Short Versions of the HCT

Subtest No.	No. of items in subtest	Victoria Revision
I	8	Items 1,4,5[a]
II	20	Items 1–5[a]
III	40	Items 1–24
IV	40	Items 1–24
V	40	Items 1–17
VI	40	Items 7–22
VII	20	0
Total	208	81

[a]Items should be administered but not scored.

Source: Sherrill (1987).

A serious problem is that impaired subjects take a long time (up to two hours) to complete the test. Short forms of the adult version of the Category Test have been developed (Boyle, 1986; Caslyn et al., 1980; Gregory et al., 1979; Russell & Levy, 1987; Victoria Revision, Labreche, 1983). Item content for the Halstead Category Test (HCT) and that for the short form by Labreche (1983; Victoria Revision) are shown in Table 3–2. The short form appears to be an excellent alternative to the long form (Sherrill, 1985, 1987). The process of problem solving across items on the abbreviated form is not significantly different from that used on the long form. It discriminates well between normal and brain-damaged populations. Moreover, the Victoria Revision (Labreche, 1983), which has 81 items, correlated well with the long form ($r = .96$). The Victoria Revision is very attractive for general clinical use, given its relatively short administration time and good predictive accuracy. In situations where time constraints are not so crucial, the full-length version of the Category Test may be preferable.

Administration

Briefly, the apparatus for presenting the test items to the subject consists of a slide projector, a console with a viewing screen, or a rear-view projector, and the examiner's control board. The purpose of the test as a whole is to find the underlying principle of each set of items. The subject responds by pressing one of four levers, numbered 1, 2, 3, and 4 (colored knobs for children), from left to right, and placed on the apparatus immediately below the screen. A correct response produces a chime; an incorrect response produces a buzzer sound.

The purpose of administering the Category Test is usually to determine the subject's ability in abstraction or concept formation. To achieve this purpose, it is necessary that the examiner elicit the best performance of which the subject is capable. We insist that each subject observe each item carefully before making a response. Usually the subject reacts to the test with interest and makes an obvious effort to respond correctly. Occasionally a patient will respond apparently at random, and in such instances the examiner must encourage the patient to make a serious effort (or, if this is not possible, to declare the test results invalid). Since the purpose is to measure the patient's concept formation ability rather than motivation for doing well, a variety of techniques may be used as necessary. Some patients need to be told repeatedly to observe the items carefully (e.g., in some instances they must be asked to describe the figures before being permitted to respond), or to state the reason for selecting a particular response. A patient who says only that he or she was "just guessing," must be encouraged not to "just guess" but to "try to figure out the principle."

As a general rule, any part of the instructions may be repeated when the examiner believes it necessary. Our purpose is to give the subject a clear understanding of the problem he or she is facing and the rules involved in its solution. The principles themselves are never given to a subject, but when working with subjects who are extremely impaired in their ability to form concepts, it may become necessary to urge them to study the picture carefully; to ask for their descriptions of the stimulus material which are then followed by examiner questions such as, "Does that give you any idea of what might be the right answer?"; to urge them to try to notice and remember how the pictures change, since this often provides clues to the underlying principle; and to try to think of the reason when they answer correctly. Subjects rarely ask the examiner to state the principle, but it is possible that in conversations such as that described above, an unwary examiner may give unwarranted reinforcement to the patient's hypotheses. Examiners should always remember that their questions and advice should be consistent with the aims of the formal instructions and should not simply provide information relevant to the solution of the problems presented by the test. The only information of this kind comes from the bell or buzzer following each response.

Most subjects are able to take the Category Test with little additional information or direction than is provided in the formal instructions. Impaired subjects sometimes find the test very trying and frustrating. The examiner should make every effort to encourage the subject to continue working at the task. If a subject shows no sign of making progress on any one of Subtests 3 through 6 in the first 20 items and *also* gives evidence of extreme frustration with the task, it is better to discontinue the subtest at this point and prorate the error scores (linear extrapolation) rather than run the risk of not being able to complete the test.

The apparatus as a whole constitutes, in effect, a multiple-choice situation. The subject's keyboard, on the front of the projection cabinet, enables the subject to indicate his or her choices objectively. The examiner's control board is set each time for the "correct" response and controls the presentation of successive items.

The test items are projected from the slide projector. The slides begin with eight roman numeral items ranging from I to IV. The keys on the subject's board are numbered; thus this first subtest serves to associate the items on the screen with the subject's keys, as well as acquainting the subject with the test procedure and relieving any test anxiety. Between each subtest or group there is one blank frame.

The master off–on switch is located on the left side of the examiner's control board. When this switch is turned on, the screen and examiner's control board are ready to use. The switch on the rear of the slide projector must also be turned on.

A hand control switch that causes the successive items to appear on the screen is located at the right of the examiner's control board. When this switch is depressed once quickly, a new item will replace the previous item on the screen. Do *not* keep the switch depressed.

A four-way control switch that corresponds to the subject's four response keys is located in the center of the examiner's control board. To set any key on the subject's board as correct (sound the chime), set the handle into the appropriate numbered slot. A prepared record blank tells the examiner the proper setting of this switch for each item.

Always set answer key before changing the slide. Some additional points should be mentioned briefly:

1. Although speed is not a factor and subjects should not be hurried, neither should they be permitted to sit and daydream or to take an unduly long time to respond. Some subjects would impair the continuity of the test if not encouraged to make reasonably prompt decisions and thus impair their prospect of making better scores.
2. The examiner should always be alert to the slide on the screen, not only to keep in touch with the subject's performance, but also to note if a slide has somehow gotten out of order, necessitating a quick change of the "answer" switch.
3. The testing room should be somewhat darkened, yet light enough for the examiner to record errors.
4. The subject should sit directly in front of the screen. The colors may be particularly difficult to see from an angle.

Adult Version: Victoria Revision

ADMINISTRATION

The adult version covers the age range 15:6 and up. Correct responses for the eight practice trials are 1, 4, 2, 1, 3, 1, 4, 2. Say to the patient: **"On this screen you** are going to see different geometrical figures and designs. Something about the pattern on the screen will remind you of a number between one and four. On the keyboard in front of you [pointing] the keys are numbered one, two, three, and four. You are to press down on the key that is the same number that the pattern on the screen reminds you of. That is, if the picture on the screen reminds you of the number one, pull key number one. If the picture on the screen reminds you of the number two, pull key number two, and so on. For example, what number does this remind you of?"

Put on the first practice slide. If the subject says "one," ask the subject which key he or she should press. After the subject has pressed the number 1 key, say: "The bell you have just heard tells you that you got the right answer. Every time you have the right answer you will hear the bell ring." Instruct the subject to try one of the other keys in order to find out what happens when an incorrect key is pressed. Then say: "The buzzer is what you hear when you have the wrong answer. In this way, you will know each time whether you have the right or wrong answer. However, for each picture on the screen you get only one choice. If you make a mistake, we just go right on to the next picture."

Proceed with the remaining practice set. Say: "Now which key would you pick for this picture?" After the practice, set, say: "That was the end of the practice set. This test is divided into four subtests. In each subtest there is one idea or principle that runs throughout the entire subtest. Once you have figured out what the idea or principle in the subtest is, by using this idea you will get the right answer each time. Now we are going to begin the first subtest. The idea in it may be the same as the practice set, or it may be different. We want you to figure it out."

Proceed with Subtest 1. After Subtest 1, say: "That was the end of the first subtest, and as you probably noticed, you don't necessarily have to see a number to have a number suggested to you. As you may or may not have noticed, in each of these subtests, there is one idea or principle that runs throughout. Once you figure out the idea, you continue to apply it to get the right answer. Now we are going to start the second subtest. The idea may be the same as the last one, or it may be different. I want to see if you can figure out what the idea is and then use it to get the right answer. Remember, the idea remains the same throughout the subtest. I will tell you when we complete one subtest and are ready to begin a new one."

Proceed with Subtest 2. In Subtest 2, after slide #6 (the first slide without numbers), say: "This is still the same group, but now the numbers are missing. The principle is still the same." After Subtests 2 and 3, say: "That was the end of that subtest. Now we are going to begin the next one. The idea in it may be the same as the last one or it may be different. We want you to figure it out."

Adult and Intermediate Standard Versions

The instructions for the standard versions are similar to those given above. For the adult version only, the following additional instructions are given: After Subtest 6, say: **"In the last subtest there is no one idea or principle that runs throughout the group because it is made up of items you have already seen in the preceding subtests. Try to remember what the right answer was the last time you saw the pattern and give that same answer again."**

Children's Version

ADMINISTRATION

This test is for use in children 8 years old and under, or in individuals suspected of being mentally retarded.

For this version of the test, the numbered key disks are replaced by colored ones. The sequence 1, 2, 3, 4 changes to red, blue, yellow, and green. **"On this screen you will see pictures of different figures and designs. Each picture will make you think of a color, either red, blue, yellow, or green. On this keyboard in front of you, you will notice that the keys are different colors. This one is red, this one is blue, this one is yellow, and this one is green [pointing]. Press down on the key that has the same color as the color you think of when you look at the picture. For example, what color does this make you think of?"**

Flash on first picture—a red circle. If the subject says "red," ask which key he or she would press. When the subject presses the key, say: **"That is the bell, which means that you got the right answer. Try another key and see what happens when you get the wrong answer."**

After the subject does this, say: **"That is the buzzer, which means you got the wrong answer. This way you will know each time whether you are right or wrong, but for each design you may press only one key. If you make a mistake we will go right on to the next one. Let's try some of these."**

After the first subtest, say: **"That completes the first group of pictures. Now we are going to start the next group. You will have to try to figure out the right reason for picking one key or another. If you are able to figure out the reason why your answers are right or wrong, it will help, because the reason stays the same all the way through the group."**

Proceed with the second subtest. Any part of the instructions may be repeated at any time, but the subject should never be told the principle. The examiner should be alert to notice what parts of the instructions need repetition. Children frequently need to be reminded to try to figure out the reason for their choices, rather than to make only haphazard guesses. When a subject has difficulty with the test, he or she should be asked to describe stimulus figures before responding, to recall what items had been presented previously, to watch how the pictures change from one to the next, and to try to figure out the reason why one system or another might be correct.

"Now we are going to start the third group. This group may be different from the one you just finished, or it may be the same. Let's see if you can figure out the right answers."

Proceed with the fourth subtest, using the same type of introductory comments as with the third subtest. Before beginning the fifth subtest, say: "Now we are going to start the last group. This group will test your memory since it is made up of pictures that you have already seen. Try to remember what the right answer was the first time you saw the picture and give the same answer again." Do not hesitate to comment favorably at any time during the test when the subject answers correctly.

Approximate Time for Administration

Standard versions require about 30–40 minutes. Abbreviated versions take about 20 minutes.

Scoring

Record the total number of errors. For sample scoring sheets, see Figures 3–1 to 3–4.

COMMENT

The odd–even split-half method and coefficient alpha have been used to calculate internal consistency values for the standard version of the Category Test. High (above .95) reliability coefficients are obtained for samples of normal and brain-damaged adults (Charter et al., 1987; Moses, 1985; Shaw, 1966). When severely impaired neurological patients are considered, the Category Test has high (above .90) retest reliability, even after intervals of two years (Goldstein & Watson, 1989; Matarazzo et al., 1974). In the case of schizophrenics, correlation coefficients are somewhat lower and range from .63 to .72 (Goldstein & Watson, 1989; Matarazzo et al., 1974). With moderately impaired neurological patients, significant changes or practice effects emerge (Dodrill & Troupin, 1975).

The Category Test shares a high loading with the Performance subtests (Block Design, Object Assembly) of the Wechsler Intelligence Scales (Klonoff, 1971; Lansdell & Donnelly, 1977). Thus, it does not distinguish an ability that is separate from nonverbal intelligence (Lansdell & Donnelly, 1977). It is almost as sensitive as the full Halstead–Reitan battery in determining the presence or absence of

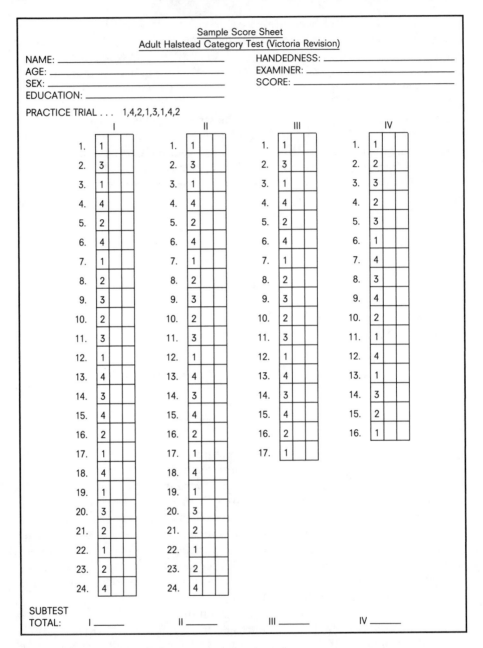

Figure 3–1. Adult Halstead Category Test (Victoria Revision) sample scoring sheet.

Sample Score Sheet
Halstead Category Test (Adult Standard Form)

NAME: _____   Date: _____

Examiner: _____   Score: _____

	I	II	III	IV	V	VI	VII
1.	1	1	1	1	1	1	1
2.	3	3	3	3	3	3	3
3.	1	1	1	1	1	1	1
4.	4	4	4	4	4	4	4
5.	2	2	2	2	2	2	2
6.	4	4	4	4	4	4	4
7.	1	1	1	1	1	1	1
8.	2	2	2	2	3	2	2
9.	E−	3	3	3	3	3	3
10.		2	2	2	2	2	2
11.		3	3	3	3	3	3
12.		1	1	1	1	1	1
13.		4	4	4	4	4	4
14.		3	3	3	3	3	3
15.		4	4	4	4	4	4
16.		2	2	2	2	2	2
17.		1	1	1	1	1	1
18.		4	4	4	4	4	4
19.		1	1	1	1	1	1
20.		3	3	3	3	3	3
21.		E−	2	2	2	2	END OF REG. TEST
22.			1	1	1	1	1
23.			2	2	2	2	2 EXTRA
24.			4	4	4	4	4 ITEMS
25.			3	3	3	3	3
26.			2	2	2	2	2
27.			4	4	4	4	
28.			3	3	3	3	
29.			1	1	1	1	
30.			4	4	4	4	
31.			2	2	2	2	
32.			1	1	1	1	
33.			3	3	3	3	
34.			1	1	1	1	
35.			3	3	3	3	
36.			2	2	2	2	
37.			4	4	4	4	
38.			3	3	3	3	
39.			4	4	4	4	
40.			2	2	2	2	
			E−	E−	E−	E−	

Figure 3–2. Halstead Category Test (Adult Form) sample scoring sheet.

Sample Score Sheet
Halstead Category Test (Intermediate Form)

Name: _____   Date: _____
Examiner: _____   Score: _____

	I	II	III	IV	V	VI
1.	1	1	1	1	1	1
2.	3	3	3	3	3	3
3.	1	1	1	1	1	1
4.	4	4	4	4	4	4
5.	2	2	2	2	2	2
6.	4	4	4	4	4	4
7.	1	1	1	1	1	1
8.	2	2	2	2	2	2
9.	E=	3	3	3	3	3
10.		2	2	2	2	2
11.		3	3	3	3	3
12.		1	1	1	1	1
13.		4	4	4	4	4
14.		3	3	3	3	3
15.		4	4	4	4	4
16.		2	2	2	2	2
17.		1	1	1	1	1
18.		4	4	4	4	4
19.		1	1	1	1	1
20.		3	3	3	3	3
21.		E=	2	2	2	E=
22.			1	1	1	
23.			2	2	2	
24.			4	4	4	
25.			3	3	3	
26.			2	2	2	
27.			4	4	4	
28.			3	3	3	
29.			1	1	1	
30.			4	4	4	
31.			2	2	2	
32.			1	1	1	
33.			3	3	3	
34.			1	1	1	
35.			3	3	3	
36.			2	2	2	
37.			4	4	4	
38.			3	3	3	
39.			4	4	4	
40.			2	2	2	
			E=	E=	E=	

Figure 3–3. Halstead Category Test (Intermediate Form) sample scoring sheet.

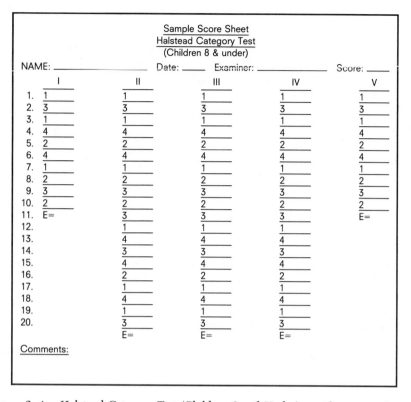

Figure 3–4. Halstead Category Test (Children 8 and Under) sample scoring sheet.

neurological damage (Adams & Trenton, 1981). However, impairment on the Category Test is not related to specific location or laterality of brain damage (Bornstein, 1986; Klove, 1974; Lansdell & Donnelly, 1977; Pendleton & Heaton, 1982), although it was originally designed to detect frontal lobe damage (Halstead, 1947).

Both the Category test and Wisconsin Card Sort Test (WCST) require, in part, the deduction of a classification principle by means of response-contingent feedback, the use of the principle while it remains effective, and the ability to abandon the principle when it is no longer effective. The two tests are not identical, however (Bond & Buchtel, 1984; King & Snow, 1981; Pendleton & Heaton, 1982). Bond and Buchtel (1984) have pointed out that the perceptual abstraction abilities that are required for the Category Test are more difficult than those required by the WCST. On the other hand, the WCST requires the subject to realize that the correct matching principle shifts periodically without warning. The Category Test makes no such demand. The WCST also provides a measure of perseverative tendencies, whereas the Category test does not do so. Additionally, the WCST has been found to be more sensitive to lesions involving the frontal lobes (Heaton, 1981; Milner, 1963), whereas the Category Test is presumably sensitive to cerebral lesions regardless of their location (Pendleton & Heaton, 1982; Reitan, 1955, 1979). The use of one or both of these tests depends on the diagnostic question. For example, if the examiner wishes to examine for perseverative tendencies, then the WCST should be chosen. On the other hand, if the examiner wishes a more difficult and sensitive measure of abstraction ability, then the Category Test is the preferred measure. The use of both tests in a comprehensive battery is desirable since it would sample a broader range of the patient's abilities and increase diagnostic efficiency. In this case, the WCST should precede the Category Test to reduce order effects (Brandon & Chavez, 1985).

Normative Data

Reitan recommends the cutoff error score of 50–51 for adults. This value appears to be appropriate for subjects under 40 years old (Fromm-Auch & Yeudall, 1983) and for people of at least average intelligence (Dodrill, 1987). For the Victoria Revision, a cutoff of 26 appears to be optimal (Labreche, 1983; Sherrill, 1987). Spreen (1988) reported scores of 19.6 (SD = 12.7) for 52 normal young adults, and of 30.2 (SD = 14.3) for 113 young adults with neurological findings and learning disability. Ranges of scores for varying degrees of impairment have been defined for both the long (Reitan & Wolfson, 1988) and Short (Sherrill, 1987) forms (Table 3–3).

Table 3–3. Severity Ranges for the Long and Short Forms of the Adult Category Test (Errors)

	Perfectly normal	Normal	Mildly impaired	Severely impaired
HCT	0–25	26–45	46–64	65+
Victoria Rev. [a]	0–11	12–22	23–33	34+

[a]Subtest II not scored.

Sources: [HCT] Reitan & Wolfson (1988); [Vict. Rev.] Sherrill (1987).

Table 3–4. Mean Number of Errors for Adult HCT (208 Items) by Age and Education

	Age			Education (years)		
	<40	40–59	60+	<12	12–15	16+
N	319	134	100	132	249	172
Mean	29.3	42.6	66.4	53.8	38.6	28.9

Note: Data are based on 553 normal individuals (396 men, 197 women) seen at three neuropsychology laboratories. Overall mean for the sample = 39.2 (SD = 25.3); age range = 15–81 (mean = 39.3; SD = 17.5); average years of education, 13.3 years.

Source: Heaton et al. (1986).

Table 3–5. Category Test (Error Score) Correction for Age and Education

Age	0	1	2	3	4	5	6	7	8	9	10	11	12	13	14	15	16	17	18	19	20	Age
															Education							
25	−13.	−11.	−8.	−6.	−3.	−1.	2.	4.	6.	9.	11.	14.	16.	18.	21.	23.	26.	28.	31.	33.	35.	25
26	−14.	−11.	−9.	−6.	−4.	−2.	1.	3.	6.	8.	11.	13.	15.	18.	20.	23.	25.	27.	30.	32.	35.	26
27	−14.	−12.	−9.	−7.	−5.	−2.	0.	3.	5.	7.	10.	12.	15.	17.	20.	22.	24.	27.	29.	32.	34.	27
28	−15.	−13.	−10.	−8.	−5.	−3.	−0.	2.	4.	7.	9.	12.	14.	16.	19.	21.	24.	26.	29.	31.	33.	28
29	−16.	−13.	−11.	−8.	−6.	−4.	−1.	1.	4.	6.	9.	11.	13.	16.	18.	21.	23.	25.	28.	30.	33.	29
30	−16.	−14.	−12.	−9.	−7.	−4.	−2.	1.	3.	5.	8.	10.	13.	15.	18.	20.	22.	25.	27.	30.	32.	30
31	−17.	−15.	−12.	−10.	−7.	−5.	−2.	−0.	2.	5.	7.	10.	12.	14.	17.	19.	22.	24.	27.	29.	31.	31
32	−18.	−15.	−13.	−10.	−8.	−6.	−3.	−1.	2.	4.	7.	9.	11.	14.	16.	19.	21.	23.	26.	28.	31.	32
33	−18.	−16.	−14.	−11.	−9.	−6.	−4.	−1.	1.	3.	6.	8.	11.	13.	16.	18.	20.	23.	25.	28.	30.	33
34	−19.	−17.	−14.	−12.	−9.	−7.	−5.	−2.	0.	3.	5.	8.	10.	12.	15.	17.	20.	22.	25.	27.	29.	34
35	−20.	−17.	−15.	−12.	−10.	−8.	−5.	−3.	−0.	2.	4.	7.	9.	12.	14.	17.	19.	21.	24.	26.	29.	35
36	−20.	−18.	−16.	−13.	−11.	−8.	−6.	−3.	−1.	1.	4.	6.	9.	11.	14.	16.	18.	21.	23.	26.	28.	36
37	−21.	−19.	−16.	−14.	−11.	−9.	−7.	−4.	−2.	1.	3.	6.	8.	10.	13.	15.	18.	20.	23.	25.	27.	37
38	−22.	−19.	−17.	−14.	−12.	−10.	−7.	−5.	−2.	0.	2.	5.	7.	10.	12.	15.	17.	19.	22.	24.	27.	38
39	−22.	−20.	−18.	−15.	−13.	−10.	−8.	−5.	−3.	−1.	2.	4.	7.	9.	11.	14.	16.	19.	21.	24.	26.	39
40	−23.	−21.	−18.	−16.	−13.	−11.	−9.	−6.	−4.	−1.	1.	4.	6.	8.	11.	13.	16.	18.	21.	23.	26.	40
41	−24.	−21.	−19.	−16.	−14.	−12.	−9.	−7.	−4.	−1.	0.	3.	5.	8.	10.	13.	15.	17.	20.	22.	25.	41
42	−24.	−22.	−20.	−17.	−15.	−12.	−10.	−7.	−5.	−2.	−0.	2.	5.	7.	9.	12.	14.	17.	19.	22.	25.	42
43	−25.	−23.	−20.	−18.	−15.	−13.	−11.	−8.	−6.	−3.	−1.	2.	4.	6.	9.	11.	14.	16.	18.	21.	24.	43
44	−26.	−23.	−21.	−18.	−16.	−14.	−11.	−9.	−6.	−3.	−2.	1.	3.	6.	8.	11.	13.	15.	18.	20.	23.	44
45	−26.	−24.	−22.	−19.	−17.	−14.	−12.	−9.	−7.	−4.	−2.	0.	3.	5.	7.	10.	12.	15.	17.	20.	22.	45
46	−27.	−25.	−22.	−20.	−17.	−15.	−13.	−10.	−8.	−5.	−3.	−0.	2.	4.	7.	9.	12.	14.	16.	19.	21.	46
47	−28.	−25.	−23.	−20.	−18.	−16.	−13.	−11.	−8.	−6.	−4.	−1.	1.	4.	6.	9.	11.	13.	16.	18.	21.	47
48	−28.	−26.	−24.	−21.	−18.	−16.	−14.	−11.	−9.	−7.	−4.	−2.	1.	3.	5.	8.	10.	13.	15.	18.	20.	48
49	−29.	−27.	−24.	−22.	−19.	−17.	−15.	−12.	−10.	−7.	−5.	−2.	−0.	2.	5.	7.	10.	12.	14.	17.	19.	49
50	−30.	−27.	−25.	−23.	−20.	−18.	−15.	−12.	−10.	−8.	−6.	−3.	−1.	2.	4.	7.	9.	11.	14.	16.	19.	50

(continued)

Table 3–5. (Continued)

Age	Education																					Age
	0	1	2	3	4	5	6	7	8	9	10	11	12	13	14	15	16	17	18	19	20	
51	−30.	−28.	−26.	−23.	−21.	−18.	−16.	−13.	−11.	−9.	−6.	−4.	−1.	1.	3.	6.	8.	11.	13.	16.	18.	51
52	−31.	−29.	−26.	−24.	−21.	−19.	−17.	−14.	−12.	−9.	−7.	−5.	−2.	0.	3.	5.	8.	10.	12.	15.	17.	52
53	−32.	−29.	−27.	−25.	−22.	−20.	−17.	−14.	−12.	−10.	−8.	−5.	−3.	−0.	2.	5.	7.	9.	12.	14.	17.	53
54	−32.	−30.	−28.	−25.	−23.	−20.	−18.	−15.	−13.	−11.	−8.	−6.	−3.	−1.	1.	4.	6.	9.	11.	14.	16.	54
55	−33.	−31.	−28.	−26.	−23.	−21.	−19.	−16.	−14.	−11.	−9.	−7.	−4.	−2.	1.	3.	6.	8.	10.	13.	15.	55
56	−34.	−31.	−29.	−27.	−24.	−22.	−19.	−16.	−14.	−12.	−10.	−7.	−5.	−2.	0.	2.	5.	7.	10.	12.	15.	56
57	−34.	−32.	−30.	−27.	−25.	−22.	−20.	−17.	−15.	−13.	−10.	−8.	−5.	−3.	−1.	2.	4.	7.	9.	12.	14.	57
58	−35.	−33.	−30.	−28.	−25.	−23.	−21.	−18.	−16.	−13.	−11.	−8.	−6.	−4.	−1.	1.	4.	6.	8.	11.	13.	58
59	−36.	−33.	−31.	−29.	−26.	−24.	−21.	−18.	−16.	−14.	−12.	−9.	−7.	−4.	−2.	0.	3.	5.	8.	10.	13.	59
60	−37.	−34.	−32.	−29.	−27.	−24.	−22.	−19.	−17.	−15.	−12.	−9.	−7.	−5.	−3.	−0.	2.	5.	7.	10.	12.	60
61	−37.	−35.	−32.	−30.	−27.	−25.	−23.	−20.	−18.	−15.	−13.	−10.	−8.	−6.	−3.	−1.	2.	4.	6.	9.	11.	61
62	−38.	−35.	−33.	−31.	−28.	−26.	−23.	−20.	−18.	−16.	−14.	−11.	−9.	−6.	−4.	−2.	1.	3.	6.	8.	11.	62
63	−39.	−36.	−34.	−31.	−29.	−26.	−24.	−21.	−19.	−17.	−14.	−12.	−9.	−7.	−5.	−2.	0.	3.	5.	7.	10.	63
64	−39.	−37.	−34.	−32.	−30.	−27.	−25.	−22.	−20.	−17.	−15.	−13.	−10.	−8.	−5.	−3.	−0.	2.	4.	7.	9.	64
65	−40.	−37.	−35.	−33.	−30.	−28.	−25.	−22.	−21.	−18.	−16.	−13.	−11.	−8.	−6.	−4.	−1.	1.	4.	6.	9.	65
66	−41.	−38.	−36.	−33.	−31.	−28.	−26.	−23.	−21.	−19.	−16.	−14.	−11.	−9.	−7.	−4.	−2.	1.	3.	5.	8.	66
67	−41.	−39.	−36.	−34.	−32.	−29.	−27.	−24.	−22.	−19.	−17.	−15.	−12.	−10.	−7.	−5.	−2.	−0.	2.	5.	7.	67
68	−42.	−39.	−37.	−35.	−32.	−30.	−27.	−24.	−23.	−20.	−18.	−15.	−13.	−10.	−8.	−6.	−3.	−1.	2.	4.	7.	68
69	−43.	−40.	−38.	−35.	−33.	−30.	−28.	−25.	−23.	−21.	−18.	−16.	−14.	−11.	−9.	−6.	−4.	−1.	1.	3.	6.	69
70	−43.	−41.	−38.	−36.	−34.	−31.	−29.	−26.	−24.	−21.	−19.	−17.	−14.	−12.	−9.	−7.	−4.	−2.	0.	3.	5.	70
71	−44.	−41.	−39.	−37.	−34.	−32.	−29.	−26.	−25.	−22.	−20.	−17.	−15.	−12.	−10.	−8.	−5.	−3.	−0.	2.	5.	71
72	−45.	−42.	−40.	−37.	−35.	−32.	−30.	−27.	−25.	−23.	−20.	−18.	−15.	−13.	−11.	−8.	−6.	−3.	−1.	1.	4.	72
73	−45.	−43.	−40.	−38.	−36.	−33.	−31.	−28.	−26.	−23.	−21.	−19.	−16.	−14.	−11.	−9.	−7.	−4.	−2.	1.	3.	73
74	−46.	−43.	−41.	−39.	−36.	−34.	−31.	−28.	−27.	−24.	−22.	−19.	−17.	−14.	−12.	−10.	−7.	−5.	−2.	0.	3.	74
75	−47.	−44.	−42.	−39.	−37.	−34.	−32.	−29.	−27.	−25.	−22.	−20.	−18.	−15.	−13.	−10.	−8.	−5.	−3.	−1.	2.	75
76	−47.	−45.	−42.	−40.	−38.	−35.	−33.	−30.	−28.	−25.	−23.	−21.	−18.	−16.	−13.	−11.	−9.	−6.	−4.	−1.	1.	76
77	−48.	−46.	−43.	−41.	−38.	−36.	−33.	−31.	−29.	−26.	−24.	−21.	−19.	−16.	−14.	−12.	−9.	−7.	−4.	−2.	0.	77
78	−49.	−46.	−44.	−41.	−39.	−37.	−34.	−32.	−29.	−27.	−24.	−22.	−20.	−17.	−15.	−12.	−10.	−7.	−5.	−3.	−0.	78

Source: Alekoumbides et al. (1987).

Table 3–6. Corrected and Standard Scores for the Category Test

A	B	A	B	A	B	A	B
156.	40.	110.	70.	64.	99.	16.	130.
155.	41.	109.	70.	63.	100.	15.	131.
154.	41.	108.	71.	62.	100.	14.	131.
153.	42.	107.	71.	61.	101.	13.	132.
152.	43.	106.	72.	60.	102.	12.	132.
151.	43.	105.	73.	59.	102.	11.	133.
150.	44.	104.	73.	58.	103.	10.	134.
149.	45.	103.	74.	57.	104.	9.	134.
148.	45.	102.	75.	56.	104.	8.	135.
147.	46.	101.	75.	55.	105.	7.	136.
146.	46.	100.	76.	54.	106.	6.	136.
145.	47.	99.	77.	53.	106.	5.	137.
144.	48.	98.	77.	52.	107.	4.	138.
143.	48.	97.	78.	51.	107.	3.	138.
142.	49.	96.	79.	50.	108.	2.	139.
141.	50.	95.	79.	49.	109.	1.	140.
140.	50.	94.	80.	48.	109.	0.	140.
139.	51.	93.	80.	47.	110.	−1.	141.
138.	52.	92.	81.	46.	111.	−2.	141.
137.	52.	91.	82.	45.	111.	−3.	142.
136.	53.	90.	82.	44.	112.	−4.	143.
135.	54.	89.	83.	43.	113.	−5.	143.
134.	54.	88.	84.	42.	113.	−6.	144.
133.	55.	87.	84.	41.	114.	−7.	145.
132.	55.	86.	85.	40.	115.	−8.	145.
131.	56.	85.	86.	39.	115.	−9.	146.
130.	57.	84.	86.	38.	116.	−10.	147.
129.	57.	83.	87.	37.	116.	−11.	147.
128.	58.	82.	88.	36.	117.	−12.	148.
127.	59.	81.	88.	35.	118.	−13.	149.
126.	59.	80.	89.	34.	118.	−14.	149.
125.	60.	79.	89.	33.	119.	−15.	150.
124.	61.	78.	90.	32.	120.	−16.	150.
123.	61.	77.	91.	31.	120.	−17.	151.
122.	62.	76.	91.	30.	121.	−18.	152.
121.	63.	75.	92.	29.	122.	−19.	152.
120.	63.	74.	93.	28.	122.	−20.	153.
119.	64.	73.	93.	27.	123.	−21.	154.
118.	64.	72.	94.	26.	124.	−22.	154.
117.	65.	71.	95.	25.	124.	−23.	155.
116.	66.	70.	95.	24.	125.	−24.	156.
115.	66.	69.	96.	23.	125.	−25.	156.
114.	67.	68.	97.	22.	126.	−26.	157.
113.	68.	67.	97.	21.	127.	−27.	158.
112.	68.	66.	98.	20.	127.	−28.	158.
111.	69.	65.	98.	19.	128.	−29.	159.
				18.	129.	−30.	159.
				17.	129.	−31.	160.

Note: A = corrected; B = standard.

Source: Alekoumbides et al. (1987).

Both age and intellectual level contribute to performance on the Category Test (Dodrill, 1987; Ernst, 1987; Leckliter & Matarazzo, 1989; Prigatano & Parsons, 1976; Seidenberg et al., 1983). Not surprisingly, performance on this measure of complex problem-solving ability is adversely affected by advancing age and lower intellectual levels. It is important to note that the norms shown in Table 3–3 for adults are derived from relatively young samples with average intellectual abilities. Use of these scores in subjects above age 40 and in those with lower than average intellectual abilities can result in erroneous diagnostic conclusions. Some normative data (means only, not standard deviations) for the standard 208-item version are available for older subjects (Heaton et al., 1986). These data are shown in Table 3–4. Alekoumbides et al. (1987) have constructed a table to correct scores on the standard version for age and education. Table 3–5 contains the numbers to be added to or subtracted from the raw score in order to obtain the corrected score. The corrected score can then be converted to a standardized score (mean = 100, SD = 15) by means of Table 3–6. The corrected scores are listed in column A and the standardized scores are in column B of the table.

A number of investigators have compiled norms for the Intermediate version. Data from Trites (1977) should probably be avoided since they were collected from referrals to a neuropsychology clinic for assessment. Both Knights (1966) and Spreen and Gaddes (1969) give data for the Intermediate version for normal school children. In the Knights (1966) report, the sample sizes at all age levels are very small. The norms provided by Spreen and Gaddes (1969), shown in Table 3–7, are more adequate in terms of sample size.

Knights (1966) also provides norms for children aged 5–8 years, based on a population of normal school children. However, the sample sizes at all age levels are very small. The normative data provided by Klonoff and Low (1974) are better since the sample sizes are larger. These data are given in Table 3–8.

Table 3–7. Total Mean Number of Errors for the Intermediate HCT (168 Items)

Age	N	Mean	SD	Range
9	22	59.5	17.7	19–93
10	56	50.0	16.9	15–84
11	50	43.3	18.5	10–79
12	72	36.2	16.5	9–89
13	52	34.6	17.2	7–84
14	43	31.3	11.1	12–53
15	41	30.6	12.3	13–61

Note: Norms are based on a population of normal school children.

Source: Spreen & Gaddes (1969).

Table 3–8. Total Mean Number of Errors for the Children's HCT (80 Items)

Age	N	Mean	SD
2–5	154	38.66	11.10
6	54	22.76	11.16
7	60	18.94	10.80
8	65	13.09	6.39

Note: Norms are based on a population of normal school children referred to pediatricians.

Source: Klonoff & Low (1974).

REFERENCES

Adams, R.L., & Trenton, S.L. (1981). Development of a paper- and -pen form of the Halstead Category Test. *Journal of Consulting and Clinical Psychology, 49,* 298–299.

Alekoumbides, A., Charter, R.A., Adkins, T.G., & Seacat, G.F. (1987). The diagnosis of brain damage by the WAIS, WMS, and Reitan battery utilizing standardized scores corrected for age and education. *International Journal of Clinical Neuropsychology, 9,* 11–28.

Bond, J.A., & Buchtel, H.A. (1984). Comparison of the Wisconsin Card Sorting Test and the Halstead Category Test. *Journal of Clinical Psychology, 40,* 1251–1254.

Bornstein, R.A. (1986). Contribution of various neuropsychological measures to detection of frontal lobe impairment. *International Journal of Clinical Neuropsychology, 8,* 18–22.

Boyle, G.L. (1986). Clinical neuropsychological assessment: Abbreviating the Halstead Category Test of brain dysfunction. *Journal of Clinical Psychology, 42,* 615–625.

Brandon, A.D., & Chavez, E.L. (1985). Order and delay effects on neuropsychological test presentation: The Halstead Category and Wisconsin Card Sorting Tests. *International Journal of Clinical Neuropsychology, 7,* 152–153.

Caslyn, D.A., O'Leary, M.R., & Chaney, E.F. (1980). Shortening the Category Test. *Journal of Consulting and Clinical Psychology, 48,* 788–789.

Charter, R.A., Adkins, T.G., Alekoumbides, A., & Seacat, G.F. (1987). Reliability of the WAIS, WMS, and Reitan Battery: Raw scores and standardization scores corrected for age and education. *International Journal of Clinical Neuropsychology, 9,* 28–32.

Dodrill, C.B. (1987). What's normal? Paper presented to the Pacific Northwest Neuropsychological Association, Seattle.

Dodrill, C.B., & Troupin, A.S. (1975). Effects of repeated administrations of a comprehensive neuropsychological battery among chronic epileptics. *Journal of Nervous and Mental Disease, 161,* 185–190.

Ernst, J. (1987). Neuropsychological problem-solving skills in the elderly. *Psychology of Aging, 2,* 363–365.

Fromm-Auch, D., & Yeudall, L.T. (1983). Normative data for the Halstead–Reitan Neuropsychological Test. *Journal of Clinical Neuropsychology, 3,* 221–238.

Goldstein, G., & Watson, J.R. (1989). Test–retest reliability of the Halstead–Reitan battery and the WAIS in a neuropsychiatric population. *Clinical Neuropsychologist, 3,* 265–273.

Gregory, R.J., Paul, J.J., & Morrison, M.W. (1979). A short form of the Category Test for adults. *Journal of Clinical Psychology, 35,* 795–798.

Halstead, W.C. (1947). *Brain and Intelligence.* Chicago: University of Chicago Press.

Heaton, R.K. (1981). *A manual for the Wisconsin Card Sorting Test.* Odessa, Fla.: Psychological Assessment Resources.

Heaton, R.K., Grant, I., & Mathews, C.G. (1986). Differences in neuropsychological test performance associated with age, education, and sex. In I. Grant & K.M. Adams (Eds.), *Neuropsychological Assessment in Neuropsychiatric Disorders* (pp. 100–120). New York: Oxford University Press.

King, M.C., & Snow, W.G. (1981). Problem-solving task performance in brain-damaged subjects. *Journal of Clinical Psychology, 38,* 400–404.

Klonoff, H. (1971). Factor analysis of a neuropsychological battery for children aged 9 to 15. *Perceptual and Motor Skills, 32,* 603–616.

Klonoff, H., & Low, M. (1974). Disordered brain function in young children and early adolescents: Neuropsychological and electroencephalographic correlates. In R. Reitan & L.A. Davidson (Eds.), *Clinical Neuropsychology: Current Status and Applications.* Washington, D.C.: V.H. Winston.

Klove, H. (1974). Validation studies in adult clinical neuropsychology. In R. Reitan & L. Davison (Eds.), *Clinical Neuropsychology: Current Status and Application.* New York: John Wiley.

Knights, R.M. (1966). Normative data on tests for evaluating brain damage in children from 5 to 14 years of age. *Research Bulletin No. 20,* Department of Psychology, University of Western Ontario, London, Canada.

Labreche, T.M. (1983). The Victoria Revision of the Halstead Category Test. Unpublished doctoral dissertation, University of Victoria, British Columbia, Canada.

Lansdell, H., & Donnelly, E.F. (1977). Factor analysis of the Wechsler Adult Intelligence Scale and the Halstead–Reitan Category and Tapping tests. *Journal of Consulting and Clinical Psychology, 3,* 412–416.

Leckliter, I.N. & Matarazzo (1989). The influence of age, education, IQ, gender, and alcohol abuse on Halstead-Reitan test battery performance. *Journal of Clinical Psychology, 45,* 484–512.

Matarazzo, J.D., Wiens, A.N., Matarazzo, R.G., & Goldstein, S.G. (1974). Psychometric and test–retest reliability of the Halstead impairment index in a sample

of healthy, young, normal men. *Journal of Nervous and Mental Disease, 158,* 37–49.

Milner, B. (1963). Effects of different brain lesions on card sorting. *Archives of Neurology, 9,* 90–100.

Moses, J.A. (1985). Internal consistency of standard and short forms of three itemized Halstead–Reitan Neuropsychological Battery Tests. *International Journal of Clinical Neuropsychology, 3,* 164–166.

Pendleton, M.G., & Heaton, R.K. (1982). A comparison of the Wisconsin Card Sorting Test and the Category Test. *Journal of Clinical Psychology, 38,* 392–396.

Prigatano, G.P., & Parsons, O.A. (1976). Relationship of age and education to Halstead test performance in different populations. *Journal of Clinical and Consulting Psychology, 44,* 527–533.

Reed, H.B.C., Reitan, R.M., & Klove, H. (1965). Influence of cerebral lesions on psychological test performances of older children. *Journal of Consulting Psychology, 29,* 247–251.

Reitan, R.M. (1955). An investigation of the validity of Halstead's measures of biological intelligence. *Archives of Neurology and Psychiatry, 42,* 615–625.

Reitan, R.M. (1979). *Manual for the Administration of Neuropsychological Test Batteries for Adults and Children.* Indianapolis: Author.

Reitan, R.M., & Davison, L.A. (1974). *Clinical Neuropsychology: Current Status and Applications.* Washington, D.C.: H.V. Winston.

Reitan, R.M., & Wolfson, D. (1988). *Traumatic Brain Injury, Volume II. Recovery and Rehabilitation.* Tucson: Neuropsychology Press.

Russell, E.W., & Levy, M. (1987). Revision of the Halstead Category Test. *Journal of Consulting and Clinical Psychology, 55,* 898–901.

Seidenberg, M., Giordani, B., Berent, S., & Boll, T.J. (1983), IQ level and performance on the Halstead–Reitan Neuropsychological Test Battery for older children. *Journal of Consulting and Clinical Psychology, 51,* 406–413.

Shaw, D.J. (1966). The reliability and validity

of the Halstead Category Test. *Journal of Clinical Psychology, 37,* 847–848.

Sherrill, R.E., Jr. (1985). Comparison of three short forms of the Category Test. *Journal of Clinical and Experimental Neuropsychology, 7,* 231–238.

Sherrill, R.E., Jr. (1987). Options for shortening Halstead's Category Test for adults. *Archives of Clinical Neuropsychology 2,* 343–352.

Spreen, O. (1988). *Learning Disabled Children Growing Up.* New York: Oxford University Press.

Spreen, O., & Gaddes, W.H. (1969). Developmental norms for 15 neuropsychological tests age 6 to 15. *Cortex, 5,* 170–191.

Trites, R.L. (1977). *Neuropsychological Test Manual.* Ottawa, Ont.: Royal Ottawa Hospital.

MATTIS DEMENTIA RATING SCALE (MDRS)

Purpose

The purpose of this scale is to provide an index of cognitive function in subjects with known or suspected dementia.

Source

The test can be ordered as a kit including manual, stimulus cards, and 25 scoring forms from Psychological Assessment Resources, Inc., P.O. Box 998, Odessa, Florida, at a cost of $45 U.S.

Description

Some patients, such as the elderly with profound cognitive impairments, may generate very few responses on such standard tests as the Wechsler Adult Intelligence Scale – Revised (WAIS-R) or Wechsler Memory Scale (WMS), making it difficult to rank them according to the magnitude of their mental impairments. The Mattis Dementia Rating Scale (MDRS) was developed to quantify the mental status of such patients (Coblentz et al., 1973; Mattis, 1976). Items are similar to those employed by neurologists in bedside mental status examinations. They are arranged hierarchically so that adequate performance on an initial item allows the examiner to discontinue testing within that section and assume that credit can be given to the patient for adequate performance on the subsequent tasks. The subtests include measures of attention (e.g., digit span), initiation and perseveration (e.g., performing alternating movements), construction (e.g., copying designs), conceptualization (e.g., similarities), and verbal and nonverbal short-term memory (e.g., sentence recall, design recognition).

Administration

See source. Briefly, the examiner asks questions or gives instructions in each area (e.g., "In what way are an apple and a banana alike?" "The same?") and records responses.

Approximate Time for Administration

The time required is approximately 10–15 minutes for normal elderly subjects. With a demented patient, administration may take 30–45 minutes to complete.

Scoring

See source. One point is given for each item performed correctly. Maximum score = 144.

Comment

When patients with a provisional diagnosis of Alzheimers are retested following a one-week interval, correlations are high (above .90) (Coblentz et al., 1973). Split-half reliability is also high (.90), indicating that the MDRS is very consistent internally (Gardner et al., 1981).

With regard to validity, the test can clearly differentiate brain-damaged patients from normal elderly subjects, but its sensitivity to early stages of dementia remains to be determined (Montgomery, 1982). Further studies are also needed with regard to predictions of mortality, independence in daily living, and prognosis for rehabilitation (Gardner et al., 1981).

Unfortunately, administration procedures are not clearly described, and the scoring criteria are imprecise. One should not focus on the summary score, except as a general indicator of degree of dementia; rather, the emphasis should be on the subtests. It is also important to note that the test is a screening device, and the clinician should follow up with more in-depth investigation.

Normative Data

Mattis (cited in Mattis, 1976; Montgomery, 1982) recommends a cutoff of 137 and indicates that a score under 100 implies that survival is doubtful over the next 20 months. However, these data are of limited value since the sample sizes on which

Table 3–9. Mean Scores on the Mattis Dementia Rating Scale for Subjects Ages 65–89 Years

	Mean	SD
Total score	137.28	6.94
Attention	35.47	1.59
Initiation & Perseveration	35.50	3.02
Construction	5.80	0.61
Conceptualization	37.25	2.58
Memory	23.28	2.12

Note: Data are derived from a well-educated group (average, 12.4 years) of healthy volunteers.

Source: Montgomery (1982).

the scores are based (Coblentz et al., 1973) are extremely small (i.e., 20 brain-damaged subjects, 11 normals).

Montgomery (1982) compiled data on 85 normal volunteers (60 women, 25 men), ranging in age from 65 to 89 (mean = 74.04), with an average educational level of 12.4 years and a mean scaled score of 13.5 on the Vocabulary subtest of the WAIS. The data for the MDRS as a whole and for the individual subsections are shown in Table 3–9. Her data would suggest a cutoff of 123 (based upon the mean ± 2 SD). Montgomery's sample is not truly representative of the elderly population since her sample is better educated, of higher socioeconomic status, and probably healthier than most elderly. Moreover, sample sizes for all age groups, especially those above age 80, are small. Consequently, one must be cautious in interpreting low scores of people with more advanced age, reduced education, and low verbal ability.

REFERENCES

Coblentz, J.M., Mattis, S., Zingesser, L.H., Kasoff, S.S., Wisniewski, H.M., & Katzman, R. (1973). Presenile dementia. *Archives of Neurology, 29*, 299–308.

Gardner, R., Oliver-Munoz, S., Fisher, L., & Empting, L. (1981). Mattis Dementia Rating Scale: Internal reliability study using a diffusely impaired population. *Journal of Clinical Neuropsychology, 3*, 271–275.

Mattis, S. (1976). Mental status examination for organic mental syndrome in the elderly patient. In L. Bellak & T.B. Karasu (Eds.), *Geriatric Psychiatry.* New York: Grune & Stratton.

Montgomery, K.M. (1982). A Normative Study of Neuropsychological Test Performance of a Normal Elderly Sample. Unpublished Master's thesis. University of Victoria, British Columbia, Canada.

NORTH AMERICAN ADULT READING TEST (NAART)
Other Test Name

The North American Adult Reading Test (NAART) is also known as the NART-R.

Purpose

The purpose of the NAART is to provide an estimate of premorbid intellectual ability.

Source

There is no commercial source. Users may refer to the following text in order to design their own material.

Description

There are a number of clinical, medicolegal, or research situations where knowledge of premorbid IQ is essential. Since premorbid test data are rarely available, methods of estimation are needed. The National Adult Reading Test, or NART (Nelson, 1982; Nelson & O'Connell, 1978), a reading test for irregularly spelled words, has promise as an assessment tool for the determination of premorbid intellectual function. Blair and Spreen (1989) have modified the test for use with North American populations and validated it against the WAIS-R. The test consists of a list of 61 words printed in two columns on both sides of an $8\frac{1}{2}'' \times 11''$ card which is given to the subject to read. The examiner records errors on a scoring sheet. A sample scoring sheet along with the correct pronunciations is given in Figure 3–5.

Administration

The following instructions are given: **"I want you to read slowly down this list of words starting here** [indicate 'debt'], **and continuing down this column and on to the next. When you have finished reading the words on the page, turn the page over and begin here** [indicate top of second page]. **After each word, please wait until I say 'next' before you read the next word. I must warn you that there are many words that you probably won't recognize. In fact,** *most* **people don't know them, so just guess at these. O.K.? Go ahead."**

The subject should be encouraged to guess, and all responses should be reinforced ("good," "that's fine," etc.). The subject may change a response if he or she wishes to do so, but if more than one version is given, the subject must decide on a final choice. No time limit is imposed.

Approximate Time for Administration

The approximate time required is 10 minutes.

NAART
Sample Scoring Sheet

Page 1

DEBT	det	SUBPOENA	sə·pē'·nə
DEBRIS	də·brē, dā·brē', dā'·brē	PLACEBO	plə·sē'·bō
AISLE	īl	PROCREATE	prō'·krē·āt
REIGN	rān	PSALM	säm, sälm*
DEPOT	dē,·pō, de'·pō	BANAL	bə·nál', bā·nal', bān'·əl
SIMILE	sim'·ə·lē	RAREFY	rār'·ə·fī
LINGERIE	lan'·zhə·rē', lon'·zhə·rā'	GIST	jist
RECIPE	res'·ə·pē	CORPS	kor, korz
GOUGE	gauj	HORS D'OEUVRE	ȯr' dərv(r)'
HEIR	ār	SIEV	siv
SUBTLE	sət'·əl	HIATUS	hī·ā·təs
CATACOMB	kat'·ə·kōm	GAUCHE	gōsh
BOUQUET	bō·kā', bü·kā'	ZEALOT	zel'·ət
GAUGE	gāj	PARADIGM	par'·ə·dīm, par'·ə·dim
COLONEL	kərn'·əl	FACADE	fə·säd'

Page 2

CELLIST	chel'·əst	LEVIATHAN	li·vī'·ə·thən
INDICT	in·dīt'	PRELATE	prel'·ət, prēl'·āt*
DETENTE	dā·tä(n)t	QUADRUPED	kwäd'·rə·ped
IMPUGN	im·pyün'	SIDEREAL	sī·dir'·ē·al, sə·dir'·ē·al
CAPON	kā'·pən, kā'·pon	ABSTEMIOUS	ab·stē'·mē·əs
RADIX	rād'·iks	BEATIFY	bē·at'·ə·fī
AEON	ē'·ən, e'·an	GOALED	jāld
EPITOME	i·pit'·ə·mē	DEMESNE	di·mān', di·mēn'
EQUIVOCAL	i·kwiv'·ə·kəl	SYNCOPE	sing'·kə·pē, sin'·k'rrn·pē
REIFY	rā'·ə·fī, rē'·ə·fi	ENNUI	an·wē'
INDICES	in'·də·sēz	DRACHM	dram
ASSIGNATE	as'·ig·nāt'	CIDEVANT	sēd·ə·vä(n)'
TOPIARY	tō·pē·er'·ē	EPERGNE	i·pərn', ā·pərn'
CAVEAT	kav'·ē·at, kāv'·ē·at,	VIVACE	vē·väch'·ā, vē·väch'·ē
	kā·vē·at'**	TALIPES	tal'·ə·pēz
SUPERFLUOUS	sú·pėr'·flü·əs	SYNECDOCHE	sə·nek'·də·kē

Figure 3–5. North American Reading Test sample scoring sheet. Pronunciation symbols follow Webster's. Single asterisk indicates correct U.S. pronunciation only. Double asterisks indicate correct Canadian pronunciation only.

Scoring

Each incorrectly pronounced word counts as one error. Slight variations in pronunciation are acceptable when these are due to regional accents. The total number of errors is tabulated. Estimated Verbal, Performance, and Full Scale IQs (VIQ, PIQ, and FSIQs) are calculated through the utilization of the following equations:

Estimated VIQ = 128.7 − .89 (NAART errors)
Estimated PIQ = 119.4 − .42 (NAART errors)
Estimated FSIQ = 127.8 − .78 (NAART errors)

The standard errors of estimate for VIQ, PIQ, and FSIQ are 6.56, 10.67, and 7.63, respectively. For VIQ and FSIQ, a positive discrepancy of 15 or more points between estimated and actual IQ scores indicates the possibility of intellectual deterioration or impairment (based on the calculation of 95% confidence levels). For PIQ, a positive discrepancy of at least 21 points between estimated and actual IQs indicates the possibility of deterioration.

Comment

Blair and Spreen (1989) report that a measure of interscorer reliability for the NAART was .99 ($p < .001$). Coefficient alpha, a measure of internal consistency, was .94. Information regarding test–retest reliability is not yet available.

In a normal sample, correlations between actual WAIS-R VIQ, PIQ, and FSIQ, and predicted IQs on the basis of NAART scores were .83, .40, and .75, respectively (Blair & Spreen, 1989). In short, the NAART is a good predictor of VIQ and FSIQ, but is relatively poor at predicting PIQ. Further, at least in normal people, prediction of IQs was more accurate with equations based on NAART scores than with demographic prediction equations developed by Barona et al. (1984). However, as indicated earlier (see Introduction), the test is not insensitive to cerebral damage, and deterioration in reading test performance does occur in patients with cerebral dysfunction; for example, in cases with moderate to severe levels of dementia (Stebbins et al., 1988, 1990a) and in patients with mild dementia who have accompanying linguistic deficits (Stebbins et al., 1990b). In short, the test is probably best regarded as providing a lower limit of the estimate of premorbid IQ (Stebbins et al., 1990a,b). Combining the NAART with demographic information should increase predictive accuracy (see Introduction). Finally, the test should not be used with aphasic or dyslexic patients, or with patients who have significant articulatory or visual acuity problems.

REFERENCES

Barona, A., Reynolds, C.R., & Chastain, R. (1984). A demographically based index of pre-morbid intelligence for the WAIS-R. *Journal of Consulting and Clinical Psychology, 52,* 885–887.

Blair, J.R., & Spreen, O. (1989). Predicting premorbid IQ: A revision of the National Adult Reading Test. *Clinical Neuropsychologist, 3,* 129–136.

Nelson, H.E. (1982). *National Adult Reading Test (NART): Test Manual.* Windsor, U.K.: NFER Nelson.

Nelson, H.E., & O'Connell, A. (1978). Dementia: The estimation of pre-morbid intelligence levels using the new adult reading test. *Cortex, 14,* 234–244.

Stebbins, G.T., Wilson, R.S., Gilley, D.W., Bernard, B.A., & Fox, J.H. (1988). Estimation of premorbid intelligence in dementia. *Journal of Clinical and Experimental Neuropsychology, 10,* 63–64.

Stebbins, G.T., Wilson, R.S., Gilley, D.W., Bernard, B.A., and Fox, J.H. (1990a). Use

Stebbins, G.T., Gilley, D.W., Wilson, R.S., Bernard, B.A., and Fox, J.H. (1990b). Effects of language disturbances on premorbid estimates of IQ in mild dementia. *The Clinical Neuropsychologist, 4,* 64–68.

RAVEN'S PROGRESSIVE MATRICES

Purpose

The purpose of Raven's Progressive Matrices is to assess reasoning in the visual modality.

Source

The test, including all levels, can be ordered from the Psychological Corporation, P.O. Box 839954, San Antonio, Texas 78204-0954 for approximately $400 U.S., or from the Ontario Institute for Studies in Education, 252 Bloor Street West, Toronto, Ontario, M5S 1V6, Canada, for about $100 Cdn.

Description

The test is a popular measure of intellectual ability because responses require neither verbalization, skilled manipulation ability, nor subtle differentiation of visuospatial information. In addition, verbal instruction is kept to a minimum (Zaidel et al., 1981). Three forms of this test have been developed. The Standard Progressive Matrices (SPM) (Raven, 1938) consist of 60 items grouped into five sets (A–E), each set containing 12 items. Each item contains a pattern problem with one part removed and from six to eight pictured inserts, one of which contains the correct pattern. Each set involves different principles of matrix transformation, and within each set the items become increasingly more difficult. The scale is intended for the entire range of intellectual development starting with the time a child is able to grasp the idea of finding a missing piece to complete a pattern. Young children, mentally defective people, and very old individuals, however, are not expected to solve more than the problems in Sets A and B of the scale and the easier problems of Sets C and D, where reasoning by analogy is not essential.

The Coloured Progressive Matrices (CPM) (Raven, 1947) provide a shorter and simpler form of the test. The test consists of 36 items, grouped into three sets (A, Ab, B) of 12 items each. It was developed for use with children (age 5.5+) and old people, for anthropological studies, and for clinical work. The test can be used with people who, for any reason, cannot understand English, or who suffer from physical disabilities, aphasias, cerebral palsy or deafness, as well as with people who are intellectually subnormal. The problems are printed on colored backgrounds in order to attract the subject's attention. The scale is arranged so that it

Table 3–10. Standard Progressive Matrices: Smoothed Summary Norms for North American Children (Ages 6.5–16.5)

%ile points	From / To	Ages (years)									
		6.03 6.08	6.09 7.02	7.03 7.08	7.09 8.02	8.03 8.08	8.09 9.02	9.03 9.08	9.09 10.02	10.03 10.09	10.09 11.02
95		30	33	36	38	40	42	44	46	47	48
90		27	30	33	36	38	40	42	44	45	46
75		21	25	28	31	34	36	38	40	41	43
50		14	17	20	23	26	29	32	34	36	37
25		12	13	14	16	18	21	24	26	28	30
10		9	10	11	13	14	16	17	19	21	23
5		7	8	9	10	11	12	13	15	17	18

Note: Data are based on a series of local systematic random samples of North American schoolchildren.

Source: Raven et al. (1986).

can be presented in the form of illustrations in a book or as boards with movable pieces. The test covers the cognitive processes of which children under the age of 11 years are usually capable. Once the intellectual capacity to reason by analogy has developed, the SPM is the more suitable scale to use.

The Advanced Progressive Matrices (APM) (Raven, 1965) were constructed as a test of intellectual efficiency that could be used with people of more than average intellectual ability and that could differentiate clearly between people of even superior ability. It is intended for those for whom the SPM are too easy—that is, for persons obtaining a raw score above about 50 on the SPM. It consists of two sets of items. In Set I, there are 12 problems designed to introduce a person to the method of working and to cover the intellectual processes assessed by the SPM. It can be used as a short 10-minute test or as a practice test before starting Set II. The 36 items in Set II are identical in presentation and reasoning with those in Set I, except that they increase in difficulty more steadily and become considerably more complex.

Administration

See source. Briefly, the subject points to the pattern piece he or she selects as correct or writes its number on an answer sheet.

Approximate Time for Administration

Both the SPM and CPM are untimed tests. The SPM requires about 40 minutes and the CPM about 25 minutes to complete. Set II of the APM can be used

Ages (years)										
11.03 11.08	11.09 12.02	12.03 12.08	12.09 13.02	13.03 13.08	13.09 14.02	14.03 14.08	14.09 15.02	15.03 15.08	15.09 16.02	16.03 16.08
49	50	51	52	53	54	55	56	56	57	57
47	48	49	50	51	52	52	53	54	55	56
44	45	46	47	48	49	49	50	51	52	53
38	39	40	41	42	43	44	45	46	47	48
32	33	34	35	36	37	38	39	40	41	42
25	27	28	30	31	32	33	35	35	36	37
19	21	22	24	26	27	28	29	29	30	31

Table 3–11. Standard Progressive Matrices: Burke's Conversion of Raw Scores into Percentiles (Ages 16–65)

Percentile rank	Ages					
	16–25 (n = 624)	26–35 (n = 882)	36–45 (n = 609)	46–55 (n = 625)	56–65 (n = 232)	65+ (n = 20)
100	59	60	58	60	59	47
95	55	54	52	51	48	44
90	54	52	50	48	45	38
85	52	51	47	45	42	36
80	51	49	46	44	40	35
75	49	48	44	42	38	30
70	48	46	42	40	36	29
65	47	45	41	38	34	24
60	46	44	40	37	32	21
55	45	43	38	35	30	20
50	44	41	37	33	29	19
45	42	40	35	31	27	19
40	41	39	33	29	26	18
35	39	37	31	26	24	17
30	38	36	29	24	22	17
25	36	34	27	22	20	16
20	33	31	24	20	18	14
15	31	28	21	18	16	13
10	28	24	19	15	14	12
5	20	19	15	12	11	10

Note: Norms are based on a population of vocational counseling and psychiatric patients admitted to a Veterans Administration hospital.

Source: Burke (1985).

Table 3–12. Colored Progressive Matrices: Smoothed Summary Norms for
North Americans (Ages 5.5–11.5)

%ile	From	Ages					
points	To	5.03 5.08	5.09 6.03	6.04 6.08	6.09 7.02	7.03 7.08	7.09 8.02
95		23	25	28	30	31	32
90		21	23	25	27	29	30
75		17	19	21	23	25	27
50		12	14	16	18	20	22
25		11	12	13	14	15	17
10		9	10	11	12	13	14
5		8	9	9	10	11	12

Note: Table is based on a series of local systematic random samples of schoolchildren.

Source: Raven et al. (1986).

without a time limit in order to assess a person's total reasoning capacity. In that
case, the subject should be shown the problems of Set I as examples to explain the
principles of the test. Allow about one hour to complete the task. To assess a
person's intellectual efficiency, Set I can be given as a short practice test followed
by Set II as a speed test. The most common time limit for Set II is 40 minutes.

Scoring

Record the total number correct.

Comment

Test–retest reliability data are acceptable (above .8), although for young children
(CPM, less than age 8; APM, less than age 11) the Raven is somewhat less reliable
(see source). The median test–retest value is about .8, although the values are
somewhat lower for retest intervals over one year. When internal consistency is
considered, reliability estimates are acceptable (above .70) (Burke, 1985).

   Although not strictly a pure measure of Spearman's g, the RPM comes as close
as many consider possible (Llabre, 1984). Concurrent validity studies show a
modest correlation (about .7) between Raven and conventional tests of intelligence
such as the Wechsler and Stanford–Binet scales (Burke, 1985; also see source).
The RPM has a relatively low correlation with tests of academic achievement
(Esquivel, 1984; Llabre, 1984)

   The bulk of the evidence suggests that focal brain damage depresses the total
score on the CPM, although there is no significant difference between average
scores of right- and left-brain-damaged individuals (e.g., Costa et al., 1969; Denes
et al., 1978; Villardita, 1985). This may reflect a lack of homogeneity of items

Ages						
8.03	8.09	9.03	9.09	10.03	10.09	11.03
8.08	9.02	9.08	10.02	10.08	11.02	11.09
33	34	35	35	35	35	35
31	32	33	33	34	34	35
29	30	31	32	32	33	34
24	26	27	28	29	30	31
19	21	22	23	24	25	26
15	16	17	18	19	20	21
12	13	14	15	16	17	18

composing the CPM (e.g., Burke, 1958; Costa, 1976). There is some evidence that left–right hemispheric differences emerge when the items of the CPM are categorized on the basis of the cognitive ability presumed to underlie their solution (Denes et al., 1978; Villardita; 1985; Zaidel et al., 1981).

In order to reduce the influence that neglect for left-sided alternatives may have on the performance of right-brain-damaged patients, the response array for each item on the CPM can be arranged vertically (Caltagirone et al., 1977; Villardita, 1985).

Normative Data

Score conversion is to percentiles. Raven scores show a significant increase with increasing years of education and socioeconomic status (Burke, 1985; also see source). Further, scores on the Raven are correlated with the subject's age (Burke, 1985; Orme, 1966; source). There appears to be an increase of ability through childhood, a period of maximum ability from adolescence to early adulthood, and then a linear decrease with age. Numerous reports of normative data have appeared in the literature (see source). Many norms are derived from studies conducted in the 1930s and 1940s. Since that time, there appears to have been an upward shift in levels of performance. Consequently, more recent normative data are preferred. In addition, given the evidence of some cultural bias, the use of local norms may be desirable (available from source). Tables giving detailed percentages are also available (Peck, 1970; see also source). Raven and his colleagues (1986), however, argue that classification into more than eight groups is unjustified. The test simply cannot support fine distinctions. Conversion of percentages to Wechsler IQ scores is also discouraged. Progressive Matrices scores are not interchangeable with those obtained from intelligence tests.

For the SPM, summary North American norms for children aged 6.5–16.5 years are given by Raven et al. (1986). These data are derived from a series of local systematic random samples of schoolchildren and are shown in Table 3–10. American norms for ages 16+ have been developed by Burke (1985) and are given in Table 3–11. The figures are based on male vocational counseling and psychiatric patients admitted to an American Veterans Administration hospital. These norms are also applicable to women since true sex differences on the Raven have not been demonstrated (Court, 1983). It should be noted that the number of subjects in the age group 65+ is quite small. Therefore, the figures for this age group are of limited value.

For the CPM, summary North American norms for children aged 5.5–11.5 years are presented by Raven et al. (1986). These data are derived from a series of local norming studies with schoolchildren and are shown in Table 3–12. Yeudall et al. (1986) tested 225 normal Canadian men and women, ages 15–40, with the CPM. At each age-group interval (e.g., 15–20, 21–25, etc.), there were few if any errors. The mean number correct for the combined group (ages 15–40) was 34.9 (SD = 1.25). Norms for the elderly, ages 65–100, have been computed by Orme (1966) and are given in Table 3–13.

Table 3–13. Colored Progressive Matrices: Smoothed Summary Norms for Normal Healthy Old People Aged 65–85 Years, Extrapolated to 90–100

Percentile points	Age in years							
	65	70	75	80	85	90	95	100
95	33	31	30	29	28	27	27	26
90	30	29	28	27	27	26	24	23
75	27	26	26	25	24	22	21	19
50	25	23	22	21	19	18	17	15
25	21	19	18	17	15	14	13	11
10	17	16	14	13	12	11	9	8
5	15	13	12	11	9	8	—	—

Note: Amended norms are based on original normative data contained in the Raven manual.

Source: Orme (1966).

Table 3–14. Advanced Progressive Matrices (Set II): Estimated Norms for Set II (Timed)

Percentile points	Age in years								
	11.5	12	12.5	13	13.5	14	20	30	40
95	16	17	18	19	20	21	24	23	21
90	14	14	15	16	17	18	21	20	17
75	8	10	11	12	13	13	14	12	9
50	—	—	—	8	9	9	9	7	—

Source: Raven (1965).

Table 3–15. Advanced Progressive Matrices (Set II): Norms for Set II (Untimed)

Total score	Percentile	Total score	Percentile
13	1	26	43
15	3	27	52
17	4	28	57
18	6	29	65
19	7	30	74
20	11	31	81
21	14	32	86
22	18	33	89
23	24	34	93
24	29	35	98
25	37	36	100

Note: Data are derived from 300 students at the University of California at Berkeley.

Source: Paul (1985).

For the APM (Set II), Raven (1965) provides norms for people of more than average intellectual ability (Table 3–14). The scores are based on an administration where working time is limited to 40 minutes. Norms for the untimed version have been compiled by Paul (1985) and are shown in Table 3–15. They are derived from 300 students attending the University of California at Berkeley.

REFERENCES

Burke, H.R. (1958). Raven's Progressive Matrices: Validity, reliability, and norms. *Journal of Psychology, 22,* 252–257.

Burke, H.R. (1985). Raven's Progressive Matrices: More on norms, reliability, and validity. *Journal of Clinical Psychology, 41,* 231–235.

Caltagirone, C., Gainotti, G., & Miceli, G. (1977). A new version of Raven's Colored Matrices designed for patients with focal hemispherical lesion. *Minerva Psichiatrica, 18,* 9–16.

Costa, L.D. (1976). Interset variability on the Raven Colored Progressive Matrices as an indicator of specific ability deficit in brain-lesioned patients. *Cortex, 12,* 31–40.

Costa, L.D., Vaughan, H.G., Horwitz, M., and Ritter, W. (1969). Patterns of behavioral deficit associated with visual spatial neglect. *Cortex, 5,* 242–263.

Court, J.H. (1983). Sex differences on Raven's Progressive Matrices: A review. *Alberta Journal of Educational Research, 29,* 54–74.

Denes, F., Semenza, C., & Stoppa, E. (1978). Selective improvement by unilateral brain-damaged patients on Raven Coloured Matrices. *Neuropsychologia, 16,* 749–752.

Esquivel, G.B., (1984). Colored Progressive Matrices. In D.J. Keyser & R.C. Sweetland (Eds.), *Test Critiques* (Vol. 1, pp. 206–213). Kansas City, Missouri: Test Corporation of America.

Llabre, M.M. (1984). Standard Progressive Matrices. In D.J. Keyser & R.C. Sweetland (Eds.), *Test Critiques* (Vol. 1, pp. 595–602). Kansas City, Missouri: Test Corporation of America.

Orme, J.E. (1966). Hypothetically true norms for the Progressive Matrices Test. *Human Development, 9,* 222–230.

Paul, S.M. (1985). The Advanced Progressive Matrices: Normative data for an American university population and an examination of the relationship with Spearman's *g*.

Journal of Experimental Education, 54, 95–100.

Peck, D.F. (1970). The conversion of Progressive Matrices and Mill Hill Vocabulary raw scores into deviation IQs. *Journal of Clinical Psychology, 26,* 67–70.

Raven, J.C. (1938). *Progressive Matrices: A Perceptual Test of Intelligence: Individual Form.* London: H.K. Lewis.

Raven, J.C. (1947). *Colored Progressive Matrices Sets A, Ab, B.* London: H.K. Lewis.

Raven, J.C. (1965). *Advanced Progressive Matrices Sets I and II.* London: H.K. Lewis.

Raven, J., Summers, B., Birchfield, M., et al. (1986). *Manual for Raven's Progressive Matrices and Vocabulary Scales.* Research

Suppl. No. 3: A Compendium of North American Normative and Validity Studies. London: H.K. Lewis.

Villardita, C. (1985). Raven's Colored Progressive Matrices and intellectual impairment in patients with focal brain damage. *Cortex, 21,* 627–634.

Yeudall, L.T., Fromm, D., Reddon, J.R., & Stefanyuk, W.O. (1986). Normative data stratified by age and sex for 12 neuropsychological tests. *Journal of Clinical Psychology, 42,* 920–946.

Zaidel, E., Zaidel, D.W., & Sperry, R.W. (1981). Left and right intelligence: Case studies of Raven's Progressive Matrices following brain bisection and hemidecortication. *Cortex, 17,* 167–186.

STROOP TEST

Source

The test can be ordered from the Neuropsychology Laboratory, University of Victoria, P.O. Box 1700, Victoria, British Columbia, V8W 3P5, at about $10 Cdn. Alternatively, users may make their own cards as described below.

Purpose

This test measures the ease with which a person can shift his or her perceptual set to conform to changing demands and suppress a habitual response in favor of an unusual one.

Description

This measure of cognitive flexibility was originally developed by Stroop (1935). His version consists of three white cards, each containing 10 rows of five items. There are four parts to the test. In Part 1, the subject reads randomized color names (blue, green, red, yellow) printed in black type. In Part 2, the subject reads the color names (blue, green, red, yellow) printed in colored ink (blue, green, red, yellow), ignoring the color of the print (the print color never corresponds to the color name). In Part 3, the subject has to name the color of dots (blue, green, red, yellow). In Part 4, the subject is given the card used in Part 2. This time, however, he or she must name the color in which the color names are printed and disregard their verbal content. Of major interest is the subject's behavior when presented with colored words printed in nonmatching colored inks. Stroop reported that normal people can read colored words printed in colored ink as fast as when the words are presented in black ink. However, the time to complete the task increases significantly when the subject is asked to name the color of the ink rather than read the word. This decrease in color-naming speed is called the "color–word interference effect."

Other versions of the Stroop Test have been developed (e.g., Golden, 1976, 1978). The Victoria version (Regard, 1981) is similar to that devised by Perret (1974). We use this version because of its short administration time and sensitivity to frontal lobe disorders. It consists of three 21.5 × 14 cm cards, each containing six rows of four items (Helvetica, 28 point). The rows are spaced 1 cm apart. In Part D, the subject has to name as quickly as possible the color of 24 dots printed in blue, green, red, or yellow. Each color is used six times, and the four colors are arranged in a pseudorandom order within the array, each color appearing once in each row. Unlike the original Stroop Test, Part W is similar to Part D, except that the dots are replaced by common words (when, hard, and, over), printed in lower case. The subject is required to name the colors in which the stimuli are printed, and to disregard their verbal content. Part C is similar to Parts D and W, but here the colored stimuli are the color names "blue, green, red, and yellow" printed in lower case so that the print color never corresponds to the color name.

Administration

In the Victoria version, the three cards are always presented in the same sequence: D, W, C. Instruct the subject to read or call out the color name as quickly as possible. Start the timer immediately after providing instruction. Instruct as follows:

PART D

"Name the colors of the dots as quickly as you can. Begin here [point], and go across the rows from left to right." Direct the patient's eyes across the rows from left to right.

PART W

"This time, name the colors of the words as quickly as you can. Begin here, and go across the rows from left to right." Clarify, if necessary: "Name the colors in which the words are printed."

PART C

"**Again, name the colors in which the words are printed as quickly as you can.**"
Clarify if necessary: "**Don't *read* the word, tell me the *color* in which the word is printed.**"

The errors in color naming are corrected immediately, if not spontaneously corrected by the patient. Then instruct the subject to go on as rapidly as possible.

Approximate Time for Administration

The approximate time required is five minutes.

Scoring

For each part, record both the time to complete and the number of errors. Score spontaneous corrections as correct. For sample scoring sheet, see Figure 3–6.

Comment

We have looked at test–retest reliability, using a one-month interval between test sessions. We found reliability estimates of .90, .83, and .91 for the three parts of the test. However, experience with the test does affect performance. Normal college students showed significant practice effects ($p < .001$). On the second administration, performance improved by about 2 points on Parts D and W, and by about five seconds on Part C.

```
                        Sample Score Sheet
                          Stroop Test
        NAME _____        DATE _____
        AGE _____
        DOTS:    G  B  Y  R               WORDS:    G  B  Y  R
                 Y  R  G  B                         Y  R  G  B
                 B  G  Y  R                         B  G  Y  R
                 B  Y  R  G                         B  Y  R  G
                 R  G  B  Y                         R  G  B  Y
                 Y  G  B  R                         Y  G  B  R

        COLORS:  G  B  Y  R
                 Y  R  G  B           ┌─────┬──────────┬──────────┐
                 B  G  Y  R           │     │   Time   │  Errors  │
                 B  Y  R  G           │  I  │          │          │
                 R  G  B  Y           │ II  │          │          │
                 Y  G  B  R           │ III │          │          │
                                      └─────┴──────────┴──────────┘
```

Figure 3–6. Stroop Test sample scoring sheet.

The Stroop Test has been studied in psychiatric and brain-damaged patients. The test is fairly effective in distinguishing between normal controls and brain-damaged patients and between psychiatric and brain-damaged samples (Golden, 1976). It also appears to be sensitive to severity of dementia (Koss et al., 1984). There is evidence that impairment on our version of the Stroop is related to the location of the cerebral lesion. Both Perret (1974) and Regard (1981) reported that the interference effect of Part C (relative to Part W) was greater for patients with left frontal lobe damage than for other patient or control groups.

Normative Data

Both age and intellectual level may contribute to performance on the Stroop Test (Comalli, 1965; Comalli et al., 1962; Das, 1970; Regard, 1981). In adults, aging appears to be linked to slowing in color naming and an increase in the Stroop interference effect.

Regard (1981) presented normative information for the Victoria version (see Table 3–16). The values are derived from a sample of young adults with average

Table 3–16. Modified Stroop Test: Mean Reading Time (in Seconds) and Errors for the 24-Item/Card Form

		Age (years)				
		20–35	50–59	60–69	70–79	80+
N		40	19	28	24	15
Name color of dots ("D")						
Seconds	M	10.10	13.74	12.71	15.00	18.87
	SD	2.01	2.58	1.90	5.07	4.67
Errors	M	0.03	—	—	0.08	0.20
	SD	0.16	—	—	0.28	0.56
Name color print of noncolor words ("W")						
Seconds	M	12.00	16.58	16.32	19.04	24.13
	SD	2.49	3.34	3.33	5.10	5.13
Errors	M	0.03	—	0.04	—	0.13
	SD	0.16	—	0.19	—	0.35
Name color print of color words ("C")						
Seconds	M	19.25	28.90	31.82	38.83	61.13
	SD	5.18	7.62	9.86	13.29	30.94
Errors	M	0.23	0.42	0.36	0.71	2.73
	SD	0.53	0.77	0.68	1.16	2.46

Note: Regard (1981) tested 40 right-handed normal people, mean age 26.7 years (range 20–35 years). We gathered data in 1989 from 86 healthy older adults, aged 50–94 years (mean = 68.5).

Sources: Regard (1981); Spreen & Strauss (unpublished data).

intellectual abilities. Recently, we compiled norms for use with older adults. The data are based on a relatively well-educated sample (n = 86; mean education = 13.2 years; SD = 3.1) of healthy elderly people, aged 50–94 (mean = 68.5; SD = 10.78). These data are also given in Table 3–16. Unfortunately, data for children are not yet available.

REFERENCES

Comalli, P.E. (1965). Cognitive functioning in a group of 80–90 year-old men. *Journal of Gerontology, 20*, 14–17.

Comalli, P.E., Jr., Wapner, S., & Werner, H. (1962). Interference effects of Stroop Color–Word Test in childhood, adulthood and aging. *Journal of Genetic Psychology, 100*, 47–53.

Das, J.P. (1970). Changes in Stroop-Test responses as a function of mental age. *British Journal of Clinical and Social Psychology, 9*, 68–73.

Golden, J.C. (1976). Identification of brain disorders by the Stroop Color and Word Test. *Journal of Clinical Psychology, 32*, 654–658.

Golden, J.C. (1978). *Stroop Color and Word Test*. Chicago, Ill.: Stoelting.

Koss, E., Ober, B.A., Delis, D.C., & Friedland, R.P. (1984). The Stroop Color–Word Test: Indicator of dementia severity. *International Journal of Neuroscience, 24*, 53–61.

Perret, E. (1974). The left frontal lobe of man and the suppression of habitual responses in verbal categorical behavior. *Neuropsychologia, 12*, 323–330.

Regard, M. (1981). Cognitive rigidity and flexibility: A neuropsychological study. Unpublished Ph.D. dissertation, University of Victoria, British Columbia.

Stroop, J.R. (1935). Studies of interference in serial verbal reaction. *Journal of Experimental Psychology, 18*, 643–662.

WECHSLER INTELLIGENCE TESTS

Other Test Names

There are three scales: the Wechsler Adult Intelligence Scale – Revised (WAIS-R), the Wechsler Intelligence Scale for Children – Revised (WISC-R), and the Wechsler Preschool and Primary Scale of Intelligence – Revised (WPPSI-R). Previous versions with similar content were the Wechsler–Bellevue Scale, the Wechsler Adult Intelligence Scale, the Wechsler Intelligence Scale for Children and the Wechsler Preschool and Primary Scale of Intelligence.

Purpose

The purpose of the Wechsler scales is to provide measures of general intellectual function.

Source

The Wechsler scales can be obtained from the Psychological Corporation, P.O. Box 839954, San Antonio, Texas 78204-0954. Each scale (WAIS-R, WISC-R,

WPPSI-R) costs about $400 U.S. The scales can also be ordered from the Psychological Corporation, 55 Horner Ave, Toronto, Ontario M8Z 4X6. The WAIS-R costs $600 Cdn., the WISC-R costs $600 Cdn., and the WPPSI-R is available for $525 Cdn.

Description

The Wechsler test is one of the most frequently used measures in neuropsychological batteries. It is a core instrument, giving information about the overall level of intellectual functioning, demonstrating the presence or absence of significant intellectual disability, and providing clues to altered functions (Lezak, 1983). The test materials for each scale (WAIS-R, WISC-R, WPPSI-R) are packaged conveniently in a case about the size of a briefcase. The complete kit contains the manual, record form booklets, cards, puzzles, and blocks that are used in the subtests. The WAIS-R (Wechsler, 1981) covers the age range 16–74 years. It is composed of 11 subtests—six verbal and five performance oriented. The verbal and performance tests can be administered separately or together to yield, respectively, a Verbal (VIQ), a Performance (PIQ), and a Full Scale IQ (FSIQ). The Verbal subtests are Information, Digit Span, Vocabulary, Arithmetic, Comprehension, and Similarities. The Performance subtests are Picture Completion, Picture Arrangement, Block Design, Object Assembly, and Digit Symbol. The items on the Information subtest assess general knowledge. Digit Span consists of two parts: Digits Forward requires the subject to repeat sequences of three to nine digits; Digits Backward sequences are two to eight numbers long, and the subject must say them in the reverse order. The Vocabulary subtest requires the subject to provide definitions of words. The Arithmetic subtest ranges from simple counting of blocks to the more complex comprehension of verbally presented mathematical problems. Items on the Comprehension subtest assess practical reasoning and the meaning of proverbs. On the Similarities subtest, the subject must explain in what way two things are alike. On the Picture Completion subtest, the subject is shown pictures in which there is an important part missing. The subject must indicate the part that is missing. Picture Arrangement consists of sets of pictures in a jumbled order. The subject is asked to arrange them in an order that tells a sensible story. On the Block Design subtest, the subject is presented with red and white blocks and is asked to construct replicas of constructions made by the examiner or of designs printed in smaller scale. Object Assembly consists of cutout figures of common objects (e.g., mannikin, animals), and the subject's task is to put the pieces of the puzzles together. The Digit Symbol substitution task consists of rows of blank squares, each printed with a randomly assigned number (1–9). A key is printed above these rows and shows each number paired with a different nonsense symbol. The subject's task is to fill the blanks with the corresponding symbols as rapidly as possible.

A simpler version of the WAIS-R, the WISC-R (Wechsler, 1974), is available for children, ranging in age from 6 years to 16 years 11 months 30 days. The IQs are calculated on the basis of five Verbal and five Performance tests: Information, Similarities, Arithmetic, Vocabulary, Comprehension (Digit Span), Picture Completion, Picture Arrangement, Block Design, Object Assembly, Coding (or Mazes). Coding (called Digit Symbol on the WAIS-R) has two forms: Coding A is for children under age 8 and Coding B is for children 8 years and older. The Maze task, which has no counterpart on the WAIS-R, requires the subject to draw paths through mazes within time limits. Digit Span on the Verbal Scale and Mazes on the Performance Scale are supplementary tests, to be administered when time permits, or to serve as a substitute if a regularly administered test cannot properly be given or is invalidated. Examiners may substitute Mazes for Coding if they wish. Wechsler (1974) recommends using Mazes for children below age 8 because it is more reliable than Coding A at ages $6\frac{1}{2}$ and $7\frac{1}{2}$ years. If Digit Span and/or Mazes are given *in addition to* the other 10 tests, they are *not* included in calculating the child's IQ.

The WPPSI-R (Wechsler, 1989) is available for children ranging in age from 3 to 7 years 3 months. It can also be used for those individuals suspected of being mentally retarded although the materials, test items, and directions were selected for their suitability for young children. The Verbal Scale consists of a simpler version of the subtests found on the WISC-R. The Sentences test is a supplementary task that substitutes for Digit Span as the test of immediate memory. The Performance Scale includes Object Assembly, Picture Completion, Mazes and Block Design. Animal Pegs (formerly Animal House) is an optional subtest that is similar in format to Digit Symbol or Coding. The child has to put colored pegs into holes under animal pictures according to the pairing of animals and colored pegs displayed in a model at the top of the pegboard. Geometric Design has two parts: part 1 requires the identification of target stimuli from an array of four designs; part 2 requires the copying of figures.

On all three tests, IQ scores compare the performance of an individual with the average scores attained by members of his or her age group. Identical IQ scores obtained by a 60-year-old and a 20-year-old reflect the same relative standing among people of the subjects' respective age groups. In one sense however, IQ scores are not identical. The reason is that test scores change with age, typically rising to a peak during young adulthood, then falling off later on. Consequently, a lower level of test performance is needed to obtain a given IQ at 60 than at 20 years of age.

Administration

See source. Briefly, the examiner asks test questions, displays pictures or puzzles to the patient, and records the patient's responses in an individual response booklet. There is a suggested order of subtest administration; however, the examiner can depart from the standard order. Also, completion of all subtests in one session is preferable, but not obligatory. The examiner can call a recess at the end of a subtest. If a subtest must be stopped in the middle, the test can usually be resumed where it had been stopped. However, the easy items on Similarities, Block Design, and Picture Arrangement provide subjects with the practice they need to succeed at more difficult items. Lezak (1983) suggests that if the examination must be stopped in the middle of any of these three subtests, the first few items should be repeated at the next session so that the patient can reestablish the set necessary to pass the harder items.

The WISC-R overlaps with the WPPSI-R for the age range 6:0:0 (years:months:days) to 7:3:0 and overlaps with the WAIS-R for the age range 16:0:0–16:11:30. In deciding which test to use, the examiner should consider the individual's estimated level of intelligence. Sattler (1988) points out that a more thorough sampling of ability can be obtained from the WPPSI-R than from the WISC-R, and from the WISC-R than from the WAIS-R, in their overlapping age ranges for children with below-average ability. Thus, a 16:8-year-old needs more successes on the WISC-R than on the WAIS-R to obtain the same scaled score. To illustrate, 13 correct WISC-R Information items but only six correct WAIS-R Information items are needed to obtain a scaled score of 5. For normal and gifted subjects, all three tests appear to provide an adequate sampling of ability.

The Wechsler Scales all contain an Information subtest that can be troublesome for subjects from other English-speaking countries because of items with U.S.-biased content. Several psychometric studies have been carried out with Canadian versions of the Information subtest (Bornstein et al., 1983; Crawford & Boer, 1985; Marx, 1984; Vernon, 1977; Violato, 1984, 1986). Although there is no firm evidence that Canadians are unduly penalized by the American items, a number of changes have been recommended in order to achieve a gain in face validity (Violato, 1986). Tables 3–17 and 3–18 show the recommended items for substitution on the WAIS-R and WISC-R, respectively. A cautionary statement is in order: For the WAIS-R, item 8 is disproportionately difficult for Canadians. For the WISC-R, items 16 and 20 are disproportionately easy for nonclinical populations, whereas for abnormal children, item 17 becomes too easy.

There have been numerous attempts to develop abbreviated forms of the Wechsler scales (see Banken & Banken, 1987, Silverstein, 1990, for review). Some procedures involve administering parts of each subtest, whereas others have relied on the administration of specific subtests (e.g., Short Form 2: Vocabulary, Block Design; Short Form 4: Vocabulary, Block Design, Arithmetic, Picture Arrangement), and transforming results by means of a formula or referring to special tables to obtain estimated IQ scores (See Sattler, 1988). Table 3–19 shows estimated WISC-R, WPPSI, and WAIS-R Full Scale IQ equivalents for the sum of scaled scores on Vocabulary and Block Design. The short forms, however, are most

Table 3–17. Recommended Items for Substitution on the Information Subtest of the WAIS-R for Canadian Subjects

Item No.	Recommended item	Acceptable answer
1.	What are the colors of the Canadian flag?	Red and white
6.	Name two men who have been prime ministers of Canada since 1950.	Any two from St. Laurent to the present
8.	Who is Gordon Lightfoot?	Singer, composer, writer
9.	In what direction would you travel if you went from Toronto to Panama?	South, southwest, southeast
13.	Who was the first prime minister following Confederation?	John A. MacDonald
14.	Who was Charles Lindbergh?	Aviator, pilot
17.	Who was Louis Riel?	Metis leader
22.	How many members of Parliament are there in the House of Commons?	285 ± 10
23.	How far is it from Paris to Toronto?	3,000–4,000 mi or 4,850–6,500 km
27.	What is the population of Canada?	24 million ± 10%

Source: Violato (1986).
Adapted from the Wechsler Adult Intelligence Scale-Revised. Copyright 1981, by The Psychological Corporation. Reproduced by permission. All rights reserved.

Table 3–18. Recommended Items for Substitution on the Information Subtest of the WISC-R for Canadian Subjects

Item No.	Recommended item	Acceptable answer
16.	Who invented the telephone?	Alexander Graham Bell, or Bell
17.	From which country did most of the settlers in Canada come?	England, Britain, Scotland, or France
19.	Name three oceans that border Canada.	Arctic and *either* Atlantic or Pacific, or both
20.	How many weeks are there in one year?	52
21.	In what continent is Sweden?	Europe
24.	How tall is the average Canadian man?	5'7" or 170–200 cm
27.	How far is it from Toronto to Vancouver? (For children living in or near Toronto, substitute Montreal for Toronto.)	2,700–4,300 km

Source: Vernon (1977).
Adapted from the Wechsler Intelligence Scale for Children-Revised. Copyright 1974 by The Psychological Corporation. Reproduced by permission. All rights reserved.

Table 3–19. Estimated WISC-R, WPPSI, and WAIS-R Full Scale IQ Equivalents for Sum of Scaled Scores on Vocabulary and Block Design

Vocabulary Plus Block Design scaled score	Estimated WISC-R Full Scale IQ	Estimated WPPSI Full Scale IQ	WAIS-R FSIQ Age group 16–17 25–44 65–74	18–24	45–64
1	45	43	—	—	—
2	48	46	50	46	48
3	51	49	52	49	51
4	54	52	55	52	54
5	56	55	58	55	57
6	59	58	61	58	59
7	62	61	64	61	62
8	65	64	66	64	65
9	68	67	69	67	68
10	71	70	72	70	71
11	74	73	75	73	74
12	77	76	78	76	77
13	80	79	80	79	80
14	83	82	83	82	83
15	85	85	86	85	86
16	88	88	89	88	88
17	91	91	92	91	91
18	94	94	94	94	94
19	97	97	97	97	97
20	100	100	100	100	100
21	103	103	103	103	103
22	106	106	106	106	106
23	109	109	108	109	109
24	112	112	111	112	112
25	115	115	114	115	115
26	117	118	117	118	117
27	120	121	120	121	120
28	123	123	122	124	123
29	126	126	125	127	126
30	129	129	128	130	129
31	132	132	131	133	132
32	135	135	134	136	135
33	138	138	136	139	138
34	141	141	139	142	141
35	144	143	142	145	144
36	146	147	145	148	146
37	149	150	148	151	149
38	152	153	150	154	152
39	155	156	—	—	—
40	158	159	—	—	—

Note: Use age-corrected scaled scores for the WAIS-R.

Source: Estimated WAIS-R Full Scale IQ equivalents are reprinted with permission of the publisher and authors from B.H. Brooker and J.J. Cyr, while WPPSI and WISC-R values are from Sattler, 1988.

Table 3–20.   Mean Performance of Children on Coding Recall Task

	Males			Females		
Age	N	Mean	SD	N	Mean	SD
8	20	5.3	2.3	30	6.3	1.8
9	45	6.2	1.5	36	6.1	1.8
10	37	6.3	1.6	37	6.2	2.2
11	32	6.5	1.7	35	7.1	1.6
12	18	7.2	1.6	15	7.7	1.1

Note: Norms are based on a population of U.S. schoolchildren.

Source: Collaer & Evans (1982).

appropriate for situations in which only rough estimates of IQ are required. Short forms might be indicated when the subject's mental status precludes the administration of the full IQ scale or when only a gross measure of intelligence is desired (Banken & Banken, 1989; Silverstein, 1990).

Finally, some clinicians adapt the Digit Symbol (or Coding) subtest to provide not only the standard performance but also a measure of incidental learning. Edith Kaplan's procedure (see Lezak, 1983) for the Digit Symbol test on the WAIS-R involves noting the number of boxes completed by the patient in the allotted time (90 seconds), but allowing the patient to continue until the end of the next-to-last row. Then without prior mention, the test sheet is folded so that only the last row shows, and the patient is then asked to fill in from memory as many of the symbols as he or she can recall. Kaplan reports that a score of 7 out of 9 symbols is at the low end of average for normal adults. Collaer and Evans (1982) use a slightly different procedure for Coding B on the WISC-R. The Coding test is completed in standard fashion, and the form is removed from view. Within 10–20 seconds of finishing the Coding subtest, and without prior warning, the child is provided with another sheet of paper containing the digits 1 through 9 and is told to fill in the associated symbols. The recall is scored as follows: One point is given for each accurately drawn *and* associated symbol, and $\frac{1}{2}$ point is given for any accurately drawn but misassociated symbol. Coding recall norms for ages 8–12 are shown in Table 3–20. These data are derived from 305 elementary schoolchildren in the United States. The values should be treated with some caution because of the small number of subjects in some of the age/sex categories.

Approximate Time for Administration

The approximate time required is one to two hours.

Scoring

See source. The record form provides space to record and score the subject's responses, to draw a profile of subtest scores, and to summarize information about the patient's behavior in the test situation. In order that scoring and qualitative features of the performance can be reviewed later, examiners should record responses to verbal subtests verbatim, or at least record each significant idea expressed by the subject. Atypical solutions on the Performance subtests should also be documented. Supplementary scoring sheets are available in order to detail performance on the Block Design and Object Assembly subtests.

All of the timed tests, except for Digit Symbol, can yield two scores: the score for the patient's response within the time limit and the score for his or her performance regardless of time. In order to describe different aspects of the patient's capacities, we change the standard procedures and give the patient an opportunity to solve problems failed under standard (timed) conditions. Usually, this means waiting an extra one to two minutes beyond the allotted time. We then use a dual scoring system, noting both the timed and untimed scores (Edith Kaplan, personal communication; Lezak, 1983).

Comment

Across the Wechsler tests, split-half reliability (with speeded tests excluded) is high (above .88) for Verbal, Performance, and Full Scale IQs (see source). Test–retest reliability data are also high for Verbal, Performance, and Full Scale IQs (see source; Lowe et al., 1987; Matarazzo & Herman, 1984; Moore et al., 1990; Snow et al., 1989). However, high test–retest correlations, even those as high as .90, can conceal large changes over time in individual scores (Ballard, 1984; Matarazzo & Herman, 1984; Moore et al., 1990). For example, scores of some children can fluctuate by as much as 25 IQ points over the school years (Richards, 1951; Sarazin & Spreen, 1986; Sontag et al., 1958). Such a situation makes predictive decisions hazardous. Moreover, over relatively short time intervals (less than two months), there are modest practice effects, with gains of about 4–10 IQ points (see source). The gains tend to be greater for the Performance scale than for the Verbal scale (Sattler, 1988).

In terms of validity, there is a substantial correlation (about .5–.8) between Wechsler IQs and other measures of intelligence and academic achievement (Carvajal et al., 1987; Lowe et al., 1987; Matarazzo, 1972; Spruill, 1984; Vernon, 1984). Typically, VIQs and FSIQs are better predictors of scholastic achievement than are PIQs. One should note, however, that the Wechsler tests do not clearly differentiate abilities at the lower or upper ends of the scale because of the range of distribution of item difficulty which concentrates on the middle range. Therefore, they may be inappropriate in the assessment of the severely mentally retarded or the very gifted (Sattler, 1982b).

Several factor-analytic studies of the Wechsler Scales have been conducted. Typically, three basic factors have been identified: a "verbal comprehension" factor, a "perceptual organization" factor, and a "memory/freedom from distractability" factor (Kaufman, 1979; Sattler, 1988a; Spruill, 1984). The "verbal comprehension" factor measures verbal knowledge and comprehension, knowledge obtained partially from formal education, and reflecting the application of verbal skills to novel situations. In general, the verbal subtests (Information, Similarities, Vocabulary, and Comprehension) constitute this factor. The "perceptual organization" factor involves perceptual and organizational dimensions and reflects the ability to interpret and organize visually perceived material within a time limit. The factor appears to measure a variable common to the Performance subtests (Picture Completion, Picture Arrangement, Block Design, and Object Assembly). The third factor, "memory/freedom from distractability", seems to measure processes related to attention, concentration, and memory. Wielkiewicz (1990) has suggested that the third factor may reflect executive and short-term memory processes involved in planning, monitoring and evaluating task performance. Arithmetic, Digit Span, and Digit Symbol (Coding B) are the major subtests for this factor.

The factor scores can be used to generate *initial hypotheses* about an individual's strengths and weaknesses (Kaufman, 1979; Sattler, 1982a). One can examine deviation quotients (e.g., Sattler, 1982b). One can also compare factor means (not IQs) to determine whether or not there is a meaningful discrepancy. Kaufman (1979) suggested that as a rule of thumb, the means should differ by 3 or more scaled score points. Sattler (1982b) provides the following example: A subject obtains scaled scores of 8, 10, 11, and 11 on the Information, Comprehension, Similarities, and Vocabulary subtests (mean = 10); scaled scores of 4, 5, 6, and 9 on the Picture Completion, Picture Arrangement, Block Design, and Object Assembly subtests (mean = 6); and scaled scores of 6, 7, and 8 on Arithmetic, Digit Span, and Coding (mean = 7). Using Kaufman's rule of thumb, there is a meaningful discrepancy between "freedom from distractability" and "verbal comprehension" $(10 - 7 = 3)$ but not between "freedom from distractability" and "perceptual organization" $(7 - 6 = 1)$. Subtest scores composing a factor should be fairly consistent. If performance is inconsistent, then the factor score may be difficult to interpret.

For years, clinicians have attempted to identify patterns of test performance typical of specific brain-damaged groups. The identification of characteristic profiles, however, has proved to be difficult, and there are no firm rules. For example, investigators have examined whether laterality of the damage (left or right hemisphere) is linked to VIQ–PIQ differences. In general, patients with unilateral left-hemisphere disease obtain lower VIQ than PIQ scores, whereas patients with unilateral right-hemisphere or bilateral disease obtain lower PIQ than VIQ scores. However, these patterns do not occur regularly enough for clinical reliability (Bornstein, 1984; Lezak, 1983). Moreover, significant differences between VIQ and PIQ are quite common among normal people (Grossman, 1983; Kaufman, 1976a; Reynolds & Gutkin, 1981; Sattler, 1982b; see below), and these discrepancies may vary as a function FSIQ. At higher FSIQ levels, there is a tendency for VIQ to be relatively high, whereas with FSIQ below 100, the Performance scale tends to be higher (Lezak, 1983; McDermott et al., 1989a; Reynolds & Gutkin, 1981).

Researchers have also been interested in determining a WAIS-R marker for dementia of the Alzheimer type (DAT). Fuld (1984) reported a profile defined by the following formula: $A > B > C \leq D, A > D$, in which A is the mean of the Information and Vocabulary subtest scores; B, of the Similarities and Digit Span subtest scores; C, of the Digit Symbol and Block Design subtest scores; and D, of the Object Assembly subtest score. All subtest scores are age corrected. The occurrence of this profile, however, does not seem specific to DAT (Logsdon et al., 1989; Satz et al., 1987).

Investigators have also tried to determine whether or not various Wechsler patterns can identify learning-disabled children. One such pattern consists of depressed scores on four subtests: It is known as the "ACID pattern," which is an acronym for Arithmetic, Coding, Information, and Digit Span. This pattern seems to be associated with a subsample, but not a majority, of learning-disabled children. Moreover, learning-disabled children who do exhibit the ACID pattern do not all have the same type of information-processing deficit (Joschko & Rourke, 1985).

In short, although there are a few performance patterns that seem to be fairly typical of specific types of clinical disorders, there are no fixed rules. In order to identify a profile as unique, one must demonstrate that the profile is not commonplace in the general population (see Normative Data). One must keep in mind, however, that pattern analysis can only provide clues about strengths and weaknesses. These ideas must then be checked against other information about the subject and must be considered in light of what is neurobehaviorally possible. Any descriptions derived from pattern analysis should be treated as initial hypotheses, not the final conclusion. Discussions of pattern analysis are available in Kaufman (1979), Lezak (1983), and Sattler (1988).

The Wechsler test should be given early in the course of the assessment since it allows the examiner to observe how the patient negotiates a wide array of tasks. In this way, the examiner can begin to develop hypotheses about the patient's spared and impaired functions that can then be tested more thoroughly during the course of the assessment.

Normative Data

Norms are presented in the Wechsler manuals and are based on large groups representative of the U.S. population.

Briefly, for the WPPSI-R or WISC-R subtests, scaled score equivalents of raw scores are provided in the test manual for each age interval covered by the scale (three-month intervals for the WPPSI, four-month intervals for the WISC-R). The sums of scaled scores are converted to Verbal, Performance, and Full Scale IQs by means of a table in the manual that is used for all ages covered by the scale. The VIQ, PIQ, and FSIQ distributions each have a mean of 100 and a standard deviation of 15. In interpreting WPPSI-R or WISC-R scores for adults, the examiner can calculate test-age equivalents for any of the subtests using the tables provided in the manuals. A test age ("mental age") represents the chronological age at which a given level of test performance is the average in a representative sample of the population.

The WAIS-R takes account of age differences when the IQ scores are computed, but not in the conversion of raw scores to scaled scores. The scaled scores, located on the front of the Record Form as well as in the test manual, are based on the performance of a reference group of young adults between 20 and 34 years of age. This particular age range was selected because performance on most tests reaches a peak during this age span (Wechsler, 1981). These scaled scores enable the examiner to compare the performance of a person of any age with that of a young segment of the working population. They are useful for questions of disability and vocational or educational planning. Age-graded subtest scaled scores are also provided in the WAIS-R manual, but are *not* to be used for computing an individual's IQ. These age-scaled scores permit a subject's score on any single test to be interpreted in relation to the performance of the subject's age peers. In general, with increasing age, additional scaled-score points are awarded primarily to the Performance Scale tests, especially the Digit Symbol test. These additional points actually reflect a decline in performance as a function of age. Lezak (1983) recommends that below age 20 and above age 35, age-graded scaled scores be used when making subtest comparisons since it is difficult to interpret many of the subtests and to perform a pattern analysis unless the age-graded scores are computed. To facilitate inter- as well as intraindividual comparisons, our standard practice is to evaluate and report both scaled and age-corrected scaled scores (see also Binder, 1987; Lezak, 1983).

When working with scaled scores, it is often helpful to translate them to percentile ranks (Sattler, 1988). Table 3–21 shows the estimated percentile ranks for each Wechsler scaled score. Scaled scores can also receive a qualitative description, and these too are shown in Table 3–21. IQs, however, should *never* be estimated on the basis of a single subtest score (Sattler, 1982b).

In evaluating significant differences between any two specific subtests,

Table 3–21.   Percentile Ranks and Suggested Qualitative Descriptions for Scaled Scores on the WPPSI, WISC-R, and WAIS-R

Scaled score	Percentile rank	Qualitative description	Educational description
19	99	very superior	superior
18	99	"	"
17	99	"	"
16	98	"	"
15	95	superior	"
14	90	"	"
13	84	high average	bright average
12	75	"	"
11	63	average/normal	average
10	50	"	"
9	37	"	"
8	25	low average	low average
7	16	"	"
6	9	borderline	slow learner
5	5	"	"
4	2	mentally retarded	educable ment. retarded
3	1	"	"
2	1	"	trainable ment. retarded
1	1	"	"

Source: Sattler (1988).

Wechsler (1967, 1974, 1981) suggested that the 15% level of significance is ample for comparisons of one test with another, and he stated that differences of 3 or more scaled score points is required for significance. However, a criterion of 3 or more points may not be defensible because, as Lezak (1983) points out, a 5% significance level is generally required when assessing the probability that an event has not occurred by chance. She recommends that clinicians consider discrepancies of 4 scaled score points as approaching significance and discrepancies of 5 or more scaled score points as significant.

Examination of test scatter on the Wechsler Scales can provide valuable information about the subject's cognitive strengths and weaknesses, along with suggestions for possible remediation. It is important to note, however, that the individual subtests are associated with adequate, but less than perfect, test–retest reliability and with standard errors of measurement of varying magnitude. For example, on the WAIS-R, average standard errors of measurement range from .61 for Vocabulary to 1.54 for Object Assembly. Further, within-test variability is characteristic of many normally functioning people and therefore may not be associated with possible pathology. One frequently used scatter index is the discrepancy between Verbal and Performance IQs. Wechsler (1974, 1981) stated that a difference of 15 or more points is important (statistically significant) and merits further investigation. However, a discrepancy may be reliable in that it is unlikely

Table 3–22.   Percentage of Normal Population Obtaining VIQ–PIQ
Differences (Regardless of Sign) on the WAIS-R, WISC-R,
and WPPSI

Percentage of population obtaining given or greater differences	Discrepancy scores for:		
	WAIS-R total sample	WISC-R total sample	WPPSI total sample
50	7	8	8
25	12	14	14
20	14	16	16
10	18	20	20
5	21	24	24
2	25	28	29
1	28	31	32
0.1	36	40	41

Sources: [WAIS-R] Grossman (1983); [WISC-R] Sattler (1982b); [WPPSI] adapted
from Sattler (1982a).

to have happened by chance but it may occur with some frequency in the normal
population. Table 3–22 shows the frequency of VIQ–PIQ difference scores, regardless of sign, for the WAIS-R, WISC-R, and WPPSI. A Verbal–Performance
discrepancy of 15 points is found in about 20–25% of the normal population
(Grossman, 1983; Kauffman, 1976a, 1976b; Matarazzo & Herman, 1984; Reynolds
& Gutkin, 1981; Sattler, 1988a; Seashore, 1951). The finding that a person functions significantly better verbally than nonverbally (or vice versa) has practical
significance, but the pattern may not be useful in supporting a diagnosis of excep-
tionality. Analyses of other scatter indexes show similar results. For example, a
scaled score range (highest minus lowest scaled score) of 5–9 points is about
average on the WISC-R or WPPSI (Kaufman, 1976b; Reynolds & Gutkin, 1981).
Similar differences (mean = 7 points) between highest and lowest scaled scores are
the norm for adults (Matarazzo & Prifitera, 1989). In other words, it is typical for
the normal person to demonstrate quite a bit of intertest scatter. Intratest scatter
(clusters of zero-point scores appearing abruptly in a string of 1- or 2-point responses) is also quite common in the normal population (Mittenberg et al., 1989).
There is also evidence that the inter- and intratest differences vary at different
points of the intelligence distribution (Matarazzo & Prifitera, 1989; Mittenberg et
al., 1989). An examination of frequency data should be a routine procedure when
interpreting scatter scores (Matarrazzo & Prifitera, 1989; McDermott et al.,
1989a, 1989b; Mittenberg et al., 1989).

Some clinicians use, in isolation, an individual's highest WAIS-R subtest score as
a measure of that person's supposedly higher level of premorbid intelligence,
and/or interpret the individual's lowest WAIS-R subtest scores as indices of impairment in the brain–behavior function presumably reflected by these low subtest

scores. Such a practice is risky (Matarazzo & Prifitera, 1989), given the high degree of subtest scatter found in the normal population (see above), the less than perfect test–retest reliabilities, and the magnitudes of the standard errors of measurement of each of the subtests.

The periodic revisions of the Wechsler scales present problems for investigators and clinicians since every Wechsler standardization sample from 1932 to the present established norms of a higher standard than did its predecessor (Flynn, 1984). As a result, the Wechsler tests get successively harder in order to compensate for the increased average performance of individuals over time. This means that the older the test, the greater the overestimation of the participant's IQ (Parker, 1986). A related implication is that one cannot directly equate performances on earlier and later versions of the test. On average, IQ shifts of 6–8 points have been reported (Wechsler, 1974, 1981) for successive versions of a scale (e.g., WAIS and WAIS-R). The amount of difference, however, between earlier and later versions of the test may vary with respect to a subject's age and ability (Feingold, 1984; Ryan et al., 1987; Wechsler, 1981). Specifically, the WAIS FSIQ tends to be about 5 points higher than the WAIS-R FSIQ in persons with high average to superior intelligence and approximately 9 points greater in persons with average intelligence; conversely, WAIS-R IQs may be slightly higher than corresponding WAIS IQs in mildly to moderately retarded individuals (Ryan et al., 1987). Further, statistical differences in content between the WAIS and WAIS-R exist and at the level of profile analysis, different versions of the scale may produce different subtest patterns for a given subject (Reitan and Wolfson, 1990). Consequently, any attempt to apply decision rules derived from a consideration of subtest patterns on one version may not be applicable when using a different version (Chelune et al., 1987). One can also not assume that patterns of performance established between other neuropsychological tests and previous editions of the Wechsler test hold for the WAIS-R (Bornstein, 1987). Additional studies are needed to address this issue.

Finally, in reporting IQ data, it is important to emphasize that there is some variability in all testing, and it is unlikely that a person would obtain exactly the same score if retested. Rather, the IQ score is best thought of as falling within a range of ±2 standard errors of measurement (SEM). Tables in the Wechsler manuals provide the standard errors of measurement of the scaled scores and of the three IQs.

REFERENCES

Ballard, K. (1984). Interpreting Stanford–Binet and WISC-R IQs in New Zealand: The need for more than caution. *New Zealand Journal of Psychology, 13*, 25–31.

Banken, J.A., & Banken, C.H. (1987). Investigation of Wechsler Adult Intelligence Scale–Revised short forms in a sample of vocational rehabilitation applicants. *Journal of Psychoeducational Assessment, 5*, 281–286.

Binder, L. M. (1987). Appropriate reporting of Wechsler IQ and subtest scores in assessments for disability. *Journal of Clinical Psychology, 43*, 144–145.

Bornstein, R.A. (1984). Unilateral lesions and the Wechsler Adult Intelligence Scale–Revised: No sex differences. *Journal of Con-*

sulting and Clinical Psychology, 52, 604–608.

Bornstein, R.A. (1987). The WAIS-R in neuropsychological practice: Boon or bust? *Clinical Neuropsychologist, 1,* 185–190.

Bornstein, R.A., McLeod, J., McClung, E., & Hutchison, B. (1983). Item difficulty and content bias on the WAIS-R Information subtest. *Canadian Journal of Behavioral Science, 15,* 27–34.

Carvajal, H., Gerber, J., Hewes, P., & Weaver, K.A. (1987). Correlations between scores on Stanford–Binet IV and Wechsler Adult Intelligence Scale-Revised. *Psychological Reports, 61,* 83–86.

Chelune, G.J., Eversole, C., Kane, M., & Talbott, R. (1987). WAIS versus WAIS-R subtest patterns: A problem of generalization. *Clinical Neuropsychologist, 1,* 235–242.

Collaer, M.L., & Evans, J.R. (1982). A measure of short-term visual memory based on the WISC-R Coding subtest. *Journal of Clinical Psychology, 38,* 641–644.

Crawford, M.S., & Boer, D.P. (1985). Content bias in the WAIS-R Information subtest and some Canadian alternatives. *Canadian Journal of Behavioral Science, 17,* 79–86.

Feingold, A. (1984). The effects of differential age adjustment between the WAIS and WAIS-R on the comparability of the two scales. *Educational and Psychological Measurement, 44,* 569–573.

Flynn, J.R. (1984). The mean IQ of Americans: Massive gains 1932–1978. *Psychological Bulletin, 95,* 29–51.

Fuld, P.A. (1984). Test profile of cholinergic dysfunction and of Alzheimer-type dementia. *Journal of Clinical Neuropsychology, 6,* 380–392.

Grossman, F.M. (1983). Percentage of WAIS-R standardization samples obtaining Verbal–Performance discrepancies. *Journal of Consulting and Clinical Psychology, 51,* 641–642.

Joschko, M., & Rourke, B.P. (1985). Neuropsychological subtypes of learning-disabled children who exhibit the ACID pattern on the WISC. In B.P. Rourke (Ed.), *Neuropsychology of Learning Disabilities* (pp. 65–88). New York: Guilford Press.

Kaufman, A.S. (1976a). Verbal–Performance IQ discrepancies on the WISC-R. *Journal of Consulting and Clinical Psychology, 44,* 739–744.

Kaufman, A.S. (1976b). A new approach to the interpretation of test scatter on the WISC-R. *Journal of Learning Disabilities, 9,* 160–168.

Kaufman, A.S. (1979). *Intelligent Testing with the WISC-R.* New York: John Wiley.

Lezak, M.D. (1983). *Neuropsychological Assessment* (2nd ed.). New York: Oxford University Press.

Logsdon, R.G., Terri, L., Williams, D.E., Vitiello, M.V., & Prinz, P.N. (1989). The WAIS-R profile: A diagnostic tool for Alzheimer's disease? *Journal of Clinical and Experimental Neuropsychology, 11,* 892–898.

Lowe, J.D., Anderson, H.N., Williams, A., & Currie, B.B. (1987). Long-term predictive validity of the WPPSI and the WISC-R with black school children. *Personality and Individual Differences, 8,* 551–559.

Marx, R.W. (1984). Canadian content and the WISC-R Information subtest. *Canadian Journal of Behavioral Science, 16,* 30–35.

Matarazzo, J.D. (1972). *Wechsler's Measurement and Appraisal of Adult Intelligence* (5th ed.). Baltimore: Williams & Wilkins.

Matarazzo, J.D., & Herman, D.O. (1984). Base rate data for the WAIS-R: Test–retest stability and VIQ–PIQ differences. *Journal of Clinical Neuropsychology, 6,* 351–366.

Matarazzo, J.D., & Prifitera, A. (1989). Subtest scatter and premorbid intelligence: Lessons from the WAIS-R standardization sample. *Psychological Assessment, 1,* 186–191.

McDermott, P.A., Glutting, J.J., Jones, J.N., & Noonan, J.V. (1989a). Typology and prevailing composition of core profiles in the WAIS-R standardization sample. *Psychological Assessment, 1,* 118–125.

McDermott, P.A., Glutting, J.J., Jones, J.N., & Kush, J. (1989b). Core profile types in the WISC-R national sample: Structure, membership, and applications. *Psychological Assessment, 1,* 292–299.

Mittenberg, W., Hammeke, T.A., & Rao, S.M. (1989). Intrasubtest scatter on the WAIS-R as a pathognomonic sign of brain injury. *Psychological Assessment, 1,* 273–276.

Parker, K.C.H. (1986). Changes with age, year-of-birth cohort, age by year-of-birth cohort interaction, and standardization of the Wechsler Intelligence Tests. *Human Development, 29,* 209–222.

Reynolds, C.R., & Gutkin, T.B. (1981). Test scatter on the WPPSI: Normative analyses of the standardization sample. *Journal of Learning Disabilities, 14,* 460–464.

Reitan, R.M., & Wolfson, D. (1990). A consideration of the comparability of the WAIS and WAIS-R. *The Clinical Neuropsychologist, 4,* 80–85.

Richards, T.W. (1951). Mental test performance as a reflection of the child's current life situation—a methodological study. *Child Development, 22,* 221–233.

Ryan, J.J., Nowak, T.J., & Geisser, M.E. (1987). On the comparability of the WAIS and WAIS-R: Review of the research and implications for clinical practice. *Journal of Psychoeducational Assessment, 5,* 15–30.

Sarazin, F.A., & Spreen, O. (1986). Fifteen-year stability of some neuropsychological tests in learning disabled subjects with and without neurological impairment. *Journal of Clinical and Experimental Neuropsychology, 8,* 190–200.

Sattler, J. (1982a). Age effects on Wechsler Adult Intelligence Scale–Revised tests. *Journal of Consulting and Clinical Psychology, 50,* 785–786.

Sattler, J. (1982b). *Assessment of Children's Intelligence and Special Abilities.* Boston: Allyn & Bacon.

Sattler, J.M. (1988). *Assessment of Children.* Third Edition. San Diego: Sattler.

Satz, P., Van Gorp, W.G., Soper, H.V., & Mitrushina, M. (1987). WAIS-R marker for dementia of the Alzheimer type? An empirical and statistical induction test. *Journal of Clinical and Experimental Neuropsychology, 9,* 767–774.

Seashore, H.G. (1951). Differences between Verbal and Performance IQs on the Wechsler Intelligence Scale for Children.

Journal of Consulting Psychology, 125, 62–67.

Snow, W.G., Tierney, M.C., Zorzitto, M.L., Fisher, R.H., & Reid, D.W. (1989). WAIS-R test–retest reliability in a normal elderly sample. *Journal of Clinical and Experimental Neuropsychology, 11,* 423–428.

Sontag, L.W., Baker, L.T., & Nelson, V.O. (1958). Mental growth and personality development: A longitudinal study. *Monograph of the Society for Research in Child Development, 23,* No. 2.

Spruill, J. (1984). Wechsler Adult Intelligence Scale–Revised. In D. Keyser & R. Sweetland (Eds.), *Test Critiques.* Kansas City, Missouri: Test Corporation of America.

Vernon, P.E. (1977). Final report on modification of WISC-R for Canadian use. *Canadian Psychological Association Bulletin, 5,* 5–7.

Vernon, P.A. (1984). Wechsler Intelligence Scale for Children–Revised. In D. Keyser & R. Sweetland (Eds.), *Test Critiques.* Kansas City: Missouri: Test Corporation of America.

Violato, C. (1984). Effects of Canadianization of American-biased items on the WAIS and WAIS-R Information subtests. *Canadian Journal of Behavioral Science, 16,* 36–41.

Violato, C. (1986). Canadian version of the Information subtests of the Wechsler Tests of Intelligence. *Canadian Psychology, 27,* 69–74.

Wechsler, D. (1989). *Wechsler Preschool and Primary Scale of Intelligence-Revised.* New York: Psychological Corporation.

Wechsler, D. (1974). *Wechsler Intelligence Scale for Children—Revised.* New York: Psychological Corporation.

Wechsler, D. (1981). *Wechsler Adult Intelligence Scale–Revised.* New York: Psychological Corporation.

WISCONSIN CARD SORTING TEST (WCST)

Purpose

The purpose of this test is to assess the ability to form abstract concepts, and shift and maintain the set.

Source

The test can be obtained from the Institute of Psychological Research, Inc., 34 Fleury Street West, Montreal, Quebec H3L 1S9, for approximately $150 Cdn., or from Psychological Assessment Resources, Inc., P.O. Box 98, Odessa, Florida, 33556-0998, for about $100 U.S. A computer version for the IBM ($295 U.S.) or Apple ($225 U.S.) is also available from this company. A computer version for the IBM is available from Multi-Health Systems, Inc., 10 Parfield Drive, Willowdale, Ontario, M2J 1B9, for approximately $280 Cdn.

Description

This test was developed by Berg and Grant (Berg, 1948; Grant & Berg, 1948) to assess abstraction ability. Heaton (1981) points out that there has been increasing interest in the test, in part because it provides information on several aspects of problem solving behavior beyond such basic indices of task success or failure. Examples of such indices include the number of perseverative responses, the number of perseverative errors, the failure to maintain set, and the number of categories achieved. Moreover, the WCST is especially sensitive to lesions of the frontal lobe (see below). Heaton (1981) standardized the test instructions and scoring procedures for the long version and formally published it as a clinical instrument. We use his method. There are, however, other versions of the test (e.g., Nelson, 1976).

The test consists of four stimulus cards, placed in front of the subject, the first with a red triangle, the second with two green stars, the third with three yellow crosses, the fourth with four blue circles on them. The subject is then given two packs, each containing 64 response cards, which have designs similar to those on the stimulus cards, varying in color, geometric form, and number. The subject is instructed to match each of the cards in the decks to one of the four key cards. The examiner explains that the object is to try to get as many right as possible and that there is no time limit to this test. The subject is told each time whether he or she is right or wrong.

Administration

See source. Briefly, the subject is given the two packs of cards and is then instructed to place each response card in a pile below one of the four stimulus cards, wherever he or she thinks it should go, and is told that the examiner will then inform him or her whether the choice was "right" or "wrong." The subject is directed to make use of this information and to try to get as many cards "right" as possible. No other cues are given. A noncorrection technique is used throughout.

The subject is required to sort first according to *color;* all other responses are called "wrong." Once 10 consecutive correct responses to color have been achieved, the required sorting principle shifts, without warning, to *form;* color responses are now "wrong." After 10 consecutive correct responses to form, the principle shifts to *number,* and then back to *color* once more. This procedure continues until the subject has successfully completed six sorting categories (i.e., color, form, number, color, form, number), or until all 128 cards have been placed.

Approximate Time for Administration

The time required is about 15 minutes.

Scoring

Performance is scored in a number of different ways. Categories achieved refers to the number of correct sorts, ranging from 0 for the subject who never gets the idea at all, to 6, at which point the test is normally discontinued. A "perseverative response" is defined as one that would have been correct on the immediately preceding stage of the test, or, as a continued response in terms of the patient's initial preference. There are, however, exceptions to this rule (see source). The perseverative response may reveal an inability to relinquish the old category for the new one, or the inability to see a new possibility. "Perseverative errors" are those perseverative responses that are also errors. The degree of perseveration (the number of perseverative responses or errors) is the most useful diagnostic measure that is derived from the test (Heaton, 1981). It is the best measure for predicting the presence or absence of brain damage and the presence of frontal involvement in focal cases.

There are a number of other measures that can be derived from the test. The nonperseverative error score can be computed by subtracting the total number of perseverative errors from the total error score. Another measure is the number of trials to complete the first category. This gives an indication of initial conceptualization before shift of set is required. The score for failure to maintain a set is the number of times the subject makes five correct responses in a row but fails to get the 10 that are required to complete the category. It indicates the inability to use a strategy that has been successful. A final score is called learning to learn, and reflects the subject's average change in efficiency across the successive stages of the WCST.

Details of scoring are outlined in the WCST manual. Recording a performance, particularly if the patient works rapidly, can be difficult. Briefly, the recording form has 128 response items, each one "CFNO" (C = color, F = form, N = number, O = other). The examiner records the patient's response by making a slash through those dimensions that are the same on the response and stimulus cards. In addition, a line is drawn under the last item when the criterion of 10 consecutive correct responses has been reached, and to indicate the new correct sorting category below that line.

Comment

See also Category Test. Information regarding test–retest, split-half, or other forms of reliability is currently unavailable. With regard to validity, Milner (1963), in her classic study with the WCST, found clear differences between patients with dorsolateral frontal excisions and those with orbitofrontal and posterior lesions. Patients with dorsolateral lesions showed an inability "to shift from one sorting principle to another, apparently due to perseverative interference from previous modes of response" (p. 99). Both Milner (1963) and Taylor (1979) suggested that the test is sensitive to function in dorsolateral areas of both frontal lobes, but more to the left than to the right side. Subsequent studies have generally confirmed that the WCST is especially sensitive to frontal lobe function, although some have reported more perseveration in patients with right as compared to left frontal lobe damage (Bornstein, 1986; Drewe, 1974; Hermann et al., 1988; Robinson et al., 1980).

It is important to note that patients with diffuse cerebral lesions perform on the WCST about the same as do focal frontal patients (Robinson et al., 1980). Therefore, the WCST cannot be used by itself to predict a focal frontal lesion, unless there is evidence from other sources that the lesion is focal and not diffuse (Heaton, 1981).

Normative Data

For the standard version, Heaton (1981) provides norms for adults below 60 years of age. Chelune and Baer (1986) give data for children, whereas we present norms for elderly people, ages 60–94. The means and standard deviations by age for three WCST variables (categories achieved, perseverative errors, failure to maintain set) are presented in Table 3–23. The table shows that children make rapid

Table 3–23. Means by Age for Three WCST Variables: Mean Number of Categories Achieved, Perseverative Errors, and Failures to Maintain Set

Children		Age (years)						
		6	7	8	9	10	11	12
n		11	14	22	16	20	12	10
Categtories achieved	M	2.73	4.07	4.05	4.81	5.61	5.58	5.70
	SD	2.10	1.94	2.01	1.47	0.75	0.79	0.95
Perseverative errors	M	40.64	25.07	23.18	18.13	13.95	15.17	12.30
	SD	28.03	18.43	13.23	11.55	6.50	13.49	16.94
Failure to maintain set	M	1.64	1.94	1.82	1.75	1.00	1.17	0.70
	SD	2.01	1.21	1.26	1.53	1.02	1.11	0.68

Adults		Age (years)					
		<40	40–49	50–59	60–69	70–79	80+
n		100	19	16	28	19	13
Categories achieved	M	5.6	4.8	5.6	5.5	5.0	4.23
	SD	1.0	1.8	1.1	1.1	1.3	1.5
Perseverative errors	M	10.4	16.0	11.3	12.25	15.9	25.77
	SD	8.0	13.9	6.9	10.91	9.8	12.23
Failure to maintain set	M	0.8	0.8	0.8			
	SD	1.3	1.5	1.1			

Note: Chelune and Baer (1986) provide normative data based on 105 school-age children with average IQ. Heaton (1981) gives norms derived from 135 adults of above-average IQ, aged <60 years. We (Strauss & Spreen, unpublished data) tested 60 well-educated healthy people aged 60–94.

gains in the number of categories achieved and significantly reduce the number of perseverative errors with advancing age. By about 10 years of age, children's performances are similar to those of young adults (see also Welsh et al., 1988). Performance appears not to decline significantly until late in life, after age 80. York Haaland et al. (1987) gave a 64-card version of the WCST to healthy elderly people. Their data are similar to our own, and they too report a significant decline only after age 80. Heaton (1981) suggests that for adults, the optimal "perseverative error" score cutoffs for predicting brain damage and focal frontal involvement, respectively, are above 13 and above 16. When using these cutoffs, the clinician should realize that many patients with focal nonfrontal lesions will be misclassified as normal (Heaton, 1981). Moreover, many normal elderly are likely to be misclassified. The perseverative error score must be adjusted upward for older patients.

Finally, both IQ and educational level show modest correlations with the WCST. Heaton (1981) recommends that the clinician give extra "leeway" to high school dropouts, especially if they have below-average IQs. The clinician may increase the impairment cutoff by five perseverative errors (or responses).

REFERENCES

Berg, E.A. (1948). A simple objective technique for measuring flexibility in thinking. *Journal of General Psychology, 39*, 15–22.

Bornstein, R.A. (1986). Contribution of various neuropsychological measures to detection of frontal lobe impairment. *International Journal of Clinical Neuropsychology, 8*, 18–22.

Chelune, G.J., & Baer, R.A. (1986). Developmental norms for the Wisconsin Card Sort Test. *Journal of Clinical and Experimental Neuropsychology, 8*, 219–228.

Drewe, E.A. (1974). The effect of type and area of brain lesion on Wisconsin Card Sort Test performance. *Cortex, 10*, 159–170.

Grant, D.A., & Berg, E.A. (1948). A behavioral analysis of degree of impairment and ease of shifting to new responses in a Weigl-type card sorting problem. *Journal of Experimental Psychology, 39*, 404–411.

Heaton, R.K. (1981). *Wisconsin Card Sorting Test Manual.* Odessa, Fla.: Psychological Assessment Resources.

Hermann, B.P., Wyler, A.R., & Richey, E.T. (1988). Wisconsin Card Sorting Test performance in patients with complex partial seizures of temporal lobe origin. *Journal of Clinical and Experimental Psychology, 10*, 467–476.

Milner, B. (1963). Effects of different brain lesions on card sorting. *Archives of Neurology, 9*, 90–100.

Nelson, H.E. (1976). A modified card sorting test sensitive to frontal lobe defects. *Cortex, 12*, 313–324.

Robinson, A.L., Heaton, R.K., Lehman, R.A.W., & Stilson, D.W. (1980). The utility of the Wisconsin Card Sorting Test in detecting and localizing frontal lobe lesions. *Journal of Consulting and Clinical Psychology, 48*, 605–614.

Taylor, L.B. (1979). Psychological assessment of neurological patients. In T. Rasmussen & R. Marino (Eds.), *Functional Neurosurgery.* New York: Raven Press.

Welsh, M.C., Groisser, D., & Pennington, B.F. (1988). A normative-developmental study of performance on measures hypothesized to tap prefrontal functions. Paper presented to the International Neuropsychological Association, New Orleans.

York Haaland, K., Vranes, L.F., Goodwin, J.S., & Garry, J.P. (1987). Wisconsin Card Sort Test performance in a healthy elderly population. *Journal of Gerontology, 42*, 345–346.

4

Cognitive Tests for Children

The neuropsychological examination of children has only recently been fully developed (Tramontana & Hooper, 1988). For the most part, downward extensions of the adult examination have been common (e.g., Reitan's "intermediate" for ages 9–14, and his "children's" battery for ages 5–8 years; Wechsler's WISC-R and WPPSI–R). Such extensions are included in the general sections on each test described in this manual.

Downward extensions are not always appropriate because item pools designed for adults may not be appropriate for children, and because the test may make different demands on a child versus an adult; for example, a cognitive test may pose primary visual, reading, or constructional problems for the child. For these reasons, even a highly simplified version of a test designed for adults may not be measuring similar functions. The construction of tests specifically designed for children would be preferable, but has been accomplished only for a few tests.

Even more serious is the lack of neuropsychological tests suitable for children under the age of 5 years. The behavioral repertoire of the younger child, of course, is more limited, and the test-taking attitude less developed the younger the child is. As a result, traditional "developmental" or intelligence tests are usually the only ones available at that age, although parts of such tests could well serve as tests of specific neuropsychological functions if they were further developed psychometrically (Aylward, 1988). For such development, newborn assessment methods such as the the Dubowitz (Dubowitz et al., 1970) and the Brazelton (1973) scale, and infant and child tests such as the Bayley (1969), the Uzgiris–Hunt (Uzgirus & Hunt, 1975; Dunst, 1980), and the Gesell (Knobloch et al., 1980) scales may provide a good starting point.

Our selection of tests specifically designed for children includes three general measures of developmental assessment: the Bayley Scale (Bayley, 1970), designed primarily for the age range 2 months to 2 years; the Stanford–Binet Scale (Thorndike, Hagen, & Sattler, 1986), covering ages 2–5 years, although it extends up to 18 years; and the Kauffman ABC (Kaufman & Kaufman, 1983), designed for ages 2:6–12:6 years, which is included because it offers a selection of tests designed along a neuropsychological theoretical model.

REFERENCES

Aylward, G.P. (1988). Infant and early childhood assessment. In M.G. Tramontana & Hooper (Eds.), *Assessment Issues in Child Neuropsychology* (pp. 225–248). New York: Plenum Press.

Bayley, N. (1969). *Bayley Scales of Infant Development*. New York: Psychological Corporation.

Brazelton, T.B. (1973). Neonatal Behavioral Assessment Scale. *Clinics in Developmental Medicine* (No. 50). Philadelphia: J.B. Lippincott.

Dubowitz, L.M.S., Dubowitz, V., & Goldberg, C. (1970). Clinical assessment of gestational age in the newborn infant. *Journal of Pediatrics*, 77, 1.

Dunst, C.J. (1980). *A Clinical and Educational Manual for Use with the Uzgiris and Hunt Scales of Infant Psychological Development*. Baltimore: University Park Press.

Kaufman, A.S., & Kaufman, N.L. (1983). *K-ABC: Kaufman Assessment Battery for Children*. Circle Pines, Minn.: American Guidance Service.

Knobloch, H., Stevens, F., & Malone, A.F. (1980). *Manual of Developmental Diagnosis*. New York: Harper & Row.

Thorndike, R.L., Hagen, E.P., & Sattler, J.M. (1986). *Stanford–Binet Intelligence Scale* (4th ed.). Chicago: Riverside Publishing.

Tramontana, M.G., & Hooper, S.R. (Eds.). (1988). *Assessment Issues in Child Neuropsychology*. New York: Plenum Press.

Uzgiris, I.C., & Hunt, J.McV. (1975). *Assessment in Infancy: Ordinal Scales of Psychological Development*. Urbana, Ill.: University of Illinois Press.

BAYLEY SCALES OF INFANT DEVELOPMENT (BSID)

Source

The Bayley Scales of Infant Development (BSID) can be ordered from the Psychological Corporation, P.O. Box 9954, San Antonio, Texas 78204-0354. The manual plus equipment, carrying case and 25 record booklets cost $790 U.S.

Description

This test by Bayley (1970) is an offshoot of the Gesell scales developed originally in 1933. It has gone through several revisions and appears to be the most popular and well established infant test for placement purposes (Damarin, 1978; Lehr et al., 1987). It is designed for infants from the age of 2 months to 2 years, and consists of three parts: (1) the mental scale, assessing sensory–perceptual acuity, discrimination and ability to respond, object constancy, memory, learning, problem solving, vocalization, early verbal communication, and the beginnings of abstract thinking (generalizations and classifications); (2) the motor scale, measuring degree of body control, coordination of larger muscles, and hand and finger manipulative skills; and (3) the infant behavior record, including behavior ratings of the child's interpersonal and affective characteristics, motivation, and interest in specific sensory experiences.

Administration

For details, see the manual. Items for both scales are numbered according to difficulty level corresponding to age expectations, and coded with a "situation code." This allows the examiner to test several items with the same situation code over several age levels as long as the child is attending sufficiently. For example, situation code C includes items using a rattle: Item 3 requires that the child responds to the rattle (any definite response is credited); item 36 requires that the child shows simple play with the rattle; item 48 involves turning of the head to the sound of the rattle; item 59 requires the recovery of the rattle in the crib after it has been dropped dropped or taken away. Situation code N refers to verbal comprehension, and ranges from listening selectively to familiar words, responding to verbal request, imitation of a word, to showing of shoes or other clothing or own toy.

Similar to the Binet method, items are numbered according to age level. A "basal level" (i.e., the level at which all items are passed) and a "ceiling level" (i.e., the level at which none of the items is passed) are established, and all items between these two levels are tested. For the experienced examiner, many responses may be observed incidentally without formal testing.

Testing is conducted under optimal conditions—that is, when the infant is fully alert, in the presence of the mother, and with constant encouragement. The first 46 items are administered with the child lying in the crib or on a comfortable supporting surface. If the child loses interest, the examiner may switch to other novel items, although as a rule the mental scale is administered first.

The infant behavior record is filled in immediately after completion of the test by choosing one statement of each set which best describes the child's behavior (i.e., "social orientation"): (1) avoiding or withdrawn, (2) hesitant, (3) accepting, (4) friendly, (5) inviting, initiating, or demanding.

Approximate Time for Administration

The time required is 45 minutes.

Scoring

The raw score for each scale is the number of items passed between basal and ceiling level, plus all items below the basal level. This score is converted into a mental (MDI) and motor (PDI) developmental index based on the child's exact age by using the appropriate tables in the manual. Age equivalents ("mental age," "psychomotor age") can also be obtained by reference to the tables. The first 24 items of the infant behavior record ratings can be compared with age-appropriate means provided in the manual to assist in judging normal or abnormal behavior.

Comment

The BSID administration and scoring techniques have been well documented in the manual, and standardized on a sample of 1,262 normal children, reasonably representative of the U.S. population distribution. Split-half reliability is reported as .88 for the MDI and .84 for the PDI. The two scales correlate modestly (.46) with each other. Tester–observer and test–retest agreement were reported as 89% and 76% for the mental scale, and as 93% and 75% for the motor scale. Concurrent validity with the Uzgiris and Hunt scales was .92 (Heffernan & Black, 1984), and with the Stanford–Binet IQ, .57 (Bayley, 1970).

Infant tests have been shown to have little predictive validity for later IQ scores (Bayley, 1970). In contrast, Ramey et al. (1973) found that in children in a relatively constant environment (i.e., attending the same day-care center), the MDI became more predictive with age (i.e., the MDI at ages 6–8, 9–12, and 13–16 months correlated with Stanford–Binet IQ at 3 years of age at a level of .49, .71, and .90, respectively, and with the Illinois Test of Psycholinguistic Abilities [ITPA] at a level of .21, .68, and .81), whereas the PDI decreased in predictive power (.77, .56, and .43, respectively, for the Stanford–Binet, and .73, .74, and .48, respectively, for the ITPA).

Means for infants with very low birth weight (<1,500 g) were lower for both MDI and PDI (102.57, 95.11) than for low-birth-weight (1,501–2,500 g; 109.52, 101.86) and normal-birth-weight children (>2,500 g; 111.34, 110.02) (Campbell et al., 1986).

Normative Data

Detailed normative data as described above are available in the manual. Campbell et al. (1986) noted, however, that in 305 normal 12-month-old North Carolina children, means for the MDI were 114 for whites and 109 for nonwhites, whereas the mean for the PDI was 110 for both groups. Even though these abnormally high scores can partly be attributed to testing in the home setting, the authors suggest that the BSID systematically overestimates the developmental progress and that restandardization may be necessary.

REFERENCES

Bayley, N. (1970). Development of mental abilities. In P.H. Mussen (Ed.), *Carmichael's Manual of Child Psychology* (3rd ed.). New York: John Wiley.

Campbell, S.K., Siegel, E., & Parr, C.A. (1986). Evidence for the need to renorm the Bayley Scales of Infant Development based on the performance of a population-based sample of 12-month-old infants. *Topics in Early Childhood Special Education*, 6, 83–96.

Damarin, F. (1978). Bayley Scales of Infant Development. In O.K. Buros (Ed.), *The Eighth Mental Measurement Yearbook* (Vol. 1, pp. 290–293). Highland Park, N.J.: Gryphon.

Heffernan, L., & Black, F.W. (1984). Use of the Uzgiris and Hunt Scales with handicapped infants: Concurrent validity of the Dunst age norms. *Journal of Psychoeducational Assessment*, 2, 159–168.

Lehr, C.A., Ysseldyke, J.E., & Thurlow, M.L. (1987). Assessment practices in model early childhood special education programs. *Psychology in the Schools*, 24, 390–399.

Ramey, C.T., Campbell, F.A., & Nicholson, J.E. (1973). The predictive power of the Bayley Scales of Infant Development and the Stanford–Binet Intelligence Test in a relatively constant environment. *Child Development*, 44, 790–795.

KAUFMAN ASSESSMENT BATTERY FOR CHILDREN (K-ABC)

Source

The complete K-ABC kit (regular edition) can be ordered from American Guidance Service, Circle Pines, Minnesota 55014 ($235.00 U.S.), or from Psycan Corporation, P.O. Box 290, Station V, Toronto, Ontario M6R 3A5 for $400 Cdn.; with plastic carrying case, $470 Cdn. Administration videotape costs $120 Cdn. The K-ABC ASSIST computer scoring manual and software cost $200 Cdn.

Description

The Kaufman and Kaufman (1983) battery covers the age range 2:6–12:6 (years:months) and is the most recently developed intelligence test which, compared to the Stanford–Binet and the Wechsler Scales, follows a different theoretical model, and also incorporates six achievement subtests. Of the 10 "mental process" subtests (the core of the battery), seven are labeled "simultaneous" and three are labeled "sequential." Six (one sequential and four simultaneous subtests) are considered "nonverbal" and therefore especially suited for children with communication handicaps. The theoretical model adopted for the construction of this

test is based on Das et al.'s (1979) notion of a sequential and simultaneous processing dichotomy, which is claimed to be related to Luria's theoretical framework. A
brief description of each of the subtests, the type of scale to which it belongs, and
the age range for which it is used follows:

1. *Magic Window* (15 items, simultaneous): This subtest measures the ability
   of the child to identify and name an object (e.g., car, girl, snake) rotated
   behind a narrow slit, which allows only partial exposure of the picture at
   any time. It is essentially a vocabulary test for young children (Goldstein
   et al., 1986). (Age range: 2:6–4:11 years)
2. *Face Recognition* (15 items, simultaneous): A face is exposed briefly, and
   the child must select the same face in a different pose from a group
   photograph. (Age range: 2:6–4:11 years)
3. *Hand Movements* (21 items, sequential): The child must copy the exact
   sequence of taps on the table with the fist, palm, or side of hand as
   demonstrated by the examiner. This test is adapted from Luria (1980). (All
   ages)
4. *Gestalt Closure* (25 items, simultaneous): The child must name or describe an ink drawing that is only partially complete (similar to the Gestalt
   Completion Test by Street, 1931). (All ages)
5. *Number Recall* (19 items, sequential): This subtest is identical to other
   digit repetition tasks. (All ages)
6. *Triangles* (18 items, simultaneous): The child has to assemble several
   identical rubber triangles (blue on one side, yellow on the other) to match
   a picture of abstract design. The test is similar to Kohs' Block Design (Age
   range: 4:0–12:6)
7. *Word Order* (20 items, sequential): The child has to point to silhouettes of
   common objects in the same order as the objects were named by the
   examiner. The test is similar to McCarthy's (1972) serial recall. (Age
   range: 4:0–12:6)
8. *Matrix Analogies* (20 items, simultaneous): The child has to select from an
   array the picture or design that best completes a 2×2 visual analogy. The
   test is similar to Raven's (1956) progressive matrices. (Age range: 5:0–
   12:6)
9. *Spatial Memory* (21 items, simultaneous): The child has to recall the
   location of pictures arranged randomly on a page. (Age range: 5:0–12:6)
10. *Photo Series* (17 items, simultaneous): The child has to arrange a series of
    photographs in proper time sequence. The test is similar to Picture Ar-
    rangement. (Age range: 6:0–12:6)
11. *Expressive Vocabulary* (24 items, achievement): The child has to name
    photographed objects correctly. The test is similar to the Peabody Picture
    Vocabulary Test. (Age range: 2:6–4:11)

12. *Faces and Places* (35 items, achievement): The child has to name fictional characters, famous persons, or well-known places (e.g., Santa Claus, pyramids, liberty bell, Fidel Castro). (All ages)
13. *Arithmetic* (38 items, achievement): The tasks begin with simple counting, recognition of shapes (triangle), numbers, comparison of two counts, verbally enclosed arithmetic ("If four of the elephants walked away, how many would be left?"), including time concepts, centered around a family visit to the zoo. (Age range: 3:0–12:6)
14. *Riddles* (32 items, achievement): The child has to infer the name of a concrete or abstract concept from several given characteristics (e.g., "What has fur, wags its tail, and barks?" "What was used by ancient Egyptians, is carved in stone, and is a form of writing?") (Age range: 3:0–12:6)
15. *Reading/Decoding* (38 items, achievement): The test indicates the child's ability to identify letters and to read and pronounce words. (Age range: 5:0–12:6)
16. *Reading/Understanding* (24 items, achievement): Reading comprehension is tested by acting out commands printed on plates. (Age range: 7:0–12:6)

Not all tests are given to children of all ages; only seven subtests are administered to 2:6-year-olds, whereas 13 subtests are given to 7.0–12.6-year-olds. With progressing age, some tests are phased out and others are added. The test comes in a durable box or carrying case. The test material, mounted on easels, has pages that can be flipped over by the examiner to move onto the next item to be shown to the subject, and that allow the examiner to read instructions on the back of the page facing him or her. The test manual includes correct answers in English and Spanish (oral instructions are given in English).

Administration

See administration and scoring manual. The usual caution of extensive training in test administration applies. The "Individual Test Record" of 12 pages assists in both administration and scoring while the battery is administered. Teaching items are included in all mental processing subtests. Items for each age are arranged in units. Similar to the "basal level" in the Stanford–Binet, a starting age for each subtest is determined by the chronological age of the child, but may require going back to easier items. The examiner then proceeds until the "stopping point" (ceiling level) or the last item of a subtest is reached. Subtests are administered in a prearranged order, but flexibility is allowed if a child shows resistance or fatigue.

Approximate Time for Administration

The time required varies from 30 minutes for 2:6-year-olds to 75 minutes for 7:0–12:6-year-olds.

Scoring

Similar to the Stanford–Binet, the raw score consists of the number of the ceiling item minus errors. This score can be translated into a scaled score with a mean of 10 and a standard deviation (SD) of 3 for mental processing subtests, and into standard scores with a mean of 100 and an SD of 15 for achievement subtests. The sums of scaled scores for the sequential and the simultaneous set of subtests, and the sum of both ("Mental Processing Composite") as well as the sum of achievement subtest standard scores can be converted into age-appropriate standard scores by the use of tables (at two-month intervals up to age 6:11). A special feature of this battery is the possibility of converting the sum of "nonverbal scales" (for children with communication impairment) into standard scores. Confidence levels for each subtest standard score and sum score can be entered into the scoring page of the test record. National percentile ranks and "sociocultural percentile ranks" (for blacks and whites) are provided as well. Finally, age equivalents for the scaled score of each of the subtests can be obtained from the tables in the manual. Significant differences between subtests indicating strengths and weaknesses of the child can also be read directly from the appended table.

Comment

Split-half reliabilities range from .62 for Gestalt Closure in 7-year-olds to .92 for Triangles in 5-year-olds; internal consistency ranges from .84 to .97; retest reliability ranges from .72 to .95 (see source). Validity has been investigated in 43 studies cited in the interpretative manual, and is based on factor-analytic, convergent, and discriminant validation (e.g., Hooper, 1986) and correlational studies, with generally positive results. Correlations of the individual subtests with the Wechsler Intelligence Scale for Children - Revised (WISC-R) ranged from .27 to .66 (with the highest correlations for the achievement subtests), and with the Stanford–Binet IQ from .10 (for Gestalt Closure) to .68 (for Riddles). The three Global Scale scores correlated with the Stanford–Binet from .15 (for Simultaneous Processing in normal preschoolers) to .79 (for Achievement in normal kindergarten children), whereas high-risk preschoolers and gifted referrals showed somewhat lower correlations. Convergent validity of the mental processing scale with the Peabody Individual Achievement Test reading recognition and comprehension was .59 and

.69, respectively, whereas discriminant validity for hyperactivity was −.51, but negligible in size for a child anxiety scale (Cooley & Ayres, 1985). Predictive validity for standard school achievement tests 12 months later was between .21 and .70 for the mental processing composite score in various groups, and between .34 and .84 for the achievement subtests. Worthington and Bening (1988) also noted that the Mental Processing Composite score predicted school achievement test scores more poorly in females than in males.

In addition to subtests familiar to most psychologists from other intelligence tests, the K-ABC strikes out into new territory by adding novel subtests (some adapted from the work of Das et al., 1979) and by using a new theoretical orientation along Das's formulations, forcing the clinician to rethink the concept of intelligence and the implications of this theory for educational and therapeutic practice. This has led to a "mixed" critical reception of the test as well as numerous studies evaluating its merits. Salvia and Ysseldyke (1985) consider the orientation "quite revolutionary," ask for a "considerably larger base of research support" (p. 458), and recommend patience and skepticism. Jensen (1984) claims that the test does not measure anything different from the WISC-R or the Stanford–Binet. Neuropsychologists may appreciate the theoretical orientation better, since the battery claims to have been constructed on the basis of neuropsychological theory (interpretative manual, p. 21) and seems to break down into left (analytic–sequential) and right (gestalt–holistic–simultaneous) -hemisphere functions (Kaufman & Kaufman, 1983, pp. 28, 29, & 232), and since it includes several subtests that are similar to specific neuropsychological tests. However, little evidence has been supplied so far that actually validates the neuropsychological implications of the sequential–simultaneous (right–left hemisphere) dimension; instead, the validity of this dimension rests on factor-analytic research, and even that has been questioned in replication studies including other tests (Goldstein et al., 1986). The dichotomy has little, if any foundation in Luria's theories about brain function; Sternberg (1984) accuses the test authors of misrepresentation of Luria's work. Sternberg also notes that all three sequential process subtests and some of the simultaneous subtests contain an "overemphasis on rote learning" (p. 275) which he feels is inappropriate in an intelligence test and which most other tests avoid. The author also suggests that the strong rote learning component of the battery is a major reason for the lack of differences among ethnic groups reported in the manual and elsewhere (e.g., Whitworth & Chrisman, 1987).

The addition of six achievement subtests to an intelligence test battery is also novel. Kaufman and Kaufman claim that the mental processing subtests measure fluid and the achievement subtests crystallized intelligence. Although this claim remains to be examined, the addition seems to create a "double-duty" test, replacing standard achievement tests to some extent. However, the limited number of items in the achievement subtests would suggest that one cannot expect more than a superficial screening of the academic achievement level of the child. Hopkins and Hodge (1984) also point out that the achievement tests do not correspond to most other achievement tests because they are not closely related to the school curriculum.

Positive features of the construction of this test include the measurement of the ability to deal with novelty, the attempt to integrate an information processing paradigm into basically psychometric testing approaches, the attempt to achieve culture-fairness by sampling minority and handicapped populations, and the attempt to ensure the subject's task comprehension by including teaching items and explicit instructions (Sternberg, 1984).

For use in neuropsychological practice, it should be remembered that the K-ABC is not equivalent to the WPPSI, the WISC-R, or the Stanford–Binet. In fact, results may be quite different, as indicated by some of the studies of concurrent validity. Nor should the construction of the test along a two-factor dimension be translated into a simple right–left hemisphere dichotomy. This is also specifically stated in the interpretative manual (p. 21). Nevertheless, the test does offer a new approach to the testing of young children, so that the comparison of K-ABC results with those of other tests may provide additional insights. Alternatively, individual subtests may be used to supplement other tests. A single subject design study (Barry & Riley, 1987) suggests how one single subtest (fist–edge–palm test; i.e., Hand Movements) can be used for rehabilitation in adult acute head injury rehabilitation patients. The interpretative manual (pp. 36–57) provides a thoughtful discussion of each test, its background (including remarks on neuropsychological significance), and a "psychological analysis" listing specific abilities that are tapped by each subtest; reading this discussion may provide the clinician with a better understanding of how each subtest may contribute to the overall clinical profile of the client. The interpretative manual also contains useful comments on remediation in children with learning problems.

Normative Data

See interpretative and scoring manuals. The battery is well standardized, based on 1,981 children representing the 1980 U.S. census in terms of geographic region, sex, socioeconomic status, race or ethnic group, and community size, with samples of approximately 200 children for each year of age. Compared to the WISC-R, the K-ABC tends to overestimate IQ scores by about 3–5 points in the average range (Naglieri & Haddad, 1984), by 8 points in a Navajo children sample (Naglieri, 1984), and by 7 points in the mentally retarded range (Naglieri, 1985). For the Hand Movement subtest only, Barry and Riley (1987) presented adult norms (Table 4–1); both age and gender effects were significant. The obtained mean scores of 17 and 15 in the younger groups correspond to scaled scores of 10 and 12 in 12-year-olds, suggesting that no further improvement with age occurs on this subtest.

Table 4–1. Adult Norms for the Hand Movements Subtest

		\multicolumn{5}{c}{Age (decade)}				
		20s	30s	40s	50s	Total
Women	n	10	10	10	10	40
	M	17.7	17.1	15.3	13.4	15.9
	SD	1.25	2.81	3.65	4.12	3.47
Men	n	10	10	10	10	40
	M	15.7	15.8	14.7	13.8	15.0
	SD	3.27	2.66	3.13	1.87	2.80

Source: Barry & Riley (1987).

REFERENCES

Barry, P., & Riley, J.M. (1987). Adult norms for the Kaufman Hand Movements Test and a single-subject design for acute brain injury rehabilitation. *Journal of Clinical and Experimental Neuropsychology, 9,* 449–455.

Cooley, E.J., & Ayres, R. (1985). Convergent and discriminant validity of the Mental Processing Scales of the Kaufman Assessment Battery for Children. *Psychology in the Schools, 22,* 373–377.

Das, J.P., Kirby, J.R., & Jarman, R.F. (1979). *Simultaneous and Successive Cognitive Processes.* New York: Academic Press.

Goldstein, D.J., Smith, K.B., & Waldrep, E.E. (1986). Factor analytic study of the Kaufman Assessment Battery for Children. *Journal of Clinical Psychology, 42,* 890–894.

Hooper, S.R. (1986). Performance of normal and dyslexic readers on the K-ABC: A discriminant analysis. *Journal of Learning Disability, 19,* 206–210.

Hopkins, K.D., & Hodge, S.E. (1984). Review of the Kaufman Assessment Battery (K-ABC) for Children. *Journal of Counselling and Development, 63,* 105–107.

Jensen, A.R. (1984). The black–white difference on the K-ABC: Implications for future testing. *Journal of Special Education, 18,* 255–268.

Kaufman, A.S., & Kaufman, N.L. (1983). *K-ABC: Kaufman Assessment Battery for Children.* Circle Pines, Minn.: American Guidance Service.

Luria, A. (1980). *Higher Cortical Functions in Man* (2nd ed.). New York: Basic Books.

McCarthy, D. (1972). *McCarthy Scales of Children's Abilities.* San Antonio, Tex.: Psychological Corporation.

Naglieri, J.A. (1984). Concurrent and predictive validity of the Kaufman Assessment Battery for Children with a Navajo sample. *Journal of School Psychology, 22,* 373–379.

Naglieri, J.A. (1985). Use of the WISC-R and the K-ABC with learning disabled, borderline mentally retarded, and normal children. *Psychology in the Schools, 22,* 133–141.

Naglieri, J.A., & Haddad, F.A. (1984). Learning disabled children's performance on the Kaufman Assessment Battery for Children: A concurrent validation study. *Journal of Psychoeducational Assessment, 2,* 49–56.

Raven, J.C. (1957). *Progressive Matrices.* London: H.K. Lewis & Co.

Salvia, J., & Ysseldyke, J.E. (1985). *Assessment in Special and Remedial Education.* Boston: Houghton Mifflin.

Sternberg, R.J. (1984). The Kaufman Assessment Battery for Children: An Information-processing analysis and critique. *Journal of Special Education, 18,* 269–279.

Street, R.F. (1931). *A Gestelt Completion Test: A Study of a Cross Section of Intellect.* New York: Bureau of Publications of Columbia Teachers College.

Whitworth, R.H., & Chrisman, S.M. (1987). Validation of the Kaufman Assessment Battery for Children comparing Anglo and Mexican-American preschoolers. *Educa-*

tional and Psychological Measurement, *47,* 695–702.

Worthington, G.B., & Bening, M.E. (1988). Use of the Kaufman Assessment Battery for Children in predicting achievement in students referred for special education services. *Journal of Learning Disabilities, 21,* 370–374.

STANFORD–BINET INTELLIGENCE SCALE–REVISED (SBISR)

Source

The Stanford–Binet Intelligence Scale (SBIS), 4th ed., can be ordered from Riverside Publishing Company, 8420 Bryn Mawr Avenue, Chicago, Illinois 60631, for $420.00 U.S.

Description

This scale (Thorndike et al., 1986a) is the most recent revision of Terman's first North American edition in 1916 of the test developed by Binet in 1905 in France. The second and third editions in 1937 and 1960 included further development, and the current edition provides a substantial revision by grouping items into 15 tests covering four broad areas—verbal reasoning, abstract/visual reasoning, quantitative reasoning, and short-term memory—and by providing normative data for each. Nine of these tests evolved from the previous edition of the test, and six were added. The test is designed for the age range 2–18 years, and provides intelligence estimates up to 23 years of age. Whereas previous editions were based primarily on the pragmatic stance of the original Binet–Simon test, the new edition follows the theoretical model of a *g*-factor comprising "crystallyzed abilities," "fluid-analytic abilities" (Cattell, 1971), and "short-term memory" as second-level factors. Within the "crystallized abilities," a distinction is made between third-level factors of verbal reasoning (including tests of vocabulary, comprehension, absurdities, verbal relations) and quantitative reasoning (including quantitative tasks, number series, equation building); the "fluid-analytic abilities" constitute only a third-level factor (including tests of pattern analysis, copying, matrices, and paper folding and cutting); "short-term memory" includes bead memory, memory for sentences, memory for digits, and memory for objects. Another difference from previous editions is that vocabulary and chronological age are used to determine the "entry level" for testing, but the subject must still pass all items at that level to establish the "basal level" (see Bayley Scales). The scales are packed in a small suitcase; much of the material is mounted on easels that allow pages to be turned over to move on to the next item facing the subject, and the back page contains instructions for the examiner.

Administration

See manual. Full familiarity and considerable practice are needed to administer this test. The examiner's handbook (Delaney and Hopkins, 1987) should be consulted since it clarifies a number of administration problems, e.g., the use of introductory explanations and/or training items when shifting to a new set of items or a different task in the determination of basal levels (Wersh and Thomas, 1990). Briefly, vocabulary is given first as a "routing test" which determines the item on each test to begin with. A "basal level" is then established for each test (passing two consecutive items), and testing is continued until the ceiling level (four consecutive failures on each test) is reached.

The test items are presented in a standardized manner, but some flexibility is acceptable; for example, the examiner may shift to another test if the subject shows fatigue or resistance to a given test. Ambiguous responses are clarified during testing or on follow-up questioning.

Of the 15 tests, only pattern analysis has definite time limits, whereas for all other tests it is left to the examiner to determine whether a satisfactory response can be elicited by allowing more time. A short description of the 15 tests follows:

1. *Vocabulary:* Picture naming (to item 14), definition vocabulary (items 15–46).
2. Comprehension: 42 questions (example: "Give two reasons why there are commercials on television").
3. *Absurdities:* 32 pictures with incongruous content ("What is wrong with this picture?") (example: girl writing with fork on paper).
4. *Verbal Relations:* 18 items with three words and a fourth word that does not fit, presented on cards and read aloud by the examiner. Subject has to find how the first three words are alike, but different from the fourth (example: boy, girl, man, but not dog).
5. *Pattern Analysis:* The first 10 items require correct block placement into holes (similar to the formboard test); items 11–42 are block design tasks with up to nine blocks (similar to the Wechsler Block Design).
6. *Copying:* For the first 12 items, examiner arranges up to four blocks in a pattern and asks the subject to copy the arrangement. For items 13–28, copying of simple geometric shapes shown on cards is required.
7. *Matrices:* A 2×2 matrix is presented on a card with three of the boxes filled with geometric designs; below are three choices. Subject has to indicate which of the three best fits into the empty box. The test increases after two items to a 3×3 matrix with up to five choices. Items 23–26 contain letter patterns instead of geometric designs.
8. *Paper Folding and Cutting:* Three line drawings of paper patterns are

presented on the top of a card. Beneath are five choices of patterns with folding marks. Subject has to indicate which of the choices looks like one of the patterns when it is unfolded. A folded sample is used to demonstrate the task if the subject does not respond correctly.

9. *Quantitative:* This test proceeds from placing blocks with varying numbers of dots correctly on a tray (12 items) to counting the number of children, pencils, etc. on cards, including simple subtraction (items 13, 14), to relations ("between," item 15), to arithmetic illustrated with pictures (items 16–23), to verbally enclosed arithmetic questions (items 24–40).

10. *Number Series:* Subject has to find the subsequent two numbers in a series printed on cards (26 items).

11. *Equation Building:* Subject has to rearrange numbers and basic arithmetic symbols to find the correct equation (18 items). Example: 2 2 7 3 × + =, subject has to find the equation $(2 \times 2) + 3 = 7$.

12. *Bead Memory:* This test proceeds from pointing out the correct colored and shaped bead in a box (as shown on a card) to arranging beads on a stick with base after the pictured pattern has been exposed for five seconds (42 items).

13. *Memory for Sentences:* Repetition of sentences ranging from two to twenty-two words (42 items).

14. *Memory* for Digits: Same-order repetition ranges from three to nine digits; repetition in reverse order is also required (14 and 12 items).

15. *Memory for Objects:* Subject has to find 2–8 objects shown previously on a multiple-choice card with distractor items in correct sequence.

For Canadian children, the use of metric equivalents for imperial measures, and the substitution of Canadian coins in the quantitative subtest are recommended (Wersh and Thomas, 1990).

Approximate Time for Administration

The time required is 60–90 minutes.

Scoring

A detailed scoring guide including examples of "pass," "query," and "fail" responses is included in the manual. The extensive (39 pp.) record booklet provides information for the examiner on item presentation and helpful guides for scoring so that the manual does not have to be consulted constantly. Raw scores for each test are converted into Standard Age Scores (SAS) by reference to the tables in the manual. The sums of raw scores for each of the four areas are converted into area SAS, based on additional tables in the manual. Finally, a composite SAS is derived from the manual by entering the sum of area SASs. The conversion tables make allowance for the possibility that some tests were not appropriate for the age of the child or may have been omitted for other reasons by providing area SASs for one, two, three, (or four) tests administered. Similarly, the composite SAS may be based on one, two, three, or four area scores.

Comment

Although many of the SBIT subtests may seem similar or identical to those used in other intelligence tests or in other tests like the Raven's or the Tactual Performance Test, it should be remembered that it was the SBIT that first developed these procedures and that tests like the WISC or WAIS were the "upstarts."

Although the use of 15 tests seemingly provides a fixed set of tasks for all ages (a serious problem of previous editions), only six of them are actually appropriate for all age levels, whereas the others cover only 7–13 years of the age span. Hence the SAS in the age range 2–6 years is based on only eight tests (with the possibility of obtaining "estimated" SAS for an additional four tests). In addition, vocabulary switches from picture naming to definition vocabulary after item 14; the task requirements for pattern analysis, copying, and quantitation also change after the first set of items.

Although the standardization of the previous edition of the SBIT has been severely criticized (Waddell, 1980), the new edition comes with an impressive "technical manual" (Thorndike et al., 1986b) documenting the development of the test, field trials for the new edition, standardization, and descriptive statistics, scaling, reliability, and validity. The standardization of this edition was accomplished on a carefully selected sample of over 5,000 children, adolescents, and young adults representative of the U.S. census in terms of gender, race, geographic distribution, and parental occupation and education. Test–retest reliability after an average of 16 weeks ranged from .71 and .51 (quantitative reasoning) to .91 and .90 for the composite score in preschoolers and elementary school children, respectively. Subtest reliability ranged from .28 (quantitative) to .86 (comprehension). It should be noted that retesting resulted in an overall gain of 7–8 points on the composite score.

In general, factor analysis bore out the authors' assumption of loadings on a g-factor and four third-level factors. However, Keith et al. (1988) point out that this is not the case for the age span 2–6 years, and that there is little support so far for the distinction of the crystallized versus fluid intelligence as a second-level factor dimension. Correlation with the previous edition was .81; with the WPPSI, .80; with the WISC-R, .83; with the WAIS-R, .91 for the appropriate groups; and with the Kaufman-ABC, between .82 and .89. The correlations with the WISC-R and WAIS-R for gifted, learning disabled, and mentally retarded populations ranged from .66 to .79. Johnson and McGowan (1984) also report that the SBIT significantly predicted school grades at age 7–9 in low-income Mexican-American children. Except for this study, research by independent investigators using this very recent edition is not yet available.

Nevertheless, the fourth edition has been criticized for the attempt to measure differential abilities as well as general intelligence, and for psychometric limitations of the four area score factorial composition, especially at younger age levels (Vernon, 1987). Wersh and Thomas (1990) report on a number of administrative and interpretative problems.

In the context of the neuropsychological assessment of children, the SBIT fills an age gap not covered by the Bayley or the WPPSI tests (ages 2–4), although the Kaufman-ABC is also designed to cover this age range. The choice between the SBIT and the K-ABC depends on the theoretical orientation of the examiner. In clinical practice, the user may also wish to utilize some of the subtests that are similar in content to some adult-specific neuropsychological tests: for example, sentence memory, matrices, copying, pattern analysis, absurdities, and comprehension. In addition, such tests may allow confirmation and a more detailed exploration of areas of deficit, or may be substituted for such tests in more severely impaired patients who cannot perform on the adult tests.

Normative Data

As previously mentioned, the standardization of this edition has been exemplary. Weighting procedures were used to simulate the U.S. census as closely as possible. This body of normative data has been used in constructing the tables for conversion of raw scores into SAS for each test, area SASs, and composite SAS. The composite SAS, of course, functions similarly to IQ scores in comparable tests. It should be noted, however, that the SBIS uses a standard deviation of 16 (as in previous editions of this test), whereas most other intelligence tests use a standard deviation of 15. Hence, if a definition of 2 SD below the mean is used to designate the mentally retarded range, the subject should obtain a score of less than 68 (not 70, as in other tests).

REFERENCES

Cattell, R.B. (1971). *Abilities: Their Structure, Growth and Action.* New York: Harcourt, Brace & Janovich.

Delaney, E.A. & Hopkins, T.F. (1987). *Examiner's Handbook: The Stanford-Binet Intelligence Scale: Fourth Edition.* Chicago: Riverside Publishing.

Johnson, D.L., & McGowan, R.J. (1984). Comparison of three intelligence tests as predictors of academic achievement and classroom behaviors of Mexican-American children. *Journal of Psychoeducational Assessment, 2,* 345–352.

Keith, T.Z., Cool, V.A., Novak, C.G., White,

L.J., & Pottebaum, S.M. (1988). Confirmatory factor analysis of the Stanford–Binet Fourth Edition: Testing the theory–test match. *Journal of School Psychology, 26,* 253–274.

Thorndike, R.L., Hagen, E.P., & Sattler, J.M. (1986a). *Stanford–Binet Intelligence Scale* (4th ed.). Chicago: Riverside Publishing.

Thorndike, R.L., Hagen, E.P. & Sattler, J.M. (1986b). *Technical Manual: Stanford-Binet Intelligence Scale: Fourth Edition.* Chicago: Riverside Publishing.

Vernon, P.E. (1987). The demise of the Stanford-Binet Scale. *Canadian Psychology, 28,* 251–258.

Waddell, D.D. (1980). The Stanford–Binet: An evaluation of the technical data available since the 1972 restandardization. *Journal of School Psychology, 18,* 203–209.

Wersh, J. & Thomas, M.R. (1990). The Stanford-Binet Intelligence Scale: Fourth Edition; observations, comments and concerns. *Canadian Psychology, 31,* 190–193.

5

Achievement Tests

This chapter considers a selection of commonly used measures of scholastic attainment. Tests such as the Peabody Individual Achievement Test (Markwardt, 1989), the Wide Range Achievement Test (Jastak & Wilkinson, 1984), and the Woodcock–Johnson Psychoeducational Battery (Woodcock & Mather, 1989) sample a large number of abilities that have neuropsychological and educational implications: sight reading, reading comprehension, mathematics, spelling, and general knowledge. However, these tests do not assess any of these abilities in great depth. The value of these tests (Hessler, 1984) is that they provide a comparison of the subject's level of development or deterioration with normative populations in the areas that they assess. These general screening measures permit the examiner to determine whether a person is in need of and qualifies for special instruction in a particular domain. Further, the progress of a person and the effectiveness of an instructional program can be assessed. The results of these tests also permit the examiner to develop hypotheses about an individual's strengths and weaknesses. But more detailed information is needed to evaluate these hypotheses and to develop instructional plans. The Stanford Diagnostic Reading Test (Karlsen, Madden, & Gardner, 1983) may be the test of choice since technical aspects are fairly adequate and it offers measures of literal and inferential comprehension. The KeyMath Test (Connolly et al., 1979) can be used for a more in-depth assessment of skills in mathematics. Since normative data are usually based on a representative U.S. sample, local or regional norms and norms for minority populations may have to be considered in the interpretation.

REFERENCES

Connolly, A.J., Nachtman, W., & Pritchett, E.M. (1979). *KeyMath Diagnostic Arithmetic Test*. Toronto: Psycan.

Hessler, G.L. (1984). Use and interpretation of the Woodcock-Johnson Psychoeducational Battery. Texas: DLM Teaching Resources.

Jastak, S., & Wilkinson, G. (1984). *The Wide Range Achievement Test–Revised*. Wilmington, Del.: Jastak Associates.

Karlsen, B., Madden, R., & Gardner, E.F. (1983). *Stanford Diagnostic Reading Test*. San Antonio, Texas: Psychological Corporation.

Markwardt, F.C. (1989). *Peabody Individual Achievement Test–Revised.* Circle Pines, Minn.: American Guidance Service.

Woodcock, R.W., & Mather, N. (1989). *Woodcock–Johnson Psycho-Educational Battery.* Allen, Tex.: DLM Teaching Resources.

KEYMATH DIAGNOSTIC ARITHMETIC TEST

Purpose

The purpose of the KeyMath is to assess strengths and weaknesses in several areas of mathematics.

Source

The combined tests (forms A and B) for KeyMath-R can be ordered from the American Guidance Service, Publishers Building, Circle Pines, Minnesota 55014 at a cost of $255 U.S. The Canadian edition is available from Psycan Corporation, P.O. Box 290, Station V, Toronto, Ontario M6R 3A5, for $375.00 Cdn. The revised U.S. version has just been published (KeyMath-R) but is not yet available to us. Consequently, the older version is described here.

Description

The KeyMath (Connolly et al., 1976, 1979) is a popular diagnostic measure, designed primarily for use from preschool through grade 6, although there is no upper age or grade limit. The test consists of 14 subtests organized into three major areas. The Content area is composed of three subtests—numeration, fractions, geometry, and symbols—which focus on basic knowledge of mathematics and concepts that are necessary to perform operations and make applications. The Operations area stresses computational processes and contains six subtests: addition, subtraction, multiplication, division, mental computation, and numerical reasoning. The Applications area contains problems involving the use of mathematics in everyday life. There are five subtests: word problems, missing elements, money, measurement, and time. A KeyMath metric supplement is also available; it covers five instructional areas: linearity, mass, capacity, area, and temperature.

The materials include the test plates bound into an easel, a manual, and a diagnostic record form. The easel presents the stimulus material to the subject and at the same time provides the examiner with instructions, test items, and the acceptable answer. Most items require the subject to respond verbally to open-ended questions presented orally by the examiner. Some items, however, require written computation. The items are sequenced in order of difficulty. The analysis of subject performance at an item level is made possible through the use of a table (Appendix A in the KeyMath manual) which describes the skill sampled by each item.

Administration

See source. Briefly, the examiner displays a test plate to the subject, asks a test question, and records the subject's response on a record form.

Approximate Time for Administration

The approximate time required is 30–40 minutes.

Scoring

See source. Briefly, to calculate the subject's raw score, count all items below the basal level as correct whether or not they were administered. To that number add one point for each additional item correctly answered prior to the ceiling.

The record form provides space to record and score the subject's responses, to draw a profile of subtest scores, and to note information about the subject's behavior in the test situation.

Comment

Split-half reliability is high, above .90 (Connolly et al., 1979; Price, 1984). Information on test–retest reliability is not available. The KeyMath is related to other measures of arithmetic achievement; however, the correlation coefficients, although significant, are not high (i.e., around .7) (Eaves & Simpson, 1984; Price, 1984).

The interpretation of errors may be facilitated by referring to the list of behavioral objectives in Appendix A and the instructional clusters in Appendix B of the KeyMath manual. This information can be used to guide teachers in the selection of appropriate procedures for remediation of arithmetic deficiencies. One should note, however, that the KeyMath objectives are each linked to only one test item. This may make it difficult to determine if one specific skill or item is truly an area

Table 5–1. KeyMath Percentile Ranks Corresponding to Total Test Raw Scores: Grades 2–6 April Testing

Standard score	Percentile rank	Grade 2	Grade 3	Grade 4	Grade 5	Grade 6
136	99	126–209	157–209	169–209	189–209	202–209
131	98	124–125	153–156	167–168	186–188	200–201
129	97	121–123	151–152	166	185	198–199
126	96	119–120	148–150	165	184	197
125	95	118	147	—	183	196
123	94	117	145–146	164	182	195
122	93	116	144	163	181	—
121	92	115	143	162	179–180	193–194
120	91	—	142	—	—	192
119	90	114	141	161	177–178	191
118	89	112–113	140	—	176	190
118	88	111	139	160	—	189
117	87	—	138	159	175	—
116	86	110	137	—	—	188
116	85	109	—	158	174	187
115	84	—	136	—	—	—
114	83	108	—	157	173	186
114	82	—	135	156	172	—
113	81	107	134	—	171	185
112	80	106	—	155	170	—
112	79	—	133	—	—	184
112	78	105	132	154	169	183
111	77	—	131	—	168	—
111	76	104	130	153	—	182
110	75	103	—	—	167	—
110	74	—	129	152	—	181
109	73	102	—	—	166	180
109	72	—	128	151	—	—
108	71	101	127	—	—	179
108	70	—	—	150	165	—
108	69	100	126	—	—	178
107	68	—	—	149	164	—
107	67	99	125	—	—	177
106	66	—	—	148	163	—
106	65	98	124	147	—	176
105	64	—	—	—	—	175
105	63	—	123	146	162	—
105	62	97	—	—	—	174
104	61	—	—	145	—	—
104	60	—	122	—	161	173
103	59	96	—	144	—	—
103	58	—	121	143	—	172
103	57	95	—	—	160	171

(*continued*)

Table 5–1. (*Continued*)

Standard score	Percentile rank	Grade				
		2	3	4	5	6
102	56	—	—	142	—	—
102	55	94	120	—	159	170
102	54	93	118–119	141	—	169
101	53	92	112	—	158	—
101	52	91	—	—	—	168
100	51	—	116	140	157	—
100	50	90	—	—	156	167
100	49	—	115	139	—	—
99	48	89	—	—	155	166
99	47	—	—	138	—	—
99	46	88	114	137	154	165
98	45	87	—	—	—	—
98	44	—	—	136	153	164
97	43	86	113	—	152	—
97	42	—	—	135	—	163
97	41	85	112	—	151	—
96	40	—	—	134	—	—
96	39	84	111	—	150	162
95	38	—	—	133	—	—
95	37	—	—	—	149	161
95	36	83	110	132	—	—
94	35	—	—	131	148	160
94	34	82	109	130	147	159
93	33	81	108	—	—	—
93	32	—	107	129	—	158
92	31	80	—	128	—	157
92	30	—	106	127	145	155–156
92	29	79	105	—	—	154
91	28	—	—	126	144	153
91	27	78	104	—	—	152
90	26	—	—	125	143	—
90	25	—	103	124	142	151
89	24	77	—	—	141	150
89	23	—	102	123	140	—
88	22	76	101	—	138–139	149
88	21	—	100	122	—	148
88	20	75	—	121	137	147
87	19	—	99	120	137	147
86	18	74	98	119	135	145–146
86	17	73	97	118	134	144
85	16	—	95–96	117	132–133	143
84	15	72	92–94	—	131	142
84	14	—	91	116	129–130	141
83	13	71	90	115	128	140
82	12	70	89	109–113	127	139
82	11	69	87–88	107–108	125–126	138
81	10	—	86	106	124	134–137

Standard	Percentile	Grade				
score	rank	2	3	4	5	6
80	9	68	85	—	—	131–133
79	8	67	84	105	123	130
78	7	66	—	104	—	—
77	6	64–65	82–83	103	122	129
75	5	62–63	81	—	121	128
74	4	60–61	78–80	102	120	122–127
72	3	59	74–77	101	119	120–121
69	2	57–58	69–73	94–100	117–118	114–119
65	1	56	68	93	116	113
64		48–50	65	89	106–109	112
63		46–47	63–64	87–88	105	111
62		45	62	86	103–104	110
61		44	61	85	102	109
60		43	59–60	83–84	100–101	108
59		42	58	82	99	106–107
58		40–41	56–57	80–81	98	105
57		39	55	79	96–97	103–104
56		38	53–54	77–78	95	102
55		36–37	52	76	93–94	100–101
54		35	50–51	74–75	92	99
53		34	49	73	91	97–98
52		33	48	72	89–90	96
51		32	46–47	70–71	88	94–95
50		30–31	45	69	86–87	93
49		29	43–44	67–68	85	92
48		28	42	66	84	90–91
47		27	41	65	82–83	89
46		25–26	39–40	63–64	81	88
45		24	38	62	79–80	86–87
44		23	37	61	78	85
43		22	35–36	59–60	77	83–84
42		21	34	58	75–76	82
41		20	33	56–57	74	81
40		19	32	55	72–73	79–80
<40		0–18	0–31	0–54	0–71	0–78

Note: Norms below the first percentile rank have been extrapolated.

Source: Connolly et al. (1983).

of need for remediation. Sometimes further assessment must be completed to make appropriate prescriptive decisions (Price, 1984).

The relative lack of reading and writing requirements makes the KeyMath attractive for individuals with poor reading skills since they are not penalized. However, people with poor receptive or expressive language deficits may not be reliably assessed by the KeyMath (Price, 1984).

Normative Data

Scores are provided for four diagnostic levels: (1) total test performance, (2) area performance in each of the clusters (content, operations, applications), (3) subtest performance within each cluster, and (4) item performance within each subtest. Total test performance provides a grade-equivalent score. The grade-equivalent scores are located on a scale at the bottom of the Diagnostic Record profile. A norm table of grade equivalent-scores is also presented in Appendix D of the KeyMath manual. Supplementary norms tables are available from the publisher for converting total-test raw scores of people in grades 2–6 to percentile ranks and standard scores. The norms reproduced in Table 5–1, are based on relatively large groups considered representative of North American schoolchildren.

One should note that the KeyMath is only a grade-referenced test, and does not allow for a comparison with age peers (Price, 1984). Moreover, the manual does not provide any information that allows the examiner to determine whether there are significant discrepancies between subtest scores (Sattler, 1982). No information on performance dispersion (e.g., standard deviation) is given.

REFERENCES

Connolly, A.J., Nachtman, W., & Pritchett, E.M. (1976). *KeyMath Diagnostic Arithmetic Test.* Circle Pines, Minn.: American Guidance Service.

Connolly, A.J., Nachtman, W., & Pritchett, E.M. (1979). *KeyMath Diagnostic Arithmetic Test/ Canadian Edition.* Toronto: Psycan.

Connolly, A.J., Nachtman, W., & Pritchett, E.M. (1983). *KeyMath Diagnostic Test— Supplementary Norms Table.* Circle Pines, Minn.: American Guidance Service.

Eaves, R.C., & Simpson, R.G. (1984). The concurrent validity of the Peabody Individual Achievement Test relative to the KeyMath Diagnostic Arithmetic Test among adolescents. *Psychology in the Schools, 21,* 165–167.

Price, P.A. (1984). A comparative study of the California Achievement Test (Forms C and D) and the KeyMath Diagnostic Arithmetic Test with secondary LH students. *Journal of Learning Disabilities, 17,* 392–396.

Sattler, J.M. (1982). *Assessment of Children's Intelligence and Special Abilities* (2nd ed.). Boston: Allyn & Bacon.

PEABODY INDIVIDUAL ACHIEVEMENT TEST – REVISED (PIAT-R)

Purpose

The purpose of this test is to provide a wide-range screening measure of achievement in the areas of mathematics, reading recognition, reading comprehension, spelling, and general information.

Source

The test can be ordered from the American Guidance Service, Inc., Publishers Building, Circle Pines, Minnesota 55014, at a cost of $175 U.S., or from Psycan Corporation, P.O. Box 290, Station V, Toronto, Ontario M6R 3A5, at a cost of $325 Cdn.

Description

The Peabody Individual Achievement Test (PIAT-R) (Dunn & Markwardt, 1970; Markwardt, 1989) is a popular screening measure of achievement, appropriate for children from kindergarten through grade 12 or ages 5:0–18:11 years. It is often administered to determine whether a more detailed diagnostic test should be given. The PIAT-R test materials include four volumes of test plates. These contain the demonstration and training exercises, the test items, and the instructions for administering the six subtests. A Written Expression Response Booklet is used by the subject for his or her responses to the Written Expression subtest. The Test Record booklet provides space for recording and scoring other test responses and plotting the profiles.

The test uses two item formats: multiple-choice and free response. The General Information subtest contains 100 open-ended questions that are read aloud by the examiner and answered orally by the subject. The items measure general encyclopedic knowledge in the content areas of science, social studies, fine arts, humanities, and recreation. The Reading Recognition subtest consists of 100 items and is an oral test of single-word reading. The initial, prereading items measure the subject's ability to recognize the sounds associated with printed letters; in subsequent items, the subject reads words aloud. The Reading Comprehension subtest consists of 82 items that measure a subject's ability to derive meaning from printed words. For each two-page item, the subject reads a sentence silently, and on the next page chooses the one picture out of four that best illustrates the sentence. The Mathematics subtest contains 100 multiple-choice items that range in difficulty from discriminating and matching tasks to geometry and trigonometry content. The examiner reads each item aloud while displaying the response choices to the subject. The Spelling subtest consists of 100 multiple-choice items. The first few items measure the subject's ability to recognize letters from their names or sounds. In subsequent items, the examiner reads a word aloud and uses it in a sentence, and the subject then selects the correct spelling for the word. The Written Expression subtest assesses the subject's written language skills at two levels: Level I tests prewriting skills (copying and writing letters, words, and sentences from dictation), whereas Level II requires the subject to write a story in response to a picture prompt.

Administration

See PIAT-R manual. Briefly, the examiner displays a test plate to the subject, asks a test question, and records the subject's responses on the record form. There is a standard order of subtest administration: General Information, Reading Recognition, Reading Comprehension, Mathematics, Spelling, Written Expression (Level I or Level II).

Approximate Time for Administration

The PIAT-R is an untimed test that takes approximately 60 minutes.

Scoring

See PIAT-R manual. The scoring criteria for the items are clearly stated with examples of correct and incorrect responses given on the examiner's side of the book of test plates. To obtain the raw score for each subtest, the errors are subtracted from the number of the ceiling item. Thus, the raw score for a subtest is the number of actual and assumed correct responses up to the ceiling item. A basal level is determined below which all items are assumed correct. Items above the ceiling item are assumed incorrect. Raw scores for each of the subtests are recorded on the test record. Composite scores summarize the subject's achievement. The Total Reading score is the sum of the Reading Recognition and Reading Comprehension raw scores and is an overall measure of reading ability. The Total Test composite raw score is the sum of the General Information, Reading Recognition, Reading Comprehension, Mathematics, and Spelling subtest raw scores. An optional Written Language composite, formed by the written Expression and spelling subtests, can also be computed.

The Scores page in the test record provides space for recording raw scores, derived scores, and confidence intervals for the first five PIAT-R subtests and the two composites. There is a separate section on the page for recording scores for Written Expression.

The test record includes two profiles for graphic representation of the PIAT-R results (except for Written Expression): The Developmental Score Profile is used for plotting either grade equivalents or age equivalents; the Standard Score Profile is used for plotting standard scores.

Comment

Markwardt (1989) reports that the PIAT-R subtests and composites show a high degree of internal consistency, with reliability coefficients reported to be above

.90. Test–retest reliability coefficients are also high (i.e., above .90), at least after intervals of about two to four weeks.

As might be expected, PIAT-R subtest and composite raw score means increase with age and grade. There is a substantial overlap between the PIAT-R and the PIAT, with correlations between scores on the two tests ranging from .46 to .97. Correlations between the PIAT-R and the Peabody Picture Vocabulary Test–Revised (PPVT-R) are modest and range from .50 to .72 (Markwardt, 1989). Factor analysis of the PIAT-R suggests three basic factors (Markwardt, 1989): Factor I seems to represent a general verbal–educational ability factor that has high loadings on General Information, Reading Comprehension, and Mathematics. Factor II has the highest loadings on Reading Recognition and Spelling and appears to define a narrower verbal factor that is more dependent on knowledge of letter–sound correspondences. Factor III has highest loadings on Reading Comprehension and Written Expression and seems to place a premium on knowledge of grammatical and syntactical structures.

Both the PIAT-R and the Woodcock–Johnson Psychoeducational Battery (WJPEB) provide a broad overview of scholastic attainment. The WJPEB is the more comprehensive measure. However, the PIAT-R may be more appropriate when the subject's verbal skills are limited. The multiple-choice pointing format on some of the subtests makes it possible to obtain an achievement measure for individuals who otherwise might be impossible to test because of their poor verbal abilities (Sattler, 1982). One should bear in mind, however, that the PIAT-R is fundamentally a screening device. It will help to spot problem areas, but it is not a diagnostic instrument. Finally, some of the arithmetic items may be problematic for subjects taught with the metric system.

Normative Data

For the first five PIAT-R subtests (General Information, Reading Recognition, Reading Comprehension, Mathematics, Spelling) and the two composite scores (Total Reading, Total Test), the following types of derived scores are provided in the PIAT-R manual: grade and age equivalents, standard scores by grade or age, percentile ranks, normal curve equivalents, and stanines. For Levels I and II of the Written Expression subtest, grade-based stanines are given; for Level II, a developmental scaled score is also provided which permits comparison with the entire standardization sample.

The PIAT-R standardization sample consisted of about 1,500 children (half males, half females), having the same proportional distribution as the U.S. population in terms of geographic region, socioeconomic status, and race or ethnic group. Because the norms are based solely on U.S. children, caution should be taken in interpreting scores of people residing outside of the United States.

REFERENCES

Dunn, L.M., & Markwardt, F.C. (1970). *Peabody Individual Achievement Test Manual.* Circle Pines, Minn.: American Guidance Service.

Markwardt, F.C. (1989). *Peabody Individual*

Achievement Test–Revised. Circle Pines, Minn.: American Guidance Service.

Sattler, J.M. (1982). *Assessment of Children's Intelligence and Special Abilities* (2nd ed.). Boston: Allyn & Bacon.

STANFORD DIAGNOSTIC READING TEST (SDRT)

Purpose

The purpose of this test is to assess strengths and weaknesses in reading.

Source

The materials include test booklets, answer sheets and scoring keys and norms booklet. These can be ordered from the Psychological Corporation, P.O. Box 839954, San Antonio, Texas 78283-3954, at a cost of $119.00 U.S., per level, or from Harcourt Brace Jovanovitch Inc., 55 Horner Avenue, Toronto, Ontario M5Z 4X6, at a cost of about $150, per level.

Description

The Stanford Diagnostic Reading Test (SDRT) third edition (Karlsen et al., 1984), was designed to provide assessment particularly of low-achieving students. It consists of four levels, with two parallel forms (G and H) at each level. At each level, a set of skills, representing the four general areas of decoding, vocabulary, comprehension, and rate, are tested. Although some skills are measured at all four levels, the ways in which these skills are measured change from level to level.

The Red Level is intended for use at the end of grade 1, in grade 2, and with extremely low-achieving pupils in grade 3. It measures skills in auditory discrimination ("Determine whether two dictated words have the same beginning, middle, or ending sound"),* phonetic analysis ("Identify the letter or letter combination that matches initial or final sounds of words"), auditory vocabulary ("Select the picture or word that best fits the word tested or the meaning of sentences"), word recognition ("Identify words that describe a particular picture"), and reading comprehension ("Identify a picture that illustrates the meaning of a printed sentence, and answer questions in a multiple-choice format after reading short passages").

The Green Level is intended for use in grades 3 and 4 and with very low-achieving pupils in grade 5. It measures skills in auditory discrimination, phonetic

---

*This and the following quotations are from the Stanford Diagnostic Reading Test: Second Edition. Copyright 1976, 1978 by Harcourt Brace Jovanovich, Inc. Reproduced by permission. All rights reserved.

analysis, structural analysis ("Analyze word parts and blend these units into words"), auditory vocabulary, and literal and inferential comprehension ("Answer the questions after reading the short passages").

The Brown Level can be used in grades 5–8 and with very low-achieving high school students. It measures skills in phonetic and structural analysis and auditory vocabulary. Literal and inferential comprehension are assessed by means of textual, functional, and recreational reading passages followed by questions. A reading rate subtest, also included in this level, requires the subject to read a passage quickly and to respond to multiple-choice questions under speeded conditions.

The Blue Level is intended for use in grades 9 through 12 and community colleges. This level measures skills in phonetic and structural analysis; reading vocabulary; literal and inferential comprehension of textual, functional, and recreational reading material; word parts ("Identify, in a multiple-choice format, the meaning of components such as affixes, root words, and word roots"); and reading rate. A scanning and skimming subtest is included in this level and consists of two parts. In Part A, subjects are presented a set of questions and are asked to find the answers in the accompanying article without reading through the article completely. In Part B, subjects are asked to extract both general and specific information about an article in a short period of time.

Administration

The test can be administered in a group or individually. Not all subtests need be given. Procedures for administration are clearly described in the SDRT manuals. Briefly, the examiner reads the instructions and the subject responds in the test booklet or answer folder.

Approximate Time for Administration

The time required is about two hours if all subtests are given.

Scoring

The test booklets or answer folders can be hand-scored using stencil keys. Alternatively, they may be processed by machine through the Psychological Corporation.

Comment

Internal consistency and alternate-form reliability are adequate, with coefficients above .7 (see source). No test–retest information is available.

One advantage of the test is that it was designed to be most useful with individuals who are experiencing reading difficulty. It was developed specifically to include very easy items at each level, so that even very low achievers would experience some success. Consequently, the SDRT is not recommended to assess the strengths and weaknesses of average to above-average readers or to monitor program gains for such individuals.

Another advantage of the test is that it provides coverage of a number of different aspects of reading, including inferential comprehension. Many brain-damaged patients have difficulty handling abstract concepts, and the inclusion of a measure of high-level conceptual abilities may be particularly revealing.

At each level, a set of component skills representing the four general areas of decoding, vocabulary, comprehension, and rate are evaluated. The authors assume a hierarchy of components in the sense that the learning of lower-level skills is prerequisite to the learning of more advanced skills later in the sequence. Some have questioned the sequencing and placement of these components (Ewoldt, 1982; Van Roekel, 1978). Others have questioned whether the skills tested are essential to the acquisition of reading (Tierney, 1985). For example, structural analysis requires selecting and arranging elements into a word (e.g., microscope) from an array of word parts (e.g., mi le cro scope). Further, although a number of different kinds of reading behaviors are sampled, the test does not sample all behaviors relevant to the reading process. In short, the test is best viewed as only a limited sample of behavior relevant to reading (Ysseldyke, 1985).

An additional feature of the SDRT that warrants some comment is the inclusion in the manual of suggestions as to how teachers might organize their classes and their instructional activities to meet individual needs. The suggestions should be regarded as speculative in nature and not drawn from a substantial data base (Tierney, 1985; Van Roekel, 1978).

Normative Data

The authors state that the test was standardized on a large number of students considered representative of the U.S. school population. However, the data supporting this claim are not detailed. A variety of different transformed scores can be obtained, including percentile ranks, stanines, grade equivalents, and scaled scores. These test results can then be summarized on either the Instructional Report Form or on the Stanine Profile.

REFERENCES

Ewoldt, C. (1982). Diagnostic approaches and procedures and the reading process. *Volta Review, 84*, 83–94.

Karlsen, B., Madden, R., & Gardner, E.F. (1984). *Stanford Diagnostic Reading Test.*

San Antonio, Texas: Psychological Corporation.

Tierney, R.J. (1985). Review of Stanford Diagnostic Reading Test, 1976 edition. In J.V. Mitchell, Jr. (Ed.), *The Ninth Mental Mea-*

surements Yearbook. Neb.: The Buros Institute of Mental Measurements.

Van Roekel, B.H. (1978). Stanford Diagnostic Reading Test. In O. Buros (Ed.), The Eighth Mental Measurements Yearbook. Highland Park, New Jersey. The Gryphon Press.

Ysseldyke, J.E. (1985). Review of Stanford Diagnostic Reading Test. Blue Level. In J.V. Mitchell, Jr. (Ed.), The Ninth Mental Measurements Yearbook. Lincoln, Neb.: The Buros Institute of Mental Measurements.

WIDE RANGE ACHIEVEMENT TEST – REVISED (WRAT-R)

Purpose

The purpose of this test is to measure reading (word recognition and pronunciation), spelling, and arithmetic.

Source

The test can be ordered from the Psychological Corporation, P.O. Box 839954, San Antonio, Texas 78204-0954, at a cost of $65 U.S., or from the Institute of Psychological Research, 34 Fleury Street West, Montreal, Quebec, H3L 1S9, for $86.95 Cdn.

Description

The Wide Range Achievement Test (WRAT) is one of the most frequently used measures of academic achievement (Sheehan, 1983) because it is quick and easy to administer and assesses three different ability areas: reading, spelling, and arithmetic (Sattler, 1982). It was originally published in 1936. Revisions appeared in 1946, 1965, 1976, 1978, and 1984. The latest revision, the WRAT-R (Jastak & Wilkinson, 1984), differs only slightly in item content from its predecessors. In addition, new record forms and norms have been provided. The complete kit consists of the administration and scoring manual, the test forms, and plastic cards containing the reading and spelling word lists.

The WRAT-R consists of two separate forms. Level 1 is designed for use with children between the ages 5:0 and 11:11. The other form, Level II, is intended for persons from 12:0 to 74:11 years. Each level is composed of three subtests: reading, spelling, and arithmetic. The reading skills that are measured include letter and word recognition. The spelling skills include copying marks, writing one's name, and writing single words from dictation. The arithmetic skills cover counting, reading number symbols, solving oral problems, and performing written computations.

Administration

See source. Briefly, the examiner presents a test card, reads aloud words and sentences, asks test questions, and records responses. The three subtests can be given in any order.

Approximate Time for Administration

The test is timed and takes about 30 minutes.

Scoring

Record the total number correct.

Comment

It is difficult to assess the reliability and validity of the WRAT-R because the data presented in the manual are very sketchy (Reid, 1986; Reynolds, 1986). Traditional measures of internal consistency are not provided. Test–retest reliabilities are reported for a small number of subjects and range from .79 to .97, but it is difficult to know to what age groups the coefficients refer. With regard to concurrent validity, the studies mentioned in the manual deal with the WRAT, not the WRAT-R, and are not directly relevant to the revision. There are modest correlations between the Wechsler Adult Intelligence Scale – Revised (WAIS-R) and Level II of the WRAT-R (Spruill & Beck, 1986a), and between the Woodcock–Johnson Achievement Test and the WRAT-R (Wilkinson, 1987). However, further research is needed to address these issues.

In addition to concerns regarding reliability and validity, there is a compound-ing problem for non-U.S. users in that there is a lack of correspondence with curricula in Canada and other English-speaking countries. The Arithmetic subtest in particular is of questionable use since students may not have been exposed to the teaching of some of the skills. Canada has gone metric, and there is much less emphasis on fractions, with more stress on decimals (Sheehan, 1983). Canadian normative data for the WRAT-R are unavailable.

The WRAT-R provides only a limited amount of information about reading, arithmetic, and spelling (Sattler, 1982). For example, reading comprehension is not assessed, only letter or word recognition. In addition, no specific breakdowns are provided to enable the user to determine the specific types of reading, arith-metic, or spelling difficulties (Sattler, 1982). Because of these issues, unresolved questions of reliability and validity, as well as shortcomings in the standardization procedures (Reid, 1986; Reynolds, 1986; Sattler, 1982; Spruill & Beck, 1986a), the test should *not* be used as a diagnostic measure of academic difficulties. However, it may be useful as a quick, but gross, screening device. Our own view is that better tests are available (e.g., Woodcock–Johnson Psychoeducational Battery – Revised; Peabody Individual Achievement Test, PIAT-R) but clinicians should be familiar with the WRAT-R, given its widespread use. If used, the formula-type arithmetic subtest should be compared with the Applied Problems subtest of the Woodcock–Johnson, and the reading recognition subtest should be supplemented with the Reading or Passage Comprehension subtests of the PIAT-R or Woodcock–Johnson.

Normative Data

Raw scores can be converted to three other types of scores: grade equivalents, percentiles, and standard scores. Grade equivalents and percentiles should be used only as rough guides to performance. Standard scores are the preferred scores to use. They are based on a mean of 100 and a standard deviation of 15. Raw scores can be converted directly to standard scores by means of norm tables listed in the WRAT-R manual. The age intervals are semiannual from ages 5:0 to 11:11 years. At Level II, the semiannual groupings continue through age 13. Thereafter, the norms are given as follows: ages 14, 15, 16–17, 20–24, 25–34, 35–44, 45–54, 55–64, and 65–74.

The standardization procedures followed for the WRAT-R are described inadequately, as is the sample (Reid, 1986; Reynolds, 1986). Thus, the current norms may not accurately reflect an individual's level of achievement relative to the general population. In short, the norms must be considered of limited value since they may result in erroneous placements or expectations.

Users should also note that the WRAT-R follows the trend for revised test scores to be lower than the test scores of earlier versions (Flynn, 1984). The standard scores for the WRAT-R are about 8–11 points lower than the corresponding WRAT (1978) scores (Spruill & Beck, 1986b). Consequently, great care should be taken when comparing test scores between current and previous editions.

REFERENCES

Flynn, J.R. (1984). The mean IQ of Americans: Massive gains 1932–1978. *Psychological Bulletin, 95,* 29–51.

Jastak, S., & Wilkinson, G. (1984). *The Wide Range Achievement Test–Revised: Administration Manual.* Wilmington, Del.: Jastak Associates.

Reid, N. (1986). Wide Range Achievement Test: 1984 Revised Edition. *Journal of Counseling and Development, 64,* 538–539.

Reynolds, D. (1986). Wide Range Achievement Test (WRAT-R) 1984 Edition. *Journal of Counseling and Development, 64,* 540–541.

Sattler, J.M. (1982). *Assessment of Children's Intelligence and Special Abilities* (2nd ed.). Boston: Allyn.

Sheehan, T.D. (1983). Re-norming the WRAT: An urban Ontario sample. *Ontario Psychologist, 15,* 16–33.

Spruill, J., & Beck, B. (1986a). Relationship between the WAIS-R and Wide Range Achievement Test–Revised. *Educational and Psychological Measurement, 46,* 1037–1040.

Spruill, J., & Beck, B. (1986b). Relationship between the WRAT and WRAT-R. *Psychology in the Schools, 23,* 357–360.

Wilkinson, G.S. (1987). *WRAT-R Monograph.* Wilmington, Del.: Jastak Associates.

WOODCOCK–JOHNSON PSYCHOEDUCATIONAL BATTERY – REVISED: TESTS OF ACHIEVEMENT (WJ-R ACH)

Purpose

This is a wide-range tool that includes measures of achievement in the areas of reading, mathematics, written language, and knowledge of science, social studies, and humanities.

Source

The achievement section of the battery can be ordered from DLM Teaching Resources, 1 DLM Park, Allen, Texas 75002, at a cost of $215 U.S., or from DLM Teaching Resources Ltd., c/o PMB Industries, Ltd., 1220 Ellesmere Road, Scarborough, Ontario M1P 2X5, at a cost of $367 Cdn. Computer scoring programs (Compuscore) are also available at additional cost ($189.00 US or $299.00 Cdn) from the publisher.

Description

The WJ-R is a revised and expanded version of the 1977 Woodcock–Johnson battery developed as a comprehensive, individually administered measure of cognitive ability, academic achievement, scholastic aptitude, scholastic/nonscholastic interests, and independent functioning. It is intended for both handicapped and nonhandicapped populations from age 2 to 90 years. Our focus here is on the Tests of Achievement (WJ-R ACH) which has two separate forms (Form A and Form B), each of which must be purchased separately. The WJ-R ACH is subdivided into a Standard Battery and a Supplemental Battery and allows for analysis of four curriculum areas: reading, mathematics, written language, and knowledge. The subtests are presented in two flip-page easel books, one for the Standard and one for the Supplemental Battery, designed to stand on the table during administration. The books contain the items for each subtest and the instructions for administration. Separate manuals provide instructions for scoring, administration, and the tables necessary for score interpretation. Response booklets are provided to record, summarize, and interpret test performance. Most of the subtests are untimed and have basal and ceiling levels established by six consecutive correct and six consecutive failed items, respectively.

The Standard Battery of the WJ-R ACH consists of nine subtests, each measuring different aspects of scholastic achievement:

Letter–Word Identification: measures the ability to identify letters and words.

Passage Comprehension: measures the subject's skill in supplying the appropriate word to complete a short passage after silently reading the passage.

Calculation: tests the subject's ability to perform calculations ranging from simple addition and subtraction to those involving trigonomic, logarithmic, geometric, and calculus operations. Procedures are specified and no application skills are required. Items are completed in a special Subject Response Booklet.

Applied Problems: measures the subject's ability to solve practical problems. The subject must recognize the correct procedure, identify the relevant data, and perform relatively simple calculations. Problems are presented visually or are read to the subject to minimize the effect of reading ability. The use of note paper is permitted.

Dictation: tests the subject's ability to respond in writing to a variety of questions requiring knowledge of punctuation, capitalization, spelling, and word usage (e.g., contractions, abbreviations, plurals).

Writing Samples: measures the subject's skill in writing responses to a variety of demands. The subject must phrase and present written sentences that are evaluated with respect to the quality of expression. The subject is not penalized for errors in basic orthography such as spelling or punctuation.

Science: tests the subject's knowledge in the biological and physical sciences. Items are read aloud by the examiner.

Social Studies: tests the subject's knowledge in geography, government, economics, and other aspects of broad social studies. Items are read aloud by the examiner.

Humanities: measures the subject's knowledge in various areas of art, music, and literature. The subject responds orally to questions that are read by the examiner.

Six tests from the Standard Battery are suitable for use as early development measures: Letter–Word Identification, Applied Problems, Dictation, Science, Social Studies, and Humanities. In addition to preschool children, this set of tests may be administered to low-functioning individuals of any age.

The WJ-R ACH Supplemental Battery can provide a more comprehensive assessment of a subject's achievement in reading, mathematics, and written language. It consists of five tests:

Word Attack: requires the subject to read nonsense words and assesses phonic and structural analysis skills.

Reading Vocabulary: measures the subject's skill in reading words and applying appropriate meanings. In Part A, Synonyms, the subject must state a word similar in meaning to the word presented. In Part B, Antonyms, the subject must state a word that is opposite in meaning to the word presented.

Quantitative Concepts: measures the subject's knowledge of mathematical concepts and vocabulary. The test does not require the subject to perform any calculations or make any application decisions.

Proofing: tests the subject's ability to read a short passage that is known to contain one and only one error. The error may be of punctuation, capitalization, spelling, or usage. The subject's task is to identify the error and to indicate how it should be corrected.

Writing Fluency: measures the subject's skill in formulating and writing simple sentences quickly. Each sentence must relate to a given stimulus picture and use a set of three words. This test has a seven-minute time limit.

In addition to these five subtests, four test scores, identified by letter names, may be derived. Scores for Punctuation and Capitalization (P), Spelling (S), and Usage (U) are determined from analysis of performance on the Dictation test in the Standard Battery and the Proofing test in the Supplemental Battery. The score for Handwriting (H) is determined from an analysis of the subject's handwriting produced during the Writing Samples test in the Standard Battery.

Although subtests are the basic components of the battery, clusters of scores (Reading, Mathematics, Written Language, Knowledge, Skills) can be derived from certain combinations of subtests. Five cluster scores can be calculated from the Standard Battery. The Broad Reading cluster is a combination of the Letter–Word Identification and Passage Comprehension tests and provides a broad measure of reading achievement. The Broad Mathematics Cluster is a combination of the Calculation and Applied Problems tests and provides a broad measure of mathematical achievement. The Broad Written Language Cluster is a combination of the Dictation and Writing Samples tests and provides a broad measure of written language achievement including both production of single-word responses and production of sentences embedded in context. The Broad Knowledge Cluster is a combination of the Science, Social Studies, and Humanities tests. The Skills cluster is a combination of the Letter–Word Identification, Applied Problems, and

Dictation tests and provides a quick screening of broad achievement. It may be used as an early development (E Dev) measure.

In addition to the cluster scores derived from the Standard Battery, six additional cluster scores can be derived using tests from the Standard and Supplemental Batteries. The Basic Reading Skills cluster is a combination of Letter–Word Identification and Word Attack and provides a measure of basic reading skills that includes both sight vocabulary and the ability to apply phonic and structural analysis skills. The Reading Comprehension cluster is a combination of Passage Comprehension and Reading Vocabulary and provides a measure of reading comprehension skills that includes both comprehension of single-word stimuli and context-embedded stimuli. The Basic Mathematics Skills cluster is a combination of the Calculation and Quantitative Concepts tests and provides a measure of basic mathematical skills, including computation skills and knowledge of mathematical concepts and vocabulary. The Mathematics Reasoning Cluster consists only of the Applied Problems test and provides a measure of the ability to analyze and solve practical math problems. The Basic Writing Skills cluster is a combination of Dictation and Proofing and provides a measure of basic writing skills, including both writing single-word responses and identifying errors in spelling, punctuation, capitalization, and word usage. Finally, the Written Expression cluster is a combination of Writing Samples and Writing Fluency and provides a measure of written expression skills, including production of simple sentences with ease and of increasingly complex sentences to meet special requirements.

Administration

See WJ-R Manual. The easel format facilitates administration. The notation of basal and ceiling rules directly on the Test Record and the uniformity of the basal (six consecutive correct responses) and ceiling (six consecutive incorrect responses) rules for most subtests also contribute to the ease of administration. Further, the use of basal and ceiling rules makes it possible to match the difficulty level of subtests to the ability of the individual being tested. Not all subtests need be given (principle of selective testing) and the subtests may be given in any order.

Approximate Time for Administration

Approximately 50–60 minutes are needed to give the nine tests of the Standard Battery. The Writing Samples test requires about 15 minutes to administer, whereas the other eight tests require an average of five minutes each. The four tests in the Supplemental Battery take about 30 minutes to give.

Scoring

See WJ-R ACH manual. The scoring criteria for the items are clear. Examples of correct and incorrect responses are presented on the examiner's side of the easel and in the examiner's manual. A variety of derived scores are available, including age equivalents, grade equivalents, relative mastery indexes (RMI), test or cluster difference scores, percentile ranks, standard scores, T-scores, stanines, and normal curve equivalents. RMIs are statements describing mastery or quality of performance. This score allows statements to be made about a subject's expected level of performance on tasks similar to the ones tested. It indicates the percentage of mastery predicted for a given subject when the reference group would perform with 90% mastery. RMIs are also interpreted by functioning levels ranging from "very superior" to "very low" (Table 4.3 in manual).

The process of obtaining derived scores is somewhat lengthy, complex, and prone to error, but may be simplified by using the Compuscore for the WJ-R. Briefly, the raw score for each subtest is associated, via a table in the Test Record, with the "W score" (which is an intermediate score needed to complete the calculations), the standard error of measurement of the W score, the age equivalent, and the grade equivalent. The Age/Grade Profiles, located on the front and back covers of the Test Record, are then completed by transferring the W scores for each subtest and cluster into the appropriate box on the front or back cover. Expected test and cluster W scores ("REF W") for age (Table B) or grade (Table C) and the standard error of measurement (SEM) for the standard scores are then entered on the Test Record, and the difference is calculated between the observed and expected scores. After difference scores have been determined, RMIs, standard scores (mean = 100, SD = 15), and percentile ranks (PR) may be obtained from norm Table D in the manual. Confidence bands for the standard scores and percentile ranks are then obtained, either directly from the Test Record (for standard scores) or from Table E in the manual (for PR). The bars on the Standard Score/Percentile Rank Profiles, found on the Test Record, are completed next and are based on 1 SEM. The degree of overlap between the confidence bands can be used to provide clues about a subject's strengths and weaknesses. If the confidence bands for any two tests or clusters overlap at all, then one can assume that no difference exists in the subject's ability for these measures. On the other hand, if the separation between the two bands is greater than the width of the wider band, then one can assume that a real difference exists in the subject's ability for these measures.

Once the scores have been derived, one can evaluate whether subjects with a significant intraachievement discrepancy exhibit specific achievement deficits. The first stage in the procedure is to determine the subject's expected score in one area of achievement based upon the average achievement levels in the other three areas of achievement. The second stage is to compare the subject's actual achievement score in the target area with the expected score, using Table F in the manual if the analysis is based on age, or Table G if the analysis is based on grade. The significance of any difference is then evaluated by obtaining the Percentile Rank and SD DIFF in Table H of the manual. The percentile rank indicates the percentage of the subject's peer group with achievement that low, or lower, compared to average achievement in the other three areas. The "SD DIFF" is the difference, in units of the standard error of estimate, between the subject's actual and expected scores.

Comment

Woodcock and Mather (1989) report impressive split-half reliability coefficients. Reliabilities are generally in the high .80s and low .90s for the tests and in the mid .90s for the clusters. Data on test–retest reliability are available only for the Writing Fluency test (.76). The concurrent validity of the WJ-R ACH, using a variety of achievement tests (e.g., KABC, PPVT, PIAT, WRAT-R), is modest, with correlations typically in the .50–.60 range. When the tests and clusters are grouped by curricular areas, the tests and clusters within the same curricular area correlate more highly with each other than with tests and clusters belonging to other curricular areas. Finally, Johnson and Mather note that the test yields the expected pattern of scores with different populations; namely, scores show a progressive increase going from the mentally retarded, learning disabled, normal to gifted populations, and there is an increase in scores with age for each type of sample.

One should note that the Reading cluster measures primarily word recognition skills, with reading comprehension only minimally assessed. Further, the reading comprehension that is evaluated is literal rather than a higher type of comprehension, such as critical or inferential (Hessler, 1984).

The WJ-R ACH is a technically excellent instrument and provides a more comprehensive measure of reading, written language, mathematics, and content knowledge, than other individually administered survey instruments [e.g., Peabody Individual Achievement Test – Revised (PIAT-R) Wide Range Achievement Test–Revised (WRAT-R)]. The PIAT-R, however, may be more appropriate when the subject's verbal skills are limited. One should also note that the WJ-R ACH is fundamentally a screening device, not a diagnostic instrument. Further testing with other instruments (e.g, KeyMath, Stanford Diagnostic Reading Test) may be necessary to provide in-depth information about a subject's skills. Further, some of the items are biased owing to their U.S. content and may be troublesome for other English-speaking populations.

Normative Data

Data provided in the WJ-R ACH manual were derived from a large sample (6,359) of normal people, ranging in age from 24 months to 95 years, residing in the United States. The norms can be considered representative in terms of U.S. census data. Since the norms are derived solely from U.S. samples, caution should be used when interpreting scores of people residing outside the United States.

REFERENCES

Hessler, G.L. (1984). *Use and Interpretation of the Woodcock–Johnson Psychoeducational Battery*. Allen, Tex.: DLM Teaching Resources.

Woodcock, R.W., & Mather, N. (1989). *Woodcock–Johnson Tests of Achievement*. Allen, Tex.: DLM Teaching Resources.

6

Attention and Memory Tests

Memory disturbance is a very common complaint which has a number of potential causes, including deficits in registration, retention, and retrieval. At a minimum, the memory examination should cover immediate or short-term retention, the rate and pattern of acquisition of new information, the efficiency of retrieval of both recently learned and remote information, and proactive and retroactive interference. Further, these component processes should be evaluated for both verbal and nonverbal domains, using both recall and recognition techniques since inferences about the relative integrity of encoding and retrieval processes are usually made by contrasting free recall and recognition performance. Evaluation of the various memory processes can play an important role in testing different diagnostic hypotheses and in facilitating efforts of rehabilitation. The reader is referred to reviews by Delis (1989), Lezak (1983), and Shimamura (1989) for more in-depth discussions of these conceptual distinctions and their neuropsychological significance.

Clinicians usually turn to an assortment of materials and procedures to evaluate meaningful components of memory. For most adults, the Wechsler Memory Scale (Wechsler, 1945) and the Wechsler Memory Scale – Revised (Wechsler, 1987) offer an important first step in the assessment of memory. Verbal memory tests, such as the Selective Reminding Test (Bushke, 1973; Bushke & Fuld, 1974) and the Rey Auditory Verbal Learning Test (Rey, 1964), can then be used to delineate further the specific component processes that are affected. These supraspan word-list learning tests include measures of immediate and long-term recall and recognition, and increased vulnerability to proactive and retroactive interference; they also reveal learning ability.

Clinical assessment of visuospatial memory typically relies on the brief presentation of visual designs followed by recall or recognition at varying length of delay. Examples of widely used tests include the Benton Visual Retention Test (BVRT;

Benton, 1974) and the Rey–Osterrieth Complex Figure (Osterrieth, 1944; Rey, 1941). The Rey Visual Learning Test (Rey, 1964) is a nonverbal analogue to the widely used supraspan word-list learning technique. Some of the tests of visuo-spatial memory confound the effects of visuoperceptual and constructional impairments with possible disorders in memory. The inclusion of both multiple-choice (e.g., BVRT, Rey Visual Design Learning Test) and copy (BVRT, Rey–Osterrieth Complex Figure) administrations may help the examiner to discriminate among perceptual, constructional, and memory disorders.

Some patients who complain of memory disorders actually have disorders of attention, concentration, or tracking. Vigilance tasks, such as the Concentration Endurance Test (D2 test) (Brickenkamp, 1975), involve visual search and scanning as well as sustained attention. More complex mental tracking tasks, such as the Paced Auditory Serial Addition Task (Gronwall & Sampson, 1974), assess the rate of information processing and sustained attention.

REFERENCES

Benton, A.L. (1974). *Revised Visual Retention Test* (4th ed.). New York: The Psychological Corporation.

Brickenkamp, R. (1975). *Test d2;/ Aufmerks-amkeits–Belastungs/Test (Handanwei-sung*, 5th ed.) Göttingen; Verlag für Psychologie Dr. C.J. Hogrefe.

Bushke, H. (1973). Selective reminding for analysis of memory and learning. *Journal of Verbal Learning and Behavior, 12,* 543–550.

Bushke, H., & Fuld, P. (1974). Evaluating storage, retention, and retrieval in disordered memory and learning. *Neurology, 24,* 1019–1025.

Delis, D.C. (1989). Neuropsychological assessment of learning and memory. In F. Boller & J. Grafman (Series Eds.) & L. Squire (Section Ed.), *Handbook of Neuropsychology* (Vol. 3, pp. 3–34). Amsterdam: Elsevier.

Gronwall, D.M. A., & Sampson, H. (1974). *The Psychological Effects of Concussion.* Auckland, N.Z.: Auckland University Press.

Lezak, M.D. (1985). *Neuropsychological Assessment* (2nd ed.). New York: Oxford University Press.

Osterrieth, P.A. (1944). Le test de copie d'une figure complex: Contribution a l'étude de la perception et de la mémoire. *Archives de Psychologie, 30,* 286–356.

Rey, A. (1964). *L'examen clinique en psychologie.* Paris; Press Universaire de France.

Rey, A. (1941). L'examen psychologique dans les cas d'encephalopathie traumatique. *Archives de Psychologie, 28,* 286–340.

Shimamura, A.P. (1989). Disorders of memory: The cognitive science perspective. In F. Boller & J. Grafman (Series Eds.) & L. Squire (Section Ed.), *Handbook of Neuropsychology.* Vol. 3, pp. 35–74. Amsterdam: Elsevier.

Wechsler, D. (145). A standardized memory scale for clinical use. *Journal of Psychology, 19,* 87–95.

Wechsler, D. (1987). *Wechsler Memory Scale – Revised.* New York: The Psychological Corporation.

BENTON VISUAL RETENTION TEST – REVISED (BVRT-R)

Other Test Name

Another test name is the Visual Retention Test (VRT)

Purpose

The purpose of this test is to assess visual memory, visual perception, and visuo-constructive abilities.

Source

The manual (fourth edition) for the drawing administrations, design cards (Forms C, D, and E bound together), and record forms can be obtained from the Psychological Corporation, P.O. Box 9954, San Antonio, Texas 78204-0954, at a cost (complete set) of $65.50 U.S. or from the Institute of Psychological Research, Inc., 34 Fleury Street West, Montreal, Quebec H3L-1S9, for $100.00 Cdn. The German manual for the multiple-choice version (Der Benton-Test), stimuli, and answer sheets can be obtained from Hogrefe and Huber Publishers, 12 Brucepark Avenue, Toronto, Ontario M4P 2S3, at a cost of about $100 Cdn.

Description

The drawing administrations of the Benton Visual Retention Test – Revised (BVRT) have three alternate forms (C, D, and E) which are roughly of equivalent difficulty. Each form is composed of 10 designs; the first two designs consist of one major geometric figure and the other eight designs consist of two major figures and a peripheral figure. Under Administration A, the standard procedure, each design is displayed for 10 seconds and withdrawn. Immediately after this, the subject is required to reproduce the design from memory at his or her own pace on a blank piece of paper. Administration B is similar to A except that each design is exposed for only five seconds. Administration C requires that the subject copy each of the designs while looking at them. In Administration D, each design is exposed for 10 seconds and the subject must reproduce each design after a 15-second delay. Two additional forms (F and G) are available to test the subject's recognition, rather than reproduction, ability (Administration M). Each of these forms consists of 15 stimulus cards, each exposed for 10 seconds, and corresponding four-choice response cards. The multiple-choice administration can be used for people with motor handicaps or for persons without motor handicaps, in order to determine whether the person's disability lies in the area of memory, perception, or drawing ability.

Administration

See manual. Briefly, for Administrations A–D, the subject is given 10 blank, white 21.5 × 14 cm pieces of paper. The subject either reproduces each design from memory (Administrations A, B, D) or copies each design (Administration C). Drawings should be numbered in the right-hand corner by the examiner after completion of the drawing in order to identify the spatial orientation of the drawing, as well as the specific design that was drawn (Wellman, 1985). For Administration M, each of the 15 stimulus cards, consisting of one to three geometric figures, is exposed for 10 seconds. Immediately after each exposure, the subject is shown a multiple-choice card with four similar stimuli; he or she must choose (point to) the one that is identical to the stimulus card.

Approximate Time for Administration

The time required is about 5–10 minutes.

Scoring

Scoring is accomplished according to explicit criteria that are detailed in the manual (see source). Briefly, two scoring systems (the number of correct reproductions and the error score) are available for the evaluation of a subject's performance on the drawing forms (Administrations A–D). The number correct score, has a range of 0–10 as each of the 10 designs is scored on an all-or-none basis and given a credit of 1 or 0. Principles underlying the scoring of the designs, together with specific scoring samples illustrating correct and incorrect reproductions, are located in the manual. The scoring of errors allows for both a quantitative and qualitative analysis of a subject's performance. Six major types of errors are noted: (1) omissions, (2) distortions, (3) perseverations, (4) rotations, (5) misplacements, and (6) size errors. Each major category contains a variety of specific error subtypes. Provision is also made for noting right- and left-sided errors. Scoring is recorded and summarized on the record form. This form allows the examiner to indicate the correct designs as well as summarize the types of errors made on each design.

Comment

For the drawing administrations of the BVRT, interscorer agreement for number correct and the total error score is high (above .95; Swan et al., 1990; Wahler, 1956). Alternate form reliability is good. Benton (1974) reports correlation coefficients ranging from .79 to .84 between the three forms (C, D, and E) of the test. There is some evidence (Benton, 1974) that Form D is slightly more difficult than Form C, with Form E occupying an intermediate position. This difference in difficulty level holds only for the memory, not the copy tasks (Benton, 1974). There is a modest relation (.41–.52) between performance levels on the copying (Administration C) and memory (Administration B) tasks (Benton, 1974). Positive correlations, ranging from .40 to .83, have also been reported between immediate (Administration A) and delayed (Administration D) reproduction versions (Benton, 1974). Retest reliability for Administration A is high (.85; Benton, 1974).

For the multiple-choice administration (M), alternate-form reliability (Forms F and G) is good (.80; Benton, 1981). Split-half reliability of the multiple-choice forms is .76 (Benton, 1981). The correlation between the multiple-choice and reproduction forms is, however, considerably lower (.55; Benton, 1981).

Although performance is intended to measure nonverbal memory, some of the geometric figures can be verbalized (Arenberg, 1978). Further, the reproduction administrations are more closely associated with visual–perceptual–motor ability than with visual memory. Factor analyses reveal that the BVRT (Administration A) loads primarily on a visual–perceptual–motor factor, and only secondarily on a memory–concentration–attention factor (Larabee et al., 1985). Finally, some of the items on the multiple-choice version of the BVRT can be correctly completed without viewing the target stimuli, merely by solving the task as an oddity problem (Blanton & Gouvier, 1985). Thus, the validity of the test may be compromised in subjects who respond strategically rather than by relying on their visual memory. The examiner should interview the subject after the test to determine the type of strategy that was used (Franzen, 1989).

A number of studies have examined the ability of the BVRT to detect brain injury (Benton, 1974; Heaton et al., 1978; Marsh & Hirsch, 1982; Schwerd & Salgueiro-Feik, 1980; Tamkin & Kunce, 1985). Overall, these studies show that the test is sensitive to the presence of brain damage, although its predictive ability is not high. The clinical impression is that patients with right posterior lesions tend to be most impaired on the reproduction administrations of the BVRT, but the evidence is inconsistent (Benton, 1974). The copying (Administration C) and multiple-choice (Administration M) versions of the BVRT also do not distinguish between hemispheric side of lesion (Arena & Gainotti, 1978). Some types of errors may, however, be of localizing significance. For example, patients with unilateral neglect may consistently omit peripheral figures appearing on one side.

The BVRT has a number of advantages (Wellman, 1985) that are worth noting.

These include short administration time, precise scoring criteria, and many alternative forms. Further, because of its multiple-choice, drawing from memory, and copying administrations, the examiner may be able to discriminate between perceptual, motor, and memory deficits. Finally, the BVRT is one of the few neuropsychological tests for which patterns of dissimulation are known (Franzen, 1989). Simulators produce more errors than brain-damaged subjects; they produce more distortions, fewer perseverations, and fewer errors than brain-damaged patients (Benton & Spreen, 1961).

Normative Data

Performance on the BVRT shows a moderate correlation with intelligence (about .7; Benton, 1974) and age (Arenberg, 1978; Benton, 1974; Benton et al., 1981; Poitrenaud & Clement, 1965). Consequently, normative data presented in the manuals (Benton, 1974; Benton & Spreen, 1981) are provided within the context of age and presumed premorbid IQ. The data were derived from relatively large samples of individuals with no history or evidence of brain damage.

For Administration A (10-second exposure, immediate reproduction), normative data are provided in the manual for subjects aged 8–64 years (Benton, 1974). Performance level on Administration A shows a progressive rise from age 8 years until a plateau is reached at age 14–15. This plateau is maintained into the 30s, and a progressive decline in performance occurs from the 40s onward. Recent studies indicate that there is a marked decline in performance, particularly after age 70 (Robertson-Tehabo & Arenberg, 1989; Benton et al., 1981). Table 6–1 shows the mean number of errors made by adults, aged 20–89 years, under Administration A.

For Administration B (five-second exposure, immediate reproduction), normative guides are available for adults, aged 16–60 years, in the manual (Benton, 1974). The examiner need only subtract 1 point from each expected Number Correct score from Administration A values.

Normative data for Administration C (copying) are also provided in the manual (Benton, 1974). For adults, only error scores are provided. In general, adults make 2 or fewer errors on this test. For children aged 7–13 years, number correct and error scores are given. Additional data gathered by Brasfield (1971) and Beames and Russell (1970) for young children, aged 5–6 years, in Victoria, are also summarized in the manual (Benton, 1974). There is a rapid rise in performance between the ages of 5 and 10, and a much slower rise between ages 10 and 13. The performance of 13-year-old children is very close to the adult level.

Benton (1974) reports that normal adults obtain number correct scores of about

Table 6–1.   Mean Number of Errors by Age, Sex, and Education

Men		No Degree			College Degree	
Age	n	mean	SD	N	mean	SD
80–89	15	11.13	4.29	40	8.15	4.25
70–79	47	7.72	3.92	139	6.03	3.20
60–69	28	6.25	2.41	123	4.66	2.81
50–59	42	5.07	2.79	156	3.67	2.57
40–49	51	3.75	2.46	155	2.94	1.89
30–39	57	3.56	3.04	181	2.49	1.87
20–29	45	2.02	1.53	92	2.47	1.87
Women		No Degree			College Degree	
Age	n	mean	SD	N	mean	SD
80–89	9	9.44	3.84	13	7.62	4.43
70–79	32	7.53	3.37	43	6.79	2.97
60–69	42	6.02	2.58	56	4.57	2.17
50–59	35	5.11	1.95	38	3.68	1.99
40–49	23	3.87	1.82	28	2.61	2.17
30–39	27	3.04	2.21	70	2.67	2.11
20–29	19	2.90	2.08	37	2.70	1.82

Source: Robertson-Tchabo & Arenberg (1989). Data are derived from volunteers in the Baltimore Longitudinal Study of Aging.

.4 point less under Administration D (10-second exposure, 15-second delay) as compared with Administration A.

For Administration M (10-second exposure, immediate multiple choice), Benton (1981) provides normative data for children aged 7–13 years, and adolescents through adults aged 14–55 years. In general, adults tend to make 2 or fewer errors. Adult levels are obtained by about age 12. Montgomery and Costa (1983) gave the test to a sample of healthy elderly subjects aged 65–89 (mean = 74.04) years. Their administration differed from the standard administration in that they used a 5-, rather than a 10-second, exposure. The data are given in Table 6–2. In contrast to the reproduction forms of the BVRT, performance did not decline significantly with age. This suggests that in the elderly, graphomotor or visuoconstructional impairments, and not memory deficits, contribute to reduced performance on the reproduction form.

It should be noted that the normative data provided in the manual (Benton, 1974) were compiled over 30 years ago and interpreted with reference to IQ levels. More recent normative data obtained with children and adults (Robertson-Tehabo & Arenberg, 1989; Brook, 1975) appear not to be significantly different from those presented in the manual. One cannot assume, however, that patterns of performance established between earlier editions of IQ tests and the BVRT hold for current editions.

Table 6–2. Performance by Elderly Subjects on the BVRT: Multiple-Choice Administration

Score	Percentile
6	2.4
7	4.7
8	12.9
9	24.7
10	42.4
11	55.3
12	82.4
13	95.3
14	100.0

Note: Montgomery and Costa's (1983) administration differed from our own in that stimulus exposure was 5, not 10, seconds. Data are based on 85 healthy, well-educated elderly volunteers, aged 65–89 years, with a mean age of 74.04.

Source: Montgomery & Costa (1983).

REFERENCES

Arena, R., & Gainotti, G. (1978). Constructional apraxia and visuoperceptive disabilities in relation to laterality of lesions. *Cortex, 14,* 463–473.

Beames, T.B., & Russell, R.L. (1970). *Normative Data by Age and Sex for Five Pre-School Tests.* Report. Neuropsychology Laboratory, University of Victoria.

Benton, A.L. (1974). *Revised Visual Retention Test* (4th ed.). San Antonio, Texas: The Psychological Corporation.

Benton, A.L. (1981). *Der Benton-Test,* transl. by O. Spreen. Berne, Switzerland: Verlag Hans Huber.

Benton, A.L., Eslinger, P.J., & Damasio, A.R. (1981). Normative observations on neuropsychological test performance in old age. *Journal of Clinical Psychology, 3,* 33–42.

Benton, A.L., & Spreen, O. (1961). Visual Memory Test: The simulation of mental incompetence. *Archives of General Psychiatry, 4,* 79–83.

Blanton, P.D., & Gouvier, W.D. (1985). A systematic solution to the Benton Visual Retention Test: A caveat to examiners. *International Journal of Clinical Neuropsychology, 7,* 95–96.

Brasfield, D.M. (1971). An investigation of the use of the Benton Visual Retention Test with preschool children. M.A. thesis, University of Victoria.

Brook, R.M. (1975). Visual Retention Test: Local norms and impact of short-term memory. *Perceptual and Motor Skills, 40,* 967–970.

Franzen, M.D. (1989). *Reliability and Validity in Neuropsychological Assessment.* New York: Plenum Press.

Heaton, R. Baade, L.E., & Johnson, K.L. (1978). Neuropsychological test results associated with psychiatric disorders in adults. *Psychological Bulletin, 85,* 141–162.

Larabee, G.J., Kane, R.L., Schuck, J.R., & Francis, D.J. (1985). Construct validity of various memory testing procedures. *Journal of Clinical and Experimental Neuropsychology, 7,* 239–250.

Marsh, G.G., & Hirsch, S.H. (1982). Effectiveness of two tests of visual retention. *Journal of Clinical Psychology, 38,* 115–118.

Montgomery, C., & Costa, L. (1983). Paper presented at the International Neuropsychological Society, Mexico City.

Poitrenaud, J., & Clement, F. (1965). La détérioration physiologique dans le Test de Retention Visuelle de Benton: Résultats obténue par 500 sujets normaux. *Psychologie Française, 10,* 359–368.

Robertson-Tehabo, E.A. & Arenberg, D. (1989) Assessment of memory in older adults. In T. Hunt & C. Lindley (Eds).

Testing older Adults. Austin, Texas: Pro-Ed.

Schwerd, A., & Salgueiro-Feik, M. (1980). Untersuchung zur Diagnostischen Validitat des Benton-test bei Kindern und Jugendlichen. *Zeitschrift für Kinder- und Jugendpsychiatrie, 8,* 300–313.

Swan, G.E., Morrison, E. & Eslinger, P.J. (1990). Interrater agreement on the Benton Visual Retention Test. *The Clinical Neuropsychologist, 4,* 37–44.

Tamkin, A.S., & Kunce, J.T. (1985). A comparison of three neuropsychological tests: The Weigl, Hooper, and Benton. *Journal of Clinical Psychology, 41,* 660–664.

Wahler, H.J. (1956). A comparison of reproduction errors made by brain-damaged and control patients on a memory-for-designs test. *Journal of Abnormal and Social Psychology, 52,* 251–255.

Wellman, M.M. (1985). Benton Revised Visual Retention Test. In D.J. Keyser & R.C. Sweetland (Eds.), *Test Critiques* (Vol. 3, pp. 58–67). Kansas City, Missouri: Test Corporation of America.

BUSCHKE SELECTIVE REMINDING TEST (BSRT)

Other Test Name

Another test name is the Selective Reminding Test (SRT).

Purpose

The purpose of the test is to measure verbal learning and memory during a multiple-trial list-learning task.

Source

There is no commercial source. Users may refer to the following text in order to design their own material.

Description

The SRT materials include a list of words, index cards containing the first two to three letters of each list word, and index cards containing the multiple-choice recognition items. The procedure (Buschke, 1973; Buschke & Fuld, 1974) involves reading the subject a list of words and then having the subject recall as many of these words as possible. Each subsequent learning trial involves the selective presentation of only those items that were not recalled on the immediately preceding trial. The SRT distinguishes between short-term and long-term components of memory by measuring recall of items that were not presented on a given trial. The rate at which subjects learn can also be evaluated.

Table 6–3.   Word List for Forms 1–4 from the Adult Version of SRT

Form 1	Form 2	Form 3	Form 4
bowl	shine	throw	egg
passion	disagree	lily	runway
dawn	fat	film	fort
judgment	wealthy	discreet	toothache
grant	drunk	loft	drown
bee	pin	beef	baby
plane	grass	street	lava
county	moon	helmet	damp
choice	prepare	snake	pure
seed	prize	dug	vote
wool	duck	pack	strip
meal	leaf	tin	truth

Source: Hannay & Levin (1985).

A number of different versions of the test exist. For adolescents and adults, our version is the same as that developed by Hannay and Levin (1985; Hannay, 1986). Briefly, the test consists of a series of 12 unrelated words presented over 12 selective reminding (SR) trials or until the subject is able to recall the entire list on three consecutive trials. Several trials are added to help identify the conditions that promote otherwise impaired memory (e.g., cueing, multiple-choice recognition) or disclose forgetting (e.g., delayed recall) (Hannay & Levin, 1985). A cued-recall trial is presented after the 12th or last selective reminding trial. The first two or three letters of each word are presented on an index card, and the subject is asked to recall the corresponding list word. Following the cued-recall trial, the examiner presents a multiple-choice recognition trial. Here the examiner presents a series of 12 index cards, each card consisting of a list word, a synonym, a homonym, and an unrelated distractor word. Finally, a delayed-recall trial is given without forewarning 30 minutes after the multiple-choice recognition trial. Four different forms of the test are available although form 1 is the most popular. Table 6–3 provides the word lists, and Tables 6–4 and 6–5 give the multiple-choice and cued-recall items for the adult versions of the test.

Similar selective reminding (SR) procedures have been developed for use with children. Clodfelter et al. (1987) developed two alternate forms for children 9–12 years old; these are given in Table 6–6. A list of 12 words is presented for eight trials or until the child recalls all 12 words for two consecutive trials. Morgan (1982) has developed three alternate forms for children aged 5–8 years; these are shown in Table 6–7. The examiner presents a list of eight words which the subject must recall, in any order. The test continues for six SR trials or until the subject is able to recall correctly the entire list on two consecutive trials.

Table 6–4. Multiple-Choice Items for Forms 1–4 of SRT

Form 1

1. bowl	dish	bell	view
2. love	poison	conform	passion
3. dawn	sunrise	bet	down
4. pasteboard	verdict	judgment	fudge
5. grand	grant	give	jazz
6. see	sting	fold	bee
7. pain	plane	pulled	jet
8. county	state	tasted	counter
9. voice	select	choice	cheese
10. flower	seed	herd	seek
11. date	sheep	wool	would
12. mill	queen	food	meal

Form 2

1. shine	glow	chime	cast
2. dispute	disappear	contour	disagree
3. fat	oil	trail	fit
4. stopwatch	affluent	wealthy	worthy
5. trunk	drunk	stoned	blunt
6. fin	peg	wake	pin
7. glass	grass	plan	lawn
8. moon	beam	spark	noon
9. propose	ready	prepare	husband
10. award	prize	pot	size
11. bark	bird	duck	luck
12. leap	ranch	blade	leaf

Form 3

1. throw	toss	through	plate
2. flower	lilt	intent	lily
3. film	movie	slave	kiln
4. waver	cautious	discreet	distinct
5. soft	loft	attic	tack
6. beet	meat	clue	beef
7. stream	street	speed	road
8. helmet	armor	bacon	velvet
9. smoke	serpent	snake	pool
10. hoed	dug	hay	dog
11. blank	bundle	pack	puck
12. ton	shirt	foil	tin

Form 4

1. egg	shell	beg	source
2. airline	runner	darling	runway
3. fort	castle	sink	fork
4. boldness	dentist	toothache	headache
5. blown	drown	float	rib
6. body	infant	middle	baby
7. larva	lava	echo	rock
8. damp	moist	hook	stamp
9. purse	clean	pure	bare
10. ballot	vote	dish	note
11. chain	peal	strip	slip
12. trust	rise	fact	truth

Source: Hannay (1986); Hannay & Levin (1985).

Table 6–5. Cued Recall Words for Forms 1–4 of SRT

Form 1	Form 2	Form 3	Form 4
BO	SH	TH	—
PA	DI	LI	RU
DA	FA	FI	FO
JUD	WEA	DI	TO
GR	DR	LO	DR
—	—	BE	BA
PL	GR	ST	LA
COU	MO	HE	DA
CH	PRE	SN	PU
SE	PR	DU	VO
WO	DU	PA	ST
ME	LE	—	TR

Table 6–6. Alternate Forms of SRT for Children Aged 9–12 Years

List 1	List 2
garden	market
doctor	palace
metal	flower
city	picture
money	dollar
cattle	river
prison	cotton
clothing	sugar
water	college
cabin	baby
tower	temple
bootle	butter

Source: Clodfelter et al. (1987).

Table 6–7. Word Lists for Three Forms of SRT for Children Aged 5–8 Years

List 1	List 2	List 3
dog	balloon	apple
horse	crayons	meat
turtle	doll	egg
lion	bicycle	candy
squirrel	paints	carrot
bear	baseball	cereal
elephant	clay	bread
rabbit	book	banana

Source: Morgan (1982).

Administration

Say to the subject: "**This test is to see how quickly you can learn a list of words. I am going to read you a list of twelve [for young children, 'eight'] words. I want you to listen carefully because when I stop, I want you to tell me as many of the words as you can recall. The words do not have to be in any particular order. When you have given me all the words that you can recall, I will tell you the words that you didn't give me from the list; then I want you to give me the entire list all over again. We do this twelve [for older children, 'eight'; for younger children, 'six'] times and each time I want you to try to give me all twelve [for younger children, 'eight'] words.**"

Read the list of words at a rate of one word per two seconds, and always present the words in the order beginning with the top of the list and working to the bottom. The presentation of words will, of course, skip over the words that were recalled correctly on the preceding trial. If the subject is able to recall correctly all 12 (for younger children, 8) words on three (for children, 2) consecutive trials, discontinue, but score as if all trials had been given. If the subject recalls words not on the list, inform the subject, and note the extra words. The total number of words on the list is not disclosed.

For the cued-recall trial, the first two to three letters of each list word are presented on an index card, and the subject is asked to say the word from the list that would begin with the first two letters on the card (see Table 6–5). The cue cards are presented one at a time in the same order as the words on the list. There is no time limit, and the subject is allowed to return to a previous card if he or she wishes. Since one word (i.e., "bee") on Form 1 can be clearly identified by the first two letters, it is omitted from cued recall, as are pin, tin, and egg in Forms, 2, 3, and 4, respectively. Cues that fail initially to evoke the list word are presented a second time after each cue has been given once. For the multiple-choice recognition trial, the subject is shown each of the 12 index cards, and is asked to identify the list word. The cued-recall and multiple-choice trials are given even if the subject has recalled the entire list on the SR trials. After a 30-minute delay, the subject is asked to recall all 12 words. The subject should be given nonverbal tasks to perform during the 30-minute delay.

Approximate Time for Administration

The adult version requires 30 minutes; the children's version takes 10 minutes.

Scoring

See samples shown in Figures 6–1 through 6–3. A number of different scores are calculated (Buschke, 1973; Buschke & Fuld, 1974; Hannay & Levin, 1985). If a

Sample SRT Score Sheet—Form 1 (Adult)

Name _____ Date _____ Examiner _____

	1	2	3	4	5	6	7	8	9	10	11	12	CR	MC	30'
bowl															
passion															
dawn															
judgment															
grant															
bee															
plane															
county															
choice															
seed															
wool															
meal															
Total Recall															
LTR															
STR															
LTS															
CLTR															
RLTR															
Reminders															
Intrusions															

Trial 1   ------
Total Recall   _____ (Number recalled over 12 trials)
LTS   _____ (Words recalled twice in a row, assumed to be in LTS from that point on.
                         Mark with red underliner, counting blanks. Compute sum over the 12 trials.)
STR   _____ (Words that are not underlined. Compute sum over the 12 trials.)
CLTR   _____ (Words that are continuously recalled. Mark with highlighter. Compute sum
                         across 12 trials.)
RLTR   _____ (Words that are underlined but NOT CLTR. Do not count blanks. Compute
                         sum across 12 trials.)
Reminders   _____ (Compute sum over 12 trials. Maximum = 144)
Intrusions   _____ (Compute sum over 12 trials.)
Cued Recall   _____ (Maximum = 11)
Mult. Choice   _____ (Maximum = 12)
30-Min Recall   _____ (Maximum = 12)

Figure 6–1. Buschke Selective Reminding Test, Form 1 (Adult) sample scoring sheet.

word is recalled on two consecutive trials, it is assumed to have entered long-term storage (LTS) on the first of these trials. Once a word enters LTS, it is considered to be in permanent storage and is scored as LTS on all following trials, regardless of the subject's subsequent recall. When a subject recalls a word that has entered LTS, it is scored as long-term retrieval (LTR). When a subject begins to recall a

Sample SRT Score Sheet—Form 1 (Children 9–12 years)

Name _____ Date _____ Examiner _____

	1	2	3	4	5	6	7	8
garden								
doctor								
metal								
city								
money								
cattle								
prison								
clothing								
water								
cabin								
tower								
bottle								
Total Recall								
LTR								
STR								
LTS								
CLTR								
RLTR								
Reminders								
Intrusions								

Total Recall	_____ (Number recalled over 8 trials)
LTS	_____ (Words recalled twice in a row, assumed to be in LTS from that point on. Mark with red underliner, counting blanks. Compute sum over the 8 trials.)
STR	_____ (Words that are not underlined. Compute sum over the 8 trials.)
CLTR	_____ (Words that are continuously recalled. Mark with highlighter. Compute sum across 8 trials.)
RLTR	_____ (Words that are underlined but NOT CLTR. Do not count blanks. Compute sum across 8 trials.)
Reminders	_____ (Compute sum over 8 trials. Maximum = 96)
Intrusions	_____ (Compute sum over 8 trials.)

Figure 6–2. Buschke Selective Reminding Test, Form 1 (Children, 9–12 Years) sample scoring sheet.

word in LTS consistently on all subsequent trials, it is also scored as consistent long-term retrieval (CLTR) or list-learning beginning on the first of the uninterrupted successful recall trials. Inconsistent LTR refers to recall of a word in LTS followed by subsequent failure to recall the word. It is scored as random long-term retrieval (RLTR) until it is recalled consistently. Short-term recall (STR) refers to recall of a word that has not entered LTS. The total recall (Sum Recall) on each

Sample SRT Score Sheet—Form 1 (Children 5–8 years)

Name _____ Date _____ Examiner _____

	1	2	3	4	5	6	7	8
dog								
horse								
turtle								
lion								
squirrel								
bear								
elephant								
rabbit								
Total Recall								
LTR								
STR								
LTS								
CLTR								
RLTR								
Reminders								
Intrusions								

Total Recall   _____ (Number recalled over 8 trials)
LTS   _____ (Words recalled twice in a row, assumed to be in LTS from that point on. Mark with red underliner, counting blanks. Compute sum over the 8 trials.)
STR   _____ (Words that are not underlined. Compute sum over the 8 trials.)
CLTR   _____ (Words that are continuously recalled. Mark with highlighter. Compute sum across 8 trials.)
RLTR   _____ (Words that are underlined but NOT CLTR. Do not count blanks. Compute sum across 8 trials.)
Reminders   _____ (Compute sum over 8 trials. Maximum = 48)
Intrusions   _____ (Compute sum over 8 trials.)

Figure 6–3. Buschke Selective Reminding Test, Form 1 (Children, 5–8 Years) sample scoring sheet.

trial is the sum of STR and LTR. The number of reminders given by the examiner before the next recall attempt is equal to 12 − Sum Recall (for young children, 8 − Sum Recall) of the previous trial. Record by number the order of the subject's recall on each trial. Intrusions of extralist words are also recorded on each trial.

Comment

It has been difficult to develop lists of equal difficulty and reliability for repeated testing of patients (Hannay & Levin, 1985; Kraemer et al., 1983; Loring & Papanicolaou, 1987). For college students, Forms 2–4 are of equivalent difficulty, whereas Form 1 is about 10 percent harder (Hannay & Levin, 1985). The separate forms for the children's version are roughly of equivalent difficulty (Clodfelter et al., 1987; Morgan, 1982). When demented subjects are given two versions of the test, with about two hours intervening between administrations, test–retest correlations range from a low of .42 for intrusions to a high of .92 for consistent retrieval (Masur et al., 1989). When normal subjects are considered, test–retest correlations are relatively low and range from .48 to .84 (Clodfelter et al., 1987; Hannay & Levin, 1985; Morgan, 1982; Ruff et al., 1988). Further, at least with normal adults, there appears to be a nonspecific practice effect with repeated administration of alternate forms (Hannay & Levin, 1985; Loring & Papanicolaou, 1987). Thus, the ability to learn how to perform a complex task, and not exclusively the ability to remember words, may be accounting for any group differences in research involving clinical populations (Loring & Papanicolaou, 1987).

The SRT is popular because it purports to parcel verbal memory into distinct component processes (e.g., LTS, LTR, CLTR, STR). However, the numerous scores that can be derived from the test tend to be highly intercorrelated, suggesting that these measures are assessing similar constructs (Kenisten, cited in Kraemer et al., 1983; Larabee et al., 1988; Loring & Papanicolaou, 1987; Paniak et al., 1989). Further, although the SR procedure offers information regarding short- and long-term memory, the operational distinction between long-term storage and retrieval is problematic (Loring & Papanicolaou, 1987). According to Bushke's definition, a word has entered LTS if it has been successfully recalled on two successive trials. By definition, failure to recall is due to a retrieval difficulty. However, the item may have been stored in a weak or degraded form and through the process of additional repetition by the examiner, the word is encoded more deeply and efficiently (Loring & Papanicolaou, 1987). Therefore, operationally defined retrieval may have little to do with retrieval itself (Loring & Papanicolaou, 1987).

The SRT has become one of the more widely used procedures for assessing memory functioning following head injury (e.g., Levin & Grossman, 1976; Paniak et al., 1989). SRT performance is impaired following severe closed head injury. Further, the severity of the injury (e.g., determined by length of unconsciousness) is related to the level of memory performance. Levin et al. (1979) have reported that the degree of long-term memory impairment one year after severe head injury corresponds to the overall level of disability in survivors. Patients who have attained good recovery (i.e., resumption of work and normal social functioning) consistently recalled words without further reminding at a level comparable to that of normal adults. In contrast, consistent recall was grossly impaired in patients who were moderately or severely disabled at the time of the study. The SRT has also proved useful in differentiating normal from demented elderly (Masur et al., 1989). The measures LTR and CLTR were most valuable in distinguishing mild dementia from normal aging. Modest correlations have been demonstrated between the SRT and other tests of verbal learning and memory (Shear & Craft, 1989). Further, there is an association between impairment of verbal learning and memory, as measured by the SRT, and left temporal lobe abnormality (Lee et al., 1989; Levin et al., 1982). It is important to note, however, that patients with diffuse cerebral lesions perform about the same as patients with focal involvement of the left temporal lobe on the SRT (Levin et al., 1982). Therefore, the SRT should not be used by itself to predict left temporal lobe abnormality.

Normative Data

Both age and sex affect performance, with age being the most salient of these two subject variables. In general, females perform better than males. Education ap-

Table 6–8. Verbal Selective Reminding Norms

	Age Groups						
Variables*	18–29	30–39	40–49	50–59	60–69	70–79	80–91
Age							
Mean	22.55	34.62	43.71	54.17	66.0	74.49	83.48
SD	(3.30)	(2.69)	(2.91)	(2.74)	(2.47)	(2.92)	(3.10)
Education							
Mean	12.88	14.90	14.71	12.92	13.40	13.46	13.22
SD	(1.73)	(2.47)	(2.72)	(1.98)	(3.57)	(3.78)	(3.76)
N	51	29	31	24	50	59	27
Femal/male	23/28	15/14	19/12	22/2	33/17	38/21	23/4
Total							
Mean	128.18	124.59	125.03	121.62	114.82	105.27	97.96
SD	(9.16)	(13.40)	(12.00)	(10.46)	(15.77)	(16.67)	(17.49)
LTR							
Mean	122.16	118.14	118.55	112.71	101.52	89.95	77.22
SD	(13.12)	(20.64)	(17.96)	(16.10)	(24.68)	(29.23)	(26.26)
STR							
Mean	6.14	6.72	6.48	8.96	13.52	17.47	20.74
SD	(4.82)	(7.59)	(6.72)	(6.40)	(9.52)	(10.41)	(9.62)
LTS							
Mean	124.00	121.62	122.45	116.67	107.00	95.54	87.48
SD	(10.47)	(18.36)	(15.64)	(14.52)	(21.79)	(24.86)	(25.26)
CLTR							
Mean	115.12	107.93	107.10	101.50	88.92	69.68	54.96
SD	(19.67)	(27.62)	(26.62)	(22.39)	(35.85)	(35.96)	(29.04)
RLTR							
Mean	8.12	10.10	11.19	10.79	14.66	20.71	22.19
SD	(9.42)	(9.73)	(11.34)	(9.25)	(11.83)	(14.37)	(10.70)

Variables*	Age Groups						
	18–29	30–39	40–49	50–59	60–69	70–79	80–91
Reminders by Examiner							
Mean	16.0	18.10	19.03	22.25	28.12	36.95	43.96
SD	(8.42)	(13.12)	(11.26)	(10.06)	(15.16)	(15.17)	(15.77)
Intrusions							
Mean	.84	.97	1.81	1.17	3.90	4.22	3.30
SD	(1.29)	(1.43)	(3.10)	(1.49)	(7.29)	(5.76)	(5.09)
Cued Recall							
Mean	—	—	—	—	9.58[a]	8.95[b]	8.16[c]
SD					(1.93)	(2.12)	(2.22)
Multiple Choice							
Mean	12.0	12.0	12.0	12.0	11.96	11.85	11.93
SD	(0.0)	(0.0)	(0.0)	(0.0)	(0.20)	(0.58)	(0.27)
Delayed Recall							
Mean	11.53	10.66	11.03	10.83	9.58	9.05	8.37
SD	(.83)	(1.97)	(1.43)	(1.40)	(2.46)	(2.62)	(2.45)

Correction values for raw scores of males (calculate before entering normative tables). Total = +5; LTR = +9; STR = −4; LTS = +7; CLTR = +13; RLTR = −5; Reminders = −5; Intrusions = 0; Cued Recall = 0; Multiple Choice = 0; Delayed Recall = +1. Caution: Do not correct LTS or CLTR if raw score is 0.

[a]$n = 31$

[b]$n = 38$

[c]$n = 19$

[d]See text for definitions of Total, LTR, STR, LTS, CLTR, RLTR, Reminders by Examiner, Intrusions, Cued Recall, Multiple Choice, Delayed Recall.

Source: Larabee et al. (1988).

pears to be relatively unimportant (Larrabee et al., 1988; Ruff et al., 1989). Larrabee et al. (1988) provide norms for the adult version (Form I) of the SRT, organized by age and sex. The data are shown in Table 6–8. The reader should note that the mean values for LTR and STR do not sum to the exact value for total correct. The same is true for the relationship of the mean values for CLTR and RLTR to LTR. These small discrepancies appeared because different gender corrections were used for these respective scores. Note too that various components (LTS, CLTR) of memory decline with age, particularly beginning after age 50.

Similar data have been reported for middle-aged adults by Ruff et al. (1988). Masure et al. (1989) also provide normative data for a large sample of elderly subjects. Their sample, however, contains a large number of nonnative English speakers. This may account for the fact that their scores are somewhat lower than those reported here.

Levin has also used Form I of the SRT with adolescents, aged 13–18 (Levin & Grossman, 1976; Levin, Benton & Grossman, 1982), and gives data for Form I for

Table 6–9.   LTS and CLTR and Adolescent Males and Females, Ages 13–18 Years

Score	Freq.	Adj. PCT	Cum. PCT	Score	Freq.	Adj. PCT	Cum. PCT	Score	Freq.	Adj. PCT	Cum. PCT
				Summation of LTS across trials							
Males											
74	1	4	4	114	2	9	43	127	2	9	78
78	1	4	9	116	1	4	48	129	2	9	87
85	1	4	13	117	1	4	52	131	1	4	91
101	1	4	17	121	1	4	57	132	1	4	96
103	1	9	26	124	1	4	61	136	1	4	100
106	1	4	30	125	1	4	65				
108	1	4	35	126	1	4	70				

Mean = 114.17   Median = 117.00   SD = 26.15

Score	Freq.	Adj. PCT	Cum. PCT	Score	Freq.	Adj. PCT	Cum. PCT	Score	Freq.	Adj. PCT	Cum. PCT
Females											
86	1	4	4	121	2	7	33	134	1	4	78
93	1	4	7	122	1	4	37	135	2	7	85
95	1	4	11	126	3	11	48	136	2	7	93
108	1	4	15	129	1	4	52	137	1	4	96
112	1	4	19	131	2	7	59	139	1	4	100
116	1	4	22	132	1	4	63				
117	1	4	26	133	3	11	74				

Mean = 123.82   Median = 129.00   SD = 14.21

Score	Freq.	Adj. PCT	Cum. PCT	Score	Freq.	Adj. PCT	Cum. PCT	Score	Freq.	Adj. PCT	Cum. PCT
				Summation of CLTR across trials							
Males											
31	1	4	4	78	1	4	39	106	1	4	74
34	1	4	9	79	1	4	43	111	1	4	78
46	1	4	13	91	1	4	48	113	1	4	83
55	1	1	17	92	1	4	52	114	1	4	87
63	1	4	22	93	1	4	57	119	2	9	96
64	1	4	26	96	1	4	61	121	1	4	100
68	1	4	30	99	1	4	65				
75	1	4	35	105	1	4	70				

Mean = 85.74   Median = 92.00   SD = 27.42

Score	Freq.	Adj. PCT	Cum. PCT	Score	Freq.	Adj. PCT	Cum. PCT	Score	Freq.	Adj. PCT	Cum. PCT
Females											
45	1	4	4	97	1	4	37	128	1	4	67
54	1	4	7	101	1	4	41	129	3	11	78
76	1	4	11	113	3	11	52	131	3	11	89
78	1	4	15	116	1	4	56	132	1	4	93
81	2	7	22	120	1	4	59	134	2	7	100
84	3	11	33	121	1	4					

Mean = 106.26   Median = 113.33   SD = 26.15

Note: Data are derived from 23 male and 27 female adolescent high school students. Adj. PCT = adjusted percent; Cum. PCT = cumulative percent.

Source: Levin & Grossman (1976).

Table 6–10. Mean Scores of Children, Ages 9–12 Years, on SRT

		Age 9–10 years (n = 28)		Age 11–12 years (n = 30)	
		List 1	List 2	List 1	List 2
LTS	M	61.92	59.32	67.10	65.80
	SD	13.92	18.29	18.65	19.81
CLTR	M	42.07	41.71	49.40	51.10
	SD	21.11	22.32	23.09	25.66
Intrusions	M	1.50	2.85	1.03	0.93
	SD	2.63	3.19	2.07	1.85

Note: Data are derived from 58 healthy children.

Source: Clodfelter et al. (1987).

Table 6–11. Mean Scores of Children, Aged 5–8 Years, on SRT

	Age 5–6 years (n = 16)		Age 7–8 years (n = 14)	
	M	SD	M	SD
Recall per trial	5.3	1.2	6.1	1.1
LTS	28.6	10.1	35.7	9.1
LTR	25.7	9.9	33.4	10.2
CLTR	18.9	11.3	27.7	13.2

Note: Scores are derived from a small group of healthy school children, ages 5–8 years, of average intelligence.

Source: Morgan (1982).

two measures, LTS and CLTR (See Table 6–9). Levin reports that there were no significant effects of age on performance between the ages of 13 and 18. Girls, however, performed at a superior level compared to boys.

Clodfelter et al. (1987) provide normative data for alternate forms of the SRT for children, aged 9–12 years. Table 6–10 presents means and standard deviations for three SRT variables (LTS, CLTR, intrusions). Normative data for parallel forms of the SRT for children aged 5–8 years have been provided by Morgan (1982). Table 6-11 presents the means and standard deviations by age for four SRT variables (recall per trial, LTS, LTR, CLTR). The tables show that children's performance increases substantially with age. It should be noted that the data presented are of limited value since the sample sizes are quite small.

REFERENCES

Buschke, H. (1973). Selective reminding for analysis of memory and learning. *Journal of Verbal Learning and Verbal Behavior,* 12, 543–550.

Buschke, H., & Fuld, P.A. (1974). Evaluating storage, retention, and retrieval in disor-dered memory and learning. *Neurology,* 24, 1019–1025.

Clodfelter, C.J., Dickson, A.L., Newton Wilkes, C., & Johnson, R.B. (1987). Alternate forms of selective reminding for children. *Clinical Neuropsychologist,* 1, 243–249.

Hannay, H.J. (1986). *Experimental Techniques in Human Neuropsychology.* New York: Oxford University Press.

Hannay, J.H., Levin, H.S. (1985). Selective Reminding Test: An examination of the equivalence of four forms. *Journal of Clinical and Experimental Neuropsychology, 7,* 251–263.

Kraemer, H.C., Peabody, C.A., Tinklenberg, J.R., & Yesavage, J.A. (1983). Mathematical and empirical development of a test of memory for clinical and research use. *Psychological Bulletin, 94,* 367–380.

Larrabee, G.J., Trahan, D.E., Curtiss, G., & Levin, H.S. (1988). *Neuropsychology, 2,* 173–182.

Lee, G.P., Loring, D.W., & Thompson, J.L. (1989). Construct validity of material-specific memory measures following unilateral temporal lobe ablations. *Psychological Assessment, 1,* 192–197.

Levin, H.S., Benton, A.L., & Grossman, R.G. (1982). *Neurobehavioral Consequences of Closed Head Injury.* New York: Oxford University Press.

Levin, H.S., & Grossman, R.G. (1976). Storage and retrieval. *Journal of Pediatric Psychology, 1,* 38–42.

Levin, H.S., Grossman, R.G., Rose, J.E., & Teasdale, G. (1979). Long-term neuropsychological outcome of closed head injury. *Journal of Neurosurgery, 50,* 412–422.

Loring, D.W., & Papanicolaou, A.C. (1987). Memory assessment in neuropsychology: Theoretical considerations and practical utility. *Journal of Clinical and Experimental Neuropsychology, 9,* 340–358.

Masur, D.M., Fuld, P.A., Blau, A.D., Thal, L.J., Levin, H.S., & Aronson, M.K. (1989). Distinguishing normal and demented elderly with the Selective Reminding Test. *Journal of Clinical and Experimental Neuropsychology, 11,* 615–630.

Morgan, S.F. (1982). Measuring long-term memory, storage and retrieval in children. *Journal of Clinical Neuropsychology, 4,* 77–85.

Paniak, C.E., Shore, D.L., & Rourke, B.P. (1989). Recovery of memory after severe closed head injury: Dissociations in recovery of memory parameters and predictors of outcome. *Journal of Clinical and Experimental Neuropsychology, 11,* 631–644.

Ruff, R.M., Quayhagen, M., & Light, R.H. (1988). Selective reminding tests: A normative study of verbal learning in adults. *Journal of Clinical and Experimental Neuropsychology, 11,* 539–650.

Shear, J.M., & Craft, R.B. (1989). Examination of the concurrent validity of the California Verbal Learning Test. *Clinical Neuropsychologist, 3,* 162–168.

Trahan, D.E., Goethe, K.E., Larrabee, G.J., & Quintana, J.W. (1989). Standardization and clinical validation of the verbal Selective Reminding Test as a measure of immediate verbal memory. *Journal of Clinical and Experimental Neuropsychology, 11,* 63.

CONCENTRATION ENDURANCE TEST (d2 TEST)

Purpose

The purpose of this test is to assess sustained attention and visual scanning ability.

Source

The manual (fifth edition in German), recording sheets, and scoring key can be obtained from Hogrefe Inc., 12–14 Brucepark Avenue, Toronto, Ontario M4P 2S3, at a cost of $23.00 U.S.

Description

This paper-and-pencil test was developed by Brickenkamp (1981) and was modeled after other cancellation tasks (Bourdon, cited in Brickenkamp, 1981). It can be given individually or as a group measure. The test is composed of 14 lines with 47 letters each (see Figure 6–4). The target is the letter "d" with two marks alternatively above, below, or separated, one mark above and one mark below. Distractors are the letter "p" with one to four marks, and the letter "d" with one, three, or four marks. The subject's task is to mark as many targets per line as possible. The time limit is 20 seconds per line.

Administration

The instructions (translated by H. Niemann) are as follows: Place the front page in front of the subject. **"Now I want to see how well you can concentrate on a task. Look down here [point to the three 'd's]. You see three 'd's, like in the word 'dash'. Each one has two dots. The first one has two dots above, the second two dots below, and the last one has one dot above and one dot below, so that makes two dots again for this letter. You should cross out all 'd's' that have two dots. Now I want you to cross out these three 'd's' in the example. Afterwards go down to the practice row below and cross out every 'd' with two dots. You should not cross out 'd's' with less or more than two dots and you should not cross out 'p's', like in 'Paul' regardless of the number of dots. Use only one slash for crossing out the correct letters. If you realize that you crossed out a wrong letter, put a second slash through it."** Demonstrate on the first four letters of the practice trial. **"Now let us see how well you did on this practice trial."** Be sure that the subject has understood the instructions before continuing the test. Before turning the page over, say: **"On the back page, you will find fourteen rows like the practice row. On every row you will be asked to go from left to right, crossing out every 'd' with two dots. After twenty seconds, I will say: 'next line!' Then you have to stop crossing out the line and start immediately at the beginning of the next line."**

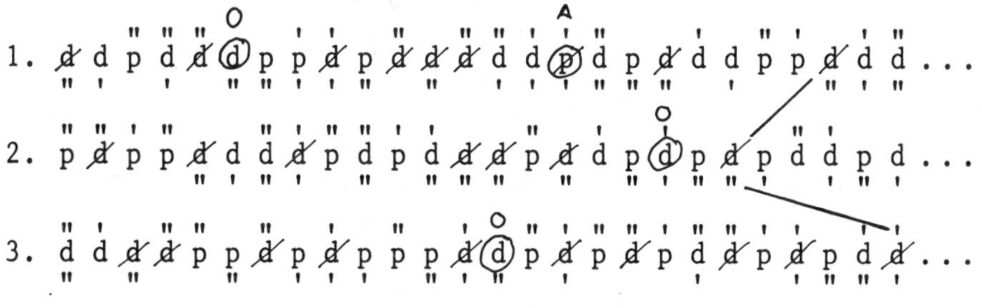

Figure 6–4.   d2 Test sample.

Work as quickly as you can, but try to be as accurate as you can. Don't make mistakes!" Turn the page over and point to the beginning of the first line and say: "Ready, go!"

Approximate Time for Administration

The time required is about 5–10 minutes.

Abbreviations

Abbreviations used in the manual are PR, Percentile Rank; SW, Standard Score; GZ, Total Score; GZ − F, Total Score minus Errors; F%, Error Percentage; SB, Fluctuations; Erw, Adults; Vo, *Volksschüler* (*innen*) (elementary school); Be, *Berufsschüler* (*innen*) (occupational school); and Ob, *Oberschüler* (*innen*) (high school).

Scoring

Several scores can be computed to evaluate the patient's speed, accuracy, persistence, and learning (see source). Briefly, the scoring is as follows:

Total Raw Score (TS; GZ in the manual) refers to the number of letters the subject has considered regardless of errors. The number of letters per line must be added together in order to derive the Total Raw Score. Counting is facilitated by the use of an overlay.

Errors: Two types of errors are recorded:
1. *Omissions* (O) refer to the number of "d's" with two dots that have been missed up to the last letter in every line that has been crossed out.
2. *Additions* (A) refer to every "d" with less or more than two dots and every "p" that has been crossed out. The sum of Omissions and Additions equals the total number of errors (E) across all rows.

Percentage of Errors (E% is equivalent to F% in the manual) is derived from the formula E% = 100 × E/TS.

Distribution of Errors:
1. Sum the number of errors on the first four rows.
2. Sum the number of errors for the last four rows.

Large differences between the first and last four rows may be due to shifts in test-taking attitude, practice effects, or fatigue.

Total Score Minus Errors (TS − E): This score, derived by subtracting the total number of errors (E) from the Total Score (TS), represents the number of correctly crossed-out letters across all rows.

Fluctuation (FL) [*Schwankungsbreite* (SB) in the manual]: This measure is derived by subtracting the score for the row with the lowest rate of production (TS) from the row with the highest rate.

Comment

Test–retest reliabilities are high, ranging from .89 to .92 for the total score after a five-hour interval, and .92 for the total score minus errors (TS − E) after a 12-month interval (Brickenkamp, 1981). With normal people, practice effects of about 25% can be expected on retesting. However, Sturm et al. (1983) did not find any practice effects after retesting a group of brain-damaged subjects following a four-week interval. The Digit Symbol subtest of the Wechsler Adult Intelligence Scale (WAIS) was the only subtest that correlated significantly with the d2 Test ($r = .45$), suggesting that it is relatively independent of factors evaluated by standardized tests of intelligence (Brickenkamp, 1981). Correlations with other tests of attention and concentration ranged from .31 to .72, depending on the sample, the comparison measure, and the score used for the statistical analysis (Niemann, 1989). Factor-analytic studies with normal people consistently report high loadings on an attentional factor, but not on factors of motor speed, motor coordination, or visual discrimination (Brickenkamp, 1981).

Cancellation tasks assess many functions (Lezak, 1983), not the least of which is the capacity for sustained attention. In addition, accurate visual scanning, and activation and inhibition of rapid responses are required. Lowered scores on cancellation tasks may reflect inattentiveness, general response slowing, poor shifting of responses, or unilateral spatial neglect.

Normative Data

Normative data given in the test manual are derived from rather large samples ($n = 3,132$) of normal students and adults, ages 9–60 years. Tables are provided for transforming the scores into percentiles, standard scores, stanines, and scaled scores. In the German school system, children 11 years of age are separated into groups of average ability and higher academic potential. In the source tables, "Vo" is equivalent to middle school, and "junior" is equivalent to secondary school. The "Be" group are those youths in vocational training settings, whereas the "Ob" group consists of students preparing for university. Consequently, when these tables are used for North American students, one should check the norms for the appropriate age at both kinds of schools.

We have collected normative data on a small group of healthy well-educated

Table 6–12. Total Raw Score and Errors for Adults on d2 Test Ages 50–85 Years

Age	Sex	N	Total raw score		Errors	
			Mean	SD	Mean	SD
50–59	m	5	470.8	79.4	26.6	35.2
	f	14	403.0	87.7	11.4	6.5
60–69	m	4	420.3	53.6	44.0	27.6
	f	23	432.0	87.7	17.9	18.1
70–79	m	9	383.6	47.9	16.1	8.1
	f	14	360.2	76.0	27.9	36.1
80+	m	5	289.2	75.3	39.0	20.9
	f	6	360.0	70.3	63.5	56.3

Note: Our data, collected in 1989, are derived from a sample of healthy, well-educated elderly volunteers.

(about 13 years) adults, aged 50–85 years. Table 6-12 shows the data for two variables, Total Raw Score and Errors, broken down by age and sex.

Sex, age, and intellectual level contribute to performance on the d2 Test. In general, females perform better than males. Scores increase with age from TS − E = 240 at age 10 years, to approximately 340–440 at age 17 years. Adult levels are reached at about 17 years of age. There is little decrement in scores until about age 40 years.

REFERENCES

Brickenkamp, R. (1981). *Test d2: Aufmerk-samkeits–Belastungs-Test* (*Handanwei-sung*, 7th ed.) [Test d2: *Concentration–Endurance Test: Manual*, 5th ed.]. Göttingen: Verlag für Psychologie Dr. C.J. Hogrefe.

Lezak, M.D. (1983). *Neuropsychological Assessment* (2nd ed.). New York: Oxford University Press.

Niemann, H. (1989). Computer-assisted retraining of head-injured patients. Unpublished Ph.D. dissertation, University of Victoria,

Sturm, W., Dahmen, W., Hartje, W., & Wilmes, K. (1983). Ergebnisse eines Trainingsprogramms zur Verbesserung der visuellen Auffassungsschnelligkeit und Konzentrationsfähigkeit bei Hirngeschädigten. [Results of a program for the training of perceptual speed and attention in brain-damaged patients.] *Archiv für Psychiatrie und Nervenkrankheiten*, 233, 9–22.

PACED AUDITORY SERIAL ADDITION TEST (PASAT)

Purpose

This test is a serial-addition task used to assess the rate of information processing and sustained attention.

Source

The tape can be ordered from the Neuropsychology Laboratory, University of

Victoria, P.O. Box 1700, Victoria, British Columbia V8W 3P5, Canada, at a cost of $10 Cdn.

Description

This test was devised by Gronwall and colleagues (Gronwall, 1977; Gronwall & Sampson, 1974; Gronwall & Wrightson, 1974) to provide an estimate of the subject's rate of information processing (or the amount of information that can be handled at one time). The subject is required to comprehend the auditory input, respond verbally, inhibit encoding of one's own response while attending to the

next stimulus in a series, and perform at an externally determined pace. A pre-recorded tape delivers a random series of 61 numbers from 1 through 9. The subject is instructed to add pairs of numbers such that each number is added to the one immediately preceding it: The second is added to the first, the third to the second, the fourth to the third, and so on. For example, if given the numbers "1,9," the answer is "10"; if the next number is "4," this is added to the previous "9" to give the answer "13"; and so on. The same 60 numbers can be presented in four different trials, each differing in their rate of digit presentation (2.4, 2.0, 1.6, 1.2 seconds). The PASAT thus increases processing demands by increasing the speed of stimulus input. The duration of each spoken digit is about 0.4 second.

Administration

Instructions are on the tape. For some very impaired subjects, the instructions may need to be expanded as follows:

ORAL AND WRITTEN DEMONSTRATION

"I am going to ask you to add together pairs of single-digit numbers. You will hear a tape-recorded list of numbers read one after the other. I will ask you to add the numbers in pairs and give your answers out loud. Although this is really a concentration task, and not a test to see how well you can add, it might help to do a little adding before I explain the task in more detail. Please add the following pairs of numbers together as fast as you can, and give your answers out loud: '3,8' [11]; '4,9' [13]; '7,8' [15]; '8,6' [14]; '8,9' [17]; '5,7' [12]; '6,5' [11]; '6,9' [15]; '4,7' [11]; '7,6' [13]. Good.

The task that I want you to do involves adding together pairs of numbers, just as you have done, except that the numbers will be read as a list, one after the other. Let me give you an example with a short, easy list. Suppose I gave you the following: '1,2,3,4'. Here is what you would do. After hearing the first two numbers on the list, which were '1,2', you would add these together and give your answer, '1 + 2 = 3'. The next number on the list is '3', so when you heard it, you would add this number to the number right before it on the list, which was '2', and give your answer, '2 + 3 = 5'. Are you following so far? The last number you heard is '4' (remember the list is '1,2,3,4'), so you would add '4' to the number right before it, which was '3', and give your answer, '3 + 4 = 7'. The important thing to remember is that you must add each number on the list to the number right before it on the list. And *not* to the answer you have just given. You can forget your answers as soon as you have said them. All you have to remember is the last digit that you have heard, and add it to the next digit that you hear. O.K.? Let's try that short list again, only this time *you* say the answers. Ready? '1,2' [3], '3', [5], '4', [7]. Now let's try another, longer practice list of numbers, this time the numbers on the list won't be in any particular order. Ready? '4,6', [10], '1', [7], '8', [9], '8', [16], '4', [12], '3', [7], '8', [11], '2', [10], '7', [9]. **Good.**"

If the subject has difficulty understanding the oral instructions, then provide a written demonstration. Instruct as follows: "**That sounds complicated. Let me show you what I mean** [write down a list of five or six numbers]:

$$5, 3, 7, 4, 2$$

You see, you add the '5' and the '3' together, and say '8'; then you have to forget the '8' and remember the '3'. When the '7' comes along, you add it to the '3', and say '10'; now you have to remember the '7'. All right. What do you say after '4'?" Continue until the subject understands what to do. Say: "**It's very easy when all the numbers are written down for you. Try it with me saying some numbers to you.**" See the above list. Discontinue if the subject is unable to get at least the first three answers from the unpaced practice list correct, after two trials.

PACED PRACTICE

"**Remember, I said the numbers would be tape-recorded? The task is not easy, and no one is expected to get all of the answers right. The hard part is keeping up with the speed of the recording. However, if you can't answer in time, don't worry. Just wait until you hear two more numbers; add them together, and go on from there. O.K.? Any questions? I'll play a practice list of numbers, and get you to give me the answers.**" Play to the end of the first practice list.

TEST TRIALS

"You see what I meant about the task measuring how well you can concentrate. It doesn't have anything to do with how smart you are. Now we'll try the first real trial. This trial is just the same as the practice trial you've just done, except that it is six times as long, so it goes on for almost two and a half minutes. Don't worry if you make adding mistakes or miss some answers. This is a difficult task. I want to see not only how long you can keep going without stopping, but also how quickly you can pick up again if you do stop. No one is expected to get all the answers. After this trial, we will take a break and then do another trial at a faster speed."

Play the first trial (2.4 seconds). Allow at least 60 seconds before playing the next trial. Warn the subject before each trial that it will be faster than the previous one.

Many patients find even the slow presentation trials (2.4, 2.0) difficult. Consequently, the two faster rates (1.6, 1.2) are given only if subjects perform adequately at the slower rates (above 20 at the pacing rate of 2.0) unless he or she scored more than 40 on the first trial (2.4-second pacing). Intensity level should be well above threshold and adjusted to a "comfortable" listening level for each subject.

FOLLOW-UP ADMINISTRATIONS (RETESTS)

Do not repeat instructions, written demonstration, or unpaced practice trial unless the subject demonstrates on the paced practice trial that he or she has forgotten what to do. Record this information.

Approximate Time for Administration

About 15–20 minutes is required if all four trials are given.

Scoring

See sample sheet in Figure 6–5. Record the number of correct and incorrect responses per trial (i.e., at the four pacing rates). To be correct, a response must be made before presentation of the next stimulus. Maximum score per trial = 60.

For subjects below the age of 40, convert the total correct scores to time per correct response, using Table 6–13. There should be no more than a 0.6-second difference between the time scores if all four trials are given. If one trial differs by more than this, discard the data from that trial. If more than one trial differs by more than 0.6 second from all other trials, the data from the whole session is unreliable.

PASAT—Record Form

NAME _____ AGE _____ DATE _____ TEST _____

2

7(9)					9(11)					2(8)				
3(10)					7(16)					7(9)				
4(7)					6(13)					5(12)				
8(12)					5(11)					9(14)				
1(9)					8(13)					2(11)				
5(6)					1(9)					3(5)				
6(11)					4(5)					9(12)				
9(15)					1(5)					7(16)				
1(10)					2(3)					4(11)				
3(4)					6(8)					5(9)				
6(9)					3(9)					7(12)				
4(10)					7(10)					6(13)				
3(7)					5(12)					8(14)				
2(5)					8(13)					1(9)				
7(9)					3(11)					3(4)				
8(15)					9(12)					1(4)				
5(13)					1(10)					9(10)				
9(14)					4(5)					2(11)				
4(13)					8(12)					5(7)				
2(6)					6(14)					6(11)				

TOTAL CORRECT   TIME/RESPONSE

2.4 sec pacing _____   _____
2.0 sec pacing _____   _____
1.6 sec pacing _____   _____
1.2 sec pacing _____   _____

TOTAL TIME _____ MEAN TIME _____

Figure 6–5. Paced Auditory Serial Addition Test sample scoring sheet.

The examiner should also compute the proportion of responses that were errors (sum across all trials). This proportion should be less 0.1. If the proportion exceeds 0.2 (i.e., 20%), the interpretation of results as a measure of attention is difficult. One can also compute the mean time score by averaging time scores for the four (or three, if one was discarded) trials.

Comment

There are significant practice effects (Gronwall, 1977). Normal subjects who are given the PASAT on two occasions, spaced one week apart, perform about 6 points higher on the second visit (Stuss et al., 1987). After the second presentation,

Table 6–13. PASAT Total Correct per Trial Converted to Time per Correct Response

N*	2.4″	2.0″	1.6″	1.2″	N*	2.4″	2.0″	1.6″	1.2″
1	144	120	96	72	31	4.7	3.9	3.1	2.3
2	72	60	48	36	32	4.5	3.8	3.0	2.3
3	48	40	32	24	33	4.4	3.6	2.9	2.2
4	36	30	24	18	34	4.2	3.5	2.8	2.1
5	28.8	24	19.2	14.4	35	4.1	3.4	2.7	2.1
6	24	20	16	12	36	4.0	3.3	2.7	2.0
7	10.6	17.1	13.7	10.3	37	3.9	3.2	2.6	2.0
8	18	15	12	9	38	3.8	3.2	2.5	1.9
9	16	13.3	10.7	8	39	3.7	3.1	2.4	1.9
10	14.4	12	9.6	7.2	40	3.6	3.0		1.8
11	13.1	10.9	8.7	6.6	41	3.5	2.9	2.3	1.8
12	12	10	8.0	6.0	42	3.4	2.9	2.3	1.7
13	11.1	9.2	7.4	5.5	43	3.3	2.8	2.2	1.7
14	10.3	8.6	6.9	5.1	44	3.3	2.7	2.2	1.6
15	9.6	8.0	6.4	4.8	45	3.2	2.7	2.1	1.6
16	9.0	7.5	6.0	4.5	46	3.1	2.6	2.1	1.6
17	8.5	7.1	5.7	4.2	47	3.1	2.6	2.0	1.5
18	8.0	6.7	5.3	4.0	48	3.0	2.5	2.0	1.5
19	7.6	6.3	5.1	3.8	49	3.0	2.5	2.0	1.5
20	7.2	6.0	4.8	3.6	50	2.9	2.4	1.9	1.4
21	6.9	5.7	4.6	3.4	51	2.8	2.4	1.9	1.4
22	6.5	5.5	4.4	3.3	52	2.8	2.3	1.9	1.4
23	6.3	5.2	4.2	3.1	53	2.7	2.3	1.8	1.4
24	6.0	5.0	4.0	3.0	54	2.7	2.2	1.8	1.3
25	5.8	4.8	3.8	2.9	55	2.6	2.1	1.7	1.3
26	5.5	4.6	3.7	2.8	56	2.6	2.1	1.7	1.3
27	5.3	4.4	3.6	2.7	57	2.5	2.1	1.7	1.3
28	5.1	4.3	3.4	2.6	58	2.5	2.1	1.7	1.2
29	5.0	4.1	3.3	2.5	59	2.4	2.0	1.6	1.2
30	4.8	4.0	3.2	2.4	60	2.4	2.0	1.6	1.2

*Number correct per trial.

Interpretation of Time Scores
N.B. Applies ONLY to ages between 14 and 40 years.
First Test: Control mean time score = 3.2 (SD = .25)
Retests: Control mean time score = 2.6 (SD = .25)

practice effects tend to be minimal (Gronwall, 1977). The PASAT's split-half relia-bility is .96, implying high internal consistency (Egan, 1988).

The PASAT is thought to measure some central information processing capacity similar to that seen on reaction time and divided attention tasks (Gronwall & Sampson, 1974). Gronwall (1977) likens the deficit on this task to the deficit a 65-year-old man would have if suddenly confronted with the work schedule he had coped with at age 25. The PASAT has been shown to be sensitive to mild concussions (Gronwall & Sampson, 1974; Gronwall & Wrightson, 1975), to relate to the patient's experience of symptoms (Gronwall, 1976), and to indicate readiness to return to work (Gronwall, 1977). Although it is a better predictor of subsequent memory difficulties than posttraumatic amnesia (Gronwall, 1981), the PASAT is not primarily a memory task itself (Gronwall & Wrightson, 1981). Further, Gronwall claims (in Gronwall & Sampson, 1974; Gronwall & Wrightson, 1981) that, although it is a cognitive task, there is only a small correlation with arithmetic ability (.28) and general intelligence (.28). Egan (1988), however, found that in healthy people the PASAT shows a modest correlation with general intelligence and numerical ability (about .68).

Overall, the PASAT appears to be a very useful measure. However, there are some weaknesses associated with the PASAT. One problem is its heavy demand on fast-speech responses, a feature that prevents its use with dysarthric or other speech-impaired patients (Weber, 1986). It is a very sensitive test of deficit in mildly brain-injured patients and it can be quite a demanding and frustrating test for normal people. Thus, it is not always appropriate cognitively or emotionally for low-functioning patients (Weber, 1986).

Normative Data

Table 6–14 shows the mean number correct at different age ranges. The normative data are based on samples of healthy adults. The data shown for young adults are similar to those reported by others (e.g., Gronwall, 1977; Weber, 1986). Examination of the table suggests that the faster the rate of presentation, the worse the

Table 6–14. Mean Number of Correct Responses for Each Age Range on the PASAT

Presentation rate (in sec)		Age in years		
		16–29 (n = 30)	30–49 (n = 30)	50–69 (n = 30)
2.4	M	47.4	43.4	43.5
	SD	10.1	10.2	13.6
2.0	M	42.0	41.9	35.6
	SD	12.5	10.2	14.6
1.6	M	36.0	33.1	30.8
	SD	13.0	12.2	15.9
1.2	M	27.4	24.6	21.2
	SD	9.9	10.6	14.4

Note: Normative data derived from a sample of healthy, relatively well-educated adults, ages 16–69 years.
Source: Stuss et al. (1988).

performance, regardless of age. Although the table suggests that performance declines with age, the correlation between age and performance on the PASAT was not significant (Stuss et al., 1987); however, performance was correlated with education: The higher the educational level, the better the performance (Stuss et al., 1987).

The average time per correct response is about 3.2 seconds (SD .25) (Gronwall, 1977; Weber, 1986). For retests, the average time score is 2.6 (SD = .25). These values apply only to adults under the age of 40 years.

REFERENCES

Egan, V. (1988). PASAT: Observed correlations with IQ. *Personality and Individual Differences, 9,* 179–180.

Gronwall, D. (1976). Performance changes during recovery from closed head injury. *Proceedings of the Australian Association of Neurologists, 5,* 72–78.

Gronwall, D.M.A. (1977). Paced Auditory Serial-Addition Task: A measure of recovery from concussion. *Perceptual and Motor Skills, 44,* 367–373.

Gronwall, D. (1981). Information processing capacity and memory after closed head injury. *International Journal of Neuroscience, 12,* 171.

Gronwall, D.M.A., & Sampson, H. (1974). *The Psychological Effects of Concussion.* Auckland, N.Z.: Auckland University Press.

Gronwall, D., & Wrightson, P. (1974). De-layed recovery of intellectual function after minor head injury. *Lancet, 2,* 605–609.

Gronwall, D., & Wrightson, P. (1981). Memory and information processing capacity after closed head injury. *Journal of Neurology, Neurosurgery, and Psychiatry, 44,* 889–895.

Stuss, D.T., Stethem, L.L., & Poirier, C.A. (1987). Comparison of three tests of attention and rapid information processing across six age groups. *Clinical Neuropsychologist, 1,* 139–152.

Stuss, D.T., Stethem, L.L., & Pelchat, G. (1988). Three tests of attention and rapid information processing: An extension. *Clinical Neuropsychologist, 2,* 246–250.

Weber, M.A. (1986). Measuring attentional capacity. Unpublished Ph.D. thesis, University of Victoria, British Columbia.

REY AUDITORY–VERBAL LEARNING TEST (RAVLT)

Other Test Name

The other test name is the Auditory–Verbal Learning test (AVLT).

Purpose

The purpose of this test is to assess verbal learning and memory.

Source

There is no commercial source. Users may refer to the following text in order to design their own material.

Description

The RAVLT is a brief, easily administered pencil-and-paper measure that assesses immediate memory span, new learning, susceptibility to interference, and recognition memory. The original version was developed by Andre Rey (1964). Taylor (1959) and Lezak (1983) altered the test and adapted it for use with English-speaking subjects. The adapted test consists of 15 nouns (List A) read aloud (with a one-second interval between each word) for five consecutive trials, each trial followed by a free-recall test. The order of presentation of words remains fixed across trials. Instructions are repeated before each trial to minimize forgetting. Upon completion of trial 5, an interference list of 15 words (List B) is presented, followed by a free-recall test of that list. Immediately following this, delayed recall of the first list is tested without further presentation of those words. After a 20-minute delay period, each subject is again required to recall words for List A. Finally, a story that uses all the words from list A is presented, either orally or in written form (depending upon the patient's reading ability), and the patient must identify words recognized from List A. Alternatively, one can test recognition in a matrix array where the patient must identify List A words from a list of 50 words containing all items from Lists A and B and 20 words phonemically and/or semantically similar to those in Lists A and B. We test recognition with the list format since there are good normative data for this version. The addition of a recognition trial permits the identification of people with suspected retrieval problems, who will score better on this trial than on free recall. A person with a generalized memory deficit will perform poorly on both free-recall and recognition trials (Bleecker et al., 1988; Lezak, 1983; Rey, 1964).

Administration

For Trial 1, give the following instructions: **"I am going to read a list of words. Listen carefully, for when I stop, you are to repeat back as many words as you can remember. It doesn't matter in what order you repeat them. Just try to remember as many as you can."**

Read List 1 words, with a one-second interval between each of the 15 words. Check off the words recalled, using numbers to keep track of the patient's pattern of recall. No feedback should be given regarding the number of correct responses, repetitions or errors.

When the patient indicates that he or she can recall no more words, the examiner rereads the list after giving a second set of instructions: **"Now I am going to read the same words again, and once again when I stop, I want you to tell me as many words as you can remember, including words you said the first time. It** doesn't matter in what order you say them. Just say as many words as you can remember, whether or not you said them before."

The list is reread for Trials 3–5, using Trial 2 instructions each time. The examiner may praise the patient as he or she recalls more words.

After Trial 5, the examiner reads List B with instructions to perform as on the first (A) list trial. Immediately after the List B trial, the examiner asks the patient to recall as many words from the first list (List A) as he or she can (Trial 6) without further presentation of those words.

After a 20-minute delay period, filled with other activity, ask the subject to recall the words from List A. On completion of the delay trial, the recognition test should be given. The recognition task requires the patient to identify as many of the list words as he or she can and, if possible, the specific list of origin. If the patient can read at least at grade 7 level, ask the patient to read the list and circle the correct words. If the patient has difficulty with reading, then the examiner should read the list to the patient.

Approximate Time for Administration

The time required is 10–15 minutes.

Scoring

See sample scoring sheet (includes correct answers) in Figure 6–6. Words that are repeated are marked R; RC, if repeated and self-corrected; RQ, if the patient questions whether he or she has repeated the words but remains unsure. Words that are not on the list are errors and are marked E.

One can derive a number of different measures. Geffen et al. (1990) provide extensive indices of aspects of memory function, only some of which are reported here. The score for each trial is the number of words correctly recalled. In addition to scores on Trials 1–5, which may be used to plot a learning curve, the RAVLT yields scores for the total number of words recalled following interference (postdistractor trial or trial 6), the number of words recalled after the 20-minute delay and the total number of words recognized from each list. Other scores, including a total score (the sum of Trials 1–5), the number of repetitions and extra-list intrusions, and the amount of loss from Trial 5 to the postdistraction recall Trial (6) can also be calculated. The percentage of words lost from Trial 5 to Trial 6 may be a particularly sensitive indicator of retroactive interference (i.e., the decremental effect of subsequent learning on the retention of previously learned material). Conversely, if learning List A significantly interferes with learning List B, then an unusually high degree of proactive interference may be occurring.

RAVLT Sample Scoring Sheet

Name: _____

Date: _____

Examiner: _____

(Note: Do not re-read List A for Recall Trial A6 or A7)

List A	Recall Trials					List B	Recall Trials			
	A1	A2	A3	A4	A5		B1	A6	A7	
drum						desk				drum
curtain						ranger				curtain
bell						bird				bell
coffee						shoe				coffee
school						stove				school
parent						mountain				parent
moon						glasses				moon
garden						towel				garden
hat						cloud				hat
farmer						boat				farmer
nose						lamb				nose
turkey						gun				turkey
color						pencil				color
house						church				house
river						fish				river

correct

Total   A1 to A5 = _____
Trial   A6 − A5 = _____
Recognition # targets correctly identified _____
              # distractors correctly identified _____

Word List for Testing RAVLT Recognition[1]

bell (A)	home (SA)	towel (B)	boat (B)	glasses (B)
window (SA)	fish (B)	curtain (A)	hot (PA)	stocking (SB)
hat (A)	moon (A)	flower (SA)	parent (A)	shoe (B)
barn (SA)	tree (PA)	color (A)	water (SA)	teacher (SA)
ranger (B)	balloon (PA)	desk (B)	farmer (A)	stove (B)
nose (A)	bird (B)	gun (B)	rose (SPA)	nest (SPB)
weather (SB)	mountain (B)	crayon (SA)	cloud (B)	children (SA)
school (A)	coffee (A)	church (B)	house (A)	drum (A)
hand (PA)	mouse (PA)	turkey (A)	stranger (PB)	toffee (PA)
pencil (B)	river (A)	fountain (PB)	garden (A)	lamb (B)

[1] Source: Lezak (1983). (A) words from list A; (B) words from list b; (S) word with a semantic association to a word on list A or B as indicated; (P) word phonemically similar to a word on list A or B.

Figure 6–6.   Rey Auditory–Verbal Learning Test sample scoring sheet.

Comment

Over one-year intervals, the test has modest test–retest reliability, with correlations of about .55 (Snow et al., 1988). Small, but significant improvements (on average, one to two words per trial) can be expected on successive administrations of the same form of the RAVLT (Crawford, 1989; Lezak, 1982). No significant improvements in performance occur when subjects are retested with a different RAVLT version (Crawford, 1989). Several investigators have provided alternative forms of the test (Crawford et al., 1989; Ryan et al. (1986). The version by Crawford et al. (1989) (Figure 6–7) seems to produce comparable scores. Age-based normative data for the alternate form are lacking, however.

The RAVLT is sensitive to laterality of brain damage and to verbal memory deficits in a variety of patient groups (Bigler, 1989; Lezak, 1983; Miceli et al.,

	Crawford Version of RAVLT			
List A		**Interference List**		
DOLL		DISH		
MIRROR		JESTER		
NAIL		HILL		
SAILOR		COAT		
HEART		TOOL		
DESERT		FOREST		
FACE		WATER		
LETTER		LADDER		
BED		GIRL		
MACHINE		FOOT		
MILK		SHIELD		
HELMET		PIE		
MUSIC		INSECT		
HORSE		BALL		
ROAD		CAR		

Recognition List				
NAIL	ENVELOPE	LADDER	FOOT	WATER
SAND	CAR	MIRROR	BREAD	JOKER
BED	FACE	SCREW	DESERT	COAT
PONY	TOAD	MUSIC	STREET	CAPTAIN
JESTER	SILK	DISH	MACHINE	TOOL
MILK	HILL	PIE	HEAD	FLY
PLATE	FOREST	WOOD	GIRL	SONG
HEART	SAILOR	BALL	HORSE	DOLL
JAIL	DART	HELMET	SOOT	STALL
INSECT	ROAD	STOOL	LETTER	SHIELD

Figure 6–7. Alternate form of the Rey Auditory–Verbal Learning Test (Crawford et al., 1989).

1981; Mungas, 1983; Rosenberg et al., 1984). Information from the test can be used to differentiate clinically among different memory disorders. Moreover, it yields information somewhat different from that provided by tests of attention/concentration, perceptual organization, and verbal intelligence. In a factor-analytic study with a diverse neurologic/psychiatric sample, the RAVLT was found to have a verbal learning and memory loading with the verbal subtests of the Wechsler Memory Scale (Ryan et al., 1984).

Normative Data

There are a few normative studies based on large samples of healthy people. The norms for Swiss people (Rey, 1964) reported in Lezak (1983) and Taylor (1959) cannot be used (see Wiens et al., 1988) since:

1. The English translations for some of the words differ from the original words.
2. The current administration differs from that used by Rey (1964), in that feedback regarding correct and incorrect words was provided, no distraction trial was given, and a different presentation rate was used.
3. Educational and cultural differences may invalidate comparison of current North American samples to those collected by Rey 40 years ago.

Table 6–15 provides recently compiled normative data derived from North American samples of school children, ages 13–16 (Munsen, 1987). Geffen et al. (1990) have recently published normative data for healthy adults, ages 16–84 years, of above average IQ. The mean recall and recognition data are shown in Tables 6–16 and 6–17 for men and women, respectively, in each of seven age groups. Bleecker et al. (1988), Ivnik et al. (1990), Read (1986), and Weins et al.

Table 6–15.   RAVLT Scores for 244 Adolescents, Age 13–16[a]

	Mean	SD
Trial A1	6.8	1.7
A2	9.5	2.0
A3	11.4	2.0
A4	12.3	1.9
A5	13.0	1.8
A6 (retention)	11.6	2.4
Distractor (List B)	6.2	1.8
Recognition	14.3	1.1
Total Words (Trials 1–5)	53.0	7.5

Note: [a]Munson (1987) gives normative data for adolescent schoolchildren. Story format (rather than list format) was used to test recognition.

Table 6–16. RAVLT Scores by Age: Males

		Age Groups						
		16–19	20–29	30–39	40–49	50–59	60–69	70+
	(n)	(13)	(10)	(10)	(11)	(11)	(10)	(10)
Trial								
1 (List A)	M	6.9	8.4	6.0	6.4	6.5	4.9	3.6
	SD	(1.8)	(1.2)	(1.8)	(1.8)	(2.0)	(1.1)	(0.8)
2		9.7	10.8	8.0	9.0	8.6	6.4	5.7
		(1.7)	(1.9)	(2.4)	(2.3)	(2.0)	(1.2)	(1.7)
3		11.5	11.3	9.7	9.8	10.1	8.0	6.8
		(1.2)	(1.6)	(2.7)	(2.0)	(1.6)	(2.6)	(1.6)
4		12.8	12.2	10.9	11.5	10.7	8.5	8.3
		(1.5)	(1.8)	(2.8)	(1.9)	(1.9)	(2.7)	(2.7)
5		12.5	12.2	11.4	10.9	11.8	8.9	8.2
		(1.3)	(2.2)	(2.6)	(2.0)	(2.6)	(2.0)	(2.5)
Total		53.2	54.9	46.0	47.5	47.6	36.7	32.6
		(5.4)	(7.0)	(10.9)	(8.3)	(8.5)	(8.4)	(8.3)
Distractor		6.9	6.5	5.3	6.1	5.0	4.9	3.5
List B		(1.9)	(1.8)	(1.6)	(2.1)	(2.3)	(1.6)	(1.3)
Trial A6		11.2	11.1	9.7	9.7	9.6	7.2	6.4
(Retention)		(1.6)	(1.7)	(2.3)	(2.5)	(2.9)	(2.8)	(1.7)
Trial A7		11.3	10.6	10.4	10.5	10.0	7.1	5.6
(Delayed Recall)		(1.7)	(2.4)	(2.3)	(2.7)	(2.6)	(3.8)	(2.6)
Recognition		14.4	14.2	13.5	14.2	13.9	12.4	11.5
List A		(0.9)	(0.8)	(1.5)	(1.0)	(0.9)	(2.8)	(2.6)
List B		8.4	8.2	4.4	6.9	4.7	4.9	3.0
		(2.8)	(2.7)	(2.0)	(2.6)	(2.9)	(2.7)	(2.7)

Source: Geffen et al. 1990

(1988) also provide normative data for healthy men and women and the values are similar to those reported here; however, fewer measures of potential interest are reported (for a more complete listing, see Geffen et al., 1990). Ivnik et al. (1990) provide normative data based on 47 healthy subjects, ages 85+. (Trial 1: M = 4.0, SD = 1.5; Trial 2: M = 6.0, SD = 1.8; Trial 3: M = 7.4, SD = 2.2; Trial 4: M = 7.9, SD = 2.4; Trial 5: M = 9.1, SD = 2.3; List B: M = 3.1, SD = 1.4; Trial 6: M = 6.2, SD = 2.6; Delayed Recall: M = 5.4, SD = 2.7; Recognition: M = 12.3, SD = 2.3)

Trial 1 may be considered an indication of immediate memory; on average, normal young adults recall seven words. In general, normal people learn about five words from Trial 1 to Trial 5; they recall about one to two fewer words on the recall trial (Trial 6) than on Trial 5. There is little forgetting over a 20-minute delay. Finally, a proactive interference effect is observed for all groups for whom recall for the second word list is inferior to initial recall of the first word list. It should be noted that age, sex, and intellectual level contribute to performance on the RAVLT (Bleecker et al., 1988; Geffen et al., 1990; Ivnik et al., 1990; Munsen, un-

Table 6–17. RAVLT Scores by Age: Females

		Age Groups						
		16–19	20–29	30–39	40–49	50–59	60–69	70+
	(n)	(13)	(10)	(10)	(11)	(11)	(10)	(10)
Trial								
1 (List A)	M	7.8	7.7	8.0	6.8	6.4	6.0	5.6
	SD	(1.9)	(1.0)	(2.0)	(1.5)	(1.5)	(2.2)	(1.4)
2		10.5	10.5	10.8	9.4	8.2	9.0	6.9
		(2.0)	(2.0)	(2.1)	(1.5)	(2.4)	(2.0)	(2.1)
3		12.3	12.2	11.5	11.4	10.2	10.8	8.9
		(1.2)	(2.3)	(1.7)	(1.7)	(2.1)	(2.0)	(1.9)
4		12.5	12.0	12.9	11.7	11.1	11.3	10.1
		(1.7)	(1.6)	(1.3)	(2.1)	(1.9)	(1.4)	(1.9)
5		13.3	12.9	12.7	12.8	11.6	11.9	10.1
		(1.5)	(1.5)	(1.3)	(1.4)	(2.1)	(1.6)	(1.2)
Total		56.5	55.3	55.9	52.1	47.6	49.0	41.6
		(6.0)	(6.6)	(6.3)	(7.1)	(7.7)	(7.1)	(6.6)
Distractor		7.7	7.9	6.5	5.2	4.6	5.3	4.2
List B		(1.3)	(2.0)	(1.5)	(1.3)	(1.9)	(1.1)	(1.9)
Trial A6		11.9	11.6	12.1	11.1	9.9	9.8	7.8
(Retention)		(2.5)	(2.5)	(1.9)	(2.4)	(2.8)	(1.6)	(1.8)
Trial A7		11.4	11.0	12.2	11.1	10.2	10.3	8.3
(Delayed Recall)		2.5	2.0	2.5	2.3	2.7	2.3	2.1
Recognition		13.8	14.4	14.2	14.4	13.7	13.8	13.6
List A		(2.0)	(0.8)	(1.7)	(0.8)	(1.1)	(1.1)	(2.0)
List B		7.8	8.0	8.9	7.4	5.7	7.5	7.5
		(3.1)	(2.9)	(4.1)	(2.8)	(2.4)	(3.6)	(3.7)

Mean (SD) number of words *recalled and recognized* according to age and trial. Number of subjects (n) is shown beneath each age group.

Source: Geffen et al. 1990

published, 1987; Query & Berger, 1980; Query & Megran, 1983; D.E. Read, unpublished, 1986; Wiens et al., 1988). Results indicate that (1) RAVLT scores decrease with advancing age; (2) recall is better at higher IQ levels; and (3) females outperform males on the recall, but not the recognition trials. Data for subjects grouped by age, sex, and intellectual level need to be gathered.

REFERENCES

Bigler, E.D., Rosa, L., Schultz, F., Hall, S., & Harris, J. (1989). Rey Auditory–Verbal Learning and Rey–Osterrieth Complex Figure Design Test Performance in Alzheimer's disease and closed head injury. *Journal of Clinical Psychology, 45,* 277–280.

Bleecker, M.L., Bolla-Wilson, K., Agnew, J., & Meyers, D.A. (1988). Age-related sex differences in verbal memory. *Journal of Clinical Psychology, 44,* 403–411.

Crawford, J.R., Stewart, L.E., & Moore, J.W. (1989). Demonstration of savings on the AVLT and development of a parallel form. *Journal of Clinical and Experimental Neuropsychology, 11,* 975–981.

Geffen, G., Hoar, K.J., O'Hanlon, A.P., Clark, C.R., & Geffen, L.B. (1990). Performance measures of 16- to 86-year-old males and females on the Auditory Verbal Learning Test. *Clinical Neuropsychologist, 4,* 45–63.

Ivnik, R.J., Malec, J.F., Tangalos, E.G., Petersen, R.C., Kokmen, S. & Kurland, L.T. (1990). The Auditory-verbal Learning Test (AVLT): Norms for ages 55 years and older. *Psychological Assessment, 2,* 304–312.

Lezak, M.D. (1982). The test–retest stability of some tests commonly used in neuropsychological assessment. Paper presented to the 5th European Conference of the International Neuropsychological Society, Deauville, France.

Lezak, M.D. (1983). *Neuropsychological Assessment* (2nd ed.). New York: Oxford University Press.

Miceli, G., Caltagirone, C., Gainotti, G., Masullo, C., & Silveri, M.C. (1981). Neuropsychological correlates of localized cerebral lesions in non-aphasic brain-damaged patients. *Journal of Clinical Neuropsychology, 3,* 53–63.

Mungas, D. (1983). Differential clinical sensitivity of specific parameters of the Rey Auditory–Verbal Learning Test. *Journal of Consulting and Clinical Psychology, 51,* 848–855.

Query, W.T., & Berger, R.A. (1980). AVLT memory scores as a function of age among general medical, neurological, and alcoholic patients. *Journal of Clinical Psychology, 36,* 1009–1012.

Query, W.T., & Megran, J. (1983). Age-related norms for the AVLT in a male patient population. *Journal of Clinical Psychology, 39,* 136–138.

Rey, A. (1964). *L'Examen Clinique en Psychologie.* Paris: Press Universitaire de France.

Rosenberg, S.J., Ryan, J.J., & Prifitera, A. (1984). Rey Auditory–Verbal Learning Test performance of patients with and without memory impairment. *Journal of Clinical Psychology, 40,* 785–787.

Ryan, J.J., Geisser, M.E., Randall, D.M., & Georgemiller, R.J. (1986). Alternate form reliability and equivalency of the Rey Auditory Verbal Learning Test. *Journal of Clinical and Experimental Neuropsychology, 8,* 611–616.

Ryan, J.J., Rosenberg, S.J., & Mittenberg, W. (1984). Factor analysis of the Rey Auditory–Verbal Learning Test. *International Journal of Clinical Neuropsychology, 6,* 239–241.

Snow, W.G., Tierney, M.C., Zorzitto, M.L., Fisher, R.H., & Reid, D.W. (1988). One-year test–retest reliability of selected neuropsychological tests in older adults. Paper presented to the International Neuropsychological Society, New Orleans.

Taylor, E.M. (1959). *The Appraisal of Children with Cerebral Deficits.* Cambridge, Mass.: Harvard University Press.

Wiens, A.N., McMinn, M.R., Crossen, J.R. (1988). Rey Auditory–Verbal Learning Test: Development of norms for healthy young adults. *Clinical Neuropsychologist, 2,* 67–87.

REY–OSTERRIETH COMPLEX FIGURE TEST

Other Test Name

Other Test names are Complex Figure (CF) and Rey Figure (RF) tests.

Purpose

The purpose of this test is to assess visuospatial constructional ability and visual memory.

Source

There is no commercial source. Users may refer to the following description in order to design their own material.

Description

The Complex Figure is a useful test since it permits assessment of a variety of cognitive processes, including planning and organizational skills and problem-solving strategies, as well as perceptual, motor, and memory functions (Waber & Holmes, 1986). It was developed by Rey (1941) and elaborated by Osterrieth (1944). The materials consist of blank pieces of paper, colored pencils, and the Rey–Osterrieth figure or an alternate version, the Taylor figure (Taylor, 1969, 1979). The drawings are shown in Figures 6–8 and 6–9. The procedure involves having the subject copy the figure and then, without prior warning, reproduce it from memory. Some investigators (e.g., Chiulli et al., 1989; Lezak, 1983; Loring et al., 1988a,b) give both immediate- and delayed-recall trials of the CF, whereas others (e.g., Bennett-Levy, 1984; King, 1981; Kolb & Whishaw, 1985; Taylor, 1969, 1979) measure only delayed recall. Further, the amount of delay varies from three minutes (e.g., Bigler, 1989) to 45 minutes (Taylor, 1969, 1979). We, like others (e.g., Chiulli et al., 1989; Kolb & Whishaw, 1985; Loring et al., 1988), use a 30-minute delay. The utility of an immediate-recall trial is unclear, and we do not include this condition since delayed recall may be more sensitive to the presence of memory deficits (Loring et al., 1990). Two measures of performance are customarily derived: a copy score, which reflects the accuracy of the original copy and is a measure of visual-constructional ability; and a recall score, which assesses amount of information retained over time.

Administration

COPY

Put a plain sheet of $8\frac{1}{2}'' \times 11''$ paper on the table so that the long edge of the paper is along the edge of the table in front of the subject. Then say: **"I am going to show you a card on which there is a design that I would like you to copy on this sheet of paper. Please copy the figure as carefully as you can. If you think you have made a mistake, don't erase it, just correct whatever you think is wrong."**

Have the subject ready, with pencil in hand before presenting the drawing. Each time the subject completes a section of the drawing, the examiner hands the subject a different colored pencil and notes the order of the colors. Alternatively, the examiner can reproduce the subject's drawing, noting the order and direc-

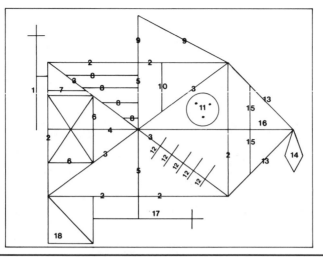

REY–OSTERRIETH COMPLEX FIGURE TEST
FORM A (Rey Figure)

Details:	COPY	DELAY
1. Cross upper left corner, outside of rectangle	____	____
2. Large rectangle	____	____
3. Diagonal cross	____	____
4. Horizontal midline of 2	____	____
5. Vertical midline	____	____
6. Small rectangle, within 2 to the left	____	____
7. Small segment above 6	____	____
8. Four parallel lines within 2, upper left	____	____
9. Triangle above 2 upper right	____	____
10. Small vertical line within 2, below 9	____	____
11. Circle with three dots within 2	____	____
12. Five parallel lines with 2 crossing 3, lower right	____	____
13. Sides of triangle attached to 2 on right	____	____
14. Diamond attached to 13	____	____
15. Vertical line within triangle 13 parallel to right vertical of a	____	____
16. Horizontal line within 13, continuing 4 to right	____	____
17. Cross attached to low center	____	____
18. Square attached to 2, lower left	____	____
TOTAL SCORE	____	____

Scoring:

Consider each of the eighteen units separately, and appraise accuracy of each unit and relative position within the whole of the design. For each unit count as follows:

Correct	⎰ placed properly	2 points
	⎱ placed poorly	1 point
Distorted or incomplete	⎰ placed properly	1 point
but recognizable	⎱ placed poorly	1/2 point
Absent or not recognizable		0 points
Maximum		36 points

Figure 6–8. Rey–Osterrieth Complex Figure Test: Form A (Rey figure) and legend.

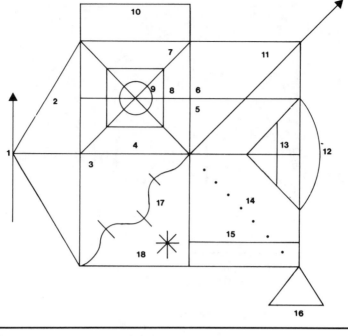

REY–OSTERRIETH COMPLEX FIGURE TEST
FORM B (Taylor Alternate Version)

Details:	COPY	DELAY
1. Arrow at left	———	———
2. Triangle at left	———	———
3. Square	———	———
4. Horizontal line	———	———
5. Vertical line	———	———
6. Horizontal in top half	———	———
7. Diagonals in top left quadrant	———	———
8. Square in top left quadrant	———	———
9. Circle	———	———
10. Rectangle	———	———
11. Arrow top right quadrant	———	———
12. Semicircle	———	———
13. Triangle line	———	———
14. Row of dots	———	———
15. Horizontal line between dots	———	———
16. Triangle at bottom of 3	———	———
17. Curves & cross bars	———	———
18. Star	———	———
TOTAL SCORE	———	———
	———	———

Figure 6–9. Rey–Osterrieth Complex Figure Test: Form B (Taylor alternate version) and legend.

tionality of each line as it is drawn. Begin timing as soon as you expose the drawing. Do not allow the subject to turn the card.

It is important to supervise the drawing carefully, particularly in the early stages (Taylor, personal communication). If drawing is careless, the patient should be reminded that he or she is to make the copy as accurate as possible. The card and the subject's copy are exposed for a maximum of five minutes and a minimum of $2\frac{1}{2}$ minutes. If by $2\frac{1}{2}$ minutes, it is obvious that the patient is drawing too slowly, he or she should be told this and asked to speed up. If the patient is finished drawing before $2\frac{1}{2}$ minutes, he or she should be told to check it over carefully to make sure it is complete.

Record the *total* time taken to complete the drawing. Subjects should normally be able to complete the drawing in no more than five minutes, unless their hands are very shaky. It is more important, however, for a subject to complete the drawing as well as he or she can, than it is to get it finished within the five minutes. For this reason, allow the subject as much time as needed to do the best copy that he or she is capable of.

Delayed Recall

The examiner waits about 30 minutes after the first administration of the CF and then requests recall of the figure. The interposed tests should be quite different from the CF, in order to avoid interference. One should especially not give any tests of drawing. Then say: **"Do you remember the design I had you copy awhile ago? I would like you to draw it again from memory as carefully and completely as you can on this sheet of paper. Again, if you make a mistake, do not erase, just correct whatever you think is wrong."**

There is *no time limit* on the delayed recall task. As in the copy trial, the order of approach should be recorded.

Approximate Time for Administration

The time required is about 10 minutes (excluding delay).

Scoring

A few preliminary remarks are in order (based on L. Taylor, personal communication, May 1989): Scoring criteria for the Complex Figure are strictly applied for both the correctness of the details and their placement, because slight drawing errors have been found to be significant in differentiating groups of patients with varying cerebral lesions. Allowance is made for the fact that it is difficult to draw a straight line without the use of a ruler, so that if there is a waver in a line or if the line descends or ascends slightly, there is no penalty for these slight inaccuracies.

Copy and memory trials are scored in the same manner. The figure is typically broken down into 18 scoreable elements, 0.5–2.0 points being awarded for each element, depending on accuracy/distortion, and also location of its reproduction (Lezak, 1983): 2 points are awarded if the unit is correct and placed properly; 1 point is awarded if the unit is correct but placed poorly; 1 point is given if the unit is distorted but placed correctly; ½ point is given if the unit is distorted and placed poorly; and 0 point is awarded if the unit is absent or not recognizable. Explicit scoring guidelines (Taylor, personal communication) are given in Table 6–18 for the Rey figure and in Table 6–19 for the Taylor figure. The highest possible score is 36. One can calculate a percent recall score [(CF recall/CF copy) × 100] in order to remove the effects of the level of performance on the copy administration from the memory performance (Lezak, 1983).

Table 6–18.   Taylor Scoring Criteria for the Rey Complex Figure

Detail 1:	The cross at the upper left corner, outside of the rectangle. The cross must come down to the horizontal midline of the rectangle and must extend above the rectangle. The line that joins the cross to the rectangle must be approximately in the middle of the cross and must come between Detail 7 and the top of the rectangle.
Detail 2:	The large retangle. The horizontal dimensions of the rectangle must not be greater than twice the vertical dimensions of the rectangle, nor must the rectangle resemble a square. As there are so many possibilities of distorting the rectangle and as it is not possible to score for position, a score of ½ point is given if the rectangle is incomplete or distorted in any way.
Detail 3:	The diagonal cross must touch each of the four corners of the rectangle and intersect in the middle of the rectangle.
Detail 4:	The horizontal midline of the rectangle must go clearly across from the midpoint of the left side of the rectangle to the midpoint of the right side of the rectangle in one unbroken line.
Detail 5:	The vertical midline must start at the midpoint of the bottom of the rectangle and go through in one unbroken line to the midpoint at the top of the rectangle. In scoring for position of 4, 5, and 6, these details should intersect at the midpoint of the rectangle. Usually, if they do not, only one detail is scored as incorrect for position. Very seldom all three are scored as incorrect for not being in position.
Detail 6:	The small rectangle must be within the large rectangle and to the left side of it. The boundaries of Detail 6 are defined by the top of the rectangle falling between lines 2 and 3 of the parallel lines that make up Detail 8, and the width of the small rectangle must be approximately one-quarter the width of the large rectangle; that is, it should come to the midpoint between the left side of the large rectangle and the vertical midpoint of the rectangle. The cross within Detail 6 must come from the four corners of the rectangle and should intersect at the midpoint of the rectangle (i.e., intersecting on Detail 4).
Detail 7:	The straight line above Detail 6 must be shorter than the horizontal aspect of Detail 6 and must fall between the top of Detail 6 and the second line of Detail 8.
Detail 8:	The four parallel lines within the rectangle in the upper left corner should be parallel, with the spaces between them approximately equal. If the lines are unduly slanted or, of course, if there are more or less than four of them, then the scoring is penalized.
Detail 9:	The triangle above the rectangle on the upper right, with the height less than the base.

Interpretation of the CF should consider not only the actual score but also qualitative aspects of performance. Some investigators have devised scoring systems to assess item distortion and misplacement, approach or style, and level of organization (Bennett-Levy, 1984; Binder, 1982; Kirk & Kelly, 1986; Loring et al., 1988b; Visser, 1973; Waber & Holmes, 1985, 1986). The designs are most commonly copied in a piecemeal fashion by younger children, and they become more configurational with increasing age. Around age 13, a shift to the base rectangle strategy occurs, where the large central rectangle is drawn first and details are added on in relation to it. In the memory production, a piecemeal strategy is very rare after age 9. In older children and adults, errors or distortions are quite common in the memory condition but are rare in the copy condition. Further, copying strategy is related to recall performance. A disorganized piecemeal approach to the copy of the figure may result in an accurate production, but recall tends to be poor.

Detail 10: The small vertical line within the rectangle just below Detail 9. The line should be clearly shifted to the left within the upper right quadrangle in the rectangle.

Detail 11: The circle with three dots must be in the lower right half of the upper right quadrangle. It must not touch any of the three sides of the triangular area in which it is placed, and the positioning of the dots should be such that there are two dots above and one below; that is, so that it resembles a face.

Detail 12: The five parallel lines that are crossing the lower right aspect of Detail 3 must all be within the lower right quadrangle. They must not touch any sides of the quadrangle, and they should be approximately equidistant from one another.

Detail 13: The triangle on the right end of the large rectangle. The height of the triangle must not be greater than half of the horizontal midline of the rectangle, and, as already mentioned, the slope of the sides of the triangle must not be a continuation of the slope of Detail 9.

Detail 14: The diamond attached to the end of Detail 13 should be diamond-shaped and must be attached to the end of Detail 13; it must not extend down below the bottom of the large rectangle, Detail 2.

Detail 15: The vertical line within triangle of Detail 13 must be parallel to the right vertical of Detail 2, the large rectangle, and it must be shifted to the left within Detail 13.

Detail 16: The horizontal line within triangle 13, which is a continuation of Detail 4 to the right, must come from the midpoint of the right side of the large rectangle and extend to the top of triangle 13. If triangle 13 is slightly askew, or if Detail 4 does not meet the midpoint of the right side of the rectangle, Detail 16 should still be scored as a full 2 points if it went to the top of the triangle from the midpoint of the right side of the rectangle.

Detail 17: The cross attached to the lower center area of the rectangle. The right side of the cross must be clearly longer than the left side of the cross but must not extend beyond the right end of the large rectangle. At its left end, it should also commence at the midpoint of the right side of the square, which is Detail 18.

Detail 18: The lower left corner of Detail 2 must clearly be a square, as opposed to the rectangular shape of Detail 6, and its sides should be the same size as the vertical aspect of Detail 6, extending halfway between the left side of the rectangle and the vertical midline of the rectangle.

Source: L. Taylor (personal communication, May 1989).

Table 6–19.   Scoring Guidelines of the Taylor (Alternate) Form of the
Rey Complex Figure

Detail 1:	Vertical arrow at the left of the figure, extending above and below the midpoints of the upper and lower quadrants of the large square, but not extending beyond the upper and lower limits of the square, and with its midpoint meeting Detail 4.
Detail 2:	Triangle whose base is the left side of the large square, with the altitude of the triangle less than half of the width of the large square.
Detail 3:	Large square, which is the basic element of the figure, and which must look like a square and not a rectangle.
Detail 4:	Horizontal midline of the large square, which extends outside the large square to midpoint of Detail 1.
Detail 5:	Vertical midline of the large square.
Detail 6:	Horizontal line bisecting the top half of the large square.
Detail 7:	Diagonal lines bisecting one another from the corners of the top left quadrant of the large square.
Detail 8:	Small square, situated in the center of the top left quadrant, one-quarter the size of the quadrant, and with the corners of the square located on the diagonals (Detail 7).
Detail 9:	Circle in the center of Detail 8, in the top left quadrant.
Detail 10:	Rectangle above the top left quadrant, with its height less than $\frac{1}{4}$ of the height of the large square.
Detail 11:	Arrow extending from the center of the large square through the top right corner of the right upper quadrant, with not more than one-third of its length outside the large square.
Detail 12:	Semicircle at the right of the figure, extending from the horizontal bisector of the top half of the base square (Detail 6) to the equivalent point in the lower half of the base square.
Detail 13:	Triangle in the right half of the base square, with the same base as the semicircle (Detail 12), and with an altitude that is one-quarter the width of the large square.
Detail 14:	Row of seven dots (not circles) in the lower right quadrant, evenly spaced in a straight line from the center of the large square to the lower right corner of the quadrant.
Detail 15:	Horizontal line in the lower right quadrant, between the sixth and seventh dots of Detail 14.
Detail 16:	Equilateral triangle whose apex is at the lower right corner of the large square and whose altitude is not more than one-quarter the height of the large square.
Detail 17:	Curved line with a cross-bar at the center of each of three sinusoids in the lower left quadrant, extending from the bottom left corner to the top right corner of the quadrant.
Detail 18:	Star, composed of eight lines radiating from a center point, and situated in the lower left quadrant, near its lower right corner.

Source: L. Taylor (personal communication, May 1989).

Comment

The strict scoring criteria described above yield a high interrater reliability (above
.95) (Bennett-Levy, 1984; Strauss & Spreen, 1990). We have found that with
repeated administration of the same figure (Rey or Taylor), practice effects occur in
normal adults. In general, normal subjects show a 10% improvement in percent
recall scores when retested after a one-month interval.

Another issue concerns the comparability of the Rey and Taylor figures. In healthy young adults, the copy administrations of the two figures are of equivalent difficulty; however, recall of the Rey figure is somewhat harder (about 5 points) than recall of the Taylor Figure (Strauss & Spreen, 1990). The greater recall difficulty of the Rey figure suggests that this measure may be more sensitive than the Taylor figure to the presence of memory deficits.

A piecemeal approach to the copying of the CF is characteristic of patients with either left- or right-hemisphere lesions (Binder, 1982; Visser, 1973). However, the drawings by the right-brain-damaged patients tend to be less accurate and more distorted than those of their left-sided counterparts (Binder, 1982). Differences between patients with parietal–occipital lesions and patients with frontal lobe lesions have also been noted on the copy trial (Lezak, 1983; Pillon, 1981; Taylor, cited in Kolb & Whishaw, 1985). Patients with posterior lesions are more likely to have difficulty with the spatial organization of the figure. Patients with frontal lobe lesions are more likely to have difficulty planning their approach to the task.

The CF is often perceived to be a test of memory. However, the test is more complex, and interpretation of the recall score must consider whether the initial copy is performed adequately. There is a tendency for patients with right-hemisphere lesions to perform more poorly on the recall trial than do patients with left-hemisphere disturbances (Loring et al., 1988b; but see King, 1981). However, the test does not provide a perfect predictor of the side of the lesion (Lee et al., 1989; Loring et al., 1988b). Analysis of qualitative features (e.g., distortion of overall configuration, major mislocation) may be helpful in distinguishing laterality of dysfunction (Loring et al., 1988b). When the initial copy is performed satisfactorily, mislocation and distortion on the recall trial tend to be characteristic of patients with right, as opposed to left, hemisphere dysfunction. Finally, information from the test may also be useful in differentiating among different memory disorders (Bigler, 1989).

Normative Data

There are a few normative studies based on large samples of healthy people. Osterrieth's (1944) data should not be used since (1) the current administration differs from that used by Osterrieth in that a 30-minute delayed recall trial was not given; (2) the data were based on 60 adults in the age range 16–60 years, and no effects of age were presented; and (3) educational and cultural differences may invalidate comparison of current North American samples to those collected by Osterrieth over 40 years ago. Kolb and Whishaw (1985) provide normative data derived from Canadian samples of school children, ages 6–15, and healthy adults, ages 16–44 and we give data for healthy, well-educated (mean = 13.2 years)

Table 6–20. Normative Data for Ages 6–85 Years on the Rey-Osterrieth Test

	Age in years						
	6	7	8	9	10	11	12
N	192	353	347	329	301	280	225
Copy	16.66	21.29	23.64	24.46	27.20	28.61	30.21
SD	7.97	7.67	8.00	6.94	7.58	7.31	6.69
30-Minute Recall	10.53	13.57	16.34	18.71	19.73	22.59	23.20
SD	5.80	6.28	6.77	6.61	6.71	6.65	6.38

	Age in years						
	12	13	14	15	16–30	31–44	50–59
N	225	237	180	116	67	26	14
Copy	30.21	32.63	33.53	33.60	35.10	33.20	35.57
SD	6.69	4.35	3.18	2.98	1.5	6.1	.76
30-Minute Recall	23.20	24.59	26.24	26.00	22.70	19.50	18.82
SD	6.38	6.29	5.40	6.35	7.00	6.70	7.37

	Age in years	
	60–69	70+
N	13	10
Copy	33.15	32.90
SD	4.02	2.69
30-Minute Recall	16.65	11.80
SD	8.70	6.20

Note: We (Strauss & Spreen, unpublished data) provide data for healthy older adults, ages 50+.

Source: Kolb & Whishaw (1985) report data that are derived from healthy schoolchildren and adults, ages 16–44, in Lethbridge, Alberta.

people, ages 50–85. The administration and scoring system is identical to that described above (see Administration and Scoring) and the data are given in Table 6–20. Similar data have been reported by Loring et al. (1990) although their scoring system is slightly different. Chiulli et al. (1989) give normative data derived from healthy elderly people and these data are similar to our own. However, their administration differs from our own in that they include an immediate-recall trial in addition to a 30-minute delayed-recall trial. In order to use their delayed-recall data, an immediate-recall trial must be given since the immediate-recall condition facilitates the delayed recall performance (Loring et al., 1990). Inclusion of an immediate-recall trial increases delayed-recall performance on average by 6 points in normal young adults. Chiulli et al. also recorded the time needed to copy the Rey figure. Elderly subjects, ages 65+, required on average 212 sec. (SD = 81 sec.) to copy the figure (Chiulli, 1990).

Both age and intellectual level contribute to performance on the CF. Inspection of the tables reveals that copy scores increase with age, with adult levels being reached at about age 13. There is little decrement in copy scores with advancing age. Scores on the delayed-recall trial attain adult levels at about age 11 and seem to show little decline until the 8th decade. Finally, scores on the CF show a modest correlation (.23–.47) with measures of general intellectual ability (Chiulli et al., 1989).

REFERENCES

Bennett-Levy, J. (1984). Determinants of performance on the Rey–Osterrieth Complex Figure test: An analysis, and a new technique for single-case measurement. *British Journal of Psychology, 23*, 109–119.

Bigler, E. (1983). Rey Auditory Verbal Learning and Rey–Osterrieth Complex Figure Design Test performance in Alzheimer's disease and closed head injury. *Journal of Clinical Psychology, 45*, 277–280.

Binder, L.M. (1982). Constructional strategies on complex figure drawing after unilateral brain damage. *Journal of Clinical Neuropsychology, 4*, 51–58.

Chiulli, S.J., Yeo, R.A., Haaland, K.Y., & Garry, P.J. (1989). Complex figure copy and recall in the elderly. Paper presented to the International Neuropsychological Society, Vancouver.

Chiulli, S.J. (1990). Personal Communication.

King, M.C. (1981). Effects of non-focal brain dysfunction on visual memory. *Journal of Clinical Psychology, 37*, 638–643.

Kirk, U., & Kelly, M.S. (1986). Scoring scale for the Rey–Osterrieth Complex Figure. Paper presented to the International Neuropsychological Society, Denver.

Kolb, B., & Whishaw, I. (1985). Fundamentals of Human Neuropsychology (2nd ed.). New York: W.H. Freeman.

Lee, G.P., Loring, D.W., & Thompson, J.L. (1989). Construct validity of material-specific unilateral temporal lobe ablations. *Psychological Assessment, 1*, 192–197.

Lezak, M.D. (1983). *Neuropsychological Assessment* (2nd ed.). New York: Oxford University Press.

Loring, D.W., Lee, G.P., Martin, R.C., & Meador, K.J. (1988a). Material-specific learning in patients with partial complex seizures of temporal lobe origin: Convergent validation of memory constructs. *Journal of Epilepsy, 1*, 53–59.

Loring, D.W., Lee, G.P., & Meador, K.J. (1988b). Revising the Rey–Osterrieth: Rating right hemisphere recall. *Archives of Clinical Neuropsychology, 3*, 239–247.

Loring, D.W., Martin, R.C., & Meador, K.J. (1990). Psychometric construction of the Rey–Osterrieth Complex Figure. *Archives of Clinical Neuropsychology, 5*, 1–14.

Osterrieth, P.A. (1944). Le test de copie d'une figure complex: Contribution à l'étude de la perception et de la mémoire. *Archives de Psychologie, 30*, 286-356.

Pillon, B. (1981). Troubles visuo-constructifs et méthodes de compensation: résultats de 85 patients atteints de lésions cérébrales. *Neuropsychologia, 19*, 375–383.

Rey, A. (1941). L'examen psychologique dans les cas d'encéphalopathie traumatique. *Archives de Psychologie, 28*, 286–340.

Strauss, E. & Spreen, O. (1990). A comparison of the Rey and Taylor Figures. *Archives of Clinical Neuropsychology, 5*, 417–420.

Strauss, E. & Spreen, O. (1990). Unpublished data.

Taylor, L.B. (1969). Localization of cerebral lesions by psychological testing. *Clinical Neurosurgery, 16*, 269–287.

Taylor, L.B. (1979). Psychological assessment of neurosurgical patients. In T. Rasmussen & R. Marino (Eds.), *Functional Neurosurgery*. New York: Raven Press.

Visser, R.S.H. (1973). *Manual of the Complex Figure Test*. Amsterdam: Swets & Zeitlinger.

Waber, D.P., & Holmes, J.M. (1985). Assessing children's copy productions of the Rey–Osterrieth Complex Figure. *Journal of Clinical and Experimental Neuropsychology, 7*, 264–280.

Waber, D.P., & Holmes, J.M. (1986). Assessing children's memory productions of the Rey–Osterrieth Complex Figure. *Journal of Clinical and Experimental Neuropsychology, 8*, 565–580.

REY VISUAL DESIGN LEARNING TEST (RVDLT)

Purpose

The purpose of this test is to assess nonverbal learning and memory.

Source

There is no commercial source. The user may refer to the following description to prepare the materials.

Description

The RVDLT is a brief, easily administered measure that assesses immediate memory span, new learning, and recognition memory. The test was developed by Rey (1964) and translated into English by Graves and Sarazin (1985) in the University of Victoria Laboratory. The test consists of 15 simple geometric forms, each on a separate stimulus card (10 × 7 cm), presented at a rate of two seconds per card. After all cards have been presented, the subject must draw all the designs that he or she can recall. This procedure is repeated five times. In the second part, the subject must identify the 15 designs from an array of 30 designs. Figure 6–10 shows the 15 designs that the subject must recall over the five trials. Figure 6–11 shows the 30 figures comprising the recognition test.

Administration

The examiner sits facing the subject and hands him or her a sheet of paper ($8\frac{1}{2}$ × 11 in), subdivided into 15 empty boxes, and a pencil. The examiner gives the instructions (below), then proceeds to present each one of the 15 stimulus cards at a rhythm of two seconds per card, being careful always to keep the same rhythm of presentation. Then the subject is instructed to draw all the designs that he or she can remember. On the first recall, the subject has 60 seconds to draw the designs, after which time the examiner removes the recall sheet. This procedure is repeated until five successive trials have been completed; each time, the examiner hands the subject a new recall sheet and gives the appropriate instructions. For the last four trials, the time allowed for execution of the drawings is 90 seconds.

For Trial 1, the examiner instructs the subject as follows: **"I am going to show you a series of cards. On each of these cards there is a design. You are to look at the cards very carefully, because when I am finished, I will ask you to draw all these designs. The order in which you draw them is not important; you are to**

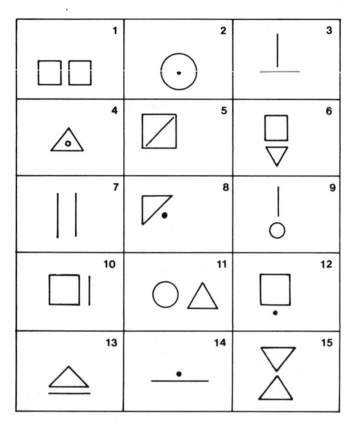

Figure 6–10. Rey Visual Design Learning Test: Part 1 (Recall).

draw one in each box, as they come to your mind. There are fifteen boxes on this sheet. There are as many boxes as there are cards. Do not worry if you do not remember all of the designs the first time. I will show them to you several times, and each time you will again draw all of the designs that you can remember. Do you understand? Yes? Then, here are the cards [present the 15 cards]. Now try to draw the designs on the sheet as I explained to you. Go ahead. [Wait one minute.] Stop! Put your pencil down!"

For Trials 2–5, say: "I am going to show you the series of cards again. Please look at them carefully, and then try to draw them on a new sheet of paper. Remember, you are to try to draw all the designs, not just the ones that you had forgotten earlier. Do you understand? Yes? Then, here are the designs." [Allow 90 seconds for drawing.] "**Stop.**"

For the Recognition test, the subject is given a blank sheet of paper and a

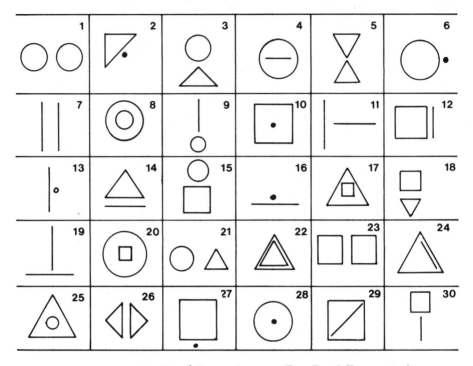

Figure 6–11.   Rey Visual Design Learning Test: Part 2 (Recognition).

pencil, and is shown the recognition sheet on which appear 30 designs. The examiner gives the instructions. There is no limit to the time of execution. As soon as the subject has finished, the examiner removes the recognition and examination sheets.

The examiner instructs the subject as follows: "On this sheet you will find all of the designs that you have just learned and others that you have not seen yet. Look over this sheet from the left to right, and from top to bottom, as if you were reading. Each time you recognize a design that you have learned, write down its corresponding number on the sheet that I have just given to you. You see, the number of each design is noted at the right-hand corner of each square. Do you understand? You are to write down only the numbers of the designs you have seen earlier on the cards. Pick up your pencil and start."

Approximate Time for Administration

The test duration is about 15 minutes.

Scoring

RECALL

In this portion, one point is given for each design reproduced correctly. The maximum possible is 15 points per trial, for a total of 75 points for the whole test. Credit is given for the following cases:

1. If the drawing is slightly distorted but recognizable
2. If it is spontaneously corrected, and the corrections clearly represent the design
3 If an incorrect drawing is crossed out clearly and replaced in the same square by the correct drawing which is then out of center
4. If the figure is correct, but placed near one side or toward an angle of the square
5. If the drawing is executed at a greater or smaller scale than that of the model, but the proportions between the two elements are respected

Specifically, the following are considered correct (see Figure 6–10):

1. On Design 3, the lines meet each other.
2. On Design 5, the diagonal of the square is traced up to the vertices.
3. On Design 9, the circle is attached to the line.
4. On Design 15, the points of the triangles are touching each other.

The following are considered incorrect (for examples, see Figure 6–12)

1. The two elements incorrectly placed with regard to each other (e.g. Designs 1, 10)
2. Reversal or rotation of the two elements with respect to each other (e.g. Designs 3, 11, 16)
3. A small circle instead of a dot (e.g. Designs 12, 14)
4. A dot used instead of a small circle (e.g. Designs 4, 9)
5. Marked distortions (e.g. Designs 1, 5)
6. All triangles having clearly faulty orientations; all angles having marked distortions; neglecting the right angle (e.g. Designs 4, 8, 11)
7. Confabulations, unrecognizable or incomplete elements, combinations of three elements, etc.

The examiner adds the scores for each of the trials and for the five trials taken together. Errors and omissions are also computed. When designs are correctly reproduced more than once, only 1 point is credited.

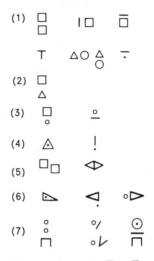

Figure 6–12. Rey Visual Design Learning Test: Examples of incorrect drawings on Recall subtest.

RECOGNITION

All correct numbers noted by the subject are scored as one point. If the subject did not follow the instructions to look over the drawings as if he or she was reading, the numbers will be out of sequence. The subject will not be penalized for this negligence. The numbers of the drawings correctly identified are 2, 5, 7, 9, 12, 14, 16, 18, 19, 21, 23, 25, 27, 28, 29.

Comment

We found that when normal young adults are retested after a one-month interval, test–retest reliability is low (total score across five trials, $r = .45$). Further, after the one-month interval, there were significant practice effects. If we consider the scores across the five trials, then normal subjects showed a gain of about 12 points on the second test administration.

Normative Data

Rey (1964) reports norms based on samples of Swiss school children, aged 9–15 years. Significant differences were observed between males and females at the ages of 10 and 11, so that separate standardizations had to be established for these two levels. Table 6–21 shows means and standard deviations for each trial for these age groups. These values establish the average curves and standard deviations.

Table 6–21. RVDLT: Mean Recall and Recognition Scores in Subjects Aged 9–15 Years

			Age in years						
			9	10	11	12	13	14	15
N			51	85	94	52	53	52	48
Trial 1	M	m	3.06	3.7	3.45	3.6	4.8	5	5.6
	SD		1.77	1.6	1.5	2	1.5	1.2	1.4
		f		3.3	3.3				
				1.6	1.4				
Trial 2	M	m	4.88	5.9	5.45	5.72	7.4	8.1	8.2
	SD		1.98	2.1	2.1	2.27	1.7	1.8	2.0
		f		4.6	5.3				
				1.77	2.14				
Trial 3	M	m	5.39	6.8	6.45	7	9.3	10.3	9.7
	SD		2.45	2.25	2.3	2.67	1.9	1.7	2.2
		f		6	6.3				
				2.8	2.5				
Trial 4	M	m	6.79	7.1	7.15	8.48	10.4	11.3	10.6
	SD		3	2.5	2.4	2.96	1.8	1.6	2.1
		f		6.6	7.3				
				2.94	2.19				
Trial 5	M	m	7.19	8.3	7.56	9	11.4	12	11.5
	SD		2.94	2.5	2.4	3.11	1.7	1.3	2.2
		f		7.7	8.3				
				2.7	2.84				
Mean total	M	m	27.27	33.55	29.95	35.35	43.8	47	45.8
	SD		10.12	7	9.66	9.4	6.9	5.8	8.8
		f		28.42	30.8				
				9.6	9.55				
Mean error over 5 trials	M	m	11.45	12.8	14.2	11.5			
	SD		7.4	7.5	7	5.2			
		f		12.5	13.5				
				5.8	6.8				
Mean recognition correct		m	12.22	12.5	13.1	12.9	13.8	13.9	13.9
		f		12.7	12.5				
False positives		m	1.94	1.66	1.2	1.3	0.8	0.4	0.5
		f		1.51	1.8				

Note: For subjects aged 9 years and subjects aged 12 years and older, scores are for combined groups of males and females.

Source: Rey (1964).

Table 6–22. RVDLT: Percentile Distributions

		Percentiles			
		10	25	50	75	90
Trial 1						
9		1	2	3	4	5
10	m	2	3	4	4	5
	f	2	2	3	4	5
11	m	2	2	3	5	5
	f	1	2	3	4	6
12		2	3	3	5	6
13		2	3	4	6	7
14		3	3	4	6	7
15		2	4	5	6	8
Trial 2						
9		2	3	5	6	7
10	m	3	4	5	7	8
	f	2	3	5	6	7
11	m	2	4	6	7	8
	f	3	4	5	7	8
12		3	4	6	7	9
13		4	5	7	9	10
14		5	6	8	9	11
15		5	7	8	10	11
Trial 3						
9		3	4	5	7	9
10	m	3	5	7	9	10
	f	2	4	6	8	10
11	m	3	4	6	8	9
	f	3	4	6	8	10
12		4	6	8	10	12
13		5	7	9	11	12
14		7	8	10	11	12
15		6	8	9	13	13
Trial 4						
9		3	5	7	9	10
10	m	3	6	8	9	10
	f	2	4	7	8	10
11	m	3	5	7	9	10
	f	4	6	7	9	10
12		4	7	9	11	12
13		5	8	10	12	13
14		8	10	11	12	14
15		7	8	11	12	13
Trial 5						
9		3	6	8	9	10

		Percentiles				
		10	25	50	75	90
10	m	4	7	8	10	11
	f	4	6	8	10	11
11	m	4	5	8	9	11
	f	5	6	8	10	12
12		6	7	10	12	13
13		8	9	11	13	14
14		9	11	12	13	14
15		7	9	11	13	14

		Percentiles											
		0	10	20	25	30	40	50	60	70	75	80	90	100
Total 5 trials														
9		4	14	18	21	22	24	25	31	34	34	35	41	51
10	m	12	16	22	24	27	31	32	34	37	37	39	44	53
	f	12	16	20	23	24	25	26	31	33	34	36	41	51
11	m	6	16	19	24	25	28	31	33	35	37	38	41	49
	f	8	17	22	23	25	29	31	33	35	39	40	42	47
12		13	18	24	31	31	32	36	38	40	42	43	44	58
13		11	31	36	39	40	43	46	47	48	49	50	53	61
14		23	37	40	42	44	46	47	48	51	52	53	56	62
15		26	30	36	36	38	43	47	50	52	53	54	60	67
Recognition														
9		2	8	11	12	12	13	13	13	14	14	14	14	15
10	m	7	9	11	11	12	13	13	13	14	14	14	15	15
	f	10	10	12	12	12	13	13	13	14	14	14	14	15
11	m	9	11	12	12	13	13	13	14	14	14	14	15	15
	f	2	10	12	12	13	13	13	14	14	14	14	14	15
12		3	10	12	12	13	13	14	14	14	15	15	15	15
13		10	12	12	13	13	13	14	14	14	14	14	14	15
14		11	12	13	13	13	13	14	14	14	14	14	15	15
15		9	12	12	13	13	13	14	14	14	14	14	15	15

Source: Rey (1964).

Percentiles are given in Table 6–22 for each of the five trials and for the total across the five trials. In addition, normative data for the recognition portion are provided. These normative data should be treated with caution since little is known about the normative samples and standardization procedures. Moreover, educational and cultural differences may make it hazardous to compare current North American samples to European ones collected by Rey 25 years ago. Rey (1964) also provides normative data for university students and elderly people, aged 60 and above. In addition to the concerns noted above, the sample size for the elderly was small ($n = 30$), and no effects of age were presented. Recently, we compiled

Table 6–23.   RVDLT: Mean Recall and Recognition Scores in Subjects Aged 20–84

		Age in years					
		20–29	30–39	40–49	50–59	60–69	70+
Trial 1	N	23	14	14	10	10	14
	M	6.09	5.36	5.64	5.00	4.70	4.29
	SD	2.11	2.10	1.91	1.56	1.16	1.64
Trial 2	N	23	14	14	10	10	14
	M	10.04	8.21	7.71	6.60	6.90	6.29
	SD	2.14	2.04	2.67	2.07	2.13	1.64
Trial 3	N	23	14	14	10	10	14
	M	11.52	9.86	10.07	8.20	7.30	6.64
	SD	2.27	2.60	2.97	1.48	1.89	2.02
Trial 4	N	23	14	14	10	10	13
	M	12.52	11.57	10.00	7.90	8.10	7.00
	SD	1.75	2.59	3.01	1.97	1.45	1.53
Trial 5	N	23	14	14	10	10	13
	M	13.48	11.64	10.93	9.30	8.20	7.46
	SD	1.70	2.21	2.92	2.16	2.62	1.66
Mean total	N	23	14	14	10	10	13
	M	53.65	46.64	44.36	37.00	35.20	31.38
	SD	8.02	9.30	12.36	7.77	7.32	6.67
Mean recognition	N	23	14	14	10	10	13
	M	14.61	14.07	14.21	13.30	13.10	13.46
	SD	0.78	1.27	0.89	1.70	0.99	2.02

Note: Our data are based on normal healthy volunteers.

Source: Strauss & Spreen, unpublished data.

normative data from healthy adult volunteers, aged 20–84, and these data are shown in Table 6–23. In general, scores for our subjects are slightly higher than those reported by Rey (1964). In contrast to the recall trials, performance on the recognition trial does not decline with age. This suggests that in the elderly, graphomotor impairments, and not memory deficits, contribute to reduced performance on the drawing trials.

REFERENCES

Graves, R.E., & Sarazin, F. (1985). Rey Visual Design Learning Test. Unpublished manuscript, University of Victoria.

Rey, A. (1964). *L'Examen Clinique en Psy-* chologie. Paris: Presse Universitaire de France.

Strauss, E. & Spreen, O. Unpublished data.

SENTENCE REPETITION

Other Test Name

This test is also known as Sentence Memory.

Purpose

The purpose of this test is the immediate oral repetition of sentences of increasing length.

Source

Tape, manual, and scoring forms can be ordered from the Neuropsychology Laboratory, University of Victoria, Victoria, B.C. V8W 3P5 Canada, at a cost of $15.00 Cdn.

Description

The test consists of two equivalent forms (A and B) of 22 tape-recorded sentences, increasing in length from one ("Look") to 26 syllables ("Riding his black horse, the general came to the scene of the battle and began shouting at his brave men") (see Figure 6–13). Grammatical structure and vocabulary have been held deliberately to simple, declarative sentences. The test is part (Test 5) of the Neurosensory Comprehensive Examination for Aphasia (Spreen & Benton, 1969, 1977). Benton and Hamsher (1983) use a similar test with only 14 items and with varying grammatical complexity.

Administration

The patient is seated about two meters from a playback loudspeaker contained in or connected with a tape recorder. Playback volume should be set at comfortable hearing level (approx. 70 db) and may be increased for hard-of-hearing patients. Say: "**I am going to play some sentences** [point to loudspeaker]. **Listen carefully, and after you have heard each sentence, repeat it as well as you can. Remember? Listen carefully, and repeat the sentence right after you heard it.**"

Repeat instructions if necessary and start tape recorder with Sentence Repetition Form A. Occasionally, the patient will not respond after hearing the first sentence. In this case, stop the tape and say: "**Would you repeat what you heard?**" If the patient responds, say: "**That's right. Do the same with each sentence you**

SENTENCE REPETITION—Form A—Sample Score Sheet   S# _____

1. Look	
2. Come here.	
3. Help yourself.	
4. Bring the table.	
5. Summer is coming.	
6. The iron was quite hot.	
7. The birds were singing all day.	
8. The paper was under the chair.	
9. The sun was shining throughout the day.	
10. He entered about eight o'clock that night.	
11. The pretty house on the mountain seemed empty.	
12. The lady followed the path down the hill toward home.	
13. The island in the ocean was first noticed by the young boy.	
14. The distance between these two cities is too far to travel by car.	
15. A judge here knows the law better than those people who must appear before him.	
16. There is a new method in making steel which is far better than that used before.	
17. This nation has a good government which gives us many freedoms not known in times past.	
18. The friendly man told us the directions to the modern building where we could find the club.	
19. The king knew how to rule his country so that his people would show respect for his government.	
20. Yesterday he said he would be near the village station before it was time for the train to come.	
21. His interest in the problem increased each time that he looked at the report which lay on the table.	
22. Riding his black horse, the general came to the scene of the battle and began shouting at his brave men.	
TOTAL SCORE	

Figure 6–13.   Sentence Repetition: Form A Sample Scoring Sheet

hear." If the patient does not respond, say: **"Listen carefully. Then repeat what you heard."** Sentences should not be repeated during the test, although the basic instructions may be repeated. Discontinue after five consecutive failures.

Approximate Time for Administration

The time required is 10–15 minutes.

Scoring

A score of 1 point is given for each sentence repeated correctly. Note that since "toward" in item 12 (Form A) is often repeated as "towards," "towards" is accepted as correct. On sentences one through 10, failure on a single sentence is disregarded if the following five sentences are correctly repeated. Poor articulation, if intelligible, should be noted, but not scored as an error. Record errors verbatim and note as omissions, alterations (substitution, change of tense, of location etc.), repetitions, or additions. Maximum raw score = 22. Subtract 1 point from the raw score if the test was administered orally instead of by tape-playback.

The following corrections for age and educational level (i.e., years of schooling or other formal education completed) are applied:

Age	Correction
<35	0
35–44	+1
45–64	+2
65+	+3

Education	Correction
Below grade 12	+2

The test score can be entered into the Neurosensory Center Comprehensive Examination for Aphasia (NCCEA) profile sheet.

Comment

Forms A and B appear equivalent in difficulty. Correlation between Forms A and B in an unselected group of 47 subjects in our sample was .79. The test correlates .88 with the repetition of words, phrases, and sentences of the Western Aphasia Battery (Shewan & Kertesz 1980). The test is sensitive to brain damage, particularly to aphasic disturbances. Percentile ranks for nonaphasic brain-damaged patients and for an unselected group of aphasics have been established (Lawriw, 1976). In a study of 23 children and 33 adolescents with closed head injury, 33% of those with severe injury and 15% with mild injury were found to score below the sixth percentile for their age (Ewing-Cobb et al., 1987); the mean for mild closed head injury patients was 48.3; for moderate and severe injury, it was 36.4%. In brain-damaged adults between 20 and 79 years, Vargo and Black (1984) did not notice any significant decrease with age ($r = -.08$) but found significant correlations with IQ (.329) and with the MQ of the Wechsler Memory Scale (.377). Their study showed the most severe impairment in patients with dementia and toxic exposure as well as with left-hemisphere lesions after cerebrovascular accident and closed head injury. In Lawriw's (1976) comparison of nonaphasic brain-damaged patients, and controls of low-average intelligence (with an aphasic population unselected as to type and severity, from referral sources in New York, Iowa City, and Victoria: $N = 208$), a mean of 12.12 (SD = 3.15) was obtained for left-brain-damaged patients (including aphasics) and of 15.75 (SD = 2.58) when aphasics were excluded. Fifty-six percent of the aphasics scored below the lowest score of normal controls with low-average intelligence. Patients with right-hemisphere lesions had a mean of 17.64 (SD = 2.12); patients with bilateral or undetermined location of brain damage had a mean of 16.84 (SD = 5.87); and moderately mentally handicapped patients had a mean of 11.88 (SD = 3.15).

Sarno (1986) reported that among closed head injury patients, those with aphasia scored at the 35th percentile for aphasics; those with subclinical aphasia and dysarthria, at the 58th percentile; and those with subclinical aphasia, at the 70th percentile. Davis et al. (1978) showed that the test is especially sensitive in cases of transcortical aphasia. Patients with dementia of the Alzheimer type showed moderately, but significantly lower scores compared to normal controls matched for age, sex, and educational level (Murdoch et al., 1987).

In 353 school-age children, Sentence Repetition formed a separate factor in a factor analysis of the 20 subtests of the NCCEA, accounting for 81% of the total variance of this factor, and was relatively independent of digit repetition (Crockett, 1974). The test contributed to the discrimination of four empirically derived subtypes of aphasia in adults; impairment of sentence repetition was especially characteristic of those individuals classed as "Type A" (good comprehension, poor attention, memory, and reproduction of speech) (Crockett, 1977). The correlation in adults with digit repetition forward was .75; with digit repetition reversed, .66; with Full Scale IQ (holding age constant), .62.

Epstein (1982) found that dyslexics lagged behind normal reading classmates by about four syllables at age 7; three at age 8; and two at age 9. Rourke (1978), on the other hand, found that 16 dyslexic children had scores in the average range, but that syntactic comprehension was impaired. Our own data (Spreen, 1988) showed that 10-year-old learning-disabled children with neurological signs were able to repeat 10.4 syllables, whereas those with minimal neurological signs repeated 11.3, and those without neurological signs 15.0 syllables. At age 25, these same subjects repeated 12.8, 13.9, and 14.0 syllables, respectively, whereas a matched control group showed a mean of 15.5.

Children with brain damage and/or epilepsy (Hamsher, personal communication, 1980) had mean scores of 9.5 at age 6; 10 at age 7; 11 at age 8; 11.5 at age 9; 12 at age 10; 12.6 at age 10; 13.2 at age 11; 13.7 at age 12; and 14.0 at age 13.

Table 6–24.   Normative Data for Adults on Sentence Repetition

Group	n	Mean age	Form A		Form B		Est. IQ	Score	Percentile rank for hospital control subjects
			M	SD	M	SD			
University students	25	24.81	21.13	1.72			120	19–22	90+
	24				20.83	1.96	120	18	80
Nurses	39	24.10	20.05	2.48	20.14		110	17	70
Controls (hospital)	52	45.92	17.21				100.45	16	58
	7	40.85			17.86			15	36
								14	14
								13	2

Note: Group 2 of students took only from B.

Source: Spreen & Benton (1977).

Normative Data

Table 6–24 shows normative data for several normal groups. Williams (1965) reported that the average adult can correctly repeat sentences of 24–25 syllables in length. However, the Benton and Hamsher (1983) normative sample of 85 non-neurological patients showed an average of only 20 syllables (16.7 points in the 22-item version).

In older, healthy, and relatively well educated adults, values similar to those by Benton and Hamsher are obtained (Age 50–55 years: mean = 19.4), although a small, but significant decrease is noted after the age of 65 even after correction for age (56–65 years: mean = 19.5, SD = 3.98; 66–75 years: mean = 18.5, SD = 4.02; 76–89 years; mean = 18.0, SD = 4.49; Read & Spreen, 1986). The nor-

Table 6–25.   Sentence Repetition, Developmental Norms for Ages 6–13, Males and Females

Age (years)	Male				Female				All normal			
	N	Mean	SD	Range	N	Mean	SD	Range	N	Mean	SD	Range
6	30	9.3	2.0	0–12	22	9.3	0.9	3–12	52	10.3	1.6	0–12
7	27	10.0	2.0	5–18	24	10.5	1.7	6–18	51	10.0	2.0	5–18
8	52	11.8	1.3	9–20	52	11.2	1.1	8–18	104	11.5	1.3	8–20
9	78	11.8	1.5	9–19	55	11.9	0.9	9–17	133	11.7	2.0	9–19
10	54	12.5	1.4	10–21	52	12.6	1.6	7–18	106	12.5	1.5	7–21
11	53	13.3	1.8	10–21	51	13.1	1.7	10–22	104	13.2	1.7	10–22
12	46	13.7	1.4	11–21	41	13.5	2.4	10–21	87	13.6	1.9	10–21
13	44	13.8	1.6	11–22	44	13.9	1.2	11–22	88	13.8	1.4	11–22

Source: Adapted from Carmichael & McDonald (1984), Gaddes & Crockett (1975), Spreen & Gaddes (1969), and merged with new data.

Table 6–26. Sentence Repetition, Percentiles for School-Age Children

Age	0	10	20	30	40	50	60	70	80	90	100
						Percentiles					
6	1–7			8		9		10		11	12
7	1–7	8			9	10		11		12	13
8	1–9	10	11				12		13	14	15
9	1–9	10	11				12		13	14	15
10	1–9	10	11			12			13	14	15
11	1–11	12			13			14		15	16
12	1–11	12			13			14		15	16
13	1–11	12			13			14		15	16

mative data also show a slightly better performance in older females as compared to men (approximately 1 point at each age range).

Table 6–25 contains the norms for normal school children merged from four different sources. No education corrections are made since they would be misleading for children. If such corrections were made, adult level of performance would be reached by age 12. Table 6–26 provides percentile equivalents for each age.

The norms for children are comparable to those presented by Epstein (1982) for Swedish children (means of 13, 16, and 17 syllables for ages 7, 8, and 9, respectively). The higher number of syllables repeated in that study was probably due to practice since the children repeated five sentences at each one-syllable increment in length. Epstein also found that children whose native tongue was not Swedish but who were taught in Swedish schools were approximately 8 syllables behind native-speaking children at age 6; however, this deficit was reduced to 6 syllables at age 7; 5 at age 8; and 3 at age 9. This finding may have some implications for the testing of children with a mother tongue other than English.

REFERENCES

Benton, A.L., & Hamsher, K.deS. (1983). *Multilingual Aphasia Examination.* Iowa City: AIA Associates.

Carmichael, J., & McDonald, J. (1984). Developmental norms for neuropsychological tests. *Journal of Clinical and Consulting Psychology, 52,* 476-477.

Crockett, D.J. (1974). Component analysis of within correlations of language skill tests in normal children. *Journal of Special Education, 8,* 361-375.

Crockett, D.J. (1977). A comparison of empirically derived groups of aphasic patients on the Neurosensory Center Comprehensive Examination for Aphasia. *Journal of Clinical Psychology, 33,* 194-198.

Davis, L., Foldi, N.S., Gardner, H., & Zurif, E.B. (1978). Repetition in the transcortical aphasias. *Brain and Language, 6,* 226-238.

Epstein, A.G. (1982). Mastery of language measured by means of a sentence span test. Unpublished manuscript, Lyngby, Denmark.

Ewing-Cobbs, L., Levin, H.S., Eisenberg, H.M., & Fletcher, J.M. (1987). Language functions following closed-head injury in children and adolescents. *Journal of Clinical and Experimental Neuropsychology, 9,* 575-592.

Gaddes, W.H., & Crockett, D.J. (1975). The Spreen-Benton aphasia tests: Normative data as a measure of normal language de-

velopment. *Brain and Language, 2,* 257-280.

Lawriw, I. (1976). A test of the predictive validity and a cross-validation of the Neurosensory Center Comprehensive Examination for Aphasia. Master's thesis, University of Victoria, British Columbia.

Murdoch, B.E., Chenery, H.J., Wilks, V., & Boyle, R.S. (1987). Language disorders in dementia of the Alzheimer type. *Brain and Language, 31,* 122-137.

Read, D.E., & Spreen, O. (1986). Normative data in older adults for selected neuropsychological tests. Unpublished manuscript, University of Victoria, British Columbia.

Rourke, B.P. (1978). Reading, spelling, arithmetic disability: A neuropsychological perspective. In H.R. Myklebust (ed.) *Progress in Learning Disabilities.* Vol. IV. New York: Wiley.

Sarno, M.T. (1986). Verbal impairment in head injury. *Archives of Physical and Medical Rehabilitation, 67,* 399-405.

Shewan, C.M., & Kertesz, A. (1980). Reliability and validity characteristics of the Western Aphasia Battery (WAB). *Journal of Speech and Hearing Disorders, 45,* 308-324.

Spreen, O. (1988). *Learning Disabled Children Growing Up.* New York: Oxford University Press.

Spreen, O., & Benton, A.L. (1969, 1977). *Neurosensory Center Comprehensive Ex-*

amination for Aphasia. Victoria, B.C.: University of Victoria, Neuropsychology Laboratory.

Spreen, O., & Gaddes, W.H. (1969). Developmental norms for 15 neuropsychological tests age 6 to 15. *Cortex, 5*, 171–191.

Vargo, M.E., & Black, F.W. (1984). Normative data for the Spreen–Benton Sentence Repetition Test: Its relationship to age, intelligence, and memory. *Cortex, 20*, 585–590.

Williams, M. (1965). *Mental Testing in Clinical Practice*. London: Pergamon.

WECHSLER MEMORY SCALE

Purpose

The purpose of this test is to provide measures of various aspects of memory function.

Source

The Wechsler Memory Scale can be obtained from the Psychological Corporation, P.O. Box 9954, San Antonio, Texas 78204-0954, at a cost (complete set) of $28.50 U.S., or from the Institute of Psychological Research, 34 Fleury Street West, Montreal, Quebec H3L 1S9, Canada, at a cost of $61.15 Cdn.

Description

The Wechsler Memory Scale (WMS) has recently undergone a major revision (WMS-R). Given the wealth of data that has accumulated with the WMS, it is likely that many clinicians will continue to use the original version. We describe first the original and then the revised version.

The WMS (Wechsler, 1945) is the most frequently used clinical measure of memory (Erickson & Scott, 1977). The complete kit contains the manual, record forms, and design cards. The test consists of seven subtests. The first two subtests, Personal and Current Information (PI) and Orientation (OR), comprise simple questions that assess whether the patient is oriented to age, date of birth, government officials, time, and place. Mental Control (MC) consists of asking the patient to count backwards, recite the alphabet, and count (by 3's or 4's) under time pressure. Logical Memory (LM) examines the ability to recall the number of ideas presented in two passages read to the patient. Memory Span (MS) requires the patient to recall digits forward and backward. Visual Reproduction (VR) requires the subject to draw from memory simple geometric figures that were exposed briefly. Associate Learning (AL) requires the patient to listen to paired associations of words and then recall the correct response to stimulus words over three trials. The patient's raw score on each subtest is summed, and an age correction factor is added to obtain a summary score, the Memory Quotient (MQ). There are two forms of the test, Form I (Wechsler, 1945) and Form II (Stone & Wechsler, 1946), although most of the published studies deal with Form I.

The validity, standardization, and general psychometric properties of the WMS have been extensively criticized (Butters et al., 1988; Erickson & Scott, 1977; Herman, 1988; Hulicka, 1966; Larrabee et al., 1985; Lezak, 1983; Loring & Papanicolaou, 1987; Prigatano, 1977; 1978). Briefly, these criticisms refer to (1) inadequate norms; (2) the fact that scores on all subtests are combined into a summary score, the MQ, which does not differentiate among various facets of memory; (3) overreliance on immediate recall with no procedures for evaluating retention over a long time period; (4) lack of control for visuoperceptive and visuomotor abilities in measures of so-called visual memory; (5) imprecise scoring criteria; (6) the fact that the scale stresses verbal as opposed to nonverbal tasks; and (7) the fact that the test assesses constructs that, although perhaps necessary for successful memory performance (e.g., orientation, mental control), are not genuine measures of memory.

In an attempt to remedy some of the limitations of the WMS, several variations of the test have been developed. Russell's (1975) system involves the administration of only the LM and VR portions of the scale. In addition to immediate recall, a 30-minute delayed recall is obtained for both portions. Three measures of verbal recall and three measures of nonverbal recall are obtained: immediate recall, delayed recall, and the percentage of the immediate recall produced after the 30-minute delay. Russell's revision is widely used. The scales differentiate demented from normal individuals and discriminate right- and left-hemisphere damage (Russell, 1988; see also Comment section). In addition, explicit scoring criteria have been developed (see Scoring), and good normative studies are available (see Normative Data).

The Montreal Neurological Institute's (MNI) revision (L. Taylor, personal communication in August 1988) retains all the elements of the original WMS but has included a 90-minute delayed recall of LM and AL (sum of both yielding a "C" score) and VR (yielding a "D" score). The "C" and "D" scores are useful in distinguishing laterality of brain lesion (Milner, 1975). However, no normative data are given, only rough clinical guidelines.

The Boston revision by E. Kaplan and her colleagues (Milberg et al., 1986) also retains all subtests from the original WMS but has added to the LM, AL, and VR subtests. LM contains an immediate recall probe asking specific questions regarding story elements (e.g., "What kind of work did this person do?"), in an attempt to assess retention rather than only spontaneous retrieval ability (Loring & Papanicolaou, 1987). A 20-minute delayed recall of LM is also given. Probe questions are administered for information not spontaneously recalled. However, normative data are not given. Unfortunately, one cannot simply use data for the Russell revision since the immediate probe may provide a rehearsal opportunity, and may lead to higher scores for delayed performance when compared to norms obtained without probe questioning. In the Boston revision, AL has been modified in three ways. First, immediately following the third standard trial, the order of each pair of words is reversed, and the patient is presented with the second pair member and asked to recall the first. This is done in order to measure the strength of the association. Patients who encode word pairs on a more superficial, phonetic level, rather than at a deeper semantic level, will often perform worse on this trial compared to the third trial because the phonemic sequence of the word pairs is altered (Delis, 1989). Second, 20 minutes later, free uncued recall of the pairs is assessed. Finally, the first word of each pair is provided as a cue, and paired recall is measured again. The immediate VR subtest has also been altered to include recognition and copy conditions. These modifications were made in order to distinguish between retention and retrieval problems and to ensure that memory disorders are not confounded with construction difficulties. In addition to a 20-minute delayed recall condition, the Boston version also includes delayed multiple-choice recognition and matching tasks. Again, no normative data are given. Data available for the Russell version cannot be used, given the additional exposure with the immediate multiple choice and copy performance (Loring & Papanicolaou, 1987).

These various innovations are useful. The Russell and MNI revisions are perhaps best used when the question is whether or not a problem exists. By contrast, the Boston version is more appropriate when one wishes to discover more about the nature of the deficit. Our procedure borrows elements from each of these approaches. All subtests in the original WMS are given. We follow Russell's procedure of interposing 30 minutes between immediate and delayed recall conditions for LM and VR. In addition, we include a 30-minute delayed recall of AL. In general, probe questions for the LM subtest are given only after the delayed (not the immediate) recall condition. Similarly, multiple-choice recognition, matching, and copying tasks are administered only after the delayed (not the immediate) VR task. In this way, we can make use of existing normative data and at the same time, assess different aspects of performance.

Administration

The instructions for most subtests of the WMS are the same as those in the manual (Wechsler, 1945). There are some changes as follows (adapted from Milberg et al., 1986; Milner, 1975; Russell, 1975; Wechsler, 1987): The examiner waits about 30 minutes after the first administration of LM, VR, and AL subtests and then requests a second recall of the material. The interposed tests should be quite different from the memory tests, in order to avoid interference. Subtests of the Wechsler Intelligence Scales are suitable tasks. One should not give drawings or other memory tests. At the end of the 30-minute period, the patient is asked to retell the stories as he or she remembers them. Say: "**Remember the stories that I read to you a few minutes ago? Tell me the stories again. Tell me all that you can.**" The stories are not read to the subject again. If either of the stories cannot be recalled at all, then say: "**Do you remember a story about a washerwoman?**" or "**Do you remember a story about a ship?**" The examiner writes both the immediate and delayed dictated stories verbatim so that scoring can be done more accurately at a later time. If the patient does not remember all of the elements of a story accurately, then the examiner should use probe questions such as those listed in Table 6–27 for Form II.

The patient is then asked to reproduce the designs again on a *blank* piece of paper. In order to permit evaluation of performance en route to the solution, no erasing is allowed. Say: "**A little while ago, I showed you some drawings on cards. You looked at each drawing and then drew it. Now draw them again on this sheet.**" If the subject does not remember any design, give a clue such as: "**Do you remember a design that looks like flags?**" (In Form II, substitute "**a cross.**") If the patient does not recall a design correctly, then the delayed recall task should be followed by the recognition task in which the correct design is displayed with four similar but slightly distorted distractors (see Figure 6–14). The patient should also be asked to copy the design. The matching task requires the patient to select the correct design from distractor items with the original stimulus present (Figure 6–14). This task should be given if there is impairment on the recognition task.

For delayed recall of AL, say: "**A little while ago, I read you pairs of words. Then I read you the first word in each pair, and you were to tell me the word that went with it. Now, I want to see how well you remember the word pairs.**" Use the list for the "Second Presentation." Say: "**What went with 'knife?'**"

Subtest 1 of the WMS, PI, contains items that can be troublesome to Canadians. Table 6–28 shows recommended substitutions.

The subtests of the WMS should be administered in one sitting. It is essential that the tasks of immediate and delayed recall be given in the same session.

Table 6–27. Logical Memory: Delayed Cued Recall

Form II: Story 1
1. Was it about cats, dogs, horses? (c)
2. Were they used in train accidents, war time, or plane crashes?
3. Were they trained to find the enemy, the wounded, or weapons?
4. Were dogs also trained to rescue hungry kittens, lost children, drowning people? (c)
5. Were they sled dogs, race dogs, police dogs?
6. Are they taught to run into water, make a flying leap, or ride in boats? (c)
7. Does leaping into the water waste energy, cause problems, or save swimming stokes?
8. Is this important for saving much money, time, or animals?
9. Does this save four seconds, valuable time, or many minutes?
10. Are the best police dogs hound dogs, bull dogs, or sheep dogs?
11. Are they English sheep dogs, German sheep dogs, or European sheep dogs?

Form II: Story 2
1. Was it about adults, children, or teachers? (c)
2. Were there a few children, many children, or 20 children?
3. Many were uninjured, killed, or sent home?
4. Did the accident occur in England, Spain, or France? (c)
5. Was it southern France, Paris, or northern France?
6. What was wrecked? A shopping mall, a schoolhouse, or a farmhouse? (c)
7. What wrecked the schoolhouse? A truck, a storm, or a shell?
8. Was the schoolhouse in a city, a village, or Paris?
9. Were the children thrown against a wall, down a hill, or into a river?
10. How far were they thrown? Three feet, a short distance, or a long distance?
11. How many children escaped uninjured? Three, none, or two?

Note: If the patient does not remember all of the elements of the story accurately, ask the corresponding multiple-choice questions. Correct only when indicated by (c). "If at any point you remember more of the story, please tell me."

Source: [Form II] Adapted from the Wechsler Memory Scale. Copyright 1945, renewed 1974 by The Psychological Corporation. Reproduced by permission. All rights reserved. Vancouver Revision (A. Carney & K. Bate).

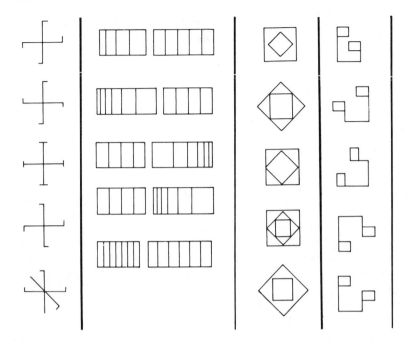

Figure 6–14. Wechsler Memory Scale: Visual Reproduction (Form II). Matching test: "POINT TO THE DESIGN THAT LOOKS LIKE THIS ONE" [point to target design]. Adapted from the Wechsler Memory Scale. Copyright 1945, renewed 1974 by The Psychological Corporation. Reproduced by permission. All rights reserved.

Table 6–28. Recommended Items for Substitution on the Personal and Current Information Subtest of the WMS with Canadian Subjects

4. Who is the prime minister of Canada?
5. Who is the premier of this province?
6. Who is the mayor of this city (or of the patient's home city)?

Finally, the examiner must remember to fold the answer sheet to cover up the AL subtest while the patient is performing the VR subtest.

Approximate Time for Administration

Our version of the WMS takes about 20–25 minutes, excluding the delay interval.

Scoring

For scoring of all the WMS subtests except Logical Memory, see the manual (Wechsler, 1945). A major criticism of the WMS is the imprecise scoring instructions for the LM subtest (Abikoff et al., 1987; Crosson et al., 1984; McCarty et al., 1980; Power et al., 1979; Prigatano, 1978; Schwartz & Ivnik, 1980). According to Wechsler (1945), the examiner should "record verbatim and score according to the number of ideas marked off in selection." There have been a number of attempts to operationalize scoring of the subtest. For example, some (Power et al., 1979) suggest ½-point credit for minor deviations from the fundamental idea or verbatim scoring (Abikoff et al., 1987). Others (Abikoff et al., 1987; Schwartz & Ivnik, 1980) have developed a specific set of "acceptable" responses that capture the gist or basic idea of each of the content units of the LM subtest. We use the gist scoring criteria of Schwartz and Ivnik (1980) and Abikoff et al. (1987) because they are reliable (.99), and norms have been developed with these systems (see Normative Data). These scoring criteria are given for Form II in Table 6–29. Story B from Form I is inherently more difficult to recall than Story A. The recall of fewer Story B items relative to Story A is expected and not due to proactive interference (Henry et al., 1990).

Note that on the delayed recall of the LM subtest, the prompt portion of the answer is not counted in the delay score, if the patient recalls the story but requires a prompt. Similarly, on the delayed VR task, if a prompt is given, then one point is deducted from the design.

When administering the immediate and delayed portions of the AL subtest, a patient may respond to "baby" with "cry" rather than "cries" and to "school" with "groceries" rather than "grocery." Give full credit for either of these responses.

Comment

Form I and Form II of the WMS are not interchangeable (Bloom, 1959; McCarty et al., 1980; Schultz et al., 1984; Stanton et al., 1984). Form II is a little easier than

Table 6–29. Detailed Scoring Criteria for WMS Form II: Logical Memory*

1. *Dogs*			*Drowning people*	
Dog	1		drowning victims	1
Canine(s)	1		the drowning	1
			people in the water	0
Are trained			swimmers	0
are taught	1		people from drowning	1
are used	1		people from water	0
go around	0		X	1
learn	0			
X	1		*Instead of running*	
			rather than running	1
To find			by running	0
to help	0		they don't run	1
to rescue	1		instead of going	0
to assist	0		X	1
to look for	1			
to locate	1		*Down to the water*	
X	1		into the water	1
			to the water	1
The wounded			in the water	1
the injured	1		to the victim	0
those hurt	1		down to the shore	1
casualties	1		X	1
people	0			
soldiers	0		*And striking out*	
X	1		setting out	1
			heading for the person	1
In the wartime			taking off	1
in war	1		lighting out	1
during the war	1		jumping in	0
in the war	1		swimming out	1
in WWII	0		diving in	0
on the battlefield	1		starting to swim	1
X	1		X	1
(Police dog)s	1(A)		*They are taught*	
dogs	0		they are trained	1
they	0		learn how to	1
			learned	0
Are also trained			X	1
are trained	1			
are taught	1		*To make*	
are used	1		to take	1
can	0		to use	1
can rescue	0		to do	1
learn	0		X	1
X	1			
			A flying leap	
To rescue			a great leap	1
to save	1		a big jump	1
to help	1		a running dive	1
to assist	1		a jump	0
to find	0		a leap	0
X	1		a dive	0
			X	1

Table 6–29. *(Continued)*

By which they save			*Children*	
in order to save	1		students	1
to save	1		pupils	1
which saves	1		kids	1
X	1		people	0
			babies	0
Many swimming strokes			youngsters	1
a lot of strokes	1		X	1
swimming strokes	0			
some strokes	1		*in (North)ern*	1
several strokes	1			
a few strokes	0		*France*	
X	1		French	1
			Frenchmen	0
And valuable			X	1
precious	1			
crucial	1		*Were killed*	
much neded	1		died	1
important	1		lost their lives	1
and many	0		were murdered	0
X	1		perished	1
			X	1
Seconds of time				
seconds	1		*Or fatally hurt*	
time	1		mortally hurt	1
minutes	0		died from their injuries	1
X	1		hurt	1
			fatalities	1
The European sheep dog			maimed	0
European shepherd	1		X	1
European dog	0			
sheep dog	0		*And others*	
German sheep dog	0		others	1
X	1		additional	1
			some	1
Makes the best			the rest	0
X	1		X	1
(Police)			*Seriously injured*	
			maimed	1
(Dog)s			hurt/wounded	
			(qualified for severity)	1
			hurt/wounded	0
2. *Many*			X	1
a lot	1			
several	1		*When a shell*	
some	1		when a bomb	1
a few	0		when a bombshell	1
X	1		after a bomb	1
			rocket	0
(school)	1(A)		when an explosion	0
			X	1

192

Wrecked		And across	
destroyed	1	across	1
hit	1	and into	0
blew up	1	over	1
ruined	1	down	0
damaged	0	X	1
severely damaged	1		
X	1	*A ravine*	
		ditch	1
The (school)house	1(A)	canyon	0
		creek	0
In their village		X	1
in their town	1		
in their city	0	*A long distance*	
in their country	0	far	1
in their community	0	far away	1
X	1	some distance	1
		a distance	1
The children		and away	0
students	1	feet, yards, etc.	1
pupils	1	X	1
kids	1		
youngsters	1	*From the (school)house*	1
people	0	past the (school)house	1
babies	0	X	
they	1		
(if "they" clearly refers to		*Only two*	
children or its synonym)		two	1
X	1	a couple	1
		several	0
Were thrown		X	1
thrown	1		
fell	0	*Children*	
went down	0	student/pupils/kids/	1
were flung	1	youngsters	
X	1	babies/people	0
		of them	1
Down a hillside		(if "of them" clearly refers to	
down a hill	1	children or its synonym)	
to the bottom of a hill	1	X	1
downhill	1		
across a hillside	0	*Escaped uninjured*	
over a hillside	0	were not hurt	1
down	0	avoided injury	1
X	1	survived	0
		were rescued	0
		escaped	0
		X	1

Note: (A) Exact wording is required for the words in parentheses. Substitution, deletion, or addition of other words is acceptable, if the essence of the block is unchanged. X: Synonym based on principles illustrated. *Double crediting is not allowed.* Each recalled word(s) will be given credit in one block only.

Source: Abikoff et al. (1987).

193

Form I (Ivison, 1988a). The differences can be reduced somewhat by adjusting the scores (Ivison, 1988a; McCarty et al., 1980), changing the scoring procedures (Abikoff et al., 1987), or interchanging the stimuli (Schultz et al., 1984). However, test–retest reliability with the same form appears adequate (.76–.89) over intervals of six months to one year (Ivison, 1988a; Snow et al., 1988). Although there is adequate reliability in terms of stability in position in group distribution, individual subjects are likely to manifest a gain in scores (4–7 points) across time (Franzen, 1989). Information regarding internal consistency in the test as a whole as well as in the subtests is sparse (Franzen, 1989). Ivinskis et al. (1971) reported that split-half reliability of the WMS is .75. Hall and Toal (1957) reported that Cronbach's coefficient alpha values ranged from .38 for Mental Control and Associate Learning to .65 for Digit Span. Cronbach's coefficient alpha for the whole test was .69.

With regard to validity, scores on the original WMS do tend to fall with increasing age, as might be predicted theoretically (Prigatano, 1978). However, the scale is not sensitive to distinctive patterns of deficits found in specific types of amnesic and demented patients (Butters, 1986). It is affected most by left-hemisphere disturbances but does not detect memory disturbances that occur with right-hemisphere lesions (Prigatano, 1978). Addition of delayed recall tasks (LN, VR, AL) improves validity. The Russell revision is not strongly related to psychopathology, as measured by the Minnesota Multiphasic Personality Inventory (MMPI), and is less strongly related to intelligence than has been reported for the original WMS (O'Grady, 1988). Demented individuals can be distinguished from normals, and the scale is sensitive to laterality of the disturbance (Bornstein, 1982; Delaney et al., 1980; Milner, 1975; Russell, 1975). However, in diffuse cases, the VR tests decline more rapidly than the verbal ones (Levin & Larrabee, 1983), a finding that must be noted in order to prevent the false assessment of right-hemisphere damage in diffuse cases (Russell, 1988). Factor analytic studies of the original WMS have generally revealed three components: Factor I (immediate learning and recall) has loadings from LM, VR, and AL; Factor II (attention and concentration) has loadings from MC and MS; Factor III (orientation and long-term Information recall) has loadings from PI and OR (for review, see Wechsler, 1987).

The factor-analytic studies do not support the unidimensional factor of memory implied in the single Memory Quotient (MQ) score of the WMS. Nonetheless, because the MQ and Wechsler Full Scale IQ (FSIQ) are linked in normal people, substantial IQ–MQ discrepancies have been interpreted as indicative of memory impairment (Milner, 1975; Prigatano, 1978). Several authors (Milner, 1975; Prigatano, 1978) have suggested that WAIS IQ–MQ differences of 12 or more points may indicate a verbal memory deficit. However, WAIS-R IQs are about 7–8 points below their WAIS counterparts, calling into question the validity of the 12-point discrepancy as an indicator of memory impairment (Larrabee, 1987; Prifitera &

Barley, 1985). Furthermore, the MQ is not sensitive to distinctive patterns of deficits, nor is it adequate in detecting mild memory problems (Butters, 1986; Squire, 1986).

The WMS should be given early in the course of the examination. It is a fairly quick and important first step in the assessment of memory. Examination of the subtests may offer clues about spared and impaired functions. More detailed assessment with other tests in the battery [e.g., Buschke, Rey Figure, Rey Auditory–Verbal Learning Test (RAVLT) and Rey Visual Design Learning Test (RVDLT)], however, is necessary in order to establish which facets of memory are impaired. One should also note, that the WMS relies heavily on verbal skills. Consequently, patients with verbal expressive problems will be penalized (Erickson & Scott, 1977).

Normative Data

The subject's raw subtest scores are summed, an age correction is added (Table 2 in the WMS manual) and this corrected score may then be converted to an MQ by means of a table (Table 3 in the WMS manual). Wechsler's (1945) original normative base was inadequate (Lezak, 1983; Prigatano, 1978) in that it was small, about 200 subjects, drawn from a restricted age range (25–50 years; although his correction scores for age extend from 20 to 64 years), and the information provided on that population was very sketchy. This deficiency has been remedied to some extent. Several investigators have derived procedures for correcting the scores for age and education (Alekoumbides et al., 1987), and others have provided tentative norms for children and the elderly (e.g., Abikoff et al., 1987; Cauthen, 1977; Curry et al., 1986; Haaland et al., 1983; Halperin et al., 1989 Hulicka, 1966; Ivinskis et al., 1971; Ivison, 1977; Kear-Colwell & Heller, 1978; Klonoff & Kennedy, 1965, 1966; Russell, 1975, 1988; Schaie & Strother, 1968). One should note that age corrections for these younger and older subjects have typically not been made, and, as a result, one cannot derive a MQ for these younger and older people. This is not necessarily a disadvantage since the concept of MQ, which reflects a unidimensional measure of memory function, has been severely criticized (see Description).

Tables 6–30 to 6–39 allow the clinician to evaluate subtest performance with reference to age-group norms. In general, the norms are based on nonneurological populations of normal intelligence. The samples however may not be representative of the North American population. Table 6–30 compiles data from four different studies (Hulicka, 1966; Ivinskis, 1977; Klonoff & Kennedy, 1966; Wechsler, 1945) for the following subtests on Form I: PCI, OR, MC, and MS.

For LM, we use the detailed gist-scoring criteria developed by Abikoff et al. (1987) and Schwartz and Ivnik (1980) (see Scoring). Normative data, broken down

Table 6–30.   Mean Scores on PCI, OR, MC, and MS Subtests by Age Group: Form I

Age	n		PCI	OR	MC	MS	
16–18	44	M	5.4	4.9	7.1	fwd	6.7
		SD	0.8	0.4	2.0		1.2
						bwd	5.0
							1.2
20–29	50	M	5.92	6.0	7.5	fwd	7.04
		SD	0.02	0.0	1.9		1.2
						bwd	5.26
							1.13
30–39	53	M	5.56				
		SD	0.72				
40–49	46	M	5.7	6.0	6.61	fwd	5.98
		SD	0.4	0.0	1.9		1.12
						bwd	4.3
							1.11
50–59	—		—		—	—	
60–69	70	M	5.47		6.24	both	9.91
		SD	1.16		2.29		1.58
70–79	46	M	5.24		5.63	both	9.91
		SD	1.03		2.46		2.51
80+	115	M	5.23	4.76	5.92	both	10.2
		SD	1.23	0.57	2.07		1.5

Note: Ivinskis et al. (1971) give norms based on a population of 16- to 18-year-old Australian schoolchildren of average intelligence. Hulicka (1966) gives norms based on a nonneurological population of hospitalized veterans, residents in homes for the aged, and members of golden age clubs. These subjects were of average intelligence and aged 30–39 and 60–79. Klonoff and Kennedy's (1966) norms are based on community-dwelling veterans, ages 80+. Wechsler's (1945) norms are derived from nonhospitalized subjects of average intelligence, ages 20–29 and 40–49. These norms apply to Form I only. PCI = Personal and Current Information; OR = Orientation; MC = Mental Control; MS = Memory Span.

by age (18–80+) and education, have been generated for this scoring system (Abikoff et al., 1987) and are given in Tables 6–31 and 6–32. The norms can be used with Form I or Form II. Both age and education have a significant impact on recall, and an accurate measure must correct for these variables. Prediction equations, presented in Table 6–33, can be used to compare obtained scores against expected scores. Abikoff et al. (1987) provide the following illustration: A 40-year-old with 12 years of schooling and an immediate gist-recall score of 17 would have an expected recall score of 21.08. This expected score is obtained by entering the person's age and education into the prediction equation for immediate gist-recall

Table 6–31. Mean Immediate and 30-Minute Delayed Recall Scores on Logical Memory Subtest by Age Group

Age	n			Immediate	Delayed
10–11	35	m	M	17.71	14.94
			SD	5.02	4.20
	41	f	M	14.61	12.05
			SD	4.36	3.96
12–13	48	m	M	18.48	15.50
			SD	5.09	4.98
	49	f	M	17.14	14.79
			SD	4.19	4.01
14–15	37	m	M	19.19	16.81
			SD	5.08	4.76
	37	f	M	17.67	15.67
			SD	4.84	4.95
18–29	74		M	22.99	19.84
			SD	6.66	6.67
30–39	67		M	24.57	22.16
			SD	6.97	7.57
40–49	41		M	23.44	21.07
			SD	5.01	5.91
50–59	54		M	23.63	20.13
			SD	6.14	6.48
60–69	56		M	20.48	17.34
			SD	6.42	6.71
70–80+	46		M	19.11	15.33
			SD	6.74	7.57

Note: The scores for the two stories have not been averaged. Curry et al. (1986) provide norms for 10- to 15-year-olds, based on a population of U.S. schoolchildren of low to high-average verbal intelligence. Note that the scores are based on the half-point scoring system developed by Power et al. (1979) and apply only to the stories on Form I. Norms for adults (ages 20+) are taken from Abikoff et al. (1987) and are derived from a normal adult U.S. population. They are based on detailed gist-scoring criteria (see Scoring) and can be used with Form I or II.

Table 6–32. Mean Gist-Recall Scores by Educational Level

Education	Immediate			Delayed		
	N	M	SD	N	M	SD
Graduate school	38	26.18	6.65	38	22.92	7.77
College graduate	63	25.13	6.12	62	22.34	6.85
Some college	136	22.65	6.17	136	19.62	6.67
H.S. graduate	81	19.90	5.30	81	16.99	5.76
Non-H.S. graduate	21	17.05	7.75	21	13.33	8.26

Note: Data apply to Forms I and II.

Source: Abikoff et al. (1987).

Table 6–33. Prediction Equations for Gist Recall Scores

Measure	Equation	SD
Immediate	6.72 + .20(age) + .93(education) − .0026(age sq.)	6.01
Delayed	3.40 + .26(age) + .90(education) − .0034(age sq.)	6.56

Note: Data apply to Forms I and II.

Source: Abikoff et al. (1989).

[Expected immediate gist-recall = 6.72 + .20(40) + .93(12) − .003(40^2) = 21.08].
Given a standard deviation of 6.01, the person's actual score of 17 is within 1 SD of
the expected score. The equations can also be used to compare recall scores across
individuals by generating standard z-scores (see Abikoff et al., 1987). Curry et al.
(1986) provide data for adolescents, aged 9.5–15.5, for the immediate and 30-
minute delayed versions of the LM subtest. Age and sex differences were documented. Table 6–31 also shows these data, separately for males and females. Note,
however, that the data apply only to Form I, and that Curry et al. did not use the
gist scoring criteria developed by Abikoff et al. (1987). Rather, LM was scored
according to the method proposed by Power et al. (1979). This system allows $\frac{1}{2}$-
point credit for minor deviations of gist (i.e., the substitution of one or more
synonyms that do not alter the fundamental idea; or the deletion of an adjective,
adverb, or article that alters the idea to only a slight degree).

Table 6–34 presents age-related norms for the immediate and 30-minute delayed versions of the Form I Visual Reproduction subtest. Age and education/IQ
also affect performance on this test. Russell (1988) has developed norms for adults
(aged 20+) which take these variables into account. In order to use this system,
one must first refer to Table 6–35 and determine whether to use education or IQ
for the correction. Russell recommends that one use the method that will give the
subject the highest estimated premorbid IQ level of correction. Next, locate the
subject's age interval and education/IQ level for each memory score. To the subject's raw test score, either add or subtract the number according to the sign (do
nothing if raw score = 0). These corrected scores are then transformed into scaled
scores by using Table 6–36. The percentage retained is calculated by dividing the
corrected score for the $\frac{1}{2}$-hour presentation by the immediate presentation and
multiplying by 100. The percentage retained can also be given a scaled score. The
"percent of normal" is an alternative to the scaled score; it is the percentage of a
normal person's memory (defined as the mean of the normal sample) that a person
can remember. Russell (1988) recommends that the following terms be adopted
for indicating the severity of impairment: 0 = above average; 1 and 1.5 = average;
2 = borderline; 2.5 = mild; 3 = mild to moderate; 3.5 = moderate; 4 = moderate
to severe; 4.5 = severe; 5 and 5.5 = severe or very severe; 6 = profound impairment or a statement that the subject could not do the test at all. He suggests that a
scaled score of 2 points be used as a cutoff point to indicate impairment.

Table 6–34. Mean Immediate and 30-Minute Delayed Recall Scores on the Visual Reproduction Subtest by Age Group: Form I

Age	n			Immediate	Delayed
10–11	35	m	M	8.86	7.48
			SD	2.72	3.09
	41	f	M	8.17	7.24
			SD	2.87	3.06
12–13	48	m	M	9.19	7.79
			SD	2.74	3.03
	49	f	M	9.98	9.20
			SD	1.94	1.95
14–15	37	m	M	10.00	8.81
			SD	2.32	3.03
	37	f	M	9.29	8.73
			SD	2.42	2.56
18–29	97		M	10.48	9.84
			SD	1.93	2.21
30–49	81		M	10.10	9.26
			SD	2.55	2.74
50–64	51		M	8.73	7.35
			SD	2.59	2.46
65–69	49		M	6.0	5.4
			SD	2.1	2.5
70–74	74		M	5.1	4.3
			SD	2.0	2.3
75–79	40		M	4.9	4.2
			SD	2.0	1.9
80+	13		M	3.3	2.8
			SD	2.3	1.9

Note: Curry et al. (1986) provide normative data for children and adolescents, based on a population of normal U.S. school children, ages 9.5–15.5 years. Trahan et al. (1988) present data derived from healthy nonhospitalized adults, ages 18–69. Haaland et al. (1983) provide norms based on a population of superior elderly individuals without chronic medical problems, ages 65+. These normative data apply to Form I only.

Some normative data are available for use with children for the AL subtest on Form I (Halperin et al., 1989; Ivinskis et al., 1971). These data are shown in Table 6–37 along with recently compiled adult norms (Strauss and Spreen, 1989) for the immediate and 30-minute delay versions of the AL subtest. For the delayed version, 1 point is given for each of the word pairs (maximum = 10).

Ivison (1988b) has provided normative data for Form II. The norms are derived from a rather large (n = 600) sample of hospitalized patients, aged 20–79 years

Table 6–35. Age and Education Corrections for Visual Reproduction Subtest: Form I

Educ.	WAIS-R FSIQ	Age interval					
		20–39	40–49	50–59	60–69	70–79	80+
		Immediate VR					
<12	<98	0	+1	+2	+3	+4	+5
12		−1	0	+1	+2	+3	+4
>12	>106	−2	−1	0	+1	+1	+2
		Delayed VR (30 min)					
<12	<98	0	+1	+2	+3	+4	+5
12		−1	0	+1	+2	+3	+4
>12	>106	−2	−1	0	+1	+2	+4
		Percent retained					
<12	<98	−3	0	+3	+7	+10	+13
12		−3	0	+3	+7	+10	+13
>12	>106	−3	0	+3	+7	+10	+13

Note: For use with Form I only.

Source: Russell (1988).

Table 6–36. Scaled Scores for the Visual Reproduction Subtest: Form I

Scaled score	Immediate VR		Delayed VR		Percent retained
	Raw score	Percent of normal	Raw score	Percent of normal	
0	13	121	11	132	93
.5	12	116	10	122	92
	12		10		88
1.0	11	110	9	107	87
	10	91	9		82
1.5	9	86	8	100	81
	9		7	82	77
2.0	8	80	6	72	76
	7	66	6		72
2.5	6	58	5	57	71
	6		5		66
3.0	5	46	4	44	65
	5		4		61
3.5	4	30	3	32	60
	4		3		56
4.0	3	16	2	20	55
	3		2		50
4.5	2	10	1	7	49
	2		1		45
5.0	1	5	0	0	44
6.0	0	0	—	—	0

Note: For use with Form I only.

Source: Russell (1988).

Table 6–37.   Mean Immediate and 30-Minute Delayed Recall
Scores on the Associate Learning (AL) Subtest by Age Group: Form I

Age	n	AL	Delayed AL
6	34	M 13.71	
		SD 3.21	
7	40	M 15.33	
		SD 2.8	
8	38	M 15.40	
		SD 3.3	
9	44	M 17.15	
		SD 2.5	
10	38	M 16.17	
		SD 2.8	
11	36	M 16.44	
		SD 2.6	
12–13	10	M 16.3	
		SD 1.9	
16–18	44	M 16.9	
		SD 2.2	
20–29	23	M 18.33	9.91
		SD 1.45	.29
30–39	13	M 18.21	9.92
		SD 2.28	.28
40–49	14	M 18.29	9.71
		SD 2.82	.61
50–59	12	M 17.30	8.92
		SD 3.34	1.17
60–69	14	M 14.30	8.64
		SD 2.52	1.74
70+	14	M 15.89	8.77
		SD 3.10	1.01

Note: Halperin et al. (1989) provide norms based on normal lower-middle-class school children in the United States aged 6–15 years. Ivinskis et al. (1971) give norms based on a population of 16- to 18-year-old Australian school children of average intelligence. We (Strauss & Spreen, unpublished data, 1989) have compiled norms based on healthy adult volunteers, aged 20–84 years.

with no known neurological or psychiatric impairment. The scores may be somewhat lower than those of community-dwelling people. In order to use the data, the raw scores for each subtest must be corrected for age and sex differences (Table 6–38). Scaled score equivalents (mean = 10, SD = 3) of corrected raw scores are given for each subtest in Table 6–39.

Several patterns emerge from examination of the tables. In general, children score below the level of adults (Curry et al., 1986; Ivinskis et al., 1971). The exception appears to be the Associate Learning subtest, where adult levels are reached by about age 7 (Halperin et al., 1989). For adults, memory function declines with age, although not all dimensions change equally (e.g., Bak &

Table 6–38. Corrections to Raw Scores for Age and and Sex Differences on Selected Subtests of Form II

Subtest		Age groups					
		20–29	30–39	40–49	50–59	60–69	70–79
PC		0	0	0	0	0	0
OR		0	0	0	0	0	0
MC	m	0	+1	+1	+1	0	+1
	f	0	+1	+1	+1	+1	+2
DSp		0	0	+1	+1	+1	+2
VR	m	0	+1	+1	+1	+3	+4
	f	+1	+2	+2	+2	+4	+4
PAL	m	0	+2	+2	+3	+4	+6
	f	−1	+1	+2	+2	+4	+4

Note: PI = Personal and Current Information; OR = Orientation; MC = Mental Control; DSp = Digit Span; VR = Visual Reproduction; PAL = Paired Associate Learning.

Source: Ivison (1988b).

Table 6–39. Scaled Score Equivalents of Corrected Raw Scores: Form II

Scaled score	PCI	OR	MC	DSp	VR	PAL
19						26
18			11	16		25.5
17						25
16				15		24
15				14	17	23.0–23.5
14			10			21–22
13				13	16	20.0–20.5
12	6				15	18–19
11			9	12	14	17.0–17.5
10		5	8	11	13	15–16
9	5		7	10	12	14.0–14.5
8					10	13
7			6	9	9	11–12
6	4		5	9	9	10.0–10.5
5		4	4	8	7–8	9
4	3		2–3		6	8
3				7	5	7
2	2	3		6	4	
1			0–1			6.5
0		0–2		0–5	0–3	0–6

Note: The data are based on 600 patients (ages 20–79) hospitalized for nonneurological or nonpsychiatric disorders. The patients are Australians, generally of lower socio-economic status.

Source: Ivison (1988b).

Greene, 1981; Haaland et al., 1983; Hulicka, 1966; Margolis & Scialfa, 1984; Zagar et al., 1984). In general, elderly subjects perform best on PCI, OR, and MC. By contrast, VR, LM, and AL prove most difficult with advancing age. Note, however, that on the delayed recall tasks, regardless of age, normal people are retaining more than 80% of their original recollections.

REFERENCES

Abikoff, H., Alvir, J., Hong, G., Sukoff, R., Orazio, J., Solomon, S., & Saravay, S. (1987). Logical Memory subtest of the Wechsler Memory Scale: Age and education norms and alternate-form reliability of two scoring systems. *Journal of Clinical and Experimental Neuropsychology, 9,* 435–448.

Abikoff, H., Alvir, J., Hong, G., Sukoff, R., Orazio, J., Solomon, S., & Saravay, S. (1989). Logical Memory subtest of the Wechsler Memory Scale: Age and education norms and alternate-form reliability of two scoring systems—a correction. *Journal of Clinical and Experimental Neuropsychology, 11,* 783.

Alekoumbides, A., Charter, R.A., Adkins, T.G., & Seacat, G.F. (1987). The diagnosis of brain damage by the WAIS, WMS, and Reitan battery utilizing standardized scores corrected for age and education. *International Journal of Clinical Neuropsychology, 9,* 11–28.

Bak, J.S., & Greene, R.L. (1981). A review of the performance of aged adults on various Wechsler Memory Scale subtests. *Journal of Clinical Psychology, 37,* 186–188.

Bloom, B.L. (1959). Comparison of the alternate Wechsler Memory Scale forms. *Journal of Clinical Psychology, 15,* 72–74.

Bornstein, R.A. (1982). Effects of unilateral lesions on the Wechsler Memory Scale. *Journal of Clinical Psychology, 6,* 17–36.

Butters, N. (1986). The clinical aspects of memory disorders. In T. Incognoli, G. Goldstein, & C. Golden (Eds.), *Clinical Application of Neuropsychological Test Batteries* (pp. 361–382). New York: Plenum Press.

Butters, N., Salmon, D.P., Cullum, C.M., Cairns, P., Troster, A.I., Jacobs, D., Moss, M., & Cermak, L.S. (1988). Differentiation of amnesic and demented patients with the Wechsler Memory Scale-Revised. *The Clinical Neuropsychologist, 2,* 133–148.

Cauthen, N.R. (1977). Extension of the Wechsler Memory Scale norms to older age groups. *Journal of Clinical Psychology, 33,* 208–211.

Crosson, B., Hughes, C.W., Roth, D.L., & Monkowski, P.G. (1984). Review of Russell's (1975) norms for the Logical Memory and Visual Reproduction subtests of the Wechsler Memory Scale. *Journal of Consulting and Clinical Psychology, 52,* 635–641.

Curry, J.F., Logue, P.E., & Butler, B. (1986). Child and adolescent norms for Russell's revision of the Wechsler Memory Scale. *Journal of Clinical Child Psychology, 15,* 214–220.

Delaney, R.C., Rosen, A.J., Mattson, R.H., & Novelly, R.A. (1980). Memory function in focal epilepsy: A comparison of non-surgical, unilateral temporal lobe and frontal lobe samples. *Cortex, 16,* 103–117.

Delis, D.C. (1989). Neuropsychological assessment of learning and memory. In F. Boller & J. Grafman (Series Eds.), L. Squire & (Topic Ed.), *Handbook of Neuropsychology* (Vol. 3, pp. 3–34). Amsterdam: Elsevier.

Erickson, R.A., & Scott, M.L. (1977). Clinical memory testing: A review. *Psychological Bulletin, 84,* 1130–1149.

Franzen, M.D. (1989). *Reliability and Validity in Neuropsychological Assessment.* New York: Plenum Press.

Haaland, K.Y., Linn, R.T., Hunt, W.C., & Goodwin, J.S. (1983). A normative study of Russell's variant of the Wechsler Memory Scale in a healthy elderly population. *Journal of Consulting and Clinical Psychology, 51,* 878–881.

Hall, J.C., & Toal, R. (1957). Reliability (internal consistency) of the Wechsler Memory

Scale and correlation with the Wechsler–Bellevue Intelligence Scale. *Journal of Consulting Psychology, 21,* 131–135.

Halperin, J.M., Healey, J.M., Zeitchik, E., Ludman, W.L., & Weinstein, L. (1989). The development of linguistic and mnestic abilities in school-age children. *Journal of Clinical and Experimental Neuropsychology, 11,* 518–528.

Henry, G.K., Adams, R.L., Buck, P., Buchanan, W.L. & Altepeter, T.A. (1990). The American Liner New York and Anna Thompson: An investigation of interference effects on the Wechsler Memory Scale. *Journal of Clinical and Experimental Neuropsychology, 12,* 502–506.

Herman, D.O. (1988). Development of the Wechsler Memory Scale-Revised. *The Clinical Neuropsychologist, 2,* 102–106.

Hulicka, I.M. (1966). Age differences in Wechsler Memory Scale scores. *Journal of Genetic Psychology, 109,* 135–145.

Ivinskis, A., Allen, S., & Shaw, E. (1971). An extension of the Wechsler Memory Scales to lower age groups. *Journal of Clinical Psychology, 27,* 354–357.

Ivison, D.J. (1977). The Wechsler Memory Scale: Preliminary findings towards an Australian standardization. *Australian Psychologist, 12,* 303–313.

Ivison, D.J. (1988a). The Wechsler Memory Scale: Relations between Form I and II. *Australian Psychologist, 23,* 219–224.

Ivison, D.J. (1988b). Normative study of the Wechsler memory Scale Form 2. Paper presented at the 24th International Congress of Psychology, Sydney, Australia.

Kear-Colwell, J.J., & Heller, M. (1978). A normative study of the Wechsler Memory Scale. *Journal of Clinical Psychology, 34,* 437–444.

Klonoff, H., & Kennedy, M. (1965). Memory and perceptual functioning in octogenarians in the community. *Journal of Gerontology, 20,* 328–333.

Klonoff, H., & Kennedy, M. (1966). A comparative study of cognitive functioning in old age. *Journal of Gerontology, 21,* 239–243.

Larrabee, G.J. (1987). Further caution in interpretation of comparisons between the WAIS-R and the Wechsler Memory Scale.

Journal of Clinical and Experimental Psychology, 9, 456–460.

Larrabee, G.J., Kane, R.L., Schuck, J.R., & Francis, D.J. (1985). Construct validity of various memory testing procedures. *Journal of Clinical and Experimental Neuropsychology, 7,* 497–504.

Levin, H.S., & Larrabee, G.J. (1983). Disproportionate decline in visuospatial memory in human aging. *Society for Neuroscience Abstracts, 9,* 21.

Lezak, M.D. (1983). *Neuropsychological Assessment.* New York: Oxford University Press.

Loring, D.W., & Papanicolaou, A.C. (1987). Memory assessment in neuropsychology: Theoretical considerations and practical utility. *Journal of Clinical and Experimental Neuropsychology, 9,* 340–358.

Margolis, R.B., & Scialfa, C.T. (1984). Age differences in Wechsler Memory Scale performance. *Journal of Clinical Psychology, 40,* 1442–1449.

McCarty, S.M., Logue, P.E., Power, D.G., Zeisat, H.A., & Rosenstiel, A.K. (1980). Alternate form reliability and age-related scores for Russell's Revised Wechsler Memory Scale. *Journal of Consulting and Clinical Psychology, 48,* 296–298.

Milberg, W.P., Hebben, N., & Kaplan, E. (1986). The Boston process approach to neuropsychological assessment. In I. Grant & K.M. Adams (Eds.), *Neuropsychiatric Disorders* (pp. 65–86) New York: Oxford University Press.

Milner, B. (1975). Psychological aspects of focal epilepsy and its neurosurgical management. *Advances in Neurology, 8,* 299–321.

O'Grady, K.E. (1988). Convergent and discriminant validity of Russell's revised Wechsler Memory Scale. *Personality, Individual Differences, 9,* 321–327.

Power, D.G., Logue, P.E., McCarty, S.M., Rosenstiel, A.K., & Zeisat, H.A. (1979). Inter-rater reliability of the Russell Revision of the Wechsler Memory Scale: An attempt to clarify some ambiguities in scoring. *Journal of Clinical Neuropsychology, 1,* 343–345.

Prifitera, A., & Barley, W.D. (1985). Cautions in interpretation of comparisons between the WAIS-R and the Wechsler Memory Scale. *Journal of Consulting and Clinical Psychology, 53*, 564–565.

Prigatano, G.P. (1977). Wechsler Memory Scale is a poor screening test for brain dysfunction. *Journal of Clinical Psychology, 33*, 772–777.

Prigatano, G.P. (1978). Wechsler Memory Scale: A selective review of the literature. *Journal of Clinical Psychology, 34*, 816–832.

Russell, E.W. (1975). A multiple scoring method for the assessment of complex memory functions. *Journal of Consulting and Clinical Psychology, 43*, 800–809.

Russell, E.W. (1988). Renorming Russell's version of the Wechsler Memory Scale. *Journal of Clinical and Experimental Neuropsychology, 10*, 235–249.

Schaie, K.W., & Strother, G.R. (1968). Cognitive and personality variables in college graduates of advanced age. In G.A. Talland (Ed.), *Human Aging and Behavior.* New York: Academic Press.

Schultz, E.E., Keesler, T.Y., Friedenberg, L., & Sciara, A.D. (1984). Limitations in equivalence of alternate subtests for Russell's revision of the Wechsler Memory Scale: Causes and solutions. *Journal of Clinical Neuropsychology, 6*, 220–223.

Schwartz, M.S., & Ivnik, R.J. (1980). Wechsler Memory Scale I: Toward a more objective and systematic scoring system of Logical Memory and Visual Reproduction subtests. Paper presented to the American Psychological Association, Montreal.

Snow, W.G., Tierney, M.C., Zorzitto, M.L., Fisher, R.H., & Reid, D.W. (1988). One-year test–retest reliability of selected neuropsychological tests in older adults. Paper presented to the International Neuropsychological Society, New Orleans.

Squire, L.R. (1986). The neuropsychology of memory dysfunction and its assessment. In I. Grant & K. Adams (Eds.), *Neuropsychological Assessment of Neuropsychiatric Disorders* (pp. 268–299). New York: Oxford University Press.

Stanton, B.A., Jenkins, C.D., Savageau, J.A., & Zyzanski, S.J. (1984). Age and educational differences on the Trail Making Test and Wechsler Memory Scales. *Perceptual and Motor Skills, 58*, 311–318.

Stone, C., & Wechsler, D. (1946). *Wechsler Memory Scale Form II.* New York: Psychological Corporation.

Strauss, E., and Spreen, O. 1989. Unpublished data.

Taylor, L. (August 1988) Personal Communication

Trahan, D.E., Quintana, J., Willingham, A.C., & Goethe, K.E. (1988). The visual reproduction subtest: Standardization and clinical validation of a delayed recall procedure. *Archives of Clinical Neuropsychology, 2*, 29–39.

Wechsler, D. (1945). A standardized memory scale for clinical use. *Journal of Psychology, 19*, 87–95.

Wechsler, D. (1987). *Wechsler Memory Scale – Revised.* New York: Psychological Corporation.

Zagar, R., Arbit, J., Stuckey, M., & Wengel, W. (1984). Developmental analysis of the Wechsler Memory Scale. *Journal of Clinical Psychology, 40*, 1466–1473.

WECHSLER MEMORY SCALE – REVISED (WMS-R)

Purpose

The purpose of this test is to provide measures of various aspects of memory function.

Source

The complete WMS-R kit can be obtained from the Psychological Corporation, P.O. Box 9954, San Antonio, Texas 78204-0954 at a cost of $220.00 U.S., or from the Institute of Psychological Research, 34 Fleury Street West, Montreal, Quebec H3L 1S9, for $390 Cnd.

Description

The complete kit of the updated version, the WMS-R (Wechsler, 1987), includes a manual, stimulus cards, record forms, and carrying case. It has altered many of the test items, administration, and scoring procedures, broadened its coverage of nonverbal visual memory, and made delayed recall a standard technique. The scale is intended for individuals aged 16–74 years. The first subtest, Information and Orientation Questions, contains simple questions covering biographical data, orientation, and informational questions such as: "Who is the President of the United States?" Mental Control requires the subject to say a series of numbers or letters. On Figural Memory, the subject looks briefly at abstract designs, and then must identify them from an array. Logical Memory I examines the ability to recall ideas in two orally presented stories. On Visual Paired Associates I, the subject is shown six abstract line drawings, each paired with a different color, and is then asked to indicate the appropriate color associated with each figure. Up to six trials are provided to learn the pairs. Verbal Paired Associates I is similar. The subject is read a group of eight word pairs. Subsequently, the first word of each pair is read, and the subject must say the second word. Up to six trials are provided to learn the pairs. On Visual Reproduction I, the subject must draw geometric designs that are exposed briefly. Digit Span consists of two parts and requires the subject to repeat digits forward and in the reverse order. The two parts of the Visual Memory Span subtest, Tapping Forward and Tapping Backward, are administered separately. The examiner, using a card printed with colored squares, touches the squares in sequences of increasing length. The subject must reproduce the sequences, in forward and reverse order. Following the administration of the above nine subtests, two verbal and two nonverbal subtests (Logical Memory II, Visual Paired Associates II, Verbal Paired Associates II, and Visual Reproduction II) are given a second time, thus providing 30-minute delayed recall measures. The first subtest, Information and Orientation Questions, is included on the scale for screening purposes. The remaining 12 subtests yield five age-corrected summary indices, each with a mean of 100 and a standard deviation of 15: one for general immediate memory, separate indexes for immediate verbal and visual memory, one for attention/concentration, and one for general delayed memory.

Administration

The instructions for the WMS-R are given in the manual (see source).

Approximate Time for Administration

The time required is about 45 minutes.

Scoring

The WMS-R manual (see source) provides detailed scoring procedures.

Comment

Wechsler (1987) presents test–retest correlation coefficients for five of the subtests and internal consistency estimates for the remaining seven subtests. The average reliability coefficients across age groups for subtests and composites ranged from .41 to .90 with a median value of .74. Several subtests have restricted score ranges that have the effect of reducing the reliability coefficients for those subtests. It should also be noted that there was an increase in scores on most of the subtests and composites from the first to the second testing. The time period between administrations ranged from four to six weeks. Scoring for most of the WMS-R is relatively simple and straightforward. Extensive scoring rules were developed for the Logical Memory and Visual Reproduction subtests. Wechsler (1987) reports that interscorer reliability coefficients for the Logical Memory and Visual Reproduction were .99 and .97, respectively. Accurate scoring of the Visual Memory Span subtest may however prove difficult for examiners who are unfamiliar with the test.

In terms of validity, Delis et al. (1988) report numerous strong correlations between the WMS-R and the California Verbal Learning Test (Delis et al., 1987). Factor analyses of the WMS-R have generally shown evidence of two major factors, general memory and attention/concentration (Bornstein & Chelune, 1988; Roid et al., 1988; Wechsler, 1987). The results of these analyses support the reporting of the two major composite scores on the WMS-R, namely the General Memory Index and the Attention/Concentration Index. It is important to note that the Attention/Concentration Index correlates highly with general intelligence, whereas memory, as measured by the WMS-R, appears to be largely independent of IQ, as measured by the Wechsler Adult Intelligence Scale – Revised (WAIS-R) (Bornstein & Chelune, 1988). This difference between the Attention/Concentration and General Memory Indices may be useful in distinguishing among certain memory disorders—for example, amnesia versus dementia (Butters et al., 1988). Furthermore, clinical investigations using the WMS-R have shown that the test is sensitive to memory disturbances and may characterize the learning and memory disorders in a number of different patient groups including those with Alzheimer's disease, Huntington's disease, multiple sclerosis, Kosakoff's, long-term alcoholism, neurotoxin exposure, schizophrenia, and depression (Butters et al., 1988; Chelune & Bornstein, 1988; Crossen & Weins, 1988; Fischer, 1988; Ryan & Lewis, 1988; Wechsler, 1987). However, simple IQ–Memory index discrepancies cannot be used in isolation to identify memory deficits (Bornstein et al., 1989). Further, the Verbal and Visual Memory Indexes cannot be used with any confidence to infer lateralized brain dysfunction (Loring et al., 1989).

The WMS-R is an improvement over the original, standard version. It does, however, have its limitations. The WMS-R takes longer to administer. There is no parallel form. Normative data for children, adolescents, and the very old (75+) are unavailable. It does not allow the awarding of scores below 50, and, as a result, some patients' scores may be inflated (Butters et al., 1988). It is still primarily a test of verbal learning (Chelune & Bornstein, 1988; Loring, 1990). The new "nonverbal" subtests are not pure measures of visual learning/memory. Moreover, when calculating the indices (General, Verbal, and Visual), verbal memory performance continues to contribute more heavily. The absence of recognition tasks also limits the capacity of the scale to differentiate among patient populations (Butters et al., 1988; Chelune & Bornstein; 1988). Further, rate of acquisition and retention are ignored (Chelune & Bornstein, 1988), as are olfactory and tactile memory and memory for previously learned skills (Holden, 1988).

Despite these limitations, the scale (WMS-R) is a fairly quick and important first step in the assessment of memory and should be given early in the course of the test session. Examination of the subtests may offer clues about spared and impaired functions. More detailed assessment, however, may be needed.

Normative Data

The WMS-R manual provides norms for individuals aged 16:0 to 74:11 years. The test was standardized on a large sample considered representative of the U.S. population.

Briefly, after obtaining the total raw scores on each WMS-R subtest, the examiner must multiply each raw score (except for scores on Information and Orientation questions) by a weight provided on the front of the record form. Subtests of weighted scores are summed; then these are transformed into their corresponding indices by means of an age-graded table in the WMS-R manual (Table C-1). Each index has a mean of 100 and an SD of 15. Examination of differences between indices may provide valuable information about the patient's strengths and weaknesses. In order to determine whether the difference between two index scores is reliable (i.e., significant at $p < .05$), the examiner should refer to Table 14 in the WMS-R manual. To facilitate comparisons among select subtests, percentile equivalents of some raw scores are given in the WMS-R manual (Tables C-4, C-5).

Scores on the Information and Orientation questions are intended primarily to identify persons for whom the meaning of scores on the rest of the scale may be questionable. Frequency distributions for raw scores on this subtest are given in Table C-2 of the WMS-R manual.

Finally, one should note that level of education is highly correlated with all five indexes (see source). Consequently, years of education is an important factor to consider and may temper interpretation of any given index score (see source).

REFERENCES

Bornstein, R.A., & Chelune, G.J. (1988). Factor structure of the Wechsler Memory Scale – Revised. *Clinical Neuropsychologist, 2,* 107–115.

Bornstein, R.A., Chelune, G.J., & Prifitera, A. (1989). IQ–Memory discrepancies in normal and clinical samples. *Psychological Assessment, 1,* 203–206.

Butters, N., Salmon, D.P., Cullum, C.M., Cairns, P., Troster, A. I., Jacobs, D., Moss, M., & Cermak, L.S. (1988). Differentiation of amnesic and demented patients with the Wechsler Memory Scale – Revised. *Clinical Neuropsychologist, 2,* 133–148.

Crosson, J.R., & Weins, A.N. (1988). Wechsler Memory Scale – Revised: Deficits in performance associated with neurotoxic solvent exposure. *Clinical Neuropsychologist, 2,* 181–187.

Delis, D.C., Cullum, C.M., Butters, N., Cairns, P., & Prifitera, A. (1988). Wechsler Memory Scale – Revised and California Verbal Learning Test: Convergence and divergence. *Clinical Neuropsychologist, 2,* 188–196.

Delis, D.C., Kramer, J.H., Kaplan, E., & Ober, B.A. (1987). *The California Verbal Learning Test.* New York: Psychological Corporation.

Fischer, J.S. (1988). Using the Wechsler Memory Scale – Revised to detect and characterize memory deficits in multiple sclerosis. *Clinical Neuropsychologist, 2,* 149–172.

Holden, R.H. (1988). Wechsler Memory Scale – Revised. In D.J. Keyser, & R.C. Sweetland (Eds.), *Test Critiques* (Vol. 7, pp. 633–638). Kansas City, Missouri: Test Corporation of America.

Loring, D.W. (1990). The Wechsler Memory Scale – Revised, or the Wechsler Memory Scale – Revisited? *Clinical Neuropsychologist, 3,* 59–69.

Loring, D.W., Lee, G.P., Martin, R.C., & Meador, K.J. (1989). Verbal and visual memory index discrepancies form the Wechsler Memory Scale – Revised: Cautions in interpretation. *Psychological Assessment, 1,* 198–202.

Roid, G.H., Prifitera, A., & Ledbetter, M. (1988). Confirmatory analysis of the factor structure of the Wechsler Memory Scale – Revised. *Clinical Neuropsychologist, 2,* 116–120.

Ryan, J.J., & Lewis, C.V. (1988). Comparison of normal controls and recently detoxified alcoholics on the Wechsler Memory Scale – Revised. *Clinical Neuropsychologist, 2,* 173–180.

Wechsler, D. (1987). *Wechsler Memory Scale – Revised.* New York: Psychological Corporation.

7

Language Tests

Because of the central importance of verbal communication deficits after brain lesions as well as delays in language development in children, numerous tests of language function have been developed, including comprehensive batteries for adults (Benton & Hamsher, 1978, 1983; Goodglass & Kaplan, 1987; Kertesz, 1980; Porch, 1971; Schuell, 1973) and children (Kirk et al., 1968) as well as "aphasia screening tests" (Reitan, 1984). In addition, tests directed more at the ability of the patient to communicate in daily life have been developed (Sarno, 1969). While readers may wish to make their own choice among these batteries (see review by Spreen & Risser, 1991), we present here a selection of highly sensitive, but brief individual tests (Token Test, Word Fluency, Boston Naming Test, Peabody Picture Vocabulary Test) as well as the Neurosensory Center Comprehensive Assessment of Aphasia (NCCEA, which includes two of these individual tests as well as the Sentence Repetition Test described in the memory section of this manual) and the Communication Abilities in Daily Living Test, both of which are given if a detailed exploration of language abilities in test performance and in daily life is desirable. The NCCEA has also been standardized for use with children.

REFERENCES

Benton, A.L., & Hamsher, K.deS. (1978, 1983). *Multilingual Aphasia Examination.* Manual of Instructions. Iowa City: University of Iowa Departments of Neurology and Psychology.

Goodglass, H., & Kaplan, E. (1987). *The Assessment of Aphasia and Related Disorders* (2nd ed.). Philadelphia: Lea & Febiger.

Kertesz, A. (1980). *Western Aphasia Battery.* London, Ont.: University of Western Ontario.

Kirk, S.A., McCarthy, J., & Kirk, W. (1968). *The Illinois Test of Psycholinguistic Abilities* (Rev. ed.). Urbana, Ill.: Illinois University Press.

Porch, B. (1971). *The Porch Index of Communicative Ability* (Vol. 2): *Administration and Scoring.* Palo Alto, Cal.: Consulting Psychologists Press.

Reitan, R.M. (1984). *Aphasia and Sensory–Perceptual Deficits in Adults.* Tucson, Ariz.: Reitan Neuropsychology Laboratory.

Sarno, M.T. (1969). *The Functional Communication Profile: Manual of Directions.* New York: New York University Medical Center-Institute of Rehabilitation Medicine.

Schuell, H. (1973). *Differential Diagnosis of Aphasia with the Minnesota Test* (2nd ed.).

Minneapolis: University of Minnesota Press.

Spreen, O., & Risser, A. (1991). Assessment of aphasia. In M.T. Sarno (Ed.), *Acquired Aphasia* (2nd ed.). New York: Academic Press.

BOSTON NAMING TEST (BNT)

Purpose

The purpose of this test is to assess the ability to name pictured objects.

Source

The test can be ordered from Lea & Febiger, 600 Washington Square, Philadelphia, PA 19106, at a cost of about $30 U.S., including scoring booklets.

Description

Because of the high incidence of naming problems in aphasia as well as in other neuropathological conditions, virtually all aphasia examinations contain a naming task. This popular test, originally published by Kaplan et al. (1978) as an experimental version with 85 items and now revised to a 60-item test (Kaplan et al., 1983), provides a detailed examination of naming abilities, well standardized across age, which is preferred when more than a brief examination is desired. It is an addition to rather than part of the Boston Diagnostic Aphasia Examination (BDAE, Goodglass & Kaplan, 1987). Sixty line drawings ranging from simple, high-frequency vocabulary ("tree") to rare words ("abacus") are presented one at a time on cards, and two prompting cues (phonemic, stimulus cue) are given if the patient does not produce the word spontaneously.

Administration

For young children and all aphasics, begin with item 1 and discontinue after six successive failures. For all other adult subjects, begin with item 30 (harmonica). If any of the next eight items are failed, proceed backward from item No. 29 until a total of eight consecutive preceding items are passed; then resume in a forward direction and discontinue the test when the subject makes six consecutive errors.

Credit is given if the item is correctly named in 20 seconds. Only in those instances where the subject has clearly misperceived the picture, the subject is told that the picture represents something else, and the subject is supplied with the bracketed stimulus cues that appear on the record form.

For example, if the response for mushroom is "umbrella," the subject is given the first (semantic) stimulus cue "something to eat." If the subject then correctly names the item within 20 seconds, a check is entered in the stimulus cue correct column. If the subject is unable to name the picture correctly within 20 seconds, a second (phonemic) cue (i.e., the underlined initial phoneme(s) of the name of the item) is offered. The response is recorded and entered in the appropriate column (phonemic cue correct, incorrect) but no credit is given.

Scoring

Recorded are (1) the number of spontaneously given correct responses, (2) the number of stimulus cues given, (3) the number of correct responses following a stimulus cue, (4) the number of phonemic cues, and (5) the number of correct and incorrect responses following phonemic cue.

A total naming score is derived from summing the number of correct responses [(1) and (3)] between the baseline item and the ceiling item, and adding that total to the number of test items that precede the baseline.

Comment

Test–retest reliability data are not available. Huff et al. (1986) divided the original version of the test into two equivalent forms and obtained between-forms correlations of .81 in healthy control subjects, and of .97 in patients with Alzheimer's disease. The coefficient alpha between the two forms was .96. A recent study (Thompson & Heaton, 1989) compared the old experimental version of 85 items, with the standard 60-item, and with the two nonoverlapping 42-item versions (Huff et al., 1986) in 49 clinical patients. The correlations between the 85-, the 60-, and the 42-item versions ranged from .96 to .92, whereas the two nonoverlapping short forms correlated .84. The authors recommend the use of the short forms, especially since they may be more suitable if repeat testing is required. Another recent study constructed an "odd-item" and "even-item" as well as an experimental version of the BNT, and found that all three short versions discriminated well between Alzheimer's disease, other dementing diseases, and normal older (mean age 73.7) subjects (Williams et al., 1989).

Construct validity in children was investigated by Halperin et al. (1989). The test loaded highly on a word knowledge, or vocabulary factor together with the

PPVT-R, but showed low loadings on a verbal fluency or a memory factor, suggesting that it is a relatively pure measure in children.

The manual provides means for aphasics with a severity level from 0 to 5 as determined by the BDAE, all of which are well below the level for normal adults. However, the range for aphasics with severity levels 2–5 extends well into the range for normals. This is not surprising since naming is not necessarily impaired in all types of aphasia. Kazniak et al. (1988) found that normal elderly subjects make one error, whereas Alzheimer's disease patients with a mild degree of impairment obtain a mean of 5.5 errors, and those with moderate impairment make about 7.5 errors. Knopman et al. (1984) reported good measurement of recovery of naming after strokes of small volume in the posterior superior temporal–inferior parietal and the insula–putamen areas.

As with other tests relying on pictorial material (e.g., Peabody Picture Vocabulary Test, PPVT), visual–perceptual integrity should be checked if errors occur. Kaplan noted that, particularly in patients with right frontal damage, "fragmentation responses" may be made (e.g., the mouthpiece on a harmonica is interpreted as a line of windows in a bus; Lezak, 1983).

Normative Data

The norms accompanying the test are based on small groups of adults aged 18–59. No age-related changes or differences between adults with 12 years of schooling or less and those with more than 12 years of education are noted. However, normative data (Table 7–1; Van Gorp et al., 1986) show a significant effect of both age and education when older subjects are included. Subjects with less than eight years of education score approximately 10 points lower, and subjects with 15 or more years of education about three points higher. These norms are consistent with those published by Taussig, Henderson, and Mack (1988) for the current version; by LaBarge et al. (1986) and Montgomery and Costa (1983) for the 85-item version; and by Villardita et al. (1985) for a 15-item version. Age-related changes occur relatively late (age 70+) on this test.

Table 7–1. Norms for Elderly Subjects on the Boston Naming Test

Age	n	M	SD	Suggested Cutoff
60–64	15	56.7	3.0	51
65–69	37	55.6	2.4	47
70–74	47	54.5	5.1	44
75–79	23	51.7	6.2	39
80–85	14	51.5	7.0	37

Source: Data derived from Van Gorp et al. (1986).

Table 7–2.　Norms for Normal School Children on the Boston Naming Test

Age	Male			Female			Total		
	N	M	SD	N	M	SD	N	M	SD
6	16	35.69	6.1	18	32.50	5.6	34	34.00	6.0
7	18	39.94	4.9	22	37.91	6.7	40	38.83	6.0
8	23	41.17	3.0	15	39.93	4.1	38	40.68	3.5
9	20	43.20	4.7	25	42.92	5.2	45	43.04	4.9
10	16	45.56	5.9	22	46.41	4.4	38	46.05	5.0
11	16	46.44	3.5	20	46.90	5.2	36	46.69	4.5
12	2	51.50	3.5	8	47.00	3.9	10	47.90	4.1

Source: From Halperin et al. (1989).

Norms for small groups of children from kindergarten to grade 5 accompany the test. The progression with age corresponds to the data presented by Kindlon and Garrison (1986) and by Wilson (personal communication) for the experimental version of the test. The Kindlon and Garrison study also shows gender differences at younger ages, with females scoring about 5 points higher at ages 6 and 7, whereas Halperin et al. (1987) failed to find sex effects. Table 7–2 presents recently developed norms for school children ages 6–12 (Halperin et al., 1989). The authors report that scores increase by two to three points after phonemic cueing.

REFERENCES

Goodglass, H., & Kaplan, E. (1987). *The Assessment of Aphasia and Related Disorders* (2nd ed.). Philadelphia: Lea & Febiger.

Halperin, J.M., Healy, J.M., Zeitschick, E., Ludman, W.L., & Weinstein, L. (1989). Developmental aspects of linguistic and mnestic abilities in normal children. *Journal of Clinical and Experimental Neuropsychology, 11*, 518–528.

Huff, F.J., Collins, C., Corkin, S., & Rosen, T.J. (1986). Equivalent forms of the Boston Naming Test. *Journal of Clinical and Experimental Neuropsychology, 8*, 556–562.

Kaplan, E.F., Goodglass, H., & Weintraub, S. (1978). *The Boston Naming Test* (exper. ed.). Boston: Kaplan & Goodglass.

Kaplan, E.F., Goodglass, H., & Weintraub, S. (1983). *The Boston Naming Test* (2nd ed.). Philadelphia: Lea & Febiger.

Kazniak, A.W., Bayles, K.A., Tomoeda, C.K., & Slauson, T. (1988). Assessing linguistic communicative functioning in Alzheimer's dementia: A theoretically motivated approach. Paper presented at the meeting of the International Neuropsychological Society, New Orleans. *Journal of Clinical and Experimental Neuropsychology, 10*, 53 (abstract).

Kindlon, D., & Garrison, W. (1986). The Boston Naming Test: Norm data and cue utilization in a sample of normal 6- and 7-year-old children. *Brain and Language, 21*, 255–259.

Knopman, D.S., Selnes, O.A., Niccum, N., & Rubens, A. (1984). Recovery of naming in aphasia: Relationship to fluency, comprehension, and CT findings. *Neurology, 34*, 1461–1470.

LaBarge, E., Edwards, D., & Knesevich, J.W. (1986). Performance of normal elderly on the Boston Naming Test. *Brain and Language, 27*, 380–384.

Lezak, M.D. (1983). *Neuropsychological Assessment* (2nd ed.). New York: Oxford University Press.

Montgomery, K., & Costa, L. (1983). Neuropsychological test performance of a normal elderly sample. Paper presented at the Meeting of the International Neuropsychological Society, Mexico City.

Taussig, I.M., Henderson, V.W., & Mack, W. (1988). Spanish translation and validation of a neuropsychological test battery: performance of Spanish- and English-speaking Alzheimer's disease patients and normal comparison subjects. Paper presented at the meeting of the Gerontological Society of America, San Francisco.

Thompson, L.L., & Heaton, R.K. (1989). Comparison of different versions of the Boston Naming Test. *Clinical Neuropsychologist, 3,* 184–192.

Van Gorp, W.G., Satz, P., Kiersch, M.E., & Henry, R. (1986). Normative data on the Boston Naming Test for a group of normal older adults. *Journal of Clinical and Experimental Neuropsychology, 8,* 702–705.

Villardita, C., Cultrera, S., Cupone, V., & Meija, R. (1985). Neuropsychological test performances and normal aging. *Archives of Gerontology and Geriatrics, 4,* 311–319.

Williams, B.W., Mack, W., & Henderson, V.W. (1989). Boston Naming Test in Alzheimer's disease. *Neuropsychologia, 27,* 1073–1079.

COMMUNICATIVE ABILITIES IN DAILY LIVING (CADL)

Purpose

The purpose of this test is to examine communicative abilities (including nonverbal communication) in normal living situations for aphasic adults and similar language-handicapped populations.

Source

The complete kit, including manual, scoring forms, and cassette training tape, can be obtained from Mind Resources Inc., P.O. Box 126, Kitchener, Ont. N2G 3W9, for $137.20 Cdn. or from Pro-Ed, 8700 Shoal Creek Blvd., Austin, TX 78758-6897 for $98 U.S.

Description

This test, developed by Holland (1980), differs from other tests designed for the evaluation of language impairment in that it measures the ability of patients to comprehend and communicate in daily living situations by whatever means remain available to them, including gestures, pointing, writing, drawing, etc. However, it does not include rating scales, another means of measuring "functional communication" (Sarno, 1969). The 68 items of this test take the patient through a variety of test methods, including actual questions, "staged" situations in a doctor's office, making telephone calls, and situations in a store and while driving simulated in pictures. Recent advances are reported by Holland (1984). An Italian version is available (Pizzamiglio et al., 1984).

Administration

The test situation is deliberately informal, and examiners are instructed to act out various roles as much as possible—for example, by changing their voice, introducing humor, etc., to increase the "contextual richness" of the situations created during the test. Although the test items follow a "natural" sequence, they can be grouped into 10 categories as follows:

1. *Reading, writing, and using numbers* are employed to estimate, calculate, and judge them. There are 21 such items which include reading signs, directions, making change, setting dates (e.g., determining from a clock drawing, how long the patient has to wait for an appointment with "Dr. Clark" at 3 PM).
2. *Speech acts*, comprising 21 items, includes pragmatic interchanges in which speech, gesture, and writing are used to convey information or intent (e.g., stating one's age within a five-year margin).
3. *Utilizing verbal and nonverbal context* consists of 17 items involving responding to an item in the context supplied by the examiner (e.g., viewing a picture of a waiting room with a nonsmoking sign and a person smoking: "What's happening in this picture?").
4. *Role playing* consists of 10 items that require a cognitive shift to an "as if" state (e.g., visiting a doctor's office).
5. *Sequenced and relationship-dependent communicative behavior* consists of nine items that require an ability to perform a sequence of behaviors (e.g., dialing a phone number).
6. *Social conventions* consists of eight items (e.g., greeting, accepting apologies, leave taking).
7. *Divergencies* comprises seven items that require responding to misleading information or proverbs (i.e., the generation of logical possibilities with a ready flow of ideas).
8. *Nonverbal symbolic communication* consists of seven items (e.g., recognizing playing cards and facial expressions of emotion).
9. *Deixis* consists of six items with movement-related or movement-dependent communicative behavior (e.g., "Show me the men's/women's room").
10. *Humor, absurdity, and metaphor* consists of four items, similar to divergencies, requiring the recognition of a humorous, or absurd, or metaphoric situation in pictures.

Approximate Time for Administration

The test duration is 30–90 minutes.

Scoring

Each item is scored as 0, 1, and 2 following detailed instructions in the manual which also contains scoring booklets for two sample cases. Usually, a score of 0 indicates an incorrect response or no response; a score of 2 points indicates a correct response, whereas a score of 1 point is given if repeating the question, or rephrasing the question elicits a response. Since the ability to communicate, not the quality of the verbal or written response, is the subject of investigation, spontaneous requests for repeating a question or grammatically incorrect, but comprehensible responses, are scored as correct.

The total score is the sum of all points obtained on the 68 items (maximum score = 136). No subscores are used, although the breakdown into areas of communication as listed above can be used as a qualitative guide to interpretation.

Comment

Reliability for 20 subjects retested after one to three weeks by a different examiner is reported by the author as .99, internal consistency as .97.

Concurrent validity (see source) with the Boston Diagnostic Aphasia Examination was .84; with the Porch Index of Communication Ability, .93; and with the Functional Communication Profile, .87. Correlations with 23 ratings by staff and family were .67. The CADL has also been shown to correlate with the number of communicative exchanges initiated by aphasics (Linebaugh et al., 1982), but not with measures of dyadic nonverbal communication (Behrmann & Penn, 1984).

Criterion validity was established by testing aphasic patients. The mean scores for subjects with different types of aphasia who were matched for age and according to whether or not they were in an institution are reported in Table 7–3 together with the appropriate scores from an Italian study (Pizzamiglio et al., 1984).

This distribution of scores for different types of aphasia follows the clinical impression of their severity. However, it should be noted that the anomic group had near-normal scores (see Normative Data, below). Aphasics living in a home situation had consistently higher scores than those living in an institution. The Italian study also showed somewhat different scores for the various types of aphasia as well as generally lower scores. This may be the result of sample selection and classification criteria, but it also suggests that scores, especially a suggested cutoff score of 120, should be interpreted with caution. Correlation between severity of

Table 7–3. Criterion Validity of the CADL in Two Studies

Type of aphasia	Holland (1980)			Pizzamiglio et al. (1984)		
	N	M	SD	N	M	SD
Anomic	14	127.21	5.57	8	104.12	28.91
Conduction	4	112.00	16.06	4	87.75	7.13
Broca's	47	106.29	22.48	42	82.55	30.27
Wernicke's	17	94.88	21.92	12	77.00	34.45
Mixed	26	79.67	28.59	—	—	—
Transcortical sensory	2	55.50	33.23	1	91.00	—
Global	20	44.25	21.38	23	41.00	18.22

aphasia and CADL score in Holland's sample was .73. It should also be noted that Sarno, Buonaguro, and Levita (1987) found that scores for fluent (Wernicke's) and nonfluent (Broca's) aphasics on the Functional Communication Profile were highly similar after controlling for age, education, and time of onset.

A group of adult mentally retarded subjects with IQs between 50 and 80 obtained scores in the aphasic range; IQ and CADL score correlated .716 (Holland, 1980). In contrast, a group of hearing-impaired subjects (with hearing aids) showed near-normal scores (Holland, 1980).

The CADL is an excellent supplement to other aphasia examinations since it allows an estimate of the patient's communication *ability* rather than his or her *accuracy* of language. The "staged" quality of some sets of items requires a certain acting ability on the part of the examiner and may not always be successful with patients who refuse to or cannot enter into such interactions; it is not clear from the manual how this affects scores, but it is probably wise to take note of a patient's inability to follow the play-acting, and make allowance for this in the interpretation of the total score. The test should also be used with caution in apraxic patients, although it may serve as a supplementary instrument in such a population (Wertz et al., 1984).

Normative Data

Based on a total population of 130 normal adults (fluent English speakers without history of mental disorder or brain damage, and with adequate vision and hearing), the manual presents means for professionals (130.34); for self-employed, clerical, and sales- and craftspersons (128.76); for operatives, homemakers, and service personnel (128.40); and for farmers and laborers (128.76). The differences between the four groups, between institutionalized and noninstitutionalized, and between males and females were not significant. However, a slight decline with age over 65 years was significant.

REFERENCES

Behrmann, M., & Penn, C. (1984). Non-verbal communication of aphasic patients. *British Journal of Disorders of Communication, 19,* 155–168.

Holland, A. (1980). *The Communicative Abilities in Daily Living: Manual.* Austin, Tex.: Pro-Ed.

Holland, A. (1984). *Language Disorders in Adults: Recent Advances.* San Diego: College-Hill Press.

Linebaugh, C.W., Kryzer, K.M., Oden, S.E., & Myers, P.S. (1982). Reapportionment of communicative burden in aphasia. In R.H. Brookshire (Ed.), *Clinical Aphasiology: Conference Proceedings.* Minneapolis: BRK Publishers.

Pizzamiglio, L., Laicardi, C., Appicciafuoco, A., Gentili, P., Judica, A., Luglio, L., Margheriti, M., & Razzano, C. (1984). Capacita communicative di pazienti afasici in situationi di vita quotidiana: Addatamento italiano. *Archivio di psicologia neurologia e psichiatria, 45,* 187–210.

Sarno, M.T. (1969). *Functional Communication Profile.* New York: Institute of Rehabilitation Medicine.

Sarno, M.T., Buonaguro, A., & Levita, E. (1987). Aphasia in closed head injury and stroke. *Aphasiology, 1,* 331–338.

Wertz, R., LaPointe, L., & Rosenbek, J. (1984). *Apraxia of Speech in Adults.* Orlando, Fla.: Grune & Stratton.

CONTROLLED ORAL WORD ASSOCIATION (WORD FLUENCY)

Other Test Names

Other test names are Word Fluency and FAS-Test.

Purpose

The purpose of the test is the spontaneous production of words beginning with a given letter or of a given class within a limited amount of time (verbal association fluency).

Source

No specific material is required. The test is also included in the Neurosensory Center Comprehensive Examination for Aphasia (NCCEA; Spreen & Benton, 1969, 1977) distributed by the Neuropsychology Laboratory of the University of Victoria.

Description

The subject is asked to produce as many words as possible beginning with a given letter in a limited period of time. As Marshall (1986) has pointed out, the label

"Word Fluency" for this test is misleading, since verbal productivity in conversation or in continuous sentences is not measured. Instead, the test measures production of individual words under restricting search conditions (i.e., a given letter of the alphabet).

F, A, and S are the most commonly used letters for this popular test, although Benton and Hamsher (1983) use C, F, L, and P, R, W. Since the test is dependent on basic spelling skills, animal (or food) names have been used for younger children, and "things in the kitchen," "things in a store," etc., have also been used. Other versions of this test require alternating naming of colors and birds (Newcomb, 1969) or written word production (Thurstone, 1938).

Administration

Use a stopwatch and have the patient comfortably seated before giving the following instructions: **"I will say a letter of the alphabet. Then I want you to give me as many words that begin with that letter as quickly as you can. For instance, if I say 'B', you might give me 'bad', 'battle', 'bed' . . . I do not want you to use words that are proper names such as 'Boston,' 'Bob', or 'Brylcreem'. Also, do not use the same word again with a different ending such as 'eat' and 'eating'. Any questions?"** [Pause.} **"Begin when I say the letter. The first letter is 'F'. Go ahead."** Begin timing immediately.

Allow one minute for each letter (F, A, and S). Say **"Fine"** or **"Good"** after each one-minute performance. If patients discontinue before the end of the minute, encourage them to try to think of more words. If there is a silence of 15 seconds, repeat the basic instructions, and the letter. For scoring purposes, write down the actual words in the order in which they are produced.

Administer all three letters: F, A, and S.

Approximate Time for Administration

The test administration takes about five minutes.

Scoring

The score is the sum of all admissible words for the three letters. Inadmissible words produced under these instructions (i.e., proper nouns, wrong words, variations, repetitions) are not counted as correct.

Comment

Interscorer reliability is near perfect; one-year retest reliability in older adults has been reported as .70 (.7 for F, .6 for A, and .71 for S; Snow et al., 1988) and retest reliability after 19–42 days in adults as .88 (desRosiers & Kavanagh, 1987). Concurrent validity has been established in several studies, generally indicating better validity for letters than for the more concrete category names such as "food" (Coelho, 1984). Correlation with age was −.19 and with education .32; correlation with the Wechsler Adult Intelligence Scale Verbal IQ (WAIS VIQ) was .14 and with Performance IQ (PIQ) .29 (Yeudall et al., 1986). Mittenberg et al. (1989) confirm a weak correlation with age (−.14) in normal control subjects between 20 and 75 years.

The test contributed mainly to Factors 1 (reading–writing) and 6 (reading–writing–sentence construction) in a factor-analytic study with children's data (Crockett, 1974). This finding is probably due to the still developing spelling skills at that age. In adults, desRosiers and Kavanagh (1987) found that the test loaded mainly on a "verbal knowledge" factor (together with Verbal IQ and Vocabulary). In children with closed head injury, 15% of those with mild injury and 35% of those with moderate or severe injury scored below the sixth centile for age and sex (Ewing-Cobbs et al., 1987). Scores for a mixed group of 200 aphasic adults ranged from 0 to 46 with a mean of 11.5; unselected brain-damaged nonaphasic patients showed scores ranging from 5 to 46+ with a mean of 28.2 (Spreen & Benton, 1977). Adults with closed head injury had mean scores of 23.8 (desRosiers & Kavanagh, 1987), and scored at the 51st centile of the normative data for aphasics of the NCCEA (Sarno, 1986). Sarno et al. (1985) found no significant difference between male and female aphasic stroke victims nor in their rate of recovery over a two-year period.

Patients with right-hemisphere lesions did not show serious impairment on this test (Cavalli et al., 1981). Miceli et al. (1981) and Bruyer and Tuyumbu (1980) reported high sensitivity of word fluency to frontal lobe damage regardless of side of lesion, whereas Parks et al. (1988), Perret (1974), Ramier and Hecaen (1970), and Regard (1981) found more impairment in patients with left frontal lesions. Benton (1968) reported the most severe impairment for bilateral frontal lesions. Patients with left pulvinotomy showed a 45% loss in word fluency (Vilkki & Laittinen, 1976). A positron emission tomography (PET)-scan study (Parks et al., 1988) with normal volunteers indicated, however, that word fluency activates bilateral temporal and frontal lobes. Welsh et al. (1988) claim that word fluency is one of the latest of prefrontal measures to mature (i.e., it develops beyond age 12, whereas other measures attain adult level as early as age 6). Spellacy and Brown (1984) found poor word fluency (together with poor achievement test scores) to be a significant predictor of recidivism in adolescent offenders.

Adams (personal communication) did not find reduced word fluency in either Alzheimer's dementia or Huntington's disease patients; however, Alzheimer's disease patients showed more intrusion (wrong letter), perseveration (repeats), and variation (fish, fishy, fishing) errors. Miller and Hague (1975) and Murdoch et al. (1987) did find reduced word fluency in Alzheimer's disease patients, whereas

Table 7–4. Controlled Word Association: Normative Data for Males and Females Stratified by Age

		15–20 (N = 62)	21–25 (N = 73)	26–30 (N = 48)	31–40 (N = 42)	15–40 (N = 225)
				Age groups		
Males						
Oral						
"F"	M	13.82	14.99	15.65	16.83	15.15
	SD	4.36	4.37	4.42	4.04	4.41
"A"	M	12.48	13.33	13.08	14.50	13.26
	SD	3.87	4.89	3.41	3.66	4.13
"S"	M	15.87	16.63	16.54	18.10	16.67
	SD	4.52	4.97	4.70	4.89	4.80
Sum of 3 trials	M	42.17	44.95	45.27	49.43	45.08
	SD	6.82	6.29	5.34	5.61	5.90
Written						
"F"	M	13.85	14.09	14.82	15.37	14.42
	SD	3.65	3.44	3.83	3.90	3.69
"A"	M	12.06	13.22	12.62	13.83	12.88
	SD	3.24	3.47	4.03	3.57	3.57
"S"	M	14.81	15.46	15.65	16.03	15.42
	SD	3.34	3.89	3.95	3.43	3.66
Sum of 3 trials	M	40.72	42.77	43.09	45.23	42.72
	SD	6.14	6.16	6.46	6.01	6.21
Females						
Oral						
"F"	M	13.60	15.14	15.25	17.25	15.03
	SD	4.29	3.90	5.16	3.64	4.31
"A"	M	11.93	13.44	13.19	14.50	13.11
	SD	3.82	4.24	3.71	2.85	3.88
"S"	M	15.93	16.31	14.75	18.44	16.29
	SD	4.31	4.94	2.91	5.72	4.68
Sum of 3 trials	M	41.46	44.89	43.20	50.19	44.43
	SD	6.71	6.86	6.27	6.43	5.73
Written						
"F"	M	14.40	15.03	15.09	15.67	14.94
	SD	3.97	3.12	4.48	3.06	3.57
"A"	M	13.00	13.69	13.64	15.00	13.66
	SD	3.15	3.51	2.58	4.29	3.41
"S"	M	15.88	16.52	15.09	17.17	16.21
	SD	3.27	4.36	2.84	3.21	3.65
Sum of 3 trials	M	42.75	45.24	43.83	47.85	44.64
	SD	6.33	6.32	6.03	5.79	6.20

Note: Subjects in this sample had relatively high education levels. Subjects with education levels below grade 12 usually achieve 4–5 words less on the sum score.

Source: Yendall et al. (1986).

Kronfol et al. (1978) found that patients with symptoms of depression mimicking dementia showed little change in word fluency.

Normative Data

Table 7–4 presents norms for the age range 15–40 years for both oral and written production. Spreen and Benton's (1977) normative data showed considerably lower scores (mean = 33); however, these norms were based on a poorly educated/low intelligence rural sample.

Table 7–5 shows norms for oral production on the FAS test for relatively well-educated, healthy elderly persons. These norms agree closely with those produced by Montgomery and Costa (1983). Other authors have found both lower and higher decreases of productivity with age: Schaie and Parham (1977) showed an age-related drop in speeded productivity on this test beginning at age 53, and found that normal adults at age 67 showed only 74% and 60% productivity compared to age 25 in the repeated measurement and in the independent random samples, respectively. Benton et al. (1981) maintained that the test shows little decline with age up to the age of 80 if a correction of 3 points is applied to subjects over 55 years of age. They found that among subjects 80–84 years old 11% fell below the corrected mean. Montgomery and Costa (1983) also reported that 82% of their elderly sample repeated one or more words, and that 40% used "wrong words" (e.g., "phone" for F, "Susan" for S).

Normative data for an unselected group of normal learning school-children are presented in Table 7–6 (Gaddes & Crockett, 1975). These data agree closely with those published by Crockett (1974). They also agree in terms of means as well as percentile distribution with those for children with epilepsy, brain damage, and learning disability in a multidisciplinary outpatient center in Milwaukee (Hamsher, personal communication, 1980), suggesting that such impairments have relatively little influence on controlled word association performance in children.

Table 7–5. Controlled Word Association in an Elderly Sample: Number of Words Produced, Stratified by Age and Education

Age group	Education: ≤12 years					Education: ≥13 years				
	n	M	SD	Range	Cutoff[a]	n	M	SD	Range	Cutoff[a]
50–54	42	41.52	12.33	16–74	17	56	41.16	11.42	21–62	18
55–59	67	37.42	9.55	17–57	18	78	45.96	11.22	23–73	24
60–64	70	37.57	10.90	14–72	16	87	40.76	9.58	18–70	22
65–69	56	39.25	11.50	12–63	16	90	44.16	10.77	19–79	23
70–74	55	36.47	13.21	10–65	10	60	41.00	10.44	22–65	20
75+	55	35.20	11.90	20–77	11	59	39.08	14.17	14–76	11

[a]Suggested cutoff score based on (M − 2 SD) rounded to the nearest whole number.

Source: Read (1987).

Table 7–6. Controlled Word Association: Children's Norms in Percentile

Age (years)	Percentiles									
	0–10	10–20	20–30	30–40	40–50	50–60	60–70	70–80	80–90	90–100
6		1	2	3	4	5	6	7–8	9–10	11–13
7	5–6	7–9	10–11	12–13	14–15	16	17–18	19–20	21–24	25+
8	1–15	16–18	19–20	21–22	23–24	25–26	27	28–30	31–33	34+
9	1–15	16–18	19–20	21–22	23–24	25–26	27	28–30	31–33	34+
10	1–15	16–18	19–20	21–22	23–24	25–26	27	28–30	31–33	34+
11	1–21	22–24	25–26	27–28	29–30	31–32	33–34	35–37	38–40	41+
12	1–21	22–24	25–26	27–28	29–30	31–32	33–34	35–37	38–40	41+
13	1–21	22–24	25–26	27–28	29–30	31–32	33–34	35–37	38–40	41+

Source: Gaddes & Crockett (1975).

Table 7–7. Performance of Normal School Children on Naming of Animals, Foods, and Words Beginning with "sh"

Age (years)	N	Animals		Foods		"Sh words"	
		M	SD	M	SD	M	SD
6	34	10.74	2.4	9.74	3.3	4.24	1.6
7	40	12.43	2.9	11.88	2.7	5.53	1.6
8	32	12.31	2.7	11.11	3.4	5.21	2.1
9	38	13.76	3.7	14.05	3.9	5.95	2.4
10	22	14.27	3.7	13.97	2.2	6.00	2.0
11	28	15.50	3.8	14.80	4.6	6.28	2.4
12	10	18.90	6.2	17.70	4.0	6.10	1.8

Source: Halperin et al. (1989).

Table 7–8. Animal-Name Fluency in Elderly Persons:
Number of Words Produced, Stratified by Age and Education

Age group (years)	Education: ≤12 years					Education: ≥13 years				
	n	M	SD	Range	Cutoff[a]	n	M	SD	Range	Cutoff[a]
50–54	42	18.64	4.06	8–33	11	56	19.98	4.08	13–32	12
55–59	67	18.81	3.83	9–31	11	78	20.88	5.14	9–34	11
60–64	70	18.61	4.49	10–30	10	87	19.97	5.00	10–31	10
65–69	56	17.75	4.02	11–29	10	90	19.13	5.01	8–35	9
70–74	55	16.35	4.36	4–28	8	60	18.28	3.58	13–28	11
75+	55	15.09	4.25	2–26	7	59	17.07	4.93	8–27	7

[a]Suggested cutoff score based on (M − 2 SD) rounded to the nearest whole number.

Source: Read (1987).

Since other word fluency tasks may occasionally be more appropriate, especially for younger children, we have included fluency for animal names, foods, and words beginning with "sh" in Table 7–7. In the animal name fluency test the subject is asked to name as many animals as possible within one minute. The scoring procedure remains the same. Animal name fluency for elderly persons is shown in Table 7–8. Table 7–9 presents norms for *written* word fluency in children.

Table 7–9. Children's Written Word Fluency

Age	Total			Female			Male		
	N	M	SD	N	M	SD	N	M	SD
6	80	9.28	4.47	40	9.85	4.58	40	8.70	4.33
7	133	15.87	8.22	72	17.22	8.20	61	14.26	8.00
8	197	21.52	9.29	85	23.72	10.34	112	19.85	8.05
9	208	25.93	10.18	90	28.41	9.93	118	24.03	10.01
10	189	29.98	11.92	86	33.16	11.83	103	27.32	11.39
11	146	37.08	11.98	75	39.03	10.57	71	35.01	13.07
12	140	40.58	13.00	84	44.52	12.98	56	34.61	10.61
13	167	45.07	14.10	76	51.37	13.65	91	39.81	12.26
14	175	48.46	14.72	85	52.64	14.30	90	44.52	14.08
15	120	47.35	15.22	51	51.57	13.28	69	44.23	15.88
16	69	48.28	13.69	28	53.43	10.54	41	44.76	14.56
17	79	49.65	17.51	37	53.65	17.63	42	46.12	16.83
18	30	61.47	15.29	18	64.22	14.98	12	57.33	15.42

Note: This test requires the subject to write as many words as possible beginning with the letter "s" in five minutes, and as many four-letter words as possible beginning with the letter "c" in four minutes. Means are totals for both sets of responses.

Source: Kolb & Wishaw (1985).

REFERENCES

Benton, A.L. (1968). Differential behavioral effects in frontal lobe disease. *Neuropsychologia, 6,* 53–60.

Benton, A.L., Eslinger, P.J., & Damasio, A.R. (1981). Normative observations on neuropsychological test performances in old age. *Journal of Clinical Neuropsychology, 3,* 33–42.

Benton, A.L., & Hamsher, K. (1983). *Multilingual Aphasia Examination.* Iowa City: AJA Associates.

Bruyer, R., & Tuyumbu, B. (1980). Fluence verbale et lésions du cortex cérébrale: Performances et types d'erreurs. Encéphale, *6,* 287–297.

Cavalli, M., De Renzi, E., Faglioni, P., & Vitale, A. (1981). Impairment of right brain-damaged patients on a linguistic cognitive task. *Cortex, 17,* 545–556.

Coelho, C.A. (1984). Word fluency measures in three groups of brain injured subjects. Paper presented at the Meeting of the American Speech–Language–Hearing Association, San Francisco.

Crockett, D.J. (1974). Component analysis of within correlations of language-skill tests in normal children. *Journal of Special Education, 8,* 361–375.

desRosiers, G., & Kavanagh, D. (1987). Cognitive assessment in closed head injury: Stability, validity and parallel forms for two neuropsychological measures of recovery. *International Journal of Clinical Neuropsychology, 9,* 162–173.

Ewing-Cobbs, L., Levin, H.S., Eisenberg, H.M., & Fletcher, J.M. (1987). Language functions following closed-head injury in children and adolescents. *Journal of Clinical and Experimental Neuropsychology, 9,* 575–592.

Gaddes, W.H., & Crockett, D.J. (1975). The Spreen–Benton aphasia tests: Normative data as a measure of normal language development. *Brain and Language, 2,* 257–280.

Halperin, J.M., Zeitchik, E., Healy, J.M., Weinstein, L., & Ludman, W.L. (1989). The development of linguistic and mnestic abilities in normal children. *Journal of Clinical and Experimental Neuropsychology, 11,* 518–528.

Kolb, B., & Wishaw, I.Q. (1985). *Fundamentals of Human Neuropsychology* (2nd ed., pp. 436, 741). New York: W.H. Freeman.

Kronfol, Z., Hamsher, K., Digre, K., & Waziri, R. (1978). Depression and hemispheric function changes associated with unilateral ECT. *British Journal of Psychiatry, 132,* 560–567.

Marshall, J.C. (1986). The description and interpretation of aphasic language disorder. *Neuropsychologia, 24,* 5–24.

Miceli, G., Caltagirone, C., Gainotti, G., Masullo, C., & Silveri, M.C. (1981). Neuropsychological correlates of localized cerebral lesions in non-aphasic brain-damaged patients. *Journal of Clinical Neuropsychology, 3,* 53–63.

Miller, E. & Hague, F. (1975). Some characteristics of verbal behaviour in presenile dementia. *Psychological Medicine, 5,* 255–259.

Mittenberg, W., Seidenberg, M., O'Leary, D.S., & DiGiulio, D.V. (1989). Changes in cerebral functioning associated with normal aging. *Journal of Clinical and Experimental Neuropsychology, 11,* 918–932.

Montgomery, K. & Costa, L. (1983). Neuropsychological test performance of a normal elderly sample. Paper presented at the Meeting of the International Neuropsychological Society, Mexico City.

Murdoch, B.E., Chenery, H.J., Wilks, V., & Boyle, R.S. (1987). Language disorders in dementia of the Alzheimer type. *Brain and Language, 31,* 122–137.

Newcombe, F. (1969). *Missile Wounds of the Brain.* New York: Oxford University Press.

Parks, R.W., Loewenstein, D.A., Dodrill, K.L., Barker, W.W., Yoshii, F., Chang, J.Y., Emran, A., Apicella, A., Sheramata, W.A., & Duara, R. (1988). Cerebral metabolic effects of a verbal fluency test: A PET scan study. *Journal of Clinical and Experimental Neuropsychology, 10,* 565–575.

Perret, E. (1974). The left frontal lobe of man and the suppression of habitual responses in verbal categorial behavior. *Neuropsychologia, 12,* 323–330.

Ramier, A.-M., & Hecaen, H. (1970). Role réspectif des attaintes frontales et la latéralisation lésionelle dans les déficits de la "fluence verbale." *Revue Neurologique (Paris), 123,* 17–22.

Read, D.E. (1987). Neuropsychological assessment of memory in early dementia: Normative data for a new battery of memory tests. Unpublished manuscript, University of Victoria, British Columbia.

Regard, M. (1981). Cognitive rigidity and flexibility, a neuropsychological study. Ph.D. dissertation. University of Victoria, British Columbia.

Sarno, M.T. (1986). Verbal impairment in head injury. *Archives of Physical and Medical Rehabilitation, 67,* 400–405.

Sarno, M.T., Buonaguro, A., & Levita, E. (1985). Gender and recovery from aphasia after stroke. *Journal of Nervous and Mental Disease, 173,* 605–609.

Schaie, K.W., & Parham, I.A. (1977). Cohort-sequential analyses of adult intellectual development. *Developmental Psychology, 13,* 649–653.

Snow, W.G., Tierney, M.C., Zorzitto, M.L., Fisher, R.H., & Reid, D.W. (1988). One-year test–retest reliability of selected tests in older adults. Paper presented at the Meeting of the International Neuropsychological Society, New Orleans.

Spellacy, F.J., & Brown, W. G. (1984). Prediction of recidivism in young offenders after brief institutionalization. *Journal of Clinical Psychology, 40,* 1070–1074.

Spreen, O., & Benton, A.L. (1969). Neurosensory Center Comprehensive Examination for Aphasia (NCCEA). Victoria: University of Victoria, Neuropsychological Laboratory.

Spreen, O., & Benton, A.L. (1977). *Neurosensory Center Comprehensive Examination for Aphasia (NCCEA).* (Revised edition). Victoria: University of Victoria, Neuropsychology Laboratory.

Thurstone, L.L. (1938). *Primary Mental Abilities.* Chicago: University of Chicago Press.

Vilkki, J., & Laittinen, L.V. (1976). Effects of pulvinotomy and ventrolateral thalamotomy on some cognitive functions. *Neuropsychologia, 14,* 67–78.

Welsh, M.C., Groisser, D., & Pennington, B.F. (1988). A normative–developmental study of measures hypothesized to tap prefrontal functioning. *Journal of Clinical and Experimental Neuropsychology, 10,* 79.

Yeudall, L.T., Fromm, D., Reddon, J.R., & Stefanyk, W.O. (1986). Normative data stratified by age and sex for 12 neuropsychological tests. *Journal of Clinical Psychology, 42,* 918–946.

NEUROSENSORY CENTER COMPREHENSIVE EXAMINATION FOR APHASIA (NCCEA)

Purpose

The purpose of this test is to provide a detailed evaluation of language abilities including reading, writing, and basic articulatory, visual, and tactile skills.

Source

The test can be ordered from the University of Victoria Neuropsychology Laboratory, P.O. Box 1700, Victoria, British Columbia V8W 3P4, Canada. The complete set, including manual, answer booklets, profile forms, tape, photos of object trays, set of 20 tokens, and stimulus cards for reading and form perception, costs $70.00 Cdn. Note that the trays and the actual objects as well as a covering screen must be purchased by the user to match the objects in the photographs.

Description

This test, originally developed by Spreen and Benton (1965) at the Neurosensory Center of the University of Iowa, was revised in 1969 and 1977; three item substitutions were made in 1987. For several of the subtests, actual objects are used which are displayed on trays. The test consists of 20 subtests and four control tests (see Administration, below). A distinctive feature of the test is the use of four sets of eight actual objects, equivalent in difficulty, rather than pictures, and the provision for constructing profiles of directly comparable percentile scores, corrected for age and education, across all 20 subtests. Subtests 5 (Sentence Repetition), 8 (Word Fluency), and 11 (Token Test) have been described in separate sections of this book since they are often administered as separate tests, and therefore, they will not be discussed here. The remaining subtests are described in the following subsections; scoring instructions for each subtest together with a sample recording sheet are included. The use of the aphasia profiles will be discussed under Normative Data at the end of the NCCEA section.

Language Tests

Test 1. Visual Naming (VN) [Trays A and B}

Administration. Present Tray A to the patient in such a way that he or she can see all of the objects without difficulty. Point to the first object (comb) listed on the answer sheet and say: "**I want you to tell me the names of these objects. What is this? Tell me the name of it.**" If the patient shows any apparent difficulty in seeing the object, the examiner may take it out of the tray and hold it up for closer inspection. However, do not allow the patient to touch the objects.

If the patient responds by giving the use of the object (e.g., "for combing hair," "for eating"), repeat instructions. If the patient responds with a generic term or a partially correct name (e.g., "silver" for spoon, "jewelry" for ring), ask the patient to give the exact name. In formulating the question, the examiner may utilize the information given in the patient's first response but must scrupulously avoid giving additional cues (e.g., the patient may say, "What is the full name of this? What kind of silver? What kind of jewelry?"). Do not ask further questions if the patient fails to improve his or her response after the first question.

The eight objects of Tray A are presented. The subtest is terminated if the patient shows either complete success or complete failure—that is, if he or she names all eight objects correctly or fails to name at least one object. If the patient makes 1–7 errors in naming the objects of Tray A, the eight objects of Tray B are presented. Thus Subtest 1 may consist of 8 or 16 items, depending upon the level of the patient's performance on Tray A.

Scoring. Detailed recording of the patient's responses is essential. The criteria for scoring and the notations to be made on the answer sheet (Fig. 7–1) are as follows: Give a score of 1 point for each correct response (i.e., those names listed on the answer sheet). Slang or childish words (e.g., "pinchers" for tweezers) are generally not acceptable. Record verbatim any incorrect response made before the correct name is produced. Make a notation, "d," if the response is delayed (i.e., produced only after five or more seconds). Spontaneously corrected misnamings are counted as correct responses. Poor articulation is disregarded as long as the word is clearly

Sample Score Sheet 7–1.
Test 1. VN–Visual Naming

(Give A. If between 1 and 7 errors occur, give B.)

Tray A	Response	Error Type	Score
comb			
ring			
key			
cup			
ashtray			
thimble			
padlock			
paper clip			
		Total A	

Tray B	Response	Error Type	Score
knife			
fork			
bottle, baby bottle			
shoelace, shoestring			
brush			
jar			
can opener, bottle opener			
tweezers			
		Total B	
		Total A & B	

Figure 7–1. NCCEA Subtest 1 (Visual Naming) sample scoring sheet.

recognizable and offers no possibility for misinterpretation. For example, "pate" for plate is acceptable, but "pape" is not; "tweeser" for tweezers is acceptable, but "stevers" is not. Incorrect responses of this type are noted as "PP" (phonemic paraphasia). Admittedly, there is a subjective element in the judgment of the examiner on this point. The guiding principle here should be whether or not a naïve observer hearing the patient's utterance would immediately know which object is being named.

Give a score of 0 for each incorrect response (no response, unrecognizable response, "don't know" response, perseveration, misnaming). Misnamings that are semantically related to the object (e.g., shaver for razor, globe for light bulb, pencil for pen, hair for comb, knife for spoon) are noted as "SP" (semantic paraphasia). If the patient indicates recognition of the incorrectness of his or her response, write "no" after the misnaming.

If the patient misnames in response to questioning of a partially correct response, score a misnaming (e.g., patient says "wire" in naming the paper clip and, when questioned, responds with "brush"). If both a misnaming and a "don't know" response are given, score as a misnaming and write "no" after it.

The Total Score for Tray A is multiplied by 2 if only the first eight items were presented. There are no corrections for age and educational level for performance on this subtest. Maximum score = 16.

TEST 2. DESCRIPTION OF USE (DU) [TRAYS C AND D]

Administration. Present the first object of Tray C. **"What do you use this for? What do you do with it?"** Do not allow the patient to touch objects. If the patient does not understand the instructions, take an object that is *not* on the tray (e.g., button on the examiner's coat), give the correct answer, and demonstrate its use at the same time (e.g., button the coat and say, "For keeping the coat closed, for buttoning the coat," etc.). If the patient responds by giving a partially correct response (e.g., light bulb "on the ceiling"), the examiner should ask for more details; in formulating questions, the examiner may use the information given in the patient's response but should avoid giving additional cues (e.g., the examiner may say, "What do you do with it on the ceiling?"). Do not ask further questions if the patient fails to improve his or her response after the first question.

All objects of Tray C are given. If 1–7 errors occur, all objects of Tray D are also administered.

Scoring. Record verbatim. The responses listed on the answer sheet (Fig. 7–2) and all responses that contain essentially the same information are scored as correct. Score 1 point for every item for which a correct description of use is given. Grammatical errors are disregarded. Multiply the score by 2 if only Tray C has been given. No corrections for age and educational level are applied in this test. Maximum score = 16.

Sample Score Sheet 7–2.
Test 2. DU–Description of Use

Tray C	Response	Score
shooting, playing		
eating		
screw it in a socket, light a room, see with it		
turn screws		
wipe, clean & soap		
measure		
season food, salt and/or pepper food		
plug into socket, use electricity		
Total C		

Tray D	Response	Score
see what time it is, tell time		
to see, read		
eating		
shaving		
light fire, cigarette, etc.		
send letter in, mail		
write		
stick, glue together, patch up		
Total D		
Total C & D		

Figure 7–2. NCCEA Subtest 2 (Description of Use) sample scoring sheet.

TEST 3. TACTILE NAMING, RIGHT HAND (TNR) [TRAYS A AND B]

Administration. Objects are presented by placing them firmly into the patient's hand under a rectangular box which is covered by a curtain on the side of the patient and which is open at the side of the examiner. **"Now I want you to put your right hand behind this curtain. I will give you an object, and I want you to feel it and tell me what it is. Handle it and feel it from all sides, but do not try to look at it."** With some apprehensive patients it is advisable to explain that the screen merely hides the object from view (demonstrate by showing the back of the box.)

The eight objects of Tray A are presented. The test is terminated if the patient shows either complete success or failure (i.e., if he or she names all eight objects correctly or fails to name at least one object correctly). If the patient makes 1–7 errors in naming the objects of Tray A, the eight objects of Tray B are presented. Thus Test 3 may consist of eight or 16 items, depending upon the level of the patient's performance on Tray A.

Scoring. Detailed recording of the patient's responses is essential, especially in the case of spontaneous corrections. The criteria for scoring and the notations to be made on the answer sheet (Fig. 7–3) are as follows: Give a score of 1 point for each correct response (i.e., those names given on the record sheet). Follow the detailed scoring rules described for Test 1 (Visual Naming).

If the patient fails to name an object correctly, but is able to identify the object clearly by a description of use, by "idiosyncratic" responses (e.g., "shaver" for razor, also "pencil" for pen *if this response was used in visual naming*), or by

---

Sample Score Sheet 7–3
Test 3. TNR–Tactile Naming, Right Hand

(Give Tray A. If between 1 and 7 errors occur, give Tray B.)

Tray A	Response	Error Type	Score
comb			
ring			
key			
cup			
ashtray			
thimble			
padlock			
paper clip			
		Total A	

Tray B	Response	Error Type	Score
knife			
fork			
bottle, baby bottle			
shoelace, shoestring			
brush			
jar			
can opener, bottle opener			
tweezers			
		Total B	
		Total A & B	

Figure 7–3. NCCEA Subtest 3 (Tactile Naming, Right Hand) sample scoring sheet.

gestures, check under Remarks and note the response verbatim. This additional score assesses tactile recognition and determines whether additional control tests (C1 and C2) should be given, as described later in this section.

Incorrect responses or mispronunciations should be noted verbatim in the Response column. The score should be multiplied by 2 if only the eight items of Tray A have been administered. No corrections for age or education are applied to this test. Maximum score = 16.

TEST 4. TACTILE NAMING, LEFT HAND (TNL) [TRAYS C AND D]

Administration. Repeat the procedure as in Test 3 for the left hand with objects of Tray C. If errors occur, use objects of Tray D.

Scoring. Score as described for Test 3. For sample score sheet, see Figure 7–4.

Sample Score Sheet 7–4
Test 4. TNL – Tactile Naming, Left Hand

Tray C	Response	Error Type	Score
pistol, gun			
plate, saucer, dish			
bulb, light bulb			
screw driver			
sponge			
ruler			
shaker, salt, pepper			
plug			
		Total C	

Tray D	Response	Error Type	Score
watch			
eyeglasses, glasses			
spoon			
razor			
matchbook, matches			
envelope			
pen, ballpoint			
scotch tape, tape			
		Total D	
		Total C & D	

Figure 7–4. NCCEA Subtest 4 (Tactile Naming, Left Hand) sample scoring sheet.

TEST 6. REPETITION OF DIGITS (DRF)

Administration. This test is administered according to the procedure of Benton and Blackburn (1957). Present the digits by tape. Start with Trial 1 of the three-digit series for all subjects. **"You will hear some numbers on the loudspeaker. Listen carefully, and when the speaker is finished, repeat the numbers just as you heard them."**

Give Trials I and II of each series, *even if the patient passes the first trial.* If the patient fails both trials of a series, proceed with the first trial of the next series. If the patient passes this trial, proceed with the second trial and then with the next series accordingly. Discontinue after failure on three consecutive trials.

Scoring. Give a score of 1 point for each trial passed. Maximum raw score = 14. Before entering these scores on the profile sheet (Fig. 7–5), apply the following corrections for both age and educational level, even if the raw score is 0.

Age	Correction
40–55	+1
56+	+2

Education	Correction
16+	−2
12–15	−1
10–11	0
6–9	+1
≤5	+2

Maximum corrected score = 18

The percentile ranks in the profiles are based on taped presentation. If digits have been presented orally, the scores are not applicable. In general, scores from oral administration will be approximately 1 raw score point higher than from the taped presentation, as shown by a recent comparative study in our laboratory.

TEST 7. REVERSAL OF DIGITS (DRR)

Administration. This test is also administered according to the procedure described by Benton and Blackburn (1957). Present the digits by tape. Start with Trial I of the two-digit series for all subjects. **"Now you will hear some more numbers, but this time when the speaker stops, I want you to say them backwards. For example, if you hear '7–1', what would you say?"** If the patient responds correctly, say: **"Here are some others."** If the patient fails the first example, correct the patient and give a second example, saying: **"Remember you**

```
Sample Score Sheet 7–5
Test 6. Repetition of Digits
```

(Record actual performance)

Digits forward	Score
5-8-2	3
6-9-4	3
6-4-3-9	4
7-2-8-6	4
4-2-7-3-1	5
7-5-8-3-6	5
6-1-9-4-7-3	6
3-9-2-4-8-7	6
5-9-1-7-4-2-8	7
4-1-7-9-3-8-6	7
5-8-1-9-2-6-4-7	8
3-8-2-9-5-1-7-4	8
2-7-5-8-6-2-5-8-4	9
7-1-3-9-4-2-5-6-8	9

SCORE	
CORRECTION	
CORRECTED SCORE	

Figure 7–5. NCCEA Subtest 6 (Repetition of Digits) sample scoring sheet.

are to say them backwards: '4–9'." After the patient's response, say: "**Here are some others,**" and start the tape. Proceed as outlined for Test 6. Discontinue after three consecutive failures.

Scoring. Give a score of 1 point for each trial passed (Fig. 7–6). Maximum score = 14. Before entering the scores into the profile sheet, apply the corrections shown:

Age	Correction
40–55	+1
56+	+2

Education	Correction
16	−2
12–15	−1
10–11	0
6–9	+1
≤5	+2

Maximum corrected score = 18

Sample Score Sheet 7–6
Test 7. DRR–Reversal of Digits

(Record actual performance)

Digits backward	Score
2-4	2
5-8	2
6-2-9	3
4-1-5	3
3-2-7-9	4
4-9-6-8	4
1-5-2-8-6	5
6-1-8-4-3	5
5-3-9-4-1-8	6
7-2-4-8-5-6	6
8-1-2-9-3-6-5	7
4-7-3-9-1-2-8	7
9-4-3-7-6-2-5-8	8
7-2-8-1-9-6-5-3	8
TOTAL SCORE	
CORRECTION	
TOTAL CORRECTED SCORE	

Figure 7–6. NCCEA Subtest 7 (Reversal of Digits) sample scoring sheet.

TEST 9. SENTENCE CONSTRUCTION (SC)

Administration. Say: "**I would like you to make up a sentence using the two words I will give you. The sentence may be short or long; just be sure it contains each word I give you. For example, If I say 'water – pool', you might say 'The water is in the pool'. Ready? 'snow – boy'. Give me a sentence with the words 'snow' and 'boy'.**"

Repeat instructions if necessary, but give no further demonstrations or help. Note the time in seconds, beginning after the presentation of each set of words. If a patient's response does not contain both words, repeat the respective set once again. In this case, the time measurement includes the first and the second attempt as well as the repetition of the words:

1. snow – boy
2. hot – summer

After these tasks, say: "**Now make a sentence with these three words**":

3. bridge – walk – man
4. hair – water – girl
5. drive – street – car

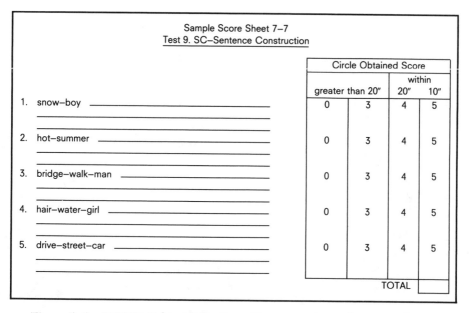

Sample Score Sheet 7–7
Test 9. SC–Sentence Construction

		Circle Obtained Score		
		greater than 20″	within 20″	10″
1. snow–boy		0	3	4	5
2. hot–summer		0	3	4	5
3. bridge–walk–man		0	3	4	5
4. hair–water–girl		0	3	4	5
5. drive–street–car		0	3	4	5
				TOTAL	

Figure 7–7. NCCEA Subtest 9 (Sentence Construction) sample scoring sheet.

Scoring. Any complete grammatically correct and meaningful sentence is given a credit of 3 points (see Fig. 7–7). The words need not be used in the order of presentation. Appropriate articles, prepositions, and adjectives must be included. Change of tense or person is accepted as a correct response. "Grammatically correct" should be interpreted liberally. For example, "ain't" is generally accepted, as is "good" for "well" in most instances, but omission of essential parts of speech (telegram style) is not. One-point credit is added if a sentence is completed within 20 seconds. Two points are added if the sentence is completed within 10 seconds. No corrections for age or educational level are necessary. Maximum score = 25.

TEST 10. IDENTIFICATION BY NAME (IN) [TRAYS A AND B]

Administration. Objects are presented on the tray, which is placed within easy reach of the patient. **"I would like you to point to the objects that I name. Which one is the comb? Point to the comb."** If the patient has difficulty in understanding the instructions, guide his or her hand to the tray and point with index finger at objects (but do not point at a specific object), repeating the word **"comb."** All words may be repeated once if the patient requests it or if the patient does not seem to understand the word. *Do not allow the patient to handle the objects.*

238

Sample Score Sheet 7–8
Test 10. IN–Identification by Name

(Give A. If between 1 and 7 errors occur, give B.)

Tray A	Response	Error Type	Score
comb			
ring			
key			
cup			
ashtray			
thimble			
padlock			
paper clip			
		Total A	

Tray B	Response	Error Type	Score
knife			
fork			
bottle, baby bottle			
shoelace, shoestring			
brush			
jar			
can opener, bottle opener			
tweezers			
		Total B	
		Total A & B	

Figure 7–8. NCCEA Subtest 10 (Identification by Name) sample scoring sheet.

Administer all objects of Tray A. If 1–7 errors occur, present all objects of Tray B.

Scoring. A score of 1 point is given for each item identified correctly (see Fig. 7–8). No correction for age or educational level is made. The obtained raw score is multiplied by 2 if only one tray has been administered. Maximum score = 16.

TEST 12. ORAL READING, NAMES (RNO)

Administration. Present the reading cards one at a time. Say: **"Read this aloud."** Instruction may be repeated. This test does not have a simple pass–fail score, and

```
┌─────────────────────────────────────────────────────────────────┐
│                    Sample Score Sheet 7–9                         │
│                 Test 12. RNO–Oral Reading (Names)                 │
│  (Give Set 1. If between 1 and 4 errors occur, give Set 2.)       │
│                                                                   │
└─────────────────────────────────────────────────────────────────┘
```

Set 1	Response	Score
pistol		
bulb		
screwdriver		
sponge		
plug		
	TOTAL SET 1	

Set 2	Response	Score
watch		
razor		
matches		
envelope		
scotch tape		
	TOTAL SET 2	
	TOTAL SETS 1 & 2	

Figure 7–9. NCCEA Subtest 12 [Oral Reading (Names)] sample scoring sheet.

the 0-1-2 scoring system (see below) must be applied during the actual administration.

If 1–4 errors occur on the first set of five cards, present the second set. The test may be discontinued after three consecutive incorrect responses.

Scoring. Score 2 points for every word pronounced correctly (see Fig. 7–9). If the word is mispronounced but is intelligible, score 1 point. Score 0 for unintelligible or incorrect responses. If the test has been discontinued because of three consecutive failures, the subsequent items receive a score of 0. Multiply the score by 2 if only one tray has been given. No correction for age or educational level is applied to this test. Maximum score = 20.

TEST 13. ORAL READING, SENTENCES (RSO)[READING CARDS, TOKENS]/
TEST 15. READING SENTENCES FOR MEANING, POINTING (RSP)[TOKENS]

Administration. Tests 13 and 15 are administered simultaneously. Display tokens in front of the patient in the order shown in Table 7–10. Present the first reading card and say: **"Read this aloud, then do what it says on the card."** If necessary, this

Table 7–10.   Display Arrangement for Tokens in Tests 13 and 15

Row 1 Large circles: red, blue, yellow, white, green
Row 2 Large squares: blue, red, white, green, yellow
Row 3 Small circles: white, blue, yellow, red, green
Row 4 Small squares: yellow, green, red, blue, white

instruction may be repeated or elaborated during the course of the test. If reading aloud presents serious difficulties, the patient should be permitted to read silently and perform all commands first; cards may then be presented again with the instruction to read aloud.

Either test may be discontinued after three consecutive failures to make a response.

Scoring.

Test 13. Score 2 points for every sentence read correctly. Articulation errors are disregarded. A single misread word if spontaneously corrected, is not counted as an error. Score 1 point if two or more mispronunciations or one other error (e.g., word substitution, unintelligible response, or omission) occurs. Score 0 for two or more errors other than spontaneously corrected misreadings. Maximum score = 16.

Test 15. The same answer sheet is used (see Fig. 7–10). Score 1 point for each part of a question performed correctly; that is, a correct performance on questions 1 and 2 receives 1 credit each; a correct performance on questions 9 through 12 ("small, white circle") receives 3 credits each. Maximum score = 17.

No corrections for age and educational level are necessary for Tests 13 and 15.

TEST 14. READING NAMES FOR MEANING, POINTING (RNP)
[TRAYS A AND B]

Administration. For the convenience of the examiner, this test may be administered after Test 12. Put Tray A in front of the patient and present the five reading cards, one at a time. Say: **"Show me this object."** This instruction may be repeated once.

```
                         Sample Score Sheet 7–10
                    Test 13. RSO–Oral Reading (Sentences)

                Test 15. Reading Sentences for Meaning (Pointing)

                                           Test 13         Test 15
          1.  Show me a circle
          2.  Show me a square
          3.  Show me a small circle
          4.  Show me a yellow square
          5.  Show me a white square
          6.  Show me a small white circle
          7.  Show me a large yellow square
          8.  Show me a small blue square
                                    TOTAL
```

Figure 7–10. NCCEA Subtest 13 [Oral Reading, Sentences)] and Subtest 15 [Reading Sentences for Meaning (Pointing)] sample scoring sheet.

If 1–4 errors occur, all cards with names of objects on Tray B should be presented. However, the test may be discontinued at any time after three consecutive incorrect responses.

Scoring. Score 1 point for every correct identification (see Fig. 7–11). If the test has been discontinued, subsequent items receive a score of 0. Multiply the score by 2 if only one set of cards has been given. No correction for age or educational level is applied to this test. Maximum score = 10.

TEST 16. VISUAL–GRAPHIC NAMING (VGN)/
TEST 17. WRITING OF NAMES (WN)

Administration. Give the patient a sheet of unruled paper and a pencil. Present the first object of Tray C. Do not handle it in any way that would indicate its use. Do not let the patient handle it. Say: **"Write the name of this object."** Encourage partial responses. If the patient wants to correct his or her response or if the word is completely illegible, instruct the patient to rewrite the word. Indicate the first attempts with brackets. Do not permit erasures. If the patient writes a word other than the first one given on the answer sheet, supply the preferred word and ask the patient to write it as well. Discontinue after three complete failures (i.e., 0 scores on Test 17).

If the patient does not respond within 30 seconds, and name-finding difficulties are suspected, supply the name and ask the patient to write it. Note that the word was supplied.

Sample Score Sheet 7–11
Test 14. RNP–Reading Names for Meaning (Pointing)

(Give Set A. If between 1 and 4 errors occur, give Set B).

Tray A	Response	Score
comb		
ring		
cup		
ashtray		
padlock		
	TOTAL A	

Tray B	Response	Score
knife		
bottle		
brush		
shoelace		
tweezers		
	TOTAL B	

Figure 7–11. NCCEA Subtest 14 [Reading Names for Meaning (Pointing)] sample scoring sheet.

If motor impairment does not permit the patient to write down with his or her preferred hand, encourage the patient to use the nondominant hand. If writing is impossible with either hand, the following substitute task may be given.

Block Letter Spelling. Present the following 13 block letters (from a set of "Scrabble") in alphabetical order: C E G I L N O P P R R S U. Present the ring, cup, sponge, ruler, and plug from Trays A and C one at a time and ask the patient to spell the name of each. If the patient does not recall the name, supply it, recording this fact as described above. Restore the alphabetical order of block letters after each response. Record the response exactly. Spelling with block letters is a substitute task that does not produce a score comparable to the written naming score of this test. The interpretation of performance is on an impressionistic basis and should be done with caution.

Scoring.

Test 16. A score of 1 point is given for each object named correctly by writing (see Fig. 7–12). Spelling errors, reversal of letters, and other writing errors are disregarded as long as the responses are intelligible. Phonetic spelling (e.g., "scicer" or "sissors" for scissors, "ruller," "Srw drive," etc.) is also accepted. Give no credit

Sample Score Sheet 7–12

Test 16. VGN–Visual–Graphic Naming			Test 17. WN–Writing of Names

(S should write the first word listed. If S writes an alternate word, he or she should then be asked to write the first word.)

Tray C	Test 16	Check if Name Supplied	Test 17
gun, pistol, revolver			
plate, saucer, dish			
bulb, light bulb			
screwdriver			
sponge			
ruler			
shaker, salt/pepper			
plug			
TOTAL SCORE			
		CORRECTION	
		TOTAL CORRECTED SCORE	

Figure 7–12. NCCEA Subtest 16 (Visual–Graphic Naming) and Subtest 17 (Writing of Names) sample scoring sheet.

for words supplied by the examiner. No correction for age and education is made on Test 16. Maximum score = 8.

Test 17. This test is a rescoring of the graphic responses of Test 16 in terms of adequacy of writing. All eight items of Tray C are scored, irrespective of whether the name was produced spontaneously or after prompting.

Score 3 points for every correct name spelled correctly (see Fig. 7–12). Compound words (e.g., egg beater, salt shaker, etc.) are acceptable if spelled as one or two words or with a hyphen. Score 2 points for words containing one spelling error; score 1 point for words with two spelling errors. Score 0 for words that are incomplete or unrecognizable, and for words with more than two spelling errors (a reversal of two letters is scored as two spelling errors). Maximum raw score = 24.

No correction for age is made. The following corrections for educational level should be made before the scores for Test 17 are entered into the profile sheet:

Education	Correction
≥8 years	0
7 years	+2
≤5 years	+4

Maximum corrected score = 28

TEST 18. WRITING TO DICTATION (WD)

Administration. Give the patient a sheet of unruled paper and a pencil. Ask the patient to write his or her name first. **"We will do some more writing now. Write down what I say."** Dictate the following text slowly one sentence at a time. Repeat parts of the text (word by word, if necessary) if the patient requests it or if it becomes obvious that the patient has missed some of the text. Do not give any aid in spelling. If the patient says that he or she does not know how to spell a given word, say: **"Just write it down as you hear it. It is not important that the spelling of every word be correct."**

Dictation text:
This is a very nice day.
This brick building was built last year.

This test may be discontinued if the patient cannot write the first four words in a recognizable manner (i.e., 0 score).

Scoring. Score 1 point for every word correctly spelled and legible. Legibility is judged generously, particularly in patients with motor disability. If the letter remains recognizable, disregard angular distortions, small additional movements, omission of *i*-dots, corrections, "dashing" (i.e., almost straight lines for lower-case letters with approximate allowance of space as in hasty writing), consistent "idio-syncratic" forms (i.e., looping, fancy strokes, failure to capitalize the first letter of a sentence).

Score $\frac{1}{2}$ point for words that are correct except for one additional up- and downstroke and for words within a sentence beginning with a capital letter. These capitalizations should be scored as $\frac{1}{2}$ point only if the capitalization is clearly recognizable. If all letters are capitalized, give a score of $\frac{1}{2}$ point for each word.

Score 0 for illegible, incomplete, or otherwise incorrect words (e.g., letter reversals, additions, and word substitutions).

Subtract 1 point for any duplicated or added words after all correctly written words are counted (see Fig. 7–13). Maximum raw score = 13.

Before the score is entered into the profile sheet, the following corrections must be applied.

Education	Correction: ≤49 years	Correction: 50+ years
<7 years	+2	+1
7–8 years	+1	+1
>8 years	0	+1

Maximum corrected score = 15

```
┌─────────────────────────────────────────────────────────────────────────┐
│                         Sample Score Sheet 7–13                           │
│                      Test 18. WD–Writing to Dictation                     │
│                                                            Score          │
│  ┌─────────────────────────────────────────────────────┬───────────────┐ │
│  │ This is a very nice day                             │               │ │
│  ├─────────────────────────────────────────────────────┼───────────────┤ │
│  │ This brick building was built last year.           │               │ │
│  ├─────────────────────────────────────┬───────────────┼───────────────┤ │
│                                  TOTAL SCORE            │               │ │
│                                     CORRECTION          │               │ │
│                       TOTAL CORRECTED SCORE             │               │ │
└─────────────────────────────────────────────────────────────────────────┘
```

Figure 7–13. NCCEA Subtest 18 (Writing to Dictation) sample scoring sheet.

TEST 19. WRITING FROM COPY (WC) [CARDS WITH TEXT]

Administration. The patient may continue on the same sheet of paper used in Test 14. Present the first card. **"I would like you to copy this. Write this sentence."** Encourage even fragmentary responses. Do not give aid.

Copying text;
Card 1: I am very hungry.
Card 2: The color of the walls is green.

The test may be discontinued if the patient cannot copy the first sentence in a recognizable manner (i.e., 0 score).

Scoring. Score 1 point for every word correctly spelled and legible. Legibility is judged generously, particularly in patients with motor disability. If the letter remains recognizable, disregard angular distortions, small additional movements, omission of *i*-dots, corrections, "dashing" (i.e., almost straight lines for lower-case letters with approximate allowances of space as in hasty writing), consistent "idio-syncratic" forms (i.e., looping, fancy strokes, failure to capitalize first letter of a sentence).

Score ½ point for words that are correct except for one additional up- and downstroke and for words within a sentence beginning with a capital letter if the capitalization is clearly recognizable. If all letters are capitalized, give full credit (in contrast to the scoring on Test 18).

Score 0 for illegible, incomplete, or otherwise incorrect words (e.g., letter reversals, additions, and word substitutions).

Subtract 1 point for each duplication after all correctly written words are counted.

```
                    Sample Score Sheet 7-14
                    Test 19. WC-Writing from Copy
                                                        Score
  I am very hungry.
  The color of the walls is green.

                                    TOTAL SCORE
                                    CORRECTION
                         TOTAL CORRECTED SCORE
```

Figure 7-14. NCCEA Subtest 19 (Writing from Copy) sample scoring sheet.

Maximum raw score = 11 (see Fig. 7-14). Before the scores are entered into the profile sheet, the following corrections must be applied.

Education	Correction: ≤49 years	Correction: 50+ years
<7 years	+2	+1
7-8 years	+1	+1
>8 years	0	+1

Maximum corrected score = 13

TEST 20. ARTICULATION (ART)

Administration. The 38 speech stimuli are presented by tape at a comfortable hearing level. The examiner says to the subject: **"You will hear some words. I would like you to repeat each word loudly and clearly."** The first three words on the tape are presented with the carrier phrase "REPEAT THE WORD. . ."

After the first 30 words (i.e., after the stimulus "understand"), the examiner should stop the tape briefly and say: **"The next words have no meaning. Just repeat them the way you hear them."**

Responses should be scored during the actual administration of the test.

Scoring. Score only the pronunciation of consonants and consonant blends listed on the record sheet. Mark errors as follows:

Circle (O) phoneme substitution (and note the substituted sound above the word).

Slash (/) through omissions.

Cross (X) through distortions.

Disregard spontaneously corrected errors.

```
                        Sample Score Sheet 7–15
                        Test 20. ART–Articulation

(Mark each of the listed consonants or blends with: / = omission, O = substitution, X =
distortion.)
```

rain	r–n	remember	r–m–mb–
tall	t–l	suddenly	s–d–nl–
nose	n–z	together	t–/–th–
tree	tr–	one thousand	/–th–s–nd
dance	d–ns	tomorrow	t–/–r–
leg	l–g	Washington	w–sh–ngt–
teacher	t–sh	animal	a–/–/–al
notice	n–/–s	direction	d–/–ksh
report	r–/–rt	natural	n–tsh–/–al
daughter	d–t–	realize	r–l–z
listen	l–sn	understand	/–/–st–nd
service	s–rv	zaratan	z–r–t–n
flower	fl–r	ladanat	l–d–n–t
shoulder	sh–ld–	tafazas	t–f–z–s
beautiful	biu–/–/–/	fazalar	f–z–l–r
continue	k–nt–nju	nataraf	n–t–r–f
condition	k–/–sh–n	saladaz	s–l–d–z
discover	d–sk–v–	dazafad	d–z–f–d
family	f–/–l–	ranasal	r–n–s–l

	SCORE	
	CORRECTION	
TOTAL CORRECTED SCORE		

Figure 7–15. NCCEA Subtest 20 (Articulation) sample scoring sheet.

The total score is the number of consonants and blends pronounced correctly
(see Fig. 7–15). Before entering the score into the profile sheet , the following
corrections are applied:

	Correction
Education: ≤8 years	+2
Age: 56–65 years	+2

Maximum raw score = 100
Maximum corrected score = 104

Control Tests

Test C1. Tactile Visual Matching, Right Hand (TMR) [Trays A and B]

Administration. Administer this test if any errors occur on Tests 3 and 4 (Tactile
Naming). Do not administer in cases of severe motor or sensory impairment of the
right hand. No corrections for age or education are necessary. *Mild* sensory loss

usually does not affect performance, but will have to be considered in the interpretation of test results.

Place objects firmly into the patient's hand under a rectangular box covered by a curtain at the side of the patient. **"Put your right hand under the curtain. I will give you an object. I want you to feel it and then point to the same object on the tray."** [*A second* set of Tray B is placed on top of the box.] **"Handle it, and feel it from all sides, but do not try to look at it."**

Give all objects of Tray A. If 1–7 errors occur, present all objects of Tray B.

Scoring. Score 1 point for each object correctly matched (Fig. 7–16). Multiply the obtained score by 2 if only Tray A has been given. Maximum score = 16.

Sample Score Sheet 7–16
Test C1. TMR–Visual Matching, Right Hand

(Give A. If between 1 and 7 errors occur, give B.)

Tray A	Response	Score
comb		
ring		
key		
cup		
ashtray		
thimble		
padlock		
paper clip		
	TOTAL A	

Tray B	Response	Score
knife		
fork		
bottle, baby bottle		
shoelace, shoestring		
brush		
jar		
can opener, bottle opener		
tweezers		
	TOTAL B	
	TOTAL A & B	

Figure 7–16. NCCEA Subtest C1 (Tactile–Visual Matching, Right Hand) sample scoring sheet.

Sample Score Sheet 7–17
Test C2. TML–Tactile-Visual Matching, Left Hand

(Give Tray C. If between 1 and 7 errors occur, give Tray D.)

Tray C	Response	Error Type	Score
pistol, gun			
plate, saucer, dish			
bulb, light bulb			
screw driver			
sponge			
ruler			
shaker, salt/pepper			
plug			
		TOTAL C	

Tray D	Response	Error Type	Score
watch			
eyeglasses, glasses			
spoon			
razor			
matchbook, matches			
envelope			
pen, ballpoint			
scotch tape, tape			
		TOTAL D	
		TOTAL C & D	

Figure 7–17. NCCEA Subtest C2 (Tactile–Visual Matching, Left Hand) sample scoring sheet.

Test C2. Tactile Visual Matching, Left Hand (TML) [Trays C and D]

Administration. Have the patient place his or her left hand into the box. Proceed as directed in Test C1, beginning with the objects of Tray C. If 1–7 errors occur, use Tray D.

Scoring. Scoring is as directed in Test C1 (Fig. 7–17). Maximum score = 16. No corrections for age or education are applied to this test.

Test C3. Visual–Visual Matching (VVM) [Trays A and B]

Administration. Administer this test if any errors occur on Visual Naming (Test 1) *or* on Tactile Visual Matching (Test C1 *or* C2).

Place Tray A in front of patient and a second set of Tray A behind it. The position of the second tray should be reversed (i.e., the side marked "examiner" should be facing the patient, whereas the first tray is placed in standard position). Say: "**Now I will point to some of the objects on this tray.**" [Point in the direction of the tray in front of the patient.] "**Can you show me the same object on the tray?**" [Point to the first object (comb) on the tray next to the patient.] If the patient does not understand the instructions, demonstrate by holding up one object and guiding the patient's hand to the same object on the tray next to him or her.

If 1–7 errors occur on Tray A, give Tray B.

Scoring. Score 1 point for each object correctly matched (see Fig. 7–18). Multiply the obtained score by 2 if only Tray A has been given. No corrections for age or education are necessary. Maximum score = 16.

Sample Score Sheet 7–18
Test C3. Visual–Visual Matching

(Give A. If between 1 and 7 errors occur, give B.)

Tray A	Response	Score
comb		
ring		
key		
cup		
ashtray		
thimble		
padlock		
paper clip		
	TOTAL A	

Tray B	Response	Score
knife		
fork		
bottle, baby bottle		
shoelace, shoestring		
brush		
jar		
can opener, bottle opener		
tweezers		
	TOTAL B	
	TOTAL A & B	

Figure 7–18. NCCEA Subtest C3 (Visual–Visual Matching) sample scoring sheet.

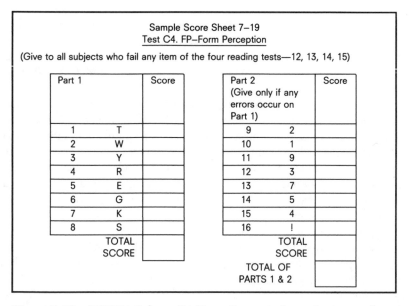

Sample Score Sheet 7–19
Test C4. FP–Form Perception

(Give to all subjects who fail any item of the four reading tests—12, 13, 14, 15)

Part 1		Score	Part 2 (Give only if any errors occur on Part 1)		Score
1	T		9	2	
2	W		10	1	
3	Y		11	9	
4	R		12	3	
5	E		13	7	
6	G		14	5	
7	K		15	4	
8	S		16	!	
	TOTAL SCORE			TOTAL SCORE	
				TOTAL OF PARTS 1 & 2	

Figure 7–19. NCCEA Subtest C4 (Form Perception) sample scoring sheet.

TEST C4. FORM PERCEPTION (FP)

Administration. Administer this test to all subjects who fail any item on the four reading tasks (Test 12: Reading Names, Oral; Test 13: Reading Sentences, Oral; Test 14: Reading Names; Test 15: Reading Sentences, Point).

Display the upper half of the multiple-choice card of letters at reading distance. Present the first letter (T) on a separate card. Say: **"Find this letter on this card."** If necessary, instructions may be given by gestures. Discontinue if no errors occur on the first eight items. If any errors occur, give items 9 through 16 (on reverse side on cards), displaying the reverse side of the multiple-choice card. Items 15 and 16 are not on the multiple-choice card.

Scoring. Give one point for every item correctly identified (see Fig. 7-19). Items 15 and 16 are scored as correct if the subject indicates that they are not on the card. Multiply by 2 if only the first part has been given. No corrections for age or education are necessary. Maximum score = 16.

Approximate Time for Administration

The time required for the NCCEA is 30–90 minutes.

Comment

One-year retest reliability in older adults for selected subtests has been reported as satisfactory (Word Fluency, .70; Visual Naming, .82; Token Test, .50; Snow et al., 1988).

Since the development of this test, a number of studies have investigated its properties and its practical usefulness. Since it was designed primarily for the examination of patients with aphasia or aphasia-type complaints, patients without language problems and normal controls tend to obtain ceiling scores. As a result, the test cannot be used to measure language ability in normals, although language development in children has been successfully measured with most subtests up to a ceiling age ranging from 8 to 13 years (Gaddes & Crockett, 1975). Because or the low ceiling of the naming tasks, the Visual Naming test can be supplemented by use of the Boston Naming Test, described in this manual.

As mentioned above, the test is not designed to yield a taxonomic diagnosis as to the type of aphasia, but rather a profile of the client's abilities and disabilities (Marshall, 1986). The order of the subtests provides a meaningful grouping into tests of name finding (Nos. 1–4), immediate verbal memory (Nos. 5–7), verbal production and fluency (Nos. 8 and 9), receptive (decoding) ability (Nos. 10 and 11), reading (Nos. 12–15), writing (Nos. 17–19), and articulation (No. 20). An empirical study with 353 children ages 5:5–13:5 (Crockett, 1974) found that seven factors—(1) reading/writing, (2) verbal memory, (3) name finding, (4) auditory comprehension, (5) syntactic fluency, (6) reversal of digits, and (7) repeating digits—described the content of the NCCEA in that population.

Construct validity was examined in two studies by Crockett (1974, 1977). The first study examined the discrimination of groups of aphasic patients based on ratings of verbal productions, and divided on the basis of the Howes/Geschwind two-type and the Weisenburg/McBride three-type typologies. Neither of the two models showed significant multivariate differences. The second study demonstrated significant differences on the NCCEA between four types of aphasia empirically derived from ratings of verbal production by hierarchical grouping analysis. Two of these four types appeared to be similar to Howes two types, a third appeared to reflect Schuell's single dimension of language disorder, whereas the fourth type seemed to be characterized primarily by memory impairment.

Predictive validity was established in a study by Lawriw (1976) which also presented a successful cross-validation among patient groups from Iowa City, New York City, and Victoria, British Columbia. Kenin and Swisher (1972) and Ludlow (1977) investigated patterns of recovery from aphasia; improvement was best reflected in writing from copy and tests of comprehension, whereas expressive performance showed least improvement. Single-word reception and production were more readily recovered than those of longer verbal units. The authors mention that items in the area of reading, writing, and oral production were not sufficiently difficult for patients at an advanced stage of recovery. In contrast, Ewing-Cobbs et al. (1987) reported that a striking percentage of a sample of 23 children and 33 adolescents with closed head injury exhibited clinically significant language impairment on the NCCEA. Visual Naming, Sentence Repetition, Word Fluency, and Writing to Dictation best discriminated between mild and moderate/severe closed head injury in children and adolescents. Sarno (1986) described significant differences between aphasic, dysarthric/subclinical, and subclinical aphasic patients on Visual Naming, Sentence Repetition, Word Fluency, and the Token Test. Patients with Alzheimer's disease scored significantly lower in the areas of verbal expression, auditory comprehension, repetition, reading, and writing, compared to age-matched nonneurological controls (Murdoch et al., 1987).

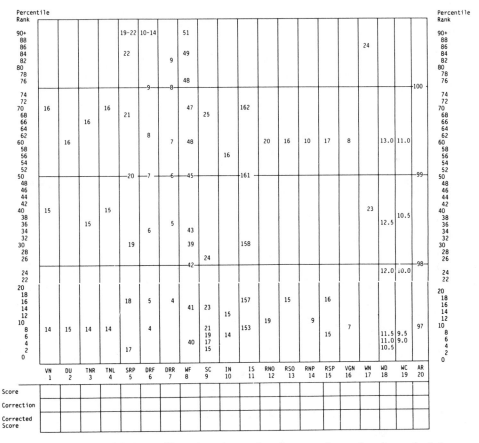

Figure 7–20. NCCEA Profile A: Normative data for normal, poorly educated adults.

It should be noted that the four trays of objects rotated throughout the test are equivalent in mean and distribution of difficulty for aphasic patients (mean percent correct: approximately 63% for all trays) and young children (mean acquisition age of names: approximately 5:8 years). Three object substitutions were made in 1987 to eliminate outdated items (Tray C: electric plug for screen door spring, salt-shaker for toy egg beater: Tray D: Bick-type shaver for safety razor).

Normative Data

For comments and normative data for Sentence Repetition (No. 5), Word Fluency (No. 8), and Identification by Sentence (Token Test, No. 11), see the separate sections in this manual. [Sentence Repetition is discussed in Chapter 6; Word

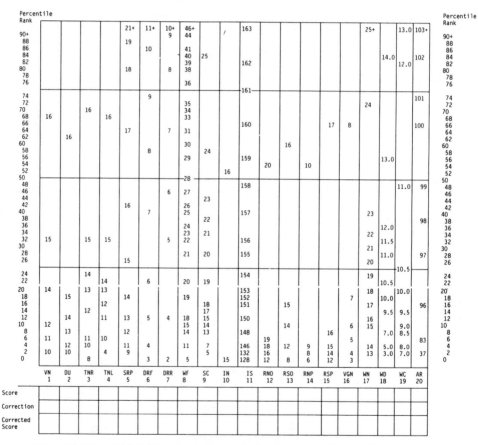

Figure 7–21. NCCEA Profile B: Normative data for an aphasic reference group.

fluency (Controlled Oral Word Association) is discussed earlier in this chapter; and the Token Test is described at the end of this chapter.]

Normative data for all subtests form the basis of Profile Sheet A (Fig. 7–20), based on a group of relatively poorly educated (grade 10) adults hospitalized for minor medical problems of a nonneurological and nonpsychiatric nature. The 1977 NCCEA normative data for an aphasic reference group Profile Sheet B (Fig. 7–21) are based on 206 unselected referrals to neuropsychological hospital/clinic services in Iowa City, Victoria, and New York City. Although the concept of "averaging" across aphasic patients disregards the different types of aphasia, this procedure allows the profiling of individual patients against this reference group; that is, an individual patient's subtype will stand out more clearly. However, if patients from another referral source (e.g., rehabilitation or patients with residual aphasia)

Percentile Rank	VN 1	DU 2	TNR 3	TNL 4	SRP 5	DRF 6	DRR 7	WF 8	SC 9	IN 10	IS 11	RNO 12	RSO 13	RNP 14	RSP 15	VGN 16	WN 17	WD 18	WC 19	AR 20	Percentile Rank
90+			16		18–22	10–12	8–10	26–46	25		157+						24–26	14.0	13.0	102+	90+
88	16	16							24		156							13.5	12.0		88
86					17	8	7	24			155					8				101	86
84				16					23	23	153							13.0			84
82								23	22		152			17					11.5		82
80					16			22	21	21	150	16					23				80
78																					78
76						7	6	21													76
—20—									—20—	—20—											—20—
74			15	15					19		147						22				74
72	15				15				18		144							12.0			72
70									17	19	141	20								100	70
68				15						18	139				7				11.0		68
66	14		14		14	6	5	16			138						21	11.0			66
64		14							16	16	137			10							64
62								15													62
60	13		13	14				14	15		134						20	10.5			60
58		13				5		13			131					6	19		10.5	99	58
56					13				14		128						18	10.0			56
54			12	13			4	12	12		122							9.5			54
52	12	12		12					11		121			16							52
50										—10—							—17—	—9.0—		—98—	50
48		11			12			11	9		119	15			5						48
46	11	10	11	11		4		10	6		114						16	8.0	10.0	97	46
44	10		10				3				102	19	14		3	15	15	7.0			44
42			9	10	11			9	5		96		13					6.5		96	42
40	9	9	8						4		93	18		15			13	6.0			40
38	8	8		9							89		12				12	5.5	9.5	95	38
36	7	7			10			8	3		81	17			2		10				36
34		6	7	8		3					76	16		14			9	5.0			34
32		5	6		9			7			64		10				8		9.0	90	32
30	6			7			2		2		58	14	9				7	4.0		89	30
28	5	4	4	5				6			56		8	12			6	3.0			28
26	4				8				1		55										26
—5—								—5—				—11—			—1—	—5—			—85—		—5—
24	3		3		2			4		15	54	10	7		11		4	2.0		84	24
22		3		4															8.0		22
20			2		7					14	53	7	5	9	10		3		7.5	76	20
18	2	2		3	6		1			13	50	5	3	8	9		2		6.0	75	18
16		1									49	4	2		5		1	1.0	5.5		16
14			1	2	5	1		3		12	46	3		7	1						14
12				1	4					11	43	2		5					3.0	67	12
10	1								2					1					2.0	65	10
8				3				1		9	42										8
6				2						8	37									44	6
4				1						4	34								1.0	41	4
2											20									29	2
0																				5	0
Score																					
Correction																					
Corrected Score																					

Figure 7–22. NCCEA Profile C: Normative data for nonaphasic, brain-damaged patients.

Table 7–11. NCCEA Norms (Percentiles) for Children, Ages 6–13 Years

Score	Age in years								Score
	6	7	8	9	10	11	12	13	
VN (Subtest 1)									
16	99.1	94	88	84	78	78	68	68	16
15	97	81	65	53	43	39	25	19	15
14	90	53	35	22	12	8	2	1	14
13	75	28	12	4	1	0.9			13
12	53	10	3	0.9					12
11	28	2							11
10	12								10
9	4								9
8	1								8
DU (Subtest 2)									
16	98	94	92	90	88	86	84	81	16
15	92	81	68	61	53	47	39	28	15
14	78	61	32	25	19	5	4	2	14
13	57	39	8	4	3				13
12	35	19	1						12
11	19	7							11
10	7	2							10
9	2								9
TNR (Subtest 3)									
16	99	95	88	78	75	75	75	72	16
15	97	81	65	53	35	35	16	8	15
14	92	61	35	25	5	5	0.8		14
13	78	39	12	7					13
12	57	19	3	1					12
11	35	5	0.8						11
10	16	1							10
9	5	0.7							9
8	1								8
TNL (Subtest 4)									
16	97	94	90	88	86	84	81	78	16
15	92	81	68	61	47	28	22	16	15
14	81	61	39	25	14	3	0.3	1	14
13	65	43	32	4	2				13
12	43	22	4	0.8					12
11	25	8	0.9						11
10	12	2							10
9	4	0.9							9
8	1								8
DRF (Subtest 6)									
10+							99+	99	10+
9				99+	99	99	98	96	9
8		99+	99	98	96	95	90	84	8
7	99+	98	96	94	86	81	75	61	7

Score	\multicolumn{8}{c}{Age in years}	Score

Score	6	7	8	9	10	11	12	13	Score
6	98	90	86	78	68	61	50	39	6
5	88	75	50	53	47	35	25	16	5
4	61	50	39	32	25	14	10	4	4
3	32	25	19	12	8	4	2	1	3
2	10	10	5	3	2	1	0.8		2
1	2	1	1	1	0.9				1
0	0.9	0.8	0.5						0

DRR (Subtest 7)

Score	6	7	8	9	10	11	12	13	Score
9+					99	99	99	99	9+
8				99	98	96	96	96	8
7			99	98	92	88	86	84	7
6			97	90	78	72	65	65	6
5		99	86	75	57	50	43	39	5
4	98	88	61	50	35	28	19	19	4
3	86	57	28	25	19	14	7	5	3
2	53	22	8	10	7	4	2	1	2
1	19	4	3	2	2	1	0.8	0.5	1
0	3	1	1	0.9	0.8	0.7			0

SC (Subtest 9)

Score	6	7	8	9	10	11	12	13	Score
25	99	92	88	78	75	75	75	75	25
24	99	88	84	72	65	61	61	57	24
23	99	86	78	61	53	50	47	39	23
22	98	81	72	53	43	35	28	22	22
21	97	75	50	43	32	25	16	12	21
20	96	72	47	35	22	16	7	4	20
19	95	65	41	25	12	10	2	1	19
18	93	61	38	19	7	5	1		18
17	92	53	35	12	4	2			17
16	88	47	28	8	2	1			16
15	86	43	22	4	1				15
14	84	35	16	3					14
13	78	32	12	1					13
12	75	25	8	1					12
11	72	19	5						11
10	65	16	4						10
9	61	12	2						9
8	53	8	1						8
7	50	7	1						7
6	47	4							6
5	39	3							5
4	35	2							4
3	32	1							3
2	25	1							2
1	22								1
0	19								0

(*continued*)

Table 7–11. *(Continued)*

Score	6	7	8	9	10	11	12	13	Score
IN (Subtest 10)									
17	84	68	61	61	61	61	61	61	16
15	35	12	10	10	1	1	1	1	15
14	3	0.7							14
RNO (Subtest 12)									
20					57	55	53	50	
19					46	48	49		
18				51					
17			54	42					
16			43						
15									
14									
13									
12									
11									
10									
9									
8									
7		54							
6		43							
5									
4									
3									
2									
1									
0.5	50								
RSO (Subtest 13)									
16			56	53	50	50	50	50	
15			49	44	47	47	47	47	
14									
13									
12									
11									
10									
9									
8		56							
7		49							
6									
5									
4									
3									
2									
1									
0.5	50								
RNP (Subtest 14)									
10			54	55	52	52	50	50	
9			44	46	45	45	42	40	

258

Score	6	7	8	9	10	11	12	13	Score
					Age in years				
8		58							
7		49							
6									
5									
4									
3									
2	52								
1	45								

RSP (Subtest 15)

Score	6	7	8	9	10	11	12	13
17			60	57	55	52	50	50
16			44	43	42	41	40	40
15								
14								
13								
12								
11								
10								
9		56						
8		50						
7		44						
6								
5								
4								
3								
2	60							
0.5	50							

VGN (Subtest 16)

Score	6	7	8	9	10	11	12	13
8					56	54	52	51
7.5			51	51	48	46	44	43
7			46	46	42			
6.5								
6								
5.5		54						
5		48						
4								
3								
2								
1	58							
0.5	50							

WN (Subtest 17)

Score	6	7	8	9	10	11	12	13
24							55	53
23						52	45	42
22					52	44		
21				56	43			
20				47				
19			58					

(*continued*)

Table 7–11. *(Continued)*

Score	6	7	8	9	10	11	12	13	Score
				Age in years					
18			47						
17									
15									
13									
11									
9		50							
7									
5									
3									
1	52								
0.5	44								

WD (Subtest 18)

Score	6	7	8	9	10	11	12	13	Score
13						57	55	52	
12.5					53	48	46	48	
12				54	47				
11			54	44					
10			44						
9									
7		54							
5		42							
3									
1									
0.5	51								

WC (Subtest 19)

Score	6	7	8	9	10	11	12	13	Score
11	90	84	81	78	72	72	72	68	11
10	75	68	43	35	19	19	5	2	10
9	65	43	12	5	1	1			9
8	53	16	1	0.5					8
7	43	4							7
6	32	1							6
5	22								5
4	14								4
3	8								3
2	4								2
1	2								1
0	1								0

ART (Subtest 20)

Score	6	7	8	9	10	11	12	13	Score
100									
99					59	59	56	56	
98			55	50	49	49	46	46	
97			45						
96		56							
95		48							
94									
93									
92	54								
91	44								
90									

are seen, the reference group may no longer be appropriate. Similarly, Profile Sheet C (Fig. 7-22) is based on a population of patients with brain lesions referred to a neuropsychological service, excluding those with diagnosed aphasia. Other patient groups (e.g., dementia of the Alzheimer type) may provide a very different referral base.

Normative data for most subtests remain stable through the age span up to age 64. Individual studies with some of the tests (Montgomery, 1982) show only a minor decline of 1 or 2 points which has been incorporated into the age and education correction rules. A study by Tuokko (1985) of elderly subjects in Vancouver, British Columbia, for example, showed a mean for Visual Naming (No. 1) of 16 for subjects below 60 years to hold up to age 79, and to drop to 15.44 for subjects 80 years and older. Similarly, Description of Use (No. 2) showed a ceiling score of 16 for subjects below 60 and up to age 74; the mean for subjects of age 75–80 and older was 15.78. Tactile Naming, Right Hand (No. 3) showed a mean of 15.66 for subjects below 60 and up to age 79, and of 14.89 for subjects 80 years and older. Tactile Naming, Left Hand (No. 4) showed a mean of 16 for subjects under 60, means between 15.14 and 15.57 for the age span 60–79, but a mean of 12.44 for subjects 80 years and older.

Normative data for children between ages 6 and 13 are presented in Table 7–11. The norms were merged from Gaddes and Crockett (1975) and Hamsher (personal communication, 1980) since the differences between these two sources (Victoria, B.C. and Milwaukee, Wisconsin) were minimal. No sex differences were found on 11 of the 20 subtests; on the remaining subtests, sex differences were transient around ages 6–7, when girls did slightly better on the writing and reading tasks, except for word fluency, on which girls were more productive between the ages of 9 and 13, and spelling of written names, where girls did better at ages 7, 9, 10, and 11.

REFERENCES

Benton, A.L., & Blackburn, H.L. (1957). Revised administration and scoring of the Digit Span test. *Journal of Consulting Psychology, 21,* 139–143.

Crockett, D.J. (1974). Component analysis of within correlations of language skill tests in normal children. *Journal of Special Education, 8,* 361–375.

Crockett, D.J. (1977). A comparison of empirically derived groups of aphasic patients on the Neurosensory Center Comprehensive Examination for Aphasia. *Journal of Clinical Psychology, 33,* 194–198.

Ewing-Cobbs, L., Levin, H.S., Eisenberg, H.M., & Fletcher, J.M. (1987). Language functions following closed head injury in children and adolescents. *Journal of*

Clinical and Experimental Neuropsychology, 9, 575–592.

Gaddes, W.H., & Crockett, D.J. (1975). The Spreen–Benton aphasia tests: Normative data as a measure of normal language development. *Brain and Language, 19,* 257–280.

Kenin, M., & Swisher, L.P. (1972). A study of patterns of recovery from aphasia. *Cortex, 8,* 56–68.

Lawriw, I. (1976). A test of predictive validity and a cross-validation of the Neurosensory Center Comprehensive Examination for Aphasia. Master's Thesis, Department of Psychology, University of Victoria, Victoria, B.C.

Ludlow, C.L. (1977). Recovery from aphasia:

A foundation for treatment. In M. Sullivan and M.S. Kommers (Eds.), Rationale for Adult Aphasia Therapy. Omaha: University of Nebraska Medical Center.

Marshall, J.C. (1986). The description and interpretation of aphasic language disorders. Neuropsychologia, 24, 5–24.

Montgomery, K.M. (1982). A normative study of neuropsychological test performance of a normal elderly sample. Master's thesis, University of Victoria, British Columbia.

Murdoch, B.E., Chenery, H.J., Wilks, V., & Boyle, R.S. (1987). Language disorders in dementia of the Alzheimer type. Brain and Language, 31, 122–137.

Sarno, M.T. (1986). Verbal impairment in head injury. Archives of Physical Medicine and Rehabilitation, 67, 402–404.

Snow, W.G., Tierney, M.C., Zorzitto, M.L., Fisher, R.H., & Reid, D.W. (1988). One-year test–retest reliability of selected neuropsychological tests in older adults. Paper presented at the meeting of the International Neuropsychological Society, New Orleans. Journal of Clinical and Experimental Neuropsychology, 10, 60 (abstract).

Spreen, O. & Benton, A.L. (1965). Neurosensory Center Comprehensive Examination for Aphasia (NCCEA). Experimental edition. Iowa City Iowa: University of Iowa, Department of Neurology.

Tuokko, H. (1985). Normative data for elderly subjects. Unpublished manuscript, University of British Columbia, Vancouver.

PEABODY PICTURE VOCABULARY TEST – REVISED (PPVT-R)

Purpose

The purpose of this test is to assess auditory comprehension of picture names.

Source

The complete test (including both forms) can be ordered from American Guidance Service, Publisher's Boulevard, Circle Pines, Minnesota 55014 at a cost of $98.00 U.S., or from Psycan, P.O. Box 290, Station U, Toronto, Ontario H6R 3A5, at a cost of $160 Cdn.

Description

This popular test (Dunn & Dunn, 1981), also part of the Florida Kindergarten Screening Battery (Satz & Fletcher, 1982), is a revision of the original 1965 edition. It was initially constructed as a test of hearing vocabulary in children, but has since been standardized for adults and used with a variety of clinical populations. The test requires the subject to choose one of four items displayed on a card as depicting the word spoken by the examiner. After five training items, 175 items of increasing difficulty can be given, but usually only 35–45 items need to be administered if a suitable entry point (six consecutive correct) is chosen; the test is discontinued after consecutive failures on six out of eight items. Two equivalent alternate forms (L and M) are available.

Approximate Time for Administration

The time required is 10–20 minutes.

Administration

See source. The test booklets fold out into an easel. The examiner explains to the subject that one of the four pictures corresponds to a word which the examiner will say, and that the subject should point to the appropriate picture. The examiner should be able to pronounce all words correctly according to the dictionary. If hearing is a problem, the word can be shown on a printed card. Entry points can be chosen by a preliminary estimate of the subject's age equivalent level and by consulting the appropriate table in the manual.

Scoring

The score on this test is simply the number of items passed, including the items prior to the entry point. The manual allows translation of these scores into "age equivalents" (previously called "mental age"), "standard score equivalents" (previously called "IQ"), stanines, and percentiles. The new terms are intended to discourage the use of the test as a measure of "verbal intelligence" (as claimed in the 1965 edition).

Comment

The new edition has been standardized on a sample of people considered representative of the U.S. population ranging in age from 2.5 to 40 years; the items have been revised or added to and correspond well to the negatively accelerating growth curve of vocabulary with age. Split-half reliability has been reported (see source) as ranging form .61 to .88 in children and adolescents, and as .82 for Form L in adults. The reliability of alternate forms ranged from .73 to .91 (source; Stoner, 1981; Tillinghast et al., 1983). Retest reliability after a minimum of nine days, with the alternate form, showed a median coefficient of .78. In children, retest stability over 11 months has been reported as .84 for the revised PPVT (Bracken & Murray, 1984), as .81 in retarded children over a period of seven months (Naglieri & Pfeiffer, 1983), and as .71 in a mixed clinical neuropsychological population after 2.6 years (Brown et al., 1989). Internal consistency (coefficient alpha) ranged from .96 to .98 in children 6–11 years old (Kamphaus & Lozano, 1984).

Construct validity of the test as a measure of scholastic aptitude is good (Hinton & Knights, 1971). Bracken and Murray (1984) report a predictive validity of .30 with spelling, .54 with reading recognition, .58 with reading comprehension, and .59 with the total Peabody Individual Achievement Test (PIAT) for the revised PPVT; similar values were reported for the first edition (Naglieri, 1981) and for mentally handicapped children with the revised edition (Naglieri & Pfeiffer, 1983). Concurrent validity with similar tests—the Bracken Basic Concept Scale, and the preschool version of the Boehm Test of Basic Concepts and its revised version—were .68, .65, and .62, respectively (Zucker & Riordan, 1988). Since vocabulary is the single most important subtest of most intelligence tests, the test also correlates strongly with measures of verbal (.87), performance (.80), and full scale IQ (.88; Crofoot & Bennett, 1980), with the McCarthy Scales in children (Naglieri, 1981), with the 1986 Stanford–Binet Intelligence Scale (Carvajal et al., 1987), and with the achievement scale of the Kaufman Assessment Battery for Children in a learning-disabled population (.78; D'Amato et al., 1987). However, Williams, Marks, and Bialer (1977) warn that the PPVT is not an adequate measure of hearing vocabulary in mentally handicapped subjects since it is also clearly related to visual decoding ability, as measured with the Illinois Test of Psycholinguistic Abilities (ITPA), and that the use of the PPVT as a measure of intelligence in the mentally handicapped person may be misleading. Hollinger and Sarvis (1984) also stress the roll of perceptual–organizational ability in PPVT performance of school-age children, and Taylor (1975) reached the same conclusion for preschool children based on a factor analysis of the Wechsler Preschool and Primary Scale of Intelligence (WPPSI) and the ITPA as well as the PPVT. Children with impaired oral language production (Rizzo & Stephens, 1981) and nonpsychotic, emotionally disturbed adolescents (Dean, 1980) also tend to produce variable results. More than one measure of auditory comprehension is needed to explore a child's abilities.

No validity studies with brain-damaged patients are available, although the test will provide an estimate of the vocabulary still available to the patient. Considering the warnings mentioned above, the visual–perceptual integrity of the patient should be carefully considered in interpreting the results of this test. Quattrochi and Golden (1983) found only small correlations with the children's version of the Luria–Nebraska Battery (Receptive Speech Scale, Visual, Arithmetic, Memory, and Intellectual Processes scales).

Normative Data

Normative data for ages 2.5 to 40 are presented in the manual. Canadian norms are available from the distributor (Psycan). Kamphaus and Lozano (1984) note that in 6- to 11-year-old children with Spanish surnames (about half of whom spoke Spanish at home), standard scores were about 12–13 points below the national norms, although they showed regular, expected increases with age.

REFERENCES

Bracken, B.A., Murray, A.M. (1984). Stability and predictive validity of the PPVT-R over an eleven-month interval. *Educational and Psychological Research, 4,* 41–44.

Brown, S.J., Rourke, B.P., & Cicchetti, D.V. (1989). Reliability of tests and measures used in the neuropsychological assessment of children. *Clinical Neuropsychologist, 3,* 353–368.

Carvajal, H., Gerber, J., & Smith, P.D. (1987). Relationship between scores of young adults on Stanford–Binet IV and Peabody Picture Vocabulary Test – Revised. *Perceptual and Motor Skills, 65,* 721–722.

Crofoot, M.J., & Bennett, T.S. (1980). A comparison of three screening tests and the WISC-R in special education evaluations. *Psychology in the Schools, 17,* 474–478.

D'Amato, R.C., Gray, J.W., & Dean, R.S. (1987). Concurrent validity of the PPVT-R with the K-ABC for learning problem children. *Psychology in the Schools, 24,* 35–39.

Dean, R.S. (1980). The use of the Peabody Picture Vocabulary Test with emotionally disturbed adolescents. *Journal of School Psychology, 18,* 172–175.

Dunn, L.M., & Dunn, L.M. (1981). *Peabody Picture Vocabulary Test – Revised Manual.* Circle Pines, MN: American Guidance Service.

Hinton, G.G., & Knights, R.M. (1971). Children with learning problems. Academic history, academic prediction, and adjustment three years after assessment. *Exceptional Children, 37,* 513–519.

Hollinger, C.L., & Sarvis, P.A. (1984). Interpretation of the PPVT-R: A pure measure of verbal comprehension? *Psychology in the Schools, 21,* 34–41.

Kamphaus, R.W., & Lozano, R. (1984). Developing local norms for individually administered tests. *School Psychology Review, 13,* 491–498.

Naglieri, J.A. (1981). Concurrent validity of the revised Peabody Picture Vocabulary Test. *Psychology in the Schools, 18,* 286–289.

Naglieri, J.A., & Pfeiffer, S.I. (1983). Stability, concurrent and predictive validity of the PPVT-R. *Journal of Clinical Psychology, 39,* 965–967.

Quattrochi, M.M., & Golden, C.J. (1983). Peabody Picture Vocabulary Test – Revised and Luria–Nebraska Neuropsychological Battery for Children: Intercorrelations for normal youngsters. *Perceptual and Motor Skills, 56,* 632–634.

Rizzo, J.M., & Stephens, M.I. (1981). Performance of children with normal and impaired oral language production on a set of auditory comprehension tests. *Journal of Speech and Hearing Disorders, 46,* 150–159.

Satz, P., & Fletcher, J. (1982). *Manual for the Florida Kindergarten Screening Battery.* Odessa, Fla.: Psychological Assessment Resources.

Stoner, S.B. (1981). Alternate form reliability of the revised Peabody Picture Vocabulary Test for Head Start children. *Psychological Reports, 49,* 628.

Taylor, L.J. (1975). The Peabody Picture Vocabulary Test: What does it measure? *Perceptual and Motor Skills, 41,* 777–778.

Tillinghast, B.S., Morrow, J.E., & Uhlig, G.E. (1983). Retest and alternate form reliability of the PPVT-R with fourth, fifth, and sixth grade pupils. *Journal of Educational Research, 76,* 243–244.

Williams, A.M., Marks, C.J., & Bialer, I. (1977). Validity of the Peabody Picture Vocabulary Test as a measure of hearing vocabulary in mentally retarded and normal children. *Journal of Speech and Hearing Research, 20,* 205–211.

Zucker, S., & Riordan, J. (1988). Concurrent validity of new and revised conceptual language measures. *Psychology in the Schools, 25,* 252–256.

TOKEN TEST

Purpose

The purpose of this test is to assess verbal comprehension of commands of increasing complexity.

Source

The manual for the 39-item form, answer sheets, and plastic tokens can be ordered from the Neuropsychology Laboratory, University of Victoria, Victoria, British Columbia V8W 3P5 Canada, at a cost of $19.50 Cdn.

Description

The test as originally developed by De Renzi and Vignolo (1962) had 61 commands. Our version uses 20 plastic tokens in five colors (red, white, yellow, blue, green), two sizes (small: approx. 2 cm in diameter; large: approx. 3 cm in diameter), and two shapes (circles and squares—squares replacing the rectangles in the original version) arranged in a fixed order in front of the patient. Thirty-nine commands of increasing length are listed on the answer sheet. Other short versions have been presented (De Renzi & Faglioni, 1978; Orgass, 1976; Spellacy & Spreen, 1969; van Harskamp & van Dongen, 1977). The Spellacy and Spreen 16-item version and the De Renzi and Faglioni short form have been specifically recommended for children for the screening of receptive language (Cole & Fewell, 1983; Lass et al., 1975). A children's version (De Simoni, 1978), a visual presentation mode (Kiernan, 1985), and a concrete object form (Martino et al., 1976) have also been described. Our version of the Token Test is also part of the Neurosensory Comprehensive Examination for Aphasia (Test 11) (Spreen & Benton, 1969, 1977) and can be used with children as well as adults.

Administration

Present tokens in the order shown in Table 7–12, and ask the first question, **"Show me a circle"**; pronounce clearly and slowly. Instructions for Parts A and B may be repeated once. No other instructions may be repeated. If the patient makes no response, he or she should be encouraged to give at least a partial response. For example, if the patient says that he or she does not remember or asks for repetition of instructions, say: **"Do it as I said. Do as much as you remember."** Discontinue after three consecutive failures (i.e., on sections A, B and C, if no part of the question received credit; on section D, if only one part; and on sections E and F, if only two parts received credit).

Table 7–12.   Token Arrangement in Front of Subject

Row 1

Large circles in order: red, blue, yellow, white, green

Row 2

Large squares in order: blue, red, white, green, yellow

Row 3

Small circles in order: white, blue, yellow, red, green

Row 4

Small squares in order: yellow, green, red, blue, white

The first section (questions 1 through 7) also provides a gross check on color blindness which might affect performance on this test. If difficulties in color recognition are noticed, further examination with the Ishihara plates or a similar test of color blindness is necessary. If gross color blindness is established both by this test and by a color-vision test, the test should be omitted.

Scoring

The questions are listed on Score Sheet Figure 7–23. Give 1-point credit for each underlined part of a question correctly performed. For example, the correct performance of questions 1–7 receives 1 credit each, the correct performance of questions 12 through 15 (*"small, white circle"*) receives 3 credits each. For questions 24–39, the verb and the preposition as well as the correct token receive credit (e.g., *"Put the red circle on the green square"* = 6 credits). Occasionally a preposition may be interpreted in several ways; for example, item 25 (i.e., "behind") may be viewed as away from the patient or as to the right of the yellow circle. In these instances, any reasonable interpretation of the preposition is accepted and scored as correct. Similarly, if the subject puts the green circle behind the red square, he or she receives 5 points of credit, since the performance shows that the five parts of the command (i.e., put, red, green, circle, square) were comprehended, but the relationship ("on") was not. If the test is discontinued, prorate the remaining items of that section on the basis of the subject's performance on the administered items. For example, if the test is discontinued after item 31 of Part F, and items 24–31 received 6 points, the remaining eight items would also be prorated with 6 points, for a total of 12 points for part F. If all or most items of sections B, C, D, E, and/or F have not been given because of previous failures, add a score of 3 points for Part B, 5 points for Part C, 6 points for Part D, 9 points for part E, and 18 points for Part F. No corrections for age and educational level are necessary. Maximum Score = 163.

Score Sheet 7–20
IDENTIFICATION BY SENTENCE (TOKEN TEST)

A. Present tokens as in Table 7–12. Instructions may be repeated once	
1. Show me a circle	
2. Show me a square	
3. Show me a yellow one	
4. Show me a red one	
5. Show me a blue one	
6. Show me a green one	
7. Show me a white one	
TOTAL A(7)	

B. Present only large tokens. Instructions may be repeated once	
8. Show me the **yellow square**	
9. Show me the **blue circle**	
10. Show me the **green circle**	
11. Show me the **white square**	
TOTAL B(8)	

C. Present all tokens as in Table 7–12. Do not repeat instructions	
12. Show me the **small white circle**	
13. Show me the **large yellow square**	
14. Show me the **large green sqaure**	
15. Show me the **small blue square**	
TOTAL C(12)	

D. Present large tokens only. Do not repeat instructions	
16. Take the **red circle** and the **green square**	
17. Take the **yellow square** and the **blue square**	
18. Take the **white square** and the **green circle**	
19. Take the **white circle** and the **red circle**	
TOTAL D(16)	

E. Present all tokens as in Table 7–12. Do not repeat instructions	
20. Take the **large white circle** and the **small green square**	
21. Take the **small blue circle** and the **large yellow square**	
22. Take the **large green sqaure** and the **large red square**	
23. Take the **large white square** and the **small green circle**	
TOTAL E(24)	

Figure 7–23.   NCCEA Subtest 11 (Token Test) sample scoring sheet.

F. Present large tokens only. Do not repeat instructions	
24. **Put** the **red circle on** the **green square.**	
25. **Put** the **white square behind** the **yellow circle.**	
26. **Touch** the **blue circle with** the **red square.**	
27. **Touch** the **blue circle and** the **red square.**	
28. **Pick up** the **blue circle OR** the **red square.**	
29. **Move** the **green square away from** the **yellow square.**	
30. **Put** the **white circle in front of** the **blue square.**	
31. **If** there is a **black circle, pick up** the **red square.**	
32. **Pick up all squares except** the **yellow one.**	
33. **Put** the **green square beside** the **red circle.**	
34. **Touch** the **squares slowly and** the **circles quickly.**	
35. **Put** the **red circle between** the **yellow square** and the **green square.**	
36. **Touch all circles, except** the **green one.**	
37. **Pick up** the **red circle—no**—the **white square.**	
38. **Instead of** the **white square, pick up** the **yellow circle.**	
39. **Together with** the **yellow circle, pick up** the **blue circle.**	

TOTAL   F(96)

TOTAL A-F (163) ☐

Figure 7–23.   (*Continued*)

Comment

This popular test was listed by 31% of speech therapists as one of their "frequently used tests" (Beele et al., 1984). Boller and Dennis (1979) reviewed the extensive literature of clinical and experimental studies. The current version of the Token Test uses a scoring system that credits almost *every word* of each item rather than assigning a score of 1 point for the *entire item*. The first four parts of the test were found to be homogeneous in a test of a probabilistic test mode, whereas the last part was different because of the greater syntactic/semantic variability that was introduced (Willmes, 1981).

For normal children above age 11 and for adults with average intelligence, ceiling scores can be expected. For this reason, one-year retest reliability in older adults has been reported as only .50 (Snow et al., 1988). Three-day retest reliability in 30 aphasics was between .92 and .94 (Gallagher, 1979). Orgass (1976) reported a retest reliability of .96.

The scoring is sensitive to even minor impairments of receptive language: Spellacy and Spreen (1969) reported a correct classification rate of 89% for unselected aphasics and of 72% for nonaphasic brain-damaged patients, using a cutoff score of 156. De Renzi and Faglioni (1978) and Cavalli et al. (1981) found virtually no difference between patients with right-hemisphere lesions and normal controls. Our own data do show a mild impairment of right-hemisphere nonaphasic patients. The difference between these two findings is probably due to our more sensitive scoring system. This contention is born out by the findings of Swisher and Sarno (1969) that patients with right-hemisphere lesions without aphasia had significantly poorer scores than controls on Parts E and F of the test, although left brain-damaged aphasics showed the highest number of errors.

De Renzi and Faglioni (1978) reported correct classification rates of 93% for aphasics as compared to 95% for patients without damage to the central nervous system. Good discrimination between aphasic and nonaphasic adults was also reported by Cohen et al. (1976), Orgass (1976), Sarno (1986), and Woll et al. (1976). Sarno, Buonaguro, and Levita (1985) found no sex differences on the Token Test between moderately and severely aphasic patients, either four to six months after stroke or in their course of recovery over a period of two years. Lang (1981) reported that the test was most sensitive in global and sensory aphasia, whereas the error percentage was lower in motor aphasia and relatively minor in amnestic aphasia. The test was also sensitive to changes in patients after ventrolateral thalamotomy, but not after pulvinotomy (Vilkki & Laitinen, 1976). McNeil (1983), on the other hand, claimed that the variability of performance as well as nonverbal deficits shown by aphasics reflects general brain damage and "oscillating biological systems" and attention deficits rather than specific linguistic or focal neurological damage. Similarly, Riedel and Studdert-Kennedy (1985) maintained that impairment on the Token Test and similar perceptual tasks in aphasics reflects a general cognitive rather than a language-specific deficit.

The test is not only sensitive to language impairment in adults; Ewing-Cobbs et al. (1987) reported that about 25% of children and adolescents with closed head injury showed impaired scores on the Token Test. Mean centile scores (using age-appropriate norms) for 5- to 10-year olds with mild injury were 46.8 and for moderate to severe injury 47.5; for 11- to 15-year-olds, the respective scores were 58.9 and 51.9. Gutbrod and Michel (1986) found good discriminative validity for aphasic children and adolescents. Lenhard (1983) found that 100 6-year-old children who had hyperbilirubinemia as infants performed significantly more poorly than normals on the Token Test, and that children who had received phototherapy in infancy did more poorly than those who had not. Tallal, Stark, and Mellits (1985) found the Token Test as well as other auditory comprehension tests to be sensitive to developmental aphasia. Naeser et al. (1987) claimed that the Token Test performance of 3-year-old children resembled that of severe Wernicke's aphasia, and that the performance of 6-year-olds was similar to that of aphasics with mild comprehension deficits and frontal–parietal perisylvian lesions (i.e., the notion of comprehension deficit in aphasia as a regression to developmental stages). A similar hypothesis was supported by a study of 10 normal elderly subjects (Emery, 1986).

A correlation of .63 between the Token Test and the Northwestern Syntax Screening Test in children 5–8 years old has been interpreted as an indicator of the validity of the Token Test for receptive language (Cartwright & Lass, 1974). Similarly, Lass and Golden (1975) reported a correlation of .71 between the Token Test and the PPVT in normal children 5–12 years old. Harris et al. (1983) found that in 104 children 6–8 years old who were followed up for the effects of different ranges of birthweight and bilirubin, low scores on the Token Test were related to poorer scores as well as a similar right-ear advantage on a dichotic consonant–vowel and a dichotic staggered spondaic word test. They interpreted these results as indicating a "lack of pronounced hemispheric dominance for language." A study by Whitehouse (1983) reported significant differences between dyslexic and normal reading adolescents (grades 7 through 12), but emphasized that 55% of the dyxlexics did not make more errors than normal readers. She concluded that errors on Part E of the Token Test reflected an impaired ability to process cognitive information. The Token Test also did not predict paragraph comprehension scores in adult aphasics (Brookshire & Nicholas, 1984). Correlation with the WISC-R Verbal and Performance IQs were reported as .42 and .47, respectively (Kitson, 1985). Fusilier and Lass (1984) reported that the Token Test showed significant correlations only with the grammatical closure and sound blending tasks of the 12 tasks of the IPTA, suggesting that the two tests measure relatively different aspects of language.

Factor-analytic validity in children was established by Niebergall et al. (1978) and Remschmidt et al. (1977), who found strong loadings on a verbal communication and language development first factor as well as high correlations with age in the younger group of children 6–14 years old. The authors interpret the factor-analytic findings as indicating that the Token Test measures more complex language abilities in addition to comprehension.

Normative Data

Table 7–13 provides our normative data for adults. The mean score for adults (and adolescents 14 years and over) is 161. Scores below 157 are virtually absent in a

Table 7–13.   Percentile Ranks for the Token Test for Normal Adults

Score	Percentile ranks
162	70
161	50
158	30
157	18
156	14
154	10
153	6
151	—

Table 7–14. Token Test Norms in Percentiles for Children Ages 6–13

Score	Centiles in children of age:								Centiles in adults
	6	7	8	9	10	11	12	13	
163	90	90	90	90	84	84	84	84	75+
162	88	86	86	86	75	75	75	75	70
161	86	84	81	78	65	61	61	57	50
160	84	78	78	72	57	50	47	39	40
159	84	75	68	65	47	35	32	19	35
158	81	72	65	53	35	25	19	8	30
157	78	68	61	47	25	16	10	2	18
156	78	61	57	39	19	8	4	0.9	14
155	75	57	53	28	12	4	2		12
154	72	53	43	22	7	2	1		10
153	72	50	35	16	4	1	0.7		6
152	68	47	28	10	2	0.8			
151	65	39	22	8	1	0.3			
150	61	35	16	4	0.9				
149	61	32	12	2	0.5				
148	57	28	7	1					
147	53	25	4	1					
146	53	19	3	0.8					
145	50	16	2	0.5					
144	47	14	1						
143	43	12	1						
142	43	10	0.7						
141	39	7							
140	35	5							
139	35	4							
138	32	4							
137	28	3							
136	25	2							
135	25	1							
134	22								
133	19								
132	19								
131	16								
130	14								
129	14								
128	12								
127	10								
126	8								
125	8								
124	7								
123	5								
122	5								
121	4								
120	4								
119	3								
118	3								
117	2								
116	2								
115	2								
114	1								

normal adult population. Tuokko (1985) reported that this cutoff also holds for elderly subjects between 60 and 85 years of age, and De Renzi and Faglioni (1978) reported a correlation with age of only −.03. Swisher and Sarno (1969) also found no significant age effect. However, De Renzi and Faglioni did recommend a correction for education [+2.36 − (.30) (years of schooling) for an item-by-item scoring], but our experience has been that such a correction is not needed for subjects with a grade 8+ education.

Normative data for children, presented in Table 7–14, are based on studies by Hamsher (personal communication, 1981) and Gaddes and Crockett (1975). The progression of scores is quite similar to that reported by Noll (1970) and Whitaker and Noll (1972). Remschmidt et al. (1977), using a pass–fail score system for each item, also found a leveling-off of the error score after age 8.

Zaidel (1977) reported mean scores of 143.7 for 5:5-year-old, and of 125.4 for 4:6-year-old children, suggesting a consistent downward extension of these norms.

REFERENCES

Beele, K.A., Davies, E., & Miller, D.J. (1984). Therapists' views on the clinical usefulness of four aphasia tests. *British Journal of Disorders of Communication, 19,* 169–178.

Boller, F. & Dennis, M. (1979). *Auditory Comprehension. Clinical and Experimental Studies with the Token Test.* New York: Academic Press.

Brookshire, R.H., & Nicholas, L.E. (1984). Comprehension of directly and indirectly stated main ideas and details in discourse by brain-damaged and non–brain-damaged patients. *Brain and Language, 21,* 21–36.

Cartwright, L.R., and Lass, N.J. (1974). A comparative study of children's performance on the Token Test, Northwestern Syntax Screening Test, and Peabody Picture Vocabulary Test. *Acta Symbolica, 5,* 19–29.

Cavalli, M., De Renzi, E., Faglioni, P., & Vitale, A. (1981). Impairment of right brain-damaged patients on a linguistic cognitive task. *Cortex, 17,* 545–556.

Cohen, R., Kelter, S., Engel, D. List, G., & Strohner, H. (1976). Zur Validität des Token-Tests. *Nervenarzt, 47,* 357–361.

Cole, K.N., & Fewell, R.R. (1983). A quick language screening test for young children. *Journal of Speech and Hearing Disorders, 48,* 149–153.

De Renzi, E., & Faglioni, P. (1978). Develop-

ment of a shortened version of the Token Test. *Cortex, 14,* 41–49.

De Renzi, E., & Vignolo, L. (1962). The Token Test: A sensitive test to detect receptive disturbances in aphasics. *Brain, 85,* 665–678.

Di Simoni, F. (1978). *The Token Test for Children.* Highman, Mass.: Teaching Resources.

Emery, O.B. (1986). Linguistic decrement in normal aging. *Language and Communication, 6,* 47–64.

Ewing-Cobbs, L., Levin, H.S., Eisenberg, H.M., & Fletcher, J.M. (1987). Language functions following closed-head injury in children and adolescents. *Journal of Clinical and Experimental Neuropsychology, 9,* 575–592.

Fusilier, F.M., & Lass, N.J. (1984). A comparative study of children's performance on the Illinois Test of Psycholinguistic Abilities and the Token Test. *Journal of Auditory Research, 24,* 9–16.

Gaddes, W.H., & Crockett, D.J. (1975). The Spreen–Benton aphasia test: Normative data as a measure of normal language development. *Brain and Language, 4,* 257–280.

Gallagher, A.J. (1979). Temporal reliability of aphasic performance on the Token Test. *Brain and Language, 7,* 34–41.

Gutbrod, K., & Michel, M. (1986). Zur klinischen Validität des Token Tests bei hirngeschädigten Kindern mit und ohne Aphasie. *Diagnostica, 32,* 118–128.

Harris, V.L., Keith, R.W., & Novak, K.K. (1983). Relationship between two dichotic listening tests and the Token Test for children. *Ear and Hearing, 6,* 278–282.

Kiernan, J. (1985). Visual presentation of the Revised Token Test: Some normative data and use in modality-independent testing. *Folia Phoniatrica, 37,* 216–222.

Kitson, D.L. (1985). Comparison of the Token Test language development and the WISC-R. *Perceptual and Motor Skills, 61,* 532–534.

Lang, C. (1981). Token-Test und Drei-Figuren-Test: Ein Vergleich zwischen zwei psychometrischen Kurztesten zur Sprachverständnisprüfung. *Diagnostica, 27,* 39–50.

Lass, N.J., De Paolo, A.M., Simcoe, J.C., & Samuel, S.M. (1975). A normative study of children's performance on the short form of the Token Test. *Journal of Communication Disorders, 8,* 193–198.

Lass, N.J., & Golden, S.S. (1975). A comparative study of children's performance on three tests for receptive language abilities. *Journal of Auditory Research, 15,* 177–182.

Lenhard, M.L. (1983). Effects of neonatal hyperbilirubinemia on Token Test performance of six-year old children. *Journal of Auditory Research, 23,* 195–204.

Martino, A.A., Pizzamiglio, L., & Razzano, C. (1976). A new version of the Token Test for aphasics: A concrete objects form. *Journal of Communication Disorders, 9,* 1–5.

McNeil, M.R. (1983). Aphasia: Neurological considerations. *Topics in Language Disorders, 3,* 1–19.

Naeser, M.A., Mazurski, P., Goodglass, H., & Peraino, M. (1987). Auditory syntactic comprehension in nine aphasic groups (with CT scan) and children: Differences in degree, but not order of difficulty observed. *Cortex, 23,* 359–380.

Niebergall, G., Remschmidt, H., Geyer, M., & Merschmann, W. (1978). Zur faktoriellen Validität des Token-Tests in einer unausgelesenen Stichprobe von Schulkin-dern. *Praxis der Kinderpsychologie und Kinderpsychiatrie, 27,* 5–10.

Noll, J.D. (1970). *The Use of the Token Test with Children: Program of the American Speech and Hearing Association.* New York: ASHA.

Orgass, B. (1976). Eine Revision des Token Tests II. Validitätsnachweis, Normierung und Standardisierung. *Diagnostica, 22,* 141–156.

Remschmidt, H., Niebergall, G., Geyer, M., & Merschmann, W. (1977). Die Bestimmung testmetrischer Kennwerte des Token-Testes bei Schulkindern unter Berücksichtigung der Intelligenz, des "Wortschatzes" und der Händigkeit. *Zeitschrift für Kinder- und Jugendpsychiatrie, 5,* 222–237.

Riedel, K., & Studdert-Kennedy, M. (1985). Extending formant transitions may not improve aphasic's perception of stop consonant place of articulation. *Brain and Language, 24,* 223–232.

Sarno, M.T. (1986). Verbal impairment in head injury. *Archives of Physical and Medical Rehabilitation, 67,* 399–404.

Sarno, M.T., Buonaguro, A., & Levita, E. (1985). Gender and recovery from aphasia after stroke. *Journal of Nervous and Mental Disease, 173,* 605–609.

Snow, W.G., Tierney, M.C., Zorzitto, M.L., Fisher, R.H., & Reid, D.W. (1988). One-year test–retest reliability of selected neuropsychological tests in older adults. Paper presented at the International Neuropsychological Society Meeting, New Orleans. *Journal of Clinical and Experimental Neuropsychology, 10,* 60 (abstract).

Spellacy, F., & Spreen, O. (1969). A short form of the Token Test. *Cortex, 5,* 390–397.

Spreen, O., & Benton, A.L. (1969, 1977). *The Neurosensory Center Comprehensive Examination for Aphasia.* University of Victoria: Neuropsychology Laboratory.

Swisher, L.P., & Sarno, M.T. (1969). Token Test scores of three matched patient groups: Left brain-damaged with aphasia; right brain-damaged without aphasia; non–brain-damaged. *Cortex, 5,* 264–273.

Tallal, P., Stark, R.E., & Mellits, D. (1985). The relationship between auditory temporal analysis and receptive language development: Evidence from studies of developmental language disorder. *Neuropsychologia, 23*, 527–534.

Tuokko, H. (1985). Norms on the Token Test for Elderly Subjects. Mimeo. Vancouver: University of British Columbia Alzheimers Clinic.

Van Harskamp, F., & Van Dongen, H.R. (1977). Construction and validation of different short forms of the Token Test. *Neuropsychologia, 15*, 467–470.

Vilkki, J., & Lattinen, L.V. (1976). Effects of pulvinotomy and ventrolateral thalamotomy on some cognitive functions. *Neuropsychologia, 14*, 67–78.

Whitaker, H.A., & Noll, J.D. (1972). Some linguistic parameters of the Token Test. *Neuropsychologia, 10*, 395–404.

Willmes, K. (1981). A new look at the Token Test using probabilistic test models. *Neuropsychologia, 19*, 631–645.

Whitehouse, C.C. (1983). Token Test performance by dyslexic adolescents. *Brain and Language, 18*, 224–235.

Woll, G., Naumann, E., Cohen, R., & Kelter, S. (1976). Kreuzvalidierung der Revision des Token Tests durch Orgass. *Diagnostica, 22*, 157–162.

Zaidel, E. (1977). Unilateral auditory language comprehension on the Token Test following cerebral commissurotomy and hemispherectomy. *Neuropsychologia, 15*, 1–18.

8

Visual, Visuomotor, and Auditory Tests

Numerous tests of "visual–perceptual" and "visuomotor" performance have been developed, especially stimulated by the notion that such tests may contribute to the riddle of dyslexia, but also aimed at subtle disorders of spatial recognition, orientation, and forms of agnosia. We include only a small selection of such tests, in an attempt to avoid duplication. Our selection was also guided by clinical experience as well as by correlational studies indicating that each of these tests makes a unique contribution to the examination of the patient.

Some tests require basic abilities of color recognition. Color blindness per se is sometimes of interest in neuropsychology, but screening for color blindness may be essential if any doubt arises regarding the patient's ability to distinguish colors. The most frequently used tests for color blindness consist of pseudoisochromatic plates (i.e., letters, numbers, or shapes printed in color on a gray background of matching darkness; these cannot be traced by color-blind persons). The tests by Ishahara (1982) and Dvorine (1953) appear to be optimal under different viewing conditions (Long et al., 1985).

Only a few specific auditory tests have been developed; however, in a wider sense many of the tests described in the language section could have been included in this section, but they are more appropriately placed in the context of these other sections of the book.

We did not include a number of other tests derived from the Seashore Tests of Musical Ability—for example, the Seashore Rhythm Test (Reitan & Wolfson, 1989), the Wepman Speech Sound Perception Test, the phoneme discrimination test (Benton et al., 1983), and the Meikle Consonant Perception Test developed in our laboratory—because in our experience these tests fail to add important specific information to the patient's disability profile, owing to their limited usefulness and/or inadequate standardization.

Prior to the administration of any of the auditory tests, a screening for auditory acuity of the patient is necessary. There is no need for a full audiologic evaluation, unless the screening indicates hearing loss. We use a standard Maico audiometer which generates a pure-tone signal calibrated in decibels (db); for each ear, fre-quencies (pitch) of 500, 1,000, 2,000, 4,000, and 6,000 Hz are tested with one ascending and one descending trial. Hearing levels between 0 and 15 db are considered normal; hearing levels of 35 db and higher indicate impairment and tend to invalidate auditory tests unless the impairment is bilateral and uniformly affects all frequencies (in this case, a stronger amplification of the test signals is indicated).

REFERENCES

Benton, A.L., Hamsher, K.deS., Varney, N.R., & Spreen, O. (1983). *Contributions to Neuropsychological Assessment*. New York: Oxford University Press.

Dvorine, I. (1953). *Dvorine Pseudo-Iso-chromatic Plates*. New York: Psychological Corporation.

Ishahara, S. (1982). *The Series of Plates Designed as a Test for Color-Blindness*. Tokyo: Kanehara.

Long, G.M., Lyman, B.J., & Tuck, J.P. (1985). Distance, duration, and blur effects on the perception of pseudoiso-chromatic stimuli. *Ophthalmic and Physiological Optics*, 5, 185–194.

Reitan, R.M., & Wolfson, D. (1989). The Seashore Rhythm Test and brain functions. *Clinical Neuropsychologist*, 3, 70–78.

CLOCK DRAWING

Purpose

This test is a clinical screening task for visuo-spatial and constructional disabilities.

Source

No material required

Description

The simple free-hand drawing of a clock face has, together with the drawing of a daisy, house—also of a person, a bicycle—been part of the brief mental status examination in neurology for a long time (Battersby et al. 1956, Critchley 1953, Goodglass and Kaplan 1972, Strub and Black 1977) and is frequently recom-mended as a screening test for dementia. In contrast to the primarily verbal content of most dementia scales, clock drawing relies on visuo-spatial, construc-tional, as well as cognitive abilities. The test requires merely a sheet of paper and a pencil, and can be given as part of a bedside examination, or in other instances when lengthy neuropsychological testing is not possible. Freehand drawing is preferred to Wolf-Klein et al.'s (1989) procedure, which uses a sheet with a printed circle, representing the shape of the clock face.

Administration

Place a standard unlined letter-size sheet of paper and a pencil in front of the patient and say: "**I want you to draw the face of a clock with all the numbers on it. Make it large.**" After completion of the clock-face, instruct as follows: "**Now, draw the hands, pointing at 20 to 4**". Instructions may be repeated or rephrased if the patient does not understand, but no other help should be given. The time taken to complete the task may be noted.

Approximate Time for Administration

5 minutes.

Scoring

A 10-point scoring system is used as follows[1]:

10 Normal drawing, numbers and hands in approximately correct positions, hour hand distinctly different from minute hand and approaching 4 o'clock.

9 Slight errors in placement of hands (not exactly on 8 and 4, but not on one of the adjoining numbers) or one missing number on clock face.

8 More noticeable errors in placement of hour and minute hand (off by one number); number spacing shows a gap.

7 Placement of hands significantly off course (more than one number); very inappropriate spacing of numbers (e.g., all on one side).

6 Inappropriate use of clock hands (use of digital display or circling of numbers despite repeated instructions); crowding of numbers at one end of the clock or reversal of numbers.

5 Perseverative or otherwise inappropriate arrangement of numbers (e.g., numbers indicated by dots). Hands may be represented, but do not clearly point at a number.

4 Numbers absent, written outside of clock or in distorted sequence. Integrity of the clock face missing. Hands not clearly represented.

3 Numbers and clock face no longer connected in the drawing. Hands not recognizably present.

[1]Adapted from Sunderland et al. (1989) and Wolf-Klein et al. (1989)

2 Drawing reveals some evidence of instructions received, but representation of clock is only vague; inappropriate spatial arrangement of numbers.

1 Irrelevant, uninterpretable figure or no attempt.

For the clinical interpretation of the clock-face drawing, special features should be noted, such as crowding of the drawing into one corner of the page, "closing in," (i.e., placing lines too close to each other), oblique shape, tremulousness, inaccurate meeting of the circle line.

Comment

Repeat test reliability has not been reported. Inter-rater reliability for drawings by elderly normals and Alzheimer's disease patients was .97, and did not differ between clinicians and nonclinicians (Sunderland et al. 1989).

Validity has been investigated in differentiating groups of normal elderly and patient groups with Alzheimer's diesase, multi-infarct dementia, and depression (Wolf-Klein et al. 1989) with a mean age of 76 years. Correct classification in normals was 97%, for Alzheimer's disease patients 87%, for multi-infarct dementia 62%, and for depression 97%.

While the significance of the test in contributing to the diagnosis of Alzheimer's disease has been established, it should be noted that this test serves many purposes, and basically provides an estimate of visuo-spatial as well as cognitive skills. The test results are seriously affected by hemianopsia and visual neglect, which is apparent in corresponding unilateral errors. It is also sensitive to more limited visuo-spatial disorders or constructional apraxia, such as those found in right or bilateral temporoparietal lesions (Critchley 1953). The appropriate interpretation should be made in the context of other test results.

Normative Data

Currently available normative data suggest (Sunderland et al. 1989, Wolf-Klein 1989) that scores between 7 and 10 should be considered normal; a score of 6 is borderline (achieved by 13% of normals and 88% of Alzheimer's disease patients; scores of 5 or less are rare in normals (.8%), but frequent in Alzheimer's disease (83%).

REFERENCES

Battersby, W.S., Bender, M.B., Pollack, M. & Kahn, R.L. (1956). Unilateral "spatial agnosia" ("inattention") in patients with cortical lesions. *Brain*, 79, 68–93.

Critchley, M. (1953). *The Parietal Lobes*. (Reprinted 1966). New York: Hafner.

Goodglass, H. & Kaplan, E. (1972). *The Assessment of Aphasia and Related Disorders*. Philadelphia: Lea & Fibiger.

Strub, R.L. & Black, F.W. (1977). *The Mental Status Examination in Neurology*. Philadelphia: F.A. Davis.

Sunderland, T., Hill, J.L., Mellow, A.M., Lawlor, B.A., Gundersheimer, J., Newhouse, P.A. & Grafman, J.H. (1989). Clock drawing in Alzheimer's disease; a novel measure of dementia severity. *Journal of the American Geriatric Association*, 37, 725–729.

Wolf-Klein, G.P., Silverstone, F.A., Levy, A.P. & Brod, M.S. (1989). Screening for Alzheimer's disease by clock drawing. *Journal of the American Geriatric Association*, 37, 730–734.

DICHOTIC LISTENING

Words

PURPOSE

This test is an indicator of language lateralization; secondarily, it is a measure of temporal lobe functional integrity.

SOURCE

Cassette tape with dichotic words, instructions, and score sheets can be obtained from the Neuropsychology Laboratory, University of Victoria, Victoria, British Columbia V8W 2Y2, Canada, for $11.50 Cdn. The original Kimura stimuli (including digits, melodies, and words are available from DK Consultants, 412 Duffrin Avenue, London, Ontario N6B 1Z6, Canada, for $160 Cdn. (with additional children's digits $200 Cdn.).

DESCRIPTION

This test was originally developed by Broadbent (1958) to investigate the ability to attend to two signals simultaneously, one to each ear. Kimura (1961) modified the task by using spoken one-syllable numbers in sets of three pairs, after which the subject was requested to repeat as many of the numbers as possible. Kimura noted that in epileptic patients with documented left-hemisphere speech dominance, right-ear recall was better than recall from the left ear. Patients with right-hemisphere speech showed the reverse. These findings are consistent with the notion that crossed auditory connections are stronger than ipsilateral pathways. Her subsequent studies also suggested a left-ear preference for the recognition of nonverbal information such as music. Numerous experimental investigations with a wide variety of stimulus material and subject populations followed these initial studies. There are a number of different tests available, including the free-recall technique (e.g., Kimura, 1961), the dichotic monitoring test (Geffen et al., 1978), and the fused-rhyme procedure (Wexler & Halwes, 1983). There is no clear evidence that one procedure is better than another in predicting speech lateralization (Strauss, 1988). More recently, the test has also been used as a measure of stimulus processing speed, assuming that the results are influenced by limitations of the immediate processing channel.

We use a free-recall technique similar to the one developed by Kimura (1961) in which six one-syllable words are presented, three to each ear. The tape prepared in our laboratory is synchronized for stimulus onset and calibrated for equal loudness in both ears. Both right- and left-ear stimuli begin with the same consonant to control voice onset time.

The apparatus consists of a high-quality stereo tape-player and amplifier, a pair of earphones plugged into the appropriate outlets, and the dichotic words tape. The right and left channel on the tape may be connected to the right or left earphone of the subject. They can be used alternately, or reversed after half of the test (to avoid bias created by poor earphone calibration), but care should be taken to note, on the answer sheet, which channel goes to which ear.

A sound-level meter (Scott or similar product) should be used in order to calibrate and balance the earphones before starting the test. The earphones should be calibrated to produce exactly equal loudness of 65–70 db for both ears.

Before administering the test, the examiner should check the subject with the audiometer to determine whether there is satisfactory hearing in both ears. Dichotic listening effects are fairly robust in the presence of minor hearing impairment (discrepancy of 5–10 db between right and left ears), but with higher discrepancies, the results should be interpreted with caution. If the discrepancy between ears is beyond 20 db, the test should not be given.

ADMINISTRATION

The subject is seated with earphones on, the earphone marked "RIGHT" on the right ear and that marked "LEFT" on the left ear. Say: **"You are going to hear some words, and I want you to repeat as many of these words as possible."** On the tape are two three-word sets of single words. The first set is heard by the right ear. After the subject repeats these words correctly, play the second set, which is heard by the left ear. These practice sets can be repeated if the subject fails to understand the instructions. If the subject completes the practice trials correctly, say: **"You will now hear words that will come into both ears at the same time. I want you to repeat all the words you hear. Each time you will hear three sets of words, and when I stop the tape, you must start repeating words immediately, as many as you can remember."**

After each set of three word pairs, stop the tape and wait for the subject to respond. Circle the words the subject remembers on the answer sheet (see Fig. 8–

```
                    Dichotic Listening–Words
                     Sample Answer Sheet
        Ear:        Track: Right          Track: Left
        Trial Set
        1.          pack tent hat         port tea cow
        2.          fame sum bond         fur sale bee
        3.          duck ship gas         deck shoe gun
        4.          vine zone mob         vane zoo meal
        5.          nose pride track      name plate trail
        6.          coast flight sake     corn fleet sunk
        7.          bowl damp good        bell deed game
        8.          shine vent zest       sheep vast zeal
        9.          mass nine pin         mill nail pace
        10.         tin cloth faith       torn clock fresh
        11.         spit belt night       speak bark need
        12.         shell guard vote      shore guest vault
        13.         there mad nick        though map note
        14.         pig teeth crust       pal tongue cream
        15.         fault sand brain      flag send blown
        16.         ditch glow shirt      dawn give shift
        17.         view this mouth       vim then mink
        18.         noon pork tan         noun pan top
        19.         cord fit stamp        coop fog style
        20.         band noise glove      birth neck grain
        21.         shoot voice than      shame verb that
        22.         mine nice cord        male nudge coop

        Total: Right Ear ____ Left Ear ____ Both Ears ____
```

Figure 8–1. Dichotic listening (Words) sample answer sheet.

1). Dubious responses should be written above the word they resemble, but *only the words on the answer sheet are accepted as correct.*

If the subject responds with only one or two words, you may say once: **"Is that all?"** or **"Are those all the words that you can remember?"** before proceeding with the next set.

APPROXIMATE TIME FOR ADMINISTRATION

About 10–20 minutes is required.

SCORING

Count 1 point for each word that is listed on the record sheet. Total each side.

COMMENT

Test–retest reliability is good (.75 to .92). No significant practice effects need be expected.

The test agrees reasonably well with speech localization as determined by the sodium amytal test (Strauss et al., 1987). In that study, patients with left-hemisphere speech lateralization obtained scores of 29.03 for the right ear, 12.95 for the left ear; the corresponding scores for patients with right-hemisphere speech were 15.20 and 21.48, and for patients with bilateral speech the scores were 19.88 and 13.24. However, the percentage of patients with right ear advantage in the three groups was 86%, 50%, and 71%. Failure to obtain a right–left ear difference suggests that language lateralization may not follow the normal pattern. In normal right-handers the test seems to underestimate the incidence of left-hemisphere speech lateralization (74%) which is consistent with Lake and Bryden's (1976) finding of 75% in right-handed males. Right-handed females apparently show even lower incidence rates for right-ear advantage (62%; Lake & Bryden, 1976). Hence firm statements about language lateralization cannot be made; the test provides clues only.

Both total score and difference scores have been investigated as measures of stimulus processing speed (Levine et al. 1986, Saccuzzo et al. 1986, Strayer et al. 1987). However, there is only a moderate correlation with tests measuring similar abilities, e.g., Test D2, Trail Making, PASAT, and the right-left difference score loads on a factor separate from an information processing factor (Spellacy and Ehle, 1990).

NORMATIVE DATA

Normative data are shown in Table 8–1. In general, the total score for recall on the full tape is approximately 40 words. The proportion of words recalled from the right ear versus the left ear is of primary interest. Failure to obtain a right-ear difference suggests that language lateralization may not follow the normal pattern.

Normative data for children from preschool to regular kindergarten up to grade 6 (Table 8–1) suggest that children of kindergarten age already show right-ear superiority, and that right–left ear differences reach adult levels by grade 3. Overall recall scores in fact exceeded those of normal adults, possibly owing to lack of clarity of the tape used in the Strauss et al. study as well as to differences in attention.

Music

PURPOSE

The purpose of this test is to determine ear advantage for musical stimuli.

SOURCE

The dichotic listening tape for music was developed by Spellacy (1970) in our laboratory and is available through the Neuropsychology Laboratory, University of Victoria, British Columbia V8W 3P5, Canada. The price is approximately $11.50 Cdn. The original (1964) version is available from D. Kimura, DK Consultants,

Table 8–1. Verbal Dichotic Lightning: Norms for Children and Adults

Grade/Age	Sex	N	Right ear	Left ear	Total
Preschool					
Age 2	f	2	13.0	5.0	18.0
	m	3	12.0	2.0	14.0
Age 3	f	9	19.1	5.6	24.7
	m	5	15.3	4.8	20.0
Age 4	f	7	24.1	8.0	31.9
	m	7	25.3	9.8	35.2
Kinderg.					
Age 5	f	10	19.6	13.1	32.7
	m	9	20.2	16.9	37.1
Elem. school					
Grade 1	f	15	24.7	12.7	37.4
	m	12	26.8	16.0	42.8
Grade 2	f	29	29.0	12.4	41.3
	m	16	30.4	13.2	43.6
Grade 3	f	19	29.6	16.9	46.5
	m	11	29.1	19.2	48.3
Grade 4	f	15	32.5	16.9	48.7
	m	16	30.0	22.6	52.6
Grade 5	f	23	33.3	20.0	53.3
	m	15	31.0	20.6	51.5
Grade 6	f	12	30.5	19.6	50.1
	m	18	32.5	20.2	52.9
Adult					
Right-handers		175	M 24.95	16.23	41.18
			SD 9.60	8.30	10.12

Note: Kosaka and Kolb used the Victoria tape for adults, reversing the headphones after half of the trials.

Source: [Children's norms] Kosaka & Kolb (unpublished data, 1977); [adult right-hander norms] Strauss et al. (1987).

412 Duffrin Avenue, London, Ontario, Canada N6B 1Z6, at a cost of $160 Cdn., including digits, words, and melodies.

DESCRIPTION

Dichotic listening with musical stimuli was first introduced by Kimura (1964) who used commonly known melodies. We use taped (short two-second excerpts) musical stimuli (original compositions for the violin, excerpted from the musical aptitude test by Gordon, 1965) which are synchronized for onset and offset and simultaneously presented to the two ears. Since subjects cannot be expected to repeat the stimuli by singing, each pair of musical stimuli is followed by a recognition foil; the subject merely indicates whether the foil is the same melody as one of the two just heard. This technique unfortunately requires a large number of trials (46) and hence makes the test somewhat lengthy.

ADMINISTRATION

The apparatus is similar to the dichotic listening words test. Care must be taken to see that the RIGHT channel is coming to the RIGHT ear, and the LEFT to the LEFT ear. As in the verbal test, the subject's hearing should be tested first and the earphones calibrated. Instruct the subject as follows: "**You are going to hear two pieces of music, one in each ear. After a short pause, you will hear one piece of music. I want you to tell me whether the second piece that you heard was the same as either one of the previous two, or whether it was completely different from either of the first two pieces.**"

SCORING

The answer sheet (Fig. 8–2) consists merely of a sheet of paper numbered from 1 to 48; the examiner records "SAME" or "DIFFERENT" as the response to each trial.

MUSIC

NAME:_____   AGE:_____

TESTER:_____   DATE OF BIRTH:_____

TOP Channel - R - L ear   DATE OF TEST:_____

BOTTOM Channel L - R ear   SCORE: RIGHT EAR_____

LEFT EAR_____

Circle Correct Response

1.	S	D	17.	S	D	33.	S	D
2.	S	D	18.	S	D	34.	S	D
3.	S	D	19.	S	D	35.	S	D
4.	S	D	20.	S	D	36.	S	D
5.	S	D	21.	S	D	37.	S	D
6.	S	D	22.	S	D	38.	S	D
7.	S	D	23.	S	D	39.	S	D
8.	S	D	24.	S	D	40.	S	D
9.	S	D	25.	S	D	41.	S	D
10.	S	D	26.	S	D	42.	S	D
11.	S	D	27.	S	D	43.	S	D
12.	S	D	28.	S	D	44.	S	D
13.	S	D	29.	S	D	45.	S	D
14.	S	D	30.	S	D	46.	S	D
15.	S	D	31.	S	D	47.	S	D
16.	S	D	32.	S	D	48.	S	D

Figure 8–2.   Dichotic Listening, Music, Sample Scoring Sheet.

COMMENT

Information regarding reliability and validity is not available. We use this test only occasionally when speech and music lateralization are of importance in the assessment. Failure to recognize melodies correctly may also be indicative of right temporal lobe lesions (Lezak, 1983) and of amusia, but such suspicions should be checked out further by use of common tunes or similar material.

NORMATIVE DATA

Spellacy (1970) reports means of 19.5 correct for the left ear and of 17.0 for the right ear in 32 young adults, for a total of 36.5 correct out of 48.

REFERENCES

Broadbent, D.E. (1958). *Perception and Communication*. Oxford: Pergamon Press.

Geffen, G., Traub, E. & Stierman, I. (1978). Language laterality assessed by unilateral ECT and dichotic monitoring. *Journal of Neurology, Neurosurgery and Psychiatry, 41*, 354–360.

Gordon, E. (1965). *Musical Aptitude Profile*. Boston: Houghton Mifflin.

Kimura, D. (1961). Cerebral dominance and the perception of verbal stimuli. *Canadian Journal of Psychology, 15*, 166–171.

Kimura, D. (1964). Left–right differences in the perception of melodies. *Quarterly Journal of Experimental Psychology, 16*, 355–358.

Lake, D.A., & Bryden, M.P. (1976). Handedness and sex differences in hemispheric asymmetry. *Brain and Language, 3*, 266–282.

Levine, G., Preddy, D., & Thorndike, R. (1987). Speed of information processing and level of cognitive ability. *Personality and Individual Differences, 8*, 599–607.

Lezak, M. (1983). *Neuropsychological Assessment* (2nd ed.). New York: Oxford University Press.

Saccuzzo, D., Larson, G., & Rimland, B. (1986). Visual, auditory and reaction time approaches to the measurement of speed of information processing and individual differences in intelligence. *Personality and Individual Differences, 7*, 659–667.

Spellacy, F. (1970). Lateral preferences in the identification of patterned stimuli. *Journal of the Acoustical Society of America, 47*, 574–578.

Spellacy, F. & Ehle, D.L. (1990). The dichotic listening test as a measure of stimulus processing speed following mild to moderate concussion. Unpublished manuscript, University of Victoria.

Strauss, E. (1988). Dichotic listening and sodium amytal: Functional and morphological aspects of hemispheric asymmetry. In K. Hugdahl (Ed.), *Handbook of Dichotic Listening*. New York: Wiley.

Strauss, E., Gaddes, W.H., & Wada, J. (1987). Performance on a free-recall verbal dichotic listening task and cerebral dominance determined by the carotid amytal test. *Neuropsychologia, 25*, 747–753.

Strayer, D., Wickens, C., & Braune, R. (1987). Adult age differences in the speed and capacity of information processing: 2. An electrophysiological approach. *Psychology and Aging, 2*, 99–110.

Wexler, B.E. & Halwes, T. (1983). Increasing the power of dichotic methods: The fused rhymed words test. *Neuropsychologia, 21*, 59–66.

DEVELOPMENTAL TEST OF VISUAL–MOTOR INTEGRATION
(VMI)
Other Test Name

Beery Test.

Source

The manual ($19.00) and booklets for the long ($195.00) and short ($139.00) forms of this test can be ordered from Psychological Assessment Resources, P.O. Box 998, Odessa, Florida 33556, or from M.D. Angus Associates, 2639 Kingsway Avenue, Port Coquitlam, British Columbia, V3C 1T5, Canada, for $168 Cdn.

Description

This copying test (Beery, 1967; Beery & Buktenica, 1967) was restandardized in 1982 and is now available in a 1989 edition. It is also part of the Florida Kindergarten Screening Battery (Fletcher & Satz, 1982). It was originally modeled after the visual perception test of Frostig (1966), and was designed primarily for the child of preschool and elementary school age. It is similar to the Bender–Gestalt Test or the copying form of the Benton Visual Retention Test, but presents the geometric designs to be copied in clearly delineated squares of space equal to the original; moreover, the 24 designs follow a developmental gradient of difficulty starting with a vertical line for 2-year-olds and progressing to three-dimensional cube and star designs for 14- and 15-year-olds. The long form allows testing up to age 14:11 and, according to the author, retains validity for older age groups and adults (Beery, 1982). The short form includes the first 15 designs for children ages 2–8 years.

Administration

See source. Briefly, the subject is told: "**Make one like that,**" and "**Make yours right here**" (i.e., in the square below the stimulus figure). The test is discontinued after three consecutive failures. There are no time limits or time scores. Group administration is possible, although in that case discontinuation rules cannot be applied.

Approximate Time for Administration

About 15–20 minutes is required for the test.

Scoring

The 1989 manual provides explicit scoring criteria and examples of acceptable and unacceptable responses together with a number of "developmental comments" on typical drawings in children of different age levels. "Lenient" scoring is recommended; that is, when in doubt about the correctness of an individual drawing, credit should be given. The raw score for the original test was obtained by counting the number of acceptable drawings up to the discontinuation of the test. The 1989 edition expands the scoring to 1–4 points per item (particularly for items for older children) for a maximum of 50 points. The raw score can be converted into an age-equivalent score, a percentile, and a standard score by use of the tables in the manual. Consultation of tables in the source based on a restandardization (Beery, 1982) is recommended. Scoring requires some training. The test author's comment that scoring can be done by classroom teachers with minimal training has been criticized (Pryzwansky, 1977), but other studies confirm good interrater reliability (>.90) in both experienced raters and teachers with no experience with the test (Lepkin & Pryzwansky, 1983).

Comment

Interrater reliability for the original form has been reported to range from .58 to .99, with a median of .93 across a number of studies (Cosden, 1985). Retest reliability ranged from .63 after seven months to .92 after two weeks, and split-half reliability was .74 (Ryckman & Rentfrow, 1971) for various populations, whereas the test manual reports a median split-half reliability of .78.

The validity studies with the VMI focus on correlations with the Bender Gestalt test and the predictive validity for academic success. Correlations with the Bender Gestalt test range from .79 in mentally retarded males (Liemohn & Wagner, 1975), to .74 for learning disabled students, to .36 for normal students (Armstrong & Knopf, 1982; Breen, 1982). The VMI tends to produce somewhat lower age-equivalent scores (7 months) than the Bender, although this may be a function of the relatively low ceiling (11 years) of the Bender compared to the Beery, which provides challenging items up to age 15. Breen (1982), using the new standardization, also reports no differences in mean scores between the two tests in emotionally disturbed boys between the age of 5:9 and 12:1 years. Porter and Binder (1981) found a correlation of .62 between the two tests and suggested that, though sharing some common variance, the two tests measure different constructs of visual–motor development. A similar conclusion is reached by DeMers and Wright (1981), who compared results with the two tests in mentally retarded children.

As part of the Florida Kindergarten Screening Battery, the VMI, given at kindergarten age, predicted school achievement in grade 5 (Gates, 1984). Whereas one study did not find good prediction in grade 2 (Flynn & Flynn, 1978), another study confirmed good predictive validity for a cohort of 299 school children (LaTorre, 1985). Prediction of school achievement on the basis of the VMI alone has been poor (Duffy et al., 1976) or moderate (Klein, 1978; Reynolds et al., 1980); correlation with school achievement has been reported as .65 (Curtis et al., 1979). Other studies suggest that the VMI is more closely correlated with the Wechsler Intelligence Scale for Children (WISC) IQ than with achievement tests such as the Wide Range Achievement Test (WRAT) (Richardson et al., 1980). In this study, the VMI did not contribute significantly to the prediction of achievement when the WISC-IQ had been partialed out. It also still remains to be clarified whether the VMI is more related to achievement in arithmetic, language skills, or spelling. Other studies by Ysseldyke et al. (1981) suggest that the test loads most strongly on an arithmetic and a reasoning factor, and predicts composite achievement scores (Colarusso et al., 1980).

The performance of physically handicapped children on the Beery is likely to be impaired (Zeitschel et al., 1979). A useful chapter on remediation is included in the test manual.

In the context of a neuropsychological evaluation, the VMI would seem to be particularly useful for the exploration of visual–perceptual and motor skills in children, especially those with learning disabilities, but also in those with other neuropsychological deficits, although studies of such populations are not available. The use with very young children (ages 2–3 years) may be questionable since only three items cover the development of this two-year age span. The use of this test for adult patients may be appropriate, but in the absence of norms, especially for elderly subjects, any deviation from near-perfect scores (raw scores of 23 or 24 are expected for 14:11-year-olds) will have to be considered as an indication of deficit.

Normative Data

The 1969 manual contains normative data for ages 2:10 through 17:11, but these norms have been criticized because serious differences between ethnic and socioeconomic groups were found (Martin et al., 1977; Schooler & Anderson, 1979). The restandardization (Beery, 1982) based on 3,090 children, stratified according to the 1980 U.S. census with respect to ethnic origin, income, residence, and sex, seems to eliminate this problem. It provides norms for ages 2:11 through 14:6. No sex differences were found.

Norms for older adolescents and adults are not available. The author (Beery, 1982) suggests, however, that for practical purposes the norms for 13- and 14-year-olds can be used for older age groups.

REFERENCES

Armstrong, B.B., & Knopf, K.F. (1982). Comparison of the Bender–Gestalt and Revised Developmental Test of Visual–Motor Integration. *Perceptual and Motor Skills, 55,* 164–166.

Beery, K.E. (1967). *Developmental Test of Visual–Motor Integration.* Administration and Scoring Manual. Chicago: Follett Publishing.

Beery, K.E., & Buktenica, N.A. (1967). *Developmental Test of Visual–Motor Integration.* Student Test Booklet. Chicago: Follett Publishing.

Beery, K.E. (1982, 1989). *Revised Administration, Scoring, and Teaching Manual for the Developmental Test of Visual–Motor Integration.* Cleveland: Modern Curriculum Press.

Breen, M.J. (1982). Comparison of educationally handicapped students' scores on the Revised Developmental Test of Visual–Motor Integration and Bender Gestalt. *Perceptual and Motor Skills, 54,* 1227–1230.

Colarusso, R., Gill, S., Plankenhorn, A., & Brooks, R. (1980). Predicting first-grade achievement through formal testing of 5-year-old high-risk children. *Journal of Special Education, 14,* 355–363.

Cosden, M. (1985). Developmental Test of Visual–Motor Integration. In D.J. Keyser & R.C. Sweetland (Eds.), *Test Critiques* (Vol. 4, pp. 229–237). Kansas City, Missouri: Test Corporation of America.

Curtis, C.J., Michael, J.J., & Michael, W.B. (1979). The predictive validity of the Developmental Test of Visual–Motor Integration under group and individual modes of administration relative to academic performance measures of second-grade pupils without identifiable major learning disabilities. *Educational and Psychological Measurement, 39,* 401–410.

DeMers, S.T., & Wright, D. (1981). Comparison of scores on two visual–motor tests for children referred for learning or adjustment difficulties. *Perceptual and Motor Skills, 53,* 863–867.

Duffy, J.B., Ritter, D.R., & Fedner, M. (1976). Developmental Test of Visual–Motor Integration and the Goodenough

Draw-A-Man Test as predictors of academic success. *Perceptual and Motor Skills, 43,* 543–546.

Fletcher, J.M., & Satz, P. (1982). Kindergarten prediction of reading achievement: A seven-year longitudinal follow-up. *Educational and Psychological Measurement, 39,* 681–685.

Flynn, T.M., & Flynn, L.A. (1978). Evaluation of the predictive ability of five screening measures administered during kindergarten. *Journal of Experimental Education, 46,* 65–70.

Frostig, M., Lefever, D.W., & Whittlesey, J.R.B. (1966). *Administration and Scoring Manual for the Frostig Developmental Test of Visual Perception.* Palo Alto: Consulting Psychologists Press.

Gates, R.D. (1984). Florida Kindergarten Screening Battery. *Journal of Clinical Neuropsychology, 6,* 459–465.

Klein, A.E. (1978). The validity of the Beery Test of Visual–Motor Integration in predicting achievement in kindergarten, first, and second grade. *Educational and Psychological Measurement, 38,* 457–461.

LaTorre, R.A. (1985). Kindergarten screening: A cross-validation of the Florida Kindergarten Screening Battery. *Alberta Journal of Educational Research, 31,* 174–190.

Lepkin, S.R., & Pryzwansky, W. (1983). Interrater reliability of the original and the revised scoring system for the Developmental Test of Visual–Motor Integration. *Psychology in the Schools, 20,* 284–288.

Liemohn, W., & Wagner, P. (1975). Motor and perceptual determinants of performance on the Bender–Gestalt and the Beery Developmental Scale by retarded males. *Perceptual and Motor Skills, 40,* 524–526.

Martin, R., Sewell, T., & Manni, J. (1977). Effects of race and social class on preschool performance on the Developmental Test of Visual–Motor Integration. *Psychology in the Schools, 14,* 466–470.

Porter, G.L.,, & Binder, D.M. (1981). A pilot study of visual–motor developmental inter-test reliability: The Beery Developmental Test of Visual–Motor Integration and the Bender Visual Motor Gestalt Test. *Journal of Learning Disabilities, 14*, 124–127.

Pryzwansky, W.B. (1977). The use of the Developmental Test of Visual–Motor Integration as a group screening instrument. *Psychology in the Schools, 14*, 419–422.

Reynolds, C.R., Wright, D., & Wilkinson, W.A. (1980). Incremental validity of the test for Auditory Comprehension of Language and the Developmental Test of Visual–Motor Integration. *Educational and Psychological Measurement, 40*, 503–507.

Richardson, E., DiBenedetto, B., Christ, A., & Press, M. (1980). Relationship of auditory and visual skills to reading retardation. *Journal of Learning Disabilities, 13*, 77–82.

Ryckman, D.B., & Rentfrow, R.K. (1971).

The Beery Developmental Test of Visual–Motor Integration: An investigation of reliability. *Journal of Learning Disabilities, 4*, 333–334.

Schooler, D.L., & Anderson, R.L. (1979). Race differences on the Developmental Test of Visual–Motor Integration, the Slosson Intelligence Test, and the ABC Inventory. *Psychology in the Schools, 16*, 453–456.

Ysseldyke, J.E., Algozzine, B., & Shinn, M. (1981). Validity of the Woodcock–Johnson Psychoeducational Battery for learning disabled youngsters. *Learning Disability Quarterly, 4*, 244–249.

Zeitschel, K.A., Kalish, R.A., & Colarusso, R. (1979). Visual perception tests used with physically handicapped children. *Academic Therapy, 14*, 565–576.

EMBEDDED FIGURES TEST

Other Test Names

Other test names include Hidden Figures and Figure-Ground Test.

Purpose

The purpose of this test is to examine visual search and tracing of a figure embedded in the background.

Source

The test (manual, 20 forms, 20 answer sheets) can be obtained from the Neuropsychology Laboratory, University of Victoria, Victoria, British Columbia V8W 3P5 Canada, at a cost of $25.00 Cdn. 20 forms for left-handers are $20.00 Cdn.

Description

Experimental versions of this test have been in use since 1960. The test (Spreen & Benton, 1969) consists of 16 straight-line drawings used as stimulus figures and presented in the left half of 5½" × 8½" sheets of paper assembled in a test booklet. The right half of each sheet contains a complex figure drawing in which the stimulus figure is embedded. Subjects are required to search for and trace the stimulus figure in the embedded design. An ordinary soft pencil is used for the tracings. The test is preceded by two demonstration items.

For left-handed subjects, placement of the stimulus figure and the embedded design is reversed; that is, the stimulus figure is shown in the right half and the embedded design in the left half of the test booklet. An equivalent parallel form of this test, Form B, is also available.

Administration

Show the subject the first demonstration item and say: **"Do you see this figure, this shape?"** [point to stimulus figure]. **"You can find it in this larger figure"** [point to embedded design]." Trace the stimulus figure in the embedded design with firm strokes so that the outline is clearly visible. **"Now let us look at another one"** [expose the second demonstration item]. **"You draw this figure in the larger figure."** If the subject draws correctly, tell the subject: **"That's right."** If the subject draws the figure too lightly, have him or her go over it, and say: **"Draw it darker. Press down with your pencil."** If the subject fails to trace the figure correctly, say: **"No, that is not quite right. Let me show you."** [Draw the embedded figure.] **"See, this figure is just like the one over here."**

Other, more detailed instructions or demonstrations are permissible if the subject fails to understand the task.

The test items are then presented individually with the instruction **"Now do this one."** Begin timing after presentation of each stimulus figure and record the time needed to complete the item in seconds. If the subject has not started to draw within 20 seconds after the presentation of an item, turn the page in the booklet to expose the next item. If the subject has begun drawing, allow him or her to finish, and record the time.

After the subject finishes an item, present the next design with the appropriate instructions. Avoid commenting on the subject's performance, except for noncommittal remarks (**"All right, let's try the next one"**).

Discontinue after five consecutive failures to draw the designs correctly.

Scoring

One point is given for every design correctly completed within 30 seconds. One additional credit point is given if the design is completed within 20 seconds. Maximum credit score for all 16 items is 32 points.

No credit is given for incorrect reproductions or for correct tracings not completed within 30 seconds. All parts of the stimulus figure have to be traced correctly in the embedded design. Poor drawing (rounded corners, sloppiness in tracing, incomplete connections between lines) is disregarded if the stimulus figure is clearly recognizable.

Special scoring rules are as follows: Design 11 is scored as correct if the K-figure is repeated. Design 15 is scored correct if the squares are drawn with interrupted lines (as in the stimulus figure).

Comment

Embedded figures have been used in many experimental studies since the time of Gottschaldt (1928). Their clinical use goes back to Poppelreuter's (1917) overlapping figures test. Some tests use shading, grids, or strong distractor figures as overlay or masking. Similar abilities are required by incomplete figures (visual closure). The figures by Witkin et al. (1971) have been used in studies of field dependence and independence. Witkin's version is designed mainly for adults, although norms for children down to the age of 10 years and reliability coefficients between .9 and .61 have been reported. No studies with neurological patients have been conducted with the Witkin test, but schizophrenics, asthmatic children, diabetics, alcoholics, enuretics, and obsessive-compulsives have been studied and show stronger field dependence. However, in recent studies the relationship with ability level has been shown to be stronger than with cognitive style (Widiger et al., 1980). Other tests have been published by Ayres (1966), Coates (1972), Mahlios and D'Angelo (1983), and Talland (1965)—all designed primarily for children of preschool and school age.

Odd–even reliability and retest reliability for most tests are usually reported as high ($r = .90$). Validity studies suggest that patients with right-hemisphere lesions do more poorly than patients with left-hemisphere lesions on tests of this type (De Renzi & Spinnler, 1966) and that patients with anterior lesions do better than

Table 8–2. Embedded Figures Test: Normative Data for Adults

Age groups	N	Total correct		Total credit	
		M	SD	M	SD
16–20	10	15.3	1.0	30.4	2.1
20–29	23	14.5	1.0	31.78	0.85
30–39	14	15.7	1.0	31.64	0.74
40–49	14	14.1	1.0	31.14	1.46
50–59	10	15.4	0.9	31.60	0.80
60–69	10	14.5	0.8	30.30	2.50
70–79	14	15.5	0.5	30.36	2.41

Table 8–3. Embedded Figures Test: Normative Data for Children (in Percentiles)

		Percentiles									
	0	10	20	30	40	50	60	70	80	90	100
Age 6 (Max. score = 16)		1–4	5–6	7	8	9	10	11	12	13–14	15–16
Age 7 (Max. score = 16)		1–4	5–6	7	8	9	10	11	12	13–14	15–16
Age 8 (Max. score = 16)		1–9	10	11	12	13	13	14	14	15	16
(Max. credit = 32)		0–16	17–18	19–20	21	22–23	24	25	26	27–28	29–30
Age 9 (Max. score = 16)		1–9	10	11	12	13	13	14	14	15	16
(Max. credit = 32)		0–16	17–18	19–20	21	22–23	24	25	26	27–28	29–30
Age 10 (Max. score = 16)		1–10	11	12	13	13	14	14	15	16	
(Max. credit = 32)		1–19	20–21	22–23	24	25	26–27	28–29	30–31	32	
Age 11 (Max. score = 16)		1–10	11	12	13	13	14	14	15	16	
(Max. credit = 32)		1–19	20–21	22–23	24	25	26–27	28–29	30–31	32	
Age 12 (Max. score = 16)					questionable < 15 > normal						
(Max. credit = 32)					questionable < 30 > normal						
Age 13 (Max. score = 16)					questionable < 15 > normal						
(Max. credit = 32)					questionable < 30 > normal						

Source: Spreen & Gaddes (1969).

Note: Credit scores are not calculated below age 9.

294

those with posterior lesions if no time limit is imposed (Egelko et al., 1988; Masure & Tzavaras, 1967), although most patients with brain damage have some difficulty with the test, dependent on the size of lesion (Corkin, 1979). This is confirmed in our own data, where brain-damaged patients in all age groups performed significantly worse than normals (average point score: 3 points; credit score: 6 points below normals); this was even more pronounced in the older (60+) age group where the differences between brain-damaged and normal performance reached 6 and 9 points, respectively.

Normative Data

Our recently compiled data show that healthy adults make very few errors on this test, as indicated in Table 8–2. The idea that older adults tend to make more errors ("return to field dependence"; Witkins et al., 1971) is not supported by our normative data for this test. Differences between males and females are negligible.

The rapid progression both in correct solutions and in time credits in children (Spreen & Gaddes, 1969) is discernible from Table 8–3. Differences between males and females are negligible. Deegener (1981) reports a strong relationship to IQ and a minor effect of visual acuity on a similar test in a population of 5-year-olds.

REFERENCES

Ayres, A.J. (1966). *Southern California Figure-Ground Visual Perception Test. Manual.* Los Angeles: Western Psychological Services.

Coates, S.W. (1972). *Preschool Embedded Figures Test.* Manual. Palo Alto: Consulting Psychologists Press.

Corkin, S. (1979). Hidden-Figures-Test performance: Lasting effects of unilateral penetrating head injury and transient effects of bilateral cingulotomy. *Neuropsychologia, 17,* 585–605.

Deegener, G. (1981). Ergebnisse mit dem Preschool Embedded Figures Test bei fünfjährigen deutschen Kindergartenkindern. *Praxis der Kinderpsychologie und Kinderpsychiatrie, 30,* 144–150.

De Renzi, E., & Spinnler, H. (1966). Visual recognition in patients with unilateral cerebral disease. *Journal of Nervous and Mental Disease, 142,* 515–525.

Egelko, S., Gordon, W.A., Hibbard, M.R., Diller, L., Lieberman, A., Holliday, R.,

Ragnarson, K., Shaver, M.S., & Orazem, J. (1988). Relationship among CT scans, neurological exam, and neuropsychological test performance in right-brain-damaged stroke patients. *Journal of Clinical and Experimental Neuropsychology, 10,* 539–564.

Gottschaldt, K. (1928). Über den Einfluss der Erfahrung auf die Wahrnehmung von Figuren. *Psychologische Forschung, 8,* 18–317.

Mahlios, M.C., & D'Angelo, K. (1983). Group embedded figures test: Psychometric data on children. *Perceptual and Motor Skills, 56,* 423–426.

Masure, M.C., & Tzavaras (1976). Perception de figures entrecroisées par des sujets atteints de lésions corticales unilaterales. *Neuropsychologia, 14,* 371–374.

Poppelreuter, W. (1917). *Die psychischen Schädigungen durch Kopfschuss im Kriege 1914/18.* Leipzig: Leopold Voss.

Spreen, O. & Benton, A.L. (1969). Embedded Figures Test. Neuropsychology Laboratory, University of Victoria, Victoria, B.C.

Spreen, O. & Gaddes, W.H. (1969). Developmental norms for 15 neuropsychological tests age 6 to 15. *Cortex*, 5, 171–191.

Talland, G.A. (1965). *Deranged Memory*. New York: Academic Press.

Widiger, T.A., Knudson, R.M., & Rorer, L.G. (1980). Convergent and discriminant validity of measures of cognitive style and abilities. *Journal of Personality and Social Psychology*, 39, 116–129.

Witkin, H.A., Oltman, P.K., & Karp, S.A. (1971). *A Manual for the Embedded Figures Test*. Palo Alto: Consulting Psychologists Press.

FACIAL RECOGNITION TEST

Purpose

The purpose of this test is to assess the ability to recognize unfamiliar human faces.

Source

The test can be ordered from Oxford University Press, 2001 Evans Road, Cary, North Carolina 27513, at a cost of $45.00 U.S. The manual (which includes 11 other tests) costs $23.95 U.S.

Description

The test (Benton et al., 1983), originally developed by Benton and Van Allen (1968), requires the subject to discriminate photographs of unfamiliar human faces. Clothing and hair are shaded out so that only facial features can be used. The full test ("long form") consists of 54 items, the Short Form (Levin et al., 1975) of 27 items. The test consists of three parts:

1. *Matching of identical front-view photographs.* The subject is presented with a single front-view photograph of a face and instructed to identify it (by pointing to it or calling its number) in a display of six front-view photographs appearing below the single photograph. In both the short and the long version of the test, three male and three female faces are presented for matching, calling for a total of six responses.
2. *Matching of front-view with three-quarter-view photographs.* The subject is presented with a single front-view photograph of a face and instructed to

locate it three times in a display of six three-quarter views, three being of the presented face and three being of other faces. In the Long Form of the test, four male and four female faces are presented for matching, calling for a total of 24 responses. In the Short Form, one male face and three female faces are presented, calling for a total of 12 responses.

3. *Matching of front-view photographs under different lighting conditions.* The subject is presented with a single front-view photograph of a face taken under full lighting conditions and instructed to locate it three times in a display of six front views taken under different lighting conditions; three photographs in the display are of the presented face and three are of other faces. In the Long Form, four male and four female faces are presented for matching, calling for a total of 24 responses. In the Short Form, two male faces and one female face are presented, calling for a total of nine responses.

Administration

See source. The test is assembled in a spiral bound booklet. Each stimulus picture and its corresponding response choices are presented in two facing pages with the single stimulus picture above the six response-choice pictures ("**You see this woman? Show me where she is on this picture**"). If they are able to do so, subjects are encouraged to hold and manipulate the test material to their best visual advantage.

The test is arranged so that the first 13 stimulus and response display pictures, which comprise the Short Form, are presented first. Following this is a page that identifies the remaining items of the 54 items of the long form.

Scoring

Record correct responses by checking the appropriate item; record errors by circling the appropriate numbers on the right side of the record form. Each correct response is assigned a score of 1 point. A minimum score of 25 may be expected on the basis of chance alone. Hence the effective range of Long Form scores may be considered to be 25–54 points. For the Short Form, the effective range may be considered to be 11–27 points.

Utilization of the record sheet will facilitate recording and scoring. If the Short Form is used, the number of correct responses on the record sheet needs to be converted to Long Form scores following a conversion table. The test manual also provides age and education corrections for the Long Form and the converted Short Form scores.

Comment

Test–retest reliability has not been reported, but correlation between Short Form and Long Form scores ranges from .88 in normals to .92 in brain-damaged subjects (Benton et al., 1983).

Although the inability to recognize familiar faces (prosopagnosia) has been recognized for some time as a special form of agnosia, standardized tests have not been available so far. The use of unfamiliar faces (as opposed to faces of actors or public figures; Warrington & James, 1967) eliminates the long-term memory component and the need for name finding. Benton et al. (1983), however, warn that patients with serious difficulties in the recognition of unfamiliar faces may well be able to recognize familiar faces since cases of true prosopagnosia are rare. The dissociation of these two abilities may suggest separate loci of brain damage (Benton, 1980; Benton & Van Allen, 1972). The test is sensitive to right parietal lobe damage, and, to a lesser extent, right temporal lobe damage (Dricker et al., 1978). Impaired performance on this test has also been reported in children with hemispherectomy regardless of the side of removal (Strauss & Verity, 1983), in patients with Parkinson's disease (Bentin et al., 1981), and in patients with severe closed head injury (Levin et al., 1977). Egelko et al. (1988) also report scores in the lowest percentile range for right-hemisphere stroke patients. The correlation between hemianopic field cut and face-recognition was .49. The computed tomography (CT) scan damage correlated highest with face recognition performance if the damage was in the parietal area. Vilkki and Laitinen (1976) reported serious deficits in face recognition after right thalamotomy. Left anterior and posterior patients with aphasia and comprehension deficits also do poorly on this test, suggesting that the test relies on linguistic functions to some extent (Hamsher et al., 1979).

Whereas Levin and Benton (1977) reported that face recognition scores in pseudoneurologic psychiatric patients were indistinguishable from those of nor-

Table 8–4.   Benton Test of Face Recognition:
Normative Standards after Correction for Age and Education

Corrected score	Percentile rank	Classification
53–54	98+	very superior
50–52	88–97	superior
47–49	72–85	high average
43–46	33–59	average
41–42	16–21	low average
39–40	8–11	borderline
37–38	3–6	defective
<37	1	severely defective

Source: Benton et al. (1983).

Table 8–5. Benton Test of Face Recognition: Age and
Education Corrections for Long Form Scores

Age	Education (years)	
	6–11	12+
16–54	0	0
55–64	3	1
65–74	4	2

Source: Benton et al. (1983).

mals, Echternacht (1986) found more defective scores in such patients and in a matched chronic psychiatric inpatient group than would be expected in normals, but less than would be expected from specific brain-damaged populations. Hence, the test may make some contribution to the discrimination of these populations.

Normative Data

Benton et al. (1983) provide score distributions for 286 normal adults with age and education correction. Test performance in old age showed some decline (Benton et al., 1981). Mittenberg et al. (1989) report a correlation of −.25 with age in normal control subjects 20–75 years of age. Table 8–4 provides a guide for test score interpretation in adults, and Table 8–5 shows the corrections to be applied to the raw score. Norms for children of average intelligence indicate a gradual improvement of face recognition ability from age 6 (mean = 33 correct) to age 14 (mean = 45 correct) when adult performance level is reached (Benton et al., 1983).

REFERENCES

Bentin, S., Silverberg, R., & Gordon, H.W. (1981). Asymmetrical cognitive deterioration in demented and parkinsonian patients. *Cortex, 17,* 533–544.

Benton, A.L. (1980). The neuropsychology of facial recognition. *American Psychologist, 35,* 176–186.

Benton, A.L., Eslinger, P.J., & Damasio, A.R. (1981). Normative observations on neuropsychological test performances in old age. *Journal of Clinical Neuropsychology, 3,* 33–42.

Benton, A.L., Hamsher, K.deS., Varney, N.R., Spreen, O. (1983). *Contributions to Neuropsychological Assessment: A Clinical Manual.* New York: Oxford University Press.

Benton, A.L., & Van Allen, M.W. (1968). Impairment in facial recognition in patients with cerebral disease. *Cortex, 4,* 344–358.

Benton, A.L., & Van Allen, M.W. (1972). Prosopagnosia and facial discrimination. *Journal of the Neurological Sciences, 15,* 167–172.

Dricker, J., Butters, N., Berman, G., Samuels, I., & Carey, S. (1978). The recognition and encoding of faces by alcoholic Korsakoff and right hemisphere patients. *Neuropsychologia, 16,* 683–695.

Echternacht, R. (1986). The performance of pseudoneurological chronic psychiatric inpatients on the test of Facial Recognition, Judgment of Line Orientation, and Aphasia Screening Test. Paper presented at the 7th Annual Meeting of the Midwest Neuropsychology Group, Rochester, Minn.

Egelko, S., Gordon, W.A., Hibbard, M.R., Diller, L., Lieberman, A., Holliday, R., Ragnarsson, K., Shaver, M.S., & Orazem, J. (1988). Relationship among CT scans, neurologic exam, and neuropsychological test performance in right-brain-damaged stroke patients. *Journal of Clinical and Experimental Neuropsychology, 10,* 539–564.

Hamsher, K.deS., Levin, H.S., & Benton, A.L. (1979). Facial recognition in patients with focal brain lesions. *Archives of Neurology, 36,* 837–839.

Levin, H.S., & Benton, A.L. (1977). Facial recognition in "pseudoneurological" patients. *Journal of Nervous and Mental Disease, 164,* 135–138.

Levin, H.S., Grossman, R.G., & Kelly, J. (1977). Impairment in facial recognition after closed head injuries of varying severity. *Cortex, 13,* 119–130.

Levin, H.S., Hamsher, K.deS., & Benton, A.L. (1975). A short form of the test of facial recognition for clinical use. *Journal of Psychology, 91,* 223–228.

Mittenberg, W., Seidenberg, M., O'Leary, D.S., & DiGiulio, D.V. (1989). Changes in cerebral functioning associated with normal aging. *Journal of Clinical and Experimental Neuropsychology, 11,* 918–932.

Strauss, E., & Verity, L. (1983). Effects of hemispherectomy in infantile hemiplegics. *Brain and Language, 20,* 1–11.

Vilkki, J., & Laitinen, L.V. (1976). Effects of pulvinotomy and ventrolateral thalamotomy on some cognitive functions. *Neuropsychologia, 14,* 67–78.

Warrington, E.K., & James, M. (1967). An experimental investigation of facial recognition in patients with unilateral cerebral lesions. *Cortex, 3,* 317–326.

HOOPER VISUAL ORGANIZATION TEST (VOT)

Purpose

This is a test of the ability to rearrange conceptually pictures that have been disarranged.

Source

The Hooper Visual Organization Test can be ordered from Western Psychological Services, 12031 Wilshire Boulevard, Los Angeles, California 90025, at a cost of $87.50 U.S.

Description

This test consists of 30 drawings of common objects on 4″ × 4″ cards in a ring-binder (test booklet). Each object is cut into two or more parts and illogically arranged in the drawing. The task is to name the object. The test is similar to other fragmented figures tests. Although originally designed to differentiate adult subjects with and without brain damage (Hooper, 1958), several studies have attempted to delimit its use more closely. The 1983 edition ("developed by the staff of Western Psychological Services", no author) is based on Hooper's original studies, but adds references to more recent studies, age- and education-corrected raw score tables, and a T-score conversion table.

Approximate Time for Administration

The time required is 10–15 minutes.

Administration

See source. With individual administration, the correct naming of each object is required. Group administration relies on written responses. The test manual stresses that in addition to the simple correct/incorrect scoring, the quality of the responses may be important.

Scoring

The score is simply the total number of correct responses, although half-credit is given for some of the items for partially correct responses (e.g., "tower" or "castle" instead of lighthouse). Qualitative scoring includes the distinctions among isolate, perseverative, bizarre, and neologistic responses.

Comment

According to Lezak (1982), a coefficient of concordance of .86 indicates good test–retest reliability after six and again after 12 months. Split-half reliability was reported as .82 (Hooper, 1948) in college students, and .80 in hospitalized adults (Gerson, 1974). Lezak (1982) also found no significant correlation with sex, education, age (except in old age), or intelligence (except at borderline defective and lower levels). However, Wentworth-Rohr et al. (1974) report correlations with intelligence of .31–.50, and with age of .04–.28 for younger subjects, and of .37–.69 for populations including subjects up to 85 years of age.

The validity of this test for "general screening for brain damage" has been hotly debated (Boyd, 1982a, 1982b; Rathbun & Smith, 1982; Woodward, 1982). Although correct classification rates of 74% between unselected brain-damaged subjects and healthy controls with a cutoff score of 25 have been reported (Boyd, 1981), and Lezak (1983) considers scores of 20–24 as "borderline," the validity of the test in detecting specific deficits as well as the localization of brain lesion would seem to be of greater importance. The face validity of the test lies in its demand on perceptual differentiation and conceptual reorganization (including mental rotation) of the fragmented objects. Rathbun and Smith (1982) point out that such functions are frequently spared in patients with right-frontal or left-hemisphere lesions, whereas impairment is most pronounced in right-posterior lesions, but such localizing value has so far been supported only by Rathbun and Smith's anecdotal report and by Wang (1977) who found only a trend toward lower scores in right-hemisphere-lesion patients; Boyd (1981) found no difference that was due to lateralization of lesion. Farver and Farver (1982) and Tamkin and Hyer (1984) interpreted age-related decline on this test as evidence of cognitive dysfunction related to right-parietal-lobe/right-hemisphere functional decline with age.

Comparing the VOT to other tests, Tamkin et al. (1984) and Tamkin and Kunce (1985) found that the Weigl Color–Form Sorting Test was most sensitive to brain dysfunction, but that the addition of the Benton Visual Retention Test and the VOT increased predictive validity. Sterne (1973), on the other hand, found that the addition of the VOT did not add to the discrimination between Veterans Administration patients classified as normal, organic, and indeterminate based on the Wechsler Adult Intelligence Scale, the Benton Visual Retention Test, and the Porteus Maze Test, whereas the addition of the Trail Making Test did.

Tamkin and Jacobsen (1984) reported that scores for 211 male psychiatric inpatients were approximately 2.5 points below average, and Gerson (1974) concluded that the test is "not sensitive to . . . thought disorders" (p. 98) and that neologisms and bizarre responses did not occur in this population at all.

We use this test only with individual patients to explore further any difficulties in perceptual organization, but not as a test confirming the presence of brain damage. Since the test requires naming, results in even mildly aphasic patients must be treated with caution.

Normative Data

See source. The published norms still seem to rely mainly on the original studies reported by Hooper (1958), although age corrections (up to age 69) and education corrections have been added. A score of 26 corresponds to a T-score of 50 (average); a score of 21, to a T-score of 60 (1 SD below average); and a score of 16, to a T-score of 70 (2 SD below average). The Victoria norms (N = 40; 22 females, 18 males; 34 right-handed, 6 left-handed; mean age = 24.7 years, SD = 4.55) agree closely (mean = 26.75; SD = 1.97). Farver and Farver (1982) report a drop of 1 point for the group 60–69 years of age, of 2 points for the group 70–79 years of age, and of 4 points for the group 80–89 years of age, compared to younger adults. This is consistent with the results of Montgomery and Costa (1983) who reported a mean of 22.5 (SD = 4.1) for 82 healthy adults 65–89 years of age, and with Farver and Farver (1982) in Boston, and Villardita et al. (1985) in Italy, although only four of the Hooper items were used in this study. Norms for children are not available.

REFERENCES

Boyd, J.L. (1981). A validity study of the Hooper Visual Organization Test. *Journal of Consulting and Clinical Psychology, 49*, 15–19.

Boyd, J.L. (1982a). Reply to Rathbun and Smith: Who made the Hooper blooper? *Journal of Consulting and Clinical Psychology, 50*, 284–285.

Boyd, J.L. (1982b). Reply to Woodward. *Journal of Consulting and Clinical Psychology, 50*, 289–290.

Farver, P.F., & Farver, T.B. (1982). Performance of normal older adults on tests designed to measure parietal lobe functions. *American Journal of Occupational Therapy, 36*, 444–449.

Gerson, A. (1974). Validity and reliability of the Hooper Visual Organization Test. *Perceptual and Motor Skills, 39*, 95–100.

Hooper, H.E. (1948). A study in the construction and preliminary standardization of a visual organization test for use in the measurement of organic deterioration. Unpublished Master's thesis, University of Southern California, Los Angeles.

Hooper, H.E. (1958). *The Hooper Visual Organization Test: Manual.* Beverly Hills, Cal.: Western Psychological Services.

Hooper Visual Organization Test (VOT). 1983 edition. Manual. Los Angeles, Calif.: Western Psychological Services.

Lezak, M.D. (1982). The test–retest stability and reliability of some tests commonly used in neuropsychological assessment. Paper presented at the meeting of the International Neuropsychological Society, Deauville, France.

Lezak, M.D. (1983). *Neuropsychological Assessment* (2nd ed.). New York: Oxford University Press.

Montgomery, K., & Costa, L. (1983). Neuropsychological test performance of a normal elderly sample. Paper presented at the meeting of the International Neuropsychological Society, Mexico City.

Rathbun, J., & Smith, A. (1982). Comment on the validity of Boyd's validation study of the Hooper Visual Organization Test. *Journal of Consulting and Clinical Psychology, 50*, 281–283.

Sterne, D.M. (1973). The Hooper Visual Organization Test and the Trail Making Test as discriminants of brain injury. *Journal of Clinical Psychology, 29*, 212–213.

Tamkin, A.S., & Hyer, L.A. (1984). Testing for cognitive dysfunction in the aging population. *Military Medicine, 149*, 397–399.

Tamkin, A.S. & Jacobsen, R. (1984). Age-related norms for the Hooper Visual Organization Test. *Journal of Clinical Psychology, 40*, 1459–1463.

Tamkin, A.S., & Kunce, J.T. (1985). A comparison of three neuropsychological tests: The Weigl, Hooper, and Benton. *Journal of Clinical Psychology, 41*, 660–664.

Tamkin, A.S., Kunce, J.T., Blount, J.B., & Magharious, W. (1984). The effectiveness of the Weigl Color–Form Sorting Test in screening for brain dysfunction. *Journal of Clinical Psychology, 40*, 1454–1459.

Villardita, C., Cultrera, S., Cupone, V., & Mejia, R. (1985). Neuropsychological test performances and normal aging. *Archives of Gerontology and Geriatrics, 4*, 311–319.

Wang, P.L. (1977). Visual organization ability in brain-damaged adults. *Perceptual and Motor Skills, 45*, 723–728.

Wentworth-Rohr, I., Mackintosh, R.M., & Fialkoff, B.S. (1974). The relationship of Hooper VOT score to sex, education, intelligence, and age. *Journal of Clinical Psychology, 30*, 73–75.

Woodward, C.A. (1982). The Hooper Visual Organization Test: A case against its use in neuropsychological assessment. *Journal of Consulting and Clinical Psychology, 50*, 286–288.

RIGHT–LEFT ORIENTATION

Purpose

The purpose of this test is to assess discrimination of left from right.

Source

Test material and scoring forms are available from the Neuropsychology Laboratory, University of Victoria, British Columbia V8W 3P5 Canada, at a cost of $5.00 Cdn. A shortened (20-item) version of Benton's test is available from Oxford University Press (1983). Record forms cost $26.95 U.S.; the manual and 12 other tests are available under the title *Contributions to Neuropsychological Assessment; A Clinical Manual* from Oxford University Press, at a cost of $23.95 U.S.

Description

We use two forms: The Benton Form was developed from items in Forms A and V in Benton (1959, pp. 14–15) and consists of 32 commands progressing from "Show me your left hand" to the indication of "Which hand is on which ear" on pictures (untimed). Since the test is fairly easy, it can be used with children and produces deficits only in seriously injured adults; an additional form was derived from Culver (1969), which requires the indication of right or left for each of 20 pictures of hands and feet in various positions (see Fig. 8–3); this test is timed.

Administration

BENTON FORM

The subject is seated across a table from the examiner and given the instructions as laid out in the answer sheet. Emphasis should be given to the capitalized words.

For the first 12 commands subjects are asked to show that they know left from right on their own bodies; for example: "**Touch your right eye with your left hand**," etc.

The following 12 items utilize a 5" wide × 7½" high, black-ink, full-length drawing of a boy. This picture is laid flat in front of the subject who is not allowed to manipulate it in any way. The subject is asked: "**Put your left hand on the boy's right ear**," etc.

The last eight items on the test use eight (5" wide × 7½" high) black-ink line drawings of the head and torso of a man. These are laid flat in front of the subject in the same manner as the drawing of the boy.

Any item may be repeated once if the subject appears hesitant or requests the examiner to do so. No time limit is imposed.

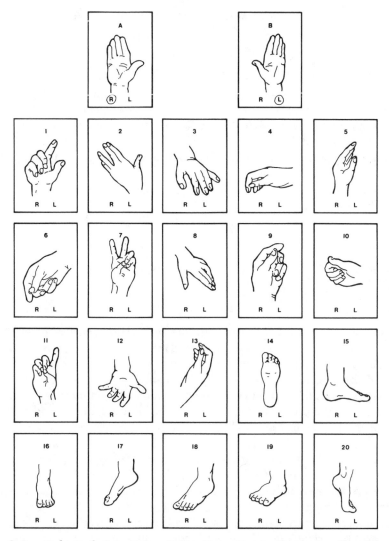

Figure 8–3. Right–Left Orientation: Culver Form, Test 1, showing hands and feet. The instructions to the subject are as follows: "THE HANDS AND FEET ON THIS PAGE ARE EITHER RIGHTS OR LEFTS. MARK ON THE ANSWER SHEET UNDER THE 'R' FOR RIGHTS AND UNDER THE 'L' FOR LEFTS. 'A' AND 'B' ARE CORRECTLY MARKED."

CULVER FORM

Present the patient with the form showing 20 pictures of hands or feet in different positions and say: "**The hands and feet on this page are either rights or lefts. On the top are two examples, 'A' and 'B', which are marked correctly. Starting with number one, as I point to each of these figures, tell me whether it is the right or the left hand or foot.**"

Stress accuracy rather than time on this test, but record time until completion of the last item.

Approximate Time for Administration

The Benton form requires 5–10 minutes; the Culver form, 2 minutes.

Scoring

BENTON FORM

Number correct. A score of 1 point is assigned to each item performed exactly as it appears on the answer sheet (see Fig. 8–4). Partially correct responses (e.g., item 17: right hand on right ear) receive no credit. If the subject changes his or her answer before the next item is given, the changed answer is recorded. For erroneous responses the subject's error is noted in the margin, next to the item. For example, if the picture shows the left hand to be on the right eye, and the subject says that the left hand is on the left eye, LL would be placed in the margin.

Reversal score. A reversal score of 1 point is assigned to each item completely reversed in orientation on confrontation testing (e.g., item 17: left hand on right ear). Reversal scores can be given to items 17 through 20 and items 25 through 32. For items 13 through 16 and 21 through 24, a reversal score is given only if right and left are consistently reversed, that is, if all four items in either of these sections are reversed in orientation. No reversal scores are assigned for orientation on the subject's own person (items 1 through 12).

Total score. The total score is either the number of items performed correctly or the reversal score, whichever is higher.

CULVER FORM

Total number correct and total time (in seconds) are recorded. Correct answers are (in order from item 1 to 20): R, L, L, R, L; R, L, L, L, R; R, L, R, L, L; L, R, L, R, L.

Answer Sheet (Benton Form)

Name: Age   Date   Examiner

Examiner to subject   Response

1. Show me your LEFT hand   1.
2. Show me your RIGHT eye   2.
3. Show me your LEFT ear   3.
4. Show me your RIGHT hand   4.
5. Touch your LEFT ear with your RIGHT hand   5.
6. Touch your RIGHT eye with your LEFT hand   6.
7. Touch your RIGHT knee with your RIGHT hand   7.
8. Touch your LEFT eye with your LEFT hand   8.
9. Touch your RIGHT ear with your LEFT hand   9.
10. Touch your LEFT knee with your RIGHT hand   10.
11. Touch your RIGHT ear with your RIGHT hand   11.
12. Touch your LEFT eye with your RIGHT hand   12.

THIS BOY (Picture 1) IS FACING YOU JUST AS I AM.
REMEMBER, HE IS FACING YOU.

		Reversal
	Response	Score
13. Point to the boy's RIGHT eye	13.	
14. Point to the boy's LEFT leg	14.	
15. Point to the boy's LEFT ear	15.	
16. Point to the boy's RIGHT hand	16.	
17. Put your RIGHT hand on the boy's LEFT ear	17.	
18. Put your LEFT hand on the boy's LEFT eye	18.	
19. Put your LEFT hand on the boy's RIGHT shoulder	19.	
20. Put your RIGHT hand on the boy's RIGHT eye	20.	

Naming:
21. E points to the boy's right hand. Which hand is this?   21.
22. E points to the boy's left ear. Which ear is this?   22.
23. E points to the boy's left hand. Which hand is this?   23.
24. E points to the boy's right eye. Which eye is this?   24.

NOW LOOK AT THESE PICTURES. I WANT YOU TO TELL ME:
25. Picture 2 (left hand–left ear). Which hand is on which ear?   25.
26. Picture 3 (right hand–left eye). Which hand is on which eye?   26.
27. Picture 4 (right hand–right ear). Which hand is on which ear?   27.
28. Picture 5 (left hand–right eye). Which hand is on which eye?   28.
29. Picture 6 (right hand–left ear). Which hand is on which ear?   29.
30. Picture 7 (right hand–right eye). Which hand is on which eye?   30.
31. Picture 8 (left hand–left eye). Which hand is on which eye?   31.
32. Picture 9 (left hand–right ear). Which hand is on which ear?   32.

Total Correct   _____

Total Reversal Score   _____

Figure 8–4. Right–Left Orientation (Benton Form) sample answer and scoring sheet.

Comment

Few studies have investigated reliability. Sarazin and Spreen (1986) report a 15-year (ages 10–25) stability of .27 in learning-disabled subjects for the Benton Form. This low value, however, should be considered minimal since it covers a large time span during development in an exceptional group.

Only a few studies have investigated the validity of right–left discrimination. Correlation with intelligence is only minimal in children (Clark and Klonoff, 1990). Using a number of different tests, McFie and Zangwill (1960) found right–left confusion in five out of eight patients with left parietal damage and in none of 21 patients with right parietal damage. Kolb and Wishaw (1985) also report more impairment in patients with left parietal lobe lesions. Semmes, Weinstein, Ghent, and Teuber (1960) and Sauguet, Benton, and Hecaen (1971) showed similar findings. Most authors point out that right–left discrimination is not a unitary function, but involves spatial orientation, mental rotation, conceptual abilities, and hand preference. Benton et al. (1983) point out that if the confronting-person parts of the test only is considered, 43% of aphasic and only 4% of nonaphasic left-hemisphere patients, but also 16% of nonaphasic right-hemisphere patients fail this part. Hence, the left parietal lobe hypothesis does not seem to apply to opposing-body parts of the test which require more mental rotation and spatial thinking. The relationship to the Gerstmann syndrome and to visual neglect has been pointed out (Benton, 1979). In comparison with the 20- to 30-year-old control group of normal learners (17.8 correct in 60.3 seconds), formerly learning-disabled subjects of the same age and normal intelligence obtained 15 correct in an average of 74.8 seconds on the Culver form, and formerly learning-disabled subjects with minimal or definite brain damage showed a mean of 16.2 in 89.5 seconds (Spreen, 1988).

In short, the Benton Form is sensitive to developmental delay, but may be useful in adults only if moderate to severe impairment is present. Performance may be affected by parietal lobe lesions in both forms, but time scores in the Culver form tend to be delayed in the presence of any CNS impairment.

Normative Data

BENTON FORM

Table 8–6 shows normative data for 8- to 15-year-old school children on the Benton Form. Benton (1959) reports that for 7-year-olds the average performance is approximately 1 point (SD = 2.81) and for 6-year-olds another 3 points (SD = 3.09) lower, although Klonoff and Low (1974) found even lower values. It is obvious that basic right–left orientation develops rapidly during early school age and that generalization of right and left to the external environment is not reached

Table 8–6. Right–Left Orientation in Children (Benton Form)

Age	Male N	Male Mean	Male SD	Female N	Female Mean	Female SD	All normals N	All normals Mean	All normals SD
6	(est.)							16.7	
7	(est.)							19.7	
8	7	24.1[a]	6.7	8	17.6	5.5	15	20.7	6.9
9	19	24.4	7.4	24	22.2	7.2	43	23.2	7.4
10	21	26.4	5.4	21	26.9	6.2	42	26.7	5.8
11	26	27.9	5.2	19	25.1	6.2	45	26.7	5.8
12	24	27.9	3.9	23	25.5	6.0	47	26.7	5.2
13	16	28.1	4.8	22	27.4	5.6	38	27.7	5.3
14	21	27.7	5.3	23	24.8	6.8	44	26.2	6.3
15	7	27.9	4.9				7	27.9	4.9
16–20	6	28.5	8.1	8	29.9	5.2	14	29.1	7.0
21–25	8	31.7	0.7	4	32.0	0.0	12	31.8	0.3
26–30				4	31.7	0.55	4	31.7	0.0
31–50	4	32.0	0.0	6	32.0	0.0	10	32.0	0.0
51–60	6	31.2	1.6	1	32.0	0.0	7	31.4	1.2
61–70	5	31.6	0.5	3	31.7	0.6	8	31.6	0.5
71–80	5	31.0	1.0	3	25.7	6.0	8	28.1	3.1

Note: Sample consists of unselected group of school children in the Greater Victoria area.

[a]Mean of the total number correct out of 32 items or the total number of reversals—whichever is higher.

Source: Spreen & Gaddes (1969).

before the age of eight years and older (Clark and Klonoff, 1990). Reversal scores occur in children 5–10 years old at an average of 14.0 (females) and 8.8 (males) points; scores drop off to 12.5 (females) and 7.5 (males) points in children 11–15 year olds; and they reach an adult level of almost 0 in females at 16–20 years of age, and in males 21–25 years of age (Victoria norms). Scores for women and for persons with less than grade 12 education are minimally lower. Data on small samples of adults show that performance on this test remains stable and at ceiling level until old age.

CULVER FORM

As Table 8–7 shows, errors are relatively rare in normal, healthy volunteers. Children show a rapid increase in performance between the ages of 5 and 15 years; the 15-year age group reaches almost adult levels on a somewhat similar test (Kolb & Wishaw, 1985). Sex differences in children are clearly in favor of males, although this difference becomes minimal in adults (Kolb & Wishaw, 1985; Snyder & Jarratt, 1989). Differences between handedness groups are also minimal but seem to favor right-handers. In an elderly population the number of correct answers drops only slightly whereas the time score rises. Mittenberg et al. (1989) report a correlation of .37 with age for this form, having sampled normal control subjects between 20 and 75 years of age. On the other hand, Farver and Farver (1982)

Table 8–7. Normative Data for
Right–Left Orientation (Culver Form)

Age	n	No. correct		Time	
		Mean	SD	Mean	SD
20–30	20	17.82	2.40	60.31	15.2
50–59	19	17.16	2.89	40.79	16.2
60–69	27	16.78	2.98	52.74	23.9
70–79	23	15.17	2.66	67.17	31.9
80+	15	15.00	2.70	69.07	26.4

Note: Sample consists of healthy adult volunteers in Greater Victoria.

found no change in total score with age in populations ranging from 40 to 89 years for a right–left orientation test including elements of the Benton and the Culver forms.

REFERENCES

Benton, A.L. (1959). *Right–Left Discrimination and Finger Localization.* New York: Hoeber.

Benton, A.L. (1979). Body-schema disturbances: Right–left orientation and finger localization. In Heilman, K.M., & Valenstein, E. (Eds.), *Clinical Neuropsychology.* New York: Oxford University Press.

Benton, A.L., Hamsher, K.deS., Varney, N.R., & Spreen, O. (1983). *Contributions to Neuropsychological Assessment: A Clinical Manual.* New York: Oxford University Press.

Clark, C.M. & Klonoff, H. (1990). Right and left orientation in children aged 5 to 13 years. *Journal of Clinical and Experimental Neuropsychology, 12,* 459–466.

Culver, C.M. (1969). Test of right–left discrimination. *Perceptual and Motor Skills, 29,* 863–867.

Farver, P.F., & Farver, T.B. (1982). Performance of normal older adults on tests designed to measure parietal lobe functions. *American Journal of Occupational Therapy, 36,* 444–449.

Klonoff, H., & Low, M. (1974). Disordered brain function in young children and early adolescents: Neuropsychological and electroencephalographic correlates. In R.M. Reitan & L.A. Davison (Eds.), *Clinical Neuropsychology: Current Status and Ap-*

plications (pp. 121–178). New York: John Wiley.

Kolb, B., & Wishaw, I.Q. (1985). *Fundamentals of Human Neuropsychology.* New York: W.H. Freeman.

McFie, J., & Zangwill, O.L. (1960). Visual–constructive disabilities associated with lesions of the left hemisphere. *Brain, 83,* 243–260.

Mittenberg, W., Seidenberg, O'Leary, D., & DiGiulio, D.V. (1989). Changes in cerebral functioning associated with normal aging. *Journal of Clinical and Experimental Neuropsychology, 11,* 918–932.

Sarazin, F.F.A. & Spreen, O. (1986). Fifteen-year stability of some neuropsychological tests in learning disabled subjects with and without neurological impairment. *Journal of Clinical and Experimental Neuropsychology, 8,* 190–200.

Sauguet, J., Benton, A.L., & Hecaen, H. (1971). Disturbances of the body schema in relation to language impairment and hemispheric locus of lesion. *Journal of Neurology, Neurosurgery and Psychiatry, 34,* 496–501.

Semmes, J., Weinstein, S., Ghent, L., & Teuber, H.L. (1960). *Somatosensory Changes After Penetrating Brain Wounds in Man.* Cambridge, Mass.: Harvard University Press.

Snyder, T.J., & Jarratt, L. (1989). Adult differences in right–left discrimination according to gender and handedness. Paper presented at the Meeting of the International Neuropsychological Society, Vancouver. *Journal of Clinical and Experimental Neuropsychology, 11,* 70 (abstract).

Spreen, O. (1988). *Learning Disabled Children Growing Up.* New York: Oxford University Press.

Spreen, O., & Gaddes, W.H. (1969). Developmental norms for 15 neuropsychological tests age 6 to 15. *Cortex, 5,* 171–191.

SOUND RECOGNITION TEST

Other Test Names

Other test names include the Acoustic Recognition Test and the Nonverbal Auditory Perception Test.

Purpose

The purpose of this test is to assess the ability to recognize familiar environmental sounds (auditory object recognition).

Source

The test can be ordered from the Neuropsychology Laboratory, University of Victoria, Victoria, British Columbia V8W 3P5 Canada. The tape, instructions, norms, pictures, and words for the multiple-choice version and 20 answer sheets cost $19.00 Cdn.

Description

The test was developed by Spreen and Benton (1963) as a procedure for assessing auditory object recognition analogous to tests for visual and tactile object recognition. The term "auditory agnosia" is often misapplied to denote the inability of a patient to understand spoken language. But the latter is a verbal disability, analogous to dyslexia in the visual realm and agraphesthesia or "tactile dyslexia" in the tactile realm; terms such as "word deafness" or "receptive aphasia" are more appropriate designations for this. If "auditory agnosia" is conceived of as being the auditory counterpart of visual object agnosia and astereognosis, it is the loss of the ability to recognize familiar nonverbal auditory stimuli. Because of the special problems posed by "amusia," such nonverbal auditory stimuli probably should not include the recognition of melodies, songs, etc.

There are two approximately equivalent forms (A and B) of the test, each consisting of 13 items. The items are listed in Tables 8–8 and 8–9 in the order in which they are presented on the sound tape. Some researchers prefer to administer both forms (26 items) to reduce the risk of false negatives (Varney & Damasio, 1986).

Table 8–8. Sound Recognition Test: Scoring Standards for Form A

Item No.	Score credits		
	3	2	0
1	cat, kitty meowing imitating a cat		
2	coughing, throat clearing, someone has cold	man*	someone's sick
3	bell, chime, church clock, outdoor clock	school bell, church*	doorbell, dinner bell
4	applause, clapping dancing	people*, crowd*	horse walking, shoes, tap
5	machine gun, automatic rifle	gun*, shooting*, bullet	
6	fog horn, boat, train whistle, ship coming in	factory whistle, whistle*	car honking
7	airplane, jet, airship	train, truck, car	factory, storm, thunder, volcano erupting
8	telephone ringing, telephone bell, calling on phone	bell*, doorbell	
9	piano, clavichord, harpsichord, organ, xylophone	chimes*, record player*, music box*, instrument*	band*, orchestra*, nursery music*, lullaby*, radio*, bells, organ grinder
10	woman, girl or boy speaking English	someone speaking English*, TV show*, church*	man or woman speaking foreign language, man speaking people talking
11	birds (any type of bird except fowl)	animals*	ducks
12	door slamming, door closing, door closing and opening	planks falling, unloading wooden boards, car door slamming, banging*	something falling, chopping wood, hitting something, hammering
13	trumpet, fanfare, any brass instrument	band*, orchestra*, record player*, movie*, show starting*, music*, end of show*, march*, instruments*, organ, any wind instrument	piano, violin, or other string instrument

Note: The underscored responses in the "3" column identify the actual source of the sound. For those items indicated by an asterisk (*), score 2 or 0 only if the answer cannot be improved upon by questioning (see Administration).

Table 8–9.   Sound Recognition Test: Scoring Standards for Form B

Item No.	Score credits		
	3	2	0
1	whistling		
2	dog barking		
3	baby or child crying		
4	auto, car, truck, bus, motor starting	cars, cars won't start	lion, jet
5	knocking or tapping on door, tapping on wood	tapping cane on floor, somebody at door, pounding desk with knuckles	hammering*, walking, tap dancing
6	dialing on telephone	banging receiver*, calling wrong number*, calling somebody on phone*	phone ringing
7	drums, drum corps	band*, Indians, soldiers, men marching	music*, train
8	typewriter		
9	thunder, thunderstorm	explosion, cannons, blast, bomb, storm, rainstorm	lightning, earthquake, gun, rain, rocket, shooting, bowling
10	faucet running, faucet water, pouring bucket of water, taking bath or shower	washing, washing machine, hose spraying, rain	steam
11	man speaking foreign language	man speaking English, they are talking*	boy speaking
12	frogs and crickets, frogs, crickets, toad	insect*, swamp noises	pigs, ducks, mud turtle, grasshopper
13	organ, church music	music*, instrument*	church*, TV*, piano, band*, orchestra*, horn, record player*

Note: Underscored responses in "3" column identify the actual source of the sound. For items indicated by an asterisk (*), score 2 or 0 only if the answer cannot be improved upon by questioning (see Administration).

Administration

STANDARD FORM

The subject is seated at a table. The playback loudspeaker is placed at a distance of about seven feet in front of the subject. The sound tape is inserted into a tape deck/amplifier. For patients with normal hearing, the volume is set at a level of approximately 70 db. For hard-of-hearing subjects, the volume may be increased or the sounds may be presented through earphones of adequate sensitivity. Instruct the subject as follows: "**We have a number of sounds recorded on this tape. I am going to play these sounds to you and I want you to guess what made these sounds, where they come from. The sounds will be loud enough for you to hear.**

Every time you hear a sound, listen carefully and then tell me what you think made the sound, where the sound came from. After each sound, there will be a pause so that you can think about it and tell me the answer. If you need more time after the sound, tell me so that I can stop the tape. If you do not know what made the sound, make a guess, give me your best guess."

Start the tape at the beginning of Series A or B. If the subject requests it, or if it is obvious that the subject will not complete his or her answer within the 15-second pause between sounds, stop the tape. If the subject gives a partially correct response or a response that is not specific enough to meet the criteria outlined in Tables 8–8 and 8–9 (responses marked with an asterisk), ask; "What was it exactly that made the sound?" or "Was that all you heard?" In formulating the question, the examiner may use the information given in the subject's response, for example: "What kind of bell?" or "How did the people make the sound?" However, the examiner should be careful not to give cues as to the correct response when posing a question. Some exceptions to this general rule are as follows: For items A9, A13, B7, and B13, if a patient indicates that it was a musical instrument, it is permissible to ask: "What kind of an instrument was it?" For items A10 and B11, if the patient indicates that it is "a voice" or "a person talking," the examiner may ask: "Was the person speaking English?" After the subject has completed an answer, continue by pushing the release button. If more than one error occurs in the series presented first, the alternate form should also be given.

MULTIPLE-CHOICE, VERBAL

This administration should be used only with patients who have difficulty to respond orally but are able to read. A multiple-choice card for each sound is used. Instructions and procedure are essentially the same as for the Standard Administration except that the subject is required to point to the response that he or she has selected from the four choices on the card.

MULTIPLE-CHOICE, PICTURES

This administration should be used only with patients who have difficulty in responding orally and who are not able to read. A multiple-choice card with four pictures for each sound is used. Instructions and procedure are essentially the same as for the Standard Administration except that the subject is required to point to the response that he or she has selected from the four choices on the card. Correct responses are the same as for the oral multiple-choice administration.

Approximate Time for Administration

The time required is 10 minutes for each form.

Scoring

The responses are scored for correct identification according to the criteria presented in Tables 8–8 and 8–9. A score of 3 points is given if the sound is identified correctly or if a response is given which was found to be equivalent in normative samples (the original source of the sounds is underscored in the left column on the tables). A score of 2 points is given for responses that are correct but too general and that cannot be improved upon questioning (center column in the tables). The right-hand column in the tables lists some incorrect responses for which a 0 score is given; a few very general responses are also included in this column.

Occasionally, a subject will give two responses without indicating a preference (the "or" response). In this case, the following scoring rules apply:

1. If both a 3-point and a 2-point response are given, a score of 2 points is given.
2. If both a 3-point response and a wrong (score 0) response are made, a score of 1 point is given.

The correct responses for the multiple-choice administration on Forms A and B (with A for upper left, B for upper right, C for lower left, and D for lower right) are:

1B	8A
2D	9C
3C	10B
4A	11B
5C	12D
6D	13A
7B	

Comment

The product–moment correlation between the two forms in a group of 79 adult control patients was found by the authors to be .73; the correlation for all adult subjects ($N = 101$) tested (including brain-damaged patients) was .68. The correlation between the two forms for a group of 97 children (ages 5–10 years) was .97.

The error rate for most brain-damaged patients tends to be low. However, Merrick, Moulthrop, and Luchins (1989) reported that with a longer (30 stimuli) and somewhat more difficult tape normal controls gave only 28 correct answers (SD = 1.8); 19 neurologically impaired (not specified) subjects obtained only 16 (SD = 6.1); and 6 Alzheimer's disease patients gave only 15 correct answers (SD = 5.7). The large standard deviations seem to indicate large variability from patient to patient. Varney (1982) found a fairly close relationship between defective sound recognition and pantomime recognition in aphasics, but suggested that sound recognition is more closely related to aural comprehension (Varney, 1980). Lezak (1983) lists defects in sound recognition as indicative of right temporal lobe lesions (Gordon, 1974; Milner, 1971). Based on autopsy results, a right temporal lesion was also most likely in a cause of auditory agnosia without aphasia (Spreen et al., 1965). In contrast, Varney and Damasio (1986) found sound recognition defects in aphasics with left-hemisphere lesions in the basal ganglia, the auditory cortex, the supramarginal gyrus, the angular gyrus, and area 37, although not all patients with lesions in these areas had sound recognition defects. Normal sound recognition in aphasics predicted rapid and almost complete recovery of even severe forms of aural comprehension deficits (Varney, 1984).

Normative Data

Normal adults almost invariably obtain near-perfect scores (38 out of a maximum of 39) on this test. In brain damaged patients, true sound agnosia is rare, so that even aphasic patients may obtain perfect scores if the multiple-choice (nonverbal) form is used.

Children seem to acquire the ability to recognize sounds only gradually. Table 8–10 shows the progression of scores with age in normal children. Klonoff and Low (1974) reported virtually no differences between children with higher and lower IQ and a similar progression with age. Although they used the same test, a different scoring method makes it impossible to compare age mean scores. Both their acute and their chronic brain damage groups scored significantly lower than did matched controls. However, the difference between matched controls and two minimal cerebral damage groups was not significant. It should be noted that Klonoff and Low used the test with children 2–5 years old and reported obtaining scores only 3 points below the 6-year-old group.

Table 8–10. Mean Sound Recognition Test Scores for Normal School Children Ages 5–10 (IQs 80–120 Inclusive)

Age	N	Form A	Form B	Mean age	Mean IQ
5	9	30.67	30.22	5.6	105.3
6	20	32.80	30.60	6.4	103.9
7	11	35.82	36.45	7.6	100.4
8	13	35.85	36.54	8.6	103.8
9	15	36.80	36.93	9.5	105.6
10	5	36.00	34.40	10.3	106.6
Total	73	34.58	34.26	—	104.1

Note: The standard administration was used.

REFERENCES

Gordon, H.W. (1974). Auditory specialization of the right and left hemispheres. In Kinsbourne, M., & Smith, W.L. (Eds.), *Hemispheric Disconnection and Cerebral Function*. Springfield, Ill.: C.C. Thomas.

Klonoff, H., & Low, M. (1974). Disordered brain function in young children and early adolescents: Neuropsychological and electroencephalographic correlates. In R.M. Reitan & L.A. Davison (Eds.), *Clinical Neuropsychology: Current Status and Applications*. New York: John Wiley.

Lezak, M.D. (1983). *Neuropsychological Assessment* (2nd ed.). New York: Oxford University Press.

Merrick, W.A., Moulthrop, M.A., & Luchins, D.J. (1989). Recall and recognition of acoustic semantic memories: Development of the acoustic recognition test (ART). *Journal of Clinical and Experimental Neuropsychology, 11*, 87.

Milner, B. (1971). Interhemispheric differences in the localization of psychologi-

cal processes in man. *British Medical Bulletin, 27*, 272–277.

Spreen, O., & Benton, A.L. (1963). A sound recognition test for clinical use. Mimeo. University of Iowa.

Spreen, O., Benton, A.L., & Fincham, R.W. (1965). Auditory agnosia without aphasia. *Archives of Neurology, 13*, 84–92.

Varney, N.R. (1980). Sound recognition in relation to aural language comprehension in aphasic patients. *Journal of Neurology, Neurosurgery, and Psychiatry, 43*, 71–75.

Varney, N.R. (1982). Pantomime recognition defect in aphasia: Implications for the concept of asymbolia. *Brain and Language, 15*, 32–39.

Varney, N.R. (1984). The prognostic significance of sound recognition in receptive aphasia. *Archives of Neurology, 41*, 181–182.

Varney, N.R., & Damasio, H. (1986). CT scan correlates of sound recognition defect in aphasia. *Cortex, 22*, 483–486.

THREE-DIMENSIONAL BLOCK CONSTRUCTION (3-D)

Other Test Name

This test is also known as the three-dimensional constructional praxis test.

Purpose

The purpose of this test is to assess visuoconstructional ability indicated by how well constructions in three-dimensional space are copied.

Source

The complete test with 100 record forms can be ordered from Oxford University Press, 2001 Evans Road, Cary, North Carolina 27513, for $185 U.S.; the manual (together with 11 other tests) can be ordered from the same source for $23.95 U.S.

Description

This is a standardized and objectively scored test of visuoconstructional ability (Benton et al., 1983) requiring the subject to reproduce three block models of increasing complexity, using 6, 8, and 15 blocks from an assortment of blocks on a tray. Two alternate forms as well as an experimental form using photographic stimuli are provided.

Administration

See source. Briefly, 29 individual blocks of different sizes and shapes are presented in a standard arrangement on a tray placed to the right or left of the subject. Only the model to be copied is set before the subject, who is instructed to "use the blocks and put some of them together so that they look like the model as you face it." Accuracy rather than speed is emphasized. The time taken for the construction of each model is recorded in seconds. A maximum of five minutes is allowed for each model.

Approximate Time for Administration

The time required is 10–15 minutes.

Scoring

One point is credited for each block placed correctly. Thus, perfect scores on the test models are 6, 8, and 15 points, respectively. A notation of the types of errors made in the construction of each model is made in addition to the overall "number correct" score.

Three types of errors are found: (1) omissions and additions; (2) substitutions; and (3) displacements (angular deviations, separations, misplacements).

An alternate scoring system counts only omissions and additions, substitutions, gross rotations, and gross misplacements. The total score is the number of blocks placed correctly on Designs I, II, and III.

If the total time taken for constructing the three designs exceeds 380 seconds, 2 points are subtracted from the total score.

Comment

Reliability data for this test are not available. Constructional praxis as required in drawing, putting together a jigsaw puzzle, or assembling a model, a bicycle, or household items, is a skill required in daily life and in many occupations. It is frequently disrupted or diminished after brain lesions, especially of the right hemisphere. Common two-dimensional tests (e.g., Kohs' Block Design, stick construction, Rey Complex Figure, Draw-A-Man, etc.) have long been known to be sensitive to such lesions. The 3-D Block Construction test is the first standardized test that uses three-dimensional constructions of wooden blocks with various shapes and sizes.

Benton (1979) discussed the possible contribution of defects of both the right and left posterior areas to constructional defects: The visuoperceptive impairment may be more frequent for both frontal and parietal right-hemisphere lesions, whereas "true," "executive" constructional impairment may be attributed only to the left parietal lesions. In either case, the defective performance is not based on primary visual or motor disorders. In Benton's study, 54% of right-hemisphere lesion patients had scores lower than 95% of normal controls, whereas only 23% of left-hemisphere lesion patients scored at that level.

Table 8–11. 3D Block Construction: Time to Construct the Three Models for Children Ages 6–12 Years

Age	N	Mean	SD	Median	Range
Model I					
6	12	36.5	13.3	29.5	12–60
7	50	36.7	37.6	29.8	15–262
8	41	29.4	15.3	26.0	13–113
9	38	25.3	10.9	22.5	15–71
10	36	20.5	7.0	18.5	10–39
11	39	18.5	6.7	17.0	10–38
12	36	18.6	11.1	15.3	9–63
Model II					
6	12	77.8	32.4	70.5	36–165
7	50	75.3	47.6	67.0	21–300
8	41	62.1	25.8	56.3	35–179
9	38	57.8	21.7	52.5	25–143
10	36	47.0	21.9	40.5	25–150
11	39	48.1	21.6	40.3	19–121
12	36	43.0	18.1	40.5	25–117
Model III					
6	12	149	37	159	85–210
7	50	160	53	142	85–295
8	41	139	46	125	72–300
9	38	120	47	110	68–290
10	36	110	76	92	52–480
11	39	89	23	87	58–153
12	36	81	29	71	51–207

Source: Spreen & Gaddes (1969).

In addition to constructional praxis, the test often reveals visual disorders such as lateral neglect or field defects by unusual constructions in which one side of the model is omitted or very poorly constructed whereas the other side is a perfect copy of the model.

Normative Data

See source. In general, normal controls (nonneurologic hospital patients with a mean age of 42 years) had scores between 26 and 29 (with only one subject scoring 25). Norms for elderly subjects are not available.

In children, a steady progression of scores from age 6 (median 21) to age 12 (median 27) has been observed (Spreen & Gaddes, 1969), suggesting that adult level scores may be reached by age 14. Time to construct each model also decreases from 180 seconds for Model III at age 6, to 71 seconds at age 12. Because time scores (measured covertly and without stressing speed of construction) may be of interest in the evaluation of developmental delay in children, Table 8–11 presents this information in detail.

REFERENCES

Benton, A.L. (1979). Visuoperceptive, visuospatial, and visuoconstructive disorders. In K.M. Heilman & E. Valenstein (Eds.), *Clinical Neuropsychology* (pp. 186–232). New York: Oxford University Press.

Benton, A.L., Hamsher, K.deS., Varney, N.R., & Spreen, O. (1983). *Contributions to Neuropsychological Assessment*. New York: Oxford University Press.

Spreen, O., & Gaddes, W.H. (1969). Developmental norms for 15 neuropsychological tests age 6 to 15. *Cortex, 5,* 170–191.

TRAIL MAKING TEST
Other Test Name

Marching Test.

Purpose

This is a test of speed for visual search, attention, mental flexibility, and motor function.

Source

The test can be purchased from Reitan Neuropsychology Laboratory, 1338 East Edison Street, Tucson, Arizona 85719. The manual of administration and 100 copies of Parts A and B for Adults cost $25.00; Parts A and B for children, $25.00 U.S.

Description

This popular test, originally part of the Army Individual Test Battery (1944) was added by Reitan to the Halstead Battery. It requires the connection, by making pencil lines, between 25 encircled numbers randomly arranged on a page in proper order (Part A) and of 25 encircled numbers and letters in alternating order (Part B). The test has two forms: the Children's ("Intermediate") Form and the Adult Form. The intermediate form is used for children 9 through 14 years of age. The adult form is used from age 15 years and older. Lewis and Rennick (1979) presented four equivalent alternative forms to be used if repeat testing is necessary, although Lezak (1983) did not report any practice effects of significant magnitude.

Administration

Part A

Sample. When ready to begin the test, place the Part A test sheet, sample side up, flat on the table directly in front of the subject, with the bottom of the test sheet approximately six inches from the subject's edge of the table. Give the subject a pencil and say: **"On this page** [point] **are some numbers. Begin at number one** [point to '1'] **and draw a line from one to two** [point to '2'], **two to three** [point to '3'], **three to four** [point to '4'], **and so on, in order, until you reach the end** [point to the circle marked 'END']. **Draw the lines as fast as you can, Do not lift the pencil from the paper. Ready! Begin!"**

If the subject makes a mistake on Sample A, point it out and explain it. The following explanations of mistakes are acceptable:

1. **"You started with the wrong circle. This is where you start** [point to '1']."
2. **"You skipped this circle** [point to the one omitted]. **You should go from number one** [point] **to two** [point], **two to three** [point], **and so on, until you reach the circle marked 'END'** [point]."
3. **"Please keep the pencil on the paper, and continue right on to the next circle."**

After the mistake has been explained, the examiner marks out the wrong part and says: **"Go on from here"** [point to the last circle completed correctly in the sequence].

If the subject still cannot complete Sample A, take the subject's hand and guide the pencil (eraser end down) through the trail. Then say: **"Now you try it. Put** your pencil, point down. Remember, begin at number one [point] and draw a line from one to two [point to '2'], two to three [point to '3'], three to four [point to '4'], and so on, in order until you reach the circle marked 'END' [point]. Do not skip around but go from one number to the next in the proper order. If you make a mistake, mark it out. Remember, work as fast as you can. Ready! Begin!"

If the subject succeeds this time, go on to Part A of the test. If not, repeat the procedure until the subject does succeed, or it becomes evident that he or she cannot do it.

If the subject completes the sample item correctly, and in a manner which shows that he or she knows what to do, say: "Good! Let's try the next one." Turn the page and give Part A of the test.

Test. Say: "On this page are numbers from one to twenty-five. Do this the same way. Begin at number one [point], and draw a line from one to two [point to '2'], two to three [point to '3'], three to four [point to '4'], and so on, in order until you reach the end [point]. Remember, work as fast as you can. Ready! Begin!"

Start timing. If the subject makes an error, call it to his or her attention immediately, and have the subject proceed from the point the mistake occurred. Do not stop timing.

If the examinee completes Part A without error, remove the test sheet. Record the time in seconds. Errors count only in the increased time of performance. Then say: "That's fine. Now we'll try another one." Proceed immediately to Part B, sample.

PART B

Sample. Place the test sheet for Part B, sample side up, flat on the table in front of the examinee, in the same position as the sheet for Part A was placed. Point with the right hand to the sample and say: "On this page are some numbers and letters. Begin at number one [point], "and draw a line from one to A [point to 'A'], A to two [point to '2'], two to B [point to 'B'], B to three [point to '3'], three to C [point to 'C'], and so on, in order until you reach the end [point to circle marked 'END']. Remember, first you have a number [point to '1'], then a letter [point to 'A'], then a number [point to '2'], then a letter [point to 'B'], and so on. Draw the lines as fast as you can. Ready! Begin!"

If the subject makes a mistake on Sample B, point it out and explain it. The following explanations of mistakes are acceptable:

1. "You started with the wrong circle. This is where you start [point to '1']."
2. "You skipped this circle* [point to the one omitted]. You should go from

---

*If it is clear that the subject intended to touch the circle but missed it, do not count it as an omission, but caution the subject to touch the circle.

one [point] **to A** [point], **A to two** [point], **two to B** [point], **B to three** [point], **and so on until you reach the circle marked 'END'** [point]."

3. "You only went as far as this circle [point]. You should have gone to the circle marked 'END' [point]."

4. "Please keep the pencil on the paper, and go right on to the next circle."

After the mistake has been explained, the examiner marks out the wrong part and says: "**Go on from here**" [point to the last circle completed correctly in the sequence].

If the subject still cannot complete Sample B, take the subject's hand and guide the pencil (eraser end down) through the circles. Then say:"**Now you try it. Remember you begin at number one** [point] **and draw a line from one to A** [point to 'A'], **A to two** [point to '2'], **two to B** [point to 'B'], **B to three** [point to '3'], **and so on until you reach the circle marked 'END'** [point]. **Ready! Begin!**"

If the subject succeeds this time, go on to Part B of the test. If not, repeat the procedure until he does succeed, or it becomes evident that he cannot do it.

If the subject completes the sample item correctly, say: "**Good. Let's try the next one.**"

Test. Turn the page over, and proceed immediately to Part B, and say: "**On this page are both numbers and letters. Do this the same way.** "**Begin at number one** point], **and draw a line from one to A** [point to 'A'], **A to two** [point to '2'], **two to B** [point to 'B'], **B to three** [point to '3'], **three to C** [point to 'C'], **and so on, in order, until you reach the end** [point to circle marked 'END']. **Remember, first you have a number** [point to '1'], **then a letter** [point to 'A'], **then a number** [point to '2'], **then a letter** [point to 'B'], **and so on. Do not skip around, but go from one circle to the next in the proper order, draw the lines as fast as you can. Ready! Begin!**"

Start timing. If the subject makes an error, immediately call it to his or her attention, and have the subject proceed from the point at which the mistake occurred. Do not stop timing.

If the subject completes Part B without error, remove the test sheet. Record the time in seconds. Errors count only in the increased time of performance.

Approximate Time for Administration

The time required is 5–10 minutes.

Scoring

For both forms, scoring is expressed in terms of the time required for Part A and Part B of the test.

Comment

Whereas Dye (1979) and Stuss et al. (1987) reported significant practice effects after a short interval and after one week for both parts of the test, Lezak (1983) found significant practice effects in the course of three administrations in six-month intervals only on Part A, but not on Part B. In the same study, reliability was reported as .98 for Part A and .67 on Part B (coefficient of concordance). Lezak also noted that the simplification of scoring achieved by using only time scores instead of both error and time scores reduces reliability since error correction may take a variable amount of time, depending on both the examiner and the examinee's ability to comprehend. Snow et al. (1988) reported a one-year retest reliability of .64 for Part A and of .72 for Part B in 100 older subjects (age 67). Goldstein and Watson (1989) found similar reliability coefficients (.69–.94 for Part A, .66–.86 for Part B) for various neurological groups, but not for schizophrenics (.36 for Part A, .63 for Part B). Charter et al. (1987) found alternate form reliability (by changing numbers and letters, but leaving the circles in place) of .89 and .92 (Parts A and B); a similar study by desRosiers and Kavanagh (1987) reported reliabilities of .80 and .81, respectively. Matarazzo et al. (1974) gave the test twice, 12 weeks apart, and reported reliability coefficients of .46 and .44 (Parts A and B) for young healthy normal males, and of .78 and .67 for 60-year-old patients with diffuse cerebrovascular disease. Dodrill and Troupin (1975) reported 6- to 12-month reliabilities for epileptics ranging between .67 and .89 for Part A, and between .30 and .87 for Part B (the highest values were obtained after four repeat administrations). When 102 adults in their early 30s were instructed to "fake brain damage," the results for Part A showed considerably faster times than those of 43 brain-damaged subjects, similar to normal controls, but this discrepancy was even more pronounced for Part B (Goebel, 1983). It seems obvious that in the fake attempt, subjects underestimated the difficulty of Part B more than that of Part A.

The test loaded on both a "rapid visual search" and a "visuospatial sequencing" factor (desRosiers & Kavanagh, 1987). Construct validity for visual search was also established by correlations (.36–.93) with an object finding test and a hidden pattern test obtained in 92 aphasic and nonaphasic patients (Ehrenstein et al., 1982). In this study, the test did not correlate with verbal tests—for example, Token Test, Peabody Picture Vocabulary Test (PPVT), and picture naming. It was highly sensitive to brain damage (Dodrill, 1978; O'Donnell, 1983), including closed head injury (desRosiers & Kavanagh, 1987) and alcoholism (Grant et al., 1984, 1987), but not to formaldehyde-exposure victims (Cripe & Dodrill, 1988). Times for a mixed neuropsychiatric population exceeded even the lowest percentile norms (Warner et al., 1987). Prigatano (1983) found significant differences between a matched control group and patients with mildly hypoxemic patients and chronic obstructive pulmonary disease, on Part B but not on Part A. Similarly, young adult learning-disabled subjects differed from controls only on Part B, but not on Part A (O'Donnell, 1983). Alekoumbides et al. (1987) reported significant differences between normals and three clinical groups with respect to correct classification rates: The percentages were (for Parts A and B): 80% and 74% for normals; 26% and 20% for patients with diffuse lesions; 95% and 94% with focal lesions; and 43% and 43% with Korsakoff's disease. Part B requires more information-processing ability than Part A; larger than normal differences between Parts A and B have been interpreted as indicative of left lateralized lesions (Lewinsohn, 1973; Wheeler & Reitan, 1963), but more recent studies have not confirmed this (Schreiber et al., 1976; Wedding, 1979). Stuss et al. (1989) report that the times required for Trails A and B showed steady and significant improvement in the course of five office visits within a three-year period for patients with traumatic head injury; this improvement was beyond the practice-effect gain in controls. Significant differences between patients with cerebral dysfunction and non-psychotic personality dysfunction (Barnes & Lucas, 1974) and psychiatric patients (Heaton et al., 1978) have not been established for this test. Performance on this test does not seem to be affected by the presence or absence of aphasia (Ehrenstein et al., 1982).

Part B is clearly the more sensitive part of the Trail Making Test. Beyond the sensitivity to brain damage, the observation of a patient's behavior on this test may be of considerable value—for example, the ability of shifting course during an ongoing activity (Pontius & Yudowitz, 1980), and the ability to deal with more than one stimulus at a time (Eson et al., 1978).

Normative Data

The use of cutoff scores designating "organic impairment," suggested by Reitan and Wolfson (1985) (e.g., >72 seconds for Part B) and Matarazzo et al. (1974) (>40 seconds for Part A, >91 seconds for Part B) has been abandoned by most authors (see Bornstein, 1986); instead, actual normative data are used.

Table 8–12 presents normative data for adults, aged 15–79 years. The age differences are only minimal for the younger age groups; the increase of time, and especially for the difference between Part A and Part B, become more pronounced with age. This has been confirmed in a study by Price et al. (1980). The norms agree reasonably well with those published by desRosiers and Kavanagh (1987), Cripe and Dodrill (1988), Dodrill (1978), Grant et al. (1984), Harley et al. (1980), Stanton et al. (1984), and Stuss et al. (1988), but not with those of Alekoumbides et al. (1987), who reported much longer times for an older sample (mean age-47 years) of 118 adults.

Scores are strongly affected by the education level of the subject. Heaton et al. (1986) reported that to complete Part B, normal adults 40–60 years old with less than 12 years of education needed 102.2 seconds; those with 12–15 years of education, 69.7 seconds; and those with 16 and more years of education, 57.9

Table 8–12. Trails Test: Time in Seconds (on Parts A and B) for Normal Control Subjects at Different Age Levels

Percentile	15–20 Years (n = 108) A	B	20–39 Years (n = 275) A	B	40–49 Years (n = 138) A	B	50–59 Years (n = 130) A	B	60–69 Years (n = 120) A	B	70–79 Years (n = 90) A	B
90	15	26	21	45	18	30	23	55	26	62	33	79
75	19	37	24	55	23	52	29	71	30	83	54	122
50	23	47	26	65	30	78	35	80	35	95	70	180
25	30	59	34	85	38	102	57	128	63	142	98	210
10	38	70	45	98	59	126	77	162	85	174	161	350

Source: Data extrapolated from Davies (1968), based on a representative British (Liverpool) sample; Fromm-Auch & Yeudall (1983); and Kennedy (1981).

seconds. Correlation coefficient between education and Trails A and B have been reported as .19 and .33 (partialing out the effect of age; Bornstein, 1985; see also Stanton et al., 1984, and Stuss et al., 1987). The effect of IQ is somewhat less pronounced, but most noticeable on Part B (Dodrill, 1987). Warner et al. (1987) reported correlations with IQ between .42 and .30 for Part A and between .48 and .42 for Part B. Alekoumbides et al. (1987) published correction equations for age and education. The effect of these corrections is briefly summarized in Table 8–13. If these corrections are used, the corrected score must be compared with the

Table 8–13. Trails Test: Summary of Corrections for Age and Education

Age	Education (grade completed) 1	5	10	12	15	20
Part A						
25	−15	−5	7	11	18	30
35	−19	−10	2	7	14	26
45	−24	−14	−3	2	9	21
55	−28	−19	−7	−2	5	16
65	−33	−23	−12	−7	8	12
75	−37	−28	−16	−12	−4	7
Part B						
25	−49	−18	21	37	60	99
35	−64	−33	6	22	45	84
45	−78	−47	−8	7	30	69
55	−93	−62	−23	−8	16	55
65	−115	−77	−38	−22	1	40
75	−122	−91	−52	−37	−14	25

Note: If corrections are used, the mean of 48.60 (SD = 23.79) for Part A and of 120.49 (SD = 78.90) for Part B of the Alekoumbides study must be referred to.

Source: Alekoumbides et al. (1987, Suppl.).

Table 8–14.   Trails Test: Normative Data for Children
(Intermediate Version): Time Score in Seconds

Age	N	Mean	SD	Median	Range
			Part A		
Male					
8	11	32.4	11.7	30.5	16–55
9	22	26.8	8.9	25.5	13–45
10	26	21.3	6.1	20.5	13–42
11	21	16.4	5.6	14.8	9–30
12	48	16.6	5.9	15.1	10–43
13	7	16.0	10.1	13.3	9–39
(14–15)[a]	5	16.0	12.0	16.0	8–30
Female					
8	12	36.4	18.7	33.5	16–86
9	19	23.1	8.1	21.0	13–48
10	25	18.2	4.6	17.8	10–28
11	30	18.0	6.6	17.2	9–37
12	44	16.0	5.4	14.7	7–32
13	7	13.7	1.9	13.3	12–18
(14–15)[a]	5	13.0	2.3	13.0	12–17
All normals					
(6)[b]	99	70	40		
(7)	101	36	11		
8	88	31	12	30.5	16–86
9	41	25.1	8.8	23.0	13–48
10	51	19.8	5.7	19.4	10–42
11	51	17.4	6.3	16.3	9–37
12	92	16.3	5.7	14.9	7–43
13	14	14.9	7.6	13.3	9–39
(14–15)[a]	10	14.6	6.2	14.6	8–30
			Part B		
Male					
8	11	77.8	34.5	76.5	32–159
9	22	58.0	21.6	57.5	22–120
10	26	51.6	14.7	52.5	18–82
11	21	43.3	20.0	38.8	25–122
12	48	39.6	13.3	37.8	14–90
13	7	34.0	12.4	34.0	17–99
(14–15)[a]	5	28.6	12.0	29.0	13–45
Female					
8	12	71.8	39.0	77.5	26–176
9	19	50.7	14.5	50.8	24–76
10	25	43.2	15.0	42.0	25–84

(*continued*)

Table 8–14. *(Continued)*

Age	N	Mean	SD	Median	Range
11	30	40.6	11.8	38.5	15–62
12	44	33.5	11.1	31.3	20–74
13	7	30.7	6.9	29.3	22–43
(14–15)[a]	5	25.0	14.6	25.0	13–50
All normals					
(6)[c]	45	133	51		
(7)	96	91	41		
8	88	72	30	76.5	26–176
9	41	54.6	19.0	51.3	22–120
10	51	47.5	15.4	45.8	18–84
11	51	41.7	15.8	38.8	15–122
12	92	35.7	12.5	34.0	14–90
13	14	30.0	19.5	29.5	17–99
(14–15)[a]	10	27.0	12.8	27.0	13–50

[a]Estimate, based on Knights & Norwood (1980).

[b]Estimate, based on Rhode Island norms and Klonoff & Low (1974).

[c]Estimate, based on Reitan (1971) and Klonoff & Low (1974).

[d]Estimate, based on Knights & Norwood (1980) and Klonoff & Low (1974).

Source: Spreen & Gaddes (1969).

means obtained in the Alekoumbides sample: Part A = 48.60 (SD = 23.79), Part B = 120.49 (SD = 78.90). The authors also present standardized scores which are not included here.

Table 8–14 presents norms for children, aged 6–15, using the intermediate form of the test. Values for children 6, 7, and 14–15 years old were extrapolated from other sources as indicated. Since the test is dependent on knowledge of number and letter sequences, norms for the youngest age groups have to be interpreted with caution. The norms presented here agree closely with those published by Klonoff and Low (1974) and by Reitan (1971). Trites (1977) reports values that are somewhat higher for all age groups, but show a similar age progression. Sex-related differences appear to be minimal for this test.

REFERENCES

Alekoumbides, A., Charter, R.A., Adkins, T.G., & Seacat, G.F. (1987). The diagnosis of brain damage by the WAIS, WMS, and Reitan Battery utilizing standardized scores corrected for age and education. *International Journal of Clinical Neuropsychology*, 9, 11–28.

Army Individual Test Battery (1944). *Manual of Directions and Scoring*. Washington, D.C.: War Department, Adjutant General's Office.

Barnes, G.W., & Lucas, G.J. (1974). Cerebral dysfunction vs. psychogenesis in Halstead–Reitan tests. *Journal of Nervous and Mental Disease, 158,* 50–60.

Bornstein, R.A. (1985). Normative data on selected neuropsychological measures from a nonclinical sample. *Journal of Clinical Psychology, 41*, 651–659.

Bornstein, R.A. (1986). Classification rates obtained with "standard" cutoff scores on selected neuropsychological measures. *Journal of Clinical and Experimental Neuropsychology, 8*, 413–420.

Charter, R.A., Adkins, T.G., Alekoumbides, A., & Seacat, G.F. (1987). Reliability of the WAIS, WMS, and Reitan Battery: Raw scores and standardized scores corrected for age and education. *International Journal of Clinical Neuropsychology, 9*, 28–32.

Cripe, L.I., & Dodrill, C.B. (1988). Neuropsychological test performances with chronic low level formaldehyde exposure. *Clinical Neuropsychologist, 2*, 41–48.

Davies, A. (1968). The influence of age on Trail Making Test performance. *Journal of Clinical Psychology, 24*, 96–98.

desRosiers, G., & Kavanagh, D. (1987). Cognitive assessment in closed head injury: Stability, validity and parallel forms for two neuropsychological measures of recovery. *International Journal of Clinical Neuropsychology, 9*, 162–173.

Dodrill, C.B. (1978). A neuropsychological battery for epilepsy. *Epilepsia, 19*, 611–623.

Dodrill, C.B. (1987). What's Normal? Presidential Address, Pacific Northwest Neuropsychological Association. Mimeo.

Dodrill, C.B., & Troupin, A.S. (1975). Effects of repeated administration of a comprehensive neuropsychological battery among chronic epileptics. *Journal of Nervous and Mental Disease, 161*, 185–190.

Dye, O.A. (1979). Effects of practice on Trail Making Test performance. *Perceptual and Motor Skills, 48*, 296.

Ehrenstein, W.H., Heister, G., & Cohen, R. (1982). Trail Making Test and visual search. *Archiv für Psychiatrie und Nervenkrankheiten, 231*, 333–338.

Eson, M.E., Yen, J.K. & Bourke, R.S. (1978). Assessment of recovery from serious head injury. *Journal of Neurology, Neurosurgery and Psychiatry, 41*, 1036–1042.

Fromm-Auch, D., & Yeudall, L.T. (1983). Normative data for the Halstead–Reitan tests. *Journal of Clinical Neuropsychology, 5*, 221–238.

Goebel, R.A. (1983). Detection of faking on the Halstead–Reitan neuropsychological test battery. *Journal of Clinical Psychology, 39*, 731–742.

Goldstein, G., & Watson, J.R. (1989). Test–retest reliability of the Halstead–Reitan battery and the WAIS in a neuropsychiatric population. *Clinical Neuropsychologist, 3*, 265–273.

Grant, I., Adams, K.M., & Reed, R. (1984). Aging, abstinence, and medical risk in the prediction of neuropsychological deficit among long-term alcoholics. *Archives of General Psychiatry, 41*, 710–716.

Grant, I., Reed, R., & Adams, K.M. (1987). Diagnosis of intermediate-duration and subacute organic mental disorders in abstinent alcoholics. *Journal of Clinical Psychiatry, 48*, 319–323.

Harley, J.P., Leuthold, C.A., Matthews, C.G., & Bergs, L.E. (1980). Wisconsin Neuropsychological Test Battery T-Score Norms for Older Veterans Administration Medical Center Patients. Mimeo. Madison: Department of Neurology, University of Wisconsin.

Heaton, R.K., Baade, L.E. & Johnson, K.L. (1978). Neuropsychological test results associated with psychiatric disorders in adults. *Psychological Bulletin, 85*, 141–162.

Heaton, R.K., Grant, I., & Matthews, C.G. (1986). Differences in neuropsychological test performance associated with age, education, and sex. In I. Grant & K.M. Adams (Eds.), *Neuropsychological Assessment of Neuropsychiatric Disorders* (pp. 100–120). New York: Oxford University Press.

Kennedy, K.J. (1981). Age effects on Trail Making Test performance. *Perceptual and Motor Skills, 52*, 671–675.

Klonoff, H., & Low, M. (1974). Disordered brain function in young children and early adolescents: Neuropsychological and electroencephalographic correlates. In R.M. Reitan & L.A. Davison (Eds.), *Clinical Neuropsychology: Current Status and Applications*. New York: John Wiley.

Knights, R.M., & Norwood, J.A. (1980). Revised Smoothed Normative Data on the Neuropsychological Test Battery for Children. Mimeo. Ottawa, Ont.: Department of Psychology, Carleton University.

Lewis, R.F., & Rennick, P.M. (1979). *Manual for the Repeatable Cognitive–Perceptual–Motor Battery.* Grosse Pointe Park, Mich.: Axon Publishing.

Lewinsohn, P.M. (1973). *Psychological Assessment of Patients with Brain Injury.* Unpublished Manuscript. Eugene, Oregon: University of Oregon.

Lezak, M.D. (1983). *Neuropsychological Assessment* (2nd ed.), New York: Oxford University Press.

Matarazzo, J.D., Wiens, A.N., Matarazzo, R.G., & Goldstein, S.G. (1974). Psychometric and clinical test–retest reliability of the Halstead Impairment Index in a sample of healthy, young, normal men. *Journal of Nervous and Mental Disease, 158,* 37–49.

O'Donnell, J.P. (1983). Neuropsychological test findings for normal, learning disabled, and brain damaged young adults. *Journal of Consulting and Clinical Psychology, 51,* 726–729.

Pontius, A.A. & Yudowitz, B.S. (1980). Frontal lobe system dysfunction in some criminal actions in a Narratives Test. *Journal of Nervous and Mental Disease, 168,* 111–117.

Price, L.S., Fein, G. & Feinberg, I. (1980). Neuropsychological assessment of cognitive function in the elderly. In L.W. Poon (ed.) *Aging in the 1980s.* Washington, D.C.: American Psychological Association.

Prigatano, G.P. (1983). Neuropsychological test performance in mildly hypoxemic patients with chronic obstructive pulmonary disease. *Journal of Consulting and Clinical Psychology, 51,* 108–116.

Reitan, R.M. (1971). Trail Making Test results for normal and brain-damaged children. *Perceptual and Motor Skills, 33,* 575–581.

Reitan, R.M., & Wolfson, D. (1985). *The Halstead–Reitan Neuropsychological Test Battery.* Tucson: Neuropsychology Press.

Schreiber, D.J., Goldman, H., Kleinman, K.M., Goldfader, P.R., & Snow, M.Y. (1976). The relationship between independent neuropsychological and neurological detection of cerebral impairment. *Journal of Nervous and Mental Disease, 162,* 360–365.

Snow, W.G., Tierney, M.C., Zorzitto, M.L., Fisher, R.H., & Reid, D.W. (1988). One-year test–retest reliability of selected neuropsychological tests in older adults. Paper presented at the International Neuropsychological Society meeting, New Orleans. *Journal of Clinical and Experimental Neuropsychology, 10,* 60 (abstract).

Spreen, O., & Gaddes, W.H. (1969). Developmental norms for 15 neuropsychological tests age 6 to 15. *Cortex, 5,* 171–191.

Stanton, B.A., Jenkins, C.D., Savageau, J.A., Zyzanski, S.J., & Aucoin, R. (1984). Age and education differences on the Trail Making Test and Wechsler Memory Scales. *Perceptual and Motor Skills, 58,* 311–318.

Stuss, D.T., Stethem, L.L., Hugenholtz, H., & Richard M.T. (1989). Traumatic brain injury: A comparison of three clinical tests, and analysis of recovery. *Clinical Neuropsychologist, 3,* 145–156.

Stuss, D.T., Stethem, L.L., & Pelchat, G. (1988). Three tests of attention and rapid information processing: An extension. *Clinical Neuropsychologist, 2,* 246–250.

Stuss, D.T., Stethem, L.L., & Poirier, C.A. (1987). Comparison of three tests of attention and rapid information processing across six age groups. *Clinical Neuropsychologist, 1,* 139–152.

Trites, R.L. (1977). *Neuropsychological Test Manual.* Ottawa, Ontario: Royal Ottawa Hospital.

Warner, M.H., Ernst, J., Townes, B.D., Peel, J., & Preston, M. (1987). Relationship between IQ and neuropsychological measures in neuropsychiatric populations: Within-laboratory and cross-cultural replications using WAIS and WAIS-R. *Journal of Clinical and Experimental Neuropsychology, 9,* 545–562.

Wedding, D. (1979). *A comparison of statis-*

tical, actuarial, and clinical models used in predicting presence, lateralization, and type of brain damage in humans. Unpublished doctoral dissertation, University of Hawaii.

Wheeler, L. & Reitan, R.M. (1963). Discriminant functions applied to the problem of predicting cerebral damage from behavioral tests: A cross-validation study. *Perceptual and Motor Skills, 16,* 681–701.

9

Tactile, Tactile–Visual, and Tactile–Motor Tests

Tactile sensitivity is part of the routine examination in neurology, typically conducted via touch with a gauze pad, pin prick, or von Frey hair stimulation. A small number of standardized techniques including calibrated stimulators have been developed since Bender et al.'s (1948) studies of extinction on double stimulation, Benton's (1959) work on right–left discrimination and finger localization, and Teuber's (i.e., Semmes et al., 1960) investigations of somatosensory changes after penetrating head injury, including the automated and highly technically refined stimulation technique of Carmon and Dyson (1967).

Neuropsychological examinations with standardized tests can and do surpass the accuracy of the clinical neurological examination. The main interest is usually on differences between the two sides (usually hands) of the body, although bilaterally raised thresholds may also be of significance. Our selection includes pure touch-threshold measurements (aesthesiometer), two-point discrimination, and the psychologically more complex functions of finger localization, stereognostic recognition (Tactile Form Perception), and the Tactual Performance Test which includes both a localization and a memory component in addition to stereognosis. We have omitted graphaesthesia (skin writing) and similar tests, which tend to overlap with the tests described here.

REFERENCES

Bender, M.B., Wortis, S.B., & Cramer, J. (1948). Organic mental syndromes with phenomena of extinction and allesthesia. *Archives of Neurology and Psychiatry, 59,* 273–291.

Benton, A.L. (1959). *Right–Left Discrimination and Finger Localization.* New York: Hoeber.

Carmon, A., & Dyson, J.A. (1967). New instrumentation for research on tactile sensitivity and discrimination. *Cortex, 3,* 406–418.

Semmes, J., Weinstein, S. Ghent, L., & Teuber, H.L. (1960). *Somatosensory Changes After Penetrating Brain Wounds in Man.* Cambridge, Mass.: Harvard University Press.

AESTHESIOMETER

Other Test Name

Another test name is Pressure Aesthesiometer, Model 1 PR-11.

Purpose

The purpose of this test is to measure tactile thresholds.

Source

The instrument can be ordered from Research Media Inc., 4 Midland Avenue, Hicksville, New York 11801, or from Stoelting Company, Oakwood Center, 620 Wheat Lane, Wood Dale, Illinois 60191, Cat. #18011, at a cost of $295.00 U.S.

Description

The test consists of 20 nylon filaments of uniform 3.8-cm length and of increasing thickness, each mounted at the end of a 13-cm plastic stick holder. The material comes with pressure weight labels as described in Semmes, Weinstein, Ghent, and Teuber (1960) attached to the holders but with only a minimum of instructions. Since the weight labels are on a relatively meaningless logarithmic scale, we have translated them into gram pressure in the scoring sheet (Fig. 9–1).

Administration

Although tactile thresholds can be tested on any part of the body, our routine administration is to test the third finger nailbed of each hand to avoid areas of hair growth and callus. Stimuli are applied slowly with enough pressure to create a 45-degree bend in the filament out of sight of the subject (preferably under a covering box) and held in that position for about one second. The subject is asked to say "touch" or otherwise indicate when he or she feels the stimulus. Reports made when there is no stimulus are scored as zero. If the examiner feels that the subject is merely slow in responding, the examiner repeats the admonition to report as soon as the stimulus is felt, and also repeats the stimulation if necessary.

```
                  Aesthesiometer
              Sample Scoring Sheet
Name:                        Date:      Age:    Examiner:
Right Hand                              Left Hand
Third Finger Nailbed                    Third Finger Nailbed
Ascending Descending    grams/pressure  Ascending Descending
                            447.0
                            281.5
                            127.0
                             75.0
                             29.0
                             15.0
                             11.7
                              8.65
                              5.50
                              3.63
                              2.06
                              1.49
                              1.19
                               .70
                               .41
                               .17
                               .07
                               .03
                               .02
                               .004
_____       Threshold Measure    _____
                         Hand Threshold

                        Mean _____
                        Median _____
                        SD _____
```

Figure 9–1. Aesthesiometer sample scoring sheet.

Begin stimulation with the dominant hand, using filament .004 and ascending in single steps until three successive touches have been reported. Begin descending order with the next lowest filament (i.e,. the second above the ascending threshold) and decrease in single steps until two successive zero scores have been obtained.

Young children often show fear of the filament, believing that they are going to be pricked or that the stimulus is painful. It is good practice to assure all subjects that the procedure is not painful, and accompany such assurance with a demonstration on the subject's and/or the examiner's forearm before screening the hand. Apply stimuli slowly since otherwise a velocity component is added to filament resistance, leading to spuriously low thresholds.

With small children, accuracy of site of stimulation is restricted to the general area between the distal joint and the fingernail.

Care should be taken to avoid experimenter cues when the stimulus is applied. The subject may be asked to look away or close the eyes.

Since the objective is to obtain a relatively stable measure, there is no objection to repeating the stimulation if necessary.

Approximate Time for Administration

The time required is 5–10 minutes for both hands.

Scoring

The threshold measure for each hand is the mean of the first ascending and the last descending touch response.

If the subject reports a touch at a low level followed by zero responses at greater pressure, the trial series should be repeated. The lowest score is taken to mean the lowest of two successive positives. The sample scoring sheet is shown in Fig. 9–1.

Comment

Reliability data are not available, although clinical observation suggests that it should be quite high.

This rather expensive equipment tends to deteriorate with frequent use. Handle with care. Although similar results may be obtained with various commercial versions of "von Frey hair" stimulators on the market, we found this test more accurate and reliable. The main value of the test is usually in discovering unilateral

Table 9–1. Aesthesiometer: Normative Data for Adults[1]

Age	N	Right Hand	SD	Left Hand	SD
Males					
20–29	8	.44	.25	.32	.23
50–59	10	.59	.42	.43	.32
60–69	12	.74	.57	.52	.41
70+	8	1.10	.52	1.01	.72
Females					
20–29	10	.17	.14	.17	.13
50–59	10	.46	.30	.27	.23
60–69	9	.45	.38	.32	.28
70+	15	.65	.48	.66	.47

[1]*Note:* Data are based on a sample of healthy volunteers from Victoria, British Columbia.

Source: Spreen & Strauss (1990)

Table 9–2. Aesthesiometer: Normative Data for Children
Ages 6–12 Years

Age	N	Mean	SD	Median	Range
6	12	0.5	0.6	0.4	0.03–2.1
7	50	0.3	0.3	0.2	0.03–1.2
8	41	0.2	0.2	0.2	0.02–0.7
9	38	0.2	0.1	0.2	0.004–0.7
10	36	0.2	0.2	0.2	0.004–0.7
11	38	0.2	0.2	0.2	0.02–0.7
12	36	0.2	0.2	0.2	0.02–0.7

Note: No meaningful differences between right and left hand or between boys and girls were found.

Source: Spreen & Gaddes (1969).

elevations in threshold. Differences of three or more steps between hands raise the possibility of a pathologically increased threshold. Larger differences are fairly reliable indicators of pathology. The possibility of peripheral lesions should be explored before central lesions are inferred. The test is surprisingly sensitive, even if the standard tactile threshold examination in neurological practice yields negative results. In some subjects attentional problems may interfere.

Normative Data

Semmes et al. (1960) reported data on head-injured patients. A 1962 publication by Weinstein listed norms for two adults subjects for the three phalanges of each finger. A recent study in our laboratory (Table 9–1) with right-handed adults indicates increasing thresholds with age. In addition, females had significantly lower thresholds then males.

Children's norms developed in our laboratory (Spreen and Gaddes, 1969) are listed in Table 9–2. As can be seen from the table, fairly stable levels are reached by age 8 which remain within the same range up to age 30.

REFERENCES

Semmes, J., Weinstein, S., Ghent, L., & Teuber, H.L. (1960). *Somatosensory Changes After Penetrating Head Wounds in Man.* Cambridge, Mass.: Harvard University Press.

Spreen, O., & Gaddes, W.H. (1969). Developmental norms for 15 neuropsycho-logical tests age 6 to 15. *Cortex,* 5, 171–191.

Spreen, O., & Strauss, E. (1990) Unpublished manuscript.

Weinstein, S. (1962). Tactile sensitivity of the phalanges. *Perceptual and Motor Skills,* 14, 351–354.

FINGER LOCALIZATION

Purpose

The purpose of this test is the identification, naming, and localization of the fingers.

Source

The test is contained in Benton, Hamsher, Varney and Spreen's (1983), *Contributions to Neuropsychological Assessment*, Oxford University Press, 200 Madison Avenue, New York, New York 10016. The manual (including 11 other tests) costs $23.95 U.S.; the test material for finger localization costs $19.95 U.S.

Description

This test is based on Benton's (1959) book and consists of 80 items in five parts:

1. Identification by name on the subject's own hand
2. Identification by name on the examiner's hand
3. Naming fingers touched by the examiner by either naming or pointing to a hand chart or to the number of the stimulated finger on the chart
4. Identification of fingers touched by the examiner while the hand is hidden under a curtained table screen
5. Identification of two simultaneously touched fingers while the hand is hidden

Only the last three parts are used in the Benton et al. (1983) sourcebook; the first two sets involve naming and are used in our laboratory as introductory material, especially with children. The last three parts can be performed without involving language.

Administration

Five trials for each hand in Parts 1 and 2 are given as introductory material. The test itself consists of 10 trials for each hand for Parts 3, 4, and 5.

Approximate Time for Administration

Ten minutes is required.

Table 9–3. Finger Localization: Normative Data for Children Aged 6–13 Years

	Normal children				Superior-IQ children		
Age	N	Right	Left	Total	N	Right	Left	Total
6	12	21	21	42	21	25	25	50
7	50	24	24	48	24	25	25	50
8	41	25	25	50	20	28	28	56
9	38	26	26	52	21	28	28	56
10	36	27	27	54	24	28	28	56
11	38	27	27	54	20	28	28	56
12	36	28	28	56	22	28	28	56
13	52	28	28	56				

Note: Standard deviations range from 3.0 at age 6, to 1.7 at age 13.

Scoring

Each of the 30 items for the left hand and the 30 items for the right hand are scored as either correct or incorrect (see source). The maximum score is 30 for each hand, with a maximum total of 60.

Comment

Attention to finger agnosia was given following Gerstmann's (1924) and Head's (1920) descriptions. Whereas unilateral finger agnosia clearly refers to a unilateral brain lesion usually with sensory or motor deficit, bilateral finger agnosia is frequent in patients with general mental impairment and aphasia, although this is by no means a regular occurrence. Reliability data are not available. Concurrent validity with finger dexterity (tapping, putting paper clips into a box) were only moderate (.26 and .21; Benton, 1959).

Finger localization develops steadily and rapidly with age before age 6 and continues to develop up to age 12. Failure to reach age-appropriate levels has been related to developmental delay and subsequent failure in reading achievement. Hutchinson (1983) found significant correlations between finger localization and matching spoken to printed words and for silent reading and retelling of a paragraph. Dysphasic children had significantly more difficulty on this task than normal-language children. Although other versions of tests for finger localization are available, we prefer this one because it is not likely to be affected by even mild aphasia, and it has a sufficient number of trials and extensive norms.

Normative Data

Benton et al. (1983) provide detailed norms for normal adults (where errors are quite rare) in relation to educational background up to the age of 65, and for children from age 3 to 12 (when adult level is reached), for both right- and left-hand performance. Differences between hands usually do not exceed 1 or 2 points (see source). Our own norms for children (Table 9–3) agree closely with those presented by Wake (unpublished, see source), but are higher than those reported by Benton et al., for both normal and superior IQ children.

REFERENCES

Benton, A.L. (1959). *Right–Left Discrimination and Finger Localization. Development and Pathology.* New York: Hoeber/Harper.

Benton, A.L., Hamsher, K.deS., Varney, N.R., & Spreen, O. (1983). *Contributions to Neuropsychological Assessment.* New York: Oxford University Press.

Gerstmann, J. (1924). Fingeragnosie: Eine umschriebene Störung der Orientierung am eigenen Körper. *Wiener Klinische Wochenschrift, 37,* 1010–1012.

Head, H. (1920). *Studies in Neurology.* New York: Oxford University Press.

Hutchinson, B.P. (1983). Finger localization and reading ability in three groups of children ages three through twelve. *Brain and Language, 20,* 143–154.

TACTILE FORM PERCEPTION

Other Test Name

The test is also known as the Stereognosis Test.

Purpose

This test is used as a measure of tactile form recognition and spatial thinking.

Source

The test is contained in Benton, Hamsher, Varney, and Spreen (1983). The manual for 12 tests can be obtained from Oxford University Press, 200 Madison Avenue, New York, New York 10016 for $23.95 U.S. The Tactile Form Perception Test material and forms cost $135.00 U.S.

Description

The test consists of two equivalent sets of 10 cards on which geometric figures of fine-grade sandpaper have been pasted. The subject feels one card at a time with one hand under a box-screen with a curtain and has to point to the corresponding figure on a multiple-choice card with 12 ink-drawn figures which is placed on top of the box.

Administration

Ten trials are given for each hand (see source).

Approximate Time for Administration

The time required is 10–15 minutes.

Scoring

Each item is scored as either correct or incorrect (see source). One set of 10 cards is used for each hand, allowing for a maximum score of 10 correct choices for each hand. One additional card is used for practice.

Comment

Alternate form reliability is reported as showing only minimal differences when both forms were given, but other reliability data are currently not available. This test is more demanding than the usual object naming or object matching tasks routinely used during neurological and neuropsychological examinations because (1) the stimuli are of an abstract nature; (2) no naming is required; and (3) it adds to the task a dimension of spatial exploration by touch. It is a more rigorous examination of stereognosis than Halstead's three-dimensional tactile form recognition test in which only four objects (cross, circle, triangle, and square) are used for both hands. Careful observation of the exploratory movements by the subject is necessary, since failure to explore may give misleading results. The test usually cannot be used in subjects with moderate sensory loss or with motor impairment.

The test authors report high sensitivity of this test for right-hemisphere lesions, although patients with left-hemisphere lesions may also show impaired performance, and the performance of patients with bilateral lesions is quite low.

Normative Data

The source provides detailed norms for adults, elderly adults, and children, and for a variety of performance patterns in patients with brain damage. The adult level of near-perfect performance (no more than one error) is usually reached by age 14, as shown in Spreen and Gaddes (1969, Table 9–4). Differences between preferred and nonpreferred hands, and between boys and girls were minimal in this study. Although under standard administration conditions, no time score is

Table 9–4. Tactile Form Perception: Norms for Children

	Number correct			Time for 10 cards (in seconds)		
Age	N	Mean	SD	N	Mean	SD
8	37	8.1	1.3	16	124.1	34.8
9	86	8.1	1.3	40	119.7	41.4
10	90	8.3	1.3	44	108.8	40.6
11	61	8.6	1.2	18	83.5	32.5
12	48	9.3	0.9			
13	38	9.3	1.0			
14	44	9.5	0.9			
15	7	9.8	0.6			

Source: Spreen & Gaddes (1969).

taken (the trial is discontinued if the subject does not respond after 45 seconds, with prompting after 30 seconds), our table shows a rapid increase in speed of performance between the ages of 8 and 11 years.

REFERENCES

Benton, A.L., Hamsher, K.deS., Varney, N.R., & Spreen, O. (1983). *Contributions to Neuropsychological Assessment.* New York: Oxford University Press.

Spreen, O., & Gaddes, W.H. (1969). Developmental norms for 15 neuropsychological tests age 6 to 15. *Cortex, 5,* 171–191.

TACTUAL PERFORMANCE TEST

Other Test Name

Other names are the Form Board Test and the Seguin–Goddard Formboard.

Purpose

The purpose of this test is to assess tactile form recognition, memory for shapes, and spatial location, as well as psychomotor problem solving.

Source

The test can be ordered from Reitan Neuropsychology Laboratory, 1338 East Edison Street, Tucson, Arizona 85719 (10- and 6-hole boards, stand, and 10 blocks: $265 U.S.; without the 6-hole board: $215 U.S.); from Stoelting Company, (10-hole board and stand: $75 U.S.); or from Technolab Industries, Ltd., 5757 Decelles Avenue, Suite 329, Montreal, Quebec, H3S 2C3, Canada (set of two boards, blocks, and stand: $432 Cdn.).

Description

This version of the Seguin Formboard is administered according to Halstead's (1947) procedure. As a test of tactile memory, it includes two trials, one for the preferred and one for the nonpreferred hand, a third using both hands. After completion of these trials, the board is concealed, the blindfold is removed, and the subject is asked to draw from memory indicating both the shape of the blocks and their placement relative to each other. Three scores are obtained: (1) total time on the tactile trials, (2) a memory score for the number of blocks correctly reproduced, and (3) a location score for the number of correctly located blocks in the drawing. There are two different formboards: the 10-hole formboard, used for subjects aged 15 and over; and the six-hole formboard, used for children below the age of 15. In addition to the formboard material, a clean, comfortably fitting blindfold (eye mask) and a stopwatch are required. Scoring forms can be easily produced. The material is sturdy and hardly ever needs replacement.

Administration

For subjects 8 years old and younger, the six-block formboard is mounted horizontally in the stand, with the cross in the upper left-hand corner. With subjects aged 9:0–14:11 years, the six-block form board is mounted vertically in the stand, with the cross in the upper right-hand corner. With subjects 15 years of age and older, the 10-block board is mounted vertically in the stand, with the cross in the upper right-hand corner.

For repeat administration, the board is set upright at the same angle as above, but the long axis of the board is vertical instead of horizontal. Instructions and procedure are exactly the same, but in scoring the subject's drawing, one must remember that the face of the board has been turned 90 degrees.

The subject is seated, squarely facing and close to the table. Two gauze pads are placed over the eyes and a blindfold is tied over them. The examiner questions the subject about his or her ability to see, especially downward. When the examiner is certain that the subject cannot see, the board is brought out. The blocks are placed in random sequence between the board and the subject. Blocks adjacent to each other on the board should not be placed next to each other on the table. Some examiners prefer to guide the subject to each block presented in standardized order, whereas our administration allows the subject to pick blocks in random order. Chavez, Schwartz, and Brandon (1982) indicated that the two modes of presentation show no differences in the results of the test.

Ask the subject to give you the preferred (dominant) hand. Take the subject's wrist and move the hand over the board and over the pieces on the table while giving the following instructions: **"In front of you on the table is a board. This is** the size and shape of it." [Move the subject's hand around the edge of the board.] **"On the face of the board are holes of various shapes and sizes."** [Move the subject's hand across the face of the board.] **"And here in front of you are blocks of various shapes and sizes."** [Pass the subject's hand over the blocks, then place the subject's hand in his or her lap.] **"You are to fit the blocks into the spaces on the board. There is a place for each block and a block for each opening. Now I want you to do the test the *first time, using only your right hand* [or '*left*', if that is the dominant hand]. You may begin whenever you are ready."**

Start the stopwatch when the subject first touches the board or blocks and stop it when the last piece has been placed. Record the time required for each hand in minutes and seconds. It is helpful to praise the subject for correctly placed blocks, and to encourage the subject if he or she is not doing well. As the blocks in front of the subject are used up, push over the others to keep a supply ready at hand. When the subject has finished, ask him or her not to remove the blindfold and suggest that the subject relax for a minute or two.

After laying out the blocks again in random order, say: **"Now I want you to do the test again, and this time you are to use *only your left hand* [or '*right*', if that is the nondominant hand]. Begin whenever you are ready."** Record the time needed for this hand.

Lay out the blocks for the third time and say: **"This time you may use *both* hands for the test."** When the subject is finished, ask the subject to leave the blindfold on for a few minutes. Record the time required for both hands; then put the board out of sight. Tell the subject to remove the blindfold.

If after 10 minutes, fewer than seven blocks are placed correctly, the trial is discontinued. If seven or more blocks have been placed, the trial should continue up to 15 minutes, and then stopped unless the patient is about to complete the task.

In front of the subject, place a sheet of white paper and a pencil, and say: **"Now on this sheet of paper, I want you to draw an *outline* of the shape of the board. On your drawing, put in the shapes of the blocks in the same place as you remember them to be on the board. Note that there are three parts to your task: the shape of the board, the shapes of the blocks, and their location on the board. Be sure to label the top of your drawing. There is no time limit on this."**

Approximate Time for Administration

The time required ranges from 15 minutes to 50 minutes.

Scoring

This test is scored by calculating the total time for the three tactile placement trials, by counting the number of blocks correctly drawn, and by counting the

```
Sample Score Sheet

        Tactual Performance Test
Trial   Hand           Circle    Time
1       dominant       R L       _____
2       nondominant    R L       _____
3       both                     _____
           Total Time   _____
           Memory       _____
           Location     _____
```

Figure 9–2. Tactual Performance Test sample scoring sheet.

number of blocks properly located in the drawings. Differences between right- and left-hand performance should be noted as shown in the sample score sheet (Fig. 9–2). For the total time, the seconds should be converted to decimal parts of a minute (Table 9–5). In counting the blocks that were correctly reproduced, count only those that are fairly accurately drawn, and indicate that the subject had a true mental picture of the block. A star of four or five points is accepted as correct. The localization score is obtained by counting the right place on the drawing in relation to the other blocks and the formboard.

Before using the normative data tables for the appropriate age of the subject, the education corrections (Table 9–6) should be applied to the raw score.

Subjects who have difficulty reproducing a shape on the drawing part of the test are given credit if they can correctly name the shape. However, they should be urged to do their best at drawing the figures. When two figures on the drawing look very similar, the examiner should ask the patient if they are the same figure. For example, the square and rectangle are often drawn very much alike. If the subject calls one a square and the other a rectangle (or a "long square"), he or she

Table 9–5. TPT: Converting Seconds to Decimal Parts of a Minute

Seconds	Score
1–3	0.0
4–8	0.1
9–15	0.2
16–20	0.3
21–27	0.4
28–32	0.5
33–39	0.6
40–44	0.7
45–51	0.8
52–56	0.9
57–60	1.0

Table 9–6.   TPT: Corrections for Number of Years of Education

Education	Preferred hand	Nonpreferred hand	Both hands	Total time	Memory
1 year	.30	.12	.55	−1.58	1
5 years	.17	.05	.29	−.64	1
10 years	.00	−.03	.03	−.08	0
12 years	−.07	−.07	−.15	+.35	0
15 years	−.17	−.12	−.35	+.80	−1
20 years	−.34	−.20	−.67	+1.53	−1

Source: Adapted from Alekoumbides et al. (1987).

is given credit for both. If two identical figures are drawn, the examiner should give credit to the one most correctly localized, even if it is not the most accurate drawing. In scoring location, the relationship of the figure to the board as well as to other shapes drawn should be considered. For example, if the triangle is drawn near the top of the board and the cross and half-circle are placed on each side of it, but another shape is drawn in above the triangle, then the triangle does not count as correctly localized. Some authors have adopted the use of a minutes-per-block score rather than a total time score (Heaton et al., 1986).

Comment

Odd–even reliability for age- and education-corrected scores in 123 young adults was reported as .60–.78 for blocks per minute, .77–.93 for time, .64 for memory, and .69 for localization; similar values were found for a "mixed sample" of normal and brain-damaged subjects (Charter et al., 1987). Schludermann and Schludermann (1983) report retest coefficients of .76 for time, .55 for location, and .60 for memory scores in a sample of 174 executives after two years, and coefficients of .91, .53, and .72, respectively, for 86 subjects in the same sample taking the test again after three years. Goldstein and Watson (1989) reported retest reliabilities after 4–469 weeks for 150 neuropsychiatric patients, ranging from .66 to .74 for time, .46 to .73 for memory, and .32 to .69 for location, with similar values for alcoholics and trauma and vascular-disorder patients and somewhat lower coefficients for schizophrenics. Dodrill (1987) reported that total time scores improved by about three minutes on retest after five years. Retest reliability in a sample of 248 8-year-old children referred because of learning disability, mental retardation, brain injury, emotional disorder, or environmental deprivation after 2.6 years was .40 for time, .48 for location, and .43 for memory (Brown et al., 1989).

Klonoff and Low (1974), Clark and Klonoff (1988), and Russell (1985) have recommended the use of the six-block formboard for adults, arguing that it cuts down the administration time by two thirds (total time, between four and five minutes). Clark and Klonoff's study with 79 right-handed males (age 55.5) undergoing coronary bypass surgery but without any neurological disorder found high reliability (internal consistency coefficients, from .80 to .63) from presurgery to 24 months post surgery. Concurrent validity with the Benton Visual Retention Test and the Block Design Test was high.

Validity for most Halstead–Reitan tests has traditionally been established by comparing scores for normal and "brain-damaged" samples, using optimal cutoff scores. Significant differences between such groups have been reported for all parts of the test by many authors (e.g., O'Donnell, 1983; Reitan & Davison, 1974); and by Bigler and Tucker (1981) between brain-damaged and control blind subjects. Barnes and Lucas (1974) found that the TPT discriminated successfully between a group of 77 "organic" patients with varying etiologies and 39 "psychogenic" patients after age and IQ effects had been statistically controlled, whereas other tests of the Reitan battery (with the exception of the aphasia test) did not. Dodrill and Clemmons (1984) found the TPT predictive for overall adjustment and independent living, but not for vocational adjustment in epileptic high school students, and the score differences between fully functioning and deficient functioning subjects in that population was not significant. Hom and Reitan (1982) reported better scores for 50 patients with trauma compared to cerebrovascular and neoplastic lesions, and for left-hemisphere lesions, especially for ipsilateral performance. Alekoumbides et al. (1987) reported a correct classification rate for normals between 73% and 79% for blocks per minute, and of 81% for memory scores, corrected for age and education, as compared to patients with diffuse lesions (20–24% for blocks per minute, and 27% for memory), with Korsakoff's disease (34–40% and 18%), and with focal lesions (31–38%, and 47%). Such "correct classification rates," although significant, are not especially convincing, and suggest that the test must be used with caution and in the context of other tests when diagnostic interpretations are sought. Heilbronner and Parsons (1989) present a detailed analysis of the performance of four patients, and conclude that the *strategies* employed by the patient deserve specific consideration, and that it is incumbent upon the psychologist to investigate the *qualitative* aspects of the many different skills required for TPT performance; such a qualitative analysis may lead to specific retraining approaches.

The test appears to be sensitive also to epileptics with and without demonstrated neurological impairment (Klove & Matthews, 1974). Dodrill (1987) found time scores for epileptics to be twice as long as for an age-matched group of normal controls, whereas memory and location scores were only 1.5 point lower in epileptics. Halstead (1947) and Reitan (1964) consider the test especially sensitive to frontal lobe lesions because of the amount of mental organization required, but patients with parietal lesions may show poor performance as well because of reduced stereognostic and tactile–kinesthetic ability, especially on the hand contralateral to the side of the lesion (Teuber & Weinstein, 1954). The test results, especially time scores, are sensitive to alcoholism (Fabian et al., 1981), but appear to show little change under conditions of state and induced depression (Harris et al., 1981) or in learning-disabled young adults (O'Donnell, 1983). Prigatano (1983) also reported significant differences for all parts of the test between controls and patients with mild hypoxemia and chronic obstructive pulmonary disease.

In an examination of deliberate "faking of brain damage," Goebel (1983) found that 102 subjects in their early 30s instructed to fake tended to obtain scores much more similar to normal controls than to actual brain-damaged patients on all parts of the test; they clearly underestimated the difficulty of the task for brain-damaged subjects.

Normative Data

A number of authors have published or distributed normative data for the TPT for adults, for healthy elderly subjects, and for various brain-damaged groups. The Wayne State norms presented by Reitan and Wolfson (1985) are very similar to those by Klove (1974) for American and Norwegian control subjects, and by Dodrill (1978, 1987) for a carefully selected representative normal sample. Age effects are quite noticeable when comparing the norms for an older sample (47 years of age; total time = 18.29 minutes, location = 2.62, memory = 6.28; Alekoumbides et al., 1987) with those of a younger one (28 years of age; total time = 13.65 minutes, location = 4.97, memory = 7.86; Dodrill, 1987). Norms for the higher age group are also confirmed by the reports of Cripe and Dodrill (1988) and Prigatano and Parsons (1976).

Dodrill (1987) investigated the effects of intelligence on TPT scores. For subjects in the 115–130 IQ range, total time was 10.8 minutes; for subjects with average IQ, it was 13.5 minutes; and for subjects with IQs in the 70–85 range, it was approximately 22 minutes. The respective means for location were 6, 5, and 3.5; for memory, 8, 8, and 6.5. Similarly, Warner et al. (1987) reported correlations of .28–.49 for various TPT scores with IQ, and of .04–.20 with number of years of education in both a U.S. (Seattle) and a British (Bristol) sample. Subjects with at least a grade 9 education did better in comparison to those with less than grade 9 education (Harley et al., 1980; Schludermann & Schludermann, 1983; Thompson et al., 1987). For subjects with less than 12 years of education, location and memory scores were approximately ½-point less, and for subjects with 16 years of education or better they were approximately ½-point higher; for these two education groups, total time was about four minutes longer and 1.5 minutes shorter, respectively (Heaton et al., 1986). Alekoumbides et al. (1987) present correction equations for both age and education.

Dodrill (1987) has pointed out that TPT scores (like scores for many neuropsychological tests) are severely skewed to the left, with approximately 95% of normal subjects completing the test within 4.0–19.0 minutes but with outliers taking as long as 47 minutes. The partial dependence of these scores on intelligence should be taken into account when results for an individual subject are interpreted.

Because of the effects of age and intelligence, we recommend the use of normative data stratified by age compiled from several sources (Table 9–7) after application of the education level correction extrapolated from Alekoumbides et al. (Table 9–6).

Kupke (1983) reported an interaction effect of sex with location and memory scores; subjects in that study tended to show significantly better scores with examiners of the opposite sex (approximately 1 point on memory, 1.5 points on location). Heaton, Grant, and Matthews (1986) also found that females tended to be about two minutes slower on the total time score compared to males, but that

Table 9–7. Normative Data for the TPT by Age

Age	N	Time, preferred hand			Time, nonpreferred hand		
		M	SD	Range	M	SD	Range
15–17	32	4.6	1.2	2.6–6.8	3.3	1.2	1.1–6.4
18–23	74	5.1	2.2	1.9–13.5	3.5	1.6	1.1–10.8
24–32	56	4.5	1.8	1.7–9.5	3.1	1.1	1.5–7.1
33–40	18	4.9	1.7	1.9–9.0	3.7	1.0	2.2–5.9
41–50	10	5.6	1.5	4.0–9.0	4.2	1.6	2.4–8.1
51–60	19	7.1	3.1	4.0–9.0	5.3	2.8	2.0–8.0

Age	N	Time, both hands			Total time		
		M	SD	Range	M	SD	Range
15–17	32	1.7	0.5	.8–3.3	9.5	2.1	4.7–14.1
18–23	130	2.1	1.3	.4–9.3	11.4	4.5	4.2–29.1
24–32	130	1.8	0.8	.5–4.6	11.4	3.0	3.8–18.8
33–40	396	2.3	0.8	1.4–4.4	11.7	2.9	5.9–19.4
41–50	224	3.0	2.1	1.4–5.5	16.0	3.6	8.3–20.6
51–60	19	3.4	2.0	1.4–6.0	16.5	5.0	8.0–21.0
65–76	125				23.0		

Age	N	Location			Memory		
		M	SD[a]	Range	M	SD[a]	Range
15–17	32	6.8	2.5	1–10	8.9	1.0	6–10
18–23	130	5.7	2.1	1–10	8.2	1.3	4–10
24–32	121	5.1	1.8	2–9	8.0	1.1	6–10
33–40	396	5.3	2.2	1–9	8.1	1.1	6–10
41–50	190	4.1	1.8	2–7	7.6	1.5	4–9
51–60	19	3.8	3.1	2–7	6.2	1.6	4–9
65–76	125	1.6	1.6	1–7	5.0	2.0	4–9

Note: For Location and Memory portions, all subjects placed 10 blocks in less than 15 minutes with the preferred, nonpreferred, and both hands.

[a]SDs are extrapolated from Bak & Green (1980) and Fromm-Auch & Yeudall (1983). Means are extrapolated from all five sources.

Sources: Extrapolated from Bak & Greene (1980); Cauthen (1978); Fromm-Auch & Yeudall (1983); Heaton, Grant & Matthews (1986); Moore, Richards, & Hood (1984).

location and memory scores needed no sex correction. In contrast, Chavez, Schwartz, and Brandon (1982) found that females had higher scores only on localization, but did not differ on other scores; finally, Fabian, Jenkins, and Parsons (1981) found that women were superior on recall, but poorer on location. Clearly, the issue of sex differences on this test is not settled as yet.

Differences between dominant and nondominant hand performance tend to be more pronounced in younger adults (20% better) than in adults over the age of 50, and higher in left-handers (30%) than in right-handers (11.7%) and in "mixed right-handers" (6.3%) (Heaton et al., 1986).

Norms for children (Table 9–8) have been compiled from our own data (including Spreen & Gaddes, 1969) and from data presented by Knights and Norwood

Table 9–8.   Normative Data for Children

	Range	Male		Female	All
Age 5 (N = 10)					
Time					
Dominant hand	12–26	M	7.0[a]	7.0	7.0
		SD	(7.5)	(7.5)	(7.5)
Nondominant hand	3–12	M	6.0	6.0	6.0
		SD	(6.5)	(6.5)	(6.5)
Both hands	2.5–19	M	5.8	5.8	5.8
		SD	(6.5)	(6.0)	(6.3)
Total time, all 3 trials	19–52	M	19.0	18.0	18.0
		SD	(12.5)	(18.4)	(15.8)
Memory	0–5	M	2.1	2.2	2.2
		SD	(1.9)	(1.3)	(1.8)
Location	0–3	M	0.7	1.3	0.9
		SD	(1.2)	(1.3)	(1.2)
Age 6 (N = 12)					
Time					
Dominant hand	2–15	M	7.6	6.3	7.0
		SD	(3.7)	(2.6)	(3.5)
Nondominant hand	1.5–15	M	5.0	6.6	5.8
		SD	(3.1)	(4.2)	(3.8)
Both hands	0.7–7.0	M	3.3	4.2	3.7
		SD	(2.0)	(2.4)	(2.2)
Total time, all 3 trials	5–45	M	15.9	17.1	16.6
		SD	(10.0)	(14.0)	(12.0)
Memory	3–6	M	4.0	3.0	3.5
		SD	(1.0)	(1.1)	(1.1)
Location	0–5	M	2.0	1.4	1.7
		SD	(1.3)	(1.0)	(1.1)

(continued)

Table 9–8. (*Continued*)

	Range	Male		Female	All
Age 7 (N = 25)					
Time					
Dominant hand	0.6–15.0	M	6.1	6.1	6.1
		SD	(6.0)	(4.9)	(5.5)
Nondominant hand	0.7–15.0	M	4.0	4.8	4.4
		SD	(3.0)	(4.9)	(4.0)
Both hands	0.5–15.0	M	2.0	1.8	1.9
		SD	(1.0)	(1.0)	(1.0)
Total time, all 3 trials	2–45	M	11.8	13.9	12.8
		SD	(9.9)	(8.9)	(9.3)
Memory	0–6	M	4.2	3.3	3.7
		SD	(1.3)	(1.1)	(1.2)
Location	0–6	M	2.5	2.6	2.6
		SD	(1.9)	(1.3)	(1.6)
Age 8 (N = 32)					
Time					
Dominant hand	0.7–15.0	M	4.4	6.5	5.3
		SD	(1.5)	(2.4)	(2.2)
Nondominant hand	0.7–15.0	M	3.1	4.0	3.8
		SD	(1.5)	(1.1)	(1.4)
Both hands	0.4–15.0	M	1.4	1.8	1.5
		SD	(2.0)	(2.0)	(2.0)
Total time, all 3 trials	1.7–45.0	M	9.7	12.0	10.8
		SD	(3.9)	(4.9)	(4.5)
Memory	2–6	M	4.3	4.3	4.3
		SD	(1.3)	(1.0)	(1.1)
Location	1–6	M	2.8	3.4	3.2
		SD	(1.3))	(2.4)	(2.1)

	Range	Male		Female	All
Age 9 (N = 71)					
Time					
Dominant hand	2–10	M	3.2	4.0	3.8
		SD	(3.0)	(2.0)	(2.2)
Nondominant hand	.9–10.0	M	3.4	4.1	3.8
		SD	(2.1)	(2.2)	(2.1)
Both hands	0.5–5.0	M	1.5	1.5	1.5
		SD	(0.8)	(0.8)	(0.8)
Total time, all 3 trials	3.1–20.0	M	9.8	9.9	9.9
		SD	(5.6)	(5.2)	(5.4)
Memory score	3–6	M	4.3	4.4	4.3
		SD	(1.3)	(1.0)	(1.1)
Location	1–5	M	2.7	3.3	8.0
		SD	(1.4)	(1.7)	(1.6)
Age 10 (N = 57)					
Time					
Dominant hand	2–12	M	3.9	3.9	3.9
		SD	(1.6)	(2.7)	(2.2)
Nondominant hand	0.5–7.0	M	2.7	3.0	2.9
		SD	(1.3)	(1.6)	(1.4)
Both hands	0.5–3.5	M	1.3	1.4	1.4
		SD	(0.7)	(0.9)	(0.8)
Total time, all 3 trials	3.3–23.0	M	8.3	9.5	9.1
		SD	(2.8)	(4.8)	(3.9)
Memory	2–6	M	4.5	4.0	4.3
		SD	(1.1)	(1.3)	(1.2)
Location	0–6	M	3.1	3.0	3.0
		SD	(1.4)	(1.7)	(1.5)

(*continued*)

Table 9–8.   *(Continued)*

	Range	Male		Female	All
Age 11 (N = 42)					
Time					
Dominant hand	1–6	M	3.1	3.0	3.0
		SD	(1.7)	(1.3)	(1.4)
Nondominant hand	1–6	M	2.2	2.4	2.3
		SD	(0.9)	(0.9)	(0.9)
Both hands	.5–3.0	M	1.2	1.2	1.2
		SD	(0.5)	(0.5)	(0.5)
Total time, all 3 trials	3–14	M	6.5	6.6	6.5
		SD	(2.5)	(2.3)	(2.4)
Memory	2–6	M	4.5	4.4	4.4
		SD	(1.0)	(1.1)	(1.1)
Location	0–6	M	3.2	3.1	3.1
		SD	(1.4)	(1.4)	(1.4)
Age 12 (N = 43)					
Time					
Dominant hand	1–8	M	2.9	3.6	3.3
		SD	(1.4)	(1.4)	(1.4)
Nondominant hand	0.5–6.5	M	2.1	2.3	2.2
		SD	(1.2)	(1.5)	(1.3)
Both hands	0.7–2.5	M	1.0	1.2	1.1
		SD	(0.5)	(0.5)	(0.5)
Total time, all 3 trials	3–15	M	6.0	7.1	6.6
		SD	(2.2)	(3.0)	(2.6)
Memory	3–6	M	5.2	4.8	5.0
		SD	(0.7)	(0.9)	(0.8)
Location	1–6	M	4.0	4.0	4.0
		SD	(1.2)	(1.3)	(1.2)

	Range	Male		Female	All
Age 13 (N = 11)					
Time					
Dominant hand	1.5–4.0	M	2.7	2.4	2.6
		SD	(1.0)	(1.0)	(1.0)
Nondominant hand	0.8–2.7	M	1.8	1.8	1.8
		SD	(0.7)	(0.5)	(0.6)
Both hands	0.5–1.5	M	0.9	1.1	1.0
		SD	(0.3)	(0.3)	(0.3)
Total time, all 3 trials	3.0–7.5	M	5.5	5.1	5.3
		SD	(1.5)	(1.0)	(1.2)
Memory	3–6	M	4.8	4.5	4.7
		SD	(1.1)	(1.2)	(1.1)
Location	1–5	M	3.5	3.4	3.5
		SD	(1.2)	(1.2)	(1.2)

Note: Children were from Victoria, B.C. and Ottawa, Ontario.

[a]Extrapolated values are in parentheses.

Sources: Knights & Norwood (1980); Spreen & Gaddes (1969); Trites (1977).

(1980) and Trites (1977). They agree fairly well with normative data by Klonoff and Low (1974). Data points in brackets have been extrapolated. The norms for younger children not only are based on small samples, but also indicate that performance at these ages is quite variable, and does not stabilize adequately until age 10. For this reason, norms can only provide guidelines. The performance of the individual young child should be evaluated qualitatively, based on the child's task organization, task orientation, and attention, and apparent sterognostic deficits. Finlayson (1978) showed that the nonpreferred hand score relative to the preferred hand score decreased significantly between the ages of 5 and 12, suggesting an increasing interhemispheric transfer effect of practice with age.

REFERENCES

Alekoumbides, A., Charter, R.A., Adkins, T.G., & Seacat, G.F. (1987). The diagnosis of brain damage by the WAIS, WMS, and Reitan Battery utilizing standardized scores corrected for age and education. *International Journal of Clinical Neuropsychology, 9,* 11–28.

Bak, J.S., & Greene, R.L. (1980). The effects of aging on a modified procedure for scoring localization and memory components of the Tactual Performance Test. *Clinical Neuropsychology, 2,* 114–117.

Barnes, G.W., & Lucas, G.J. (1974). Cerebral dysfunction vs. psychogenesis in Halstead–Reitan tests. *Journal of Nervous and Mental Disease, 158,* 50–60.

Bigler, E.D., & Tucker, D.M. (1981). Comparison of verbal IQ, tactual performance, Seashore rhythm and finger oscillation tests in the blind and brain-damaged. *Journal of Clinical Psychology, 37,* 849–851.

Brown, S.J., Rourke, B.P., & Cicchetti, D.V. (1989). Reliability of tests and measures used in the neuropsychological assessment of children. *Clinical Neuropsychologist, 3,* 353–368.

Cauthen, N. (1978). Normative data for the tactual performance test. *Journal of Clinical Psychology, 34,* 456–460.

Charter, R.A., Adkins, T.G., Alekoumbides, A., & Seacat, G.F. (1987). Reliability of the WAIS, WMS, and Reitan Battery: Raw scores and standardized scores corrected for age and education. *International Journal of Clinical Neuropsychology, 9,* 28–32.

Chavez, E.L., Schwartz, M.M., & Brandon, A. (1982). Effects of sex of subject and method of block presentation on the Tactual Performance Test. *Journal of Consulting and Clinical Psychology, 50,* 600–601.

Clark, C., & Klonoff, H. (1988). Reliability and construct validity of the six-block Tactual Performance Test in an adult sample. *Journal of Clinical and Experimental Neuropsychology, 10,* 175–184.

Cripe, L.I., & Dodrill, C.B. (1988). Neuropsychological test performance with chronic low-level formaldehyde exposure. *Clinical Neuropsychologist, 2,* 41–48.

Dodrill, C.B. (1978). A neuropsychological battery for epilepsy. *Epilepsia, 19,* 611–623.

Dodrill, C.B. (1987). What's normal? Presidential address, Pacific Northwest Neuropsychological Association, Seattle.

Dodrill, C.B., & Clemmons, D. (1984). Use of neuropsychological tests to identify high school students with epilepsy who later demonstrate inadequate performances in life. *Journal of Consulting and Clinical Psychology, 52,* 520–527.

Fabian, M.S., Jenkins, R.L., & Parsons, O.A. (1981). Gender, alcoholism, and neuropsychological functioning. *Journal of Consulting and Clinical Psychology, 49,* 138–140.

Finlayson, M.A.J. (1978). A behavioral manifestation of the development of interhemispheric transfer of learning in children. *Cortex, 14,* 290–295.

Fromm-Auch, D., & Yeudall, L.T. (1983). Normative data for the Halstead–Reitan neuropsychological tests. *Journal of Clinical Neuropsychology, 5,* 221–238.

Goebel, R.A. (1983). Detection of faking on the Halstead–Reitan neuropsychological test battery. *Journal of Clinical Psychology, 39,* 731–742.

Goldstein, G., & Watson, J.R. (1989). Test–retest reliability of the Halstead–Reitan battery and the WAIS in a neuropsychiatric population. *Clinical Neuropsychologist, 3,* 265–273.

Halstead, W.C. (1947). *Brain and Intelligence: A Quantitative Study of the Frontal Lobes.* Chicago: University of Chicago Press.

Harley, J.P., Leuthold, C.A., Matthews, C.G., & Bergs, L.E. (1980). T-Score Norms: Wisconsin Neuropsychological Test Battery (CA 55-79). Mimeo.

Harris, M., Cross, H., & VanNieuwkerk, R. (1981). The effects of state depression, induced depression and sex on the finger tapping and tactual performance tests. *Clinical Neuropsychology, 3(4),* 28–34.

Heaton, R.K., Grant, I., & Matthews, C.G. (1986). Differences in neuropsychological test performance associated with age, education, and sex. In I. Grant & K.M. Adams (Eds.), *Neuropsychological Assessment of Neuropsychiatric Disorders.* New York: Oxford University Press.

Heilbronner, R.L., & Parsons, O.A. (1989). The clinical utility of the Tactual Performance Test (TPT): Issues of lateralization and cognitive style. *Clinical Neuropsychologist, 3,* 250–264.

Hom, J., & Reitan, R.M. (1982). Effect of lateralized cerebral damage upon contralateral and ipsilateral sensorimotor performance. *Journal of Clinical Neuropsychology, 4,* 249–268.

Klonoff, H., & Low, M. (1974). Disordered brain function in young children and early adolescents: Neuropsychological and electrophysiological correlates. In R.M. Reitan & L.A. Davison (Eds.), *Clinical Neuropsychology: Current Status and Applications* (pp. 121–178). New York: John Wiley.

Klove, H. (1974). Validation studies in adult clinical neuropsychology. In R.M. Reitan & L.A. Davison (Eds.), *Clinical Neuropsychology: Current Status and Applications* (pp. 211–236). New York: Wiley.

Klove, H., & Matthews, C.G. (1974). Neuropsychological studies of patients with epilepsy. In R.M. Reitan & L.A. Davison

(Eds.), *Clinical Neuropsychology: Current Status and Applications* (pp. 237–266). New York: Wiley.

Knights, R.M., & Norwood, J.A. (1980). Revised Smoothed Normative Data on the Neuropsychological Test Battery for Children. Mimeo. Department of Psychology, Carleton University, Ottawa, Ontario.

Kupke, T. (1983). Effects of subject sex, examiner sex, and test apparatus on Halstead Category and Tactual Performance Tests. *Journal of Consulting and Clinical Psychology, 51*, 624–626.

Moore, T.E., Richards, B., & Hood, J. (1984). Aging and the coding of spatial information. *Journal of Gerontology, 39*, 210–212.

O'Donnell, J.P. (1983). Neuropsychological test findings for normal, learning disabled and brain damaged young adults. *Journal of Consulting and Clinical Psychology, 51*, 726–729.

Prigatano, G.P. (1983). Neuropsychological test performance in mildly hypoxic patients with chronic obstructive pulmonary disease. *Journal of Consulting and Clinical Psychology, 51*, 108–116.

Prigatano, G.P., & Parsons, O.A. (1976). Relationship of age and education to Halstead Test performance in different populations. *Journal of Consulting and Clinical Psychology, 44*, 527–533.

Reitan, R.M. (1964). Psychological deficit resulting from cerebral lesions in man. In J.M. Warren & K. Akert (Eds.), *The Frontal Granular Cortex and Behavior.* New York: McGraw-Hill.

Reitan, R.M., & Davison, L.A. (Eds.). (1974).

Clinical Neuropsychology: Current Status and Applications. New York: John Wiley.

Reitan, R.M., & Wolfson, D. (1985). *The Halstead–Reitan Neuropsychological Test Battery.* Tucson: Neuropsychology Press.

Russell, E. (1985). Comparison of the TPT-10- and 6-hole form board. *Journal of Clinical Psychology, 41*, 68–81.

Schludermann, E.H., & Schludermann, S.M. (1983). Halstead's studies in the neuropsychology of aging. *Archives of Gerontology and Geriatrics, 2*, 49–172.

Spreen, O., & Gaddes, W.H. (1969). Developmental norms for 15 neuropsychological tests age 6 to 15, *Cortex, 5*, 171–191.

Teuber, H.L., & Weinstein, S. (1954). Performance on a formboard task after penetrating brain injury. *Journal of Psychology, 38*, 177–190.

Thompson, L.L., Heaton, R.K., Matthews, C.G., & Grant, I. (1987). Comparison of preferred and nonpreferred hand performance on four neuropsychological motor tasks. *Clinical Neuropsychologist, 1*, 324–334.

Trites, R.L. (1977). Neuropsychological Test Manual. Mimeo. Ottawa, Ontario: Royal Ottawa Hospital.

Warner, M.H., Ernst, J., Townes, B.D., Peel, J. and Preston, M. (1987). Relationship between IQ and neuropsychological measures in neuropsychiatric populations: Within-laboratory and cross-cultural replications using WAIS and WAIS-R. *Journal of Clinical and Experimental Neuropsychology, 9*, 545–562.

TWO-POINT DISCRIMINATION

Other Test Name

The other name for this test is Two-Point Aesthesiometer.

Purpose

The purpose of this test is to measure the two-point discrimination threshold.

Source

The instrument can be ordered from Lafayette Instrument Company, P.O. Box 5729, Lafayette, Indiana 47903, Order #16011, at a cost of approximately $65.00 U.S. or from TechnoLab, Succursale St. Laurent, C.P. 5195, Montreal, Quebec H4L 4Z8, for $78.40 Cdn.

Description

The test consists of simple sharp-point calipers which can be varied in distance from each other. The instrument is calibrated in $\frac{1}{16}$ of an inch (1 inch = 2.52 cm)

Administration

Although two-point discrimination can be tested on any part of the body, the standard administration introduced by Weinstein (1961) and by Corkin et al. (1970) uses the center of the palm of each hand. If there is a known unilateral impairment, begin with the unimpaired side; otherwise start with the preferred hand.

First, demonstrate the calipers to the subject and explain what you will be doing, that you will be touching the hand gently. Ask the subject to place the hand under a cover screen, palm up and hand open. Touch the center of the palm with the points of the instrument, taking care that for two-point stimulation both points touch simultaneously.

Start with the widest setting. Touch the hand with one or two points in the sequence given on the sample answer sheet (Fig. 9–3) for each trial. For example, for the trial of 2.8 cm between points, touch the preferred hand with two points of the calipers, then with one point, again one, then two, etc. The next trial is conducted at the same width with the nonpreferred hand. Ask the subject to indicate verbally or with the fingers whether one or two points have been touched. If the subject is accurate for all touches of the 2.85-cm width ($^{18}/_{16}''$), skip the next trial, and proceed to 2.5-cm width ($^{16}/_{16}''$). Continue with every alternate setting down to 1.8-cm width or until errors occur. Then give all trials in sequence until three errors have been made on two consecutive trials for each hand. Discontinuation criteria are used separately for each hand: If the subject makes three errors on two consecutive trials for the "bad" hand, continue with the other hand until you reach the discontinuation criterion.

The threshold is the last trial before a trial with three errors.

Answer Scoring Sheet

Two-Point Discrimination (in fractions of inches and cm in brackets)

												Errors
18/16″ (2.85)	Preferred Hand	2	1	1	2	1	1	1	2	2	2	
	Non-Preferred	1	2	1	1	1	1	2	2	2	2	
17/16″ (2.70)		1	2	2	1	2	2	2	1	1	1	
		1	2	2	2	1	1	1	2	2	1	
16/16″ (2.54)		1	2	1	2	1	2	1	1	2	2	
		1	1	2	1	2	1	1	2	2	2	
15/16″ (2.38)		2	1	2	1	2	2	2	1	1	1	
		2	1	1	1	2	1	2	1	2	2	
14/16″ (2.22)		1	2	1	2	1	1	2	2	2	1	
		2	2	1	2	1	1	2	2	1	1	
13/16″ (2.06)		1	1	1	2	1	1	2	2	2	2	
		2	1	2	2	2	1	2	1	1	1	
12/16″ (1.90)		1	2	1	1	2	1	2	2	1	2	
		2	2	1	2	2	2	1	1	1	1	
11/16″ (1.75)		1	2	1	2	2	2	1	1	2	1	
		1	1	1	2	2	2	2	1	2	1	
10/16″ (1.59)		2	2	1	1	1	2	2	2	1	1	
		1	2	2	2	1	1	1	1	2	2	
9/16″ (1.42)		1	2	2	1	1	2	1	1	2	2	
		1	2	2	2	2	1	1	2	1	1	
8/16″ (1.27)		2	1	1	2	1	2	1	1	2	2	
		2	2	2	2	1	1	2	1	1	1	
7/16″ (1.11)		1	2	1	1	2	1	2	2	1	2	
		1	2	2	1	2	2	2	1	1	1	
6/16″ (0.95)		2	2	1	1	1	1	1	2	2	2	
		2	2	2	1	2	1	1	1	2	1	
5/16″ (0.79)		2	2	1	1	2	2	1	1	1	2	
		1	1	2	1	2	1	1	2	2	2	
4/16″ (0.64)		1	2	2	1	2	2	2	1	1	1	
		2	2	2	1	2	1	1	1	1	2	
3/16″ (0.48)		2	1	1	2	1	2	1	2	1	2	
		2	1	1	1	2	1	2	2	2	1	
2/16″ (0.32)		1	2	2	1	1	1	2	1	2	1	
		1	1	2	2	2	1	1	2	1	2	

Figure 9–3. Two-Point Discrimination sample scoring sheet.

Approximate Time for Administration

Ten minutes is required.

Comment

Information on reliability is not available, although in our experience retest reliability has been adequate. Some examiners erroneously substitute this procedure

Table 9–9. Normative Data for Adults (in $1/16'' = 0.16$ cm) (cm in brackets)

Age	N	Preferred hand	SD	Non-preferred hand	SD
20–30	16	4.31 (0.68)	1.08	4.87 (0.77)	1.25
50–59	14	4.93 (0.78)	1.38	5.46 (0.87)	1.13
60–69	13	5.15 (0.81)	1.28	5.31 (0.84)	1.65
70+	10	5.30 (0.84)	1.16	5.60 (0.89)	1.65

for the Weinstein Aesthesiometer. It should be noted that it measures a different function: discrimination of two points at relatively strong pressure compared to the tactile threshold measurement. The results of the two procedures are likely to correlate highly in healthy persons, but may differ greatly if sensory functions are defective since the two functions rely on somewhat different pathways. We use this procedure only if tactile thresholds are elevated or if detailed exploration of the tactile sense is indicated. The original procedure described by Semmes et al. (1960) included directional judgments with simultaneous or successive stimulation in two (and three) different points of an eight-spoked pattern of dots printed on the subject's palm.

Defective scores were found mainly in subjects with parietal lesions invading the postcentral gyrus of the contralateral hemisphere, but were extremely rare if the postcentral gyrus was spared or if the lesion was in other areas of the brain.

Normative Data

Table 9–9 shows norms for adults recently compiled in our laboratory. The right hand tends to have slightly lower thresholds. Thresholds tend to rise slightly, but not significantly, in an older population. There are no sex-related differences. The means obtained for younger adults agree closely with those reported by Corkin et al. (1970). Normative data for children are not available.

REFERENCES

Corkin, S., Milner, B., & Rasmussen, T. (1970). Somatosensory thresholds. *Archives of Neurology, 23,* 41–58.

Semmes, J., Weinstein, S., Ghent, L., & Teuber, H.L. (1960). *Somatosensory Changes After Penetrating Head Wounds in Man.*

Cambridge, Mass.: Harvard University Press.

Weinstein, S. (1962). Tactile sensitivity of the phalanges. *Perceptual and Motor Skills, 14,* 351–354.

10

Motor Tests

A number of measures are especially useful for identifying subtle motor impairment and making inferences about the functional integrity of the two cerebral hemispheres. These include measures of three somewhat separate aspects of handedness, namely, preference (e.g., Annett Handedness questionnaire), strength (e.g., Hand Dynamometer), and dexterity (e.g., Finger Tapping, Purdue Pegboard). In general, performance with the preferred hand is slightly superior to that with the nonpreferred hand; however, there is considerable variability in the normal population, and the preferred hand is not necessarily the more proficient one (e.g., Benton et al., 1962; Satz et al., 1967). Patterns of performance indicating equal or better performance with the nonpreferred hand occur with considerable regularity in the normal population, and neurological disturbance should not be inferred from an isolated lack of concordance. Further, even fairly large intermanual discrepancies on one motor task are quite common in the normal population. On the other hand, discrepant performances that are consistent across several tests are quite rare in the normal population and thus are more likely to suggest a lesion in the contralateral hemisphere (Bornstein, 1986; Thompson et al., 1987).

REFERENCES

Benton, A.L., Meyers, R., & Polder, G.J. (1962). Some aspects of handedness. *Psychiatrica et Neurologica Basel, 144,* 231–337.

Bornstein, R.A. (1986). Consistency of intermanual discrepancies in normal and unilateral brain lesion patients. *Journal of Consulting and Clinical Psychology, 54,* 719–723.

Satz, P., Achenbach, K., & Fennell, E. (1967). Correlations between assessed manual laterality and predicted speech laterality in a normal population. *Neuropsychologia, 5,* 295–310.

Thompson, L.L., Heaton, R.K., Mathews, C.G., & Grant, I. (1987). Comparison of preferred and nonpreferred hand performance on four neuropsychological motor tasks. *Clinical Neuropsychologist, 1,* 324–334.

FINGER TAPPING TEST (FTT)

Other Test Name

The other test name is the Finger Oscillation Test.

Purpose

The purpose of this test is to measure the motor speed of the index finger of each hand.

Source

The finger tapper (manual tapper) can be ordered from the Reitan Neuropsychology Laboratory, 1338 East Edison Street, Tucson, Arizona 85179, at a cost of $95 U.S. Because children below 9 years of age have difficulty manipulating the arm of the finger tapper, an electric finger tapper was devised that can also be ordered from the Reitan Neuropsychology Laboratory (see above) at a cost of $165 U.S. There are a number of other tapping devices on the market. However, different levels of performance may be obtained when subjects are tested with devices other than the Reitan apparatus (Snow, 1987). If another device is used, the examiner should ensure that comparable results are obtained with the new finger tapping unit.

Description

The Finger Tapping Test (FTT) (Reitan, 1969) was originally called Finger Oscillation Test (FOT) and was part of Halstead's (1947) test battery. Using a specially adapted tapper, the subject is instructed to tap as fast as possible using the index finger of the preferred hand. A comparable set of measurements is then obtained with the nonpreferred hand.

Administration

Have the subject place the preferred hand, palm down, with fingers extended and the index finger placed on the key. Direct the subject to tap as quickly as he or she can, moving only the index finger, not the whole hand or arm. The subject is given five consecutive 10-second trials with the preferred hand. The procedure is then repeated with the nonpreferred hand. Five 10-second trials are given for each hand except when the results are too variable from one trial to another. Specifically, the test procedure requires that the five consecutive trials for each hand are within a 5-point range from fastest to slowest. If one or more of the trials exceed this range, additional trials are given, and the scores of the deviant trial(s) discarded. This procedure is used in order to avoid instances in which a single deviant score unduly influences the score. A maximum of 10 trials with each hand is allowed (Bornstein, 1985, 1986a).

Fatigue may affect performance, and a brief rest period should be given after each trial. Even when no sign of fatigue is apparent, a rest period of one to two minutes is required after the third trial. A practice trial is given before the test begins so that the subject may get a "feel" for the apparatus.

Do not allow the subject to move the whole hand from the wrist. With young children and poorly coordinated adults, this requirement is difficult, and may be relaxed as long as it is clear that the score is obtained by index finger oscillation and not by movement of the whole hand.

The number on the counter is recorded when the examiner says "Stop," not when the subject in fact stops.

Approximate Time for Administration

The time required is 10 minutes.

Scoring

The finger tapping score is computed separately for each hand and is the mean of five consecutive 10-second trials within a range of five taps. A maximum of 10 trials with each hand is allowed, and if the above criterion is not met, the score is the mean of the best five trials.

Comment

Performance with each hand is quite stable over time, even with lengthy intervals between retest sessions (e.g., two years). Reliability coefficients ranging from .58 to .93 have been reported with both normal and neurologically impaired subjects (Brown et al., 1983; Dodrill & Troupin, 1975; Gill et al., 1986; Goldstein & Watson, 1989; Morrison et al., 1979; Provins & Cunliffe, 1972; but see Matarazzo et al., 1974, for somewhat lower values). Some investigators have reported that the differences between hands are consistent ($r = .70$) (Provins & Cunliffe, 1972). Others, however, have indicated that the differences between hands are not highly reliable (.50) (Morrison et al., 1979).

Finger tapping measures are included in neuropsychological examinations to assess subtle motor impairment. The measure is sensitive to the presence and laterality of brain lesions (Barnes & Lucas, 1974; Bigler & Tucker, 1981; Dodrill, 1978; Finlayson & Reitan, 1980; Hom & Reitan, 1982; York Haaland & Delaney, 1981). Given the crossed nature of the motor system, performance tends to be worse in the hand contralateral to the lesion. Typically, the performances of the preferred and nonpreferred hands are compared to determine if there is consistent evidence of poor performance with one hand relative to the other. The most frequently reported guideline is that the preferred hand should perform about 10% better than the nonpreferred hand (Reitan & Wolfson, 1985). In general, performance with the preferred hand is superior to that with the nonpreferred hand (Bornstein, 1985, 1986a; Thompson et al., 1987). However, there is considerable variability in the normal population, and the preferred hand is not necessarily the faster one, especially when left-handed people are considered (Bornstein, 1986a; Trahan et al., 1987; Thompson et al., 1987). Patterns of performance indicating equal or better performance with the nonpreferred hand occur with considerable regularity in the normal population (about 30%), and neurological involvement should not be inferred from an isolated lack of concordance. Fairly large discrepancies between the hands on the Finger Tapping Test alone also cannot be used to suggest unilateral impairment since large-magnitude discrepancies are not uncommon (about 25%) in the normal population (Bornstein, 1986a; Thompson et al., 1987; Trahan et al., 1987). Greater confidence in the clinical judgment of impaired motor function with one or the other hand can be gained from consideration of the consistency of intermanual discrepancies across several motor tasks since truly consistent, deviant performances are quite rare in the normal population (Bornstein, 1986a, 1986b; Thompson et al., 1987).

Normative Data

Conventional cutoff scores (Reitan & Wolfson, 1985) should not be used since high false-positive rates are likely to occur (Bornstein, 1986c). Table 10–1 provides recently compiled cross-sectional normative data for adults, stratified on the basis of age, sex, and education (Bornstein, 1985). Right-handers comprised 91.5% of the sample. Fromm-Auch and Yeudall (1983), Goldstein and Braun (1974) and Trahan et al. (1987) also give normative data for healthy men and women. Their values are slightly higher than those reported here; however, their data were not stratified according to education. Finlayson and Reitan (1976) give normative data for right-handed boys and girls at each of six age levels, and these data are shown in Table 10–2. A comparison with Klonoff and Low's (1974) norms show fairly good agreement; however, their data are not specified for each sex separately. Spreen and Gaddes (1969) also provide data for a small group of normal children. Their

Table 10–1. Mean Performance of Adults for Finger Tapping

Age group	Education: <grade 12			Education: >grade 12		
	N	M	SD	N	M	SD
Males						
Preferred hand						
20–39	21	49.7	6.0	86	48.5	6.5
40–59	13	42.3	5.2	17	43.4	7.9
60–69	16	39.1	5.7	23	43.0	4.7
Nonpreferred hand						
20–39	21	47.0	5.5	86	44.8	6.4
40–59	13	39.8	3.6	17	39.5	5.8
60–69	16	35.2	5.2	23	39.3	6.2
Females						
Preferred hand						
20–39	13	45.2	6.0	49	44.3	5.8
40–59	22	36.3	7.8	43	40.5	7.1
60–69	22	29.7	6.2	34	32.2	6.0
Nonpreferred hand						
20–39	13	40.7	5.0	49	40.6	5.6
40–59	22	35.2	5.8	43	37.8	6.0
60–69	22	29.8	5.6	34	32.0	4.9

Note: The sample consisted of 365 healthy individuals from the general population of a large Canadian city.

Source: Bornstein (1985).

version of the test is slightly different from the one presented here in that a 50-tap warmup period and five 10-second trials (prorated to six trials) were given. Their data, however, are fairly consistent with those reported by Finlayson and Reitan (1976).

When each hand is considered separately, several trends emerge from the normative data. In general, better performance is associated with the preferred hand, male sex, younger age, and more years of education (Bornstein, 1985; Finlayson & Reitan, 1976; Fromm-Auch & Yeudall, 1983; Harris et al., 1981; Heaton et al., 1986; Trahan et al., 1987). Dodrill (1979) suggests that the observed sex difference for finger tapping may be attributed to sexual dimorphism in body and hand size rather than to a neuropsychological mechanism.

The findings regarding sex differences in intermanual difference scores is inconsistent: Some studies report greater between-hand differences for males than for females (Bornstein, 1986b; Fromm-Auch & Yeudall, 1983) and others do not (Thompson et al., 1987). There is some evidence that right-handers show larger

Table 10–2. Mean Performance of Children for Finger Tapping

Age	N	Male		Female	
		Right hand	Left hand	Right hand	Left hand
6	20	35.60 (4.06)[a]	32.00 (4.32)	33.10 (4.07)	30.10 (3.45)
7	20	37.00 (3.83)	33.40 (3.34)	36.90 (5.57)	32.50 (5.06)
8	20	39.90 (5.15)	35.20 (5.09)	38.80 (4.95)	33.30 (4.55)
12	20	41.00 (6.34)	36.40 (4.95)	41.40 (5.83)	35.50 (3.92)
13	20	45.80 (3.99)	38.90 (5.36)	40.70 (5.17)	35.40 (4.33)
14	20	47.30 (7.13)	40.70 (6.72)	44.70 (4.83)	39.30 (4.95)

Note: The data were derived from 120 normal right-handed children, 20 at each of six age levels, with boys and girls being equally represented.

[a]SD in parentheses.

Source: Finlayson & Reitan (1976).

intermanual differences than left-handers (Thompson et al., 1987). Age and years of education do not seem to have a strong relationship with measures of intermanual difference (Bornstein, 1986b; Heaton et al., 1986; Thompson et al., 1987).

REFERENCES

Barnes, G.W., & Lucas, G.J. (1974). Cerebral dysfunction vs. psychogenesis in Halstead–Reitan tests. *Journal of Nervous and Mental Disease, 158,* 50–60.

Bigler, E.D., & Tucker, D.M. (1981). Comparison of verbal IQ, tactual performance, seashore rhythm and finger oscillation tests in the blind and brain damaged. *Journal of Clinical Psychology, 37,* 849–851.

Bornstein, R.A. (1985). Normative data on selected neuropsychological measures from a nonclinical sample. *Journal of Clinical Psychology, 41,* 651–659.

Bornstein, R.A. (1986a). Normative data on intermanual differences on three tests of motor performance. *Journal of Clinical and Experimental Neuropsychology, 8,* 12–20.

Bornstein, R.A. (1986b). Consistency of intermanual discrepancies in normal and unilateral brain lesion patients. *Journal of Consulting and Clinical Psychology, 54,* 719–723.

Bornstein, R.A. (1986c). Classification rates obtained with "standard" cut-off scores on selected neuropsychological measures. *Journal of Clinical and Experimental Neuropsychology, 8,* 413–420.

Brown, S.J., Rourke, B.P., & Cicchetti, D.V. (1989). Reliability of tests and measures used in the neuropsychological assessment of children. *Clinical Neuropsychologist, 3,* 353–368.

Dodrill, C.B. (1978). A neuropsychological battery for epilepsy. *Epilepsia, 9,* 611–623.

Dodrill, C.B. (1979). Sex differences on the Halstead–Reitan Neuropsychological Battery and on other neuropsychological measures. *Journal of Clinical Psychology, 35,* 236–241.

Dodrill, C.B., & Troupin, A.S. (1975). Effects of repeated administrations of a comprehensive neuropsychological battery among chronic epileptics. *Journal of Nervous and Mental Desease, 161,* 185–190.

Finlayson, M.A., & Reitan, R.M. (1976). Handedness in relation to measures of motor and tactile–perceptual function in normal children. *Perceptual and Motor Skills, 43,* 475–481.

Finlayson, M.A.J., & Reitan, R.M. (1980). Effect of lateralized lesions on ipsilateral and contralateral motor functioning. *Journal of Clinical Neuropsychology, 2,* 237–243.

Fromm-Auch, D., & Yeudall, L.T. (1983). Normative data for the Halstead–Reitan neuropsychological tests. *Journal of Clinical Neuropsychology, 5,* 221–238.

Gill, D.M., Reddon, J.R., Stefanyk, W.O., & Hans, H.S. (1986). Finger tapping: Effects of trials and sessions. *Perceptual and Motor Skills, 62,* 675–678.

Goldstein, S.G., & Braun, L.S. (1974). Reversal of expected transfer as a function of increased age. *Perceptual and Motor Skills, 38,* 1139–1145.

Goldstein, G., & Watson, J.R. (1989). Test-retest reliability of the Halstead–Reitan battery and the WAIS in a neuropsychiatric population. *Clinical Neuropsychologist, 3,* 265–273.

Halstead, W.C. (1947). *Brain and Intelligence.* Chicago: University of Chicago Press.

Harris, M., Cross, H., & Van Nieuwkerk, R. (1981). The effects of state depression, induced depression and sex on the finger tapping and tactual performance tests. *Clinical Neuropsychology, 3,* 28–34.

Heaton, R.K., Grant, I., & Mathews, C.G. (1986). Differences in neuropsychological test performance associated with age, education, and sex. In I. Grant & K.M. Adams (Eds.), *Neuropsychological Assessment of Neuropsychiatric Disorders* (pp. 100–120). New York: Oxford University Press.

Hom, J., & Reitan, R.M. (1982). Effect of lateralized cerebral damage upon contralateral and ipsilateral sensorimotor performances. *Journal of Clinical Neuropsychology, 4,* 249–268.

Klonoff, H., & Low, M. (1974). Disordered brain function in young children and early adolescents: Neuropsychological and electroencephalographic correlates. In R. Reitan and L.A. Davidson (Eds.), *Clinical Neuropsychology: Current Status and Applications.* Washington, D.C.: V.H. Winston.

Matarazzo, J.D., Weins, A.N., Matarazzo, R.G., & Goldstein, S.G. (1974). Psychometric and clinical test–retest reliability of the Halstead Impairment Index in a sample of healthy, young, normal men. *Journal of Nervous and Mental Disease, 158,* 37–49.

Morrison, M.W., Gregory, R.J., & Paul, J.J. (1979). Reliability of the Finger Tapping Test and a note on sex differences. *Perceptual and Motor Skills, 48,* 139–142.

Provins, K.A., & Cunliffe, P. (1972). The reliability of some motor performance tests of handedness. *Neuropsychologia, 10,* 199–206.

Reitan, R.M. (1969). *Manual for Administration of Neuropsychological Test Batteries for Adults and Children.* Indianapolis University Medical Center: Unpublished Manuscript.

Reitan, R.M., & Wolfson, D. (1985). *The Halstead–Reitan Neuropsychological Test Battery: Theory and Interpretation.* Tucson: Neuropsychology Press.

Snow, W.G. (1987). Standardization of test administration and scoring criteria: Some shortcomings of current practice with the Halstead–Reitan Test Battery. *Clinical Neuropsychologist, 1,* 250–262.

Spreen, O., & Gaddes, W.H. (1969). Developmental norms for 15 neuropsychological tests age 6 to 15. *Cortex, 5,* 170–191.

Thompson, L.L., Heaton, R.K., Mathews, C.G., & Grant, I. (1987). Comparison of preferred and nonpreferred hand performance on four neuropsychological motor tasks. *Clinical Neuropsychologist, 1,* 324–334.

Trahan, D.E., Patterson, J., Quintana, J., & Biron, R. (1987). The finger tapping test: A re-examination of traditional hypotheses regarding normal adult performance. Paper presented to the International Neuropsychological Society, Washington, D.C. *Journal of Clinical and Experimental Neuropsychology, 9,* 52 (abstract).

York Haaland, K., & Delaney, H.D. (1981). Motor deficits after left or right hemisphere damage due to stroke or tumor. *Neuropsychologia, 19,* 17–27.

HAND DYNAMOMETER
Other Test Name

Another test name is Grip Strength.

Purpose

The purpose of this test is to measure the strength or intensity of the voluntary movements of each hand.

Source

The Smedley dynamometer can be ordered from the Stoelting Company, Oakwood Center, 620 Wheat Lane, Wood Dale, Illinois 60191, at a cost of $190.00 U.S.

Description

This frequently used measure of hand strength (Reitan & Davison, 1974) requires the subject to hold the upper part of the dynamometer in the palm of the hand and to squeeze the stirrup with the fingers as hard as he or she possibly can.

Administration

Briefly, the length of the dynamometer stirrup must be adjusted to the size of the subject's hand (see Instrument Manual). Illustrate the use of the instrument to the subject. Indicate that the lower pointer will register the grip, so that the subject does not have to continue gripping while the scale is read. Then place the dynamometer in the subject's preferred hand (palm down), and instruct the subject to hold his or her arm down at the side and away from the body. The subject is then told to squeeze the dynamometer as hard as he or she can, taking as much time as needed to squeeze to the maximum. Allow one practice trial and two recorded trials with each hand, preferred and nonpreferred alternately, with 10-second pauses between each trial to avoid excessive fatigue. If either an increase or a decrease of more than 5 kg occurs on the second trial for either hand, provide a third trial.

Approximate Time for Administration

The time required is approximately 5 minutes.

Scoring

The amount (in kilograms) registered at each trial is recorded, and the mean is calculated for each hand separately.

Comment

The performance of each hand is quite stable over time, even with lengthy intervals between retest sessions (e.g., 30 months). Reliability coefficients ranging from .52 to .96 have been reported with both normal and neurologically impaired subjects (Brown et al., 1989; Dodrill & Troupin, 1975; Dunn, 1978; Matarazzo et al., 1974; Provins & Cunliffe, 1972; Reddon et al., 1985). The differences between hands, however, are not highly reliable, and variations in performance from time to time may be influenced by variations in motivation (Provins & Cunliffe, 1972; Sappington, 1980).

Grip strength measures are included in neuropsychological examinations to assess subtle motor impairment, and to permit inferences about the cerebral speech pattern and the functional integrity of the two cerebral hemispheres. The measure has proven useful in discriminating epileptic patients with left-hemisphere speech from those with right-hemisphere speech (Strauss & Wada, 1988), in differentiating brain-damaged from normal people, and in detecting the laterality of brain lesion (Bornstein, 1986b; Dodrill, 1978; Finlayson & Reitan, 1980; Hom & Reitan, 1982; York Haaland & Delany, 1981). Dodrill (1978) reports that the dynamometer correctly identified the lateralization of brain lesions with higher accuracy than either the Finger Tapping Test or Tactual Performance Test. Given the crossed nature of the motor system, right-hemisphere lesions tend to depress performance on the left hand, whereas left-hemisphere lesions tend to lower performance on the right hand. The assumption is often made that right-handed people should perform better on the dynamometer with their right hand and that left-handed people should perform better with their left hand (e.g., Reitan & Wolfson, 1985). In general, performances with the preferred hand is superior to that with the nonpreferred hand (Bornstein, 1985, 1986a). However, there is considerable variability in the normal population, and the preferred hand is not necessarily the stronger one, especially when left-handed people are considered (Benton et al., 1962; Koffler & Zehler, 1985; Lewandowski et al., 1982; Satz et al., 1967; Smiljanic-Colanovic, 1974). Even fairly large discrepancies between the hands (more than 1 SD from the mean) are not uncommon (about 25%) in the normal population (Bornstein, 1986a; Koffler & Zehler, 1985; Thompson et al., 1987). Rather, greater confidence in the clinical judgment of impaired motor function with one or the other hand can be derived from consideration of the consistency of intermanual discrepancies across several motor tasks (Bornstein, 1986b; Thompson et al., 1987; for a more complete discussion, see Introduction).

Normative Data

There are several normative studies based on relatively large samples of healthy people. Table 10–3 provides recently compiled cross-sectional normative data for adults, stratified on the basis of age, sex, and education (Bornstein 1985). Right-handers comprised 91.5% of the sample. Ernst (1988), Fromm-Auch and Yeudall

Table 10–3. Mean Performance of Adults for Grip Strength in kg

Age group	Education: <grade 12			Education: >grade 12		
	N	M	SD	N	M	SD
Males						
Preferred hand						
20–39	21	50.8	11.5	86	49.9	8.4
40–59	13	39.8	6.0	17	48.2	7.3
60–69	16	38.7	5.9	22	44.5	5.6
Nonpreferred hand						
20–39	21	47.7	11.7	86	46.4	7.6
40–59	13	38.2	6.5	17	46.4	9.1
60–69	16	37.2	5.4	22	39.3	5.5
Females						
Preferred hand						
20–39	13	32.7	8.7	50	31.0	5.4
40–59	22	27.7	5.9	43	29.8	5.8
60–69	22	25.6	5.3	34	25.0	4.9
Nonpreferred hand						
20–39	13	31.2	8.0	50	28.7	5.0
40–59	22	24.9	6.7	43	26.9	5.4
60–69	22	24.0	6.0	34	22.8	4.8

Note: The sample consisted of 365 healthy individuals from the general population of a large Western Canadian city.

Source: Bornstein (1985).

Table 10–4. Mean Performance of Children for Grip Strength in kg

| Age | N | Male | | Female | |
		Right hand	Left hand	Right hand	Left hand
6	20	10.40 (2.80)[a]	9.45 (2.87)	9.05 (2.50)	7.90 (2.34)
7	20	11.95 (2.10)	11.10 (2.27)	9.30 (1.75)	8.80 (1.80)
8	20	12.25 (2.36)	11.40 (2.08)	11.55 (2.36)	10.15 (2.46)
12	20	21.95 (3.10)	19.55 (3.88)	23.05 (5.36)	19.10 (5.04)
13	20	28.30 (4.15)	27.55 (5.47)	25.00 (5.21)	23.25 (4.29)
14	20	35.25 (8.95)	33.80 (7.29)	28.30 (2.98)	25.65 (4.30)

Note: The data were derived from 120 normal right-handed children, 20 at each of six age levels, with boys and girls being equally represented.

[a]Standard deviation (SD) in parentheses.

Source: Finlayson & Reitan (1976).

(1983), and Koffler and Zehler (1985) also provide normative data for healthy men and women. Their values are similar to those reported here; however, their data were not stratified according to education. Table 10–4 gives normative data for right-handed boys and girls at each of six age levels (Finlayson & Reitan, 1976). A comparison with Spreen and Gaddes's (1969) norms and those provided with the instrument (from Stoelting Company) show relatively good agreement; however, their data are given for combined groups of right- and left-handed children and not according to preferred and nonpreferred handedness.

When each of the hands is considered separately, several trends emerge from the studies. First, performance tends to be better with the preferred than with the nonpreferred hand. Strength is related to sex, with males being stronger than females. There is a positive correlation between grip strength and height and weight, and also between grip strength and education. Finally, strength is also related to age. Longitudinal assessments of age changes in physical strength suggest that the decline in the older age groups is greater than is indicated by cross-sectional comparisons of different age groups. The underestimation of strength loss in cross-sectional estimates probably occurs because relatively fewer weak individuals are represented in older healthy samples (Clement, 1974).

Age and education do not affect the magnitude of intermanual differences (Bornstein, 1986a; Ernst, 1988). The findings regarding sex differences in intermanual difference scores are inconsistent; some studies find sex-related differences (i.e., greater between-hand differences for males than for females) (Bornstein, 1986a) whereas others do not (Ernst, 1988; Fromm-Auch & Yeudall, 1983; Thompson et al., 1987). There is also some evidence that right-handers show larger intermanual differences than do left-handers (Thompson et al., 1987).

REFERENCES

Benton, A.L., Meyers, R., & Polder, G.J. (1962). Some aspects of handedness. *Psychiatrica et Neurologia (Basel), 144,* 321-337.

Bornstein, R.A. (1985). Normative data on selected neuropsychological measures from a nonclinical sample. *Journal of Clinical Psychology, 41,* 651-659.

Bornstein, R.A. (1986a). Normative data on intermanual differences on three tests of motor performance. *Journal of Clinical and Experimental Neuropsychology, 8,* 12-20.

Bornstein, R.A. (1986b). Consistency of intermanual discrepancies in normal and unilateral brain lesion patients. *Journal of Consulting and Clinical Psychology, 54,* 719-723.

Brown, S.J., Rourke, B.P., & Cicchetti, D.V. (1989). Reliability of tests and measures used in the neuropsychological assessment of children. *Clinical Neuropsychologist, 3,* 353-368.

Clement, F.J. (1974). Longitudinal and cross-sectional assessments of age changes in physical strength as related to sex, social class, and mental ability. *Journal of Gerontology, 29,* 423-429.

Dodrill, C.B. (1978). The Hand Dynamometer as a neuropsychological measure. *Journal of Consulting and Clinical Psychology, 46,* 1432-1435.

Dodrill, C.B., & Troupin, A.S. (1975). Effects of repeated administrations of a comprehensive neuropsychological battery among chronic epileptics. *Journal of Nervous and Mental Disease, 161,* 185-190.

Dunn, J.M. (1978). Reliability of selected psychomotor measures with mentally retarded adult males. *Perceptual and Motor Skills, 46,* 295-301.

Ernst, J. (1988). Language, grip strength, sensory-perceptual, and receptive skills in a normal elderly sample. *Clinical Neuropsychologist, 2,* 30-40.

Finlayson, M.A., & Reitan, R.M. (1976). Handedness in relation to measures of motor and tactile-perceptual functions in normal children. *Perceptual and Motor Skills, 43,* 475-481.

Finlayson, M.A., & Reitan, R.M. (1980). Effect of lateralized lesions on ipsilateral and contralateral motor functioning. *Journal of Clinical Neuropsychology, 2,* 237-243.

Fromm-Auch, D., & Yeudall, L.T. (1983). Normative data for the Halstead–Reitan Neuropsychological Tests. *Journal of Clinical Psychology, 5,* 221-238.

Hom, J., & Reitan, R.M. (1982). Effect of lateralized cerebral damage upon contralateral and ipsilateral sensorimotor performances. *Journal of Clinical Neuropsychology, 4,* 249-268.

Koffler, S.P., & Zehler, D. (1985). Normative data for the hand dynamometer. *Perceptual and Motor Skills, 61,* 589-590.

Lewandowski, L., Kobus, D.A., Church, K.L., & Van Orden, K. (1982). Neuropsychological implications of hand preference versus hand grip performance. *Perceptual and Motor Skills, 55,* 311-314.

Matarazzo, J.D., Wiens, A.N., Matarazzo, R.G., & Goldstein, S. (1974). Psychometric and clinical test–retest reliability of the Halstead Impairment Index in a sample of healthy, young, normal men. *Journal of Nervous and Mental Disease, 158,* 37-49.

Provins, K.A., & Cunliffe, P. (1972). The reliability of some motor performance tests of handedness. *Neuropsychologia, 10,* 199-206.

Reddon, J.R., Stefanyk, W.O., Gill, D.M., & Renney, C. (1985). Hand dynamometer: Effects of trials and sessions. *Perceptual and Motor Skills, 61,* 1195-1198.

Reitan, R.M., & Davison, L.A. (1974). *Clinical Neuropsychology: Current Status and Applications.* Washington, D.C.: V.H. Winston.

Reitan, R.M., & Wolfson, D. (1985). *The Halstead–Reitan Neuropsychological Test Battery: Theory and Interpretation.* Tucson: Neuropsychology Press.

Sappington, J.T. (1980). Measures of lateral dominance: Interrelationships and temporal stability. *Perceptual and Motor Skills, 50,* 783-790.

Satz, P., Achenbach, K., & Fennel, E. (1967). Correlations between assessed manual laterality and predicted speech laterality in a normal population. *Neuropsychologia, 5,* 295-310.

Smiljanic-Colanovic, V. (1974). The measurement of different aspects and degrees of hand dominance. *Studiae Psychologica, 16,* 204–208.

Spreen, O., & Gaddes, W.H. (1969). Developmental norms for 15 neuropsychological tests age 6 to 15. *Cortex, 5,* 170–191.

Strauss, E., & Wada, J. (1988). Hand preference and proficiency and cerebral speech dominance determined by the carotid amytal test. *Journal of Clinical and Experimental Neuropsychology, 10,* 169–174.

Thompson, L.L., Heaton, R.K., Mathews, C.G., & Grant, I. (1987). Comparison of preferred and nonpreferred hand performance on four neuropsychological motor tasks. *Clinical Neuropsychologist, 1,* 324–334.

York Haaland, K., & Delaney, H.D. (1981). Motor deficits after left or right hemisphere damage due to stroke or tumor. *Neuropsychologia, 19,* 17–27.

HAND PREFERENCE TEST

Other Test Name

This test is also known as the Annett Handedness Questionnaire.

Description

Investigators often report their patient's hand preference since this may provide clues regarding the cerebral representation of speech and/or the location of hemispheric disturbance (Rasmussen & Milner, 1977; Satz et al., 1988). Measures of hand preference are diverse and include questionnaires, behavioral tests, and verbal self-report about hand preference or about the hand used for writing (Chapman & Chapman, 1987). The Annett (1970) questionnaire consists of 12 items, six of which are designated "primary" and six of which are designated "secondary" items. We use the six primary items of the Annett (1970) questionnaire—that is, writing, throwing a ball, holding a racket, holding a hammer, holding a toothbrush, and striking a match.

Administration

Because problems may arise when answers given on questionnaires are compared with actual behavior (Raczkowski et al., 1974), the patient's behavior is observed while he or she is performing each of the tasks. Performance items, using real objects, should be presented to the patient in such a way as to give neither hand an obvious preference. Say to the patient: "**Show me how you**"

1. **write a letter legibly?**
2. **throw a ball to hit a target?**
3. **hold a tennis racket**
4. **hammer a nail into wood?**
5. **hold a match while striking it?**
6. **hold a toothbrush while cleaning your teeth?**

In addition, the patient is asked if any close relatives are left-handed. This final question is not scored.

Approximate Time for Administration

This test requires 5 minutes.

Scoring

Annett (1970) has emphasized that preferences vary continuously although the information can be used to classify subjects. If all six actions are carried out by the same hand (all six right or all six left), then the subject is classified as right-handed or left-handed. If the patient is not uniformly right or left-handed for all six items, then the subject is classified as mixed-handed.

Comment

A person's writing hand does not always predict an individual's behavior on other unimanual tasks (Annett, 1970; Benton et al., 1962; Crovitz & Zener, 1962; Provins & Cunliffe, 1972; Satz et al., 1967). Consequently, many investigators determine the consistency of a person's hand preference either by asking the subject a series of questions concerning which hand he or she prefers to use in a range of selected activities, or by asking the subject to perform a number of tasks and noting the hand employed in each case. The better known questionnaires include those by Annett (1970), Crovitz and Zener (1962), Oldfield (1971), and Raczkowski, Kalat, and Nebes (1974). There is considerable repetition in the items used to determine hand preference by the various investigators, and the choice of questionnaire is somewhat arbitrary (Chapman & Chapman, 1987).

   McMeekan and Lishman (1975) had normal subjects complete the paper-and-pencil version of the 12-item Annett questionnaire on two separate occasions, about 14 weeks apart. Test–retest reliability was satisfactory (kappa coefficient, .80). Raczkowski, Kalat, and Nebes (1974) gave a 23-item questionnaire, including all six primary items in Annett's questionnaire, to undergraduates on two separate occasions, one month apart. Test–retest reliability was high (.89 and above). Chapman and Chapman (1987) reported similar findings.

The test is easy to administer and score. An association analysis carried out by Annett (1970) found that the six "primary" items in her handedness questionnaire clustered together. Geffen and Caudry (1981) have shown that the relation between handedness (as measured by the six primary items of the Annett questionnaire) and speech lateralization [determined by electroconvulsive therapy (ECT) or the carotid amytal test] is statistically significant. However, hand preference, by itself, does not provide an adequate basis for predicting cerebral speech dominance for the individual (Annett, 1972; Geffen & Caudry, 1981; Rasmussen & Milner, 1977; Satz et al., 1988; Strauss & Wada, 1983, 1988).

Normative Data

About 70% of normal people give consistent right-hand responses, whereas about 5% are consistently left-handed. The remainder show a mixed hand-preference pattern. Handedness varies as a function of sex. When sex differences are found, they tend to be small, with a higher precentage of men as opposed to women shown to be left-handed (Annett, 1972; Porac & Coren, 1981). Handedness also varies as a function of age. Although infants appear to exhibit inherent hand preferences at an early age, these asymmetries increase in consistency with a gradual shift toward habitual right-handedness with increasing age (Porac & Coren, 1981). Finally, there appears to be an elevated incidence of consistent left-handedness and mixed-handedness in homosexual men (Lindesay, 1987); this appears to be true also for dyslexic children (Annett & Kilshaw, 1984) and other atypical groups (e.g., mentally retarded).

REFERENCES

Annett, M. (1970). A classification of hand preference by association analysis. *British Journal of Psychology, 61*, 303–321.

Annett, M. (1972). The distribution of manual asymmetry. *British Journal of Psychology, 63*, 343–358.

Annett, M., & Kilshaw, D. (1984). Lateral preference and skill in dyslexics. *Journal of Child Psychology and Psychiatry, 25*, 357–377.

Benton, A.L., Meyers, R., & Polder, G.J. (1962). Some aspects of handedness. *Psychiatrica et Neurologia, (Basel) 144*, 321–337.

Chapman, L.J., & Chapman, J.P. (1987). The measurement of handedness. *Brain and Cognition, 6*, 175–183.

Crovitz, H.F., & Zener, K. (1962). A group-test for assessing hand-and-eye dominance. *American Journal of Psychology, 73*, 271–276.

Geffen, G., & Caudry, D. (1981). Reliability and validity of the dichotic monitoring test for language laterality. *Neuropsychologia, 19*, 413–423.

Lindesay, J. (1987). Laterality shift in homosexual men. *Neuropsychologia, 25*, 965–969.

McMeekan, E.R.L., & Lishman, W.A. (1975). Retest reliabilities of the Annett Hand Preference Questionnaire and the Edinburgh Handedness Inventory. *British Journal of Psychology, 66*, 53–59.

Oldfield, R.C. (1971). The assessment and analysis of handedness: The Edinburgh Inventory. *Neuropsychologia, 9*, 97–113.

Porac, C., & Coren, S. (1981). *Lateral Preferences and Human Behavior.* New York: Springer-Verlag.

Provins, K. A., & Cunliffe, P. (1972). The reliability of some motor performance tests. *Neuropsychologia, 9*, 97–113.

Raczkowski, D., Kalat, J.W., & Nebes, R. (1974). Reliability and validity of some handedness questionnaire items. *Neuropsychologia, 12*, 43–47.

Rasmussen, T., & Milner, B. (1977). The role of early left-brain injury in determining lateralization of cerebral speech functions. *New York Academy of Sciences, 299*, 355–379.

Satz, P., Achenbach, K., & Fennell, E. (1967). Correlations between assessed manual laterality and predicted speech laterality in a normal population. *Neuropsychologia, 5*, 295–310.

Satz, P., Strauss, E., Wada, J., & Orsini, D.L. (1988). Some correlates of intra- and interhemispheric speech organization after left focal brain injury. *Neuropsychologia, 26*, 345–350.

Strauss, E., & Wada, J. (1983). Lateral preferences and cerebral speech dominance. *Cortex, 19*, 165–177.

Strauss, E., & Wada, J. (1988). Hand preference and proficiency and cerebral speech dominance determined by the carotid amytal test. *Journal of Clinical and Experimental Neuropsychology, 10*, 169–174.

PURDUE PEGBOARD TEST

Purpose

The purpose of this test is to measure finger and hand dexterity.

Source

The pegboard, manual, and record forms can be ordered from Lafayette Instrument Company, Inc., P.O. Box 5729, Sagamore Parkway, Lafayette Indiana 47903, at a cost of $90 U.S., or from Technolab Industries Ltd., 5757 Decelles Avenue, Suite 329, Montreal, Quebec H3S 2C3, Canada, at a cost of $149 Cdn.

Description

The Purdue Pegboard was developed in the 1940s as a test of manipulative dexterity for use in personnel selection (Tiffin, 1968; Tiffin & Asher, 1948). In addition to its use in personnel selection, the Purdue Pegboard has been used in neuropsychological assessment to assist in localizing cerebral lesions and deficits (Reddon et al., 1988). The board contains two parallel rows of 25 holes each. Pins (pegs), collars, and washers are located at the extreme right-hand and left-hand cups at the top of the board. Collars and washers occupy the two middle cups. In the first three subtests, the subject places as many pins as possible in the holes, first with the preferred hand, then with the nonpreferred hand, and finally with both hands, within a 30-second time period. To test the right hand, the subject has to insert as many pins as possible in the holes, starting at the top of the right-hand row. The left-hand test uses the left row. Both hands then are used together to fill both rows top to bottom. In the fourth subtest, the subject uses both hands alternately to construct "assemblies," which consist of a pin, a washer, a collar, and another washer. The subject must complete as many assemblies as possible within one minute.

Administration

The instructions are described in the test manual. Briefly, the subject is required to take pins with the preferred (e.g., right) hand from the right-hand cup and place them as quickly as possible in the right column of holes, during a 30-second period. The pins are allowed to remain in the holes, and the same procedure is repeated with the nonpreferred hand. The pins are then removed, and the test is repeated with the subject using both hands simultaneously. Again the trial period is 30 seconds. The pins are then removed, and the subject is asked to form "assemblies." The subject is asked to use continuous alternating movements of the right and left hands, one picking up a pin, one a washer, one a collar, and so on. The time allowed is 60 seconds. Demonstration and practice are provided prior to each subtest. Examiners may repeat each task three times; however, most of the recent normative data are based on a single-trial administration.

Scoring

Scores are derived for each part of the test. The scores for the pin (peg) placement subtests consist of the number of pins inserted in the time period for each hand. The score for the bimanual condition consists of the total number of pairs of pins inserted. The assembly score refers to the number of parts assembled (see source).

Comment

In normal people, moderate test–retest reliabilities, ranging from .63 to .82, have been obtained by correlating the scores for one trial on each of the subtests, with the one-trial scores obtained by giving the subtests one to two weeks later (Reddon et al., 1988; Tiffin, 1968). However, there are practice effects, with scores improving on subsequent trials (Reddon et al., 1988; Wilson et al., 1982). Right–left difference scores or ratios tend not to be very reliable, with correlations ranging from .22 to .61 (Reddon et al., 1988; Sappington, 1980).

Factor-analytic studies (Fleishman & Ellison, 1962; Fleishman & Hempel, 1954) have shown that the Purdue Pegboard loads on a finger dexterity factor which is defined as "the ability to make rapid, skillful, controlled manipulative movements of small objects, where the fingers are primarily involved." However, the assembly test appears to measure some skill besides finger dexterity and also loads on a manual dexterity factor that is defined as "the ability to make skillful, controlled arm–hand manipulations of larger objects." Finally, the peg placement portion of the Purdue Pegboard Test appears to be sensitive to the presence of brain damage and may provide information of lateralizing significance (Costa et al., 1983; Gardner & Broman, 1979; Rapin et al., 1966; Vaughan & Costa, 1962). Because changes in performance occur over time, right–left differences (or ratios) on the Purdue Pegboard may have diagnostic value only when differences are also found on other tests (Reddon et al., 1988).

Normative Data

In general, performance is better with the preferred than the nonpreferred hand; females perform better than males, and performance changes with age (Gardner & Broman, 1980; Mathiowetz et al., 1986; Sattler & Engelhardt, 1982; Wilson et al., 1982; Yeudall et al., 1986; but see Costa et al., 1963, who did not find sex-related differences). Education appears to be unrelated to performance (Costa et al., 1963; Yeudall et al., 1986). Tables 10–5 through 10–7 provide normative data for children and young adults, stratified on the basis of age (5–40 years) and sex (Gardner & Broman, 1979; Yeudall et al., 1986). Table 10–8 provides normative data (Strauss & Spreen, unpublished data) for a largely right-handed group of healthy, well-educated (mean = 13.2 years) older adults, ages 50–85. These tables are based on an administration of one trial per subtest. Mathiowetz et al. (1986) give normative data, based on a three-trial administration, for subjects 14–19 years of age. Wilson et al. (1982) modified the pegboard by shortening the board, so that it could be used with preschoolers. They compiled data on right-handed children, ages 2½–6 years, for the peg placement portions only.

Table 10-5. Performance of Children on Purdue Pegboard: Means and Standard Deviations

Age	N	Preferred hand		Nonpreferred hand		Both hands		Assembly	
		Mean	SD	Mean	SD	Mean	SD	Mean	SD
Boys									
5:0–5:5	30	9.33	1.81	8.40	1.33	6.73	1.17	14.10	3.29
5:6–5:11	30	9.93	1.51	8.83	1.95	6.97	1.54	15.57	3.56
6:0–6:5	30	9.77	1.57	9.13	1.83	7.30	1.53	15.93	2.94
6:6–6:11	30	11.57	1.45	10.17	2.17	8.23	1.77	19.20	3.84
7:0–7:5	30	11.67	1.67	11.00	1.70	8.77	1.41	19.23	4.95
7:6–7:11	30	12.07	1.95	11.23	1.68	9.57	1.59	20.40	4.10
8:0–8:5	30	12.70	1.60	12.17	1.51	9.83	1.51	22.20	3.80
8:6–8:11	30	13.90	2.19	12.57	1.85	10.90	1.73	24.47	5.35
9:0–9:5	30	13.33	1.60	12.43	1.59	10.50	1.48	24.57	3.75
9:6–9:11	30	13.87	1.91	12.87	2.05	11.33	1.65	27.37	4.55
10:0–10:5	30	14.03	1.88	12.87	1.72	10.93	1.84	26.37	6.15
10:6–10:11	30	14.93	1.51	13.90	1.84	11.77	1.65	28.17	5.38
11:0–11:5	30	14.93	1.86	14.00	1.98	11.30	1.68	29.53	6.19
11:6–11:11	30	14.83	1.60	13.93	1.60	12.27	1.41	31.13	5.19
12:0–12:5	30	14.83	1.78	13.67	2.02	11.67	1.52	31.13	5.78
12:6–12:11	30	15.37	2.81	14.00	2.38	11.87	1.87	30.13	6.08
13:0–13:5	40	15.15	1.92	13.90	2.00	11.85	1.58	33.73	5.00
13:6–13:11	30	14.87	1.72	14.10	1.47	11.53	1.80	34.57	5.88
14:0–14:5	30	15.67	1.47	14.40	1.57	12.03	1.67	33.97	6.58
14:6–14:11	30	14.70	1.49	14.33	1.65	12.20	1.61	31.37	7.24
15:0–15:5	30	15.57	1.50	14.87	1.50	12.57	1.48	32.20	6.21
15:6–15:11	23	15.09	1.50	14.30	1.61	12.65	1.30	33.04	6.24
Girls									
5:0–5:5	30	10.00	1.53	8.50	1.36	6.97	1.25	14.70	2.55
5:6–5:11	30	9.30	1.73	9.13	1.59	6.77	1.28	14.37	4.02
6:0–6:5	30	11.43	1.33	10.23	1.52	8.53	1.46	18.03	3.54
6:6–6:11	30	11.87	1.68	10.47	1.38	8.67	1.79	20.63	4.27
7:0–7:5	30	12.03	1.65	10.47	2.08	8.83	1.80	19.77	4.49
7:6–7:11	30	12.47	1.53	11.50	1.80	9.50	1.70	20.20	4.61
8:0–8:5	30	13.07	1.78	12.03	1.40	10.10	1.81	21.93	4.31
8:6–8:11	30	13.77	1.63	12.30	1.26	10.43	1.59	24.50	5.83
9:0–9:5	30	13.37	1.79	11.83	2.12	9.83	1.62	24.97	6.81
9:6–9:11	30	14.40	1.52	13.03	1.67	11.60	1.65	29.07	6.01
10:0–10:5	30	15.13	1.48	13.20	1.35	11.33	1.42	27.90	5.10
10:6–10:11	30	15.47	1.59	13.63	1.33	12.27	1.46	31.70	6.02
11:0–11:5	30	14.90	1.79	14.00	2.00	11.67	1.63	32.77	5.50
11:6–11:11	30	15.70	1.84	13.83	1.88	12.00	1.82	33.47	7.24
12:0–12:5	30	15.57	1.65	14.20	1.73	12.00	1.23	34.57	5.20
12:6–12:11	30	15.40	1.96	14.07	1.66	12.03	1.65	34.70	7.52
13:0–13:5	40	15.55	1.69	14.15	1.64	12.03	1.44	34.85	5.57
13:6–13:11	32	15.38	1.58	14.09	1.44	12.13	1.31	37.40	5.34
14:0–14:5	30	16.33	1.73	14.93	1.78	12.63	1.61	36.43	6.76
14:6–14:11	30	16.03	1.77	14.83	1.66	12.40	1.94	34.17	6.62
15:0–15:5	28	16.68	1.49	14.89	1.40	12.89	1.64	36.89	7.75
15:6–15:11	31	16.42	1.84	15.29	2.04	12.77	1.45	37.35	8.24

Note: Data were derived from 1,334 normal schoolchildren.

Source: Gardner & Broman (1979).

Table 10-6. Performance of Children on Purdue Pegboard: Percentiles

Age	N	10	20	30	40	50	60	70	80	90
Percentiles for boys: Preferred hand										
5:0–5:5	30	7.0	8.0	8.0	9.0	9.0	10.0	10.0	11.0	11.0
5:6–5:11	30	8.0	9.0	9.0	10.0	10.0	10.0	11.0	11.8	12.0
6:0–6:5	30	7.1	9.0	9.0	9.0	9.5	10.0	11.0	11.0	11.9
6:6–6:11	30	9.1	10.2	11.0	11.0	12.0	12.0	12.0	13.0	13.0
7:0–7:5	30	9.1	10.2	11.0	11.4	12.0	12.0	12.7	13.0	13.9
7:6–7:11	30	9.0	10.0	11.0	12.0	12.0	12.6	13.0	14.0	14.0
8:0–8:5	30	11.0	12.0	12.0	12.0	13.0	13.0	14.0	14.0	14.0
8:6–8:11	30	11.1	12.0	12.3	13.0	14.0	15.0	15.0	16.0	17.0
9:0–9:5	30	11.0	12.0	12.0	13.0	13.0	14.0	15.0	15.0	15.0
9:6–9:11	30	12.0	12.0	13.0	13.0	14.0	14.6	15.0	15.0	15.9
10:0–10:5	30	11.1	12.2	13.0	14.0	14.0	15.0	15.0	15.8	16.9
10:6–10:11	30	13.0	13.2	14.0	14.0	15.0	15.0	15.0	16.0	17.0
11:0–11:5	30	13.0	13.0	13.0	14.0	14.5	16.0	16.0	16.8	17.0
11:6–11:11	30	13.0	14.0	14.0	14.0	15.0	15.0	15.0	16.8	17.0
12:0–12:5	30	13.0	13.0	14.0	14.0	14.5	15.0	15.7	16.0	17.9
12:6–12:11	30	13.0	13.2	15.0	15.0	15.0	15.0	16.0	17.0	18.9
13:0–13:5	40	12.1	14.0	14.0	15.0	15.0	15.0	16.0	16.8	18.0
13:6–13:11	30	13.0	13.0	14.0	14.4	15.0	15.0	16.0	16.0	17.0
14:0–14:5	30	14.0	14.0	14.3	15.0	16.0	16.0	17.0	17.0	17.9
14:6–14:11	30	13.0	13.0	14.0	14.4	15.0	15.0	15.0	16.0	16.9
15:0–15:5	30	14.0	14.0	14.0	15.0	15.5	16.0	16.7	17.0	18.0
15:6–15:11	23	13.0	14.0	14.0	15.0	15.0	15.0	16.0	17.0	17.0
Percentiles for boys: Nonpreferred hand										
5:0–5:5	30	6.1	7.0	8.0	8.0	8.5	9.0	9.0	9.0	10.0
5:6–5:11	30	6.1	8.0	8.0	8.0	9.0	9.6	10.0	10.0	11.0
6:0–6:5	30	6.0	8.0	9.0	9.0	9.0	10.0	10.0	10.0	12.0
6:6–6:11	30	7.1	8.2	9.0	10.0	10.5	11.0	11.7	12.0	13.0
7:0–7:5	30	9.0	10.0	10.0	11.0	11.0	11.0	12.0	12.0	12.9
7:6–7:11	30	9.1	10.0	10.0	11.0	11.0	11.0	12.0	13.0	13.9
8:0–8:5	30	10.0	11.0	11.0	12.0	12.5	13.0	13.7	13.0	15.9
8:6–8:11	30	10.1	11.0	11.0	12.0	12.0	13.0	13.7	14.0	15.9
9:0–9:5	30	10.0	11.0	11.3	12.0	13.0	13.0	13.7	14.0	14.0
9:6–9:11	30	10.0	11.2	12.0	12.0	12.0	13.0	14.0	15.0	16.0
10:0–10:5	30	10.1	12.0	12.0	13.0	13.0	13.6	14.0	14.0	15.0
10:6–10:11	30	11.0	12.2	13.0	13.0	14.0	14.0	15.0	15.8	17.0
11:0–11:5	30	12.0	13.0	13.0	13.0	13.5	14.0	15.0	15.8	16.9
11:6–11:11	30	11.1	13.0	13.0	14.0	14.0	14.0	15.0	15.0	16.0
12:0–12:5	30	12.0	13.0	13.0	13.0	14.0	14.0	15.0	15.0	16.0
12:6–12:11	30	11.0	12.2	13.0	13.4	14.0	14.0	15.0	16.0	16.9
13:0–13:5	40	11.0	11.2	13.0	14.0	14.0	15.0	15.0	16.0	16.0
13:6–13:11	30	12.0	13.0	13.0	14.0	14.0	14.0	15.0	15.8	16.0
14:0–14:5	30	12.1	13.0	14.0	14.0	14.5	15.0	15.7	16.0	16.0
14:6–14:11	30	11.2	13.2	14.0	14.0	14.5	15.0	15.0	15.8	16.0
15:0–15:5	30	13.0	14.0	14.3	15.0	15.0	15.0	16.0	16.0	16.9
15:6–15:11	23	12.0	13.0	13.0	14.0	15.0	15.0	15.0	16.0	16.6

Age	N	10	20	30	40	50	60	70	80	90
Percentiles for boys: Both hands										
5:0–5:5	30	5.1	6.0	6.0	6.0	7.0	7.0	7.0	8.0	8.0
5:6–5:11	30	5.0	6.0	6.0	6.4	7.0	7.0	8.0	8.0	9.0
6:0–6:5	30	5.0	6.0	6.3	7.0	7.0	7.6	8.0	9.0	9.0
6:6–6:11	30	6.0	7.0	8.0	8.0	9.0	8.6	9.0	9.0	10.9
7:0–7:5	30	7.0	8.0	8.0	8.0	8.0	9.0	10.0	10.0	10.0
7:6–7:11	30	8.0	8.0	8.0	9.0	9.5	10.0	10.7	11.0	12.0
8:0–8:5	30	8.0	8.0	9.0	9.0	10.0	10.0	11.0	11.0	12.0
8:6–8:11	30	9.0	9.2	10.0	10.0	11.0	11.0	12.0	12.8	13.0
9:0–9:5	30	8.1	9.0	10.0	10.0	10.0	11.0	11.0	12.0	12.0
9:6–9:11	30	9.1	10.0	10.0	11.0	11.0	11.6	12.0	13.0	13.9
10:0–10:5	30	9.0	9.0	10.0	10.4	11.0	11.0	11.0	12.8	13.9
10:6–10:11	30	10.0	10.2	11.0	11.0	12.0	12.0	12.0	13.0	14.0
11:0–11:5	30	9.0	10.0	10.3	11.0	11.0	12.0	12.7	13.0	13.0
11:6–11:11	30	11.0	11.0	12.0	12.0	12.0	13.0	13.0	13.8	14.0
12:0–12:5	30	9.1	11.0	11.0	11.0	12.0	12.0	12.0	12.8	14.0
12:6–12:11	30	9.1	10.2	11.0	12.0	12.0	12.6	13.0	13.8	14.0
13:0–13:5	40	9.1	11.0	11.0	11.4	12.0	12.0	13.0	13.0	14.0
13:6–13:11	30	9.1	10.0	11.0	11.0	11.0	12.0	12.0	13.0	14.0
14:0–14:5	30	10.1	11.0	11.0	11.0	12.0	12.0	13.0	14.0	14.0
14:6–14:11	30	10.0	11.0	11.0	12.0	12.0	12.0	13.0	14.0	15.0
15:0–15:5	30	10.1	11.0	12.0	12.0	13.0	13.0	13.0	14.0	14.9
15:6–15:11	23	11.0	11.8	12.0	12.0	13.0	13.0	13.0	14.0	14.0
Percentiles for boys: Assembly										
5:0–5:5	30	10.0	11.2	12.0	13.0	14.0	14.6	16.0	16.0	17.0
5:6–5:11	30	10.1	12.2	14.0	15.0	16.0	16.0	17.7	18.0	20.0
6:0–6:5	30	12.1	14.0	15.0	15.0	16.0	16.0	17.0	19.0	20.0
6:6–6:11	30	14.0	16.2	18.0	18.0	19.5	20.6	22.0	22.8	24.0
7:0–7:5	30	12.1	16.0	17.3	18.4	19.0	20.6	21.7	23.0	26.7
7:6–7:11	30	16.0	17.2	18.3	19.4	21.0	22.0	22.7	24.0	25.0
8:0–8:5	30	19.0	20.2	21.0	22.4	23.5	24.0	24.0	26.8	28.9
8:6–8:11	30	18.0	20.0	20.3	23.4	24.0	25.0	27.1	30.0	32.0
9:0–9:5	30	20.0	21.2	23.0	24.0	24.0	26.0	26.0	27.0	28.0
9:6–9:11	30	21.1	24.0	24.3	25.4	26.0	29.2	30.7	31.8	32.0
10:0–10:5	30	19.1	20.2	24.0	25.0	26.0	26.0	28.7	30.0	35.7
10:6–10:11	30	22.0	24.0	25.3	28.4	29.0	30.0	30.0	31.0	33.8
11:0–11:5	30	22.0	22.2	26.0	27.4	28.0	31.0	32.0	34.6	39.9
11:6–11:11	30	25.1	27.0	28.6	30.0	31.0	32.6	33.7	35.0	39.0
12:0–12:5	30	25.0	26.0	27.0	29.0	29.0	32.6	35.4	36.0	40.9
12:6–12:11	30	23.1	25.4	28.0	29.0	30.5	32.2	34.0	35.8	37.0
13:0–13:5	40	27.0	30.0	31.0	32.0	34.0	34.8	36.0	37.0	40.9
13:6–13:11	30	27.1	30.0	30.0	33.0	34.5	35.6	36.7	39.8	43.8
14:0–14:5	30	26.1	29.2	31.0	32.0	34.0	36.0	38.7	40.0	41.0
14:6–14:11	30	23.0	25.2	26.3	29.0	30.5	32.0	34.7	35.8	45.4
15:0–15:5	30	24.0	26.0	28.0	31.4	33.5	35.6	36.0	37.8	39.9
15:6–15:11	23	24.4	26.8	29.4	32.0	33.0	34.4	35.8	39.0	42.0

(continued)

Table 10–6. *(Continued)*

Age	N	10	20	30	40	50	60	70	80	90
Percentiles for girls: Preferred hand										
5:0–5:5	30	8.0	8.2	9.3	10.0	10.0	10.6	11.0	11.0	12.0
5:6–5:11	30	7.0	8.0	8.0	9.0	9.5	10.0	11.0	11.0	11.0
6:0–6:5	30	9.1	10.2	11.0	11.0	11.5	10.0	12.0	12.0	13.0
6:6–6:11	30	10.1	11.0	11.0	11.0	11.0	12.0	3.0	14.0	14.0
7:0–7:5	30	10.0	11.0	11.0	12.0	12.0	12.0	13.0	13.0	14.9
7:6–7:11	30	10.1	11.0	12.0	12.0	13.0	13.0	13.0	14.0	14.0
8:0–8:5	30	11.0	12.0	12.0	12.4	13.0	13.0	14.0	14.8	15.9
8:6–8:11	30	12.0	12.0	13.0	13.0	14.0	14.0	14.7	15.0	16.9
9:0–9:5	30	10.1	12.0	13.0	13.0	13.0	14.0	14.0	15.0	16.0
9:6–9:11	30	12.0	13.0	14.0	14.0	14.0	15.0	15.0	16.0	16.9
10:0–10:5	30	13.0	14.0	14.0	15.0	15.0	15.0	16.0	16.0	17.9
10:6–10:11	30	13.1	14.0	14.8	15.0	15.5	16.0	16.0	16.8	17.9
11:0–11:5	30	12.0	13.2	14.0	15.0	15.0	15.0	15.7	16.8	17.0
11:6–11:11	30	14.0	14.0	15.0	15.0	16.0	16.0	17.0	17.0	18.0
12:0–12:5	30	14.0	14.0	14.0	15.0	15.0	16.0	17.0	17.0	17.9
12:6–12:11	30	12.1	13.2	15.0	15.0	16.0	16.0	16.0	17.0	18.0
13:0–13:5	40	14.0	14.0	15.0	15.0	16.0	16.0	16.0	17.0	18.0
13:6–13:11	30	13.3	14.0	14.0	15.0	15.0	15.0	16.0	17.0	18.0
14:0–14:5	30	14.1	15.0	15.0	16.0	16.0	16.0	17.0	17.8	19.0
14:6–14:11	30	14.0	14.0	15.0	15.0	16.0	16.6	17.0	17.0	18.9
15:0–15:5	30	15.0	15.0	16.0	16.0	17.0	17.0	18.7	18.0	19.0
15:6–15:11	23	14.0	15.0	15.6	16.0	16.0	17.0	17.4	18.0	19.0
Percentiles for girls: Nonpreferred hand										
5:0–5:5	30	7.0	7.0	8.0	8.0	9.0	9.0	9.0	10.0	10.0
5:6–5:11	30	7.0	7.2	8.0	8.4	9.0	10.0	10.0	11.0	11.0
6:0–6:5	30	8.0	8.2	9.3	10.0	10.0	11.0	11.0	11.8	12.0
6:6–6:11	30	9.0	9.2	10.0	10.0	10.0	11.0	11.0	12.0	12.0
7:0–7:5	30	8.0	9.0	10.0	10.0	11.0	11.0	11.0	12.0	13.0
7:6–7:11	30	9.0	10.0	10.3	11.0	11.0	12.0	13.0	13.0	14.0
8:0–8:5	30	10.0	11.0	11.0	12.0	12.0	12.0	12.7	13.0	14.0
8:6–8:11	30	11.0	11.0	12.0	12.0	12.0	12.6	13.0	13.8	14.0
9:0–9:5	30	9.0	10.0	11.0	11.0	11.5	12.6	13.0	14.0	14.9
9:6–9:11	30	11.0	11.0	12.0	12.0	13.0	13.6	14.0	14.8	15.0
10:0–10:5	30	11.0	12.0	13.0	13.0	13.0	13.6	14.0	14.8	15.0
10:6–10:11	30	11.2	13.0	13.0	13.4	14.0	14.0	14.0	14.8	15.0
11:0–11:5	30	10.2	12.4	14.0	14.0	14.0	15.0	15.0	15.0	16.8
11:6–11:11	30	11.0	12.0	13.0	14.0	14.0	14.0	15.0	15.0	16.0
12:0–12:5	30	12.0	13.0	13.3	14.0	14.0	14.0	15.0	16.0	16.9
12:6–12:11	30	12.0	13.0	13.0	13.0	14.0	14.0	15.0	15.0	16.9
13:0–13:5	40	12.1	13.0	13.0	13.4	14.0	14.0	15.0	16.0	16.0
13:6–13:11	30	12.0	13.0	14.0	14.0	14.0	15.0	15.0	15.0	16.0
14:0–14:5	30	13.0	13.0	14.0	15.0	15.0	15.0	15.7	16.0	17.0
14:6–14:11	30	13.0	13.2	14.0	14.0	15.0	15.0	16.0	16.8	17.0
15:0–15:5	30	12.9	14.0	14.0	14.6	15.0	15.4	16.0	16.0	17.0
15:6–15:11	23	13.0	13.0	14.0	14.0	15.0	16.0	16.4	17.8	18.0

Age	N	10	20	30	40	50	60	70	80	90
Percentiles for girls: Both hands										
5:0–5:5	30	5.0	6.0	6.0	7.0	7.0	7.6	8.0	8.0	8.0
5:6–5:11	30	5.0	6.0	6.0	6.4	7.0	7.0	7.7	8.0	8.0
6:0–6:5	30	6.1	7.2	8.0	8.0	9.0	9.0	9.0	10.0	10.0
6:6–6:11	30	6.1	8.0	8.0	8.0	8.0	8.6	9.7	10.0	12.0
7:0–7:5	30	6.0	7.2	8.0	9.0	9.0	9.0	10.0	10.8	11.0
7:6–7:11	30	7.0	8.0	9.0	9.0	9.5	10.0	10.7	11.0	11.0
8:0–8:5	30	8.0	8.2	9.0	10.0	10.0	11.0	11.0	11.0	12.0
8:6–8:11	30	8.0	9.0	10.0	10.0	10.5	11.0	11.0	12.0	12.9
9:0–9:5	30	8.0	8.0	9.0	9.4	10.0	10.0	11.0	11.0	12.0
9:6–9:11	30	9.0	10.0	11.0	12.0	12.0	12.0	13.0	13.0	13.0
10:0–10:5	30	10.0	10.0	11.0	11.0	11.0	11.6	12.0	12.0	13.0
10:6–10:11	30	11.0	11.0	11.3	12.0	12.0	12.0	13.0	13.8	14.9
11:0–11:5	30	9.1	10.0	11.0	11.4	12.0	12.0	12.7	13.0	13.0
11:6–11:11	30	9.1	10.2	11.0	11.0	13.0	13.0	13.0	14.0	14.0
12:0–12:5	30	10.0	11.0	12.0	12.0	12.0	12.0	12.0	13.0	14.0
12:6–12:11	30	10.0	10.2	11.0	12.0	12.0	12.0	13.0	13.8	14.0
13:0–13:5	40	10.0	11.0	11.0	12.0	12.0	12.0	13.0	13.0	14.0
13:6–13:11	30	10.3	11.0	11.9	12.0	12.0	12.0	13.0	13.0	13.7
14:0–14:5	30	11.0	11.0	12.0	12.0	12.0	13.0	13.0	14.8	15.0
14:6–14:11	30	9.1	11.0	11.3	12.0	12.0	13.0	13.7	14.0	15.0
15:0–15:5	30	11.0	11.0	12.0	12.0	13.0	13.0	14.0	14.0	16.0
15:6–15:11	23	11.0	11.0	12.0	13.0	13.0	13.0	13.4	14.0	14.0
Percentiles for girls: Assembly										
5:0–5:5	30	11.1	13.0	13.0	14.0	15.0	15.6	16.0	17.0	18.0
5:6–5:11	30	9.0	11.0	12.3	13.4	14.0	15.6	16.0	17.0	20.0
6:0–6:5	30	14.0	16.0	16.0	16.0	17.0	18.0	20.0	22.0	23.9
6:6–6:11	30	16.0	17.0	18.0	19.0	20.0	21.0	22.7	25.6	27.8
7:0–7:5	30	14.0	15.2	17.0	18.0	19.5	21.6	22.0	24.0	24.9
7:6–7:11	30	14.0	16.0	17.0	18.4	19.5	21.6	23.4	25.8	26.9
8:0–8:5	30	16.0	17.0	20.0	21.0	22.0	23.0	23.0	24.8	28.9
8:6–8:11	30	18.0	19.2	20.3	21.4	23.0	24.6	27.4	31.8	32.0
9:0–9:5	30	18.0	19.0	20.3	22.0	23.5	26.0	29.0	31.8	16.0
9:6–9:11	30	22.1	23.2	26.0	27.0	28.0	31.0	32.0	34.8	37.9
10:0–10:5	30	20.3	23.2	26.0	27.0	28.0	29.0	29.7	30.8	35.8
10:6–10:11	30	24.1	27.0	28.3	29.4	30.5	31.6	35.7	37.8	39.8
11:0–11:5	30	25.1	28.0	29.3	31.4	32.5	34.0	35.7	37.0	40.9
11:6–11:11	30	22.2	25.4	28.3	31.0	34.5	37.0	39.0	40.0	41.0
12:0–12:5	30	28.0	31.0	32.0	34.0	34.0	34.6	36.7	39.0	43.6
12:6–12:11	30	24.0	28.0	30.3	32.8	35.0	36.0	38.7	41.7	45.7
13:0–13:5	40	27.0	31.2	32.3	33.4	35.0	37.6	38.0	39.0	41.9
13:6–13:11	30	29.5	33.0	34.9	36.4	38.0	38.0	40.0	42.0	44.1
14:0–14:5	30	25.3	30.2	34.0	34.0	36.0	38.0	40.7	43.0	45.9
14:6–14:11	30	27.1	28.2	30.3	32.0	33.0	35.2	37.7	40.8	44.9
15:0–15:5	30	28.7	29.8	31.7	33.6	35.5	38.4	41.3	43.2	50.2
15:6–15:11	23	23.2	29.4	33.0	36.8	39.0	40.0	41.0	43.0	47.8

Note: Data were derived from 1,334 normal schoolchildren.

Source: Gardner & Broman (1979).

Table 10–7. Mean Performance of Young Adults for the Purdue Pegboard

		Age groups				
		15–20	21–25	26–30	31–40	15–40
Females						
N		30	36	16	16	98
Preferred hand	M	16.69	16.64	17.25	15.94	16.64
	SD	2.16	2.31	1.88	1.61	2.10
Nonpreferred hand	M	16.10	15.89	16.13	15.63	15.95
	SD	1.57	1.79	1.50	1.89	1.68
Both hands	M	13.76	13.75	13.31	13.13	13.58
	SD	1.41	1.54	1.45	1.31	1.45
Assemblies	M	41.83	42.47	40.44	41.44	41.77
	SD	5.08	5.43	5.90	5.75	5.42
Males						
N		32	37	32	26	127
Preferred hand	M	15.56	15.44	16.22	15.35	15.65
	SD	1.52	1.71	1.81	1.72	1.71
Nonpreferred hand	M	15.09	15.08	15.41	15.12	15.17
	SD	1.42	1.98	2.08	1.77	1.82
Both hands	M	12.59	12.97	12.94	12.42	12.75
	SD	1.56	1.18	1.29	1.65	1.42
Assemblies	M	40.25	38.89	39.13	37.50	39.01
	SD	4.64	6.60	3.58	3.64	4.92

Note: Data were compiled from 225 healthy adults, largely right-handed (87.7%), with above average IQ, residing in a large city in Western Canada.

Source: Yeudall et al. (1986).

REFERENCES

Costa, L.D., Vaughan, H.G., Levita, E., & Farber, N. (1963). Purdue Pegboard as a predictor of the presence and laterality of cerebral lesions. *Journal of Consulting Psychology, 27,* 133–137.

Costa, L.D., Scarola, L.M., & Rapin, I. (1983). Purdue Pegboard scores for normal grammar school children. *Perceptual and Motor Skills, 18,* 748.

Fleishman, E.A., & Ellison, G.D. (1962). A factor analysis of fine manipulative tests. *Journal of Applied Psychology, 46,* 96–105.

Fleishman, E.A., & Hempel, W.E., Jr. (1954). A factor analysis of dexterity tests. *Personnel Psychology, 7,* 15–32.

Gardner, R.A., & Broman, M. (1979). The Purdue Pegboard: Normative data on 1334 school children. *Journal of Clinical Child Psychology, 8,* 156–162.

Mathiowetz, V., Rogers, S.L., Dowe-Keval, M., Donahoe, L., & Rennels, C. (1986). The Purdue Pegboard: Norms for 14 to 19-year-olds. *American Journal of Occupational Therapy, 40,* 174–179.

Rapin, I., Tourk, L.M., & Costa, L.D. (1966). Evaluation of the Purdue Pegboard as a screening test for brain damage. *Developmental Medicine and Child Neurology, 8,* 45–54.

Reddon, J.R., Gill, D.M., Gauk, S.E., & Maerz, M.D. (1988). Purdue Pegboard:

Table 10–8. Mean Performance of Older Adults for the Purdue Pegboard

		Age Groups		
		50–59	60–69	70+
Males				
N		10	12	8
Preferred hand	M	14.7	14.2	11.4
	SD	2.2	2.8	2.0
Nonpreferred hand	M	14.4	13.6	10.9
	SD	2.0	2.8	1.5
Both hands	M	12.1	10.1	8.4
	SD	1.9	.7	1.5
Assemblies	M	30.6	27.2	21.9
	SD	6.7	5.9	5.4
Females				
N		11	9	15
Preferred hand	M	14.5	14.7	13.2
	SD	1.9	1.0	1.5
Nonpreferred hand	M	14.0	14.0	12.6
	SD	2.2	1.9	2.0
Both hands	M	13.3	11.3	11.4
	SD	1.8	1.5	1.6
Assemblies	M	28.3	28.9	24.9
	SD	5.1	7.1	3.2

Note: Data were compiled from healthy volunteers living in Victoria, British Columbia.
Source: Strauss & Spreen (1990).

Test–retest estimates. *Perceptual and Motor Skills, 66,* 503–506.

Sappington, T.J. (1980). Measures of lateral dominance: Interrelationships and temporal stability. *Perceptual and Motor Skills, 50,* 783–790.

Sattler, J.M., & Engelhardt, J. (1982). Sex differences on Purdue Pegboard norms for children. *Journal of Clinical Child Psychology, 11,* 72–73.

Tiffin, J. (1968). *Purdue Pegboard: Examiner Manual.* Chicago: Science Research Associates.

Tiffin, J., & Asher, E.J. (1948). The Purdue Pegboard: Norms and studies of reliability and validity. *Journal of Applied Psychology, 32,* 234–247.

Vaughan, H.G., & Costa, L.D. (1962). Performance of patients with lateralized cerebral lesions: II. Sensory and motor tests. *Journal of Nervous and Mental Disease, 134,* 237–243.

Wilson, B.C., Iacovello, J.M., Wilson, J.J., & Risucci, D. (1982). Purdue Pegboard performance of normal preschool children. *Journal of Clinical Neuropsychology, 4,* 19–26.

Yeudall, L.T., Fromm, D., Reddon, J.R., & Stefanyk, W.O. (1986). Normative data stratified by age and sex for 12 neuropsychological tests. *Journal of Clinical Psychology, 42,* 918–946.

11

Adaptive Behavior and Personality Tests

Although an accurate description of a patient's abilities based on test results is of primary importance for the neuropsychologist in the diagnostic and rehabilitation process, relatively little can be inferred from such tests about the ability of the patient to function in the daily living situation at home, in new situations, or even in hospital or long-term care facilities. For the assessment of such abilities, other factors such as the functional capability to dress, eat, and cook for oneself, as well as personality variables including the premorbid personality features, the reaction to illness and disability, and direct personality alteration as a result of the brain lesion must be taken into account.

Adaptive behavior assessment is frequently (and expertly) done informally by the occupational therapist who relies on home visits, observation of the patient's behavior, and information provided by the primary caretaker (spouse, nurse, group home staff etc.). The development of formal instruments to assess adaptive behavior was first started in the field of mental retardation (Doll, 1935) and has more recently resulted in relatively sophisticated instruments: for example, the American Association on Mental Retardation (AAMR) Adaptive Behavior Scale (Fogelman, 1974; Nihira et al., 1969), the revised Vineland Adaptive Behavior Scales (Sparrow et al., 1984); and the System of Multicultural Pluralistic Assessment (SOMPA) (Mercer, 1977), which includes the Adaptive Behavior Inventory for Children in a comprehensive system of assessment stressing culture-fairness. The importance of adaptive behavior is stressed in all recent definitions of mental retardation which require significantly subnormal functioning in both intelligence *and* adaptive behavior (Grossman, 1983; Heber, 1959). Similar weight of adaptive behavior has usually not been placed on definitions of dementia and other neuropsychological disorders by neuropsychologists although it is of crucial importance in making recommendations about appropriate settings of care, in rehabilitative efforts, and in compensation litigation as well as in rating the severity of dementia. We recommend the use of the Vineland scales when such questions arise.

The assessment of the personality of the brain-damaged patient, on the other hand, has a long history in neuropsychology, dating back to descriptions of the "frontal lobe syndrome," the "catastrophic reactions of patients with missile wounds" or the search for "the epileptic personality." The need to consider the premorbid personality and the emotional reaction to the handicap (which is often related to premorbid personality features) has been recognized for some time. The need to make a distinction between the superficially similar behavior of patients with depression and dementia has led to further work in this field in more recent years. Yet, no generally accepted instrument covering these specific neuropsychological problems has been developed. Our selection covers the most useful instruments currently available, ranging from the traditional Rorschach Test, the Thematic Apperception Test (TAT), and the Minnesota Multiphasic Personality Inventory (MMPI), to two specific depression scales and the Personality Inventory for Children. None of these are administered routinely; rather a selection is made based on the nature of the presenting problem and the complaints and behavior of the patient during testing and interview.

REFERENCES

Doll, E.A. (1935). A genetic scale of social maturity. *American Journal of Orthopsychiatry, 5,* 180–188.

Fogelman, C. (Ed.). (1974). *Manual for the AAMD Adaptive Behavior Scales: 1974 Revision.* Washington, D.C.: American Association on Mental Deficiency.

Grossman, H.J. (1983). *Manual on Terminology and Classification in Mental Retardation* (Rev. ed.). Washington, D.C.: American Association on Mental Retardation.

Heber, R. (1959). *A Manual on Terminology and Classification in Mental Retardation.*

Monograph Suppl. *American Journal of Mental Deficiency.*

Mercer, J.R. (1977). *System of Multicultural Pluralistic Assessment.* New York: Psychological Corporation.

Nihira, K., Foster, R., Shellhaas, M., & Leland, H. (1969). *Adaptive Behavior Scales.* Washington, D.C.: American Association on Mental Deficiency.

Sparrow, S.S., Balla, D.A., & Cicchetti, D.V. (1984). *Vineland Adaptive Behavior Scales.* Circle Pines, Minn.: American Guidance Service.

BECK DEPRESSION INVENTORY (BDI)

Purpose

The purpose of this test is to screen for depression by self-report statements.

Source

The test can be ordered from the Psychological Corporation. P.O. Box 9959, San Antonio, Texas 78204-0959, or from Psychological Corporation, 55 Horner Avenue, Toronto, Ontario M8Z 4X6, Canada. Manual and 25 forms cost approximately $55 U.S. or $65.20 Cdn.

Description

The patient checks 21 four-choice statements presented on a single page [or on a 13-item short form (items with asterisks) by Beck & Beck, 1972] for the choice or choices most appropriate to him or her. The statements refer to the following areas:

*1. Sadness
*2. Pessimism/Discouragement
*3. Sense of Failure
*4. Dissatisfaction
*5. Guilt
6. Expectation of Punishment
*7. Self-Dislike
8. Self-Accusation
*9. Suicidal Ideation
10. Crying
11. Irritability

*12. Social Withdrawal
*13. Indecisiveness
*14. Unattractiveness
*15. Work Inhibition
16. Insomnia
*17. Fatigability
*18. Loss of Appetite
19. Weight Loss
20. Somatic Preoccupation
21. Loss of Libido

An example of the four-choice items follows:**

9. (0) I don't have any thoughts of killing myself.
   (1) I have thoughts of killing myself, but I would not carry them out.
   (2) I would like to kill myself.
   (3) I would kill myself if I had the chance.

Administration

Say to the patient: "**This questionnaire consists of twenty-one groups of statements. After reading each group of statements carefully, circle the number— zero, one, two, or three—next to the one statement in each group that best describes the way you've been feeling in the** *past week,* **including** *today.* **If several statements within a group seem to apply equally well, circle each one. Be sure to read all the statements in each group before making your choice.**"

At this point, hand a copy of the questionnaire to the patient and say: "**Here is a copy for you, so that you can follow along as I read.**" Read the entire group of statements in the first category (do not read the numbers appearing before the statements), then say: "**Now, which one of the statements best describes the way you have been feeling in the *past week*, including *today*?**"

If the patient indicates his or her choice by responding with a number, read back the statement corresponding to the number given by the patient, to clarify exactly which statement the examinee has selected. When the patient responds, "The first statement," he or she may mean (0) or (1). After it is apparent that the patient understands the numbering system, the numerical answer should be sufficient to indicate his choice.

The BDI may be given to the patient for self-administration or group administration, but it should be verified that the patient understands the purpose and the answering method for the test as outlined above.

Approximate Time for Administration

The time required is 5–10 minutes.

Scoring

The total score is obtained by adding the highest score circled for each of the 21 items. The maximum score is 63. Item 19 (weight loss) was designed to assess anorexic symptoms. If the patient responds affirmatively to the supplementary question "Are you trying to lose weight by eating less?" the score on that group is *not* added to the total score.

Comment

The BDI is just one of a score of depression scales (e.g., Hamilton, 1967; Lubin, 1965; Radloff, 1977; Zung, 1965) developed to detect depression in routine screening or research. It was selected because of its simplicity of administration, scoring, and interpretation. Since the items are very similar to many MMPI items, it need not be given if the MMPI is administered. Moreover, depression has been recognized as a multidimensional disorder. Bolon and Barling (1980), for example, extracted three factors (ideational depression, physiological depression, behavioral depression); Zung (1972) derived five factors from the Zung scale; and the MMPI delivers several subscales (pure depression, subjective depression, psychomotor retardation, physical malfunctioning, mental dullness, brooding), in addition to the D-scale† (Scale 2), that allow differential diagnostic considerations which screening inventories cannot provide because of their brevity.

†See note p. 399.

Test–retest reliability with 38 patients was above .90 and tended to follow the trend for each patient on depth of depression (Beck, 1970). Spearman–Brown reliability was .93, and internal consistency for test items .86 (Reynolds & Gould, 1981).

Concurrent validity coefficients with Lubin's Depression Adjective Checklist were .38–.50 for psychiatric patients and .66 in normals; with the Zung Self-Rating Depression scale, .79 in psychiatric patients and .54 in college students (Kerner & Jacobs, 1983); with the MMPI D-Scale, .75; with the Hamilton Rating Scale, and .78 and .82 in psychiatric patients (Schwab et al., 1967; Williams et al., 1973). Marsella et al. (1974) described correlations ranging from .32 to .74 with four other depression scales including the MMPI D-Scale (.63 in male, .73 in female Caucasian students). Beck (1970) also reported correlations of .66 between the BDI and psychiatric ratings of university students. The test also overlapped with the Beck anxiety checklist (.60) and the Maudsley obsessive–compulsive index (.49; Dent & Salkovskis, 1986) in nonclinical populations. It had only a modest negative correlation (−.41) with Rotter's (1966) Internalizing–Externalizing Scale and with Duttweiler's (1984) Internal Control Index (−.37), suggesting less depression in persons with internal control (Meyers & Wong, 1988). M. Ehrenberg (personal communication, 1990) reported a strong correlation (.68) with scales of self-efficacy in adolescents.

One disadvantage of the test is its obvious face validity, which is also apparent to the patient and hence makes dissimulation easy. It is not clear whether self-administration or administration by an examiner leads to different results.

For use in a neuropsychological setting, it should be noted that the BDI is not specifically designed to evaluate depression in elderly populations, and its value for the differential diagnosis of dementia versus depression has not been established. Plumb and Holland (1977) and Cavenaugh et al. (1983) recommend the use of the first 13 items as a cognitive affective subscale for estimating depression in patients with vegetative/somatic complaints, whereas the remaining 8 items tend to measure somatic/performance complaints.

Knight (1984) reports significant increases of the short form BDI scores with age in males, but not in females in their 70s and 80s, based on a survey of a small New Zealand community. We recommend the use of the Geriatric Depression Scale (Brink et al., 1982) for elderly subjects (see the following description). A report comparing the Geriatric Depression Scale with the BDI in 68 geriatric medical outpatients (Norris et al., 1987) and a study of depression in alcoholics (Tamkin et al., 1987) accurately identified patients with depression using both instruments. However, it was noted that the BDI's multiple-choice format makes it more difficult for elderly patients to respond, that some somatic content items make the BDI less suitable for them, and that neither instrument has been validated in patients with cognitive or sensory impairment.

Table 11–1. Interpretation Guidelines for the BDI

Short / Long form		
0–4	0–9	Normal range
5–7	10–15	Minimal depression (cutoff = 10.9[a], SD = 8.1)
8–11	16–19	Mild–moderate depression (cutoff = 18.7, SD = 10.2)
11–15	20–29	Moderate-to-severe depression (cutoff = 25.4, SD = 9.6)
16+	30–63	Severe depression (cutoff = 30.0, SD = 10.4)

[a]Cutoff points are based on Marsella et al. (1974) and Beck (1987).

Normative Data

There is no arbitrary score that can be used for all purposes to classify different degrees of depression. However, Table 11–1 provides suggested guidelines to interpret the full scale (Beck, 1987) and the short form (Beck & Beck, 1972). Some confirmation for these norms comes from a study with Dutch students (Bosscher, 1986) and British nonclinical populations (Dent & Salkovskis, 1986).

The BDI has not been used with children, but a well-researched, separate Children's Depression Inventory is available (Finch et al., 1985; Kovacs, 1983). In adolescents, an increase in scores on the long form from 8.9 to 12.3 between ages 13 and 17 has been reported (Baron, 1986; M. Ehrenberg, personal communication, 1990); scores for females were consistently higher than for males. An inference from a study by Kerner and Jacobs (1983) suggests that scores drop gradually with increasing age (mean for college freshmen, 8.8; seniors, 6.5). Marsella et al. (1974) reported similar values for college students which remained consistently higher for females; they were also consistently higher for Japanese and Chinese than for Caucasian students.

REFERENCES

Baron, P. (1986). Sex differences in the Beck Depression Inventory scores of adolescents. *Journal of Youth and Adolescence, 15*, 165–171.

Beck, A.T. (1970). *Depression: Causes and Treatment.* Philadelphia: University of Pennsylvania Press.

Beck, A.T. (1987). *Beck Depression Inventory: Manual.* San Antonio, Tex.: Psychological Corporation.

Beck, A.T., & Beck, R.W. (1972). Screening depressed patients in family practice. *Postgraduate Medicine, 52*, 81–85.

Bolon, K. & Barling, J. (1980). The measurement of self-rated depression: A multidi-

mensional approach. *Journal of Genetic Psychology, 137*, 309–310.

Bosscher, R.J. (1986). Reliability and validity of the BDI in a Dutch college population. *Psychological Reports, 58*, 696–698.

Brink, T.L., Yesavage, J.A., Owen, L., Heersema, P.H., Adey, M., & Rose, T.L. (1982). Screening tests for geriatric depression. *Clinical Gerontology, 1*, 37–43.

Cavenaugh, S.V., Clark, D.C., & Gibbons, R.D. (1983). Diagnosing depression in the hospitalized medically ill. *Psychosomatics, 24*, 809–815.

Dent, H.R., & Salkovskis, P.M. (1986). Clinical measures of depression, anxiety, and obsessionality in non-clinical populations. *Behavioral Research and Therapy, 24*, 689–691.

Duttweiler, P.C. (1984). The Internal Control Index: A newly developed measure of locus of control. *Educational and Psychological Measurement, 44*, 209–221.

Finch, A.J., Saylor, C.F., & Edwards, G.L. (1985). Children's Depression Inventory: Sex and grade norms for normal children. *Journal of Consulting and Clinical Psychology, 53*, 424–425.

Hamilton, M. (1967). Development of a rating scale for primary depressive illness. *British Journal of Social and Clinical Psychology, 6*, 278–296.

Kerner, S.A., & Jacobs, K.W. (1983). Correlation between scores on the Beck Depression Inventory and the Zung Self-Rating Depression Scale. *Psychological Reports, 53*, 969–970.

Knight, R.G. (1984). Some general population norms for the short form Beck Depression Inventory. *Journal of Clinical Psychology, 40*, 751–753.

Kovacs, M. (1983). The Children's Depression Inventory: A Self-Rated Depression Scale for School-Aged Youngsters. Unpublished manuscript, University of Pittsburgh.

Lubin, B. (1965). Adjective check lists for the measurement of depression. *Archives of General Psychiatry, 12*, 57–62.

Marsella, A.J., Sanborn, K.O., Kamboka, V., Shizuri, L., & Brennan, J. (1974). Cross-validation of self-report measures of depression among normal populations of Japanese, Chinese, and Caucasian ancestry. *Journal of Clinical Psychology, 30*, 281–287.

Meyers, L.S., & Wong, D.T. (1988). Validation of a new test of Locus of Control: The Internal Control Index. *Educational and Psychological Measurement, 48*, 753–761.

Norris, J.T., Gallagher, D., Wilson, A., & Winograd, C.H. (1987). Assessment of depression in geriatric medical outpatients: the validity of two screening measures. *Journal of the American Geriatrics Society, 35*, 989–995.

Plumb, M.M., & Holland, J. (1977). Comparative studies of psychological function in patients with advanced cancer. I: Self-reported depressive symptoms. *Psychosomatic Medicine, 39*, 264–279.

Radloff, L.S. (1977). The CES-D scale: A new self-report depression scale for research in the general population. *Applied Psychological Measurement, 1*, 385–401.

Reynolds, W.M., & Gould, J.W. (1981). A psychometric investigation of the standard and short form Beck Depression Inventory. *Journal of Consulting and Clinical Psychology, 49*, 306–307.

Rotter, J.B. (1966). Generalized expectancies for internal versus external control of reinforcement. *Psychological Monographs, 80* (Whole No. 609).

Schwab, J.J., Bialow, M.R., & Holzer, C.E. (1967). A comparison of two rating scales for depression. *Journal of Clinical Psychology, 23*, 45–46.

Tamkin, A.S., Carson, M.F., Nixon, D.H., & Hyer, L.A. (1987). A comparison among some measures of depression in male alcoholics. *Journal of Studies on Alcohol, 48*, 176–178.

Williams, J.G., Barlow, D.H., & Agras, W.S. (1973). Behavioral measurement of severe depression. *Archives of General Psychiatry, 16*, 321–325.

Zung, W.W.K. (1965). A self-rating depression scale. *Archives of General Psychiatry, 12*, 63–70.

Zung, W.W. (1972). How normal is depression? *Psychosomatics, 13*, 174–178.

GERIATRIC DEPRESSION SCALE

Other Test Name

Another test name is the Mood Assessment Scale.

Purpose

This test is a screening instrument to measure depression in the elderly.

Description

The GDS (Brink et al., 1982; Yesavage et al., 1983) consists of 30 yes/no questions designed for self-administration. The directionality of answers scored for depression changes randomly. The purpose of the scale is partially disguised by the title "Mood Assessment Scale" at the top of the questionnaire.

Administration

The examiner requests the patient to complete a simple questionnaire (Fig. 11–1) referring to changes in mood, and to answer the questions by circling yes or no, whichever appropriately describes his or her feelings at that time. Alternatively, the questions can be read to the patient, if there is any question about his or her ability to read or comprehend reading material.

Approximate Time for Administration

About 5–10 minutes is required.

Scoring

One point is given for each of the answers marked in bold in Scale 11–1.

Comment

The GDS was developed specifically for elderly subjects. It deliberately omits items dealing with guilt, sexuality, and suicide, which the authors considered inappropriate for elderly subjects. It includes items dealing with perceived locus of control that makes this test more suitable for hospitalized and long-term care subjects. The original item pool also included 12 items focusing on psychosomatic complaints, which were dropped because of poor item-total correlation. The item–total correlations of the current scale range from .32 to .83 with a mean of .56; internal consistency (alpha) was .94, and split-half reliability was .94. Retest reliability after one week was .85 (Koenig et al., 1988). Parmelee, Lawton, and Katz (1989) reported very similar internal consistency and reliability values in a group of 806 institutionalized persons between 61 and 99 years.

Mood Assessment Scale

1.	Are you basically satisfied with your life?	Yes/**No**
2.	Have you dropped many of your activities and interests?	**Yes**/No
3.	Do you feel that your life is empty?	**Yes**/No
4.	Do you often get bored?	**Yes**/No
5.	Are you hopeful about the future?	Yes/**No**
6.	Are you bothered by thoughts that you can't get out of your head?	**Yes**/No
7.	Are you in good spirits most of the time?	Yes/**No**
8.	Are you afraid that something bad is going to happen to you?	**Yes**/No
9.	Do you feel happy most of the time?	Yes/**No**
10.	Do you often feel helpless?	**Yes**/No
11.	Do you often get restless and fidgety?	**Yes**/No
12.	Do you prefer to stay home rather than go out and doing new things?	**Yes**/No
13.	Do you frequently worry about the future?	**Yes**/No
14.	Do you feel you have more problems with memory than most?	**Yes**/No
15.	Do you think it is wonderful to be alive now?	Yes/**No**
16.	Do you often feel downhearted and blue?	**Yes**/No
17.	Do you feel pretty worthless the way you are now?	**Yes**/No
18.	Do you worry a lot about the past?	**Yes**/No
19.	Do you find life very exciting?	Yes/**No**
20.	Is it hard for you to get started on new projects?	**Yes**/No
21.	Do you feel full of energy?	Yes/**No**
22.	Do you feel that your situation is hopeless?	**Yes**/No
23.	Do you think that most people are better off than you are?	**Yes**/No
24.	Do you frequently get upset about little things?	**Yes**/No
25.	Do you frequently feel like crying?	**Yes**/No
26.	Do you have trouble concentrating?	**Yes**/No
27.	Do you enjoy getting up in the morning?	Yes/**No**
28.	Do you prefer to avoid social gatherings?	**Yes**/No
29.	Is it easy for you to make decisions?	Yes/**No**
30.	Is your mind as clear as it used to be?	Yes/**No**

Figure 11–1. Geriatric Depression Scale. (*Source:* Brink et al., 1982; Yesavage et al., 1983.)

Factor analysis established a major factor of dysphoria (unhappiness, dissatisfaction with life, emptiness, downheartedness, worthlessness, helplessness) and minor factors of worry/dread/obsessive thought, and of apathy/withdrawal (Parmelee et al., 1989). Concurrent validity was established by correlations of .73 with the BDI (Hyer & Blount, 1984), of .84 with the Zung scale, and of .83 with the Hamilton scale (Yesavage et al., 1983, 1986). Similar correlations were obtained in elderly subjects 65–89 years old, using the Zung (.86) and the Gilleard scales (.89; Gilleard et al., 1981), although the wording of the GDS was found less confusing than for the other two scales (Hickie & Snowdon, 1987). Staff rating of depression correlated only moderately (.34; Parmelee et al., 1989).

Criterion validity was measured against the Research Diagnostic Criteria and reported as .82 (Yesavage & Brink, 1983). The age range for the populations studied by the authors of the scale has not been reported, except that subjects were specified as over 55 years old. Weiss et al. (1986) point out that further validation in elderly subjects over 75 years of age is needed since people at the higher age ranges show specific problems that are absent in younger subjects. Parmelee et al. (1989) found good agreement with ratings of minor, major, and no depression that were based upon clinical diagnoses and symptom checklists, although the false-negative rate in minor depression was fairly high (17.4%).

Yesavage et al. (1981) found the GDS useful in elderly subjects with physical illness (arthritis; mean for depressed subjects, 13.1, for nondepressed subjects, 5.10). Discrimination between mildly demented depressed and nondepressed subjects was satisfactory in three studies (Snowdon and Donnelly 1986, Stebbins and Hopp 1990, Yesavage 1987), but Brink (1984) admits that the test loses some validity in more severe dementia. Age and length of institutionalization did not affect the GDS scores (Parmelee et al., 1989). Discriminant validity for dementia versus depression was investigated in a study by Folstein et al. (1975). Depressed demented elderly showed a mean score of 14.72 (SD = 6.13), whereas nondepressed demented elderly had a mean score of only 7.49 (SD = 4.26). The difference between the two groups was significant ($p < .001$). No information about potential differences between self-administration and oral administration is available.

Normative Data

Table 11–2 lists normative data for the GDS, including sensitivity (correct classification of depressives) and specificity (correct classification of normals). It should be remembered that the GDS, like the BDI, is a screening instrument and not a diagnostic tool. The following cutoff points are recommended: normal, 0–9; mild depressives, 10–19; and severe depressives, 20–30. These values agree with those published by Hickie and Snowdon (1987).

Table 11–2. Geriatric Depression Scale: Normative Data for Elderly Subjects

Subjects	N	Mean	SD
Mild depression	26	15.05	4.34
Severe depression	34	22.85	5.07
Controls	40	5.75	4.34

	Cutoff scores		
	>8	>10	>13
Sensitivity	90	84	80
Specificity	80	95	100

Note: The distinction between mild and severe depression is based on Research Diagnostic Criteria (Spitzer et al., 1978).

Sources: Brink et al. (1982); Yesavage et al. (1983).

REFERENCES

Brink, T.L., Yesavage, J.A., Lum, O., Heersema, P.H., Adey, M., & Rose, T.S. (1982). *Clinical Gerontologist, 1,* 37–43.

Brink, T.L. (1984). Limitations of the GDS in cases of pseudodementia. *Clinical Gerontology, 2,* 60–61.

Folstein, M.F., Folstein, S.E., & McHugh, P.R. (1975). Mini Mental State: A practical method for grading the cognitive state of patients for the clinician. *Journal of Psychiatric Research, 12,* 189–198.

Gilleard, C.J., Willmott, M., & Vaddadi, K.S. (1981). Self-report measures of mood and morale in elderly depressives. *British Journal of Psychiatry, 138,* 230–235.

Hickie, C., & Snowdon, J. (1987). Depression scales for the elderly: GDS, Gilleard, Zung. *Clinical Gerontologist, 6,* 51–53.

Hyer, L., & Blount, J. (1984). Concurrent and discriminant validities of the GDS with older psychiatric patients. *Psychological Reports, 54,* 611–616.

Koenig, H.G., Meador, K.G., Cohen, H.J. & Blazer, D.G. (1988). Self-rated depression scales and screening for major depression in older hospitalized patients with medical illness. *Journal of the American Geriatrics Society, 36,* 699–796.

Parmelee, P.A., Lawton, M.P., & Katz, I.R. (1989). Psychometric properties of the Geriatric Depression scale among the institutionalized aged. *Psychological Assessment, 1,* 331–338.

Snowdon, J. & Donnelly, N. (1986). A study of depression in nursing homes. *Journal of Psychiatric Research, 20,* 327–333.

Spitzer, R.L., Edicott, J., & Robins, E. (1978). Research diagnostic criteria: Rationale and reliability. *Archives of General Psychiatry, 35,* 773–782.

Stebbins, G. & Hopp, G. (1990). Elderly residents' depression levels at admission and post admission to a long-term care facility. Unpublished manuscript, University of Victoria.

Weiss, I.K., Nagel, C.L., & Aronson, M.K. (1986). Applicability of depression scales to the old-old person. *Journal of the American Geriatrics Society, 34,* 215–218.

Yesavage, J. (1987). The use of self-rating depression scales in the elderly. In L.W. Poon (Ed.) *Handbook for Clinical Memory Assessment of Older Adults,* pp. 213–217. Washington, D.C.: American Psychological Association.

Yesavage, J., & Brink, T.L. (1983). Development and validation of a geriatric depression scale: A preliminary report. *Journal of Psychiatric Research, 17,* 37–49.

Yesavage, J.A., Brink, T.L., Rose, T.L., & Adey, M. (1986). The geriatric depression rating scale: Comparison with other self-report and psychiatric rating scales. In L. Poon (Ed.). *Handbook of Clinical Memory Assessment of Older Adults* (pp. 153–167). Washington, D.C.: American Psychological Association.

Yesavage, J.A., Brink, T.L., Rose, T.L., Lum, O., Huang, V., Adey, M.B., & Leirer, V.O. (1983). Development and validation of a geriatric depression rating scale: A preliminary report. *Journal of Psychiatric Research, 17,* 37–49.

Yesavage, J.A., Rose, T.L., & Lapp, D. (1981). *Validity of the Geriatric Depression Scale in Subjects with Senile Dementia.* Palo Alto, Cal.: Veterans Administration Medical Clinic.

MINNESOTA MULTIPHASIC PERSONALITY INVENTORY (MMPI)

Purpose

This test is a general personality assessment with objective questions.

Source

The MMPI manual, reusable booklets in English, French, or Spanish, scoring keys for basic and supplementary scales, and answer sheets can be ordered from the Institute of Psychological Research, Inc., 34 Fleury Street West, Montreal, Quebec H3L 1S9, Canada, for approximately $100 Cdn. or from National Computer Systems, P.O. Box 1416, Minneapolis, Minnesota 55440 for approximately $70 U.S. Tape-recorded questions and hand-scoring keys for 76 supplementary scales as well as computer scoring and interpretation services are also available. The MMPI-2 (described below) is available from both distributors for approximately $230 U.S. for the complete set.

Description

The MMPI is a self-administered test consisting of 566 true/false questions, published first by Hathaway and McKinley in 1943. Patients mark their answers on the two sides of the standard answer sheet which is then scored by overlay scoring keys for a variety of scales. Sixteen questions are repeated to facilitate the (now obsolete) op-scan computer scoring. Since the original 14 scales use only a portion of the total number of questions, a short version with 399 questions has been in use for some time. However, if use of any of the additional scales is intended, the long form is still required. Other more abbreviated forms of the MMPI were found not to be suitable as a substitute in patients with head injury (Alfano & Finlayson, 1987). A new addition is the "neurocorrected" MMPI-NC44 (Alfano et al. 1990) in which 44 items referring to potential valid manifestations of neurologic disorder were eliminated.

Numerous subscales and new scales have been developed over the years; the *MMPI Handbook* (Dahlstrom et al., 1975) lists over 550 scales, including some with neuropsychological content.

The MMPI-2 (Butcher et al., 1989) will probably gradually replace the MMPI in future years. The revision contains 567 items, uses the same (slightly revised) validity and clinical scales as well as the critical item list, but adds two new validity scales (response consistency scales) and a new set of 15 content scales, and eliminates duplicate, nonworking, objectionable, or outmoded items, and rewords 14% of the items in more modern language.

Administration

Instructions are printed on the front of the booklet. Briefly, patients are instructed to read each statement and to decide whether it is true or false as applied to themselves. Patients are then asked to mark their answers on the answer sheet, and are encouraged to answer all items. Reassurance may be given by stating that there are no right or wrong answers, and that the patient should answer each statement spontaneously and without lengthy deliberation. It is recommended that the test administrator check, during the initial 45 items and, if necessary, later during the test, whether the patient is following the item numbering correctly, since skipping items may invalidate the whole test. This is less likely in the lapboard booklet version, where the scoring sheet corresponds directly to the questions.

For poor readers, tape-recorded versions are available. Generally, a grade 7 reading ability is considered minimal (Ward & Ward, 1980). Butcher and Hosteller (1990) provide a detailed discussion of abbreviated MMPI and MMPI-2 administrations.

Approximate Time for Administration

The time required is 40–90 minutes.

Scoring

The test comes complete with overlay scoring keys for the original four validity and 10 clinical scales. Additional scoring keys for various subscales and newly developed research and clinical scales can be obtained (see source; also Psychological Assessment Resources Inc., P.O. Box 98, Odessa, Florida 33556) or made up by the user. Each scale produces a sum of answers relevant to that scale. These raw scores can then be transferred to the standard profile sheet which also provides corrections for some scales that are affected by a concealing attitude or by attempting to appear in a favorable light (K-Scale). Corrected scores, when plotted on the profile sheet, directly translate into T-scores based on the original standardization of the test in the 1940s.

Computer scoring by professional scoring services (e.g., Testscor, Inc., 2312 Snelling Avenue South, Minneapolis, Minnesota 55404; Institute of Psychological Research) as well as for personal computers (Williams, 1981), and a variety of computer interpretation services (e.g., National Computer Systems, which charges $3.65 to $4.60 depending on the number of cases) are available.

Comment

The MMPI has been criticized on the basis of its outdated standardization; its disregard of age effects; its poor item selection; and the phrasing, redundancy, and heterogeneity of its scales; as well as the overlap in its item content; however, the test continues to remain the most widely used personality test in the world, as documented by over 9,000 publications in 1977 (Graham, 1977) and by numerous foreign-language adaptations. Most reviewers agree that with adequate safeguards in interpretation, the test remains the most useful of currently existing personality tests.

Administration and interpretation of the MMPI require considerable training and reasonable familiarity with the literature. Several books are available for introduction and reference (e.g., Colligan et al., 1983; Dahlstrom & Welsh, 1960, 1975; Gilberstadt & Duker, 1965; Graham, 1977; Greene, 1980; Lanyon, 1968).

Reliability varies from scale to scale, but test–retest reliability has been reported as ranging from .50 to .90 (Buros, 1978), depending on whether they are reflecting "mood" or more "characterological" content, and the time elapsed between testing (Fekken & Holden, 1987; Hunsley et al., 1988). Retest reliability for the MMPI-2 after seven days is reported in the manual to range from .51 to .92; internal consistency estimates range from .24 to .91.

Validity has been investigated in numerous studies and also varies from scale to scale. The original validation was based on the discrimination between various psychiatric groups and normal subjects in the Minnesota area. However, discriminant validity for individual scales cannot be assumed; Davies et al. (1987), for example, found that Scale 8 (Sc) did not show significant differences between psychotic and normal adolescents. Instead, the profile as a whole is usually considered for interpretation. Subscales and new scales were in part based on construct (factor-analytic) as well as criterion validity. A recent study showed good discriminant validity between *DSM-III*-diagnosed* schizophrenia, major depression, and paranoid disorders (Patrick, 1988) and *DSM-III*-diagnosed personality disorders (Morey et al., 1988). Simulation of psychopathology is relatively easy to detect; however, many disturbed subjects can simulate normal profiles (Archer et al., 1987).

Rather than using the test for assigning diagnostic labels, most users interpret the high-point scales descriptively. DeMendonca (1984) summarized the most commonly used descriptor terms for the clinical scales:

Scale 1 (Hs): Immature, self-centered, complaining, demanding†

Scale 2 (D): Pessimistic, withdrawn, slow, timid, shy

Scale 3 (Hy): Immature, egotistical, suggestible, friendly

*DSM-III: Diagnostic and Statistical Manual of Mental Disorders, third edition.

†Note: The full names of the scales are: 1 Hypochondriasis (Hs); 2 Depression (D); 3 Hysteria (Hy); 4 Psychopathic Deviance (Pd); 5 Male-Female Scale (MF); 6 Paranoia (Pa); 7 Psychasthenia (Pt); 8 Schizophrenia (Sc); 9 Mania (Ma); and 0 Social Introversion (Si). The validity scales are: L Lie Scale; K Correction; and F Conformity. Since these terms are somewhat misleading or outdated, the scales are usually referred to only by number, abbreviation, or letter.

Scale 4 (Pd): Rebellious, resentful, impulsive, energetic, irresponsible

Scale 5 (Mf) (male): Fussy, idealistic, submissive, sensitive, effeminate

Scale 5 (Mf) (female): Aggressive, dominant, masculine

Scale 6 (Pa): Suspicious, hostile, rigid, distrustful

Scale 7 (Pt): Worrying, anxious, dissatisfied, sensitive, rigid

Scale 8 (Sc): Confused, imaginative, individualistic, impulsive, unconventional

Scale 9 (Ma): Energetic, enthusiastic, active, sociable, impulsive

Scale 0 (Si) Aloof, sensitive, inhibited, timid

In addition, the author lists possible descriptors for high-point scores on the three validity scales as follows:

L-Scale: Conventional, rigid, self-controlled

F-Scale: Restless, changeable, dissatisfied, opinionated

K-Scale: Defensive, inhibited

Another clinical use frequently recommended is an item-by-item check of 38 "critical Items" (Grayson, 1951) which require follow-up in subsequent interviews since they bear on serious symptoms, impulses, or experiences. The item numbers are 20, 27, 33, 37, 44, 48, 66, 69, 74, 85, 114, 121, 123, 133, 139, 146, 151, 156, 168, 179, 182, 184, 200, 202, 205, 209, 215, 251, 275, 291, 293, 334, 337, 339, 345, 349, 350, and 354.

Within the context of the neuropsychological examination, the most frequent indications for the use of the MMPI are differential diagnostic considerations (e.g., between psychosis and organic disorder), the question of functional disorders accompanying or resulting from brain damage, personality alterations after brain damage, and questions relating to the personality that may be relevant to the design of rehabilitation programs. For example, Gass and Russell (1986) found that elevation of the MMPI depression scale did not affect performance on the Wechsler Adult Intelligence Scales (WAIS) Digit Span subtest or on the Wechsler Memory Scale (WMS), whereas brain damage did. Similarly, Query and Megran (1984) found that MMPI-defined depression affected only the first trial of the Rey Auditory–Verbal Learning Test, but did not affect subsequent recall and recognition.

Diagnosis of "organicity," though attempted by some authors, is not a question that can or should be answered by the MMPI. For example, Hovey's (1964) five-item scale failed to discriminate among organic impairment, functional disorder, schizophrenics, alcoholics, and normals (Chaney et al., 1977; Maier & Abidin, 1967; Watson, 1971; Weingold et al., 1965). The "pseudoneurologic scale" (Shaw &

Matthews, 1965), designed to identify patients with neurological complaints not supported by neurological findings also failed to show adequate discriminating power (Watson, 1971). Similarly, the Psychiatric–Organic (P-O) Scale (Watson & Plemel, 1978) did not sufficiently discriminate between patients with functional and those with organic disorders (Golden et al., 1979). Recently, limited support for the validity of the P-O scale and Russell's MMPI key (Russell, 1975) in differentiating brain-damaged and schizophrenic patients has been reported (Carpenter & LeLieuvre, 1981; Horton & Wilson, 1981; Trifiletti, 1982). Meyerink et al. (1988) isolated items that are affected by the physical symptoms of multiple sclerosis and pointed out that the neurological disease process can artificially inflate four of the clinical scales (Scales 1, 2, 3, and 8).

Discrimination between anterior and posterior lesions has been attempted with the Parietal–Frontal (Pf) (Friedman, 1950) and the Caudality Scale (Williams, 1952), but a study by Reitan (1976) found inadequate support for this claim. More recently, however, Black and Black (1982) found qualified support for the "caudality" hypothesis of increased MMPI abnormality in posterior lesions if cognitive, motor, and sensory defects are controlled for. Moehle and Fitzhugh-Bell (1988) confirmed two earlier studies indicating that the MMPI is not sensitive to lateralization of lesion in brain-injured adults, although Cullum and Bigler (1988) found somewhat higher D-scale scores in adults with lesions in the left-hemisphere and in the posterior right hemisphere; in contrast, Gass and Russell (1987) found mild elevations of the D-scale in patients with right-hemisphere lesions although no left-hemisphere control group was used in this study.

A number of MMPI items, primarily scored in scales 1, 3, and 8, ask for symptoms that reflect potential neurological damage or dysfunction. Recently, Alfano et al. (1990) suggested that these 44 items be deleted when neurologically impaired clients are tested. The resulting "neurocorrected MMPI-NC44" showed somewhat lower clinical and F scales in neurological patients; the high-point remained unchanged in 46%, but the two-point code remained the same in only 29%, suggesting that the full-length MMPI should be interpreted with caution when given to neurological patients.

Since the MMPI-2 has only recently been published, studies regarding neuropsychologically relevant questions are not yet available.

Normative Data

T-score norms are automatically obtained by plotting raw scores into the (male or female) profile form, the most common base for interpreting the MMPI. These norms are based on data collected from friends and relatives of patients at the University of Minnesota as well as high school graduates, workers employed in the U.S. work program in the late 1930s, and general medical patients in the early

1940s. No allowance for age or education corrections is made. Traditionally, clinicians have learned to modify their interpretation of the profile on the basis of books, publications, teaching, and experience. For example, elevated clinical scales are quite common in college students 20–25 years of age.

Colligan et al. (1983, 1989) has published new norms based on 1,408 usable MMPIs collected from randomly selected households in Minnesota, Iowa, and Wisconsin. From these, 335 females and 305 males aged 18–99 years were drawn to constitute a census-matched subsample. The authors published new norms classified by sex and age groups (18–19, 20–29, 30–39, 40–49, 50–59, 60–69, 70+ years). In general, the new T-scores are 3–7 points above the original means. In normal elderly subjects, increases in Hs, D, and L scales were noted. Previous studies had shown these elevations, but also elevations in the K, Hy, and Sc scales (Lezak, 1987). Even larger changes were observed in a recent restandardization of the MMPI for teenagers (age 13–17), based on 691 girls and 624 boys (Archer, 1987; Colligan & Offord, 1989). Norms for 15- and 18-year-olds have also been published by Gottesman et al. (1987). Although far from ideal because of the geographic and racial (predominantly white) restriction, these norms are preferable and can and should be plotted on the profile to facilitate interpretation. Colligan and Offord (1987, 1988a, 1988b) also updated norms for Barron's Ego-Strength Scale, McAndrew's Alcoholism Scale, the A-Scale (anxiety/ maladjustment), the R-Scale (repression/control), and the Wiggins Content Scale. Gapinski et al. (1987) provided updated norms for the Augmented Purdue Content Scales; these are 10 scales that represent direct item content in the following areas: (1) anxiety/tension, (2) somatic complaints, (3) cognitive/sensory deficits, (4) paranoid ideation, (5) sensorimotor disturbance, (6) emotional lability, (7) interpersonal conflicts, (8) personal/social inadequacy, (9) stereotypic feminine interests, and (10) brooding/distractibility. They also updated norms for 30 direct-content subscales within the validity and clinical scales. Again, norms for adolescents have become available (Colligan et al., 1988). Normative data for other scales and subscales often remain unreplicated, and have not been updated.

The MMPI-2 has been restandardized for a randomly chosen sample of 2,600 adults between 18 and 90 years of age, which was representative of the 1980 U.S. census in terms of age, ethnic origin, sex, education, socioeconomic status, and geographic distribution. Uniform T-scores were prepared for all scales, but age-appropriate norms are not available. Comparability with the original MMPI has been maintained as far as possible.

REFERENCES

Alfano, D.P., & Finlayson, M.A. (1987). Comparison of standard and abbreviated MMPIs in patients with head injury. *Rehabilitation Psychology, 32,* 67–76.

Alfano, D.P., Finlayson, M.A.J., Stearns,

G.M., & Neilson, P.M. (1990). The MMPI and neurologic dysfunction: profile configuration and analysis. *Clinical Neuropsychologist, 4,* 69–79.

Archer, R.P. (1987). *Using the MMPI with Ad-*

olescents. Hillsdale, N.J.: Lawrence Earlbaum.

Archer, R.P., Gordon, R.A., & Kirchner, F.H. (1987). MMPI response-set characteristics among adolescents. *Journal of Personality Assessment, 51*, 506–516.

Black, F.W., & Black, I.L. (1982). Anterior–posterior locus of lesion and personality: Support for the caudality hypothesis. *Journal of Clinical Psychology, 38*, 468–477.

Buros, O.K. (1978). *The Eighth Mental Measurement Yearbook*. Highland Park, N.Y.: Gryphon Press.

Butcher, J.N., Dahlstrom, W.G., Graham, J.R., Tellegen, A.M., & Kaemmer, B. (1989). *MMPI-2: Minnesota Multiphasic Personality Inventory – 2*. Manual for Administration and Scoring. Minneapolis: University of Minnesota Press.

Butcher, J.N. & Hostetler, K. (1990). Abbreviating MMPI administration: What can be learned from the MMPI for the MMPI-2? *Psychological Assessment: A Journal of Consulting and Clinical Psychology, 2*, 12–21.

Carpenter, C.B., & LeLieuvre, R.B. (1981). The effectiveness of three MMPI scoring keys in differentiating brain damaged women from schizophrenic women. *Clinical Neuropsychology, 3*, 18–20.

Chaney, E.F., Erickson, R.C., & O'Leary, M.R. (1977). Brain damage and five MMPI items with alcoholic patients. *Journal of Clinical Psychology, 33*, 307–308.

Colligan, R.C., Greene, R.L., Gapinski, M.P., Archer, R.P., & Lingoes, J.C. (1988). MMPI Subscales and Profile Interpretation: Harris and Lingoes Revisited. Mimeo. Symposium, 96th Annual APA Convention.

Colligan, R.C., & Offord, K.P. (1989). The aging MMPI: Contemporary norms for contemporary teenagers. *Mayo Clinic Proceedings, 64*, 3–27.

Colligan, R.C., Osborne, D., Swenson, W.M., & Offord, K.P. (1983). *The MMPI: A Contemporary Normative Study of Adults*. New York: Praeger. [2nd ed. (1989). Odessa, Fla.: Psychological Assessment Resources.]

Colligan, R.R., & Offord, K.P. (1987). Resilience reconsidered: Contemporary MMPI Normative data for Barron's ego strength scale. *Journal of Clinical Psychology, 43*, 467–472.

Colligan, R.C., & Offord, K.P. (1988a). Changes in MMPI factor scores: Norms for the Welsh A and R dimensions from a contemporary sample. *Journal of Clinical Psychology, 44*, 142–148.

Colligan, R.C., & Offord, K.P. (1988b). Contemporary norms for the Wiggins Content Scales: A 45-year update. *Journal of Clinical Psychology, 44*, 23–32.

Cullum, C.M., & Bigler, E.D. (1988). Short-form MMPI findings in patients with predominantly lateralized cerebral dysfunction: Neuropsychological and computerized axial tomography-derived parameters. *Journal of Nervous and Mental Disease, 176*, 332–342.

Dahlstrom, W.G., & Welsh, G.S. (1960, 1975). *An MMPI Handbook: A Guide To Use in Clinical Practice and Research* (Vols. 1 & 2). Minneapolis: University of Minnesota Press.

Davies, A., Lachar, D., & Gdowski, C. (1987). Assessment of PIC and MMPI scales in adolescent psychosis: A caution. *Adolescence, 22*, 571–577.

DeMendonca, M., Elliott, L., Goldstein, M. McNeill, J. Rodriguez, R., & Zelkind, I. (1984). An MMPI-based behavior descriptor/personality trait list. *Journal of Personality Assessment, 48*, 483–485.

Fekken, G.C., & Holden, R.R. (1987). Assessing the person reliability of an individual MMPI protocol. *Journal of Personality Assessment, 51*, 123–132.

Friedman, S.H. (1950). *Psychometric Effects of Frontal and Parietal Lobe Damage*. Unpublished doctoral dissertation, University of Minnesota, Minneapolis.

Gapinski, M.P., Colligan, R.C., & Offord, K.P. (1987). A new look for the old MMPI scales: Contemporary norms for the augmented Purdue subscales. *Journal of Clinical Psychology, 43*, 669–682.

Gass, C.S., & Russell, E.W. (1986). Differential impact of brain damage and depression on memory test performance. *Journal of Consulting and Clinical Psychology, 54*, 261–263.

Gass, C.S., & Russell, E.W. (1987). MMPI correlates of performance intellectual deficits in patients with right hemisphere lesions. *Journal of Clinical Psychology, 43,* 484–489.

Gilberstadt, H., & Duker, J. (1965). *A Handbook for Clinical and Actuarial MMPI Interpretation.* Philadelphia: W.B. Saunders.

Golden, C.J., Sweet, J.J., & Osmon, D.C. (1979). The diagnosis of brain damage by the MMPI: A comprehensive evaluation. *Journal of Personality Assessment, 43,* 138–142.

Gottesman, I.I., Hanson, D.R., Kroeker, T.A., & Briggs, P.F. (1987). New MMPI normative data and power-transformed T-score tables for the Hathaway–Monachesi Minnesota cohort of 14,019 15-year-olds and 3,674 18-year-olds. In R.P. Archer (Ed.), *Using the MMPI with Adolescents* (pp. 241–297). Hillsdale, N.J.: Lawrence Earlbaum.

Graham, J.R. (1977). *The MMPI: A Practical Guide.* New York: Oxford University Press.

Graham, J.R. (1987). *The MMPI: A Practical Guide* (2nd ed.). New York: Oxford University Press.

Graham, J.R. (1990). *The MMPI-2: A Practical Guide.* New York: Oxford University Press.

Grayson, H.M. (1951). *A Psychological Admissions Testing Program and Manual.* Los Angeles: Veterans Administration Center, Neuropsychiatric Hospital.

Greene, R.L. (1980). *The MMPI: An Interpretive Manual.* New York: Grune & Stratton.

Hathaway, S.R., & McKinley, J.C. (1943). *Booklet for the Minnesota Multiphasic Personality Inventory.* New York: Psychological Corporation.

Horton, A.M., & Wilson, F.M. (1981). Cross-validation of the Psychiatric–Organic (P-O) special scale of the MMPI. *Clinical Neuropsychology, 3,* 1–3.

Hovey, H.B. (1964). Brain lesions and five MMPI items. *Journal of Consulting Psychology, 28,* 78–79.

Hunsley, J., Hanson, R.K., & Parker, K.C. (1988). A summary of the reliability and stability of MMPI scales. *Journal of Clinical Psychology, 44,* 44–46.

Lanyon, R.I. (1968). *A Handbook of MMPI*

Group Profiles. Minneapolis: University of Minnesota Press.

Lezak, M.D. (1987). Norms for growing older. *Developmental Neuropsychology, 3,* 1–12.

Maier, L.R., & Abidin, R.R. (1967). Validation attempt of Hovey's five-item MMPI index for central nervous system disorder. *Journal of Consulting Psychology, 31,* 542.

Meyerink, L.H., Reitan, R.M., & Selz, M. (1988). The validity of the MMPI with multiple sclerosis patients. *Journal of Clinical Psychology, 44,* 764–769.

Moehle, K.A., & Fitzhugh-Bell, K.B. (1988). Laterality of brain damage and emotional disturbance in adults. *Archives of Clinical Neuropsychology, 3,* 137–144.

Morey, L.C., Blashfield, R.K., Webb, W.W., & Jewell, J. (1988). MMPI scales for *DSM-III* personality disorders: A preliminary validation study. *Journal of Clinical Psychology, 44,* 47–50.

Patrick, J. (1988). Concordance of the MCMI and the MMPI in the diagnosis of three *DSM-III* Axis I disorders. *Journal of Clinical Psychology, 44,* 186–190.

Query, W.T., & Megran, J. (1984). Influence of depression and alcoholism on learning, recall, and recognition. *Journal of Clinical Psychology, 40,* 1097–1100.

Reitan, R.M. (1976). Neurological and physiological bases of psychopathology. *Annual Review of Psychology, 27,* 189–216.

Russell, E.W. (1975). Validation of a brain-damage vs. schizophrenia MMPI key. *Journal of Clinical Psychology, 31,* 659–661.

Shaw, D.J., & Matthews, C.G. (1965). Differential MMPI performance of brain-damaged vs. pseudo-neurologic groups. *Journal of Clinical Psychology, 21,* 405–408.

Trifiletti, R.J. (1982). Differentiating brain damage from schizophrenia: A further test of Russell's MMPI key. *Journal of Clinical Psychology, 38,* 39–44.

Ward, L.C., & Ward, J.W. (1980). MMPI readability reconsidered. *Journal of Personality Assessment, 44,* 387–389.

Watson, C.G. (1971). An MMPI scale to separate brain-damaged from schizophrenics. *Journal of Consulting and Clinical Psychology, 36,* 121–125.

Watson, C.G., & Plemel, D. (1978). An MMPI scale to separate brain-damaged from functional psychiatric patients in neuropsychiatric settings. *Journal of Consulting and Clinical Psychology, 36,* 121–125.

Weingold, H.P., Dawson, J.G., & Kael, H.C. (1965). Further examination of Hovey's "index" for identification of brain lesions: Validation study. *Psychological Reports, 16,* 1098.

Williams, H.L. (1952). The development of a caudality scale for the MMPI. *Journal of Clinical Psychology, 8,* 293–297.

Williams, R.J. (1981). User's Manual and Interpretive Guide for "MMPI/TRS-80 Computer Program" MMPI Subscales and Selected Research Scales. Unpublished manuscript.

PERSONALITY INVENTORY FOR CHILDREN (PIC)

Purpose

This test is a personality evaluation through a parent questionnaire.

Source

Revised manuals, administration booklets, answer sheets, and scoring keys can be obtained from Western Psychological Services, 12031 Wilshire Boulevard, Los Angeles, California 90025, at a cost of about $175 U.S. Computer scoring and interpretation disks are available from the same source. A young children's version (ages 3–6 years) is also available, but will not be discussed in this context.

Description

The PIC (Wirt et al., 1984) is a true/false statement questionnaire for the parent, modeled along lines similar to the MMPI. The full-length version contains 600 statements (e.g., "My child has little self-confidence," "Other children look upon my child as a leader"). The revised format booklet allows the scoring of four broad factor dimensions of childhood psychopathology (externalizing behavior, internalizing behavior, social incompetence, cognitive dysfunction), based on the first 131 items (Part I) only. The first 280 items (Parts I and II) allow scoring of abbreviations of the four dimensions and 12 clinical scales (achievement, intellectual skills, development, somatic concerns, depression, family relations, delinquency, withdrawal, anxiety, psychosis, hyperactivity, social skills). The first 421 items (Parts I, II, and III) allow scoring of all scales in full, whereas the 600-item version is needed if scoring of research scales is desired.

Administration

Since the PIC is designed for self-administration by the parent, instructions are presented on the front of the question booklet. Briefly, the test is introduced as an inventory of statements about children and family relationships. The parent or primary caregiver is asked to read each statement and decide if it is true or false as applied to the child, and to mark the answer sheet accordingly.

Approximate Time for Administration

The test requires 1–1½ hours unless one of the shortened versions is used.

Scoring

The 12 clinical scales, the three validity scales (assessing dimensions of underreporting, random reporting, or exaggeration), the one screening scale ("adjustment," for any type of psychopathology) and the four factor scales are scored by using overlay templates and counting the total number of items of each scale marked in the appropriate direction. The clinical scales reflect concern on the part of the parent about the following areas: (1) Achievement, (2) Intellectual Screening (scored separately for ages 6 through 10+), (3) Development, (4) Somatic Concern, (5) Depression, (6) Family Relations, (7) Delinquency, (8) Withdrawal, (9) Anxiety, (10) Psychosis, (11) Hyperactivity, and (12) Social Skills. The totals for each scale are inserted into the profile form which automatically converts the scores into T-scores similar to the MMPI.

Comment

The PIC should be filled out by both parents independently. Use of the 421- or the 280-item version is recommended. Use of the full-length version allows the scoring (also computer scoring) of several research scales that may be of interest in individual cases: ACDM (Assessment of Career Decision Making), BCAS (Barclay Classroom Assessment System), DP-II (Developmental Profile II, ISI (Interpersonal Style Inventory), LBC (Louisville Behavior Checklist), MSI (Marital Satisfaction Inventory), MDQ (Menstrual Distress Questionnaire), MKAS (Meyer–Kendall Assessment Survey), MDI (Multiscore Depression Inventory), PHCSC (Piers–Harris Children's Self-Concept Scale), TSCS (Tennessee Self-Concept Scale), TSCS:DC (Tennessee Self-Concept Scale – Diagnostic Classification Report), VII (Vocational Interest Inventory). An interpretative guide is available (Lachar & Gdowski, 1979).

The reliability, reported in the manual, is good (mean alpha of .74 in a heterogeneous clinic sample of 1,226 clients), and does not drop seriously when the short form is used. The average retest correlation after 4–72 days was .86 (lowest correlation of .46 for Defensiveness); the values were similar for the shortened versions. Retest reliability in normals after two weeks was .89 (range .70 to .93); for preschoolers with the short form, retest reliability after two weeks ranged from .77 to .92, with the exception of somatic concerns (.59) and defensiveness (.31) (Keenan & Lachar, 1988). Between-parents agreement defined as scores within 10 T-scale points was 75% for normals, but less in parents of clinical cases. Father-produced profiles appear to have limited validity. However, psychopathology of the mother (as measured by the MMPI) does not appear to limit the predictive accuracy of the PIC (Lachar et al., 1987).

Validity was originally established by selecting items that correlated highly with criterion group membership, then further refined to achieve maximum correlation. Sex effects on 18 of the scales led to the construction of profiles for males and females. Since its first publication in 1977, numerous studies have supported the validity of the PIC. Davies et al. (1987), however, point out that the profile as a whole should be considered for interpretation since the psychosis scale alone did not significantly discriminate between psychotic and normal adolescents. Nor should the other clinical scales be interpreted as diagnostic for specific types of pathology. T-scores of 79 and higher are considered as indicating significant concern in the respective area.

Correlations between parent checklists on behavioral observations and PIC scales are generally good, whereas those with checklists filled out by professionals and teachers tend to be poorer. Correlational validity with other instruments, such as the Child Behavior Checklist and the MMPI, is high for several of the PIC scales. Discrimination between impaired and normal preschoolers was high (91% correct classifications; Keenan & Lachar, 1988). Kline et al. (1987b) reported good discriminant validity when the PIC was used to predict intellectual, academic, and classroom placement, as well as attentional deficit and emotional impairment. Similarly, Clark et al. (1987) reported good identification of salient personality and cognitive features in learning-disabled, emotionally disturbed, and intellectually handicapped children.

The cognitive scales of the PIC are no substitute for the measurement of intelligence. Beck and Spruill (1987) found only minimal correlations with the WISC-R (.24–.46) and with the Arithmetic score on the Wide Range Achievement Test (WRAT; .06–.29), although correlations with WRAT Reading and Spelling were significant (.29–.41). Cognitive impairment in preschoolers was detected with some success (correlation with the McCarthy Scales, .38–.59), but correct classification of normal preschoolers was poor (Byrne et al., 1987). On the other hand, Kline et al. (1987a) report 90% correct classification between groups of children with autism, mental retardation, and pervasive developmental disorder, and Clark et al. (1987) found correlations of .56, .49, and .56 between the Wechsler Intelligence Scale for Children – Revised (WISC-R) and the achievement, intellectual screening, and development scales, respectively. These latter results are probably due to the wide range of intelligence sampled in these studies.

In neuropsychological settings, it is important to remember that, like the MMPI, the PIC is not designed to detect neurological impairment in children. It also, of course, reflects only the parent's perception of their child's problems, and does not objectively measure the child's problems directly. The PIC should therefore be used as a supplement to the parent interview, and as a screening instrument to point up areas of parental concern and potential emotional and behavioral problems. An attempt to discriminate between groups of normal children and children with somatoform, neurologic, and chronic medical disorders (Pritchard et al., 1988) found significant group differences, but failed to distinguish among the three groups with disorders. The hyperactivity scale is an adequate substitute for specific questionnaires for attention deficit syndrome with hyperactivity (e.g., Conners, 1973); in fact, it may be superior to such scales because of the availability of validity scales in the PIC.

Normative Data

The normative data from which the profiles were created are based on a sufficiently large data base that exists for children 6–16 years old; this data base takes into account the U.S. census in terms of race and socioeconomic status.

REFERENCES

Beck, B.L., & Spruill, J. (1987). External validation of the cognitive triad of the Personality Inventory for Children: Cautions on interpretation. *Journal of Consulting and Clinical Psychology, 55,* 441–443.

Byrne, J.M., Smith, D.J., & Backman, J.E. (1987). Cognitive impairment in preschoolers: Identification using the Personality Inventory for Children. *Journal of Abnormal Child Psychology, 15,* 239–246.

Clark, E., Kehle, T.J., Bullock, D., & Jenson, W.R. (1987). Convergent and discriminant validity of the Personality Inventory for Children. *Journal of Psychoeducational Assessment, 2,* 99–106.

Conners, C.K. (1973). Rating scales for use in drug studies with children. *Psychopharmacology Bulletin, 3,* 24–29.

Davies, A., Lachar, D., & Gdowski, C. (1987). Assessment of PIC and MMPI scales in adolescent psychosis: A caution. *Adolescence, 22,* 571–577.

Keenan, P.A., & Lachar, D. (1988). Screening preschoolers with special problems: Use of the Personality Inventory for Children (PIC). *Journal of School Psychology, 26,* 1–11.

Kline, R.B., Lachar, D., & Boersma, D.C. (1987a). A personality inventory for children (PIC) profile typology: III. Relationship to cognitive functioning and classroom placement. *Journal of Psychoeducational Assessment, 4,* 327–339.

Kline, R.B., Maltz, A., Lachar, D., Spector, S., & Fischhoff, J. (1987b). Differentiation of infantile autistic, child-onset pervasive developmental disorder, and mentally retarded children with the Personality Inventory for Children. *American Journal of Child Psychiatry, 15,* 839–843.

Lachar, D. & Gdowski, C.L. (1979). *Actuarial Assessment of Child and Adolescent Personality: An Interpretive Guide for the Personality Inventory for Children.* Los Angeles: Western Psychological Services.

Lachar, D., Kline, R.B., & Gdowski, C.L. (1987). Respondent pathology and interpretive accuracy of the Personality Inventory for Children: The evaluation of a "most reasonable" assumption. *Journal of Personality Assessment, 51,* 165–177.

Pritchard, C.T., Ball, J.D., Culbert, J., & Faust, D. (1988). Using the Personality Inventory for Children to identify children with somatoform disorders: MMPI findings revisited. *Journal of Pediatric Psychology, 13,* 237–245.

Wirt, R.D., Lachar, D., Klinedinst, J.K., & Seat, P.D. (1984). *Multidimensional Description of Child Personality: A Manual for the Personality Inventory for Children – Revised.* Los Angeles: Western Psychological Services.

RORSCHACH TEST

Purpose

This is a projective test requiring interpretation of (free association to) black and colored inkblots.

Source

The boxed plates can be ordered from Psychological Assessment Resources, Inc., P.O. Box 998, Odessa, Florida 33556, for $70 U.S. Location charts are available for $16.00 U.S. An alternate form, the Behn–Rorschach Test, is available from the Swiss publisher Hans Huber, Länggass-Strasse 78, Berne.

Description

This "classic" test consists of 10 stimulus cards. Each card contains symmetrical "inkblot" shapes in black, black and red, or several colors. We prefer this test over similar tests with larger numbers of cards in which only one response per card is allowed (Holtzman et al., 1970).

Administration

Administration of the Rorschach Test should not be attempted without previous instruction and supervised experience with the test. Various authors differ slightly in their administration procedure. Our administration generally follows Klopfer (1954) and Klopfer and Davidson (1977). Other manuals are by Aaronow and Reznikoff (1984), Exner (1974), and Phillips and Smith (1980). The test administration is deliberately unstructured, forcing the individual to deal with the situation in his or her own manner. After some rapport has been established with the patient, a brief introductory statement is made—for example: **"I will show you some cards and I would like you to tell me what you see. There are no right or wrong answers on this test. Just tell me everything you see."** The first card is presented and the subject is asked: **"Tell me what you see on this card. Tell me what this could be. Tell me everything you see."** Questions directed by the subject to the examiner should be answered as noncommittally as possible ("That is entirely up to you"; Klopfer, 1954, p. 7), and conversations and discussions during testing should be avoided. For anxious subjects, some reassurance ("good," "fine") may·be given. During the presentation of the first three cards, the subject should be encouraged to give as many responses as possible, and to rotate the plates. If the subject produces a very large number of responses, it should be pointed out that it is not important to see how many responses the individual can produce. Occasionally, it may be necessary actually to limit the number of responses.

After completion of the last card, the examiner should explain to the subject that the cards will be presented again to allow the examiner to see exactly where on the card each response of the subject was seen. Repeat the response to the subject, and inquire by asking the subject to outline the figure with his or her finger on the card (e.g., "You said this was a pretty bear rug. Please show me where on the card you saw this"). Additional scoring sheets with all 10 cards in miniature form are available from the publisher and allow the examiner to make notations, circle the parts outlined by the subject, etc. At the same time, the inquiry subtly extends to the determinants of each response (i.e., form, color, etc.) unless it is quite clear from the first answer (e.g., "What made it look like a bear rug? Does this also belong to it? What makes it look pretty?").

Approximate Time for Administration

The time required is 15–30 minutes.

Scoring

The examiner should prepare recording sheets (standard size paper held sideways not lengthwise) by folding (or dividing by lines down the page) blank paper into three approximately equal sections. The left-hand section is used to keep a protocol of everything said by the subject, the time in minutes and seconds for the presentation of each card, and the time when the first response is given, the rotated position of the card, as well as any interjections or instructions made by the examiner. The second column is used for recording of the responses given during the inquiry. The simple example (Fig. 11–2) (left column) illustrates the method of recording. The third column of the page is used for scoring of the responses. For an experienced practitioner, a preliminary scoring can be combined with the inquiry process; the attempted scoring may lead to additional questions during the inquiry (e.g., "Is it moving? What makes you think of a butterfly"), particularly when the possibility of color, shading, movement, or unusual (original) responses or response combinations needs to be explored. Although formal scoring of each response with either Klopfer's, Beck et al.'s (1961), or Exner's (1974, 1978, 1982) system is desirable, many practitioners have abandoned the practice of calculating the many totals and percentage values in a tabulation sheet (e.g., animal percentage, F+ percentage, popular response percentage, etc.), which are highly dependent on the total number of responses. (For a proposed adjustment, see Morey, 1982). Instead, they view the Rorschach protocol as a reflection of the cognitive processes of the individual, observing rather than calculating cognitive flexibility or rigidity, perseverative tendencies, emotional reaction to color or shading, the ability to recoup after a delayed color response (see responses 3, 4, and 5 in the example above), to free-associate some of the more common responses, the accuracy of form, especially in novel ("original") responses, and the presence of responses suggestive of psychopathology.

Comment

Interscorer agreement was reported as .87 (De Cato, 1983, 1984). Retest reliability for 6-year-old children after 24 months ranged from .86 for active movement to .13 for inanimate movement; for adults after 36–39 months, from .87 for human movement to .31 for inanimate movement; for adults after seven days, from .91 for active movement to .28 for inanimate movement; and for 8-year-olds after three to four days, from .94 for active movement to .27 for inanimate movement (Exner, 1980; Haller & Exner, 1985). Odd–even split-half reliabilities ranged from .89 for the total number of responses to .39 for form movement (Wagner et al., 1986). A meta-analysis by Parker (1983) reported predictive and correlational validity co-

Response Record	Inquiry	Explanation of Response Record (Col. 1)
I. 8.50–20″		I = Card 1
		8.50–20″ Card 1 was presented at 8:50 a.m. + 20 seconds.
1./\ 20″ The wings of a bat.	At first I saw only those wings, but then the whole thing seemed like a bat.	1. First response. 20″ It took 20 seconds before participant responded to this card. /\ Card in upright position
2.>	A large-winged animal ready to pounce down on its prey.	Just this upper part, wings and head raised, claws down here.	2. Second response > Card in rotated position
II. 8.52–10″		II. 8.52–10″ Time when second card was presented
3./\ 45″ There are two red things,	They are here on the side, just blotches, I can't think of what it could be.	3. /\ 45″ It took 45 seconds to produce first response. (consecutively numbered #3) to this card.
4. 5.	Two black things, and Another red thing.	Like shadow images of people. Could be a butterfly.	4. No upright signs needed if patient does not rotate card.

Figure 11–2. Rorschach Test sample response record/scoring sheet.

efficients of .45–.50 and higher. Garwood (1978) reported good predictive validity for success in psychotherapy within 30 weeks. For a more recent approach to scoring, interpretation, and data on construct validity and reliability, see Lerner (1980).

The long history of this test has led to many suggested usages, including the "screening for organicity" (Oberholzer, 1931; Piotrowski, 1937). Numerous publications have dealt with the application of the test for purposes of psychoanalytic usage, for personality and psychiatric diagnoses, and for the detection of specific organic disorders. Norms for "organic," schizophrenic, normals, and even for reading-disabled children (Alheidt, 1980) and adult offenders (Prandoni & Swartz, 1978) have been published. Because of the multiple determination of the responses, the open-ended, free-association response form, and the deliberate ambiguity of the stimuli, severe criticism has been expressed about the validity of the test in terms of strict psychometric standards, and its suitability for statistical analysis. However, more recently the test has been reevaluated as a sensitive measure of clinical interaction, which may be an indispensable tool in the hands of the skilled clinician and which may be suitable for research with both a psychometric and a cognitive approach (Weiner, 1977) or as a "type of structured interview" (Howes, 1981). A meta-analysis by Atkinson (1986) of studies with the Rorschach and the MMPI suggested that there is no difference between the two tests in conceptually designed validity studies.

In relation to neuropsychological assessment, Lezak (1983) mentions that the test can be evaluated as a measure of the patient's perceptual abilities, as a test of processing and integrating multiple stimuli, as a measure of the patient's certainty of his or her own perceptions, and as a measure of reaction time. Although all of these factors are aspects of the Rorschach protocol, many other neuropsychological tests provide more specific and more accurate measures of these abilities.

We use the test only secondarily for the measurement of these basic features, and, instead, treat it as a measure of changes of cognitive style and personality as well as an indicator of primary or secondary functional disorders of personality. For example, impoverished thinking in dementia frequently results in very few, poorly perceived, perseverative responses; neurotic or psychotic intrusions are frequently noted in unusual reactions to some of the plates and "poor original" responses on many cards or even in an isolated response or two. Disinhibition and other frontal lobe disorders may be evident in inappropriate or overly aggressive or destructive responses or in numerous small detail responses that often bear no resemblance to the stimuli presented.

Normative Data

Normative data for preschool (Takeuchi, 1986) and for inner-city children from age 3 to 12 years (Krall et al., 1983), college-student twin pairs and sex differences

(Rice et al., 1976), and numerous other groups have been published. Although such norms show trends, they are of limited value for the interpretation of individual cases because of the large variability of Rorschach responses. However, textbook authors such as Beck, Exner, and Klopfer list both age-appropriate responses and response summaries for children as well as "optimal" response patterns (including "popular" responses) for healthy adults and for elderly subjects that may serve as a guide. Lezak (1987) reports that in the few studies with normal elderly subjects, fewer responses, decreased creativity (more stereotyped content, fewer complex and original percepts), and constriction (fewer movement and color responses) have been noted.

REFERENCES

Aaronow, E., & Reznikoff, M. (1984). *A Rorschach Introduction: Content and Perceptual Approaches.* Los Angeles: Western Psychological Services.

Aldheidt, P. (1980). The effect of reading ability on Rorschach performance. *Journal of Personality Assessment, 44,* 3–10.

Atkinson, L. (1986). The comparative validity of the Rorschach and the MMPI: A meta-analysis. *Canadian Psychology, 27,* 238–249.

Beck, S.J., Beck, A.G., Levitt, E.E., & Molish, H.B. (1961). *Rorschach's Test: Basic Processes.* New York: Grune & Stratton.

DeCato, C.M. (1983). Rorschach reliability: Cross validation. *Perceptual and Motor Skills, 56,* 11–14.

DeCato, C.M. (1984). Rorschach reliability: Toward a training model for interscorer agreement. *Journal of Personality Assessment, 48,* 58–64.

Exner, J.E. (1974, 1978, 1982). *The Rorschach: A Comprehensive System* (Vols. 1–3). New York: John Wiley.

Exner, J.E. (1980). But it's only an inkblot. *Journal of Personality Assessment, 44,* 563–576.

Garwood, J. (1978). Six-month prognostic norms derived from studies of the Rorschach prognostic rating scale. *Journal of Personality Assessment, 42,* 22–26.

Haller, N., & Exner, J.E. (1985). The reliability of Rorschach variables for inpatients presenting symptoms of depression and/or helplessness. *Journal of Personality Assessment, 49,* 516–521.

Holtzman, W.H., Thorpe, J.S., & Swartz, J.D. (1970). *Inkblot Perception and Personality: Holtzman Inkblot Technique.* Austin: University of Texas Press.

Howes, R.J. (1981). The Rorschach: Does it have a future? *Journal of Personality Assessment, 45,* 339–351.

Klopfer, B. (1954). *Developments in the Rorschach Technique* (Vols. 1–3). Yonkers-on-Hudson: World Book Company.

Klopfer, B., & Davidson, H.H. (1977). *The Rorschach Technique: An Introductory Manual.* Los Angeles: Western Psychological Services.

Krall, V., Sachs, H., Lazar, B., Rayson, B., Growe, G., Novar, L., & O'Connell, L. (1983). Rorschach norms for inner city children. *Journal of Personality Assessment, 47,* 155–157.

Lerner, P. (Ed.). (1980). *Handbook of Rorschach Scales.* New York: International Universities Press.

Lezak, M.D. (1983). *Neuropsychological Assessment* (2nd ed.). New York: Oxford University Press.

Lezak, M.D. (1987). Norms for growing older. *Developmental Neuropsychology, 3,* 1–12.

Morey, L.C. (1982). An adjustment for protocol length in Rorschach scoring. *Journal of Personality Assessment, 46,* 286–288.

Oberholzer, E. (1931). Zur Differentialdiagnose psychischer Folgezustände nach Schädeltraumen mittels des Rorschachschen Formdeutversuchs. [On differential diagnosis of psychological sequelae after head trauma by means of the Rorschach form interpretation experiment.] *Zeit-*

schrift für die Gesamte Neurologie und Psychiatrie, 136, 596–629.

Parker, K. (1983). A meta-analysis of the reliability and validity of the Rorschach. Journal of Personality Assessment, 47, 227–230.

Phillips, L., & Smith, J.G. (1980). Rorschach Interpretation: Advanced Technique. Los Angeles: Western Psychological Services.

Piotrowski, Z. (1937). The Rorschach ink blot method in organic disturbances of the central nervous system. Journal of Nervous and Mental Diseases, 86, 525–537.

Prandoni, J.R., & Swartz, C.P. (1978). Rorschach protocols for three categories of adult offenders: Normative data. Journal of Personality Assessment, 42, 115–120.

Rice, D.G., Greenfield, N.S., Alexander, A.A., & Sternbach, R.A. (1976). Genetic correlates and sex differences in Holtzman inkblot technique responses of twins. Journal of Personality Assessment, 40, 122–129.

Takeuchi, M. (1986). Educational productivity and Rorschach location responses of preschool Japanese and American children. Psychology in the Schools, 23, 368–373.

Wagner, E.E., Alexander, R.A., Roos, G., & Adair, H. (1986). Optimum split-half reliabilities for the Rorschach: Projective techniques are more reliable than we think. Journal of Personality Assessment, 50, 107–112.

Weiner, I. (1977). Approaches to Rorschach validation. In M.A. Rickers-Ovsiankina (Ed.), Rorschach Psychology. Huntington, N.Y.: R.E. Krieger.

THEMATIC APPERCEPTION TEST (TAT)

Purpose

This is a projective test of thought content, emotions, and conflicts through storytelling based on pictures.

Source

The manual and 31 cards can be ordered from Western Psychological Services, 12031 Wilshire Boulevard, Los Angeles, California 90025, for $115 U.S.

Description

The TAT consists of individual pictures of which the client is instructed to make up a story. The basic set includes 10 pictures. The remaining set contains 10 pictures designated for children, males, and females, and one "picture" as a blank page, resulting in a total of 31 pictures. A separate "Children's Apperception Test" (Bellak, 1949) is also available.

Administration

Adequate rapport and knowledge of some basic personal data are required prior to administration. The full test is normally given in two sessions (pictures 1–10, 11–20) on separate days, although many examiners prefer to make a selection of only a few pictures which may be presented in one session; in this case, however, the examiner should be very familiar with the client so that pictures relevant to the client's problem areas can be selected in advance. Typical general selections recommended for all clients are cards 1, 2, 3BM*, 4MF, 6BM, 7BM, 8BM, 10, 11, 13MF, 14, 16, & 20 (Arnold, 1962); cards 2, 3GF, 4, 6GF, 7GF for females; and cards 2, 3BM, 4 6BM, 7BM for males (Dana, 1956).

Instruction A for adolescents and adults with at least average intelligence are as follows: "**We have here a test to study fantasy. I will show you some pictures, and for each picture I want you to make up as dramatic a story as you can. Please look at the picture and tell me what happens in the picture at the moment—what the people in the picture are thinking, feeling, planning to do. Please make a complete story, inventing how it came to this situation, what happened before, how it developed further, and how it came out in the end. You cannot make a mistake in this test; it is only necessary to let your fantasy play and to invent a dramatic story. You can take about five minutes for each story. Here is the first picture.**"

Instruction B for children and adults with low intelligence or education is: "**I have here a story-telling test. I will show you some pictures; and for each picture you make up a story. Tell me what is happening in the picture, and what happened before. Then tell me also how the story goes on and how it ended. You can tell any story you wish, just as it comes to your mind.**"

If the client does not observe all parts of the instruction, the client should be told what he or she did right, and what he or she has not done yet (e.g., "**Tell me how it came out in the end**"). Otherwise, the test administrator should interfere as little as possible, except for occasional encouraging remarks when the client hesitates or when long pauses occur. Neutral questions (avoiding any suggestions) may be asked during the test to encourage continuity and avoid awkward pauses. If the client asks what a particular part of the picture is, he or she should be informed that that is entirely up to him- or herself, that the client can make out of it whatever he or she wishes.

Scoring

The examiner tries to keep a verbatim protocol of everything that was said during the test, including exclamations and other initial reactions that are not part of the

*M and F refer to male and female; B and G, to boys and girls.

story, and the "response latency"—that is, the time from card presentation to response. This should be done unobtrusively in a note-taking manner, although in some cases tape-recording may be necessary to keep pace with the client's story. Most authors agree that asking the client to write the stories reduces productivity and should be avoided.

A supplementary interview ("inquiry") is often recommended: In this case, the examiner reads the story back to the client, and asks the client to elaborate, and to explain whether the story is based on or reminiscent of personal experiences, books, or shows. If such sources are mentioned, the details should be noted carefully. Frequently, the examiner will ask the client to point out the most and least favorite card. Finally, the inquiry can be used as a base for free associations by the examiner who is trained in psychotherapy.

The evaluation of the protocol is a complex process that requires considerable training and experience. As a guide to interpretation, Murray (1943) suggests noting the following "press" and "need" factors (rated from 1 to 5) for each of the stories:

1. Affiliation
   a. Social
   b. Emotional
2. Aggression
   a. Affective or verbal
   b. Physical and social
   c. Physical and asocial
   d. Destruction of property
3. Dominance
   a. External force
   b. Interference by others
   c. Influence or persuasion
4. Nurturance
   a. Includes feeding, protecting, encouragement, consolation, help or forgiving.
5. Rejection
6. Lack or loss
   a. Lack of recognition, happiness, success, family, poverty, etc.
   b. Loss as in (a)
7. Physical damage by nonhuman factors
   a. Active
   b. Loss of solid foundation (drowning, ship, or airplane accident etc.)
8. Physical injury

For each story, the key figure ("hero") should be established, which is most likely the one with whom the client identifies. Other "figures" (father, mother, sibling, teacher) should be noted for each story.

The stimulus value of each card is different and has been discussed by several authors. Since this is of importance for both card selection and interpretation, the following list (abbreviated from Murray, 1943) may be useful:

Card 1: Young boy contemplating violin on table: need for achievement, autonomy, particularly with respect to parents and authorities, self- versus other-motivation.

Card 2: Country scene: family relations, separation and individuation, achievement values and aspirations, pregnancy issues.

Card 3BM: Boy huddled on floor with revolver: depression, helplessness, suicide, guilt, impulse control, handling of aggression.

Card 3GF: Woman standing with downcast head: depression, loss, suicide, guilt.

Card 4: Woman clutching shoulders of man: male–female relationships, sexuality, infidelity, interpersonal control, dominance, and conflict.

Card 5: Middle-aged woman looking into a room: attitude toward mother or wife, guilt, autonomy issues, fear of intruders, paranoia.

Card 6BM: Elderly woman with back towards young man: mother–son relations, loss and grief, separation–individuation.

Card 6GF: Young woman sitting, looking at older man with pipe: daughter–father or male–female relationships, heterosexual relationships, interpersonal trust, employer–employee relationship.

Card 7BM: Gray-haired man looking at younger man: father–son relationship, employer–employee relationship, authority issues.

Card 7GF: Older woman sitting close to young girl: mother–daughter relationship, rejection issues, child-rearing attitudes and experiences.

Card 8BM: Adolescent boy with rifle, and surgery in background: aspirations and achievement, handling of aggression, guilt, fears of being harmed, oedipal issues.

Card 8GF: Young woman looking off into space: diverse themes, aspirations, thoughts of future.

Card 9BM: Four men lounging on grass: homosexuality, male–male relationship, work attitude, social prejudice.

Card 9GF: Young woman observing woman in party dress: female–female relationships, rivalry, jealousy, sexual attack, trust versus suspicion, suicide.

Card 10: Young woman resting head against man's shoulder: marital or parents' relationship, intimacy, loss or grief.

Card 11: Road between cliffs and dragon: unknown, threatening forces, attack and defense, aggression.

Card 12M: Young man on couch and elderly man stretching out hands above: health, homosexuality, father–son relationship, issues of control, response to psychotherapy.

Card 12F: Young woman and weird old woman grimacing in background: mother and mother-in-law relationship, guilt and superego conflict, good and evil.

Card 12BG: Rowboat drawn up on river bank: loneliness, nature, peace, imaginal capacities, suicide.

Card 13MF: Young man with head downcast and woman lying on bed: sexual conflict and attitude, heterosexual relations, guilt, handling of provocative stimuli, aggression.

Card 13B: Boy sitting on doorstep of log cabin: loneliness, abandonment, childhood memories.

Card 13G: Little girl climbing winding stairs: childhood memories, loneliness.

Card 14: Silhouette of man or woman against bright window: wishes and aspirations, depression, suicide, loneliness, burglary, intrapersonal concerns.

Card 15: Gaunt man among gravestones: death, religion, fantasy, aggression.

Card 16: Blank card: varied themes, handling of unstructured situations, imaginal capacities, optimism versus pessimism.

Card 17BM: Naked man clinging to rope: achievement and aspirations, homosexuality, optimism and pessimism, danger, escape, competitiveness.

Card 17GF: Female leaning over river bridge railing: loneliness, suicide, intrapersonal concerns.

Card 18BM: Man clutched from behind by three hands: alcoholism, drunkenness, homosexuality, aggression, paranoia, helplessness.

Card 18GF: Woman with hands squeezed around throat of another woman: aggression, particularly mother–daughter, rivalry, jealousy, conflict.

Card 19: Cloud formations overhanging snow-covered cabin: varied themes, imaginal capacities.

Card 20: Figure of man or woman at night leaning against lamppost: loneliness, fears, aggression.

A variety of scoring methods (reviewed by Murstein, 1963), including quantitative and nonquantitative systems and rating scales have been developed. Experienced clinicians frequently prefer to review the stories without quantitative evaluation, keeping in mind the "normal" responses to each card based on stimulus properties.

Subjects with a low educational level and elderly subjects (Fogel, 1967) tend to produce shorter and less elaborate stories.

Comment

Despite Murray's (1938) somewhat outdated personality theory underlying the construction of the TAT, the test has found continuing use up to today, with more than 2,000 papers and books published. Validity and reliability data are scarce, leading Swartz (1978) to remark that "if the TAT were published today with the same amount of information on its reliability, validity and standardization, it is very doubtful that it would ever attain anywhere near its present popularity" (p. 1127). He adds, however, that Murray described the test as "an aid to the exploration of personality, and as such, of course, it must be rated an overwhelming success" (p. 1127).

The TAT is not a diagnostic instrument, but a projective technique suitable for the exploration of specific problems, conflicts, fears, and needs of the individual at the conscious and at a more subliminal level. Stories may reflect mere recent experiences at a superficial level (e.g., recently viewed movies), the current situational problems of the individual at work or at home, as well as more persistent personal motivation, needs, fears, etc., and even more subliminal (i.e., to the individual not immediately apparent) past experiences and other personality features. For these reasons, thorough training of the interpreter of the test and of the person conducting the inquiry, and a background in personality theory and psychotherapy are necessary.

In the context of a neuropsychological examination, the TAT can be used in a manner similar to the Rorschach Test or other story-telling techniques—that is, it provides information about (1) general response-time delays in brain-damaged patients; (2) ability to organize a story sequentially; (3) paucity of ideas (concrete description of picture rather than making up a story; or stories with few characters and little action); (4) misinterpretation of pictures or parts of pictures due to confusion, simplification, or vagueness (Lezak, 1983); (5) perseveration of content or phrasing; (6) word-finding difficulties; and (7) inability to interpret the picture as a whole. In addition the TAT may reflect the personal reaction to injury or deficit, "catastrophic reactions," indications of a posttraumatic stress syndrome, feelings of failure, as well as insights into premorbid or postmorbid reactive mechanisms, and may guide the examiner into current problem content.

REFERENCES

Arnold, M.B. (1962). *Story Sequence Analysis.* New York: Columbia University Press.

Bellak, L. (1949). *Children's Apperception Test.* Los Angeles: Western Psychological Services.

Dana, R.H. (1956). Selections of abbreviated TAT sets. *Journal of Clinical Psychology, 12,* 36–40.

Fogel, M.L. (1967). Picture description and interpretation in brain-damaged subjects. *Cortex, 3,* 433–448.

Lezak, M.D. (1983). *Neuropsychological Assessment* (2nd ed.). New York: Oxford University Press.

Murray, H.A. (1938). *Explorations in Personality.* New York: Oxford University Press.

Murray, H.A. (1943). *Thematic Apperception Test: Manual.* Cambridge, Mass.: Harvard University Press.

Murstein, B.I. (1963). *Theory and Research in Projective Techniques* [emphasizing the TAT]. New York: John Wiley.

Swartz, J.D. (1978). Thematic Apperception Test. In Buros, O.K. (Ed.), *The Eighth Mental Measurement Yearbook* (Vol. 1, pp. 1127–1130). Highland Park, N.J.: Gryphon Press.

VINELAND ADAPTIVE BEHAVIOR SCALES

Purpose

The purpose of this test (Sparrow et. al., 1984) is to assess social and personal adaptive abilities in daily living.

Source

The complete set can be ordered from American Guidance Service, Inc., Circle Pines, Minnesota 55014-1796, for $95.00 U.S.; in Canada from Psycan Corporation P.O. Box 290, Station V, Toronto, Ontario, M6R 3A5 for $140.00 Cdn. Also available are cassette training tape, automated system for scoring and interpreting standardized tests, technical and interpretative manual, and a Spanish test version.

Description

The survey form consists of 297 items; the expanded form includes an additional 280 items which are presented to the primary caretaker in a semistructured interview similar to Doll's (1935) original Vineland Social Maturity Scales. The test is not administered directly to the subject, but rather to the person most familiar with him or her. The items cover four domains: communicative, daily living skills, socialization, and motor skills. There are subdomains within domains: for communicative—receptive, expressive, and written communication; for daily living—personal, domestic, and community; for socialization—interpersonal relationship, play and leisure time, and coping skills; for motor—gross and fine. In addition, an optional set of items covers maladaptive behavior (e.g., bedwetting, inappropriate impulsiveness, crying or laughing). The scales are designed to cover ages 3:0–18:11 years (when presumably an adult ceiling is reached). The expanded form is designed to serve as a systematic basis for preparing educational, habilitative, and treatment programs by means of a separate booklet ("Program Planning Report"). A "Classroom Edition" of 244 items, which is simply completed by the teacher, differs considerably from the interview edition and has been criticized because it requires "guesstimates" on many items that are not known to the teacher (Kamphaus, 1987).

Administration

The approximate age starting points for nonhandicapped individuals are indicated in the record booklet for each domain. Considerable time can be saved by beginning the interview at a level estimated as appropriate for the patient's estimated "adaptive age" equivalent. After establishing rapport with the respondent, it is explained that the purpose of the interview is to determine what the client does to take care of him- or herself and to get along with others, and what others usually do for the client. Then begin with the items, for example: "speaks in full sentences," uses "a" and "the" in phrases or sentences, follows instructions in "if–then" form," etc. The items are presented in a general form, but are followed by probe questions for clarification as needed. Extensive training in administration is essential, since many items may require probing. Refer to the manual for details.

Approximate Time for Administration

The time required is 20–60 minutes for the survey form or 60–90 minutes for the expanded form.

Scoring

A simple scoring system of 2 points (activity performed satisfactorily and habitually), 1 point (emerging or sometimes correctly performed skill), and 0 is used for each item, following the criteria appended to the manual. Sums of total raw scores for each subdomain and domain are calculated. These can be transferred into standard scores appropriate for age (with confidence interval), percentile ranks, adaptive levels, and age equivalents by the use of tables in the manual, and plotted in a standard score profile.

Comment

This "revision" of the Doll scales resulted in a virtually new test, although the interview technique remained the same. The standardization is based on 3,000 normal individuals chosen from all parts of the country to represent the 1980 U.S. census. However, Evans and Bradley-Johnson (1988) point out weaknesses in the number of subjects used to represent socioeconomic status, geographic distribution, and urban–rural residence. Interrater reliabilities are .74 for the composite score, and between .62 and .78 for domain scores (see source). Split-half reliability for a variety of handicapped groups ranges from .83 for the Motor Skill domain to .94 for the Adaptive Behavior composite (see source). Retest reliability after an interval of two to four weeks (based on 484 subjects) was .90 for children up to age 6, .80 for older subjects, and .98 for the whole range across domains (see source).

Construct validity is documented by a satisfactory increase with age in each domain, and by the extraction of one significant factor, accounting for 55–70% of the variance, dependent on age level. The test also correlates only .12–.37 with the Peabody Picture Vocabulary Test (PPVT), indicating its relative independence from a measure of verbal ability. The correlation of the Communications domain with the Kaufman Assessment Battery for Children (Kaufman & Kaufman, 1983) was highest with the Achievement portion of that test (.52). Because the scales are designed to provide a profile of developmental delay, criterion validity relies on the quality of standardization. Correlational validity with the original Vineland is reported as .55, with the Adaptive Behavior Inventory for Children (Mercer & Lewis, 1978) as .58, and with the AAMD Adaptive Behavior Scale as between .40 and .70. Systematic investigations of patients with dementia or other forms of brain damage are not available as yet.

Its tendency toward "statistical overkill"—provision of too many different scores (Holden, 1984)—can easily be avoided by using the score that is most familiar to the examiner and that is comparable to other scores used in testing.

Normative Data

As mentioned above, the test was standardized on 1,500 males and 1,500 females representative of the geographic and racial composition of the United States. The manual presents detailed domain standard scores and bands of error from age 0:0 to 18:11 years and older, in increments of three months or less, as well as supplementary norms for maladaptive behavior in seven handicapped groups.

REFERENCES

Doll, E.A. (1935). A genetic scale of social maturity. *American Journal of Orthopsychiatry, 5,* 180–188.

Evans, L.D., & Bradley-Johnson, S. (1988). A review of recently developed measures of adaptive behavior. *Journal of Clinical Psychology, 44,* 276–287.

Holden, R.H. (1984). Vineland Adaptive Behavior Scales. In D.J. Keyser & R.C. Sweetland (Eds.), *Test Critiques* (Vol. 1, pp. 715–719). Kansas City, Missouri: Test Corporation of America.

Kamphaus, R.W. (1987). Critiques of school psychological materials. *Journal of School Psychology, 25,* 97–98.

Kaufman, A.S., & Kaufman, N.L. (1983). *Kaufman Assessment Battery for Children.* Circle Pines, Minn.: American Guidance Service.

Mercer, J.R., & Lewis, J.F. (1978). *Adaptive Behavior Inventory for Children.* New York: Psychological Corporation.

Sparrow, S.S., Balla, D.A. & Cicchetti, D.V. (1984) Vineland Adaptive Behavior Scales. Circle Pines, Minn.: American Guidance Service.

Name Index

Aaronow, E., 408, 412
Abidin, R.R., 398, 402
Abikoff, H., 190, 193, 194, 195, 196, 197, 198, 203
Achenbach, K., 359, 370, 374
Adair, H., 413
Adams, K.M., 221, 329
Adams, R.L., 31, 37
Adey, M., 389, 394
Adkins, T.G., 31, 37, 203, 328, 329, 353
Agnew, J., 156
Agras, W.S., 390
Aldheidt, P., 412
Alekoumbides, A., 35, 36, 37, 195, 203, 325, 326, 328, 329, 345, 353
Alexander, A.A., 413
Alfano, D.P., 395, 399, 400
Algozzine, B., 291
Alheidt, P., 411
Allen, S., 204
Alvir, J., 203
Anderson, H.N., 70
Anderson, R.L., 289, 291
Annett, M., 371, 372
Apicella, A., 226
Appicciafuoco, A., 219
Arbit, J., 205
Archer, R.P., 397, 400
Arena, R., 121, 124
Arenberg, D., 121, 122, 123, 124
Armstrong, B.B., 288, 290
Arnold, M.B., 414, 419
Aronson, M.K., 138, 394
Asher, E.J., 375, 383

Atkinson, L., 411, 412
Aucoin, R., 330
Aylward G.P., 77, 78
Ayres, A.J., 74, 293, 295
Ayres, R., 85, 87

Baade, L.E., 124, 329
Backman, J.E., 406
Baer, R.A., 74, 75, 76
Bak, J.S., 201, 203, 348, 353
Baker, L.T., 71
Baker, W.W., 226
Ball, J.D., 407
Balla, D.A., 385, 422
Ballard, K., 63, 69
Banken, C.H., 59, 62, 69
Banken, J.A., 60, 62, 69
Barley, W.D., 195, 204
Barling, J., 387, 389
Barlow, D.H., 390
Barnes, G.W., 325, 328, 346, 353, 362, 364
Baron, P., 389
Barona, A., 19, 20, 44
Barry, P., 86, 87
Battersby, W.S., 277, 279
Bayles, K.A., 214
Bayley, N., 77, 78, 80, 81, 85, 88
Beames, T.B., 122, 124
Beck, A.G., 412
Beck, A.T., 385, 388, 389
Beck, B., 108, 109, 110
Beck, B.L., 405, 406
Beck, R.W., 385, 389
Beck, S.J., 409, 412

Beele, K.A., 269, 273
Beery, K.E., 287, 288, 289, 290
Behrmann, M., 217, 219
Bellak, L., 413, 419
Bender, M.B., 279, 332
Bening, M.E., 85, 88
Bennett, T.S., 264, 265
Bennett-Levy, J., 158, 163, 164, 167
Bentin, S., 298, 299
Benton, A.L., 118, 121, 122, 123, 124, 135,
    177, 181, 183, 210, 219, 220, 221, 223, 226,
    228, 261, 262, 266, 274, 276, 277, 279, 291,
    295, 296, 298, 299, 300, 304, 308, 310, 311,
    317, 318, 319, 320, 332, 337, 338, 339, 341,
    359, 367, 369, 372, 373
Berent, S., 38
Berg, E.A., 72, 76
Berger, R.A., 156, 157
Bergs, L.E., vii, 329, 354
Berman, G., 299
Bernard, B.A., 20, 44
Bialer, I., 264, 265
Bialow, M.R., 390
Bigler, E.D., 153, 156, 158, 165, 167, 346, 353,
    362, 364, 399, 401
Binder, D.M., 288, 290
Binder, L.M., 66, 69, 163, 165, 167
Birchfield, M., 52
Biron, R., 365
Black, F.W., 80, 81, 179, 183, 277, 279, 399,
Black, I.L., 399, 401
Blackburn H.L., 261
Blair, J.R., 17, 20, 42, 44
Blanton, P.D., 121
Blashfield, R.K., 402
Blau, A.D., 138
Blazer, D.G., 394
Bleecker, M.L., 98, 154, 155, 156
Bloom, B.L., 190, 203
Blount, J.B., 303, 392, 394
Boer, D.P., 59, 70
Boersma, D.C., 406
Boll, T.J., 38
Bolla-Wilson, K., 156
Boller, F., 269, 273
Bolon, K., 389, 391
Bond, J.A., 31, 37
Bornstein, R.A., 31, 37, 59, 65, 69, 74, 76, 194,
    203, 207, 208, 325, 326, 359, 361, 362, 363,
    364, 367, 368, 369, 370

Bosscher, R.J., 389
Bourdon, 302
Bourke, R.S., 329
Boyd, J.L., 301, 302, 303
Boyle, G.L., 22, 37
Boyle, R.S., 183, 226, 262
Bracken, B.A., 263, 264
Bradley-Johnson, S., 421
Brandon, A.D., 32, 37, 342, 349, 353
Brasfield, D.M., 122, 124
Braun, L.S., 362, 365
Braune, R., 286
Brazelton, T.B., 77, 78
Breen, M.J., 288, 290
Brennan, J., 390
Brickenkamp, R., 118, 141, 142
Briggs, P.F., 402
Brink, T.L., 230, 388, 389, 391, 392, 393, 394
Broadbent, D.E., 280, 286
Brod, M.S., 280
Broman, M., 376, 377, 382
Brook, R.M., 123, 124
Brooks, R., 290
Brookshire, R.H., 271, 273
Brown, G., 21
Brown, S.J., 263, 345, 353, 361, 364, 367, 370
Brown, W.G., 136, 221
Bruyer, R., 221, 226
Bryden, M.P., 283, 286
Buchtel, H.A., 31, 37
Buktenica, N.A., 287, 290
Bullock, D., 406
Buonaguro, A., 218, 219, 227, 270, 274
Burke, H.R., 47, 48, 49, 51
Buros, O.K., 397, 401
Buschke, H., 117, 118, 125, 137
Butcher, J.N., 395, 396, 401
Butler, B., 203
Butters, N., 185, 194, 195, 203, 207, 208, 209
Byrne, J.M., 406

Cairns, P., 203, 205
Caltagirone, C., 48, 49, 51, 226
Campbell, F.A., 80, 81
Campbell, S.K., 80, 81
Carey, S., 299
Carmichael, J., 183
Carmon, A., 332
Carpenter, C.B., 399, 401
Carson, M.F., 390

Cartwright, L.R., 271, 273
Carvajal, H., 63, 70, 264
Caslyn, D.A., 22, 37
Cattell, R.B., 88, 92
Caudry, D., 373, 374
Cauthen, N.R., 195, 203, 348, 353
Cavalli, M., 221, 226, 269, 273
Cavenaugh, S.V., 388, 389
Cermak, L.S., 203
Chaney, E.F., 37, 398, 401
Chang, J.Y., 226
Chapman, J.P., 371, 372, 373
Chapman, L.J., 371, 372, 373
Charter, R.A., 27, 37, 203, 324, 328, 329, 345, 353
Chastain, R., 20, 44
Chavez, E.L., 32, 37, 342, 349, 353
Chelune, G.J., 69, 70, 74, 75, 76, 207, 208
Chenery, H.J., 183, 226, 262
Chirsman, S.M., 85, 87
Chiulli, S.J., 158, 166, 167
Christ, A., 291
Church, K.L., 370
Cicchetii, D.V., 264, 353, 364, 370, 385, 422
Clark, C.M., 308, 309, 310, 345
Clark, C.R., 156
Clark, D.C., 389
Clark, E., 405, 406
Caltagirone, C., 157
Clement, F.J., 82, 124, 369, 370
Clemmons, D., 346, 354
Clodfelter, C.J., 126, 128, 133, 137
Coates, S.W., 293, 295
Coblentz, J.M., 39, 40, 41
Coelho, C.A., 226
Cohen, H.J., 394
Cohen, R., 270, 273, 329
Colarusso, R., 289, 290, 291
Cole, K.N., 266, 273
Coleho, C.A., 221
Collaer, M.L., 62, 70
Colligan, R.C., 397, 400, 401, 402
Collins, C., 214
Comalli, P.E., 55, 56
Conners, C.K., 406
Connolly, A.J., 94, 95, 96, 97, 100
Cool, V.A., 92
Cooley, E.J., 85, 87
Coren, S., 373, 374
Corkin, S., 214, 295, 356, 358

Cosden, M., 288, 290
Costa, L.D., 49, 51, 123, 124, 213, 214, 223, 226, 302, 303, 376, 383
Court, J.H., 48, 51
Craft, R.B., 134, 138
Cramer, J., 332
Crawford, J.R., 17, 19, 20, 98, 132, 133
Crawford, M.S., 59, 70, 153, 156
Cripe, L.I., 324, 325, 329, 347, 354
Critchley, M., 180, 183, 226, 252, 261, 273, 274, 277, 279
Crockett, D.J., 180, 181, 182, 224, 226, 252, 261
Crofoot, M.J., 264, 265
Cross, H., 354, 365
Crossen, J.R., 157, 208, 209
Crosson, B., 190, 209
Crovitz, H.F., 372, 373
Culbert, J., 407
Cullum, C.M., 203, 209, 214, 399, 401
Cultreta, S., 303
Culver, C.M., 185, 304
Cunliffe, P., 361, 365, 367, 370, 372, 374
Cupone, V., 214, 303
Currie, B.B., 70
Curry, J.F., 195, 197, 198, 199, 201, 203
Curtis, C.J., 289, 290
Curtis, G., 138

Dahlstrom, W.G., 395, 397, 401
Dahmen, W., 142
Damarin, F., 78, 81
Damasio, A.R., 124, 226, 299
Damasio, H., 312, 316, 317
D'Amato, R.C., 264, 265
Dana, R.H., 414, 419
D'Angelo, K., 293, 295
Das, J.P., 55, 56, 82, 85, 87
Davidson, H.H., 408, 412
Davies, A., 326, 329, 397, 401, 405, 406
Davies, E., 273
Davis, L., 180, 183
Davison, L.A., 20, 21, 38, 346, 355, 366, 370
Dawson, J.G., 403
Dean, R.S., 264, 265
De Cato, C.M., 409, 412
Deegener, G., 295
Delaney, E.A., 89, 92
Delaney, H.D., 362, 365, 367, 371
Delaney, R.C., 194, 203

Delis, D.C., 56, 117, 118, 186, 203, 207, 209
DeMendonca, M., 397, 401
DeMers, S.T., 288, 290
Denes, F., 49, 51
Dennis, M., 269, 273
Dent, H.R., 388, 389
De Paolo, A.M., 274
De Renzi, E., 226, 262, 269, 270, 273, 293, 295
De Simoni, F., 262
des Rosiers, G., 221, 226, 324, 325, 329
DiBenedetto, B., 291
Dickson, A.L., 86, 137
DiGiulio, D.V., 226, 300, 310
Digre, K., 226
Diller, L., 295, 299
Di Simoni, F., 273
Dodrill, C.B., 27, 32, 37, 324, 325, 326, 329,
    345, 347, 353, 361, 362, 363, 364, 367, 370
Dodrill, K.L., 226
Doll, E.A., 384, 385, 419, 422
Donahoe, L., 382
Donnelly, N., 393, 394
Donnely, E.F., 27, 31, 38
Dowe-Keval, M., 381, 382
Drewe, E.A., 74, 76
Dricker, J., 298, 299
Duara, R., 226
Dubowitz, L.M.S., 77, 78
Dubowitz, V., 78
Duffy, J.B., 289, 290
Duker, J., 397, 402
Dunn, J.M., 367, 370
Dunn, L.M., 101, 104, 262, 265
Dunst, C.J., 77, 78
Duttweiler, P.C., 388, 390
Dvorine, I., 276, 277
Dye, O.A., 324, 329
Dyson, J.A., 332

Eaves, R.C., 96, 97
Echternacht, R., 299
Edicott, J., 394
Edwards, D., 214
Edwards, G.L., 390
Egan, V., 148, 149
Egelko, S., 295, 298, 299
Ehle, D.L., 283, 286
Ehrenberg, M., 388, 389
Ehrenstein, W.H., 324, 325, 329
Eisenberg, H.M., 183, 223, 261, 273

Elliott, L., 401
Ellison, G.D., 376, 382
Emery, O.B., 270, 273
Empting, L., 41
Emran, A., 226
Engelhardt, J., 376, 383
Epstein, A.G., 182, 183
Erickson, R.A., 185, 195, 203
Erickson, R.C., 401
Ernst, J., 32, 37, 330, 355, 368, 369, 370
Eslinger, P.J., 124, 125, 226, 299
Eson, M.E., 325, 329
Esquivel, G.B., 48, 51
Evans, J.R., 62, 70
Evans, L.D., 421, 422
Eversole, C., 70
Ewing-Cobbs, L., 179, 183, 221, 226, 253, 261,
    270, 273
Ewoldt, C., 106
Exner, J.E., 408, 409, 411, 412

Fabian, M.S., 346, 349, 354
Faglioni, P., 226, 266, 269, 270, 273
Farber, N., 382
Farver, P.F., 302, 303, 309, 310
Farver, T.B., 302, 303, 309, 310
Faust, D., 407
Fedner, M., 290
Fein, G., 330
Feinberg, I., 330
Feingold, A., 70, 71
Fekken, G.C., 397, 401
Fennell, E., 359, 370, 374
Fewell, R.R., 266
Fialkoff, B.S., 303
Finch, A.J., 389, 390
Fincham, R.W., 317
Finlayson, M.A.J., 353, 354, 362, 363, 364,
    367, 368, 369, 370, 395, 400
Fischer, J.S., 208, 209
Fischhoff, J., 407
Fisher, L., 41
Fisher, R.H., 71, 157, 205, 227, 262, 274, 330
Fitzhugh-Bell, K.B., 399, 402
Fleishman, E.A., 376, 382
Fletcher, J.M., 183, 226, 262, 265, 273, 287,
    290
Flynn, J.R., 69, 70, 109
Flynn, L.A., 289, 290
Flynn, T.M., 289, 290

Fogel, M.L., 418, 419
Fogelman, C., 384, 385
Foldi, N.S., 183
Folstein, M.F., 17, 20, 393, 394
Folstein, S.E., 17, 20, 394
Foster, R., 385
Fox, J.H., 20, 44
Francis, D.J., 124, 204
Franzen, M.D., 121, 122, 124, 194
Friedenberg, L., 205
Friedland, R.P., 56
Friedman, S.H., 399, 401
Fromm, D., 52, 227, 383
Fromm-Auch, D., 32, 37, 329, 348, 354, 362, 363, 364, 368, 369, 370
Frostig, M., 287, 290
Fuld, P.A., 70, 117, 118, 125, 137, 138
Fusilier, F.M., 271, 273

Gaddes, W.H., 36, 39, 79, 184, 223, 224, 226, 252, 261, 273, 274, 286, 294, 295, 296, 309, 311, 319, 320, 336, 340, 349, 353, 355, 362, 365, 369, 371
Gainotti, G., 51, 121, 124, 157, 226
Gallagher, A.J., 269, 273
Gallagher, D., 390
Gapinski, M.P., 400, 401, 402
Gardner, E.F. 94, 106
Gardner, H., 183
Gardner, R., 40, 41
Gardner, R.A., 376, 377, 382
Garrison, W., 214
Garry, J.P., 76, 167
Garwood, J., 411, 412
Gass, C.S., 398, 399, 401
Gates, R.D., 289, 290
Gauk, S.E., 383
Gdowski, C.L., 401, 405, 406, 407
Geffen, G., 151, 154, 155, 156, 280, 286, 373, 374
Geffen, L.B., 155, 156
Geisser, M.E., 71, 157
Gentili, P., 219
Georgemiller, R.J., 157
Gerber, J., 70, 265
Gerson, A., 301, 302, 303
Gerstmann, J., 338, 339
Geyer, M., 274
Ghent, L., 308, 310, 332, 336, 358
Gibbons, R.D., 389

Gilberstadt, H., 397, 402
Gill, D.M., 361, 364, 370, 383
Gill, S., 290
Gilleard, C.J., 394
Gilley, D.W., 20, 44
Giordani, B, 38
Glutting, J.J., 70
Goebel, R.A., 324, 329, 347, 354
Goethe, K.E., 138, 205
Goldberg, C., 78
Golden, C.J., v, vii, 53, 55, 56, 264, 265, 399, 402
Golden, S.S., 271, 274
Goldfader, P.R., 330
Goldman, H., 330
Goldstein, D.J., 85, 87
Goldstein, G., 324, 329, 345, 354, 362, 364
Goldstein, M., 401
Goldstein, S.G., 27, 37, 38, 330, 361, 364, 365
Goodglass, H., v, vii, 210, 211, 214, 274, 277, 279
Goodwin, J.S., 76, 203
Gordon, E., 284, 286
Gordon, H.W., 299, 316, 317
Gordon, R.A., 401
Gordon, W.A., 295, 299
Gottesman, I.I., 400, 402
Gottschaldt, K., 293, 295
Gould, J.W., 388, 390
Gouvier, W.D., 121, 124
Grafman, J.H., 280
Graham, J.R., 397, 401, 402
Grant, D.A., 72, 76
Grant, I., 37, 324, 325, 329, 347, 348, 354, 355, 359, 365, 371
Graves, R.E., 168, 176
Gray, J.W., 265
Grayson, H.M., 398, 402
Greene, R.L., 203, 353, 397, 401, 402
Greenfield, N.S., 413
Gregory, R.J., 22, 37, 365
Grisell, J., 21
Groisser, D., 76, 227
Gronwall, D.M.A., 118, 143, 146, 147, 148, 149
Grossman, F.M., 65, 68, 70
Grossman, H.J., 384, 385
Grossman, R.G., 133, 135, 136, 300
Growe, G., 412
Gundersheimer, J., 280

Gutbrod, K., 270, 273
Gutkin, T.B., 17, 21, 65, 68, 71

Haaland, K.Y., 167, 195, 199, 203
Haddad, F.A., 86, 87
Hagen, E.P., 78, 93
Hague, F., 221, 226
Hall, J.C., 194, 203
Hall, S., 156
Haller, N., 409, 412
Halperin, J.M., 195, 199, 201, 204, 212, 214, 224, 226
Halstead, W.C., 20, 21, 31, 37, 342, 346, 354, 360, 365
Halwes, 281, 286
Hamilton, M., 387, 390
Hammeke, T.A., vii, 70
Hamsher, K.deS., 109, 177, 181, 183, 210, 220, 223, 226, 261, 273, 277, 298, 299, 300, 310, 320, 337, 339, 341
Hannay, H.J., 133
Hannay, J.H., 125, 126, 127, 132, 133, 138
Hans, H.S., 364
Hanson, D.R., 402
Hanson, R.K., 402
Harley, J.P., vii, 325, 329, 347, 354
Harris, J., 156
Harris, M., 347, 354, 363, 365
Harris, V.L., 271, 274
Hartje, W., 142
Hathaway, S.R., 395, 402
Head, H., 338, 339
Healey, J.M., 204, 214, 226
Heaton, R.K., 20, 31, 32, 36, 37, 72, 73, 74, 75, 76, 121, 124, 212, 215, 325, 329, 345, 347, 348, 349, 354, 355, 359, 363, 365, 371
Hebben, N., 204
Heber, R., 384, 385
Hécaen, H., 221, 226, 308, 310
Heersema, P.H., 389, 394
Heffernan, L., 80, 81
Heilbronner, R.L., 346, 354
Heister, G., 329
Heller, M., 195, 204
Hempel, W.E., Jr., 376, 382
Henderson, V.W., 212, 215
Henry, R., 190
Herman, D.O., 63, 68, 70, 185, 204
Hermann, B.P., 70, 74, 76
Hessler, G.L., 94, 115, 116

Hewes, P., 70
Hibbard, M.R., 295, 299
Hickie, C., 392, 393, 394
Hill, J.L., 280
Hinton, G.G., 264, 265
Hirsch, S.H., 121, 124
Hoar, K.J., 157
Hodge, S.E., 86, 87
Holden, R.H., 208, 209, 421, 423
Holden, R.R., 397, 401
Holland, A., 215, 216, 218, 219
Holland, J., 388, 390
Holliday, R., 296, 299
Hollinger, C.L., 264, 265
Hulicka, Ì.M., 185, 195, 196, 203, 204
Hunt, W.C., 203

Iacovello, J.M., 383
Ishahara, S., 276, 277
Ivinskis, A., 194, 195, 196, 201, 204
Ivison, D.J., 194, 195, 199, 202, 206
Ivnik, R.J., 154, 155, 157, 190, 195

Jacobs, D., 203, 209
Jacobs, K.W., 388, 389
Jacobsen, R., 302, 303
James, M., 288, 300
Jarman, R.F., 87
Jarratt, L., 309,. 311
Jastak, S., 94, 107, 109
Jenkins, C.D., 205, 330
Jenkins, R.L., 349, 354
Jensen, A.R., 85, 87
Jenson, W.R., 406
Jewell, J., 402
Johnson, D.L., 92
Johnson, K.L., 124, 329
Johnson, R.B., 137
Jones, J.N., 70
Joschko, M., 65, 70
Judica, A., 219

Kael, H.C., 403
Kaemmer, B., 401
Kahn, R.L., 279
Kalat, J.W., 372, 373, 374
Kalish, R.A., 291
Kamboka, V., 390
Kamphaus, R.W., 263, 264, 265, 420, 422
Kane, M., 70

Kane, R.L., 124, 206
Kaplan, E., v, vii, 41, 62, 68, 185, 204, 209, 210, 211, 214, 277, 279
Karlsen, B., 94, 106
Karp, S.A., 296
Kasoff, S.S., 41
Katz, I.R., 391, 394
Katzman, R., 41
Kaufman, A.S., 64, 68, 70, 78, 81, 85, 87, 421, 422
Kaufman, N.L., 78, 81, 85, 87, 421, 422
Kavanagh, D., 221, 226, 324, 325, 329
Kazniak, A.N., 213, 214
Kear-Colwell, J.J., 195
Keenan, P.A., 405, 406
Keesler, T.Y., 205
Kehle, T.J., 406
Keirnan, J., 274
Keith, R.W., 274
Keith, T.Z., 91, 92
Kelly, J., 300
Kelly, M.S., 163, 167
Kelter, S., 273, 275
Kenin, M., 252, 261
Kenisten 133
Kennedy, K.J., 331
Kennedy, M., 195, 196, 204
Kerner, S.A., 388, 389, 390
Kertesz, A., v, viii, 179, 183, 210
Kiernan, J., 266
Kiersch, M.E., 215
Kilshaw, D., 373
Kimura, D., 280, 281, 284, 286
Kindlon, D., 216
King, M.C., 31, 38, 158, 165, 167
Kirby, J.R., 87
Kirchner, F.H., 401
Kirk, S.A., 163, 167, 210
Kirk, U., 163, 167
Kirk, W., 210
Kitson, D.L., 271, 274
Klein, A.E., 289, 290
Kleinman, K.M., 330
Kline, R.B., 405, 406, 407
Klinedinst, J.K., 407
Klonoff, H., 27, 36, 38, 195, 196, 204, 308, 309, 310, 317, 328, 329, 345, 353, 354, 362, 365
Klopfer, B., 408, 409, 412
Klove, H., 31, 38, 346, 347, 354

Knesevich, J.W., 214
Knight, R.G., 388, 390
Knights, R.M., 36, 38, 264, 265, 330, 349, 353, 355
Knobloch, H., 77, 78
Knopf, K.F., 288, 290
Knopman, D.S., 213, 214
Knudson, R.M., 296
Kobus, D.A., 370
Koenig, H.G., 391, 394
Koffler, S.P., 367, 369, 370
Kokmen, S., 157
Kolb, B., 158, 165, 166, 167, 225, 226, 284, 308, 309, 310
Koss, E., 55, 56
Kovacs, M., 389, 390
Kraemer, H.C., 132, 133, 138
Krall, V., 411, 412
Kramer, J.H., 122
Kroeker, T.A., 402
Kronfol, Z., 223, 226
Kryzer, K.M., 219
Kunce, J.T., 121, 124, 302, 303
Kupke, T., 348, 355
Kurland, L.T., 157
Kush, J., 70

Labarge, E., 213, 214
LaBreche, T.M., 22, 32, 38
Lacher, D., 401, 405, 406, 407
Laicardi, C., 219
Laitinen, L.V., 221, 270, 298, 300
Lake, D.A., 283, 286
Lang, C., 274
Lansdell, H., 27, 31, 38
Lanyon, R.I., 397, 402
LaPointe, L., 219
Lapp, D., 394
Larabee, G.J., 121, 124, 133, 135, 138, 185, 194, 204
Larson, G., 286
Lass, N.J., 266, 271, 273
LaTorre, R.A., 289, 290
Lattinen, L.V., 227, 275
Lawlor, B.A., 280
Lawriw, I., 180, 183, 252, 261
Lawton, M.P., 391, 394
Lazar, B., 412
Leckliter, I.N., 32, 33
Ledbetter, M., 209

Lee, G.P., 122, 134, 138, 165, 167
Lefever, D.W., 290
Lehman, R.A.W., 76
Lehr, C.A., 78, 81
Leirer, V.O., 394
Leland, H., 385
LeLieuvre, R.B., 399, 401
Lenhard, M.., 270, 273
Lepkin, S.R., 288, 290
Lerner, P., 411, 412
Leuthold, C.A., vii, 329, 354
Levin, H.S., 125, 126, 127, 132, 133, 134, 135,
    136, 138, 179, 183, 194, 204, 226, 261, 273,
    296, 298, 300
Levine, G., 283, 286
Levita, E., 218, 219, 227, 270, 274, 382
Levitt, E.E., 412
Levy, A.P., 280
Levy, M., 22, 38
Lewandowski, L., 367, 370
Lewinsohn, P.M., 325, 330
Lewis, C.V., 208, 209
Lewis, J.F., 421, 422
Lewis, R.F., 321, 330
Lezak, M.D., 17, 20, 57, 59, 62,63, 65, 66, 67,
    70, 117, 118, 141, 142, 150, 152, 153, 154,
    157, 158, 162, 163, 165, 167, 185, 195, 209,
    213, 214, 286, 301, 303, 316, 317, 321, 324,
    330, 400, 402, 411, 413, 418, 419
Lieberman, A., 295, 299
Liemohn, W., 288, 290
Light R.H., 138
Lindesay, J., 373, 374
Linebaugh, C.W., 217, 219
Lingoes, J.C., 401
Linn, R.T., 203
Lishman, W.A., 372, 374
Llabre, M.M.,48, 51
Loewenstein, D.A., 226
Logsdon, R.G., 65, 70
Logue, P.E., 203, 204
Long, G.M., 276, 277
Loring, D.W., 132, 133, 138, 158, 163, 165,
    166, 167, 185, 186, 187, 204, 208, 209
Low, M., 36, 38, 310, 317, 328, 329, 345, 353,
    354, 362, 365
Lowe, J.D., 63, 70
Lozano, R., 263, 264, 265
Lubin, B., 387, 390

Lucas, G.J., 325, 328, 346, 353, 362, 364
Luchins, D.J., 315, 317
Ludlow, C.L., 252, 261
Ludman, W.L., 204, 214, 226
Luglio, L., 219
Lum, O., 394
Luria, A., 85, 87
Lyman, B.J., 277

McCarthy, D., 85, 87
McCarthy, J., 210
McCarty, S.M., 190, 194, 204
McClung, E., 66
McDermott, P.A., 65, 68, 70
McDonald, J., 183
McFie, J., 308, 310
McGowan, R.J., 92
McHugh, P.R., 20, 394
McKinley, J.C., 395, 402
McLeod, J., 66
McMeekan, E.R.L., 372, 374
McMinn, M.R., 157
McNeil, M.R., 270, 274
McNeill, J., 401
Mack, W., 213, 215
Mackintosh, R.M., 303
Madden, R., 94, 106
Maerz, M.D., 383
Magharious, W., 303
Mahlios, M.C., 293, 295
Maier, L.R., 398, 402
Majia, R., 305
Malec, J.F., 157
Malone, A.F., 78
Maltz, A., 409
Manni, J., 292
Margheriti, M., 221
Margolis, R.B., 203, 204
Marks, C.J., 152, 199
Markwardt, F.C., 94, 95, 101, 102, 103, 104
Marsella, A.J., 388, 389, 390
Marsh, G.G., 121, 124
Marshall, J.C., 219, 226, 252, 262
Martin, R., 289, 290
Martin, R.C., 122, 167
Martino, A.A., 266, 274
Marx, R.W., 59, 70
Masullo, C., 157, 226
Masur,, D.M., 133

Masure, M.C., 135, 138, 295
Matarazzo, J.D., 17, 20, 27, 32, 38, 63, 68, 69, 70, 324, 325, 330, 361, 365, 370
Matarazzo, R.G., 27, 32, 330, 365, 367, 370
Mather, N., 94, 95, 115, 116
Mathews, C.G., vii, 37, 329, 346, 348, 354, 355, 359, 365, 371, 376, 399, 402
Mathiowetz, V., 382
Mattis, S., 17, 20, 39, 40, 41
Mattson, R.H., 203
Mazurski, P., 274
Meador, K.J., 122, 167
Meador, K.G., 394
Megran, J., 156, 157, 398, 402
Meija, R., 215
Mellits, D., 270, 275
Mellow, A.M., 280
Mercer, J.R., 384, 385, 421, 422
Merrick, W.A., 315, 317
Merschmann, W., 274
Meyerink, L.H., 399, 402
Meyers, D.A., 156
Meyers, L.S., 388, 390
Meyers, R., 359, 370, 373
Miceli, G., 51, 153, 157, 221, 226
Michael, J.J., 290
Michael, W.B., 290
Michel, M., 270, 273
Milberg, W.P., 185, 187, 204
Miller, D.J., 273
Miller, E., 221, 226
Milner, B., 32, 38, 74, 76, 112, 113, 114, 185, 187, 194, 204, 316, 317, 358, 371, 373, 374
Mitrushina, M., 71
Mittenberg, W., 68, 70, 157, 221, 226, 299, 300, 309, 310
Moberg, P.J., 21
Moehle, K.A., 399, 402
Molish, H.B., 412
Monkowski, P.G., 203
Montgomery, C., 123, 124
Montgomery, K.M., 40, 41, 213, 214, 223, 226, 261, 262, 302, 303
Moore, J.W., 63, 156
Moore, T.E., 355
Morey, L.C., 397, 402, 409, 412
Morgan, S.F., 126, 128, 133, 137
Morrison, M.W., 37, 125, 361, 365
Morrow, J.E., 265

Moses, J.A., 27, 38
Moss, M., 122, 203
Moulthrop, M.A., 315, 317
Mungas, D., 154, 157
Munsen, 154, 155
Murdoch, B.E., 180, 183, 221, 226, 253, 262
Murray, A.M., 263, 264
Murray, H.A., 415, 416, 418, 419
Murstein, B.I., 417, 419
Myers, P.S., 219

Nachtman, W., 94, 97
Naeser, M.A., 270, 274
Nagel, C.L., 394
Naglieri, J.A., 86, 87, 263, 264, 265
Naumann, E., 275
Nebes, R., 372, 373, 374
Neilson, P.M., 400
Nelson, H.E., 17, 20, 42, 44, 72, 76
Nelson, V.O., 71
Newcomb, F., 220, 226
Newhouse, P.A., 280
Newton Wilkes, C., 86, 137
Niccum, N., 214
Nicholas, L.E., 271, 273
Nicholson, J.E., 81
Niebergall, G., 271, 274
Niemann, H., 141, 142
Nihira, K., 384, 385
Nixon, D.H., 390
Noll, J.D., 273, 274, 275
Noonan, J.V., 70
Norris, J.T., 388, 390
Norwood, J.A., 330, 349, 353, 355
Novak, C.G., 92
Novak, K.K., 274
Novar, L., 412
Novelly, R.A., 203
Nowk, T.J., 71

O'Connell, A., 17, 20, 42, 44
O'Connell, L., 17, 412
O'Donnell, J.P., 324, 325, 330, 346, 347, 355
O'Grady, K.E., 194, 204
O'Hanlon, A.P., 156
O'Leary, D.S., 226, 300, 310
O'Leary, M.R., 37, 401
Ober, B.A., 56, 122
Oberholzer, E., 411, 412

Oden, S.E., 219
Offord, K.P., 400, 401, 402
Oldfield, R.C., 372, 374
Oliver-Munoz, S., 41
Oltman, P.K., 296
Orazem, J., 295, 299
Orazio, J., 203
Orgass, B., 264, 269, 270, 274
Orme, J.E., 49, 50, 51
Orsini, D.L., 374
Osborne, D., 401
Osmon, D.C., 402
Osterrieth, P.A., 118, 158, 165, 167
Owen, L., 389

Paniak, C.E., 133, 138
Papanicolaou, A.C., 132, 133, 138, 185, 186, 204
Parham, I.A., 136, 223
Parker, K.C., 69, 70, 402, 409, 413
Parks, R.W., 221, 226
Parmelee, P.A., 391, 392, 393, 394
Parr, C.A., 81
Parsons, O.A., 32, 38, 346, 347, 349, 354, 355
Patrick, J., 397, 402
Patterson, J., 365
Paul, J.J., 37, 365
Paul, S.M., 48, 51
Peabody, C.A., 138
Peck, D.F., 49, 52
Peel, J., 330, 355
Pelchat, G., 149, 330
Pendleton, M.G., 31, 32, 38
Penn, C., 217, 219
Pennington, B.F., 76, 227
Peraino, M., 274
Perret, E., 53, 55, 56, 221, 226
Peterson, R.C., 157
Pfeiffer, S.I., 263, 264, 265
Phillips, L., 408, 413
Pillon, B., 165, 167
Piotrowski, Z., 411, 413
Pizamiglio, L., 216, 217, 219, 274
Plankenhorn, A., 290
Plemel, D., 399, 403
Plumb, M.M., 388, 390
Poirier, C.A., 149, 330
Poitrenaud, J., 82, 124
Polder, G.J., 359, 370, 373
Pollack, M., 280

Pontius, A.A., 325, 330
Poppelreuter, W., 293, 295
Porac, C., 373, 374
Porch, B., v, viii, 210
Porter, G.L., 288, 290
Pottebaum, S.M., 93
Power, D.G., 190, 197, 198, 204
Prandoni, J.R., 411, 413
Preddy, D., 286
Press, M., 291
Preston, M., 330, 355
Price, L.S., 325, 330
Price, P.A., 96, 97
Prifitera, A., 68, 69, 70, 122, 157, 194, 204
Prigatano, G.P., 32, 38, 185, 190, 194, 195, 205, 324, 330, 347, 355
Prinz, P.N., 70
Pritchard, C.T., 406, 407
Pritchett, E.M., 94, 97
Provins, K.A., 361, 365, 367, 370, 372, 374
Pryzwandky, W.B., 288, 290, 291
Pursich, A.D., vii

Quattrochi, M.M., 265
Quayhagen, M., 138
Query, W.T., 156, 157, 398, 402
Quintana, J.W., 138, 205, 365

Raczkowski, D., 371, 372, 373, 374
Radloff, L.S., 387, 390
Ragnarsson, K., 295, 299
Ramey, C.T., 80, 81
Ramier, A.M., 221, 226
Randall, D.M., 157
Rao, S.M., 71
Rapin, I., 376, 382
Rasmussen, T., 358, 371, 373, 374
Rathbun, J., 301, 302, 303
Raven, J.C., 20, 45, 46, 47, 50, 52, 87
Rayson, B., 412
Razzano, C.A., 219, 274
Read, D.E., 154, 156, 181, 183, 223, 225, 227
Reddon, J.R., 52, 136, 364, 367, 370, 375, 376, 382
Reed, H.B.C., 21, 38
Reed, R., 329
Regard, M., 53, 55, 56, 221, 227
Reid, D.W., 71, 157, 205, 227, 262, 274, 330
Reid, N., 108, 109
Reitan, R.M., 20, 21, 32, 38, 69, 71, 77, 210,

276, 277, 321, 325, 328, 330, 331, 346, 347,
354, 355, 360, 362, 363, 364, 365, 366, 367,
368, 369, 370, 399, 402
Remschmidt, H., 271, 273, 274
Rennels, C., 382
Renney, C., 370
Rennick, P.M., 321, 330
Rentfrow, R.K., 288, 291
Rey, A., 117, 118, 150, 154, 157, 158, 167, 172,
173, 175, 176
Reynolds, C.R., 17, 20, 44, 65, 68, 71, 108,
109, 289, 291
Reynolds, D., 66, 108
Reynolds, W.M., 388, 390
Reznikoff, M., 408, 412
Rice, D.G., 412, 413
Richard, M.T., 330
Richards, B., 355
Richards, T.W., 63, 71
Richardson, E., 289, 291
Richey, E.T., 76
Riedel, K., 154, 268
Riley, J.M., 86, 87
Rimland, B., 286
Riordan, J., 264, 265
Risser, A., 211
Risucci, D., 383
Ritter, D.R., 290
Ritter, W., 51
Rizzo, J.M., 264, 265
Robertson-Tehabo, E.A., 122, 123, 124
Robins, E., 394
Robinson, A.L., 74, 76
Rodriguez, R., 401
Rogers, S.L., 382
Roid, G.H., 207
Roos, G., 413
Rorer, L.G., 296
Rosa, L., 156
Rose, J.E., 138
Rose, T.L., 389, 394
Rosen, A.J., 203, 214
Rosenbaum, G., 21
Rosenberg, S.J., 154, 157
Rosenbuck, J., 219
Rosenthal, A.K., 204
Roth, D.L., 203
Rotter, J.B., 390
Rourke, B.P., 65, 70, 138, 181, 183, 265, 353,
364, 370

Rourke, D., 21
Rubens, A., 214
Ruff, R.M., 133, 135, 138
Russell, E.W., 22, 38, 185, 187, 194, 195, 198,
200, 205, 345, 355, 398, 399, 401, 402
Russell, R.L., 122, 124
Ryan, J.J., 69, 71, 153, 154, 157, 208
Ryckman, D.B., 288, 291

Saccuzzo, D., 283, 286
Sachs, H., 412
Salgueiro-Feik, M., 121, 125
Salkovskis, P.M., 388, 389
Salmon, D.P., 203, 208
Salvia, J., 85, 87
Sampsom, H., 118, 143, 147, 148, 149
Samuel, S.M., 274
Samuels, I., 299
Sanborn, K.O., 390
Sappington, J.T., 367, 370, 376, 383
Saravay, S., 203
Sarazin, F.A., 63, 71, 308, 310
Sarno, M.T., 168, 176, 180, 183, 210, 211, 215,
219, 221, 227, 253, 262, 270, 273, 274
Sarvis, P.A., 264, 265
Sattler, J.M., 59, 60, 63, 64, 65, 66, 67, 68, 78,
93, 97, 103, 104, 107, 108, 109, 376, 383
Satz, P., 65, 71, 215, 261, 262, 265, 287, 290,
359, 367, 370, 371, 372, 373, 374
Sauguet, J., 308, 310
Savageau, J.A., 207, 330
Saylor, C.F., 390
Scarola, L.M., 382
Schaie, K.W., 195, 205, 223, 227
Schludermann, E.H., 345, 347, 355
Schludermann, S.M., 345, 347
Schooler, D.L., 289, 291, 355
Schreiber, D.J., 325, 330
Schuck, J.R., 124, 204
Schuell, H., 210, 211
Schultz, E.E., 190, 194, 205
Schultz, F., 156
Schwab, J.J., 388, 390
Schwartz, M.M., 342, 349, 353
Schwartz, M.S., 190, 195, 205
Schwerd, A., 121, 125
Scialfa, C.T., 203, 204
Sciara, A.D., 205
Scott, M.L., 185, 195, 203
Seacat, G.F., 37, 203, 328, 329, 353

Seashore, H.G., 68, 71
Seat, P.D., 407
Seidenberg, M., 32, 38, 226, 300, 310
Seigel, E., 81
Selz, M., 402
Semenza, C., 51
Semmes, J., 308, 310, 332, 336, 358
Sewell, T., 290
Shaver, M.S., 295, 299
Shaw, D.J., 27, 39, 398, 402
Shaw, E., 204
Shear, J.M., 134, 138
Sheehan, T.D., 107, 108, 110
Shellhaas, M., 385
Sheramata, W.A., 226
Sherrill, R.E., Jr., 22, 32, 39
Shewan, C.M., 178, 183
Shimamura, A.P., 117, 118
Shinn, M., 291
Shizuri, L., 390
Shore, D.L., 138
Siegel, E., 81
Silverberg, R., 299
Silveri, M.C., 158, 226
Silverstein, 59, 62
Silverstone, F.A., 280
Simcoe, J.C., 274
Simpson, R.G., 96, 97
Slauson, T., 214
Selnes, O.A., 214
Smiljanic-Colanovic, V., 367, 371
Smith, A., 301, 302, 303
Smith, D.J., 406
Smith, J.G., 408, 413
Smith, K.B., 87
Smith, P.D., 265
Snow, W.G., 31, 38, 63, 71, 153, 157, 194, 205,
    220, 227, 252, 262, 269, 274, 324, 330, 360,
    365
Snowdon, J., 392, 393, 394
Snyder, T.J., 309, 311
Soloman, S., 203
Sontag, L.W., 63, 71
Soper, H.V., 71
Sparrow, S.S., 384, 385, 422
Spector, S., 407
Spellacy, F.J., 221, 227, 266, 269, 274, 283, 286
Sperry, R.W., 52
Spinnler, H., 293, 295
Spitzer, R.L., 394

Spreen, O., 17, 32, 36, 39, 42, 44, 63, 71, 122,
    124, 164, 165, 167, 176, 177, 180, 181, 184,
    199, 201, 205, 210, 211, 219, 221, 222, 227,
    228, 262, 266, 269, 274, 277, 291, 294, 295,
    296, 299, 308, 309, 311, 316, 317, 319, 320,
    330, 335, 336, 337, 339, 340, 349, 353, 355,
    362, 365, 369, 371
Spruill, J., 63, 64, 71, 108, 109, 110, 406
Squire, L.R., 197, 205
Stanton, B.A., 190, 205, 325, 326, 330
Stark, R.E., 270, 275
Stearns, G.M., 400
Stebbins, G.T., 17, 20, 44, 393, 394
Stefanyuk, W.O., 52, 227, 364, 370, 383
Stephens, M.I., 264, 265
Sternbach, R.A., 413
Sternberg, R.J., 85, 86, 87
Sterne, D.M., 302, 303
Stethem, L.L., 149, 330
Stevens, F., 78
Stewart, L.E., 156
Stierman, I., 286
Stilson, D.W., 76
Stone, C., 184, 205
Stoner, S.B., 263, 265
Stoppa, E., 51
Strauss, E., 164, 165, 167, 176, 199, 201, 205,
    281, 283, 286, 298, 300, 335, 367, 371, 373,
    374
Strayer, D., 283, 286
Street, R.F., 87
Stroop, J.R., 20, 52, 56
Strother, G.R., 195, 205
Strub, R.L., 277, 279
Stuckey, M., 205
Studdert-Kennedy, M., 270, 275
Sturm, W., 142
Stuss, D.T., 146, 148, 149, 324, 325, 326, 330
Sukoff, R., 203
Summers, B., 52
Sunderland, T., 279
Swan, G.E., 120, 125
Swartz, J.D., 413, 418, 419
Swartz, C.P., 411, 412
Sweet, J.J., 17, 19, 21, 402
Swenson, W.M., 401
Swisher, L.P., 252, 261, 273, 274

Takeuchi, M., 411, 413
Talbott, R., 70

Tallal, P., 270, 275
Talland, G.A., 293, 296
Tamkin, A.S., 121, 125, 302, 303, 388, 390
Tangalos, E.G., 157
Taussig, I.M., 213, 215
Taylor, E.M., 150, 154, 157
Taylor, L.B., 74, 76, 157, 158, 161, 163, 164
    165, 167, 185, 205
Taylor, L.J., 264, 265
Teasdale, G., 138
Tellegen, A.M., 401
Terri, L., 70
Teuber, H.L., 308, 310, 332, 336, 346, 355, 358
Thal, L.J., 138
Thomas, M.R., 89, 90, 92, 93
Thompson, J.L., 138, 167
Thompson, L.L., 212, 215, 347, 355, 359, 362,
    363, 365, 367, 368, 369, 371
Thorndike, R.L., 78, 88, 91, 93, 286
Thorpe, J.S., 412
Thurstone, L.L., 220, 227
Thurlow, M.L., 81
Tierney, M.C., 71, 157, 205, 227, 262, 274,
    330
Tierney, R.J., 106, 107
Tiffin, J., 375, 376, 383
Tillinghast, B.S., 263, 265
Tinklenberg, J.R., 138
Toal, R., 194, 203
Tomoeda, C.K., 214
Tourk, L.M., 382
Tovian, S.M., 21
Townes, B.D., 330, 355
Trahan, D.E., 138, 199, 362, 363, 365
Tramontana, M.G., 77, 78
Traub, E., 286
Trenton, S.L., 31, 36
Trifiletti, R.J., 399, 402
Trites, R.L., viii, 36, 39, 328, 330, 353, 355
Troster, A.I., 122, 203
Troupin, A.S., 27, 37, 324, 329, 361, 364, 367,
    370
Tuck, J.P., 277
Tucker, D.M., 346, 353, 362, 364
Tuokko, H., 262, 273, 275
Tuymubu, B., 221, 226
Tzavaras, 295

Uhlig, G.E., 265
Uzgiris, I.C., 77, 78, 80

Vaddadi, K.S., 394
Van Allen, M.W., 296, 298, 299
Van Dongen, H.R., 266, 275
Van Gorp, W.G., 71, 213, 215
Van Harskamp, F., 266
Van Harskamp, G., 275
VanNieuwkerk, R., 354, 365
Van Orden, K., 370
Van Roekel, B.H., 106, 107
Vargo, M.E., 179, 184
Varney, N.R., 277, 299, 310, 312, 316, 317,
    320, 337, 339
Vaughan, H.G., 51, 376, 382, 383
Verity, L., 298, 300
Vernon, P.E., 59, 60, 63, 71, 92, 93
Vignolo, L., 266, 273
Vilkki, J., 221, 227, 266, 270, 275, 298, 300
Villardita, C., 49, 52, 213, 215, 302, 303
Violato, C., 59, 60, 71
Visser, R.S.H., 163, 165, 167
Vitale, A., 226
Vitiello, M.V., 70
Vranes, L.F., 76

Waber, D.P., 158, 163, 167
Wada, J., 286, 367, 371, 373, 374
Waddell, D.D., 91, 93
Wagner, E.E., 409, 413
Wagner, P., 288, 290
Wahler, H.J., 120, 125
Waldrep, E.E., 87
Wang, P.L., 302, 303
Wapner, S., 56
Ward, J.W., 396, 402
Ward, L.C., 396, 402
Warner, M.H., 324, 326, 347, 355
Warrington, E.K., 298, 300, 330
Watson, C.G., 398, 402, 403
Watson, J.R., 27, 37, 324, 329, 345, 354, 361,
    365
Waziri, R., 226
Weaver, K.A., 70
Webb, W.W., 402
Weber, M.A., 148, 149
Wechsler, D., 17, 21, 57, 58, 66, 67, 69, 71,
    117, 118, 148, 149, 184, 187, 190, 194, 195,
    205, 206, 207, 208
Wedding, D., 325, 330
Weiner, I., 411, 413
Weingold, H.P., 398, 399, 402

Weinstein, S., 308, 310, 332, 336, 346, 355, 356, 358
Weintraub, S., 214
Weiss, L.K., 393, 394
Wellman, M.M., 121, 125
Welsh, G.S., 397, 401
Welsh, M.C., 75, 76, 221, 227
Wengel, W., 205
Wentworth-Rohr, I., 301, 303
Werner, H., 56
Wernicke, C., 218
Wersh, J., 89, 90, 92, 93
Wertz, R., 218, 219
Wexler, B.E., 281, 286
Wheeler, L., 325, 331
Whishaw, I., 99, 101, 166, 225
Whitaker, H.A., 273, 275
White, L.J., 92
Whithouse, C.C., 271, 275
Whitman, D., 21
Whittlesey, J.R.B., 290
Whitworth, R.H., 85, 87
Wickens, C., 286
Widiger, T.A., 293, 296
Wielkiewicz, 64
Wiens, A.N., 38, 122, 154, 156, 157, 208, 330, 365, 370
Wienstein, L., 204, 214, 226
Wilkinson, G.S., 94, 107, 108, 109, 110
Wilkinson, W.A., 291
Wilks, C., 226
Wilks, V., 183, 262
Williams, A.M., 70, 264, 265
Williams, B.W., 215
Williams, D.E., 70
Williams, H.L., 399, 403
Williams, J.G., 388, 390
Williams, M., 184
Williams, R.J., 396, 403
Willingham, A.C., 205
Willmott, M., 394
Wilmes, K., 142, 269, 275
Wilson, A., 390
Wilson, B.C., 376, 383
Wilson, F.M., 399, 402
Wilson, J.J., 383
Wilson, R.S., 17, 20, 21, 44

Winograd, C.H., 390
Wirt, R.D., 403, 407
Wishaw, I.Q., 102, 135, 158, 165, 167, 308, 309
Wisniewski, H.M., 41
Witkin, H.A., 293, 295, 296
Wolf-Klein, G.P., 278, 279, 280
Wolfson, D., 32, 38, 69, 71, 276, 277, 325, 330, 347, 355, 362, 365, 367, 370
Woll, G., 270, 275
Wong, D.T., 388, 390
Woodcock, R.W., 95, 115, 116
Woodward, C.A., 301, 303
Worthington, G.B., 85, 88
Wortis, S.B., 332
Wright, D., 288, 290, 291
Wrightson, 143, 146, 148, 149
Wyler, A.R., 76

Yen, J.K., 329
Yeo, R.A., 167
Yesavage, J.A., 138, 389, 391, 392, 393, 394
Yeudall, L.T., 32, 37, 50, 52, 221, 222, 227, 329, 344, 348, 362, 363, 364, 368, 369, 370, 376, 382, 383
York Haaland, K., 75, 76, 362, 365, 367, 370
Yoshi, F., 226
Ysseldyke, J.E., 81, 85, 87, 106, 289, 291
Yudowitz, B.S., 326, 330

Zagar, R., 203, 205
Zaidel, D.W., 45, 49, 52
Zaidel, E., 52, 273, 275
Zangwill, O.L., 308, 310
Zehler, D., 367, 369, 370
Zeisat, H.A., 204
Zeitchik, E., 204
Zeitschel, K.A., 289, 291
Zeitschick, E.S., 214, 226
Zelkind, I., 401
Zener, K., 372, 373
Zingesser, L.H., 41
Zorzitto, M.L., 71, 157, 205, 227, 262, 274, 330
Zucker, S., 264, 265
Zung, W.W.K., 387, 390
Zurif, E.B., 183
Zyzanski, S.J., 207, 330

Test and Subject Index

abbreviations, list of, xiii
abstraction ability, 20, 27, 72
achievement tests, 85, 94, 289
Acoustic Recognition Test, 311
acronyms, list of, xiii
adaptive behavior, 384
Adaptive Behavior Inventory for Children, 421
Adaptive Behavior Scale, 384, 421
Aesthesiometer, 332, 333
agnosia, 276
alcoholism, 346
Alzheimer's disease, 40, 65, 180, 208, 212, 253, 289, 315
amusia, 286
Annett Handedness Questionnaire, 359, 371
Army Individual Test Battery, 321
articulation, 252
Assessment of Career Decision Making, 398
attention and concentration, 118, 138, 141, 142, 147, 207, 320
attention tests, 117
audiometer, 276
auditory acuity, 276
auditory agnosia, 311
auditory tests, 276

Barclay Classroom Assessment System, 404
Barona equation, 18
Bayley Scale, 77, 78, 92
Beck Anxiety Checklist, 388
Beck Depression Inventory, 385, 392
Beery Test, 287
Bender Gestalt Test, 287, 288

Benton Visual Retention Test, 117, 118, 287, 346
Block Design Test, 346
Boehm Test of Basic Concepts, 264
Boston Diagnostic Aphasia Examination, 211, 213, 217
Boston Naming Test, 211, 212
Bracken Basic Concept Scales, 264
Brazelton Scales, 77
Buschke Selective Reminding Test, 117, 125, 195

California Verbal Learning Test, 194
cancellation tasks, 141
Category Test, 20, 74
    adult and intermediate versions, 26
    children's version, 26
    Victoria revision, 22
Child Behavior Checklist, 205
children, cognitive tests, 77
Christensen-Luria Tests, v
Clock Drawing, 277
closing-in, 279
cognitive tests for children, 77
color recognition, 276
Communication Abilities in Daily Living, 210, 215
Concentration Endurance Test, 118, 138
conceptual ability, 18, 308
constructional disorders or apraxia, 157, 168, 184, 185, 276, 279, 317
Controlled Oral Word Association. *See* Word Fluency

coordination, 141
crystallized abilities, 88

D2 Test, 118, 138, 282
dementia, 41, 133, 185, 194, 277, 388, 393, 411
depression, 385, 390, 398
Depression Adjective Checklist, ·388
Developmental Profile, 404
Developmental Test of Visual-Motor
    Integration, 287
dexterity, 359, 374
dichotic staggered spondaic word task, 271
dichotic fused-rhyme procedure, 280
dichotic consonant-vowel task, 271
Dichotic Listening, music, 283
    free-recall technique, 280
    words, 281
dissimulating, 121, 324, 397
Draw-a-Man Test, 319
Dubowitz Scales, 77
Dynamometer. See Hand Dynamometer
dyslexia, 276
dysphoria, 392

Embedded Figures Test, 291
extinction, on double tactile stimulation, 332

Facial Recognition Test, 296
faking brain damage, 324, 347
Figure-Ground Test, 291
finger agnosia, 338
finger dexterity, 338, 374
Finger Localization, 332, 337
Finger Oscillation, 360
Finger Tapping, 360, 367
flexibility, cognitive, 20, 52, 320
Florida Kindergarten Screening Battery, 262,
    287, 289
fluency, 252
fluid-analytic abilities, 88
Functional Communication Profile, 215, 217

g-factor, 47, 55, 91
Geriatric Depression scale, 388, 390
Gerstmann syndrome, 308, 338
Gesell Scales, 78
Giannetti On-Line Psychosocial History, 9
Gilleard Scales, 392
graphaesthesia, 332
grip strength. See Hand Dynamometer

Halstead-Reitan Test Battery, v, 21, 321, 346
Hamilton Rating Scale, 388, 392
Hand Dynamometer, 359, 365
Hand Preference Test, 359, 371
Handedness Questionnaire. See Hand
    Preference Test
hearing loss, 276
hemianopsia, 279
hidden figures, 291
history taking, 1, 3
    computer based, 8
Hooper Visual Organization Test, 300
hyperactivity, 406

Illinois Test of Psycholinguistic Abilites, 80, 264
incomplete figures tests, 293
infant and child tests, 293
information processing, rate of, 142, 147
intelligence, 17, 122, 148, 154, 155, 166, 198,
    207, 218, 326, 346, 347
    premorbid, 17, 18, 41, 44, 68, 122
inference, proactive, 117, 151
    retroactive, 117, 151
intermanual discrepancies, 369
Internal Control Index, 388
Internalizing-Internalizing Scale, 388
Interpersonal Style Inventory, 404
interpretation, blind, vii
interpretative process, 10
interview, 8

Kauffman Assessment Battery for Children, 78,
    81, 92, 215, 264, 421
    hand movements, 86
Key-Math Diagnostic Arithmetic Test, 94, 95,
    115
Kohs Block Design, 319
Korsakoff's disease, 325

language lateralization, 279
language comprehension, 252, 268, 269
language tests, 210
long-term memory, 117, 125, 129
Louisville Behavior Checklist, 404
Luria-Nebraska Battery, 264
Luria theory, 85

Marching Test, 320
Marital Satisfaction Inventory, 404
Mattis Dementia Rating Scale, 17, 39

Maudley Obsessive-Compulsive Index, 388
McCarthy Scales for Children, 264
Meikle Consonant Perception Test, 276
memory, immediate verbal, 150, 155, 177, 252
    tests, 117
Menstrual Distress Questionnaire, 404
mental status examination, 277
Meyer-Kendall Assessment Survey, 404
Mini-Mental State Examination, 17
Minnesota Multiphasic Personality Inventory,
    194, 385, 387, 394, 403, 405, 406, 411
    neurocorrected, 395, 399
Mood Assessment Scale. See Geriatric
    Depression Scale
motor speed, 141, 320, 359
motor tests, 359, 420
Multiscore Deression Inventory, 405

name finding, 252
National Adult Reading Test, 18
Neurosensory Center Comprehensive
    Examination for Aphasia, 177, 210, 227,
    266
newborn assssment methods, 77
Nonverbal Auditory Perception Test, 311
nonverbal learning and memory, 118, 121, 154,
    158, 168, 206
North American Adult Reading Test, 18, 41
Northwestern Syntax Screening Test, 270

Paced Auditory Serial Addition Task, 118, 142
parent questionnaire, 403
Peabody Individual Achievement Test, 84, 94,
    109, 115, 264
Peabody Picture Vocabulary Test, 103, 115, 210,
    213, 262, 271, 421
perseveration, 32, 72, 74, 141, 418
Personality Inventory for Children, 385, 403
personality tests, 385
Phoneme Discrimination Test, 276
Piers-Harris Children's Self-Concept Scale,
    405
Porch Index of Communication Ability, 217
Porteus Maze Test, 302
post-traumatic stress syndrome, 405
Pressure Aesthesiometer, 333
prosopagnosia, 298
pseudoisochromatic plates, 276
Purdue Pegboard Test, 359, 374

Raven's Progressive Matrices, 20, 45, 91
reaction times, auditory, 276
reading, 227, 252
Research Diagnostic Criteria, 392
Rey Auditory-Verbal Learning Test, 117, 149,
    195, 398
Rey Complex Figure, 118, 157, 195, 319
    Taylor scoring criteria, 17-33
Rey Visual Design Learning Test, 118, 168, 195
right-left discrimination, 332
Right-Left Orientation, 303
    Benton form, 304
    Culver form, 306
Rorschach Test, 387, 407, 418

scanning, 138
scores, standard, 10
    and percentile ranks, 10
    and standard deviations, 10
    T-scores, 10
    z-scores, 10
Seashore Rhythm Test, 276
Seashore Tests of Musical Abilities, 276
Seguin-Goddard Formboard, 341
Sentence Repetition Test, 177, 210, 228
sequential processing, 82, 85
short-term memory, 117, 125, 133
simultaneous processing, 82, 85
somatosensory changes, 332
Sound Recognition Test, 311
spatial orientation, 276, 308
spatial recognition, 276, 341
Spearman's g. See g-factor
speech lateralization, 279, 282, 367, 371, 373
Stanford Diagnostic Reading Test, 94, 104, 115
Stanford-Binet Intelligence Scale, 12, 77, 80,
    81, 83, 86, 88, 264
Stereognosis Test, 34, 332
stereognosis, 346
stick construction, 319
story-telling techniques, 418
Stroop Test, 20, 52
System of Multicultural Pluralistic Assessment,
    384

Tactile Form Perception, 332, 339
tactile memory, 342
tactile tests, 332
tactile thresholds, 332, 333, 336, 358
tactile-kinesthetic ability, 346

tactile-motor tests, 332
tactile-visual tests, 332
Tactual Performance Test, 91, 332, 341, 367
Taylor Figure, 165
Tennessee Self-Concept Scale, 405
test results, summary, 10
   profile, 10
Thematic Apperception Test, 385, 413
3-D Test, 317
Three-Dimensional Block Construction, 317
Token Test, 210, 228, 252, 266
tracking, 118
Trail Making Test, 283, 302, 320
Two-Point Discrimination (Aesthesiometer), 332,
   355

Uzgiris-Hunt Scales, 77, 80

verbal learning and memory, 117, 133, 149,
   154, 206, 207
verbal production, 252
Vineland Adaptive Behavior Scales, 384, 419
visual neglect, 276, 308, 320
visual search, 291, 320, 324
visual tests, 276
visuomotor tests, 157, 276, 319
visuo-spatial disorders, 157, 276, 279
visuo-spatial sequencing, 324
von Frey hair, 332, 335

Wechsler Adult Intelligence Scale, 398
Wechsler Intelligence Scales, 17, 27, 39, 48, 56,
   81, 86, 91, 108, 141, 180, 194, 207, 221,
   264, 289, 405
   ACID pattern, 65
   Canadian items, 59
   factor scores, 64
   pattern analysis, 64, 66, 68
   scatter, 67
   short forms, 60
Wechsler Memory Scale, 39, 117, 154, 179,
   184, 398
   Boston revision, 185
   MNI revision, 185
   Revised, 205
   Russell revision, 185, 194, 205
Weigl Color-Form Sorting Test, 302
Wepman Speech Sound Perception Test, 276
Western Aphasia Battery, 179, 405
Wide Range Achievement Test, 94, 100, 107,
   115, 289
   for non-U.S. users, 108
Wisconsin Card Sorting Test, 20, 71
Woodcock-Johnson Psychoeducational Battery,
   94, 103, 109, 110
Word Fluency, 210, 219, 228, 252
writing, 227, 252

Zung Self-Rating Depression Scale, 387, 392